lonely planet

Trekking in the Nepal Himalaya

Stan Armington

Trekking in the Nepal Himalaya

7th edition

Published by

Lonely Planet Publications

Head Office: PO Box 617, Hawthorn, Vic 3122, Australia
Branches: 150 Linden St, Oakland, CA 94607, USA
              10a Spring Place, London NW5 3BH, UK
              71 bis rue du Cardinal Lemoine, 75005 Paris, France

Printed by

Colorcraft Ltd, Hong Kong

Photographs by

Stan Armington	Richard I'Anson
Glenn Beanland	Margaret Jung
Sara Jane Cleland	Glenn Tempest/Open Spaces Photography
Greg Elms	Tony Wheeler

Front cover: Prayer flags at a base camp near Kanchenjunga, eastern Nepal
Lisl Dennis (The Image Bank)

First Published

April 1979

This Edition

September 1997

Although the authors and publisher have tried to make the information as accurate as possible, they accept no responsibility for any loss, injury or inconvenience sustained by any person using this book.

National Library of Australia Cataloguing in Publication Data

Armington, Stan.
    Trekking in the Nepal Himalaya.

    7th ed.
    Includes index.
    ISBN 0 86442 511 2.

    1. Hiking - Himalaya Mountains - Guidebooks. 2. Nepal -
    Guidebooks. 3. Himalaya Mountains - Guidebooks. I. Title.
    (Series : Lonely Planet walking guide).

915.496

text © Stan Armington 1997
maps © Lonely Planet 1997
photos © photographers as indicated 1997
Pokhara climate chart compiled from information supplied by Patrick J Tyson, © Patrick J Tyson, 1997

Stan Armington

Stan has been organising and leading treks in Nepal since 1971. A graduate engineer, he has also worked for the US National Park service in the Yellowstone and Olympic parks as well as serving as a guide on Mt Hood in Oregon. Stan is a director of the American Himalayan Foundation, a fellow of the Royal Geographical Society and the Explorers Club, and a member of the American Alpine Club and the Alpine Stomach Club. He lives in Kathmandu, where he runs a trekking company and tries to keep up with all the changes to trekking routes.

From the Author

A word of thanks to the many people who encouraged and assisted me with writing this book. Brian Weirum, Keith and Shanan Miller, Bob Peirce, Chuck McDougal, Leo Murray, Kanak Dixit, Yangdu Gombu, Bruce Klepinger, Gil Roberts, Erica Stone, Dana Keil, Harka Gurung, Elizabeth Hawley, Jim Williams, Lila Bishop, Richard Irvin, Ann Sainsbury, Sergio Fitch Watkins, Sushil Upadhyay, Daniel Tamang, Jim Fisher, Jay Ullin, Richard Brown, Alison Stone and Jungly John were all a great help. They provided me with information about recent changes, places I had not been or things I did not understand, and they checked my version of facts for accuracy. Hundreds of trekkers have helped me by asking questions I would never have thought of otherwise. Tsering Dorje Lama and Surendra Malla collected and double checked a multitude of facts and figures. Professor Trilok Chandra Majupuria assisted with research, mapping and illustrations.

This book could never have been written without the help of the many sherpas who led me up and down hills and patiently answered my questions about what we were seeing. Nawang Chuldim, 'big' Dawa Lama, Lila Tamang, 'small' Dawa Lama, Ramesh Ohja and Norbu Lama helped with this edition.

David Shlim's medical chapter gives a first-class analysis of the medical problems of a trek. David's wife, Jane Gallie, helped with the sections on women's issues and trekking with children. Lewis Underwood

wrote the many Flora & Fauna sections throughout the book. Ang Rita Sherpa of the Makalu-Barun Conservation Project reviewed the eastern Nepal chapter and made many suggestions and corrections. Thanks to Scott Yost and Dr Raju Tuladhar for allowing me to reproduce their comments on porters, and to Ken Bauer of the WWF Nepal Program for letting me verify some facts with the draft management plan for Shey Phoksumdo National Park.

Many people provided assistance and information about the Mustang trek. Broughton Coburn accompanied the one week dash to Lo Manthang when permits cost $500 per week or part thereof. Thomas Laird provided hospitality, introductions and a bottle of scotch in Lo Manthang. The Lo raja and his secretary, Tashi Wangel, were particularly helpful and patient with all my queries.

During trips to Tibet, Karchung of Ngari Travels kept us going, as did our guide, Kelsang. Choying Dorje, better known as 'Kailash Dorje', assisted in Darchan and later helped correct the information about Ngari. During that trip our sirdar, Bhakta Gurung, managed to keep us moving and our cook, Babu Ram Bhattarai, prepared many outstanding meals under truly appalling conditions. Our Humli guide, Kunga Dorje, provided great insight and assistance.

Once again, thanks to Tony and Maureen Wheeler, who pushed me to tackle this project and continue to provide suggestions on how to improve it. Tony is also responsible for the tipping guidelines for group trekkers and the cautionary tale on reconfirming your flight out of Kathmandu.

Thanks to Cambridge University Press for permission to quote four lines from *Nepal Himalaya*, by HW Tilman, and to Art Lange from Trimble Navigation, who helped me understand the complications of the Global Positioning System and provided equipment that allowed me to produce accurate readings. Thanks also to Sierra Club Books for permission to quote Tom Hornbein's reflections on Nepal from *Everest, the West Ridge*.

From the Publisher

This 7th edition of *Trekking in the Nepal Himalaya* was edited by Nick Tapp with help from Brigitte Barta, Andrew McKenna and Paul Harding. Lyn McGaurr assisted with proofing and Peter D'Onghia lent a hand with the language section. Cartography and design were by Andrew Smith, with help from Glenn Beanland, who conjured up the colour wraps; Louise Klep, who worked on the route profiles; and Chris Klep. Joanna Macfadyen assisted with preparing the artwork. Nick compiled the index. Adam McCrow designed the cover and did the back cover cartography. Rob Flynn and Grant Baxter facilitated the book's several electronic journeys to and fro between author in Kathmandu and editor in Melbourne. Thanks to all.

Thanks

Many thanks to the trekkers who used the last edition and wrote to us with useful advice and interesting anecdotes. Malcolm Donne and Andrew Simon, in particular, sent detailed letters with lots of suggestions and corrections. Others who wrote were:

Geoff Bennett, Heather Canerow, Henry Cazalet, David DeWit, Roy Ealinton, Greg Kennedy, Charlie Moore, Paul Nickodem, Sue Pickering, Pat Quinn, Alan Smith, Gail Stein, Diane Truyens.

Trekking Disclaimer

Although the authors and publisher have done their utmost to ensure the accuracy of all information in this guide, they cannot accept any responsibility for any loss, injury or inconvenience sustained by people using this book. They cannot guarantee that the tracks and routes described here have not become impassable for any reason in the interval between research and publication.

The fact that a trip or area is described in this guidebook does not mean that it is safe for you and your trekking party. You are ultimately responsible for judging your own capabilities in the light of the conditions you encounter.

Warning & Request

Things change. Prices go up, schedules change, good places go bad and bad places go bankrupt – nothing stays the same. So, if you find things better or worse, recently opened or long since closed, please tell us and help make the next edition even more accurate and useful.

We value all the feedback we receive from travellers. Julie Young coordinates a small team who read and acknowledge every letter, postcard and email, and ensure that every morsel of information finds its way to the appropriate authors, editors and publishers.

Everyone who writes to us will find their name in the next edition of the appropriate guide and will also receive a free subscription to our quarterly newsletter, *Planet Talk*. The very best contributions will be rewarded with a free Lonely Planet guide.

Excerpts from your correspondence may appear in new editions of this guide; in our newsletter, *Planet Talk*; or in updates on our Web site – so please let us know if you don't want your letter published or your name acknowledged.

Contents

Boxed Asides

MT EVEREST REGION
Jiri to Namche Bazaar p 178
Lukla to Everest Base Camp pp 188-9
Namche Bazaar p 193
Around Namche Bazaar p 195
Lukla p 205
Barahbise to Shivalaya p 211

ANNAPURNA REGION
Pokhara p 217
Annapurna Panorama &
 Ghandruk Loop p 220
Tatopani Loop p 220
Annapurna Sanctuary
 & Jomsom Trek pp 224-5

Ghandruk p 242
Around Annapurna pp 246-7
The Royal Trek Route p 261

LANGTANG & HELAMBU
Langtang & Helambu Treks pp 266-7

EASTERN NEPAL
Makalu Base Camp & Solu
 Khumbu to Hile pp 290-1
Kanchenjunga Treks pp 306-7

WESTERN NEPAL
Jumla to Rara Lake p 323
Jumla to Dolpo pp 328-9

Baglung to Dolpo p 344

RESTRICTED AREAS
Restricted Areas Map Index p 349
Mustang Trek p 355
Lo Manthang p 358
Around Manaslu pp 362-3
Humla p 376
Taklakot (Tibet) p 383
Mt Kailas & Manasarovar (Tibet) p 384
Mt Kailas Circuit (Tibet) p 385
Rivers from Mt Kailas p 386

CHINA
(TIBET)

▲ Mt Kailas

Western Nepal (p 318)

Annapurna Region (p 214)

Dhaulagiri ▲

▲
Annapurna Manaslu

Langtang &
Helambu (p 263)

Mt Everest Region (p 168)

Eastern Nepal (p 285)

Mt Everest

Makalu

Kanchenjunga

● Pokhara
(p 217)

✪ KATHMANDU
(pp 76-8)

Trekking Regions
Map Index

0   100   200 km

INDIA

80°E   82°E   84°E   86°E   88°E

32°N

30°N

28°N

26°N

Map Legend

BOUNDARIES

.... International Boundary
.... State Boundary

ROUTES

.... Freeway
.... Highway
.... Major Road
.... Minor Road
.... 4WD Track
.... Walking Track
.... Walking Route
.... Described Trek
.... City Road
.... City Street
.... Railway
.... Chair Lift

AREA FEATURES

.... Parks
.... Building
.... Built-Up Area
.... Reef
.... Beach or Desert
.... Rocks

HYDROGRAPHIC FEATURES

.... Coastline
.... River, Creek
.... Intermittent River or Creek
.... Rapids, Waterfalls
.... Lake, Intermittent Lake
.... Canal
.... Glacier

SYMBOLS

✪ **CAPITAL**		.... National Capital
◉ **Capital**		.... State Capital
CITY		.... Major City
● **City**		.... City
● **Large Town**		.... Large Town
● Town		.... Town
■	▼	.... Place to Stay, Place to Eat
�’	▮	.... Cafe, Pub or Bar
✉	☎	.... Post Office, Telephone
❶	❸	.... Tourist Information, Bank
◔	**P**	.... Transport, Parking
🏛	⚑	.... Museum, Youth Hostel

⌂	▲	.... Caravan Park, Camping
⛪	✚	.... Church, Cathedral
⊕	★	.... Hospital, Police Station
✈	✝	.... Airport, Airfield
📡	⌂	...... Satellite TV Dish, Picnic Site
⛽	A25	..... Petrol Station, Route Number
⌒	◙	.... Cave, Hut
▲	⊞	.... Mountain or Hill, Lookout
◪	⍗	.... Mosque, Temple
)(	◎	.... Pass, Spring
〿		.... Cliff or Escarpment, Ridge
		.... Train Station

Note: not all symbols displayed above appear in this book

Preface

To travel in the remote areas of Nepal today offers much more than superb mountain scenery. It provides an opportunity to step back in time and meet people who, like our ancestors many centuries ago, lived free of complications, social, economic and political, which beset the developed countries. To the Nepal peasant, his life revolves around his homestead, his fields and, above all, his family and neighbours in the little village perched high on a Himalayan mountainside. Here we can see the meaning of community, free of the drive of competition. We see human happiness despite – or because of – the absence of amenities furnished by our modern civilisation.

Change will come to the Nepalese way of life, but it behoves travellers from the modernised countries to understand and respect the values and virtues of life today in rural Nepal. They have much to teach us about how to live.

John Hunt

Lord Hunt was the leader of the 1953 Mt Everest expedition when Edmund Hillary and Tenzing Norgay Sherpa scaled the peak for the first time.

Introduction

The Himalaya, the 'abode of snows', extends from Assam in eastern India west to Afghanistan. It is a chain of the highest and youngest mountains on earth and it encompasses a region of deep religious and cultural traditions and an amazing diversity of people. Nowhere is this diversity more apparent and the culture more varied and complex than in Nepal. This book concentrates on trekking in Nepal – not quite the same experience as trekking in the Himalaya of India, Pakistan or China, even though the landscape may be similar.

A trek in Nepal is a special and rewarding mountain holiday. Do not lose sight of this as you read about the problems you may encounter and the formalities you must cope with to arrange a trek. These sound worse than they really are.

If you trek on your own, remember that you will be far from civilisation as you know it (including medical care, communication facilities and transport), no matter how many local hotels or other facilities may exist. It is only prudent to take the same precautions during a trek in Nepal as you would take on a major hiking or climbing trip at home, and carry a basic medical kit. There will often be nobody but your own companions to help you if you should fall sick or be injured. Dr Shlim's excellent Health & Safety chapter will help you prepare for many possible problems.

Tourism is a major source of foreign exchange in Nepal and is important for the country's continued economic development. The government encourages tourists to visit Nepal because they spend money. The people in the hills expect to gain a bit of income from every traveller. Even the poorest porter in the hills buys an occasional cup of tea from local inns and purchases rice from villagers. I have made a few suggestions on how to arrange a trek in a manner that is economically beneficial to both you and Nepal, with a minimum of hassle.

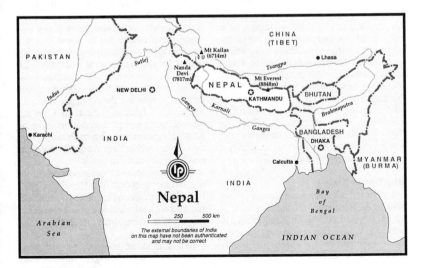

11

The information here is based on my experiences in leading and organising treks and living in Nepal since 1970. A lot of my opinions have crept in, especially relating to trekking equipment and cultural interaction. If you've done a lot of hiking, you will certainly have developed preferences for the gear you need to be comfortable. Read my suggestions about equipment, then make your own decisions.

People of various means and temperaments read and use this book. Be aware that there are many ways to approach a trek. If you have booked a group trek, it may amaze you that there should be any need to discuss the relative merits of carrying a sleeping bag. A trekker on a tight budget may find this discussion useful, yet consider it preposterous that anyone would pay US$100 per day or more to trek. There is room for both attitudes (and a lot in between) in Nepal and you will certainly meet 'the other half' during your trek. This book is your introduction to these diverse opinions and styles.

I have tried to avoid preaching about how to behave on a trek. Obviously, you should pay for what you eat and drink, bury your faeces, avoid the use of firewood, respect local customs and attitudes and try to interact gently with Nepal. Some trekkers do not do this, and it is unlikely that anything I write will change that. In rare cases, an innkeeper might overcharge you, abuse you, refuse food or accommodation or insult you. Filthy hotels, camp sites and latrines may disgust you along some popular trekking routes. If this happens, it is because someone (probably the person who stayed there last night) contributed to the problem. You have the choice of continuing to escalate the mess or doing your own small part to make Nepal more pleasant for those who follow.

Why Trek in Nepal?

Just as New York is not representative of the USA, so Kathmandu is not representative of Nepal. If you have the time and energy to trek, don't miss the opportunity to leave Kathmandu and see the spectacular beauty and the unique culture of Nepal. Fortunately

for the visitor, there are still only a few roads extending deeply into the hills, so the only way to truly visit the remote regions of the kingdom is in the slowest and most intimate manner – walking. It requires more time and effort, but the rewards are also greater. Instead of zipping down a freeway, racing to the next 'point of interest', each step provides new and intriguing viewpoints. You will perceive your day as an entity rather than a few highlights strung together by a ribbon of concrete. For the romanticist, each step follows the footsteps of Hillary, Tenzing, Herzog and other Himalayan explorers. If you have neither the patience nor the physical stamina to visit the hills of Nepal on foot, a helicopter flight provides an expensive and unsatisfactory substitute.

Trekking in Nepal will take you through a country that has captured the imagination of mountaineers and explorers for more than 100 years. You will meet people in remote mountain villages whose lifestyle has not changed in generations. Most people trust foreigners. Nepal is one of only a handful of countries that have never been ruled by a foreign power.

Many of the values associated with a hiking trip at home do not have the same importance during a trek in Nepal. Isolation is traditionally a crucial element of any wilderness experience, but in Nepal it is not possible to get completely away from people except for short times or at extremely high elevations. Environmental concerns must include the effects of conservation measures on rural people and the economic effects of tourism on indigenous populations. Even traditional national park management must be adapted because there are significant population centres within Sagarmatha (Mt Everest) and Langtang national parks.

Trekking does not mean mountain climbing. While the ascent of a Himalayan peak may be an attraction for some, you need not have such a goal to enjoy a trek. Throughout this book, trekking always refers to walking on trails.

While trekking you will see the great diversity of Nepal. Villages embrace many ethnic groups and cultures. The terrain changes from tropical jungle to high glaciated peaks in the space of only 150 km. From the start, the towering peaks of the Himalaya provide one of the highlights of a trek. As your plane approaches Kathmandu these peaks appear to be small clouds on the horizon. The mountains become more definable and seem to reach impossible heights as you get closer and finally land at Kathmandu's Tribhuvan airport.

During a trek, the Himalaya disappears behind Nepal's continual hills, but dominates the northern skyline at each pass. Annapurna, Manaslu, Langtang, Gauri Shankar and Everest will become familiar names. Finally, after weeks of walking, you will arrive at the foot of the mountains themselves – astonishing heights from which gigantic avalanches tumble earthwards in apparent slow motion, dwarfed by their surroundings. Your conception of the Himalaya will alter as you turn from peaks famed only for their height to gaze on far more picturesque summits that you may never have heard of – Kantega, Ama Dablam, Machhapuchhare and Khumbakarna.

The beauty and attraction of the Nepal Himalaya emanates not only from the mountains themselves, but also from their surroundings. Nepal is a country of friendly people, picturesque villages and a great variety of cultures and traditions that seem to exemplify many of the attributes we have lost in our headlong rush for development and progress in the West.

Avoiding the Crowds

It's true, the hills of Nepal can be crowded with trekkers. But there are still many ways to avoid the crowds. There are three excellent times for trekking when you will often have camp sites or lodges to yourself and can usually rely on good weather. These secret trekking seasons are the first two weeks of December, the entire month of February, and the second half of September.

You can trek to many places in Nepal where no trekkers go, but you'll have to bring an entire support team, because there are no hotels in those places. However, there is a little-used trek route where you can find excellent hotels every night and will often be the only Westerner in a village. Because many people now fly in and out of Lukla, the classic trek from Jiri to Lukla has been almost totally abandoned. There are some long, steep hills, but this route has excellent lodges and passes through great trekking country.

Facts about the Country

HISTORY

What is now Nepal was once a collection of feudal principalities sandwiched between Moghul India and Tibet. You can see the palaces of these ancient rulers as you trek through Nepal at places such as Sinja near Jumla, Besi Sahar (Lamjung) near Dumre, Lo Manthang, Gorkha and, of course, the Kathmandu Valley. Many of these small kingdoms had little or no contact with Kathmandu. The early history of the Kathmandu Valley, with its Licchavi dynasty from the 3rd to the 13th century and the Malla reign from the 13th to the 18th century, had little effect on the remote hill regions.

In 1769 Prithvi Narayan Shah, the ruler of the House of Gorkha, unified these diverse kingdoms and established the general shape of the present borders of Nepal. He also founded the Shah dynasty, defeated the Newar kings of Kathmandu, Patan and Bhaktapur, and established the capital in Kathmandu. King Birendra Bir Bikram Shah Dev is a direct descendant of Prithvi Narayan Shah.

In 1814 the British East India Company declared war on Nepal. After a fierce war with imperial India, Nepal conceded a large part of its territory, which now comprises the northern areas of the Indian states of Kashmir, Himachal Pradesh, West Bengal, Bihar and Uttar Pradesh. Nepal also agreed to allow a British 'resident' in the country, but he was not permitted to leave the Kathmandu Valley. The old British residency is now the British Council building on Kantipath.

Rana Prime Ministers

In 1846 the prime minister, Jung Bahadur Rana, conspired with the queen regent to gain control of the country. He invited the top political and military leaders to a party and ambushed them in what is known in Nepali history as the Kot Massacre. The site of the massacre, the Kot, still stands near Hanuman Dhoka in Durbar Square. Following the massacre, Jung Bahadur decreed that the post of prime minister was to be hereditary, and took the precaution of ensuring that the title passed to a younger brother if the ruler had no qualified son. The Ranas adopted the title 'maharaja' and ruled the country for 104 years. Jung Bahadur visited England and France and was received with all the honours due a head of state.

Despite Jung Bahadur's refusal to adopt European practices which conflicted with his Hindu beliefs, he was fascinated with European architecture. The profusion of white stucco neoclassical palaces in Kathmandu was inspired by this journey. The largest of these, Singha Durbar, now houses the parliament and secretariat.

Re-Emergence of the Monarchy

In 1950 King Tribhuvan, assisted by the Indian embassy in Kathmandu, fled to India. The rule of the Shah kings was reinstated through an armed people's revolution led by the Nepal Congress Party. King Tribhuvan instituted political reforms and, until the 1990 revolution, was credited with being the father of democracy in Nepal.

During a period of political squabbling, the number of political parties in Nepal grew to more than 60. In 1960 Tribhuvan's son, King Mahendra, engineered a bloodless palace coup, declared a new constitution, jailed all the leaders of the government and announced a ban on political parties. He established a partyless *panchayat* ('five councils') system that was answerable only to the monarch.

The political system was described as 'partyless panchayat democracy' and allowed direct election of local leaders and representatives to the Rastrya Panchayat, the National Assembly. Although the council of ministers was made up of members of the Rastrya Panchayat, the king retained the right to appoint a quota of legislators, effectively retaining control.

King Birendra succeeded to the throne in 1972. After a period of political unrest, he declared that a national referendum would decide whether the country would adopt a multiparty system or retain the panchayat system 'with suitable reforms'. The 1980 referendum endorsed the panchayat system by a narrow margin and was thereafter cited as the will of the people.

The 1990 Revolution

Being a landlocked country, Nepal depends on its neighbour India for most of its manufactured goods and for access to the sea. In March 1989 the Trade & Transit Treaty between Nepal and India expired. Pride and protocol prevented the two countries from reaching any agreement on an extension. The issue was further complicated by Nepal's recent purchase of hundreds of truckloads of military supplies from China. India reduced the number of entry points into Nepal to the minimum required by international law, raised tariffs on goods from Nepal and severely limited the supply of petroleum products. Nepal's economy and quality of life declined and there was considerable popular unrest with the government's inability to resolve the issue.

This unrest reached a crescendo in the spring of 1990 when the 'illegal, banned' political parties began to severely criticise the panchayat system for corruption, human rights violations and incompetence. The various opposition factions coalesced into a united force, bent on the restoration of democracy in Nepal under the leadership of Nepal's new 'father of democracy', Ganesh Man Singh. The government replied with a show of force that escalated from arrests to public beatings and shootings. After the resignation of several ministers forced the issue, the king reconstituted the Cabinet and promised that grievances would be reviewed and appropriate changes made.

But the people were not mollified. In a spectacular display of unity, more than 200,000 people took to the streets of Kathmandu on 6 April 1990, chanting pro-democracy slogans. After they had exercised restraint throughout most of the day, the police attacked the demonstrators, first with bamboo staves and then with guns. Hundreds of people were killed or wounded. The army took control of the city. During a tense weekend curfew, the king negotiated with opposition leaders, then late in the evening of 8 April proclaimed that the ban on political parties was lifted.

The next day the country erupted in an outpouring of joy. The interim council of ministers appointed in the aftermath of the revolution included leaders of various parties, many of whom had spent time in jail as political prisoners. One of the major accomplishments of the new government was the restoration of friendly relations with India. Imports of Indian goods, especially fuel, and the export of Nepali goods to India resumed. A new constitution was written and promulgated in 1990, and Nepal became a constitutional monarchy with sovereignty vested in the people.

Democratic Elections

In the elections of 1991, the Nepal Congress Party gained a majority and formed a government. The mood of the public was upbeat for a while, but the inexperience, sometimes coupled with sheer incompetence, of the elected government demoralised the average Nepali. The various communist parties banded together to organise several crippling strikes and demonstrations against the ruling Nepal Congress Party. The government cracked down on the communists with brutal force and dozens of agitators were killed by the police. The political squabbling continued, and in 1994 parliament was dissolved and new elections were called.

In the November 1994 elections, no party gained a majority. The United Marxist-Leninist Party (CPN-UML) won the most seats in parliament, so it formed a communist government that lasted 10 months before the Nepal Congress Party and the resurgent royalist parties of the panchayat era formed a new coalition government.

The next coalition government was led by the Young Turks of the Nepal Congress Party. It was a tenuous liaison at best, with charges and countercharges being thrown around. The communist opposition party was in disarray, its top leaders fighting amongst themselves to hold rein over party politics and policies.

The CPN-UML formed an alliance with a disgruntled faction of the royalist (Panchayat) party and tabled a vote of no confidence against the Congress prime minister in January 1997. This was defeated, but in March the prime minister called for another vote of confidence in his government. He lost the motion by two votes and had to resign. Three days later the royalist and communist coalition garnered the required 103 votes to form a new government. The prime minister is the same person who presided over the country during the revolution of 1990.

HISTORY OF TREKKING

The first trekker in Nepal was Bill Tilman, who somehow wrangled permission from the maharaja in 1949 to make several treks, including the Kali Gandaki, Helambu and Everest. His exploits are described in *Nepal Himalaya*, a mountaineering classic that has been reprinted by the Seattle Mountaineers as part of a Tilman collection, *The Seven Mountain-Travel Books*. Another early visitor was Maurice Herzog, who led a French expedition to Annapurna in 1950.

During King Tribhuvan's visits to India, the king met Boris Lissannivich, a Russian ballet dancer who was running a club in Calcutta. Boris convinced the king that people would like to visit Nepal and would actually pay for the experience. Soon a few well-heeled ladies flew from Patna to Kathmandu's Gaucher ('cowfield') airport in an Indian Airlines Dakota. Boris accommodated them in his new establishment, the Royal Hotel. The women were charmed by Boris and the exotic kingdom of Nepal. Thus Nepali tourism was born. The Royal Hotel and its Yak & Yeti bar became the meeting place for climbers from the 1950s until 1971, when the Royal Hotel was closed.

Colonel James OM Roberts was the first person to realise that trekking would appeal to tourists. 'Jimmy' Roberts had spent years in Nepal attached to the British residency and accompanied Tilman on his first trek. In 1965 he took a group of ladies up the Kali Gandaki and founded Mountain Travel, the first of Nepal's trekking companies and the inspiration for the adventure travel industry.

GEOGRAPHY

Nepal is a small, landlocked country, 800 km long and 200 km wide. In the longitudinal 200 km, the terrain changes from glaciers along the Tibetan border to the flat jungles of the Terai, barely 150m above sea level. The country does not ascend gradually from the plains. Rather, it rises in several chains of hills that lie in an east-west direction, finally terminating in the highest hills in the world – the Himalaya. Beyond the Himalaya is the 5000m high plateau of Tibet. Despite the height of the Himalaya, the peaks do not form a continental divide. Though most rivers flow southward from the glaciers of the Nepal Himalaya to join the Ganges in India, several rivers do flow from Tibet through deep gorges in the main Himalayan range. These rivers have scarred the country with great gorges in both north-south and east-west directions and created a continual series of hills, some of which are incredibly steep.

From east to west, the geographic division of the kingdom is less clearly defined, though there are clear political divisions. Nepal is divided into 14 zones, several of which extend across the country from the Terai to the Tibetan border.

The primary difference between eastern and western Nepal is that the influence of the monsoon is less in the west. In the east the climate is damp and ideal for tea growing, the conditions being similar to those in Darjeeling in India. In the far west the climate is quite dry, even during the monsoon season.

Another influence on the east-west division is the large rivers that flow southward in deep canyons. These rivers often limit east-west travel as they wash away bridges during the monsoon. For this reason the major trade routes are from south to north, from Indian border towns to hill villages in Nepal and then across high mountain passes to Tibet.

Despite the steepness of the country, there is extensive farming on thousands of ancient terraces carved into the hills. Pressure from the increasing population is forcing people to bring even the most marginal land into cultivation. This has resulted in erosion, flooding and landslides.

Extensive systems of trenches and canals provide the irrigation necessary for food production. Houses are near family fields, and a typical Nepali village extends over a large area. The hilly terrain often creates an elevation differential of several hundred metres or more between the highest and lowest homes in a village.

Physiographic Regions

Geographers divide the country into three main physiographic regions, or natural zones: the Terai, the Middle Hills and the Himalaya.

The Terai The Terai is the southernmost region of Nepal and is an extension of the Gangetic plains of India. Until 1950 this was a malarial jungle inhabited primarily by rhinoceros, tiger, leopard, wild boar and deer. Now, with malaria controlled, farming and industrial communities cover the Terai. The region supports about 47% of Nepal's population and encompasses the majority of the country's cultivable land. The Terai includes the big cities of Nepalgunj, Birganj, Janakpur, Bhairawa and Biratnagar, but most of the region is dotted with small villages – clusters of 40 or 50 houses in the centre of a large area of cultivated fields.

Just north of the Terai is the first major east-west chain of hills, the Siwalik (or Churia) Hills, and then comes the Mahabharat Range. In some parts of Nepal only farmers live in these hills, but in other parts they are the sites of large and well-developed villages such as Ilam, Dhankuta and Surkhet.

The Middle Hills The Middle Hills, a band only 60 km wide, are home to about 45% of the population. This is the home of the ancient ethnic groups of Nepal. Kathmandu, Patan, Bhadgaon, Pokhara, Gorkha and Jumla are all in the Middle Hills. Kathmandu lies in the largest valley of the kingdom, and according to legend the valley was once a huge lake. Other than the Kathmandu and Pokhara valleys, the Middle Hills region is all steep hillsides.

The Himalaya The Himalaya and its foothills make up only a small portion of the kingdom along the northern border. This inhospitable region is the least inhabited part of Nepal. Less than 8% of the population lives here. Most of the villages sit between 3000m and 4000m elevation, although there are summer settlements as high as 5000m. Winters are cold, but the warm sun makes most days comfortable. Because of the short growing season, crops are few and usually small, consisting mostly of potatoes, barley and a few vegetables. The primary means of support are trading and the herding of sheep, cattle and yaks. The part of this region known as Solu Khumbu is the home of the Sherpas. Mountaineering expeditions and trekking have a large influence on the economy of this area.

In the west the Himalayan region is an area of Tibetan influence and parts of this region are on the north side of the main Himalayan range. This is the trans-Himalaya, a high desert region similar to the Tibetan Plateau. This area encompasses the arid valleys of Mustang, Manang, Dolpo and Limi, as well as the Tibetan marginals (the fourth range of mountains that sweep from central to northwestern Nepal, averaging below 6000m in height). The trans-Himalaya is in the rain shadow of the main Himalayan range and receives significantly less precipitation than the southern slopes. Uneroded crags, spires, and formations like crumbling fortresses are typical of this stark landscape.

GEOLOGY

Imagine the space Nepal occupies as an open expanse of water, once part of the Mediterranean Sea, and the Tibetan Plateau, or 'roof of the world', as a beachfront property. This was the prehistoric setting until 60 million years ago, before the Indo-Australian plate's collision with the Eurasian continent. As the former was pushed under Eurasia, the earth's crust buckled and folded and mountain-building began.

The upheaval of mountains caused the temporary obstruction of rivers that once flowed unimpeded from Eurasia to the sea. However, on the southern slopes of the young mountains, new rivers formed as trapped, moist winds off the tropical sea rose and precipitated. As the mountains continued to rise and the gradient became steeper, these rivers cut deeply into the terrain.

The continual crunching of the two plates, augmented by phases of crustal uplifting, created yet newer mountain ranges and once again the rivers' courses were interrupted. If the forces of erosion eventually prevailed, long east-west valleys were formed. If not, lakes resulted.

The colossal outcome was the formation of four major mountain systems running from north-west to south-east and incised by the north-south gorges of not only new rivers, but the original ones with watersheds in Tibet that are older than the mountains themselves. In conjunction with the innumerable rogue ridges that jut out from the main ranges, the terrain can be likened to a complex maze of ceilingless rooms.

The mountain-building process continues today, not only displacing material laterally, but sending the ranges yet higher and resulting in natural erosion, landslides, silt-laden rivers, rock faults and earthquakes.

CLIMATE

Nepal has four distinct seasons. Spring, from March to May, is warm and dusty with rain showers. Summer is from June to August, and much of this season is dominated by the monsoon, when the hills turn lush and green. Autumn, from late September to November,

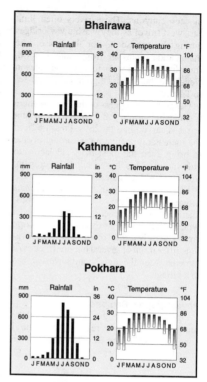

is cool with clear skies, and is the most popular trekking season. In winter, from December to February, it is cold at night and can be foggy in the early morning, but afternoons are usually clear and pleasant, though there is occasional snow in the mountains.

Because Nepal is quite far south (at the same latitude as Miami and Cairo) the weather is warmer and winter is much milder at lower elevations, including Kathmandu at 1400m. It rarely snows below 2000m.

The monsoon in the Bay of Bengal governs the weather pattern. The monsoon creates a rainy season from mid-June to mid-September. It is hot during the monsoon and it rains almost every day, but it is a considerate rain, limiting itself mostly to the night. During this season, trekking in most of Nepal is difficult and uncomfortable. Clouds usually hide the mountains and the trails are muddy and infested with leeches.

It usually does not rain for more than a few days during the entire autumn season from mid-October to mid-December. During winter and spring there may be a week or so of rainy days, and occasional thunderstorms blanket the hills with snow. The Himalaya makes its own localised weather, which varies significantly over a distance of a few km. Despite the sanguine assurances of Radio Nepal that the weather will be '...mainly fair throughout the kingdom', always expect clouds in the afternoon and be prepared for occasional rain.

Most of the precipitation in the Himalaya occurs during the summer monsoon. There is less snow on the mountains and on many of the high trails during winter. Everest itself is a mass of black rock during the trekking season, becoming snow-covered only during summer. There are always exceptions to this weather pattern, so be prepared for extremes. Winter snowstorms in December and January may make an early spring pass crossing difficult and can present an avalanche danger, especially on the approach to the Annapurna Sanctuary. During the spring, sudden violent thunderstorms accompanied by high winds blow down trees and tents and cause streams to swell.

In Kathmandu, spring and autumn days are comfortable and the evenings are cool, usually requiring a light jacket or pullover. Winter in Kathmandu brings cold, foggy mornings and clear evenings, but pleasant daytime temperatures with brilliant sunshine most days after the morning fog has lifted. It never snows in Kathmandu, though there is frost on cold nights in January and February. The hottest month is May, just before the rains start.

ECOLOGY & ENVIRONMENT

Except for a few manufacturing centres, agriculture dominates the economy. In the hill regions people have cultivated every possible piece of land except where the hillsides are too steep or rocky to carve out even the smallest terrace. Much of the land between the Himalaya and the Terai has been worked and sculpted over the centuries to provide space for crops, animals and houses. Because of this, forests lying within the inhabited zone, especially on the southern slopes, have been lopped, cut and cleared.

Conservation

As long as Nepali people marry early, feel uncertain about infant survival and desire sons to look after them in their old age and perform funeral rites, the population of Nepal will continue to burgeon. With population tension, the forests will continue to be depleted, erosion caused by humans will compound that which is natural, water supplies will dry up and floods will inundate the lowlands.

The visitor should not, however, adopt the role of the vociferous critic. Nepal is making positive changes, but traditional societies require long lead times for change. There are various alternative energy schemes under way throughout the hills, the largest and most successful of which is the Austrian hydroelectric project near Thami that serves the Khumbu region. The Annapurna Conservation Area Project (ACAP) is also an innovative approach, incorporating not only other alternative energy developments, forest conservation and environmental education, but an effective strategy of getting the Nepali people directly involved in determining their own destiny. Another success story is the Sagarmatha Pollution Control Committee (SPCC) in the Everest region. Faced with criticism from trekkers and a potential loss of tourist income, the Sherpas created their own organisation to cope with the environmental pressures of both visitors and a growing local population.

Conservation is typically a concept of affluent countries with land and resources to spare, a luxury unknown in the Third World. With dwindling space and forests, it is difficult for a farmer to grasp why land should be set aside for tigers and rhino, especially when they ravage crops, kill domestic animals, and generally make a hard life even harder.

Visitors should ensure that they minimise their impact on the environment. Trekking groups or individuals staying in lodges should insist that kerosene, as opposed to firewood, is used for cooking meals and heating water. One should also minimise the use of nonbiodegradable products (especially plastic and batteries) as there are no facilities for their disposal. One potential nightmare is the trend to sell water in plastic bottles, which are expensive and completely unnecessary if you carry your own water bottle and iodine. See the Facts for the Trekker chapter for more information on minimising your impact on the environment. Also, see the Books section in that chapter for a list of supplementary reading on flora, fauna and national parks.

National Parks
The first national park in Nepal was the Royal Chitwan National Park in the Terai, established in 1973. There are now eight national parks, five wildlife reserves and two conservation areas, though many of these are in the Terai. If you are trekking, you will almost certainly enter one of the mountain national parks: Sagarmatha, Langtang, Rara, Shey Phoksumdo and Makalu-Barun.

Conservation Areas
The idea of a conservation area to protect a populated area originated in Nepal, and the Annapurna Conservation Area has become a recognised model of community involvement in preservation efforts. The Annapurna Conservation Area was created in 1986 by the King Mahendra Trust for Nature Conservation in an effort to balance the needs of the local population, trekking tourism and the environment. It is not a national park since such a designation would have prohibited many types of land use, but conservation of the natural and cultural heritage is a primary goal. Roughly 40,000 people, mostly farmers, live in the region and over 30,000 trekkers visit the area each year, which has led to many environmental problems. Some

of these are deforestation, water pollution, poor sanitation, litter and expansion of agriculture to meet tourist needs. A priority of the Annapurna Conservation Area is to increase the local economic benefits of tourism and reduce the environmental and social costs.

The Makalu-Barun Conservation Area was established in 1991 to provide a buffer zone around the national park of the same name. It is co-managed by the Mountain Institute (a North American-based nongovernmental organisation) and the Department of National Parks & Wildlife Conservation.

Endangered Species
Many of the endangered species in Nepal are found in the Terai; these include the Bengal tiger, Asian elephant, one-horned rhinoceros, Gaur bison, swamp deer and Gangetic dolphin. In the hills, the snow leopard, clouded leopard, red panda, wild yak, musk deer, great Tibetan sheep and hispid hare are on the International Union for Conservation of Nature (IUCN) list of endangered or vulnerable species. Nepal's Department of National Parks & Wildlife Conservation is working with international organisations like the World Wide Fund for Nature (WWF, known in the USA and Canada as the World Wildlife Fund) to ensure the preservation of these animals.

Plant Use
The Terai is considered the rice bowl of Nepal, though rice is usually grown up to 2000m, or even higher in the west. It is usually planted before the advent of the monsoon, transplanted soon after and harvested in the autumn. The rich, vibrant greens of the rice plant during the monsoon contrast with the subtle, diffused tones as it ripens.

If possible, wheat is planted in the cleared rice fields and harvested in spring. Fields of yellow-flowering mustard are planted for making cooking oil. Corn is planted in spring, especially on the hillsides, while millet is grown above the rice zone. Barley is sown in the higher altitudes, as well as buckwheat with its pink-and-white flower cluster. The Sherpas grow potatoes up to 4000m, and have been doing so since the crop was introduced, probably from Darjeeling in the middle of the last century. Besides providing an important food staple, potatoes and the prosperity attained from trading them allowed Sherpas to begin building their *gompas* (temples) and enabled their culture to flourish.

Amongst the crops, on the berms dividing the plots, various other food crops are grown, including soya beans, lentils, sesame and chilli peppers. The bright red-and-yellow plants with clustered seed heads seen amidst the shades of greens are *Amaranthus*, once an important food and medicinal grain for the Aztecs and Incas.

To keep animals out of crops, Nepali farmers use assorted spiny or unpalatable exotics as natural barriers. Besides prickly pear cactus and agave, there are several euphorbias used, such as the red-flowering crown of thorns, spurge and physic nut.

There are numerous trees planted around villages and fields, all for some kind of purpose, be it for shade, fruit, fodder or medicine. Bananas, mangoes, papaya, citrus fruits, peaches and apples have all brought new income to the remote hill areas.

Fodder such as rice stalks and corn sheaves are often dried and stored in trees, while seed corn is stored under the eaves of houses. A variety of fig trees provide shade for pilgrims and travellers. The magnificent mushrooming canopies of banyan and pipal tress are unmistakable, and are usually found together atop a stone *chautaara* (platform) designed for accommodating porters' loads. The banyan has hanging aerial roots and leathery elliptical leaves, while the pipal has a heart-shaped leaf with a long spur. The Buddha is believed to have received enlightenment under a pipal tree, and Hindus revere the banyan as an embodiment of Lakshmi, the goddess of wealth, and the pipal as an embodiment of Narayan (Vishnu).

Bamboo grows under a variety of conditions and is found throughout Nepal. Giant bamboo is common in the tropics and dwarf bamboo in the temperates. This grass species is used for basketry and, where forests are depleted, particularly in the east, for building. The Rais work bamboo into everything from water vessels to entire houses.

Kitchen gardens are common features in villages and comprise greens, beans, turnips, radishes, pumpkins, cucumbers, taro and squash. Bauhinia, with its distinctive camel-hoof leaves and orchid-like flowers, is grown near houses; the leaves are used for fodder and the flowers cooked or pickled. In the west, tobacco is a commonly seen plot in villages, as are fields of cannabis grown for hemp. In addition, stinging nettles are picked with thongs, anaesthetised by boiling and eaten as greens. Eupatorium is a red-stemmed daisy with heart-shaped leaves called *ban mara* ('death of forest') in Nepali. A native of Latin America introduced into the Himalaya during the last century, it invades subtropical and temperate zones, and is widespread. Covering deforested hillsides, it is unpalatable, even for sheep and goats, and is a prime indicator of environmental degradation.

Animal Husbandry

Bovines play an important role in rural and urban Nepal. Cows are sacred and are not slaughtered, nor used as beasts of burden – they bear calves and provide milk and, of course, multipurpose dung. The beasts of burden on the lowlands are usually castrated bulls, or oxen. In the Kathmandu Valley, the cows wandering and sleeping in the streets have been let loose by pious Hindus. Because the bull is Shiva's steed, and Pashupatinath is a major Shaivite temple, bulls are also considered holy and generally are not used to pull ploughs in the valley.

Water buffaloes belong to a different genus, but are still lumped with the bovines. These animals lose their body hair as they mature, and must wallow to dissipate heat and for protection from the sun. The males are used as beasts of burden and are butchered. The females produce a creamy milk, some of which is converted into yoghurt. These animals tend to be skittish, a trait probably inherited from their wild ancestors, and those at the Koshi Tappu Reserve in the eastern Terai are considered aggressive and dangerous.

The long-haired yaks, no longer found in the wilds of Nepal, are also very temperamental and are mostly used for stud service. What one generally sees are hybrids, which have confusing names. First of all, the female yak is called a *nak*. The nak or yak can be crossbred with cattle, which produces a more docile creature suitable for carrying loads. Locally, the male is called a *zopkiok* or *dzopkyo* and the female a *zhum* or *dzum*. The dzum lactates well and produces a better quality milk than the nak. The second generation of these hybrids is sterile.

In the Kali Gandaki and, more recently, on the southern approaches to the Everest region, donkeys and mules are being used as pack animals. These beasts are often adorned with headgear of dyed plumes and mirrors, and collars of bells. Also, in autumn, during the prime festival season, herds of goats and sheep are driven down from Tibet to be sold for ritual slaughter and the subsequent feasts.

FLORA

There are 6500 known species of trees, shrubs and wild flowers in Nepal. In the temperate areas the flowers emerge as winter recedes and the rivers swell with snow melt, while in the subtropics the bloom is triggered by warmer temperatures and spring showers. Americans and Europeans will recognise many of the species in the temperate areas, and residents of South-East Asia will recognise many of the subtropical species.

The height of floral glory can be witnessed in March and April when rhododendrons burst into colour. The huge magnolias of the east with their showy white flowers borne on bare branches are also spectacular, as are the orchids (there are over 300 varieties in Nepal). Not far behind is the blossoming of a variety of shrubs, while on the ground, blue irises and lavender primulas appear. The succession of flowers continues higher up as the monsoon approaches.

To see wild flowers in bloom, it is necessary to visit the temperate and alpine areas

during the monsoon season. In order to do this, one must be prepared to sacrifice comfort and views. However, this is the time to see the true colours of the Himalaya. The southern slopes and the inner valleys are particularly lush at this time. Mints, scrophs, buttercups, cinquefoils, polygonums and composites abound in these areas, while in the alpine areas, dwarf rhododendrons, junipers, ephedras, cotoneasters, saxifrages and primulas paint the bleak landscape.

Western Nepal, particularly the Dolpo area, is reminiscent of Kashmir in its rich variety of flora. Being in the rain-shadow area, monsoon conditions are more amenable for visitors – the region is drier and free of leeches. In order to witness the full regalia, the time to visit is July and August. From Jumla east one may recognise ground orchids, edelweiss, corydalis, campanulas, anemones, forget-me-nots, impatiens and roses. Higher up in the alpine areas, larkspurs, geraniums, poppies, sedums and saxifrages proliferate.

In the trans-Himalaya, common vegetation is primarily from the legume family, such as the spiny caragana and astragalus, as well as from the honeysuckle family (eg lonerica).

In the postmonsoon season, when most people choose to visit, the flowers of summer are all but gone, save for some straggler blooms and those not palatable to grazing animals. However, in the subtropical and lower temperate areas, some wild flowers are fortunate and survive environmental degradation, such as the pink luculia, mauve osbeckia and yellow St John's wort. Flowering cherry trees also add colour to the autumn village scenes as do blue gentians in the temperate areas. Otherwise, one can enjoy the autumn yellows of withering maples and ginger, and the reds of barberry shrubs. When the dark temperate forests are back lit, the moss appears luminescent, and the epiphytic ferns and orchids shine like tiny paper lanterns.

In the Kathmandu Valley, Australians will find the familiar silky oak with its spring golden inflorescence, and bottlebrush and eucalyptus. Though the first and last are fast-growing timber species in their native country, in the valley these trees are planted as ornamentals along with cherry, poplar and jacaranda. The latter, with its lavender blossoms, is from South America, as are the bougainvillea and giant poinsettia. Historically, people in Nepal have been avid gardeners of such exotics as hibiscus, camellia, cosmos, salvia and marigold.

FAUNA
Birds

More than 800 species are known in Nepal, more birds than in Canada and the USA combined, or nearly 10% of the world's species! Resident bird numbers are augmented by migratory species, as well as winter and summer visitors.

Eight species of stork, some as tall as 150 cm, have been identified along the watercourses of the Terai. Cranes are similar in appearance, but not as well represented save for the demoiselle cranes that fly down the Kali Gandaki and Dudh Kosi for the winter before returning in spring to their Tibetan nesting grounds. Herons and egrets are quite common in the tropics and subtropics, and are distinguished in flight by their curved-neck posture, as opposed to the outstretched necks of storks and cranes.

Most of the waterfowl are migratory. Many can be seen at the Kosi Barrage in the eastern Terai and in the Chitwan and Bardia areas. The swift-flying bar-headed goose has been observed flying at altitudes of nearly 8000m.

Raptors, or birds of prey, are found in all sizes in the Himalaya, and are especially prevalent with the onset of winter. One of the first raptors to leave is the small Eurasian kestrel, which must flap its wings at regular intervals, or rapidly when hovering. By comparison, the Himalayan griffon is a heavy bird that must wait for thermal updraught to allow its soaring, gliding flight. The griffon and the lammergeier, with wingspans of nearly three metres, are carrion eaters, though often mistaken for eagles. There are, however, true eagles, including the resident

The golden eagle *(Aquila chrysaeetos)* can have a wing span of up to three metres.

golden eagle common in the Khumbu, as well as other species that are known to migrate in large numbers in the Kali Gandaki region. Many medium-sized raptors have highly variable plumages and are difficult to identify in the sky.

There are six species of pheasant in Nepal, including the national bird, the impeyan pheasant, the male of which has a plumage of iridescent colours. These birds are known as downhill fliers, as they do not fly, per se, and must walk uphill! When flushed they will cant and swerve downhill to evade enemies such as the golden eagle. The cheer and koklas pheasants are only found west of the Kali Gandaki, while the kalij pheasant is common throughout, but with different colour phases.

Nepal hosts 17 species of cuckoo, which are characterised by their distinctive calls. Arriving in March, they herald the coming of spring. The call of the Indian cuckoo is recognisable as *'kaphal pakyo'*, which is Nepali for announcing that the fruit of the box myrtle is ripe. The common hawk cuckoo has a repetitious call that sounds like 'brain fever' and rises in a crescendo – aptly described by British sahibs as they lay sweating with malarial fevers. Most cuckoos are social parasites, meaning they lay their eggs in the nests of other species.

One of the most colourful, varied and

Vegetation Zones
In western Nepal, forests usually extend to higher elevations than elsewhere in the country due to drier conditions and a more northerly latitude. Above the cultivation zone the forests are less disrupted, although they do come under pressure from summer herders and wood-gatherers.

Tropical Zone (up to 300m) Sal, a broad-leafed, semideciduous hardwood, dominates here. The leaves are used for 'disposable' plates, and the wood is used for construction. It varies little from east to west and is a climax species.

There is also a deciduous moist forest in this zone, of acacia and rosewood, as well as open areas of tall elephant grass. The grass areas are burned off in winter, which helps preserve them – otherwise they would be succeeded by a moist forest. These two habitats are known as seral communities, because if they are left undisturbed, they would both be replaced by the sal climax forest.

The silky cotton tree with its thorny trunks when young, and smooth-buttressed trunk bases when older, has leafless limbs that burst into bright red flowers in early spring. It is also a part of the moist forest. The cotton or 'kapok' from these trees is used for stuffing cushions and mattresses.

These forest types are typical of the Churia Hills and Inner Terai, though sal and silky cotton are also found in the subtropical zone.

Subtropical Zone (1000m to 2000m) The dominant species east of the Kali Gandaki are the true chestnuts and a member of the tea family, the schima. The spiky flower clusters of the chestnuts appear in the fall, while the fragrant white flowers of the schima bloom in late spring. Due to chestnut wood's popularity as a source of fuel, it is often depleted.

In the west, the chir pine is found on all aspects. The species has long needles in bundles of three and is also found in the east, but confined to drier southern slopes.

Cone and foliage of the chir pine *(Pinus roxburghii)*

Lower Temperate Zone (1700m to 2700m) Evergreen oaks are indigenous to this zone. In the east, the oaks of the wet forests are festooned with moss and epiphytes and have dense understoreys. In the west, another oak preferring dry conditions is present, as well as on the sunny slopes of the east.

A common wet forest that occurs mostly on north and west faces in western Nepal consists of horse chestnut, maple and walnut. Alder and birch are prevalent along watercourses.

Homogeneous blue-pine forests occur extensively in the west, mostly on south faces, and range to the tree line. This species is hardy and fire resistant, thriving well in habitats modified by humans. It is also found throughout the east, but to a lesser extent. The blue pine is distinguished from the only

Horse chestnut *(Aesculus indica)*

vocal families is that of the timalids, or babblers and laughing thrushes, common from the tropical Terai to the upper temperate forest. They are from eight to 33 cm in size and live in both terrestrial and arboreal habitats. They are found individually or in large foraging parties, and can often be identified by their raucous calls. The black-capped other pine in Nepal, the chir pine, by its shorter needles in bundles of five, and long, pendulous cones. Both species are used for carpentry and roofing, while the resin is converted to turpentine.

Upper Temperate Zone (2400m to 4000m)

Another evergreen oak widespread throughout the dry forests two types of leaves, the young ones spiny, while older leaves have smooth edges. In the east, this species is confined to southern slopes, but is heavily cut for fodder and fuel.

The spectacular wet rhododendron forests are interspersed with hemlock and fir. *Rhododendron arboreum*, the national flower, reaches heights of 18m and ranges in colour from red to white. There are more than 30 species of rhododendron in Nepal, but these are found more extensively in the east than the west. Unfortunately, this tree is felled for fuel or turned into charcoal.

There is also a high conifer forest where blue pine is found in pure stands. In the west it occurs with fir and spruce; in the east, firs, hemlocks and yews associate with blue pine. Firewood and roofing shingles are the common uses for these species. A mixed broad-leafed forest of maple and laurel is also typical of this zone.

Subalpine Zone (3000m to 4000m)

Silver fir mixed with oak and birch extend to the tree line in the west. East of the Kali Gandaki, only birch is found to the tree line, though under wetter conditions, dwarf bamboo and shrub rhododendron may replace it. In dry areas, juniper species occur to the tree line.

Alpine Zone (4000m to Snow Line)

In this realm above the tree line, vegetation must cope with extremes in ground temperatures, and moisture gradients that range from nothing in winter to profuse in summer. Only the most tenacious of wild flowers thrive here, generally by being hirsute or having thick underground stems (rhizomes). A successful example is stellara, common above 5500m.

In the trans-Himalaya, vegetation is restricted to the arid-adapted species of the Tibetan Plateau. ∎

Rhododendron *(Rhododendron sp)*

Himalayan birch *(Betula utilis)*

sibia with its constant prattle and ringing song is an integral part of the wet temperate forests. The spiny babbler is Nepal's only endemic species.

There are three pairs of species amongst the crow family; their appearance and behaviour are virtually identical, but each species occupies a different altitudinal range.

The black-capped sibia *(Heterophasia capistrata)* is often seen in oak and rhododendron forests of the temperate zones.

The red-billed blue magpies are residents of the subtropical zone, while the yellow-billed species are found in the temperates. The Indian tree pie prefers the tropics while the Himalayan species lives in the subtropics and temperates. Above the tree line, two species of chough are prevalent, congregating in large flocks in winter. Though they often overlap in range, the yellow-billed chough is found at greater altitudes and is known to enter mountaineers' tents high on Everest. Another of the crow family, also bold and conspicuous in the trans-Himalayan region, is the large raven.

Besides such families as kingfishers, bee-eaters, drongos, minivets, parakeets and sunbirds, there are a host of other passerines, or perching birds, throughout Nepal. These include 30 species of flycatchers and nearly 60 species of thrushes and warblers. Many smaller species congregate in heterogeneous flocks, not only for feeding purposes but also for protection.

In the Kathmandu Valley, sparrows and pigeons demonstrate adaptability to urban centres by their sheer numbers. Dark kites, hawk-like birds with forked tails, are often seen over the city. At sunset, loose groups of crows, mynas, egrets and kites fly to their respective roosts. After dark, the noisy ruckus of spotted owlets substitutes for the cacophony of car horns. The robin dayal, with its cocked tail, is the common songster of early mornings. Pulchowki, Nagarjun and

Shivapuri are excellent areas for finding birds of subtropical and temperate habitats, while the Gokarna Safari Park offers a cross section of species typical of the valley floor.

In the Pokhara region, the Indian roller is conspicuous when it takes flight and flashes the iridescent turquoise on its wings. Otherwise, while perched, it appears as a plain brown bird. Local superstition has it that if someone about to embark on a journey sees a roller going their way, it is a good omen. If they see a crow, however, it is a bad omen and the trip is aborted. Many trips must be destined for delay thanks to the presence of the common crow.

Mammals

As one might expect, due to habitat degeneration from both natural and human causes, opportunities for seeing wildlife are usually restricted to national parks, reserves and western Nepal, where population is sparse. Wildlife numbers have also been thinned due to poaching for pelts or other parts that are considered to be delicacies or medicinally valuable. In addition, animals are hunted because of the damage they inflict on crops and domestic animals.

At the top of the food chain is the royal Bengal tiger, the most magnificent cat, which is solitary and territorial. Males have territorial ranges that encompass those of two or three females and may span as much as 100 sq km. The Royal Chitwan National Park of the Inner Terai and the Royal Bardia National Park in the western Terai protect sufficient habitat to sustain viable breeding populations.

The spotted leopard is an avid tree climber and in general more elusive than the tiger. These nocturnal creatures, like tigers, have been known to become human-eaters when they have grown old or been maimed. Not only are humans easy prey, but once the animals acquire the taste for human flesh, they lose interest in their natural prey. Local people have likened them to evil spirits because of their success at evading hunters.

The snow leopard is often protected from hunters, not only by national parks, but also by inhabiting inhospitable domains above the tree line as well as sensitive border regions. Its territory depends upon the ranges of ungulate herds, its prey species, as well as breeding females. Packs of wolves compete directly and when territories overlap, the solitary snow leopard will be displaced.

The one-horned rhinoceros is the largest of the three Asian species of rhino and is a totally different genus from the two-horned African varieties. It has poor eyesight and, though weighing up to two tonnes, is amazingly quick. Anyone who encounters a mother with its calf is likely to be charged, a disconcerting experience even if you are atop an elephant. The rhino is a denizen of the grasslands of the Inner Terai, specifically the Chitwan Valley, although it has also been reintroduced to the Royal Bardia National Park.

The Asian elephant, like the one-horned rhino, is starkly different from its African relative, belonging to a separate genus. The only wild elephants known to exist in Nepal are in the western part of the Terai and Churia Hills, though individuals often range across the border from India. Elephants are known to maintain matriarchal societies, and females up to 60 years old bear calves. Though elephants are able to reach 80 years of age, their life spans are determined by dentition. Molars are replaced as they wear down, but only up to six times. When the final set is worn, the individual dies of starvation.

Male elephants, and occasionally females, periodically enter a 'musth' condition that makes them excitable and highly aggressive. While in this agitated state they have been known to trample villages. When a herd goes on the rampage outsiders, or non-Hindus, are often summoned as the elephant is considered a holy animal because of the much-loved Ganesh, the elephant-headed god of the Hindu pantheon.

There are several species of deer, but most of them are confined to the lowlands. The spotted deer is probably the most beautiful, while the sambar is the largest. The *muntjak*, or barking deer, which usually makes its presence known by its sharp, one-note alarm

call, is found at elevations up to 2400m, while the unusual musk deer, with antelope-like features and only 50 cm high at the shoulder, ranges even higher.

There are two primates: the rhesus macaque and the common langur. The rhesus is earth-coloured with a short tail and travels on the ground in large, structured troops, unafraid of humans. The langur is arboreal, with a black face, grey fur, and long limbs and tail. Because of Hanuman, the monkey god in the Hindu epic the *Ramayana*, both species are considered holy and are well protected. The rhesus ranges from the Terai up to 2400m, while the langur goes higher, up to 3600m.

At the Swayambhunath and Pashupatinath temples in the Kathmandu Valley, rhesus macaques take advantage of their holy status and relieve worshippers of their picnic lunches and consecrated food.

Two even-toed hoofed mammals are found in the alpine regions. They are the Himalayan tahr, a near-true goat, and the blue sheep, or bharal, which is genetically stranded somewhere between goats and sheep. The male tahr poses majestically in its flowing mane on the grassy slopes of inner valleys, while the blue sheep turns a bluish grey in winter and is found in the trans-Himalayan biotope.

The Himalayan black bear is omnivorous and a bane to corn crops in the temperate forests. Though it rarely attacks humans, its poor eyesight may lead it to interpret a standing person as making a threatening gesture and to attack. If so, the best defence is not to run, but to lie face down on the ground – particularly effective when one is wearing a backpack. Nepal's bears are known to roam in winter instead of hibernating.

There are some prominent canines, though they are fairly shy. The jackal, with its eerie howling that sets village dogs barking at night, ranges from the Terai to alpine regions. It is both a hunter and scavenger, and will take chickens and raid crops.

The pika, or mouse-hare, is the common guinea pig-like mammal of the inner valleys, often seen scurrying nervously between

The loud whistle of the marmot *(Marmota himalayana)* can be heard over a distance of several kilometres.

rocks. The marmot of western Nepal is a large rodent; it commonly dwells in the trans-Himalayan zone. The marmot is also found in Sikkim and Bhutan, but not eastern Nepal; such gaps in speciation are not uncommon across the Himalaya.

Noisy colonies of flying foxes or fruit bats have chosen the trees near the Royal Palace in Kathmandu and the chir pines at the entrance to Bhaktapur as their haunts. They are known to fly great distances at night to raid orchards before returning at dawn. They have adequate eyesight for their feeding habits and do not require the sonar system of insectivorous bats.

Pulchowki, Nagarjun and Shivapuri are good areas for possible sightings of small mammals. The Gokarna Safari Park contains introduced deer species.

Reptiles

There are two indigenous species of crocodile: the gharial and marsh mugger. The gharial inhabits rivers and is a prehistoric-looking fish-eating creature with bulging eyes and a long, narrow snout. The marsh mugger prefers stagnant water and is omnivorous, feeding on anything within reach. Because of the value of its hide and eggs, the gharial was hunted to the brink of extinction, but it has increased in numbers since the establishment of a hatchery and rearing centre in Chitwan. Both crocodiles inhabit the Terai.

Though venomous snakes such as cobras, vipers and kraits are present, the chance of encountering one is small, not only because of their usual evasive tactics, but also because they are indiscriminately slaughtered. The majority of species are found on the Terai, though the mountain pit viper is known higher up, along with a few other nonvenomous species.

GOVERNMENT & POLITICS

The November 1990 constitution established Nepal as a parliamentary democracy with King Birendra Bir Bikram Shah Dev as a constitutional monarch. The parliament is based on the British system of two houses. The lower house consists of representatives directly elected from Nepal's 205 constituencies. Of the 60 members of the upper house, 10 are appointed by the king, 35 are elected by the lower house, and 15 are elected from Nepal's five development zones.

There are 75 districts in Nepal, each with a Chief District Officer (CDO) appointed by the central government. One of the long-term development goals of the government is to establish telephone and road service to each district headquarters, no matter how remote.

Politics in Nepal has always been confrontational. Strikes are often called by the opposition party and demands are made of the government. The general populace seems to be fed up with these leaders and may send more royalist party members to parliament in the next round of elections scheduled to be held sometime late in 1999. On the other hand, the political situation may deteriorate to the extent that the king has to call midterm elections

ECONOMY

Isolation and political pressures have combined to make Nepal one of the poorest and least developed countries. The per capita income is estimated to be about US$170 and the 1994 gross domestic product was US$3.5 billion. More than 90% of the economy is related to agriculture and there is very little industrialisation. Nepal exports carpets, ready-made garments, jute and handicrafts. Tourism is a major source of employment and foreign exchange. Foreign aid plays a large part in Nepal's economy and foreign grants and loans account for 50% of the national budget.

POPULATION & PEOPLE

Nepal's population of more than 21 million is growing at an alarming rate of 2.3% per year. Almost half of the people live in the Terai, and most of the rest are spread throughout the country in small hill villages. The bright lights and perceived opportunities for wealth in the Kathmandu Valley are attracting many village people, and the valley's population has grown to an estimated 1.8 million.

Because you will encounter people living in tiny villages that blanket the hills throughout the country, trekking in Nepal is not a wilderness experience. Even in the high mountains, small settlements of stone houses and yak pastures dot every possible flat space. Much of the fascination of a trek is the opportunity to observe and participate in the life of these villages. People truly live off the land, using only a few manufactured items such as soap, kerosene, paper and matches, all of which are imported in bamboo baskets carried by barefoot porters.

It is difficult for most Westerners to comprehend this aspect of Nepal until they actually visit the kingdom. Our preconception of a roadless area is strongly influenced by the places we backpack or hike to at home – true wilderness, usually protected as a national park or forest. In the roadless areas of Nepal there is little wilderness up to an elevation of 4000m. The average population density in Nepal is more than 142 people per sq km. But much of the country is high mountains and steep hillsides, so the true population density is much higher. It is estimated that only about 12% of the population lives in cities. The size and type of rural settlements vary widely, but most villages have from 15 to 75 houses, a population of 200 to 1000 and cover an area of several sq km.

Rather than detract from the enjoyment of a trek, the hill people, particularly their traditional hospitality and fascinating culture, make a trek in Nepal a special kind of mountain holiday unlike any other in the world.

Anthropologists divide the people of Nepal into about 60 'ethnic groups'. This is a convenient term to encompass the various categories of tribe, clan, caste and race. Each ethnic group has its own culture and traditions. Everyone is proud of their heritage and there is no need for embarrassment when asking someone about their ethnicity (*jaat* or *thar* in Nepali). Often it's not even necessary to ask, as many people use the name of their ethnic group, caste or clan as a surname.

While some groups are found only in specific regions, many groups are spread throughout the country. Nepal has historically been a nation of traders, acting as intermediaries for transactions between India and Tibet, so there is a history of extensive travel and resettlement.

The caste system has many 'occupational castes' and these groups have also spread throughout the country. Potters (Kuhmale), butchers (Kasain), blacksmiths (Kami), tailors (Damai), cobblers (Sarki), goldsmiths (Sunar), clothes washers (Dhobi) and others have travelled throughout Nepal to ply their trade.

Most ethnic groups have their own language; at least 49 mother tongues have been identified. Almost everyone speaks Nepali – the *lingua franca* or trade language of the country – as a second language.

As the hill population has increased, many hill and even Himalayan people have migrated to lower elevations and the Terai in order to improve their lot. The following regional classification is, therefore, a bit artificial, but it does represent the traditional environment of each group.

People Found throughout Nepal

Brahmans The Brahmans (or Bahuns in Nepali) are the traditional Hindu priest caste

Nepali Folk Songs

You are almost certain to hear folk songs in the hills. If you are travelling with sherpas and porters your own crew will probably entertain themselves – and you – with songs and dances to the accompaniment of a two-headed drum called a *madal*. If you are staying in hotels the entertainers may be villagers, a trekking group's porters or the children of the hotel owner.

Most songs consist of an endless series of verses and a chorus. One or two people who know the words to verses usually take the lead and everyone joins in the chorus. Here are two of the most popular songs and a rough translation of the lyrics.

Resham Pheeree Ree

Resham pheeree ree, Resham pheeree ree
Udeyra jaunkee dandaa ma bhanjyang
Resham pheeree ree
My heart is fluttering like silk in the wind
I cannot decide whether to fly or sit on the hilltop

Ek naley bunduk, dui naley bunduk, mriga lai takey ko
Mriga lai mailey takey ko hoeina, maya lai dankey ko
One-barrelled gun, two-barrelled gun? targeted at a deer?
It's not the deer that I am aiming at, but at my beloved

Chorus:
Resham pheeree ree, Resham pheeree ree
Udeyra jaunkee dandaa ma bhanjyang
Resham pheeree ree

Kukur lai kutti kutti, biralo lai suri
Timro hamro maya priti dobato ma kuri
To the dog it's puppy, puppy, to the cat it's meow meow
Our love is waiting at the crossroads

Repeat chorus

Saano ma sano gaiko bachho bhirai ma, Ram Ram
Chodreh jana sakena mailey, baru maya sanghai jaun
The tiny baby calf is in danger at the precipice
I couldn't leave it there, let's go together, my love

Repeat chorus

Kodo charyo, makai charyo, dhan chareko chhaina
Pachi, pachi na au Kanchi, manpareko chaina
Millet is planted, corn is planted, but not the rice
Don't follow me little girl, because I don't like you

Repeat chorus

Paan Ko Paat

Paan ko paat
Maya timi lai samjhanchhu deen ko raat
Marsyangdi sa la la
Beetle leaf
Sweetheart, I keep you in mind for days and nights
Like the flow of the Marsyangdi

Timro hamro bhet bhako deena, bhet bhako deena
Saanglo paani dhamilo mun keena, paan ko paat
On the day we met, the day we met
The water was clear, why then was the heart so murky

Chorus: Paan ko paat
Maya timi lai samjhanchhu deen ko raat
Marsyangdi sa la la
Beetle leaf
Sweetheart, I keep you in mind for days and nights
Like the flow of the Marsyangdi

Maya bhaye auw aggi sarey ra, auw aggi sarey ra
Chhaina maya jau maya marey ra, paan ko paat
If you love me, come forward, come forward
If you don't love me, dismiss it and go

Repeat chorus

Phewa tal ma sanglo chha paani, sanglo chha paani
Yo ramailo chhodera kahan janey, paan ko paat
The water in lake Phewa is clear, the water is clear
Where would you want to go and abandon this delight

and speak Nepali as their first language. They are distributed throughout the country in both the Terai and Middle Hills and traditionally plaster their houses with red earth. Many Brahmans are influential business people, landowners, moneylenders and government workers. They are very conscious of the concept of *jutho*, or ritual pollution, of their home and food. Always ask permission before entering a Brahman house and never enter a Brahman kitchen. Brahmans traditionally do not drink alcohol.

Chhetris The other major Hindu group is the Chhetri caste. In villages Chhetris are farmers, but theirs is the warrior caste. They are known for being outstanding soldiers, and a large part of the Nepal army is made up of Chhetris. Thakuris are a group of Chhetris descended from the Rajputs in India and have the highest social, political and ritual status. The Chhetri clans include the Ranas; the ruling family of Nepal, the Shahs, are Thakuris.

Newars The original inhabitants of the Kathmandu Valley are the Newars. To this day they remain concentrated in the valley in the cities of Kathmandu, Patan, Bhaktapur and Kirtipur and in smaller towns. Newars have a rich cultural heritage and are skilled artisans; a lot of the traditional art of Nepal and Tibet is Newar crafted. There are both Buddhist and Hindu Newars. In the hills you are likely to meet Newars as government officers and merchants.

Musalman Nepal's Muslim population is known as Musalman. They live in the Kathmandu Valley, the eastern Terai and throughout the western hills. They migrated to Nepal from India, predominantly from Kashmir and Ladakh. Musalman are traditionally traders and dominate Kathmandu's trade in handicrafts, souvenirs, shoes and bangles.

Tibetans Tibetans are found mostly at Boudhanath and Jawalakhel in Kathmandu and in the Himalayan border regions. Often called Bhotia, this group includes both recent migrants and Tibetans who settled here long ago. The Sherpas, Dolpo people and other groups were originally from Tibet, but settled in Nepal so long ago that they have built up their own traditions and culture. There are significant Tibetan settlements in the hills at Solu Khumbu, Jumla, Dhorpatan, Dolpo, Hile and Pokhara.

People of the Middle Hills

Tamangs You will encounter Tamangs, one of the most important groups in the hills, on almost every major trek. Tamangs speak a Tibeto-Burman language among themselves and believe they originally came from Tibet. They practise a form of Tibetan Buddhism and there are Buddhist temples in many Tamang villages, though they have no monks, nuns or monasteries. Tamang priests are usually married and participate in regular day-to-day activities. Most Tamangs are farmers and live at slightly higher elevations than their Hindu neighbours, but there is a lot of overlap. Tamang women wear gold decorations in their noses and the men traditionally wear a *bokkhu*, a sleeveless woollen jacket. The rough black-and-white blankets, called *rari*, that you see in homes in the hills and in shops in Kathmandu are a Tamang speciality.

Ta-mang literally means 'horse soldier'. Tamang legend says they migrated to Nepal at the time of Genghis Khan as cavalry troops. Though they are primarily hill people, many Tamangs have moved to Kathmandu, where they are employed as weavers of Tibetan rugs and as painters of high-quality *thangkas*. They also work as rickshaw drivers and porters; the 'sherpa' on your trek is more likely to be Tamang than Sherpa.

Rais Like the Tamangs and Sherpas, Rais speak a Tibeto-Burman language of their own and have a very unusual culture. They practise an indigenous animistic religion that is neither Buddhist nor Hindu, though it has a fair amount of Hindu influence. Rais have

A Rai woman from the hills of eastern Nepal

very characteristic Mongoloid features which make them easy to recognise.

Some Rai villages are extremely large and boast 200 to 300 households. Typically, Rai villages are spread out over the hillside with trails leading in every direction. Finding the right route in these villages is always a challenge. Rais are skilled in using bamboo for many purposes, including construction of houses, baskets, fences and water pipes.

Rai people are very independent and individualistic. The 200,000 or so Rais in the eastern hills speak at least 15 different languages which, although seemingly closely related, are mutually unintelligible. When Rais of different areas meet they must converse in Nepali.

Rais (along with Limbus, Magars and Gurungs) are one of the ethnic groups which supply a large proportion of the recruits for the well-known Gurkha regiments of the British and Indian armies.

An unusual sight, to Western eyes, in regions of Rai influence is the *dhami*, a shaman who is a diviner, spirit medium and medicine man. Occasionally you will see dhamis in villages, but more often you will encounter them on remote trails, dressed in elegant regalia and headdresses of pheasant feathers. The rhythmic sound of the drums that a dhami continually beats while walking echoes throughout the hills. Most Rais live between the Dudh Kosi and Arun rivers. You will meet them on treks to Everest, Makalu and from Khumbu to Hile.

Limbus The Rais and Limbus are known collectively as Kiranti. The Kiranti are the earliest known population of Nepal's eastern hills where they have lived for at least 2000 years. Early Hindu epics such as the *Mahabharata* refer to the warlike Kirantis of the eastern Himalaya. From the 7th century CE (the Common Era or AD), the Arun valley was the site of fierce fighting between Tibetan and Assamese warlords. The Kiranti only joined the Gurkhali kingdom in 1774.

Many Limbus have adopted Subba as a surname and many men serve either in Gurkha regiments or in the Nepal army. Limbus are the inventors of *tongba*, a tasty, but very potent, millet beer that is sipped through a bamboo straw. Their religion is a mixture of Buddhism and shamanism and they have their own dhamis. Most Limbu people live in the region east of the Arun River. You will be in Limbu country during a trek to Kanchenjunga.

Gurungs Gurungs often serve in the Nepal army and the Nepal police, as well as in the Gurkha regiments of both the British and Indian armies. It is not unusual to meet ex-soldiers on the trail who have served in Malaysia, Singapore, Hong Kong and the UK. The stories of their exploits, told in excellent British-accented English, provide fascinating trailside conversation. An important source of income in most Gurung villages is the salaries and pensions of those in military service. The remaining income is from herding, particularly sheep, and agriculture – rice, wheat, corn, millet and potatoes. Access to many high pastures, including the Annapurna Sanctuary, is possible because of trails built by Gurung sheep herders.

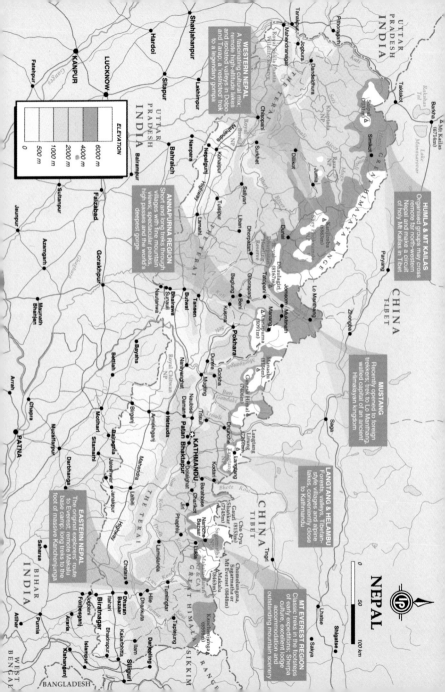

NEPAL

ELEVATION

6000 m
4000 m
2000 m
1000 m
500 m
0

WESTERN NEPAL
A fascinating cultural mix; remote high-altitude lakes and isolated valleys in Dolpo and Tarap; a restricted trek to a legendary gompa

HUMLA & MT KAILAS
Organised groups may cross remote far north-western Nepal en route to holy Mt Kailas in Tibet

ANNAPURNA REGION
Short and long treks through villages; with fine mountain views; spectacular peaks, high passes and the world's deepest gorge

MUSTANG
Recently opened to foreign trekkers; trek to Lo Manthang, walled capital of an ancient Himalayan kingdom

LANGTANG & HELAMBU
Fertile valleys, alpine lakes and villages conveniently close to Kathmandu.

EASTERN NEPAL
The original explorers' route to Everest; remote Makalu base camp; long treks to the foot of massive Kanchenjunga

MT EVEREST REGION
Classic treks in the footsteps of early expeditions; Sherpa culture, excellent lodge accommodation and outstanding mountain scenery

0   50   100 km

RICHARD I'ANSON

STAN ARMINGTON

STAN ARMINGTON

GREG ELMS

STAN ARMINGTON

People of Nepal

Top Left: Limbu   Middle Right: Brahman
Bottom Left: Gurung   Bottom Right: Loba
Top Right: Rai

Gurungs are Mongoloid in feature and trace their ancestry to Tibet. The second storey of Gurung houses is usually whitewashed. Many men still wear the traditional short blouse tied across the front and short skirt of white cotton material, or often a towel, wrapped around their waist and held by a wide belt. In the Ghandruk area near the Annapurna Sanctuary, Gurung men fashion a backpack out of a piece of coarse cotton looped across the shoulders.

The Gurung funeral traditions and dance performances (the latter staged at the slightest excuse) are particularly exotic, and it is often possible to witness such aspects of Gurung life during a trek in Gurung country. You will find Gurungs throughout the Annapurna region as well as at major settlements in the east, including Rumjatar, south of Jiri.

Magars You will find Magars throughout Nepal, generally living south of their Gurung neighbours. Traditionally they are farmers and stonemasons, but many Magars serve as soldiers in Gurkha regiments and in the Nepal army. Magars can be either Hindu or Buddhist. Hindu Magars practise the same religion as the Brahmans and Chhetris and employ Brahmans as priests. Magar women often wear necklaces of Indian silver coins. Magars constitute the largest ethnic group in the country and you will encounter them on most treks in Nepal. They are often integrated into villages dominated by other groups.

Sunwars One of the dominant groups in the region east of Kathmandu, particularly in the villages of Ramechhap, Charikot and Okhaldunga, is the Sunwars. The women wear gold ornaments in their nose and ears and the men often join the Nepal army. They live in whitewashed stone houses with black window frames. They worship their own gods, but often employ Brahmans as priests. You will be in Sunwar country at the start of the trek from Jiri to Everest.

Jirels A small subgroup of the Sunwars who live in and near Jiri are known as Jirels. Unlike the Sunwars, they use Buddhist lamas as their priests.

Thakalis The Thakalis originally came from the Kali Gandaki (Thak Khola) valley, but they have migrated wherever business opportunities have led. They are traditionally excellent business people and hoteliers and have created hotels, inns and other businesses throughout Nepal. Their religion is a mixture of Buddhism, Hinduism and ancient shamanistic and animistic cults, but they claim to be more Hindu than Buddhist. Despite their history of trade with Tibet, the Thakalis are not of Tibetan ancestry. They are related to the Tamangs, Gurungs and Magars.

Himalayan People

Sherpas The most famous of Nepal's ethnic groups is the Sherpas, even though they form only a tiny part of the total population and live in a small and inhospitable region of the kingdom. Sherpas first came to international prominence when the 1921 Mt Everest reconnaissance team hired them. The expedition started from Darjeeling in India and travelled into Tibet. Because many Sherpas lived in Darjeeling, it was not necessary to travel into 'forbidden' Nepal to hire them.

The Sherpa economy has become highly dependent on tourism and many Sherpas have developed Western tastes and values. This Western influence has made wages and other costs higher and non-negotiable in areas of Sherpa influence. It has given Sherpas the reputation among many independent trekkers for being rather grasping and difficult to deal with. You will find, however, that once fees and conditions are agreed to, or a trekking company has done the negotiating for you, Sherpas are reliable, charming and helpful. Sherpa-run hotels have fixed prices and do not entertain bargaining.

Though the most famous Sherpa settlements are in Khumbu, near Everest, Sherpas are found throughout the eastern part of Nepal. There are Sherpa villages all the way from Helambu, north of Kathmandu, to the Indian border. There are also large Sherpa populations in both Darjeeling and Sikkim in India. Most Sherpa villages are at elevations above 2500m or 3000m.

Sherpas frequently name their children after the day of the week on which they were born. Sunday is Nima and the following days are Dawa, Mingma, Lakpa, Phurba, Passang and Pemba. They often add the prefix 'Ang' to the name (similar to the English suffix 'son' or abbreviation 'Jr'). You would call Ang Nima 'Nima' for short, but never 'Ang'.

Manangis Manang, the region north of Annapurna, is the home of the Manangis. A decree by King Rana Bahadur Shah in 1784 gave them special trading privileges, which they continue to enjoy. These privileges originally included passport and import and export concessions not available to the general population of Nepal. Beginning long ago with the export of live dogs, goat and sheepskins, yaks' tails, herbs and musk, the trade expanded into the large-scale import of electronic goods, cameras, watches, silk, clothing, gems and other high-value items in exchange for gold, silver, turquoise and other resources available in Manang.

The trade network of the Manang people extends throughout South-East Asia and as far away as Korea. It is not uncommon to see large groups of. Manang people jetting to Bangkok, Singapore and Hong Kong. Manangis call themselves Nye-shang, but many Manang people adopt the surname Gurung on passports and travel documents even though they are more closely related to Tibetans than to Gurungs.

Dolpo People The isolation of the Dolpo people in the remote region north of Dhaulagiri has made them one of the most undeveloped and traditional groups in the kingdom. They are traders, specialising in the exchange of sheep, yaks and salt between Nepal and Tibet. You will meet them in Dolpo, especially in Do Tarap and Ringmo villages. Dolpo people have a reputation for

staying continuously occupied, particularly with spinning wool by hand as they walk.

Loba The people of Lo live in the fabled and once forbidden region of Mustang. They compete with the Thakalis for trade in salt and wool, and keep yaks, donkeys, mules and herds of sheep. They have close ties with Tibet and travel extensively on horseback. The region was once ruled by the Lo Gyelpo, or raja of Mustang, but since 1952 his position has been only honorary. He has the rank of lieutenant colonel in the Nepal army.

Baragaunle The upper Kali Gandaki valley, including Kagbeni and Muktinath, is the traditional home of the Baragaunle – the people of '12 villages'. They are of Tibetan ancestry and practise a kind of Tibetan Buddhism that has been influenced by ancient animistic and pre-Buddhist Bon-po rituals. The elegantly dressed women you will see near Muktinath are from this group.

People of the Terai

Tharus The largest and probably the oldest group in the Terai is the Tharu. Now mostly peasant farmers, they once lived in small settlements of single-storey thatched longhouses within the jungle, which gained them a reputation for being immune to malaria. They have their own tribal religion based on Hinduism. Tharu women have a special dignity and play an important role in Tharu society. You will meet Tharus in Biratnagar, Nepalgunj and Royal Chitwan National Park.

Dhanwar, Majhi & Darai These three related groups live along the Terai's river valleys and are among the poorest and least educated of Nepal's ethnic groups. Majhi traditionally live by fishing and operate dugout canoe ferries throughout the country.

Other Groups The Satar, Dhangar, Rajbansi, Koche and Tajpuri are other Terai groups. You are not likely to meet these people during a trek.

Nonethnic Groups

Sherpa Guides Since the first expedition to Mt Everest in 1921, Sherpas have been employed on treks and mountaineering expeditions. Their performance at high altitude and their selfless devotion to their jobs impressed members of early expeditions. Later expeditions continued the tradition of hiring Sherpas as high-altitude porters. Most of the hiring was done in Darjeeling or by messages sent through friends and relatives into the Solu Khumbu region of Nepal (where most Sherpas live).

The practice continues to the present day, with trekking organisations hiring Sherpas either as permanent employees or on a per-trek basis. The emphasis shifted from Darjeeling to Kathmandu and to the Solu Khumbu region itself as these areas became accessible to foreigners.

It is confusing to discuss the role of Sherpas on an expedition or a trek because 'sherpa' can refer both to an ethnic group and to a function or job on a trek. Sherpa with a capital 'S' refers to members of that ethnic group, while on a trek or expedition the word sherpa (lower-case 's') usually refers to a trekking guide or mountaineer. Traditionally, sherpas are Sherpas, but there are many exceptions. In this book, 'Sherpa' always refers to a member of that ethnic group. I have also used the words sherpa and guide interchangeably.

Generally a sherpa is reasonably experienced in dealing and communicating with Westerners and can speak some English. The job of sherpa comprises several roles: *sirdar* (trail boss), cook, kitchen boy, guide or high-altitude porter. The head sherpa on a trek or expedition is the sirdar and he is responsible for all purchases and for hiring porters. In the lowlands, a sherpa acts as a trekking guide, asking directions from the locals, as necessary, to find the best trail to a destination. Cooks and kitchen boys can produce amazing trailside meals. The term 'kitchen boy' is used for an assistant cook or kitchen hand, but women and men of all ages can fill the position.

The term 'sherpa' does not imply a high degree of technical mountaineering skill. Although they live close to the high Himalayan peaks, Sherpas used rarely to set foot on those peaks except to cross high passes on trade routes. This changed when the British introduced them to the sport of mountaineering. Many trekking sherpas have served as high-altitude porters on mountaineering expeditions, carrying loads along routes already set up by technically proficient mountaineers. The Nepal Mountaineering Association school in Manang now provides mountaineering training to Nepali guides. If you are looking for experienced mountaineering sherpas, be sure that they have attended this course.

Sherpas are not the only high-altitude climbers. Sambhu Tamang reached the summit of Everest with the Italian expedition in 1973, becoming the first non-Sherpa Nepali to reach the summit of a major Himalayan peak. Numerous other Nepalis of various ethnic groups have now climbed peaks throughout the country.

Porters carry loads, and their job finishes once that load reaches camp. Once the group is in camp, the job of the sherpa begins. A porter may be a member of any ethnic group. Many Rais, Tamangs and Magars spend almost their entire lives on the trails serving as porters. They carry loads, not only for trekkers, but also to bring supplies to remote hill villages. Expeditions use either the term 'high-altitude porter' or 'sherpa' to denote those who carry loads to high camps on the mountain.

Gurkhas Nepalis who enlisted in the British and Indian armies became known as Gurkhas. The name is derived from the ancient town of Gorkha, which was the home of Prithvi Narayan Shah, the founder king of Nepal. The British army applied the name Gurkha to all people in Nepal and coined the name Gurkhali for the Nepali language.

In the old British army there were 10 Gurkha rifle regiments, but when India gained independence in 1947 it took six of the regiments and the UK retained four. The UK still maintains Gurkha recruiting centres at Pokhara and near Jawalakhel in Kathmandu. Most Gurkhas are Rais, Limbus, Gurungs and Magars in roughly equal number, though the Gurkha regiments also accept recruits from other ethnic groups. The Nepali word for Gurkha soldier is *lahure*.

Sahibs Nepali people in the hills tend to call Western (or Japanese) men *sahib* (pronounced like 'sob'). A Western woman is a *memsahib* and a porter is a *coolie*. These terms no longer hold the derogatory implications that they did during the British Raj, though many Nepalis now use the more polite term *bhaaria* (load carrier) to refer to a porter. In a peculiar turnabout, the locals call a lone trekker a 'tourist' and someone with a trekking group a 'member'.

SOCIETY & CONDUCT

Nepal represents a culture far older and in many ways more sophisticated than Western culture, but you are not visiting a museum. Rather, you are visiting a country that is vibrantly alive, where many people live more comfortably and, in many cases, more happily than in the West. The more you listen and observe, the more you will learn and the more people will accept you. If you must try to teach Nepali hill people something, try teaching them English. English is a key to upward mobility for employment in, or the running of, any business that deals with foreigners. This is the one element of Western culture that everyone desires – the English language. Spending your time conversing with a sherpa or porter in English as you stroll the trail together will be a good start towards a lasting friendship.

When trekking you will have a chance to meet and become acquainted with Sherpas and members of other Nepali ethnic groups. The background of these people is completely different from what you are familiar with in the West. Treks are a fascinating cultural experience, but are most rewarding when you make some concessions to the customs and habits of Nepal.

Traditional Culture

As you would expect, the people in the hills are more traditional and conservative than those who live in Kathmandu. Nepal is a very family-oriented society, and the majority of people are basically farmers. Most rural Nepali families are self-sufficient in their food supply, raising all of it themselves and selling any excess in the few places, such as Kathmandu and Pokhara, that do not have a strictly agricultural economy. In return, the villagers buy mostly nonfood items that they cannot raise or produce themselves. These include sugar, soap, cigarettes, tea, salt, cloth and jewellery.

Throughout Nepal this exchange of goods creates a significant amount of traffic between remote villages and larger population and manufacturing centres. In the roadless hill areas, porters transport goods in bamboo baskets that they carry with a tumpline across their foreheads. During the many days they travel, porters either camp alongside the trail and eat food that they have brought from home or purchase food and shelter from homes along the trail or from tea shops, called *bhattis*. Often porters travel in groups and take turns cooking food that they carry themselves. Many of these porters are simply farmers carrying rice and other items they have raised themselves to sell in the market. Once they sell their wares, they will return home carrying goods that they have bought.

Second in importance to the transportation of goods is the flow of people between the colder Himalayan regions and the warmer climates of the Terai. Some of the movement is caused by seasonal migrations, but many people move permanently because of the pressures of increasing population in the hills. People also travel extensively in connection with weddings, funerals, festivals, pilgrimages, school and government or military business.

Several of the hundreds of festivals that occur annually in Nepal require people to visit the homes of their relatives. Of particular importance is the Dasain festival in October, during which time thousands of

Has Trekking Changed Nepal?

Tom Hornbein was a member of the first American Everest Expedition. In his book *Everest, the West Ridge*, which he wrote in 1963, he described life in the hills of Nepal and wondered how change would affect it.

From the beginning we had seen virtually no wilderness. Rice terraces had climbed thousands of feet up hillsides, prayer flags flapped at passes; paths occasionally edged with mani walls crisscrossed the country. For all the size, for all the intransigent power of the ice-encrusted wall to the north, wilderness, as western man defines it, did not exist. Yet there was no impression of nature tamed. It seemed to me that here man lived in continuous harmony with the land, as much and as briefly a part of it as all its other occupants. He used the earth with gratitude, knowing that care was required for continued sustenance. He rotated crops, controlled the cutting of wood, bulwarked his field against erosion. In this peaceful co-existence, man was the invited guest. It was an enviable symbiosis. The expedition surely must have affected this balance: a thousand porters living off the produce of the land, a mixing of peoples, the economic stresses, the physical impact itself. Although we touched each place for only a day and then moved on, I wondered how many such passings could be made before the imprint would become indelible.

In answer to this question of a third of a century ago, Dr David Shlim replied:

We visited the Khumbu last fall. I believe the annual visitor count in Sagarmatha National Park is about 12,000 per year. It was wonderfully clean, and in general flavour unchanged from past visits. One is struck, however, that there are virtually no homes along the trail; every home has been converted to a lodge of some sort. Namche is virtually urban, with stacks of lodges in the heart of the 'city'. Electrification has improved the quality of life through lighting, blenders, microwaves, stoves and telephones. Whether videos represent an improvement is up for grabs. I was struck by a comment made last year by an American consular officer who had gone up to Namche to help with the evacuation of trekkers trapped by last November's big storm. He phoned to say that he was having trouble getting lists of the rescued trekkers down 'because there is only one copy machine in Namche'. Imagine dreaming that comment up in 1963!

My wife and four year old son and I sat at some outside tables at the edge of Khumjung, Ama Dablam massively at our backs, sipping cappuccino and eating fresh baked pizzas from a large electric oven. It was different than sharing boiled potatoes around the hearth of a Sherpa home, but it was hard to say that it was less pleasant.

The Sherpa village way of life is certainly threatened by tourism, but there is a prosperity, compared to other parts of Nepal, that I'm sure the Sherpas appreciate. The bigger threat, in the long run, is not tourists visiting Khumbu, but Sherpas living most of their lives in Kathmandu. Many of the kids don't learn Sherpa language anymore, and can't imagine themselves living full time in Khumbu. This is going to be the ultimate demise of the Sherpa land that we knew. But it certainly is not our right to say that Sherpas can only be mountain guides and grow potatoes.

I guess Khumbu cannot remain an anthropologic reserve for the benefit of future generations of Westerners. However, it feels as if it is making the transition to an Alpine-style mountain environment, with more creature comforts. I believe it can be enjoyed for a long time to come as this style progresses. ∎

people from a wide variety of economic and social backgrounds travel from urban centres to hill villages in a style that befits their standing. Their mode of travel may range from trailside camps, similar to those of porters, to service by an entire household staff. It is certainly rare, but still possible, to see porters carrying a woman in a sedan chair or basket.

Men who were born in hill villages and served in a Gurkha regiment in the British or Indian army return home to their villages on leave or upon retirement. They often have a huge retinue of porters to carry items they have collected during their assignments in Singapore, Hong Kong, Brunei or the UK.

Therefore, a wide variety of modes of travel exists on the trails of Nepal. Whatever their means of travel and whatever their economic status, travellers make a direct contribution to the economy of most villages through which they pass. In some cases, it is through the purchase of food; in others it is the buying of necessary goods or services;

and in yet others it is the hiring of local people to serve as porters for a few days. The inhabitants of villages along major trails have come to expect and depend on this economic contribution – in much the same way as our cafes, roadhouses, motels and petrol stations rely on highway travellers of all sorts to provide their income.

Another phenomenon in the hills is that people come into continual personal contact with others. There are no trail signs, few hotel signs and no maps available locally. So no matter how shy a person may be, travellers must continually ask for directions or help in finding food and other items. They must also ask for information about places to stay, how far it is to the next village etc. Many Westerners seem to have lost this ability, and rely on the isolation of a car to insulate them from strangers. They rarely need to ask directions because of the abundance of road signs and maps. The passing scene becomes merely another picture, framed by a car window.

Because Nepalis are constantly talking and exchanging important information, conversation often develops into long exchanges of pure chitchat or useless information. When trekking, you will hear the most commonly learned English phrases: 'What time is it?', 'What is your name?' and 'Where are you going?'. A traveller may spend an hour or two discussing trail conditions, where they have been, politics, the weather, crop conditions, the price of rice in a neighbouring village, who has just married (and who isn't, but should be), who died recently or hundreds of other topics – all with a complete stranger whom they may never meet again. This is an important part of life in the hills as there are no telephones, newspapers or TVs and few radios. Most news comes from travellers. It certainly is more stimulating to hear first-hand experiences than a radio news broadcast. Once a family has planted the crops for the season, there isn't much to do beyond the day-to-day activities of house cleaning, cooking and taking care of children, until harvest time. Besides their economic importance, travellers offer a valu-

able diversion, a source of information and a glimpse into a new and different world.

Dos & Don'ts

Nepali people are traditionally warm and friendly and treat foreigners with a mixture of curiosity and respect. 'Namaste' ('Hello, how are you?') is a universal greeting, accompanied by placing the hands in a prayerlike position. Most Nepalis speak at least some English, though smiles and gestures work well where language is a barrier.

Always double-check when asking for information or directions. As Nepalis hate to say 'no', they will give you their individual versions whether they know the answer or not. Their intention is not to mislead you; it is only to make you happy that you received an answer. You can often circumvent this problem by asking questions in a way that require a choice of alternatives rather than yes or no answers.

The following section offers some more suggestions and considerations that will make your trek more enriching. You will find many of these suggestions repeated on your trekking permit, in ACAP and national park information, and even on the arrival card that you fill out on the plane before you arrive in Kathmandu. Yet many people still ignore these suggestions. There are many tourists in Nepal, and the people in the hills have seen every kind of cultural faux pas. They will not chastise you if you flaunt your sexuality, bathe naked, litter, refuse to pay for food you have eaten or act disrespectfully in temples. But they will be embarrassed, will talk about you, make fun of you and probably act rudely to you in return.

Visiting a Temple Nepal is a Hindu country, although the Sherpas and most other high mountain people are Buddhists. In Kathmandu, you will be refused entry to a Hindu temple if you are wearing leather shoes or a leather belt. There are other temples such as Pashupatinath in Kathmandu that you will not be allowed to visit at all. Buddhist temples (gompas) are less restrictive, but you should still ask permission to enter and remove your shoes when you do – and leave an offering in the donation box. Definitely ask permission before photographing religious festivals, cremation grounds and the inside of temples.

If you meet the head lama inside a Buddhist gompa it is appropriate to present him with a white silk scarf called a *kata*. It is traditional to include a donation to the gompa inside the folded kata. The lama will remove the money and either keep the kata or place it around your neck as a blessing. Place the kata you are offering on the table or in the hands of the lama; do not place it around his neck. Monetary offerings should be in odd numbers like Rs 101; a donation of an even amount like Rs 100 is inauspicious.

Mani Walls & Chortens Along many trails you will see *mani* walls. These are stones covered with the Tibetan Buddhist inscription *'om mani padme hum'*, usually translated as 'hail to the jewel in the lotus', though its true translation is much more complex and mysterious. In villages in areas of Tibetan influence you will see *chat-dar*, poles decorated with long prayer flags, and *chortens*, stone monuments, in the middle of the trail. You should walk to the left side of all of these as the Buddhists do.

Photographing People During a trek you will have many opportunities to photograph local people. Some people, however, will not want you to photograph them. Always ask before photographing women. There are always cases of shyness that you can overcome with a smile or a joke or by using a telephoto lens, but don't pay people for taking their picture. Some people are afraid that a camera might 'steal their soul', but more often they are concerned about how photographs will eventually be used. Many photographs of hill people in Nepal, especially Sherpas, have been printed in books, magazines and brochures. The Sherpas, in particular the women, are afraid that a photo of them will be reproduced in quantity and eventually burned, thrown away or even used as toilet paper. This is a major reason

that many local people will refuse photographs, and it is a valid fear that should be respected.

Environmental Considerations There are a number of things the visitor can do to prevent pollution and other forms of environmental degradation. (See also the Facts for the Trekker chapter, and 'The ACAP Minimum Impact Code' in the Annapurna chapter.)

- Pick up papers, film wrappers and other junk.
- Use locally made toilets *(charpi)* whenever available, no matter how revolting they might be.
- Burn all your toilet paper and bury your faeces.
- Don't make campfires, as wood is scarce in Nepal.

Dress & Behaviour These are also important considerations for the trekker, and points to observe include the following:

- Nudity is completely unacceptable and brief shorts on either men or women are not appreciated. Men should always wear a shirt.
- Public displays of affection are frowned upon.
- Don't pass out balloons, candy and money to village children as it encourages them to beg. Trekkers are responsible for the continual cries of children for *mithai* (candy), *paisa* (money) and 'boom boom' (balloon). Well-intentioned trekkers thought they were doing a service by passing out pens for use in school, so clever kids now ask for pens.
- Don't tempt people into thievery by leaving cameras, watches and other valuable items around a hotel or trekking camp. Keep all your personal belongings in your hotel room or tent. This also means that you should not leave laundry hanging outside at night.

Food & Etiquette Most Nepalis eat with their hands. They use only their right hand for eating and will expect you to do the same. If you eat with your hand, manners dictate that you wash it before and after eating. A jug of water is always available in restaurants for this purpose. In small tea shops you may not be offered a spoon, but one is often available if you ask.

- Don't touch food or eating utensils that local people will use. Any food that a (non-Hindu) foreigner has touched becomes *jutho* ('polluted') and cannot be eaten by a Hindu. This problem does not apply to Sherpas, however.

- Do not put more food on your plate than you can eat. Once it has been placed on your plate, food is considered polluted.
- Don't throw anything into the fire in any house – Buddhist or Hindu. In most cultures the household gods live in the hearth.
- When you hand something to a Nepali, whether it is food, money or anything else, use your right hand.
- A Nepali person will not step over your feet or legs. If your outstretched legs are across a doorway or path, pull them in when someone wants to pass. Similarly, do not step over the legs of a Nepali.
- The place of honour in a Sherpa home is the seat closest to the fire. Do not sit in this seat unless you are specifically invited to do so.

RELIGION

In Nepal, Hinduism and Buddhism are mingled into a complex blend which is often impossible to separate. The Buddha was actually born in Nepal but the Buddhist religion first arrived in the country around 250 BCE (Before Common Era or BC), introduced, so it is said, by the great Indian Buddhist emperor Ashoka himself. Buddhism later gave way to Hinduism, but from around the 8th century CE, the Tantric form of Buddhism practised in Tibet also began to make its way across the Himalaya into Nepal. Today Buddhism is mainly practised by the people of the high Himalaya, such as the Sherpas, and also by Tibetans who have settled in Nepal. Several ethnic groups, including the Tamangs and Gurungs in the Middle Hills and the Newars in the Kathmandu Valley, practise both Buddhism and Hinduism.

Officially Nepal is a Hindu country, but in practice the religion is a strange blend of Hindu and Tantric Buddhist beliefs. A pantheon of Tantric deities is tagged onto the list of Hindu gods or, in many cases, inextricably blended with them. Thus Avalokitesvara, the prime Bodhisattva of this Buddhist era, becomes Lokesvara, a manifestation of the Hindu god Shiva, and then appears as Machhendranath, one of the most popular gods of the Kathmandu Valley. Is he Hindu or Buddhist? Nobody can tell.

The vast majority of the population is Hindu, and Buddhists make up most of the balance. There are also small groups of Muslims and a few Christians. The Muslims are mainly found close to the border with India, and in the odd isolated village. Some ethnic groups, such as the Tharus and the Rais, have their own form of religion and worship the sun, moon and trees, though their practices still retain many Buddhist and Hindu influences.

Hinduism

India, the Indonesian island of Bali, the Indian Ocean island of Mauritius, and possibly Fiji, are the only places apart from Nepal where Hindus predominate, but Hinduism is the largest religion in Asia in terms of the number of adherents. It is one of the oldest extant religions, with firm roots extending back to before 1000 BCE.

The Indus valley civilisation developed a religion which shows a close relationship to Hinduism in many ways. It developed further on the subcontinent through the combined religious practices of the Dra-

Hinduism's four *Vedas* are said to have emerged from the four mouths of Brahma.

Hindus believe that the ninth incarnation of Vishnu, the preserver, was the Buddha.

The home of Shiva, the destroyer and creator, is Mt Kailas, in Tibet.

vidians and the Aryan invaders who arrived in the north of India around 1500 BCE. Around 1000 BCE, the Vedic scriptures were introduced and gave the first loose framework to the religion.

Hinduism today has a number of holy books, the most important being the four *Vedas*, or 'Divine Knowledge', which are the foundation of Hindu philosophy. The *Upanishads* are contained within the *Vedas* and delve into the metaphysical nature of the universe and soul. The *Mahabharata* is an epic poem describing in over 220,000 lines the battles between the Kauravas and Pandavas. It contains the story of Rama, and it is probable that the most famous Hindu epic, the *Ramayana*, was based on this. The *Bhagavad Gita* is a famous episode of the *Mahabharata* where Krishna relates his philosophies to Arjuna.

Hinduism postulates that we will all go through a series of rebirths, or reincarnations,

that eventually lead to *moksha*, the spiritual salvation which frees one from the cycle of rebirths. With each rebirth you can move closer to or further from eventual moksha; the deciding factor is your *karma*, which is literally a law of cause and effect. Bad actions during your life result in bad karma, which ends in a lower reincarnation. Conversely, if your deeds and actions have been good you will reincarnate on a higher level and be a step closer to eventual freedom from rebirth.

Dharma is the natural law that defines the total social, ethical and spiritual harmony of your life. There are three categories of dharma, the first being the eternal harmony which involves the whole universe. The second category is the dharma that controls castes and the relations between castes. The third dharma is the moral code which an individual should follow.

The Hindu religion has three basic practices. They are *puja* (worship), the cremation of the dead, and the rules and regulations of the caste system. There are four main castes: the Brahman, or priest caste; the Chhetris, or soldiers and governors; the Vaisyas, or tradespeople and farmers; and the Sudras, or menial workers and craftspeople. These basic castes are then subdivided, although this is not taken to the same extent in Nepal as in India. Beneath all the castes are the Harijans, or untouchables, the lowest, casteless class for whom all the most menial and degrading tasks are reserved. Westerners and other non-Hindus are outside the caste system and, being therefore unclean, are not allowed to enter many Hindu temples. Any food that is touched by a Westerner, or put on their plate, becomes 'polluted' and must be discarded.

Westerners have trouble understanding Hinduism principally because of its vast pantheon of gods. In fact you can look upon all these different gods simply as pictorial representations of the many attributes of a god. The one omnipresent god usually has three physical representations. Brahma is the creator, Vishnu is the preserver and Shiva is the destroyer and reproducer. All three gods are usually shown with four arms, but Brahma has the added advantage of four heads.

Each god has an associated animal known as the 'vehicle' on which they ride, as well

Gurus & Sadhus

A guru is not so much a teacher as a spiritual guide, somebody who by example or simply by their presence indicates what path you should follow. In a spiritual search one always needs a guru. A sadhu is an individual on a spiritual search. They're an easily recognised group, usually wandering around half-naked, smeared in dust with their hair and beard matted. Sadhus most often follow Shiva and generally carry his symbol, the trident or *trisul*.

Sadhus are often people who have decided that their business and family life have reached their natural conclusions and that it is time to throw everything aside and go out on a spiritual search. They may previously have been the village postal worker, or a businessperson. Sadhus perform various feats of self-mutilation, and wander all over the subcontinent, occasionally coming together in great pilgrimages and other religious gatherings. Important pilgrimage sites for sadhus are Pashupatinath in Kathmandu, and the sacred sites of Gosainkund and Muktinath. Many sadhus are, of course, simply beggars following a more sophisticated approach to gathering in the paisa, but others are completely genuine in their search. ■

as a consort with certain attributes and abilities. Generally each god also holds symbols; you can often pick out which god is represented by the vehicle or symbols. Most temples are dedicated to one or other of the gods, but most Hindus profess to be either Vaishnavites (followers of Vishnu) or Shaivites (followers of Shiva). A variety of lesser gods and goddesses also crowd the scene. The cow is, of course, the holy animal of Hinduism.

Hinduism is not a proselytising religion since you cannot be converted. You're either born a Hindu or you are not; you can never become one. Similarly, once you are a Hindu you cannot change your caste – you're born into it and are stuck with it for the rest of that lifetime. Nevertheless Hinduism has a great attraction for many Westerners, and India's 'export gurus' are numerous and successful. Because proselytising and conversion are not part of Hindu tradition, Nepali law prohibits these practices, so Nepal has been spared the influence of missionaries and evangelists.

Buddhism

Strictly speaking, Buddhism is not a religion, since it is not centred on a god, but a system of philosophy and a code of morality. Buddhism was founded in northern India about 500 BCE when Siddhartha Gautama, born a prince, achieved enlightenment. Gautama Buddha was not the first Buddha but the fourth, and is not expected to be the last 'enlightened one'. Buddhists believe that the achievement of enlightenment is the goal of every being so eventually we will all reach Buddhahood.

The Buddha never wrote down his dharma or teachings, and a schism later developed so that today there are two major Buddhist schools. The Theravada or Hinayana, 'doctrine of the elders' or 'small vehicle', holds that the path to nirvana, the eventual aim of all Buddhists, is an individual pursuit. In contrast, the Mahayana, or 'large vehicle', school holds that the combined belief of its followers will eventually be great enough to encompass all of humanity and bear it to

salvation. To some, the less austere and ascetic Mahayana school is a 'soft option'. Today it is chiefly practised in Vietnam, Japan and China, while the Hinayana school is followed in Sri Lanka, Burma (Myanmar) and Thailand, and by the Buddhist Newars in the Kathmandu Valley. There are other, sometimes more esoteric, divisions of Buddhism, including the Tantric Buddhism of Tibet, which is the version found in the Himalayan regions of Nepal. Tibetan Buddhism was influenced by the ancient animistic Bon-po tradition, and there are a few pockets of Bon-po remaining in Nepal, especially in Dolpo.

The Buddha renounced his material life to search for enlightenment but, unlike other prophets, found that starvation did not lead to discovery. Therefore he developed his rule of the 'middle way' – moderation in everything. The Buddha taught that all life is suffering, but that suffering comes from our sensual desires and the illusion that they are important. By following the 'eightfold path' these desires will be extinguished and a state of nirvana, where they are extinct and we are free from their delusions, will be reached. Following this process requires going through a series of rebirths until the goal is eventually reached and no more rebirths into the world of suffering are necessary. The path that takes you through this cycle of births is karma, but this is not simply fate. Karma is a law of cause and effect; your actions in one life determine the role you will play and what you will have to go through in your next life.

In India Buddhism developed rapidly when it was embraced by the great emperor Ashoka. As his empire extended over much of the subcontinent, so Buddhism was carried forth. Later, however, Buddhism began to contract in India because it had never really taken a hold on the great mass of people. As Hinduism revived, Buddhism in India was gradually reabsorbed into the older religion.

Buddhism is more tolerant of outsiders than is Hinduism; you will be welcome at most Buddhist temples and ceremonies. In

Important Figures of Tibetan Buddhism

The following is a brief guide to some of the gods and goddesses of the Tibetan Buddhist pantheon. It is neither exhaustive nor scholarly, but it may help you to recognise a few of the statues you encounter in gompas during a trek.

Padmasambhava – the 'lotus-born' Buddha – assisted in establishing Buddhism in Tibet in the 8th century. He is regarded by followers of Nyingmapa Buddhism as the second Buddha. He is also known as Guru Rimpoche.

Avalokitesvara – 'glorious gentle one' – one of the three great saviours or Bodhisattvas. He is the Bodhisattva of compassion and is often pictured with 11 heads and several pairs of arms. His Tibetan name is Chenresig and the Sherpas call him Pawa Cherenzig.

Manjushree – the 'princely lord of wisdom' – is regarded as the first divine teacher of Buddhist doctrine. He is also known as Jambyang. Manjushree is said to have made the cleft in the mountains that drained the lake that once flooded the Kathmandu Valley.

Vajrapani – 'thunderbolt in hand' – is one of the three great saviours or Bodhisattvas. He is also known as Channadorje. The thunderbolt represents power and is a fundamental symbol of Tantric faith; it is called a *dorje* in Tibetan and *vajra* in Sanskrit.

Sakyamuni – the 'historical Buddha' – born in Lumbini in southern Nepal in the 5th century BCE, he attained enlightenment under a pipal (Bo) tree and his teachings set in motion the Buddhist faith. In Tibetan-style representations he is always pictured sitting cross-legged on a lotus-flower throne.

Milarepa – was a great Tibetan magician and poet who is believed to have attained the supreme enlightenment of Buddhahood in the course of one life. He lived in the 11th century and travelled extensively throughout the Himalayan border lands, including Kailas, Shey Gompa, Nupri and Nelam near Kodari on the road from Kathmandu to Lhasa. Most images of Milarepa picture him smiling, holding his hand to his ear as he sings.

Maitreya – the 'Buddha of the future'. He is passing the life of a Bodhisattva and will return to earth in human form 4000 years after the disappearance of Buddha (Sakyamuni).

Tara – 'the saviouress' – has 21 different manifestations or aspects. She symbolises fertility and is believed to be able to fulfil wishes. Statues of Tara usually represent Green Tara, who is associated with night, or White Tara, who is associated with day. You can recognise statues of White Tara because she has seven eyes, including one on her forehead, each palm and the sole of each foot. ■

Kathmandu and in the hills there are Buddhist monasteries that are willing to provide spiritual training and advice to Westerners.

Buddhism prohibits any form of killing, a contrast to Hinduism in which some forms of the religion require animal sacrifices to appease the goddess Kali.

FESTIVALS

It is said that there are more festivals in Nepal than there are days in the year. Most Nepali festivals are celebrated in homes and there is often little to see or photograph. Festivals complicate treks, however, because government offices close, so you cannot get a trekking permit, and porters disappear home, occasionally leaving you at the side of the trail with your baggage.

Festivals are scheduled in accordance with the Nepali calendar and the phase of the moon, so they can vary over a period of almost a month with respect to the Gregorian (Western) calendar. Nepali months overlap Western months. The annual festival cycle through the Nepali year is:

Baisakh – April to May

Naya Barsa & Bisket Jatra The Nepali New Year always falls in mid-April. The people of Bhaktapur celebrate the Bisket Jatra (Death of the Snake Demons Festival) on this day. Two chariots are drawn pell-mell through the narrow alleyways of the town and a mighty tug of war ensues. The winners draw the chariots to their locale. A huge lingam pole is erected in the middle of the town by drunken revellers.

Mata Tirtha Aunsi Mother's Day is the day when children offer gifts, money and sweets to their mother and literally look at their mother's face. Those whose mother is dead make a ritual pilgrimage to Mata Tirtha Aunsi near Thankot.

Rato Machhendranath Jatra The Red (Rato) Machhendra festival, also known as Bhota Jatra or the Festival of the Vest, is held annually in Patan just before the monsoon on a date decided by astrologers. Both Hindus and Buddhists celebrate the festival. The idol of Machhendra is brought from Bungmati village to Pulchowk and paraded on a huge, tottering chariot through the alleys of Patan to Jawalakhel. On an auspicious day, the king and queen of Nepal, along with top government officials and thousands of devotees, descend upon Jawalakhel to catch a glimpse of the jewel-encrusted *bhoto* (vest) that Machhendra has been safeguarding for centuries.

Buddha Jayanti The main festival celebrating the full moon of Buddha's birth is held in Lumbini, the birthplace of Buddha. Similar festivals are held at Swayambhunath and Boudhanath. Processions carry the Buddha's image and all through the night, glowing butter lamps and blazing electric lights celebrate Buddha's birth.

Shrawan – July to August

Ghanta Karna or Ghatemangal On the Night of the Witch, street urchins set up barricades all over the city and solicit donations from motorists, cyclists and even pedestrians. A mock funeral procession is held later in the day, followed by a feast. Effigies of the devil, made of bamboo poles and leaves, are erected on every crossroads of the city.

Nag Panchami On the Day of the Snake God, Brahman priests are hired by all households to cleanse their houses by pasting a picture of the *naga* (snake) over their doorways. Pujas are performed and offerings of milk and honey are left for the snake gods. The nagas are pacified through prayers and their protection and blessings are sought.

Gokarna Aunsi Father's Day is similar to Mother's Day. People offer sweets, money and gifts to their fathers and look at their father's face. Those without fathers go to the Bagmati River at Gokarna to bathe and have their father's soul blessed.

Janai Purnima The Festival of the Sacred Thread is also known as Raksha Bhandhan and is celebrated on the full moon day of August. Higher caste Hindu men change the sacred thread they wear around their chests. In the hills of Nepal, devotees descend upon Shiva temples with a *jhankri* (medicine man) leading the throngs from each village.

Gai Jatra During the Festival of the Sacred Cows, children and adults dressed as cows pass through the city streets to honour the souls of their relatives who have recently died. It is also the day on which newspapers are legally allowed to defame and slander any and all persons.

Bhadra – August to September
Krishna Jayanti Krishna's birthday is celebrated with a huge festival at the stone temple of Krishna in Patan Durbar Square. Hymns and religious songs are sung all night by devotees. The king and queen of Nepal pay their respects to Krishna at the Krishna Mandir.

Teej Brata On the day of fasting for wives, all Nepali wives fast from sunup to midnight to ensure that their husbands have good fortune and a long life. Heavily bejewelled women wearing red saris descend upon Pashupatinath to dance and sing the day away. Colourfully attired hill women trek down to Kathmandu for this festival.

Indra Jatra The Festival of the King of Gods is an eight day festival at Kathmandu Durbar Square. The purpose of the festival is to ask Indra for postmonsoon showers for the harvest of the rice crop. This is the day the Living Goddess, or Kumari, of Kathmandu presides over a colourful ceremony attended by the king and queen, government officials and foreign diplomats.

Kartik – October to November
Dasain (Durga Puja) The 10 day festival of Dasain, celebrating Durga's triumph over evil, is the biggest festival in Nepal. All creeds and castes participate. People visit their families all over the country to rejoice over the goddess Durga's triumph. Banks and government offices are closed and most of the country comes to a standstill for the duration of this festival. It is difficult to start a trek during Dasain because buses and planes are jammed and porters are totally unavailable.

Tihar (Diwali) The 'festival of lights' is the second-most important festival in Nepal. During it people pay homage to Laxmi, the goddess of wealth. Houses are given new coats of paint, hundreds of oil lamps and candles are lit, firecrackers are recklessly tossed into the streets and most households are packed with men gambling the night away. The goddess blesses gamblers who have made her happy.

Poush – December to January
Seto Machhendranath Snan Kathmandu's version of Patan's Rato (Red) Machhendra is the Seto (White) Machhendra. The chariot of Machhendra is built on Durbar Marg and dragged to Ratna Park. On the day deemed auspicious by astrologers, the Living Goddess presides over a function where Machhendra is bathed by priests.

Magh – January to February
Maghey Sankranti The first day of the Nepali month of Magh, marking the end of winter, is an important festival all over the country. The Sankhamul Ghat in Patan is alive with devotees taking ritual baths in the Bagmati River, even though this is one of the coldest days of the year!

Falgun – February to March
Losar A two week festival of drunken revelry commemorates the Tibetan New Year in February. Though it's strictly a Buddhist affair, Hindus (such as Tamangs) who believe in both religions also participate. The Sherpas are likely to be in a drunken stupor for two weeks, so treks tend to be difficult to arrange at this time.

Shiva Ratri On the sacred night dedicated to Shiva, thousands of pilgrims descend upon Pashupatinath, the holiest Hindu temple in the world – the abode of Shiva. Bonfires burn throughout the night to seek Shiva's blessings. All wood that is not nailed down is stolen by urchins who then spend all night basking in the glow of Shiva's glorious bonfires.

Holi Nepal's water-throwing festival is a merry affair during which people douse each other with buckets of scarlet liquid and daub red powder on their faces. The youngsters nowadays use acrylic paint and sewer water to enjoy themselves. Hashish cakes and *bhaang* (a cannabis-flavoured drink) are legally sold on this day.

Chaitra – March to April
Ghora Jatra The Nepal army takes over the Tundikhel parade ground in Kathmandu on horse racing day to display its skills in warfare, acrobatics, motorcycle stunts and horse racing. Legend has it that the horses are raced to trample devils who may rise out of the ground to create havoc.

Balaju Jatra Thousands of pilgrims keep an all-night vigil at the Swayambhunath Temple. The following day they trek to the 22 waterspouts at Balaju for a ritual bath.

LANGUAGE
Nepali is the working tongue of Nepal and is understood by almost everyone in the country. Newars, Tamangs, Gurungs, Rais, Sherpas and many other ethnic groups have their own language which they speak among themselves, but they use Nepali outside their own region. Nepali is the first language of the Brahmans, Chhetris and Thakuris – the highest castes in Nepal. It belongs to the Indo-Aryan family of languages, derived from Sanskrit. Its nearest relative today is Kumaoni, spoken in a region of north-west India. Nepali has much in common with Hindi, the official language of India, which has the same origins. It has also taken many words from Persian, through Hindi.

It's not difficult to learn a bit of the language, and it can add greatly to your enjoyment of trekking. Nepalis aren't fussy about the language and will appreciate an effort to learn it. You'll find a little Nepali can go a long way.

Since Nepali, like Hindi, uses the Devanagari script, for English-speakers it must be transliterated into Roman script. There are many systems of transliteration, but the one used here is from Meerendonk's *Basic Gurkhali* dictionary. To make it easier to see the difference in pronunciation, I have used 'aa' where he uses 'a'.

Lonely Planet's *Nepali phrasebook* also gives a handy introduction to the language.

Pronunciation
a	as in	*up*
aa	as in	f*a*ther
e	as in	caf*e*
i	as in	r*i*m
o	as in	g*o*
u	as in	f*u*ll
ai	as in	*ai*sle

A big key to the correct pronunciation of Nepali is the 'a' and 'aa' sound. The sound represented here by a single 'a' is like the 'u' sound in 'up' and the sound of 'aa' is a true 'a' sound as in 'car' or 'far'. For example, *chhang* is pronounced to rhyme with 'bung' or 'rung', not with 'clang' or 'bang'.

Another difficulty is the 'h' sound, which almost vanishes in Nepali pronunciation, particularly when it follows a consonant. Ask a Nepali to pronounce *dhungaa* (stone) and *dungaa* (boat); they will probably sound the same to you, as will *ghari* (wristwatch) and *gaari* (automobile). To a Westerner, *mahango* (expensive) sounds like 'mungo', but a Nepali includes (and hears) the 'h' sound. In the transliteration used here, 'ch' is pronounced as in the English 'chin', while 'chh' sounds like a combination of 'ch' plus 'h'. The letter 'r' is rolled and is pronounced almost like 'dr'; some transliteration systems replace the 'r' with a 'd' or combine them as 'dr'.

Why isn't the language written as it sounds? Each of these sounds is a different letter or character in the Devanagari script used to write Nepali, and in Nepali they are

RICHARD I'ANSON

STAN ARMINGTON

Festivals & Religion
Top: Monks prepare for the Mani Rimdu festival in Tengpoche.
Bottom: Ritual dances during Mani Rimdu, for which the monks don elaborate costumes, dramatise the triumph of Buddhism over the ancient animistic religion of Tibet.

GLENN BEANLAND

RICHARD I'ANSON

TONY WHEELER

Village Life
Top: Small village near Pokhara
Middle: Magar home in Sikha
Bottom: Small village in the Annapurna region

distinct letters and sounds – even if they sound the same to Westerners. Nepali has more vowels than English, so English letters must be combined to represent these sounds.

In Nepali, the verb is placed at the end of a sentence. Grammatically, questions are identical to statements. The differentiation is made by the intonation pattern of the voice. For example, *thik chha?* (with a rising tone) means 'Are you OK?', while *thik chha!* answers 'Yes, I'm OK!'.

Greetings & Civilities

Hello/Goodbye.	*namaste*
Thank you.	*dhanyabaad* (not commonly used)
Where are you going?	*tapain kahan jaane?*
What is your name?	*tapainko naam ke ho?*
My name is ...	*mero naam ... ho*
How are you?	*tapailai kasto chha?*
I am well.	*sanchai chha*
What is this?	*yo ke ho?*
It is cold today.	*aaja jaaro chha*
It is raining.	*paani parchha*
That's OK.	*thik chha*
I know.	*thaahaa chha*
I don't know.	*thaahaa chhaina*

Trekking Words & Phrases

house	*ghar*
latrine	*charpi*
left	*baayaan*
right	*daahine*
shop	*pasal*
steep uphill	*ukaalo*
steep downhill	*oraalo*
straight ahead	*sidha*
tired	*thaakyo*
cold (weather)	*jaaro*
warm (weather)	*garam*

This river is cold.
   yo kholaa chiso chha
Which trail goes to ...?
   kun baato ... jaanchha?
Is the trail steep?
   baato ukaalo chha?
Where is my tent?
   mero tent kahaan chha?

What is the name of this village?
   yo gaaunko naam ke ho?
Where is a shop?
   pasal kahaan chha?
How many hours to Namche Bazaar?
   Namche Bazaar kati gantaa laagchha?

Food Words & Phrases

beer (local)	*chhang/jaanr*
bread	*roti*
cabbage	*banda kobi*
cauliflower	*kauli or phul kobi*
chicken (meat)	*kukhoroko maasu*
chilli	*khorsaani*
corn	*makai*
egg	*phul*
food	*khaanaa*
hot	*taato*
hot (spicy)	*piro*
lentils	*daal or kodo*
local inn	*bhatti*
meat	*maasu*
mustard	*tori*
potatoes	*aalu*
radish	*mula*
rice (cooked); also food in general	*bhaat*
soybeans	*baatamaas*
tasty	*mitho*
tea	*chiyaa*
turnips	*gyante mula*
spinach; also vegetable in general	*saag*
cooked vegetable	*tarkaari*
water	*paani*
hot water	*taato paani*
cold water	*chiso paani*
boiled water	*umaleko paani*
whisky (local)	*rakshi*
yams	*sutaani*

Please give me a cup of tea.
   ek cup chiyaa dinuhos
Do you have food (rice) now?
   aile bhaat chha?
It is enough.
   pugchha
Is the food good?
   khaana mitho chha?

Other Useful Words

big	*thulo*
cheap	*sasto*
clean	*saaph or saphaa*
dirty	*mailo*
enough	*pugyo*
expensive	*mahango*
good	*ramro*
not good	*naraamro*
happy	*khushi*
heavy	*gahrungo*
here	*yahaan*
his, hers	*unko*
maybe	*hola*
mine	*mero*
no (it is not ...)	*hoina*
small	*sano*
this	*yo*
that	*tyo*
there	*tyahaan*
where	*kahaan*
which	*kun*
yes (it is ...)	*ho*
yours	*timro*

Family

mother	*aamaa*
father	*baabu*
son	*chhoro*
daughter	*chhori*
elder brother	*daai*
younger brother	*bhaai*
elder sister	*didi*
younger sister	*bahini*
friend	*saathi*

Animals & Crops

bird	*charo*
chicken	*kukhoro*
cow	*gaai*
dog	*kukur*
horse	*ghoraa*
pig	*sungur*
water buffalo	*bhainsi*
male yak	*yak*
female yak	*nak*

barley	*jau*
buckwheat	*paapad*
millet	*kodo*

field rice	*dhaan*
husked rice	*chaamal*
tobacco	*surti*
wheat	*gahun*

Places

alpine pasture	*kharka*
alpine hut	*goth*
hills	*lek*
hill/mountain	*daanda*
snowy mountains	*himal*
trail	*baato*
mountain pass:	
Nepali	*bhanjyang*
Tibetan	*la*
western Nepal	*laagna*
the plains	*terai*
landing place, ferry	*ghat*
river	*kholaa*
major river	*kosi*
small stream	*naalaa*
stream (in Hindi)	*nadi*
lake	*kund, pokhari, taal*
village	*gaon*
resting place	*chautaara*
Buddhist monument	*chorten*
arch-shaped chorten	*kani*
Tibetan Buddhist temple	*gompa*
Hindu temple	*mandir*
wall or stone carved with prayers	*maani*

Time & Dates

day	*din*
morning	*bihaana*
night	*raat*
today	*aaja*
yesterday	*hijo*
tomorrow	*bholi*
day after tomorrow	*parsi*
sometime	*bholi-parsi*

What time is it (now)?
  (aile) kati bajyo?
Five o'clock.
  paanch bajyo

Numbers

1	*ek*	16	*sohra*
2	*dui*	17	*satra*
3	*tin*	18	*athaara*
4	*chaar*	19	*unnaais*
5	*paanch*	20	*bis*
6	*chha* (some say *chhe*)	25	*pachchis*
7	*saat*	30	*tis*
8	*aath*	40	*chaalis*
9	*nau*	50	*pachaas*
10	*das*	60	*saathi*
11	*eghaara*	70	*sattari*
12	*baahra*	80	*ashi*
13	*tehra*	90	*nabbe*
14	*chaudha*	100	*ek say*
15	*pandhra*	1000	*ek hajaar*
		100,000	*ek lakh*

Nepalese numerals

१ २ ३ ४ ५
1 2 3 4 5

६ ७ ८ ९ १०
6 7 8 9 10

Facts for the Trekker

General Information

PLANNING

There are a tremendous number of factors that can influence your plans for a trek in Nepal. Most trekkers come in the autumn; springtime is the second-most popular season. About 60% of the trekkers use local facilities and the rest book their trek in advance. The costs of a trek can vary from less than $5 a day to more than $200 a day depending on the destination and style of trek that you choose. Though you can rent or buy trekking gear in Nepal, most trekkers bring their equipment with them from home. The two simplest ways to organise a trek are either to call an adventure travel company and put yourself into its hands, or merely to fly to Kathmandu, pick up a permit and start walking. This chapter should help you handle either of those alternatives and all the other options in between.

WHEN TO TREK

The traditional trekking season in Nepal is from October to May, with October and November generally recognised as having the best weather for trekking. There are two major factors to weigh as you decide when to trek: crowds and weather. As a general rule, the better the weather, the more people come to Nepal to go trekking. It's the high tourist season during the time of best weather in the autumn. At this time flights and hotels are fully booked, and hotels and trails in the hills can be horrendously busy.

During autumn the nights are cold in the mountains, but the bright sun makes for pleasant daytime temperatures – in the high 20s°C, falling to 5°C at night, between 1000m and 3500m. At higher altitudes tem-

---

Leeches

Leeches are more of an annoyance than a health hazard, but they do make a mess and leave an uncomfortable itching wound once they have drunk their fill of your blood. During the monsoon, leeches are everywhere, hanging from twigs and leaves and trying to find a warm body to attach to. They thrive at elevations between 1500m and about 3500m and vanish surprisingly quickly as soon as the monsoon stops. They also can appear equally quickly in the spring after a spell of several days of rain. If you trek on a major trekking route during the normal trekking season from October to May, you will probably not encounter a leech.

Leeches usually stay close to the ground and gain entry to your body over the top, or through the eyelets, of your boots. Once inside, they can easily bore through the fabric of your socks. You often do not notice them until your shoes start squishing with bloated leeches and blood-soaked socks. Be especially careful if you make a toilet stop in the bushes during leech season.

Leeches secrete a novocaine-like substance so that you do not notice when they poke a hole in you. They then fill themselves with blood and, once satiated, drop off to digest their dinner.

There are numerous folk remedies for leeches, all designed to prevent them from attaching themselves to you. Salt, lemon juice, mosquito repellent and kerosene may all be rubbed into the ankles or socks. Whether the mess that these repellents cause is worse than the occasional leech is open to question. If a leech has just arrived on your shoe, it is often possible to just flick it off with your finger or, if you are squeamish, a stick. Once a leech has attached itself to you it may be pulled off, or made to drop off by torturing it with a pinch of salt or a small flame or burning cigarette. Leeches are not like ticks; they do not leave any part of themselves behind, so it is perfectly safe to simply pull them off. Local folklore says that if you rub your feet with ashes from the fire, it will prevent leeches. There is a herbal leech repellent made in Nepal that works surprisingly well. There's also a Gurung solution – a small bag of salt tied to the end of a short stick. You wet the bag and tap it on a leech when it attaches itself to your shoe and it's supposed to drop off. ■

Trekking in the Monsoon

Because of the monsoon, the recognised trekking season in Nepal is October through May. A monsoon trek is still possible, and can be rewarding if you're ready to put up with a few problems. The monsoon is not a continual downpour. Most of the rain falls after sunset, and it often rains hard throughout the night. This makes living in a tent fairly miserable, so unless you're trekking in the Himalayan rain shadow, you should plan on staying in lodges if you undertake a monsoon trek. During the day there are often long periods without rain, and the sun filtering through the clouds gives a striking Gauguin lighting effect to the bright green of the rice terraces and surrounding valleys. Trails are wet and slippery, but they often dry out during the day.

There's a tremendous amount of water both in the streams and running down the trails. Giant waterfalls shoot off the hillsides. You will have to put up with muddy and wet shoes, and should bring along enough socks to change them a few times a day. Leeches are a problem above 1500 metres, but there are numerous home-grown remedies to combat them (see the boxed aside on page 52 for more about leeches). You probably won't see the mountains, but if they do appear, it will be magical, with clouds surrounding peaks that are draped in snow.

You'll have your choice of lodges, but nobody bakes apple pie in the monsoon season. It will be hot in the lowlands, and the humidity will keep you sweating. You'll need to drink lots of water, so bring a water bottle and iodine for water purification. You may have to wade some streams, and a landslide or serious flood is always a possibility. These problems may force you to change your route, but such problems happen during the normal trekking season as well. Flights operate to Lukla, Jomsom and other hill airstrips during the monsoon, though they are even less regular than in the autumn season, if such a thing is possible. Be sure that you have a few extra days in case of severe flooding, landslides, washed-out roads or torrential rain.

If you get into the rain shadow in places like Manang, Mustang and Humla, things will be drier, but there will still be clouds and drizzles during the day, and possibly rain at night. The snow line is very high; even Thorung La is free of snow in the summer. You can camp near meadows at 5000m in a panorama of alpine flowers. ■

peratures range from about 20°C down to -10°C. Mornings are usually clear, and clouds build up during the afternoon, disappearing at night to reveal spectacular starry skies. During winter it is about 10 degrees colder.

Early December usually has a lull in tourist arrivals and is a good time for trekking. The Christmas period is cold, but this is the holiday season. Japanese and Australians arrive in droves and fill up flights and hotels through to the end of January. High passes, especially Thorung La on the Around Annapurna trek, Ganja La in Langtang and Laurebina Pass on the Gosainkund trek are usually closed from late November to March. February is still cold, though less so as the spring trekking season of March and April approaches. The Middle Hills, especially around Pokhara, are full of dust and haze in April and May, but the high country is usually clear. Trekking tapers off in the heat of May except at high elevations.

The monsoon season from June to September is a good time to visit Kathmandu, but there are few trekkers among those who come. A monsoon trek is possible if you are willing to put up with the rain, leeches, slippery trails and lousy mountain views. Flights operate throughout the monsoon to Lukla, Jumla and Jomsom, so it is possible to fly in and trek above the 'leech line'.

Many of the new treks to recently opened restricted areas are good summer options. Mustang, Simikot and Dolpo are in the Himalayan rain shadow, so trekking conditions are good throughout the monsoon season. Most of the restricted-area treks are snowbound during the winter.

SUGGESTED ITINERARIES

In this book many treks are described in detail and there are numerous suggestions for side trips, short cuts and extensions. The table on pages 98-9 outlines the major factors that you might weigh as you choose a trek: length, difficulty, elevation, cost, season and facilities along the way. The classic Everest and Annapurna treks are spectacular and worth doing, but for the 'real Nepal' you need to get into some of the more remote regions where tourist facilities don't exist.

STYLE OF TRIP

A trek in Nepal may be a camping trip or else rely on the local accommodation that is available in the hills; see Types of Trek later in this chapter for details. In some areas, either because of government regulation or lack of facilities, only camping treks are possible. In other areas, your choice will depend on how much you are prepared to spend, on how confident you are walking in remote regions, and on how much comfort you desire. You should not trek alone. Unless you have a friend to trek with, or are prepared to take a chance on finding a companion in Kathmandu, booking a group trek may be a good option. There is no 'best' way to trek, and whichever style you choose will provide you with cultural insight, a good physical workout and spectacular mountain views.

If you do not already have a travelling companion, then you should find one in Kathmandu. You can hire a guide, look on bulletin boards, check with the office of the Kathmandu Environmental Education Project (KEEP; see Information Sources later in this chapter for details), or just chat with someone who sits next to you in a restaurant and decide to travel together. Many times it's useful to have someone to watch your pack – when you have to run off the trail into the bushes, or even when you are in a lodge and go out to the toilet. It's also good to have someone around in case you injure yourself or fall sick while walking. The few recent incidents of violent crime have all been directed at trekkers travelling alone; a companion could help convince a would-be thief to direct his attention elsewhere.

MAPS

The best series of maps of Nepal is the 1:50,000 series produced by Erwin Schnei-der for Research Scheme Nepal Himalaya and originally printed in Vienna. Most sheets are in their 3rd edition (1987) and are now published by Nelles Verlag in Munich, Germany. They cover the Kathmandu Valley and the Everest region from Jiri to the Hongu valley and have a contour interval of 40m. There are 1:100,000 Schneider maps of Annapurna and Langtang; these have a contour interval of 100m. They're available from many map shops overseas and at many bookshops in Kathmandu. The fantastically coloured maps are also fantastically expensive – each sheet is Rs 1000 in Nepal and £8.50 at Stanfords in London – but if you are doing any serious trekking they are worth it. If you are planning a climb, they are absolutely necessary.

The excellent Survey of India series (an inch equals a mile, or 1:63,360) are restricted and hard to obtain because in India maps are secret documents. The US Army Map Service produced a set of maps in the 1950s (Series U502 at 1:250,000) based on the Survey of India maps. Though they are outdated, the topography is quite accurate except in north-western Nepal. Stanfords bookshop in London has reprinted the entire series.

Other maps are available as blueprints of traced maps produced in Nepal. They aren't really very accurate, but they will give you some idea of where you are going and are the only maps available for some regions. Several quite good printed maps are produced in Kathmandu. One series is published by Mandala Maps. A 1:250,000 series is edited by Paolo Gondoni and published by Nepa Maps; these cost Rs 200 each.

Both the Royal Geographical Society and the National Geographic Society have made special maps of the Everest region. The Nepal Police Adventure Foundation has also produced a series of maps. The Nepal Mountaineering Association sells a map that shows the location of, and routes to, all the peaks open for climbing.

All of these maps are available at bookshops in Kathmandu and many are stocked by speciality map shops overseas.

TOURIST OFFICES

Nepal has no tourist offices abroad, though Nepal embassies and consulates try to maintain a supply of the brochures that the department of tourism prepares.

The department of tourism operates an office in the Kathmandu airport that has leaflets and maps. The tourist information office (☎ 220818) on New Rd in Kathmandu, near Basantapur, has government publications and an information counter. Most Nepalis who have lived all their lives in Kathmandu are not well informed about life in the hills, so you may not get much sophisticated trekking information from the people who staff the tourist office counters.

DOCUMENTS

Visas

Nepal's immigration rules are complex, cumbersome and, above all, expensive. All foreigners, except Indians, must have a visa. Visas are issued by Nepal embassies and consulates overseas, or they can be issued on the spot when you arrive in Nepal, either at the Kathmandu airport or at a road border with India or Tibet. If you stay in Nepal for longer than the duration of your original visa, you will require a visa extension. To trek, you must obtain a trekking permit from the immigration office specifying the time and route of your trek.

To obtain a visa when you arrive in Kathmandu you must fill in an application form; in theory you should have a photograph, though this requirement is overlooked if you don't have one. Visa application forms are available on a table in the arrival hall; airlines do not normally provide this form on the flight. You can choose between the following visas:

Duration	Type	Cost
15 days	single entry	US$15
30 days	single entry	US$25
30 days	double entry	US$40
60 days	multiple entry	US$60

The double and multiple entry visas are useful if you are planning a side trip to Tibet

or India. At Kathmandu airport the fee is payable only in US dollars cash. If you arrive with some other currency, you may be sent back to the bank to change your money into US dollars.

Don't overstay a visa. You can pay a fine of US$2 per day at the airport if you've overstayed less than seven days. If you've overstayed longer, you might not be allowed to board your departing flight. In such cases you must go back to the immigration office and settle the situation there.

There is no advantage to having a visa in advance except for the time you may save at the airport when you arrive – though sometimes the visa-on-arrival queue moves faster than the queue for those who have a visa. If you are arriving by road, it might save some hassle and delay if you already have a visa, but you can get one at any road border, even the funky Kodari checkpost on the road to Tibet. A Nepal visa is valid for entry for three months from the date of issue. Do not apply too soon or it will not be valid when you arrive in Kathmandu.

Visa Extensions

To get a visa extension or trekking permit in Kathmandu, go to the central immigration office (☎ 418573, 412337), near the Royal Palace on Tridevi Marg at the entrance to Thamel. The immigration office accepts applications Sunday to Thursday from 10.30 am to 2 pm and on Friday from 10.30 am to noon. The office is closed on Saturday and holidays. Visa extensions and trekking permits are normally available the same day, but during the busy season you should allow up to three working days for an extension to be processed. At peak times the queues are long and the formalities are tedious.

A large sign at the entrance to the immigration office details the latest rules and regulations. For a fee, trekking and travel agencies can assist with the visa extension process and can usually save you the time and tedium of queueing.

Every visa extension or trekking permit requires your passport, money, photos and an application form. Collect all these before you join the queue. There are several instant photo shops near the immigration office, but Polaroid photos are expensive. If you plan ahead, there are many photographers who will provide passport photos within a day. Kathmandu is a good, inexpensive place to stock up on extra photos of yourself for future travels.

Prior to October 1993 you were required to produce bank receipts to prove you had changed US$20 per day into local currency for every day of visa extension. This requirement has been replaced by a US$1 per day fee, but it's worthwhile to collect bank receipts when you change money in case of a switch back to the old rules. You can extend your visa up to a total stay of 120 days without undue formality; the next 30 days of extension require a special application. You are allowed to stay in Nepal for a maximum of 150 days per year (which is counted as January to December) on a tourist visa.

Trekking Permits

A Nepal visa is valid only for the Kathmandu Valley, Pokhara and those parts of Nepal accessible by road. To travel into the roadless areas you need a trekking permit. The permit has your photograph and specifies the places you may visit and the duration of your trek. Long ago, a trekking permit cost Rs 1 and served as a translation of your passport into Nepali so that officials in the hills could read it. Now the fees have increased, there is no Nepali at all on the permit and the issuance of trekking permits has become a large-scale industry. Theoretically you can leave your passport in a hotel safe during a trek, because a trekking permit is sufficient documentation to travel throughout Nepal. See the section on Trekking Permits on pages 91-2 for details of the formalities involved.

Re-Entry Permits

If you are travelling from Nepal to India or Tibet and returning to Kathmandu within 30 days you should either buy a double entry visa or else get a re-entry permit before you leave Nepal. This is an easy process at the immigration office and costs US$25. Don't overlook it or you may be obliged to pay excessive visa fees on your return.

Onward Tickets

You don't need to show an onward ticket for entry into Nepal, but if you are travelling in the high season, you would do well to have a ticket – and a confirmed seat – before you arrive. Airfares to some destinations from Nepal are quite competitive, so you can sometimes book a flight in Kathmandu at bargain prices during the low season.

Travel Insurance

Travel agents and adventure travel companies can offer a travellers' insurance policy. Coverage varies from policy to policy, but will probably include loss of baggage, sickness and accidental injury or death. Most policies also cover the reimbursement of cancellation fees and other costs if you must cancel your trip because of accident or illness, or the illness or death of a family member. It's probably worth purchasing this inexpensive protection, especially if you are travelling on nonrefundable advance purchase plane tickets.

Be sure that the policy does not exclude mountaineering or alpinism or you may have a difficult time settling a claim. Although you will not engage in such activities, you may not be able to convince a flatland insurance company of this fact. It would be prudent to check the policy to be sure that it specifically covers helicopter evacuation.

If you purchase insurance and have a loss, you must submit proof of this loss when you make an insurance claim. If you have a medical problem, you should save all your bills and get a physician's certificate stating that you were sick. If you lose something covered by insurance, you must file a police report, no matter how remote the location. No insurance company considers a claim without such documentation. Police checkposts in Nepal will provide a police report if there is a major theft. They are all familiar with this bit of bureaucracy.

Two companies offer rescue insurance in Nepal. The Oriental Insurance Company

(☎ 221448, 223419; fax 223419), Jyoti Bhavan, Kantipath, has a scheme that covers medical expenses and cost of rescue up to US$10,000. The premium is US$52 for seven to 14 days and $98 for 30 days of coverage. Himalayan General Insurance Co (☎ 226604, 226634; fax 223906), Durbar Marg, in Kathmandu, offers a mountain rescue insurance policy in association with International Health Insurance of Denmark. The premium depends on your age and the length of coverage you arrange; it's expensive, approximately $200 for 30 days of coverage if you're in your 30s.

Rescue insurance is important. If you are injured and unable to travel, you can ask for a rescue helicopter or charter flight from a remote airstrip only if you have some definite proof that you can pay for it. It costs more than US$1500 for a helicopter evacuation from 4000m near Mt Everest and up to US$5000 for a rescue in the far west of Nepal. In the past, helicopters have saved the lives of several people who left Nepal without paying the bill for the rescue flight. The Royal Nepal Army, which operates the service, now refuses to send a chopper unless they have cash in hand. All trek organisers have an agreement in Kathmandu that guarantees payment for helicopter evacuations. They pay a cash deposit to the helicopter operator and collect the money from you once you have been rescued. It's then up to you to obtain reimbursement from your insurance company. For more on helicopter rescue, see the Rescue section in the Health & Safety chapter.

Other Documents

It's useful to carry extra passport photos. If you go rafting, you'll need a rafting permit, or you may decide to stay longer and need a visa extension or take another trek. All these formalities require photos. If you have photos made in Kathmandu, get about 20 extra. Make a photocopy of the important pages of your passport and carry it separately. This will expedite replacement in case of loss.

EMBASSIES

Nepal's embassies and consulates abroad issue the same collection of visas that are available in Nepal, though the cost is often higher than the fees charged at Kathmandu airport. In many countries, Nepal has appointed honorary consuls who are not employees of the government of Nepal. When honorary consuls issue visas they often levy a service charge to cover the expense of maintaining a visa office on behalf of the Nepal government. The following list identifies the honorary consuls.

Nepal Embassies & Consulates Abroad

Australia
> Christine Gee, Honorary Consul, 441 Kent St, Sydney, NSW 2000 (☎ 02-9264-5909; fax 9261-1974)
> WA Johns, Honorary Consul, Moncroft House, 93 Rose St, Essendon, Melbourne, Vic 3040 (☎ 03-9337-0444; fax 9331-1378)
> Lillian Roberts, Honorary Consul, Suite 2, 16 Robinson St, Nedlands, WA 6009 (☎ 08-9386-2102; fax 9386-3087)

Bangladesh
> United Nations Rd, Road No 2, Baridhara Diplomatic Enclave, Dhaka (☎ 601890, 602091; fax 886401)

Belgium
> 21 Avenue Champel, B-1640, Rhode St Genese, Belgium (☎ 02-358-5808, 358-5822; fax 358-3384)

China
> No 1, Sanlitun Xi Liu Jie, Sanlitun Ku, Beijing (☎ 532-1795; fax 532-3251)
> Norbulingka Rd 13, Lhasa, Tibet Autonomous Region (☎ 36890, 22881)

Denmark
> Ole Janus Larsen, Honorary Consul, 2 Teglgaardstraede, 1452 Copenhagen K (☎ 3312-4166, 3940-0136)

Finland
> Gustav Mattson, Honorary Consul, Kaisaniemenkarul B, 00100 Helsinki (☎ 1311-6230)

France
> 45, bis Rue des Acacias, 75017 Paris (☎ 01 46 22 48 67; fax 01 42 27 08 65)

Germany
> Im Hag 15, D-5300 Bonn (☎ 0228-343097; fax 856747)

India
> 1 Barakhamba Rd, New Delhi 110001 (☎ 011-332-9969, 332-7361; fax 332-6857)
> 19 Woodlands, Sterndale Rd, Alipore, Calcutta

700027 (☎ 033-479-1224, 479-1085;
fax 479-1410)

Italy
Anselmo Previdi, Honorary Consul, Piazzale
Medaglie d'Oro 20, 00136 Rome (☎ 348176,
341055)

Japan
14-9 Tokoroki 7-chome, Setagaya-ku, Tokyo 158
(☎ 03-3705-5558; fax 3705-8264)

Myanmar (Burma)
16 Natmauk Yeiktha, Yangon (☎ 250633,
253168; fax 239803)

Netherlands
Casper De Stoppelaar, Honorary Consul,
Keizersgracht 463, 1017 DK Amsterdam
(☎ 020-250388; fax 624-6173)

Pakistan
House No 506, Street No 84, Attaturk Ave,
Ramna G-6/4, Islamabad (☎ 210642, 212754;
fax 217875)

Russia
2nd Neopalimovsky pereulok 14/7, Moscow
(☎ 095-244-7356, 241-9311)

Spain
Lluis Belvis, Honorary Consul, Mallorca 194
Pral 2A, 08036 Barcelona (☎ 93-323-1323)

Sweden
Claes-Olof Livijn, Honorary Consul, Eriksbergs-
gatan 1A, S-11430 Stockholm (☎ 08-679-8039)

Switzerland
1, rue Frederic-Amiel, 1203 Geneva
(☎ 022-344-4441; fax 344-4093)
Dr Hans Ulrich Vetsch, Honorary Consul,
Asylstrasse 81, 8030 Zurich (☎ 01-475993)

Thailand
189 Soi 71 Sukhumvit, Bangkok (☎ 391-7240,
390-2280; fax 381-2406)

UK
12A Kensington Palace Gardens, London W8
4QU (☎ 0171-229-1594, 229-6231;
fax 792-8861)

USA
2131 Leroy Place NW, Washington, DC 20008
(☎ 202-667-4550; fax 667-5534)
820 Second Ave, Suite 202, New York, NY 10017
(☎ 212-370-4188; fax 953-2038)
Mary B Sethness, Honorary Consul, 1500 Lake
Shore Drive, Chicago, Illinois 60610
(☎ 312-787-9199)
Richard Blum, Honorary Consul, Suite 400, 909
Montgomery St, San Francisco, California
94133 (☎ 415-434-1111)
Lucille G Murchison, Honorary Consul, 16250
Dallas Parkway, Suite 110, Dallas, Texas 75248
(☎ 214-931-1212)
Josephine Crawford Robinson, Honorary
Consul, 212 15th St NE, Atlanta, GA 30309
(☎ 404-892-8152)

Foreign Embassies & Consulates in Nepal

Officials of all embassies in Nepal stress the benefits of registering with them, telling them where you are trekking, and reporting in again when you return. In the aftermath of the avalanches in November 1995 (see the boxed aside for details) Kathmandu's embassies were flooded with requests from anxious parents and friends, yet they had very little information available. The offices of KEEP and the Himalayan Rescue Association (HRA; see Information Sources later in this chapter for details) have forms from most embassies, so it's simple to provide the information and keep the folks at home from worrying if there is an emergency.

Some embassies will guarantee helicopter payments. If you are going on an extended trek, ask about their policy on rescues when you register with your embassy.

Australia
Bansbari (☎ 419264, 417566, 413076;
fax 417533)

Bangladesh
Naxal (☎ 414943; fax 414265)

Belgian Consulate
Lal Durbar (☎ 228925, 214730; fax 223310)

China
Baluwatar (☎ 411740, 411958, 415383;
fax 414045)

Denmark
Baluwatar (☎ 413010, 413020; fax 411409)

Finland
Lazimpat (☎ 416636, 417221; fax 416703)

France
Lazimpat (☎ 412332, 413839, 414734;
fax 419968)

Germany
Gyaneshwor (☎ 412786, 416527, 416832;
fax 416899)

India
Lainchaur (☎ 410900, 411940, 414990;
fax 413132)

Israel
Lazimpat (☎ 411811, 413419; fax 413920)

Italy
Baluwatar (☎ 412743, 412280; fax 413879)

Japan
Pani Pokhari (☎ 426680; fax 228638)

Myanmar (Burma)
Patan Gate (☎ 521788, 524788; fax 523402)

Netherlands Consulate
Patan (☎ 522915; fax 523155)

Avalanche!

On 9 November 1995, at the height of the autumn trekking season, a storm swept into Nepal from the Bay of Bengal and dumped as much as two metres of wet snow onto the mountains in 36 hours. This is a tremendous amount of snowfall in a short time, and because this snow was wet, it was unstable.

Hundreds of avalanches started crashing down throughout the mountains. A Japanese trekking group was buried in their dining tent at Pangka, just above Machhermo on the way to Gokyo. The entire group, including sherpas, was killed and a trekking lodge was buried. Several members of another Japanese group were killed in an avalanche near Gunsa on the way to Kanchenjunga. An American group was avalanched on Mera Peak and another group was hit in the Barun Valley near Makalu base camp, but they escaped without injury. The rain also set off a huge mudslide that roared through the village of Bagarchhap on the way to Manang, wiping out two lodges and killing several people. The deep snow made it impossible to travel, and both individual and group trekkers were stranded in Gokyo, the Everest base camp area and near both Island Peak and Mera Peak. One group of Island Peak climbers suffered severe frostbite, and one sherpa died of exposure, when they tried to descend through the soft snow. The official toll was 63 dead, of whom 22 were foreign trekkers.

The Nepal government mounted a major rescue effort using army and civilian helicopters, including the big Russian MI-17s that can operate as high as Everest base camp. The relief task force rescued 299 Nepalis and 250 foreign trekkers between 11 and 16 November. Helicopters rescued people from Gokyo, Na, Machhermo, Gorak Shep, Lobuje, Pheriche, Langtang, Larkya, Manang, Samagaon, Hodku, Chukudga, Cholang, Dhunsa and Pangma, as well as base camps on Kanchenjunga, Makalu, Everest, Manaslu and Dhaulagiri.

This was an unusual storm, but was a repeat of a cyclone in 1985 when a group was snowed in at Tilicho Lake. The groups that were avalanched were camped in places that normally would not be subject to avalanche danger. There was so much snow that it came off the mountains in all directions. In October 1996 there was a similar situation in Dolpo, where a trekking party was buried in their tents under two metres of snow. ■

New Zealand Consulate
  Bagh Bazaar (☎ 412436; fax 414750)
Pakistan
  Pani Pokhari (☎ 411421; fax 419113)
Russia
  Baluwatar (☎ 412155, 411063; fax 416571)
Sri Lanka
  Baluwatar (☎ 417406; fax 410525)
Swiss Consulate
  Patan (☎ 523468; fax 525358)
Thailand
  Maharajgunj (☎ 420410, 420411; fax 420408)
UK
  Lainchaur (☎ 410583, 411281, 411590;
  fax 411789)
USA
  Pani Pokhari 9 (☎ 411179, 413890, 411613;
  fax 419963)

CUSTOMS
Arrival

Nepal's customs formalities were liberalised in 1995 with the introduction of a 'green channel'. All hand baggage is x-rayed when you enter the customs hall and checked baggage is x-rayed as you pass through the green channel. Electronic goods attract attention; there's no problem with laptop computers and video cameras, though customs officials often write the details in your passport to ensure that you re-export them. Other so-called luxuries, such as video players and TVs, require an import licence. If you are carrying such items they will be impounded and kept in customs bond until you depart. Things often get lost or broken in the customs bond facility, so it's best to avoid carrying anything that might end up there.

The duty-free allowance includes 200 cigarettes, 20 cigars and one bottle of liquor. There is a duty-free shop in the arrival hall of Kathmandu airport. Personal effects, including trekking equipment, are permitted free entry. Excessive amounts of film, 16 mm movie equipment, firearms or food and gear for mountaineering expeditions are subject to special restrictions.

Nepal controls the import and export of gold and a substantial part of the efforts of customs inspectors is to detect smuggled gold.

You may not import Nepal rupees, and only nationals of Nepal and India may import Indian currency. There is no restriction on bringing in either cash or travellers' cheques, but the amount taken out at departure should not exceed the amount brought in. The rules say that you should declare cash or travellers' cheques in excess of US$2000, or the equivalent.

Departure

Baggage is also inspected when you leave the country. Checked baggage is x-rayed and the security check for hand luggage doubles as a customs check. Nepal prohibits the export of antiques. Items that look old should have a certificate from the Department of Archaeology. Other prohibited exports are gold, silver, precious stones, wild animals and their skins and horns and all nonprescription drugs, whether processed or in their natural state. You will be hassled if you carry out a fancy statue without a certificate stating that it is not an antique.

Warning

There is considerable money to be made by smuggling gold, drugs and foreign currency into or out of Nepal. Nepali people may approach you in Kathmandu or Hong Kong offering you money, free air tickets or other incentives to carry goods for them. The penalties are severe, informants are everywhere and the jails in Nepal are dreary. Forget it!

MONEY
Costs

If you stay in lodges as you trek, estimate your costs at Rs 250 to Rs 400 per day for food, Rs 20 to Rs 50 per day for dormitory lodging and Rs 30 to Rs 100 for private rooms, though some fancy lodges charge up to Rs 500 for a room. Add 50% or 60% to these costs when you trek above 3500m. Local trekking companies charge US$30 to US$75 per day for a camping trek and US$20 to US$40 per day for a lodge trek. If you book a trek overseas it will cost you US$100 or more per day, often more if the trip includes the services of a Western leader.

How to Organise Money

Before You Go You can carry either cash or travellers' cheques for your expenses in Nepal. US dollars are the most acceptable, though banks and moneychangers are also happy with pounds sterling, Australian dollars and most European currencies. (Note that Scandinavian money is sometimes difficult to change.) US cash dollars are the primary medium of exchange for hotels, airlines and the government. Visa fees, hotel rates and airline tickets are all priced in US dollars, so you will have less hassle everywhere if you carry greenbacks. US$100 notes are subject to special scrutiny and confirmation by the bank because of a rash of counterfeit bills. Travellers' cheques are fine in Kathmandu and Pokhara, but are rarely accepted in the hills.

Credit cards are slowly gaining acceptance in Kathmandu, but are worthless in the hills. If you are an American Express cardholder, you can get US dollar travellers' cheques with a personal cheque at the American Express office. Nepal Grindlays Bank can provide a cash advance in Nepal rupees or US dollar travellers' cheques against a Visa card. The Alpine Travel office in Thamel can provide a cash advance for both Visa card and MasterCard holders. Both American Express and Visa have refund facilities in Kathmandu. The only automatic teller machine (ATM) in Nepal is for the local Himalayan Bank and does not handle overseas transactions.

You are supposed to pay for Kathmandu hotel accommodation and airline tickets in foreign currency. Most larger hotels will accept credit cards, but in smaller hotels and for domestic flights it will have to be foreign cash or travellers' cheques. Royal Nepal Airlines does not accept credit cards, though some other domestic airlines and travel agencies do accept them. If you plan to fly back from Lukla, Shyangboche, Pokhara or Jomsom at the end of a trek, be sure you have enough foreign currency, preferably in US dollars, to purchase a plane ticket. Even if you do not plan to fly, you should carry enough cash on a trek to buy a plane ticket in case you need one in an emergency.

On the Trek If you will be trekking on your own, you should carry enough money in rupees to cover all your expenses. It is often difficult to change foreign currency except in Kathmandu or Pokhara and major trekking villages like Namche Bazaar and Jomsom. Carry the largest stash of money safely in the bottom of your rucksack and keep only a small amount on hand. Flashing a pile of money around at a tea stall invites night-time theft.

The money you take on the trek should be in smaller denomination notes. It may be difficult to find change for Rs 1000 notes in the hills, though hotels in Namche and Jomsom can usually handle them. If you have big notes, you can get change at banks in Namche, Chame, Jomsom, Dhunche and Pokhara. If you are going to a particularly remote area such as the Arun River or the far west of Nepal, you should carry stacks of Rs 5 and Rs 10 notes, but this is not necessary on the more popular routes. Consider yourself lucky that paper money is now accepted throughout Nepal. The 1953 Everest expedition had to carry all its money in coins. The money alone took 30 porter loads!

Currency
There are banknotes of Rs 1, 2, 5, 10, 20, 50, 100, 500 and 1000. Coins are Rs 1, 2 and 5 plus aluminium coins for fractions of a rupee. There are 100 paisa (p) in a rupee. In the hills, shopkeepers often do their calculations in units of 50 paisa, called a *mohar* – Rs 1.50 equals three mohar. In Kathmandu, virtually everything is rounded to the next higher rupee.

Currency Exchange
The Nepal Rastra Bank (the national bank of Nepal) determines the value of the Nepal rupee (Rs) against a 'basket of currencies' and fixes exchange rates daily against all major currencies. Radio Nepal, Nepal Tele-

vision, Nepali and English newspapers all announce the rates every morning. In June 1997 the exchange rates were:

Australia	A$1	=	Rs 43
France	FF1	=	Rs 10
Germany	DM1	=	Rs 36
India	Rs 1	=	Rs 1.6
UK	UK£1	=	Rs 94
USA	US$1	=	Rs 57

Changing Money
You can change money officially at banks, exchange counters and moneychangers authorised by the Nepal Rastra Bank. Hotels in Kathmandu and Pokhara are also licensed to change foreign currency; rates are almost the same as at the bank. When you change money, be sure to get a receipt that bears the stamp of the moneychanger. They don't always volunteer to give you this, but if you plan to exchange any money back to foreign currencies when you leave Nepal, you must have a receipt. At the airport on the way out of the country, you can reconvert only 15% of the total amount supported by exchange receipts.

Black Market
Nepal has liberalised its foreign exchange restrictions, so the black market in currency has declined. Touts around Thamel in Kathmandu and the lakeside in Pokhara still offer to change money, but the premium over the official rate is usually less than 5%, so it's hardly worth the risk of getting counterfeit money. It's still illegal, of course, and the money is often used in the drug trade.

Tipping
Waiters in Kathmandu expect tips of Rs 5 to Rs 10 in smaller restaurants and from 5% to 10% in hotels. Bellhops and cleaning staff are happy to receive about Rs 10. Trek and travel guides expect substantially more. Taxi drivers don't expect tips, but it is OK to leave them loose change.

Trekking lodges, which are generally owner-operated, do not solicit tips, but they certainly do not refuse them. Sherpas and porters on camping treks expect a generous tip, called baksheesh, at the conclusion of a trek. A tip of between 10% and 25% of the total wage is the norm. See the suggestions in the boxed aside.

Bargaining

Before you bargain, try to establish a fair price by talking to locals and other travellers. Paying too much feeds inflation, while paying too little denies the locals a fair return for their efforts and investments. Not all transactions are subject to bargaining: respect standard food, accommodation and entry charges and follow the going rate for services. Bargaining in lodges and teahouses on treks is seldom tolerated; competition has already driven prices about as low as possible.

Bargaining should never be treated as a matter of life and death importance – it's usually regarded as an integral part of a transaction and is, ideally, an enjoyable

social exchange. Nepali people do not ever appreciate aggressive behaviour. A good deal is when both parties are happy. Try to remember that Rs 10 might make quite a difference to the seller, but in hard currency it amounts to only 20 US cents.

POST & COMMUNICATIONS

The GPO is at Sundhara (The Golden Tap) in Kathmandu. It is open Sunday to Friday from 10 am to 5 pm.

The Foreign Post Office sends and receives parcels and is next to the GPO. Parcels sent to Nepal must be cleared through customs. This can be a tedious, complicated and disappointing process. Do not allow anyone to send a package to you in Nepal, and think twice before sending a Nepali a package larger than an envelope.

There is a postal service throughout the hills of Nepal. You will find post offices and letter boxes in many remote villages. It can

---

Tips for a Trekking Crew

If there is one thing that seems certain to cause endless confusion for trekkers, particularly those on an organised trek, it's the question of tipping. Tipping, or more correctly baksheeshing, the trekking crew has become an expected custom, but doing it right is far from easy. If you're trekking by yourself, of course, it's not a problem. If you've just got a single guide or porter it's also quite easy – you simply tip about 10% of the amount you pay, or about one day's pay for every week you walk.

The real confusion comes when you have a big group with lots of trekkers and, therefore, an even bigger team with sirdar, sherpas, cooks, kitchen crew and porters. Apart from the sheer number of people involved there will also be all sorts of questions of rank and pay scales. In this situation it's going to be virtually impossible for each individual trekker to tip each individual member of the trekking crew; the best system is to pool the money and pay each person individually but as a single tip from the entire group.

Try to tip about one day's pay for each week of the walk. Starting with porters, this means about Rs 150 for a seven-day trek. The kitchen crew should then get about Rs 400, the sherpas or guides about Rs 500, and the cook and the sirdar about Rs 800. That may seem reasonably straightforward, but the bigger the trekking party the more complicated the sub-rankings and the more delicate the nuances of privilege and importance. The cook may have an assistant cook, the sherpas may be junior and senior, there may be an assistant sirdar and the 'fifth kitchen boy' may not be a kitchen boy at all but a porter whose brother happens to be in the kitchen crew. Also the numbers can vary; just when you've worked out there are 10 porters, two of them may be dropped off because you've eaten all the food they've been carrying. Or another porter may be added along the way.

It's best to have all this worked out, at least approximately, before the trek starts. If there are 10 porters to tip Rs 150 each you need to have 10 notes of Rs 100 and 10 of Rs 50 to hand when the time for the final payout rolls round. And be ready to baksheesh 12 porters if you discover at the last moment there were 12, not 10. It's also a good idea to conduct the final operation with military efficiency. Don't try and hand out money to a milling mob; line those porters up and get them to step forward one at a time. Otherwise, you'll certainly be getting the third kitchen boy and fifth porter confused! Don't worry about it too much, you've been providing solid, reliable employment, and though your trekking crew may work hard, you're unlikely to see anything but smiling faces when the trek is over. ■

be fun to mail postcards and letters from these facilities, but don't be frustrated if they don't reach their destination.

Postal Rates

Air-mail rates (in Rs) for the first 20 grams are:

Destination	Letter	Postcard
USA, Canada, Australia	20	15
Africa, Europe, Japan, Korea	18	12
Asia excluding SAARC	15	10
SAARC (excluding Nepal and India)	10	8
Nepal and India	1	1

Sending Mail

As with all mail in Asia, you, or someone you trust, should personally take outgoing letters to the post office and watch the postal clerk cancel the stamps. The post office can be chaotic. Unless you are collecting letters from poste restante, it's better to employ someone to mail your letters. Most hotels will do this, and Pilgrims Book House in Thamel offers a mailing service for a reasonable fee. There are several private 'postal care' and communications companies that will also mail letters and parcels reliably.

The only practical way to send letters to Nepal is by air mail. Surface mail (by sea via Calcutta) takes months. The mail service to and from Nepal is not particularly reliable, so send important letters by registered mail. Never send cheques through the mail. If someone is sending you money, it should be done through a bank.

Receiving Mail

Poste restante at the GPO is reasonably efficient; they will want to see your passport when you collect letters. A more reliable way to collect mail is to arrange to have it sent to a company that has a post office box. Many embassies will receive mail on your behalf. American Express has an office in Kathmandu that handles client mail. You can also make arrangements with most communica-

tions companies for them to receive mail for you.

Telephone

International telephone calls, telexes and telegrams are coordinated through the Central Telegraph Office, about two blocks south of the GPO. The international telephone and telegraph counter is open around the clock. Hotels will book overseas calls and send faxes for a service charge. You can make reverse-charge (collect) calls only to the UK, Japan and Canada.

Sabha-Doot, in an upstairs office near KC's restaurant in the Thamel area of Kathmandu, is run by the owners of the Kathmandu Guest House and offers a full range of telex, fax, mail, photocopy and telephone services around the clock. Similar establishments have sprung up throughout Kathmandu and Pokhara. In Kathmandu, Pokhara and many hill villages you can also make both domestic and international calls. Look for signs advertising STD/ISD services.

Nepal has a sophisticated new international communications system and is within easy reach of almost any place on the international direct dialling system. Nepal's IDD code is ☎ 977 and its telex code is 891. For outgoing IDD calls the international access number is 00, and this is followed by the country code.

There are few public telephone booths, but most small shops will allow you to make local calls from their phone for two or three rupees.

There is a direct dial service within Nepal to Pokhara, most cities in the Terai and many hill villages. In the hills the telephone service is often a single line for the entire community. Where telephone service does not exist you can send domestic telegrams, but they are sent in Nepali, so there is a good chance of confusion by the time they have been translated.

Domestic STD Codes The following list includes cities, towns and many trailheads and remote trekking destinations that now have telephone service:

Baglung	068
Besi Sahar	066
Bhairahawa	071
Biratnagar	021
Birgung	051
Charikot	049
Dhading	010
Dhankuta	026
Dumre	065
Gorkha	064
Hile	026
Kathmandu	01
Kusma	067
Lukla	038
Nepalgunj	081
Pokhara	061

Fax, Telex & Email

Fax has virtually replaced telex in Nepal for both domestic and international communications. Most hotels, travel agencies and trekking companies have fax facilities and charge for both sending and receiving. Faxes, both incoming and outgoing, often get garbled, but you still must pay for the transmission.

There are several email bureaus in Thamel and in Pokhara. All charge by the kilobyte for sending and receiving; bring the message on a diskette for cheaper rates. There's a cybercafe, *K@mandu*, on Kantipath that charges Rs 350 per half-hour for Internet access. Two companies offer email service; you can arrange an email account in Nepal in advance by sending a message to postmaster@wlink.com.np or to cybercafe@mos.com.np.

BOOKS

There are hundreds of books about Nepal, Tibet and the Himalaya, some dating back to the 1800s. A trip to your local library will provide you with an armload of fascinating books. The following list includes publications that are historically important and describe many aspects of trekking in Nepal. Most are recent enough to be available in large libraries. You can buy many of these books, and others not available in the West, in Kathmandu. Speciality mountaineering bookshops also have an extensive stock of books on Nepal available by mail order. In the US, contact Chessler Books (☎ 800-654-8502), PO Box 399, Kittredge, CO 80457, and in the UK try Himalayan Books (☎ 0171-607-5575), 41 Thornhill Road, London N1 1JS.

Another good source of material about Nepal is the (American) *National Geographic* magazine. Over the years, about 10 issues have had some material on Nepal and the Himalaya. Also look for copies of the *Himalayan Journal*, an annual publication of the Himalayan Club in Bombay, India. The *American Alpine Journal* records details of all major mountaineering expeditions in Nepal.

Kathmandu has some of the best and least expensive bookshops in Asia. In addition to a huge variety of books about Nepal and Tibet, there are thousands of new and used paperbacks available at moderate prices. A paperback book is very useful on a trek, both to relieve boredom while waiting for meals, buses and planes, and as a source of emergency toilet paper.

Good shops for books about Nepal are Pilgrims Book House in Thamel, Himalayan Booksellers and Mandala Book Point. New and used paperbacks are available from bookshops everywhere. Kailas Bookshop near the Yak & Yeti Hotel is affiliated with Pilgrims and has a huge stock of books about Nepal, Tibet and Eastern religions. By special arrangement you can visit the 3rd floor, which houses a fascinating rare-book section. Here you can probably find any out-of-print book on the Himalaya, though the prices are greatly inflated.

Most books are published in different editions by different publishers in different countries. As a result, a book might be a hardcover rarity in one country while it's readily available in paperback in another. Fortunately, bookshops and libraries search by title or author, so your chosen bookshop or library is best placed to advise you on the availability of the following recommendations. The list includes general books about trekking and Nepal. Books that specifically relate to individual treks or regions of Nepal are listed in the appropriate chapters.

Lonely Planet

Nepal, 3rd edition, by Tony Wheeler, Richard Everist & Hugh Finlay, is a complete guidebook to Nepal.

Guidebooks

Nepal Namaste, by Robert Rieffel, is a good general guidebook written by a long-term resident of Kathmandu with a great eye for interesting detail.

Trekking in Nepal: A Traveler's Guide, by Stephen Bezruchka, has cross-cultural suggestions and detailed information about how to organise a backpacking or lodge trek. There are many route descriptions that include walking times.

Trekking in Nepal, West Tibet & Bhutan, by Hugh Swift, has route descriptions that are not as detailed, but cover a larger area than other books and reflects the author's unique view of the Himalaya and its people.

Treks on the Kathmandu Valley Rim, by Alton C Byers III, describes one-day and overnight treks near Kathmandu.

Trekking in the Himalayas, by Tomoya Iozawa, is a well-illustrated trekking guidebook with lots of hand-drawn maps and sketches.

Nepal Trekking, by Christian Kleinert, is a set of route descriptions in a fancy plastic cover that you can carry while trekking. The book suggests some very ambitious routes and schedules. It's out of print.

Trekking in Nepal, by Toru Nakano, has descriptions, maps and photographs of many remote treks that Nakano made when he travelled with mountaineering expeditions.

The Trekking Peaks of Nepal, by Bill O'Connor, is an excellent reference for anyone thinking about doing any climbing in Nepal.

Travel & Mountaineering

Nepal Himalaya, by HW Tilman, is one of my favourites. It's a delightful book filled with Tilman's dry wit and describes the first treks in Nepal in 1949 and 1950. The book is out of print and hard to find, but it is part of a Tilman anthology, *The Seven Mountain-Travel Books*, published by the Seattle Mountaineers.

Americans on Everest, by James Ramsey Ullman, is the official account of the 1963 US expedition.

Vignettes of Nepal, by Harka Bahadur Gurung, provides personal accounts of treks throughout Nepal. The book includes good historical and geological background information and many maps.

Himalayan Pilgrimage, by David L Snellgrove, is an account of a Tibetan scholar's explorations of Nepal. It contains lots of information about Dolpo, Mustang and Nupri.

Travels in Nepal, by Charlie Pye-Smith, is a travel account and an interesting study of the impacts and benefits of foreign aid to Nepal.

Escape from Kathmandu, by Kim Stanley Robinson, is an off-the-wall romp around Nepal. There's an effort to free a captured yeti, an illegal ascent of Everest with a reincarnate lama and an encounter with Jimmy Carter.

The Ascent of Rum Doodle, by WE Bowman, is the classic spoof of mountaineering books. It's a good diversion after reading a few expedition accounts that take themselves too seriously.

Natural History

Birds of Nepal, by Robert L Fleming Sr, Robert L Fleming Jr & Lain Bangdel, has been out of print for years (there are rumours of a reprint), but is still the definitive work on the hundreds of species of birds in Nepal. It contains many outstanding colour paintings.

A Guide to the Birds of Nepal, by Carol & Tim Inskipp, is only available in a hardcover edition and is too large to be used as a field guide but is an excellent reference book.

Trees and Shrubs of Nepal and the Himalayas, by Adrian & Jimmie Storrs, gives good information about the trees of Nepal, including their economic and cultural significance.

Flowers of the Himalaya, by Oleg Polunin & Adam Stainton, is highly technical and very detailed and is the recognised reference book for Nepal's flowers.

Himalayan Flowers & Trees, by Dorothy Mierow & Tirtha Bahadur Shrestha, is the recognised field guide to the plants of Nepal.

Geography
Nepal – the Kingdom in the Himalayas, by Toni Hagen, is still the definitive documentation of the geology and people of Nepal, with many fine photos.

Mount Everest, the Formation, Population & Exploration of the Everest Region, by Toni Hagen, GO Dyhrenfurth, C Von Fürer Haimendorf & Erwin Schneider, is a shortened version of material in Hagen's book, combined with other works describing the Solu Khumbu region in detail. The maps are good.

People & Society
Himalayan Traders, by C Von Fürer Haimendorf, studies the change in trading patterns and culture among Himalayan peoples throughout Nepal.

People of Nepal, by Dor Bahadur Bista, gives an excellent overview of the various ethnic groups in Nepal. Bista is Nepal's foremost anthropologist.

Faces of Nepal, by Jan Salter & Harka Gurung, is a collection of drawings of 20 of the ethnic groups in Nepal. Dr Gurung's text describes the history and traditions of each group.

The *Festivals of Nepal*, by Mary M Anderson, describes the important festivals of Nepal and provides a lot of background information on the Hindu religion.

Fatalism & Development – Nepal's Struggle for Modernization, by Dor Bahadur Bista, is a controversial analysis of Nepali society and the dynamics that operate within it. There is a very good historical introduction, and the author looks especially critically at the role of the caste system in Nepali life. This book provides very useful

background if you expect to have extensive dealings with Nepali business people or government officials.

Nepali Aama: Life Lessons of a Himalayan Woman, by Broughton Coburn, is an account of a US Peace Corps volunteer's encounters with an elderly Gurung woman. Coburn later took her on a trip to the USA; this trip is described in a sequel, *Aama in America: A Pilgrimage of the Heart*.

Language
Lonely Planet's *Nepali phrasebook*, by Mary-Jo O'Rourke & Bimal Man Shrestha, is a handy phrasebook with a good section on trekking.

LP's *Tibetan Phrasebook*, by Sandup Tsering, is useful to have along in Mustang, Dolpo and on the trek to Mt Kailas.

Basic Gurkhali Grammar, by M Meerendonk, is a good introductory text on Nepali, which the British army calls Gurkhali. It was written for the army, so it teaches a slightly strange military vocabulary, eg 'lo, the postilion was struck by lightning'.

Basic Gurkhali Dictionary, by M Meerendonk, is a pocket-sized dictionary of the Nepali language. It is quite useful once you understand the rudiments of the grammar.

Trekkers Pocket Pal, compiled by the Summer Institute of Linguistics, is yet another phrasebook for trekkers.

Sherpa Nepali English, by Phinjo Sherpa, is the first Sherpa phrasebook.

Nepali for Trekkers, by Stephen Bezruchka, is a Nepali phrasebook with a good tape.

Tibet
Freedom in Exile is the autobiography of His Holiness the Dalai Lama and provides insight into the factors that influenced the present status of Tibet.

The Secret War in Tibet, by Michel Peissel, is a one-sided description of the resistance of Khampa warriors against the Chinese in Tibet. It was published in England as *Cavaliers of Kham*.

Seven Years in Tibet, by Heinrich Harrer, is a best-selling book describing Harrer's adventures in Tibet before the Chinese occupation. It also contains commentary on Harrer's discussions with the Dalai Lama. There is a feature movie based on this book.

Health

Medicine for Mountaineering & Other Wilderness Activities, by James A Wilkerson, is an outstanding reference book for the lay person. It describes many of the medical problems typically encountered in Nepal. One copy of this book should accompany every trekking party.

Mountain Medicine, by Michael Ward, is good background reading on the subject of cold and high-altitude problems.

Where There is No Doctor: A Village Health Care Handbook, by David Werner, is also a good lay person's medical guide with lots of application to Nepal.

Altitude Sickness, by Peter Hackett, is required reading for anyone who treks above 4000m.

ONLINE SERVICES

There is a lot of material about Nepal available on the Internet. Nepali students studying in the USA have created several useful World Wide Web sites, and Mercantile Communications, Nepal's Internet provider, maintains a site with Nepal newspapers and magazines online. Numerous adventure travel companies maintain Web pages, and several photographers and trekkers have established sites with their photos and advice.

The usenet groups rec.travel.asia and soc.culture.nepal often have discussion about treks in Nepal. J Mario Pires in Portugal collects these and archives them in *Stego's FAQ on Nepal Travel*. In the spring of 1995 three Everest expeditions had Web sites that carried later and more accurate news of the successful ascents and subsequent deaths on the mountain than was available in any other medium, including television. The *Outside* magazine Web site maintains up-to-date expedition news as does the Expedition News site.

For up-to-date links to material on trekking in Nepal on the Web, link to http://www.lonelyplanet.com/dest/ind/nep.htm.

NEWSPAPERS & MAGAZINES

The *Rising Nepal* is the official daily English-language newspaper. There are other daily and weekly papers in both English and Nepali. Since the 1990 revolution, the constitution has guaranteed freedom of the press, so these publications now actually carry some news. The *Kathmandu Post* and *Everest Herald*, both of which are private English-language dailies, and the weekly *Independent* offer nongovernmental viewpoints.

Nepal Traveller is a monthly magazine that is distributed free to all passengers on arrival at the airport. It has an excellent Kathmandu city map, a description of the current festivals and usually contains good current advice about trekking.

For political and economic commentary, buy a copy of *Spotlight*, a weekly English-language news magazine published in Kathmandu. *Himal South Asia* is also published in Kathmandu and devotes itself to important social, economic and environmental issues throughout South Asia.

RADIO & TV

Radio Nepal broadcasts from 6 am until 11 pm and uses short-wave frequencies to reach the remote hill areas. Frequencies are 5005, 7165 and 792 kHz in Kathmandu and 684 kHz in Pokhara. It broadcasts the news in English at 8 am and 8 pm. During the climbing season a special mountaineering weather report follows the English news. There is a commercial FM station at 100 MHz that provides local programming and music in a mixture of Nepali and English.

Even without a radio, you should have no problem listening to Radio Nepal in the hills. As a gesture of generosity, most Nepali people try to entertain the entire village by playing the radio at high volume.

Nepal Television broadcasts in Kathmandu, Pokhara and several Terai towns. In 1985 Nepal became one of the last countries in the world to begin TV broadcasts. The news is broadcast in English at 10 pm. Satellite Television for the Asia Region (STAR TV) broadcasts from Hong Kong with a satellite footprint that extends from Korea to the Middle East. Shangri La Channel and Space Time Network rebroadcast satellite programmes in Kathmandu, so in many hotels you can watch BBC or CNN news, sports, MTV and cartoons day and night.

PHOTOGRAPHY & VIDEO
Film & Equipment
Film is available in Kathmandu, but it is a bit more expensive here than it is abroad and it may have been through an airport x-ray machine before reaching Nepal. Photo shops in Thamel and throughout Kathmandu can probably supply any kind and quantity of film you require. Take as much film as you think you will need on the trek; once you get into the hills, you will probably find only colour print film, and that will most likely be what another trekker sold when he ran out of money. On a two or three week trek, 20 rolls of 36 exposure film is not too much.

There are many colour print processing facilities in Kathmandu. Hicola (☎ 410200) in Lazimpat, Das Photo (☎ 213621), Nepal Colour Lab (☎ 211290) and Photo Concern (☎ 223275) are fairly reliable and can handle colour prints and E-6 or Ektachrome slides. Several of these companies have branches in Thamel and throughout Kathmandu. Colour enlargements are produced in Kathmandu at reasonable prices. Ganesh Photo Lab (☎ 216898), in an alley behind Hanuman Dhoka, and Print Maker (☎ 416971) in Lazimpat are the places to go for B&W processing.

Photo Concern on New Rd is the best place to go for batteries, accessories and camera repairs. You can also buy a second-hand camera from many photo shops. Some surprisingly high quality cameras show up on their shelves at bargain prices (read the later section on theft if you are wondering where they come from). New cameras are available in shops in Bishal Bazaar, the supermarket complex on New Rd.

You can buy blank VHS and video-8 cassettes at supermarkets and shops on New Rd. It's almost impossible to rent video cameras in Nepal.

Technical Tips
Remember to allow for the exceptional intensity of mountain light when setting exposures at high altitude. At the other extreme it's surprising how often in Nepal you find the light is insufficient. Early in the morning, in deep valleys on the trek, or in gloomy temples and narrow streets, you may often find yourself wishing you had high-speed film.

A flash is often necessary inside temples or to fill in shots of sculptures and reliefs.

Be sure to protect your camera from dust and rain. Dust is a real problem in Kathmandu and on treks to the Kali Gandaki, Mustang and Tibet.

Restrictions
Nepal has very complicated and expensive regulations governing commercial filming. If you plan to make a 16 mm movie or commercial video, you will certainly need the help of a trekking company in Nepal and should plan far ahead. Eight millimetre movie and 'handycam' type video cameras are not subject to any restrictions.

There are no special restrictions on what you may photograph, but it would be prudent to avoid taking pictures of army camps.

Photographing People
Most Nepali people in Kathmandu are content to have their photograph taken, but you should always ask for permission first. People in the hills can be very camera-shy. Also, be aware that if someone poses for you (especially those saintly *sadhus*), they may insist on being given some baksheesh for doing so.

Respect people's privacy and bear in mind that most Nepalis are extremely modest. Although people carry out many activities in public (they have no choice), it does not follow that passers-by have the right to watch or take photographs. Riverbanks and village wells, for example, are often used as bathrooms, but the users expect as much consideration and privacy as you would in your own house.

Religious ceremonies are also often private affairs, so first ask yourself whether it would be acceptable for a tourist to intrude and to take photographs at a corresponding ceremony in your home country, and then get explicit permission from the senior participants. The behaviour of many would-be *National Geographic* photographers at places like Pashupatinath (the most holy cremation site in Nepal) is horrendous. Imagine the outrage a bus load of scantily clad, camera-toting tourists would create if they invaded a family funeral in the West.

Airport Security

Hand luggage and checked baggage go through an airport x-ray on both entry and exit. Security officials are usually cooperative if you request that they inspect your film by hand.

TIME

Nepal has one time zone which is five hours and 45 minutes ahead of GMT/UTC. When it is noon in Kathmandu, standard time is 6.15 am in London, 4.15 pm in Sydney, 1.15 am in New York and 10.15 pm the previous night in San Francisco. The odd 15 minute difference is said to be a reflection of the exact time at the summit of Gauri Shankar.

If you drive or fly to Tibet, the time change can be fun. Tibet is on Beijing time, so when you cross the border at Kodari or Taklakot, set your watch ahead two hours and 15 minutes.

During winter the days are short – first light is about 6 am and it gets dark at about 6 pm. Nepal has no summer time, but by March the days are about two hours longer, so you could trek from 5 am to 7 pm if you wished.

ELECTRICITY

Nepal's electricity is nominally 220V, 50 Hz, but fluctuations are severe and unpredictable. You must use a voltage stabiliser to protect all sensitive electronic equipment.

There is a power shortage in Nepal, so there is occasional load shedding. During thunderstorms, transformers blow up and the power goes off for periods of between a few minutes and a day or more. Until new generating capacity is provided, the electricity supply will continue to be unstable, but many large hotels now have generators.

There are many kinds of plugs used in Nepal, mostly the Indian round-pin variety that come in three sizes and tend to burn out. Rather than carry a collection of plugs, stop in at a local electric shop in Kathmandu and have them make up an adapter that connects whatever plug you have to whatever socket your hotel has. It should cost less than Rs 50 for a custom-made connector.

There is locally generated electricity in a surprising number of villages throughout the hills. It is mostly in the 220V range, but it's unstable and usually on only at night except in the Khumbu region, where electricity is abundant and is used during the day for cooking. You can charge batteries in many villages for a fee of about Rs 50 per hour. A good solar charger is a cheaper and more versatile solution if you plan to rely on a battery-powered appliance when trekking.

WEIGHTS & MEASURES

Nepal has adopted the metric system, though in the hills shopkeepers often use an ancient system of weights and measures. In the hill system there are eight *maanas* to a *paathi*, a unit of volume equivalent to about 4.5 litres. The old unit of weight is the *dharni*, about 2.4 kg, which is divided into 12 *pau*. Often, however, the unit of measurement is whatever container is most convenient. Kerosene and cooking oil are usually sold by the bottle – a 650 ml beer bottle. A 'tin' usually refers to a 19 litre mustard-oil tin, but I have seen sherpas flummoxed by a shopkeeper who used a fruit tin that held only about five potatoes.

While counting and talking figures, the words *lakh* (100,000) and *crore* (10 million, or 100 lakh) are commonly used. You may often see figures written using this system: 1,02,00,000 equals one crore and two lakhs.

LAUNDRY

Most hotels in Kathmandu and Pokhara can arrange to wash your clothes. In small lodges the room attendant will do the washing; in such cases the price is not really fixed. In trekking lodges there is no formal laundry service, but the hotel keeper may be able to arrange for someone to wash your clothing. Most trekkers do their own laundry on the trail and hang their clothing over the back of their rucksack to dry during the day. When you do wash clothes, be careful to keep soap out of streams. Don't soap up your laundry and beat it on a rock as the locals do. Do your bit to minimise pollution and borrow a large bowl or bucket from the lodge to wash in.

If you are on a group trek, a sherpa may agree to wash your clothes, but this is an extra service and some sort of payment is expected.

If you want to have a sleeping bag cleaned in Kathmandu, try My Shop on Putali Sadak.

TOILETS

There are very few public toilets in Nepal, even in Kathmandu, but most hotels and restaurants in Kathmandu and Pokhara have facilities. The better hotels in the hills have outhouses with Asian-style squat toilets. In many places, however, there are no facilities at all, so it's off to the bushes. Be sure to enquire first about where the *charpi* (toilet) is, because it's important to encourage sanitary facilities, no matter how primitive, wherever they exist. If you go in the bushes, be sure to bury your faeces and burn your toilet paper. If you use a toilet in a lodge, put your used tp in the container provided, not down the loo.

Trekking groups dig toilet holes and erect toilet tents; if you are with a group, encourage the sherpas to fill in the hole completely when you break camp.

WOMEN TREKKERS

Jane Gallie provided the following viewpoint on the issues affecting women travellers in Nepal.

Women the world over have to be concerned about safety from assault and sexual harassment. Nepal, unfortunately, is joining the rest of the world as a place where a single woman cannot be guaranteed safety in the trekking environment. Although this comes as a disappointment to travellers who remember the time, less than a decade past, when a Western woman could feel comfortable travelling anywhere in Nepal, it is remarkable to think that there was ever a time when a foreign woman could feel perfectly safe in remote areas of a developing country. The reasons that attacks may have been increasing are multiple, and the trend probably has as much to do with the changes taking place in Nepali society as with the comportment and dress of visiting Western women.

Safety

It makes sense these days never to trek alone. A lone trekker away from a village is a tempting target for opportunistic thieves, and physical assault has sometimes been added needlessly to robbery. Sexual assault and harassment have been reported at lodges. Two or more people walking together are a less likely target for random assault or sexual harassment.

Travelling with a reliable male guide can help ensure safety, but be sure you do have a reliable person before you go. Occasionally a guide himself has become obnoxious and harassing during the trek. The bigger name trekking agencies are more likely to provide reliable guides than an off-the-street tout.

What to Wear

The question of appropriate dress for women while trekking tends to stir the blood of those who, despite the urgings of the anthropologically sensitive types that they should show respect for the local culture, feel they should be able to dress any way they please. There is, however, a practical reason for dressing conservatively while trekking: you will be treated better, and may even be more comfortable. Nepali culture is uncomfortable with the display of the female leg, and of large expanses of flesh in general. Although, as a tourist and a source of income, you will still be waited on politely in lodges, the owners and workers will be inwardly uncomfortable around you if you are inappropriately dressed. Demonstrating an effort to be culturally sensitive will gain you the kind of rapport with the local people, especially with local women, that many female trekkers are seeking.

Experienced women trekkers have sung the praises of the lightweight cotton mid-calf length skirt that can be worn by itself in hot weather and layered over tights or bicycle shorts as the altitude increases. Sleeveless tops are acceptable in hot weather, but bikini tops or revealing halter tops are not the right idea. In the highest mountain areas, as the weather becomes the major factor, pants are perfectly OK, and in fact are seen on increasing numbers of local hill women. Along busy trekking trails the skirt can make discreet toilet stops easier. Make sure that you seek privacy for changing clothes, and try not to expose yourself needlessly to local people. Pay attention to how the local women behave, and take your clues from them.

Other Hints for Women

Getting to know local people, and local women in particular, can be one of the most rewarding aspects of trekking. Two welltested icebreakers are photos of your family back home, and attractive jewellery – but don't wear expensive jewellery while you trek.

Trekking for an extended length of time means having to deal with menstruation. Bring a plastic bag, and carry used pads with you until an opportunity arises to dispose of them properly. Do not just discard them along the trail. Since tampons and pads are virtually indestructible, do not dispose of them in outhouses; the material in outhouses is often eventually used as fertiliser, and stained pads are an unwelcome sight for villagers. Household fires are considered sacred in Nepal, and are not used for burning garbage. Trekking groups occasionally build fires for burning garbage, and these are acceptable for burning pads. Some doctors prescribe birth-control pills to prevent a menstrual period while trekking. This

method, while effective, is not wise. It may throw off your cycle for a while, and birthcontrol pills can increase the risk of serious blood clots to your lungs or brain while trekking at high altitude.

Bring dark-coloured underpants; bring plenty of pairs if you like to feel more clean while trekking. Don't use toilet paper after urinating, and then you won't have to worry about disposing of it.

Useful Organisations

Chhetri Sisters Guest House at the lakeside in Pokhara specialises in arranging female guides and porters for women travellers.

TREKKING WITH CHILDREN

Thanks to David Shlim, Jane Gallie and Matthew (aged six, and a trekker since he was eight months old) for their advice in this section.

Trekking with children can be a thoroughly enjoyable experience if the parents are already comfortable with backcountry travel and are realistic in their expectations of what children can tolerate in the trekking environment. If parents are nervous about Third World travel, and uncomfortable living in tents, it is unlikely that they will relax enough to enjoy the experience with their children. The most successful parents trekking with children already have a lot of Third World experience, either through their own travels or from residing abroad. Read the following suggestions, go on at least one short test trip at home before you commit yourself to a long Asian holiday or trek, and remember: a first trek with a child is better too short than too long.

Children's Health

All parents experience emotions ranging from mild concern to terror when their child becomes ill, even in their home country. These concerns become magnified when transferred to a developing country with a poor medical infrastructure, where remoteness can put any medical help at least 24 hours away. Parents who have had extensive experience with their own cases of diarrhoea, flu and skin conditions while travelling are likely to be more relaxed when confronting these conditions in their children. These parents will be more comfortable with making their own diagnoses and starting treatment when appropriate. If possible, parents should spend time with their child's medical practitioner before the trip to obtain a list of appropriate medications to carry and the indications for using them. Parents should try to maintain hygiene on the trek, washing the child's hands frequently and limiting, if possible, the number of local people who handle the child. It is imperative to know exactly what your options are in regard to obtaining medical help or evacuation if you should need it; see also the Travel Insurance section earlier in this chapter.

Choosing an Age-Appropriate Itinerary

The factors to consider are altitude, cold and the difficulty and length of the trek. In choosing a trek with a child who will be carried, try to determine the nature of the trails you will be travelling on. Most trails in Nepal are quite safe, and the likelihood of a fall is small. However, some trails are carved into the sides of cliffs, built out on sticks from a hillside or subject to rock fall. The quality of many bridges in Nepal ranges from merely unsafe to horrifying. If the prospect of watching your child sitting precariously on a porter's back as he inches along a cliff above a 100m drop makes little hairs on your neck stand up, make sure you know where you are going before your trek starts.

Three Months to Three Years We don't recommend going trekking with an infant before three months, and preferably six months, of age. Children this young can become ill rapidly, with few signs to indicate how serious the illness is. It is difficult to ascertain if they are suffering from altitude illness, as they can't always tell you whether they have headache, loss of appetite etc. It is better to plan treks under 3000m with children this age. In addition, children this young cannot easily be kept warm in the very cold conditions that are often encountered at

higher altitudes. They will need to be carried virtually all of the time, either by a parent or by a specially selected porter. Porter baskets, called *dokos*, can be modified to include seats, padding and footrests for children, making being carried much easier. Children two years and older can generally sit in a doko, but younger ones will need to be in a child's backpack. Treks with very young children should be kept shorter, usually under seven days, as children may not have as much fun as their parents for an extended period of time. Dress the child more warmly than you would yourself, as he or she will not be generating as much body heat while being carried as you will while walking. Synthetic pile or fleece is the ideal fabric for children: warm, lightweight and rapidly drying. If the child is in nappies (diapers), it usually works better to bring an ample supply of disposables, as there is rarely an opportunity while trekking to wash and dry cloth nappies. Carry the soiled nappies in a plastic bag until you find an appropriate place to dispose of them or burn them.

Three to Six Years Children in this age group can start to tell you more about how they are feeling, and can be kept warm more easily. Thus, depending on the level of experience of their parents, they can be taken to higher altitudes. However, be careful to allow extra days in the itinerary for acclimatisation if there should be any doubt at all as to how the child is adapting. In this regard it is important to be in the company of other adults who understand that the trek is revolving around the children's pace. Make sure that others are as committed to your children as you are before teaming up for a trek. In this age group, it is ideal to go with another family who have children of a similar age. Be sure to bring toys, games and comfort foods familiar to the child, who may not adapt readily to the local fare. Carry surprise presents, and bring them out as needed when the child hits a low point. The children will want to walk at least part of the time, but it is still important to have a child porter available as few children in this age group can walk extensively. A good child porter, or *doko dai*, can develop a warm relationship with the child, carrying them when needed, and holding the child's hand and chatting along the trail when the child needs some exercise.

Six to 12 Years As the children get older, they will be able to walk most or all of the way. Children eight years and up should not need a child porter. In this age group, companions are even more important. Keep the walking days shorter than you might choose for yourself, and make sure you have games, books and treats for distraction, as the kids may not be as thrilled with the Himalayan views as you would wish them to be. Surprise presents are still appropriate. Prepare the children for the experience of being stared at and doted upon, as this can be overwhelming to a shy child. Fair-skinned children are still a relative rarity in the mountains and attract a lot of positive attention.

13 to 18 Years If children this age still want to go on a holiday with you, count yourself a lucky parent. Make sure that the kids really want to do this type of holiday before committing them to a three week trek. Sullen, cold, and bored children can be a ball and chain around the legs of the most enthusiastic parents. Again, if they have companions whom they like, the trip will be much easier. Health concerns are beginning to ease at this age, as the children are physically similar to adults in their ability to withstand illness and to give you a good history of their symptoms.

Choosing a Style of Trekking
The two main options are a lodge trek or an organised camping trek with a trekking company. If you travel on an organised trek, you are a self-contained unit. You can develop a family-like atmosphere with your staff, control meal times and types of food, and have built-in support in Kathmandu through your trekking agency if an emergency arises. The choice is an individual one, based on personal experience, but if you

have doubts, choose an organised trek for your first trek with children.

DANGERS & ANNOYANCES
Personal Safety & Theft
In 1974 I wrote: '...there is virtually nothing to fear in Nepal from thieves, hijackings or the other horrors of our urban civilisation'. Unfortunately, this has changed, and it pays to be cautious about your companions – whether fellow trekkers or porters – and your belongings, especially when you camp. There are frequent reports of items being stolen from the tents and hotel rooms of trekkers, even in the most remote villages. There have even been incidents of violent crime, something previously unheard-of in Nepal.

The US Embassy in Kathmandu makes the following suggestions:

While Nepali people are generally friendly and present no threat to trekkers, the number of violent incidents in recent years against trekkers has unfortunately increased. Crime, while still low by Western standards, does exist on the trails. Westerners have been the victims of murder and violent assaults; there were several cases of assault in 1996 in the forests between Ghorapani and Ghandruk. All the victims have been travelling alone or as a couple. The general motive seems to have been robbery, even though the possessions of some of the victims were insignificant by American standards. To help you enjoy your trek and to minimise the risk of unpleasant incidents, the embassy recommends that you take the following precautions:

- Register with the consular section, giving the trek itinerary and dates of the trek.
- Do not travel alone. Join up with other Westerners going along the same trail if you are alone in Nepal.
- Do take a porter or guide. Backpacking by yourself may seem the noble thing to do but it is dangerous. You will also be doing a disservice to Nepal by not contributing to the local economy.
- Arrange for porters and guides through a reputable trekking agency, friends or the embassy so that they can be traced if you have trouble. Do not just pick up a porter or guide off the street, no matter how friendly he may appear.
- Do not make ostentatious displays of your cash or possessions. Store all valuable items in Kathmandu at your hotel or lodge. Be sure to obtain a detailed receipt of your items from the hotel or lodge.

- If possible, camp at night near other trekkers. Do not walk along trails after dark.
- Don't leave your passport as collateral for renting trekking equipment. You may need it if an emergency should arise.
- Be sure to register at all the police and immigration posts along the trail and go only on the route prescribed in your trekking permit.
- If you encounter problems along the trail, report them to the nearest police or immigration post. When you return to Kathmandu, report any unresolved problems to the appropriate trekking agency or hotel as well as the police and the Ministry of Tourism.
- The embassy recommends that you do not take night buses in Nepal. There have been serious problems recently with bandits holding up these buses.

Despite this caution, you will find most Nepalis friendly, helpful and honest. It is, however, *essential that you trek with a well-chosen companion* – either another Westerner or a guide – for your own safety. The chance of theft is still remote, but a sprained ankle, debilitating illness or other misfortune can occur at any time. It is only common sense, applicable to a hiking trip anywhere, that you should not travel alone in the mountains. Women should be aware of possible sexual harassment; clothing and actions that seem totally innocent are viewed as open invitations by many Nepali youths. If you bathe topless you are asking for serious trouble.

Looking after Valuables on a Trek There is at least one roving gang of thieves who watch trekkers and go after those who display valuable items or who have large amounts of cash. Most thefts have been from those who had things we would recognise as worth stealing – with the possible exception of boots. Boots are high on the list of desirable items (along with money and cameras). Don't leave your boots near the door of your tent or outside a hotel room. Thefts occur most frequently in Naudanda, Ghandruk, Dhampus and Hyangja on the Annapurna Trek. Another danger spot is the Chisopani/Shivapuri area at the beginning of the Helambu Trek, but it pays to be cautious everywhere. Always be especially cautious

within two or three days of a road on which buses might offer a quick getaway. If you are camping, be warned that thieves often cut tents in the night and reach inside to grab whatever is handy.

Animals & Plants Most of the animals you will encounter on a trek are domesticated, so they present very little danger. But don't be foolish. There is rabies around, so don't pet dogs. Don't get downhill of a runaway yak or water buffalo – they can move fast. There are few mosquitoes in the hills, but malaria is endemic in the Terai, so take precautions if you are visiting a jungle lodge. You will rarely encounter a snake, but poisonous species do exist, particularly in the lowlands.

Nettles can inflict a nasty sting. Learn to recognise them and stay clear.

Strikes & Demonstrations
Nepal's political process involves frequent communist-style demonstrations and strikes. They are generally peaceful, but any large gathering of people can cause problems. Often there are processions in the street and meetings in Tundikhel, the parade ground in the centre of Kathmandu. If you come across a large group of slogan-chanting youths, it's best to avoid them in case you end up on the downstream side of a police *lathi* charge (a team of police wielding bamboo staves) or worse.

A normal procession or demonstration is a *julus*. If things escalate there may be a *chakka jam* ('jam the wheels'), in which all vehicles stay off the street, or a *bandh*, in which case not only do vehicles not ply the roads, but all shops, schools and offices are closed. If you're unlucky enough to have booked a flight during one of these events, you may end up walking to the airport or travelling in a bicycle rickshaw at an outrageous price.

Traffic & Pollution
Traffic on the streets of Kathmandu is a rumpus of pollution-belching two, three and four-wheel vehicles wending their way around a mass of people and a variety of

animals. Doomsters compare Kathmandu's air pollution to that of Mexico City. Sergio, the Mexican trek leader, assures everyone that it's nowhere near that bad. But the combination of ancient vehicles, low-quality fuel and lack of emission controls makes the streets of Kathmandu particularly dirty, noisy and unpleasant. Traffic rules do exist, but are rarely enforced; be especially careful when crossing streets and riding a bicycle. Traffic is supposed to travel on the left side of the road, but many drivers simply choose the most convenient side. Left turns are allowed without stopping, even at controlled intersections with red lights; beware of vehicles racing around a corner when you cross a road. Consider bringing a face mask to filter out dust and emission particles if you plan to ride a bicycle in Kathmandu.

The worst of the pollution and traffic problems are confined to central Kathmandu. Fortunately, you're going trekking. Other than enduring a day or two of pollution while you get your trekking permit, you won't have to deal with the problem much. There are a few smoky houses, but otherwise the air on a trek is crystal clear and the only traffic jams are caused by yaks and buffaloes.

BUSINESS HOURS

Saturday is the weekly holiday. The working week is Sunday to Friday, though many offices work only a half-day on either Friday or Sunday. Government offices open at 10 am and close at 5 pm (4 pm in winter when the days are short). Shops are usually open from 9.30 am to 7.30 or 8 pm. Banks, offices and most shopping areas are closed on Saturday and on most festival days and religious holidays.

Punctuality is not habitual in Nepal, but if you are dealing with a government office or a diplomatic functionary you should try to arrive within five to 10 minutes of the appointed time.

PUBLIC HOLIDAYS

In addition to festivals (see the Facts About the Country chapter), there are numerous public holidays. These tend to be more in line with the Western calendar and include:

10 January
Birth-anniversary of His Late Majesty King Prithvi Narayan Shah
18 February
National Democracy Day
14 April
New Year's Day
9 November
Constitution Day
28 December
Birthday of His Majesty the King

ACCOMMODATION
Kathmandu

Hotels in Kathmandu range from the luxurious to the downright depressing. The Hotel Association of Nepal has a reservation desk at the airport, and touts from small hotels meet every arriving flight, often offering free transportation to their hotel. Except at the budget end, Kathmandu hotel rates are expensive for what you get. Government tax adds considerably to the cost; it is charged on a sliding scale from 10% to 14% depending on the rating of the hotel. If you arranged your trek with an adventure travel company, the cost probably includes accommodation at one of the more expensive hotels.

The well-known hotels in all price ranges are booked solid during the trekking season, so you may have to do a bit of shopping, or take advantage of the airport touts, if you arrive without a reservation. There is an oversupply of hotel rooms in Kathmandu in both the budget and luxury categories, so you can always find a room somewhere.

Kathmandu's budget accommodation is centred around the Thamel area. Hotels include the famous Kathmandu Guest House and the lesser known but adequate Tibet Guest House, Star, Garuda, Utse, Mustang Holiday Inn and Shakti hotels. Mountaineers gather at the Potala Guest House and the Manang. Costs are in the US$10 to US$30 per night range. When you choose a hotel, check the room for street noise. Nepali drivers use their horn more than their brakes, so streetside rooms tend to be intolerable.

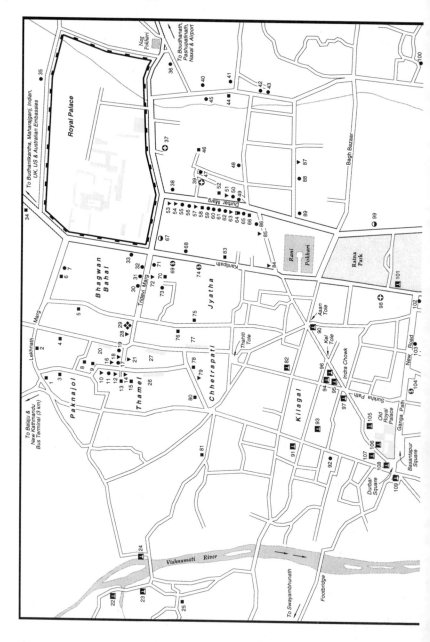

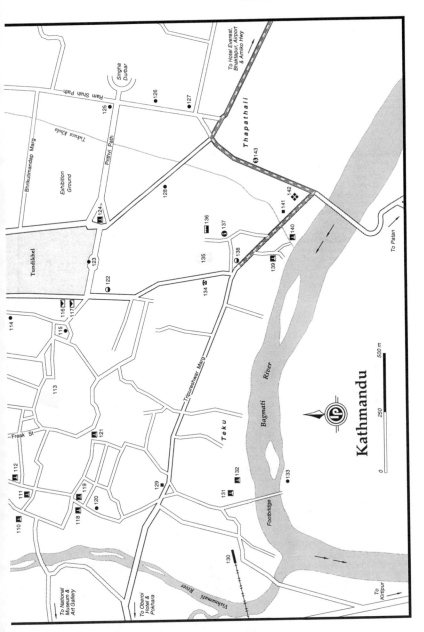

Kathmandu

PLACES TO STAY
1 Hotel Manang
2 Hotel Gauri Shanker
3 Hotel Marsyangdi
4 Pilgrims Hotel
5 Shakti
6 Hotel Malla
8 Hotel Shree Tibet
9 Hotel Garuda
13 Kathmandu Guest House
15 Star
25 Hotel Vajra
34 Hotel Ambassador
44 Marco Polo Business Hotel
46 Yak & Yeti Hotel
52 Hotel Sherpa
58 Hotel de l'Annapurna
66 Hotel Woodlands
70 Mustang Holiday Inn
75 Utse Hotel
76 Hotel Blue Diamond
78 Potala Guest House
80 Tibet Guest House
81 Sita Guest House
83 Hotel Yellow Pagoda
129 Hotel Valley View
141 Blue Star Hotel

PLACES TO EAT
10 Northfield Cafe
12 G's Terrace
14 Le Bistro
16 La Dolce Vita
18 KC's
21 Pumpernickel Bakery
28 Old Vienna
51 Tansen
53 Wimpys
54 Hot Breads
57 Baan Thai
63 Nirula's
64 Nanglo Pub
72 Fire & Ice
79 Narayan's Restaurant
84 Aroma Restaurant
85 Kathmandu Kitchen
87 Bhanchha Ghar Restaurant

OTHER
7 Northwest Airlines & KLM
11 Pilgrims Book House
17 Tashi's Trekking Shop
19 Alpine Travel Service
20 Trekking Equipment Shops
22 Shobabaghwati Temple
23 Bijeshwari Temple
24 Indrani Temple
26 Trekking Equipment Shops
27 Trekking Equipment Shops
29 Best Shopping Centre
30 Himalayan Rescue Association
31 Asian Airways
32 Immigration Office
33 Kaiser Library
35 Manakamna Airways
36 Nepal Mountaineering Association
37 Nepal International Clinic
38 Pakistan International Airlines
39 CIWEC Clinic
40 Nepal Airways
41 Krishna Loaf
42 Swissair
43 Cathay Pacific
45 Air India, Indian Airlines
47 Kailas Books
48 China Southwest Airlines
49 Ecotel Nepal
50 Private Car Booking Office
55 Singapore Airlines & Delta Airlines
56 Everest Air
59 Thai International
60 British Airways
61 Air France
62 Lufthansa
65 Qantas
67 Bus Stop for Pokhara Tourist Buses
68 British Council
69 Grindlays Bank
71 SAARC Secretariat
73 KEEP & Himalayan Explorers Club
74 Nabil Bank
77 Trekking Equipment Shops
82 Ikha Narayan Temple
86 American Express
88 Aeroflot
89 Clocktower
90 Annapurna Temple
91 Nara Devi Temple
92 Yatkha Bahal
93 Yitum Bahal
94 Jana Bahal Temple
95 Shiva Temple
96 Sweta Machhendranath Temple
97 Akash Bhairab Temple
98 Bir Hospital
99 City Bus Station
100 Necon Airways
101 Mahakala Temple
102 RNAC (international & domestic tourist flights)
103 US Library & Informtion Service
104 Nepal Bank
105 Taleju Temple
106 Jagannath Temple
107 Krishna Temple
108 Maju Deval
109 Kasthamandap
110 Bhimsen Temple
111 Hari Shankar Temple
112 Adko Narayan Temple
113 Vegetable Market
114 RNAC (other domestic flights)
115 Bhimsen Tower
116 Foreign Post Office (parcels)
117 Main Post Office
118 Ram Chandra Mandir
119 Jaisa Deval Temple
120 Takan Bahal
121 Machhendranath Temple
122 Buses for Pharping & Dakshinkali
123 Martyrs' Memorial Gate
124 Bhadrakali Temple
125 Duty Free Centre
126 Supreme Court
127 National Archives
128 Army Headquarters
130 Cableway Station
131 Pachali Bhairab
132 Tindeval Temple
133 Raj Ghat
134 Central Telegraph Office
135 National Stadium
136 Swimming Pool
137 Ministry of Tourism
138 Bhaktapur Trolley-Bus Terminus
139 Tripureshwar Mahadev Temple
140 Kalmochan Temple
142 Bluebird Supermarket
143 Nepal Rastra Bank

Ecotel Nepal (☎ 228210, 248591; fax 229380) offers a booking service for budget hotels in Thamel.

Bottom-End Hotels Hotels and guesthouses in this category range from US$10 to US$30 plus 10% or 11% tax and include:

Hotel Blue Diamond, Jyatha (☎ 226320; fax 226392)
Hotel Garuda, Thamel (☎ 416340; fax 413614)
Hotel Gauri Shanker, Sallaghari, Thamel (☎ 411605, 417181)
Hotel Manaslu, Lazimpat (☎ 413470; fax 416516)
Hotel Shree Tibet, Thamel (☎ 419902, 211092; fax (977) 1-419361)
Kathmandu Guest House, Thamel (☎ 418733, 413632; fax 417133)
Pilgrims Hotel, Thamel (☎ 416910; fax 22983)
Potala Guest House, Thamel (☎ 226566, 220467)
Tibet Guest House, Chetrapati (☎ 414383, 214951; fax 220518)
Utse Hotel, Thamel (☎ 226946, 228952; fax 226945)

Mid-Range Hotels Hotels and guesthouses in this category range from US$30 to US$80 plus 13% tax and include:

Hotel Ambassador, Lazimpat (☎ 414432, 410432; fax 413641)
Hotel Blue Star, Tripureshwore (☎ 228833; fax 226820)
Hotel Manang, Thamel (☎ 410993, 419247; fax 415821)
Hotel Marsyangdi, Thamel (☎ 412129, 414105; fax 410008)
Hotel Vajra, Swayambhunath (☎ 272719, 271545)
Hotel Woodlands, Durbar Marg (☎ 222683, 220123; fax 225650)
Hotel Yellow Pagoda, Kantipath (☎ 220337; fax 228914)
Marco Polo Business Hotel, Kamal Pokhari (☎ 415984, 415432; fax 413641)
Summit Hotel, Kupondole (☎ 521894, 524694; fax 523737)

Top-End Hotels Hotels in this category range from US$80 to US$125 plus 13% tax, and include the following:

Hotel Himalaya, Kupondole (☎ 523900; fax 523909)
Hotel Malla, Lekhnath Marg (☎ 418385; fax 418382)
Hotel Narayani, Pulchowk (☎ 521442, 521711; fax 521291)
Hotel Shangri La, Lazimpat (☎ 412999; fax 414184)
Hotel Shanker, Lazimpat (☎ 410151/2; fax 412961)

Hotel Sherpa, Durbar Marg (☎ 227000; fax 222026)
Kathmandu Hotel, Maharajganj (☎ 418984, 410786; fax 414091)

Over-the-Top Hotels Hotels in this bracket range from US$125 and up, plus 14% tax:

Hotel de l'Annapurna, Durbar Marg (☎ 221711; fax 225236)
Hotel Everest International, Naya Baneshwore (☎ 220567; fax 226088)
Hotel Yak & Yeti Durbar Marg (☎ 413999; fax 227782)
Soaltee Holiday Inn Crowne Plaza Tahachal (☎ 272550, 272555; fax 272205)

Hotels in the Hills

Local inns or *bhattis* have existed for centuries in the hills. A bhatti is usually a wooden or maybe even a bamboo structure close to the trail, with the large house of the owners some distance away. It usually has a simple mud stove with a pot of milk and another pot of hot water to make tea. There is usually a jug or two of *chhang* or *rakshi* in the back room to provide a bit of alcoholic diversion for the village elders and the few overnight guests who happen along. Where trekking has not developed, these reasonably primitive establishments are still the only hotel facilities available.

As trekking increased and as Nepali travellers began to have a bit more money, facilities improved and new hotels were built and developed into the extensive system of lodges that now serves major trekking routes. Most hotels in the hills are family-run affairs that started in the living room and grew as more and more trekkers appeared. Many have private rooms for guests, but some are still living-room affairs at which the family that operates the inn eats and sleeps in the same building, and often the same room, that it offers to guests.

Only since the mid-1970s have trekkers become an important source of income in the hills, so most of the hotels that cater to trekkers opened after 1979 or 1980. The proliferation of lodges is still continuing at a frantic pace, with each one trying to outdo the other. There have been 15 years of continual hotel

What to Expect in a Trekking Lodge

A typical trekkers' lodge in the hills has a central dining room with wooden tables and plank seats or, in some lodges, chairs. The kitchen is either at one end of the dining room or in a separate, adjacent room. In either case, smoke from a wood fire or the roar of a kerosene stove often permeates the eating area. The kitchen doubles as the lodge owners' family room, so meals for the elders and kids of the house are prepared – and often served – alongside yours. Despite the proximity of the family, there's not much opportunity for conversation or cultural interaction because of all the rushing around preparing food for hotel guests and the family.

If you opt for dormitory facilities, you'll usually get a narrow wooden cot and share the room with other trekkers and, in some places, local porters. The porters may entertain you with their drinking, card playing or radios. If the hotel has private rooms, the rooms will usually be the minimum size to accommodate two beds. The walls and door will be wood, or in more rustic lodges, bamboo mats or even curtains. Some places provide a cotton quilt and hard pillow, but don't count on finding these everywhere. There may be a table, and you can always ask the lodge owner for a candle, but that's usually the extent of the amenities. Some up-market facilities feature double beds, private toilets and hangers for clothing, but these are not common.

Beds are wooden bench-like structures with either a cotton or foam mattress, usually covered with a sheet that in the better establishments will be freshly laundered. The common toilet is usually in a shed outside; in most places it will be of the Asian squatting variety and will usually have a tin for collection of used toilet paper, which the lodge keeper will burn rather than risk clogging up the loo. There will also be a bucket of water or a tap (faucet) should you choose to clean up in the local manner – using your left hand. Most hotels keep their toilets surprisingly clean.

Trekkers seem to thrive on hot showers, so almost all lodges offer this facility. This is usually provided in a small shed with rustic plumbing which allows the one bucket of warm water you have been allocated to dribble over you. You should avoid those shower facilities that use wood fires to heat the water since this is a flagrant waste of a scarce resource. There are a growing number of solar-heated showers in the hills, and some lodges have a piping system that runs through the kitchen stove, automatically heating water at the same time food is cooked. Try to schedule your showers around these 'green' facilities. Americans should note that the door marked 'bathroom' leads to the shower; if nature is calling, choose the door marked 'toilet'.

Remember that all trekking lodges are 'mom and pop' operations, with the owners trying their best to make you comfortable. Some lodge owners have had a bit of training from ACAP or the hotel training centre in Kathmandu, but most are operating from instinct and trying to manage with limited supplies and in somewhat primitive conditions. The reason so many lodges have copycat facilities and menus is because everyone imitates the most successful operation they have seen. Try to be gentle, helpful and understanding as you deal with hotel keepers. Your assistance and advice can help them improve their facilities and service, and thereby earn more money to support their families. ∎

construction on the Everest and Annapurna treks, and it's a rare visit to the villages of Ghandruk and Namche Bazaar during which you are not subjected to the sounds of hammering by rock masons and carpenters. Features such as pavement cafes, sun rooms, private rooms, indoor Western-style toilets and electric lights abound. Hotels compete for the attention of your stomach with offerings of cake, pie, pizza, steaks, tacos, enchiladas and spaghetti bolognese. Someone commented that every house along the trail from Jiri to Gorak Shep and all the way around Annapurna was now a hotel. That's probably an overstatement, but cer-

tainly more than 50% of the houses on both those routes do cater to either trekkers or locals.

The primary incentive for operating a hotel in the hills is to turn locally produced food, labour and firewood into cash. The hills of Nepal are increasingly becoming a cash-oriented society. There are few ways to earn this cash, other than operating a hotel, that allow people to remain at home and tend to the house, children, livestock and crops. The prices at most hotels in the hills are artificially cheap for this reason. Intense competition and the lack of an alternative way to secure cash keeps prices ridiculously low. It certainly is not profitable to sell a cup of tea with sugar for Rs 3 (about five US cents) when sugar is Rs 24 per kg, tea is Rs 34 per 200g packet and it takes a full day to fetch a load of firewood. The Annapurna Conservation Area Project (ACAP) helped encourage an effort to standardise rates for food and accommodation, with the result that most hotels in a particular village charge the same. There are committees of lodge owners in both the Annapurna and Langtang regions that meet to establish minimum rates. The cost of accommodation is very low, so hotel-keepers expect you to eat in their establishments so they can earn a bit more money.

Often the husband of the house is away trading or working as a porter or trekking guide. Usually the wife manages things, but sometimes hotels are left in the care of children. Some pretty weird meals and service can result when a six or eight-year-old tries to deal with customers. In remote areas that trekkers do not frequent, the 'hotel' may exist only in the mind of the proprietor and will consist of sharing the eating and living accommodation with a family.

It is a bit pretentious to call some of these village establishments hotels, but the most common word in Nepali for restaurant or eating place is 'hotel'. Since the word hotel has, therefore, been pre-empted, Nepalis use the word 'lodge' for a sleeping place or inn. Thus in the hills of Nepal a 'hotel' has food, but may not provide a place to sleep, while a 'lodge' always offers accommodation. Many innkeepers specify the services they provide by calling their establishments 'Hotel & Lodge'. In reality you can almost always find food and some kind of accommodation at any trailside establishment.

There are still numerous bhattis that are not westernised. These normally cater to porters and Nepali travellers and usually do not have any signboard at all. In remote regions, these are the only facilities available, and conditions can be pretty rough. On routes where trekkers' hotels exist, the local-style teahouses are where the locals and porters eat, drink and sleep. Trekkers are

more than welcome in these places, and a night in a local inn can be a great experience (and a good time warp back to what trekking was like in the 1970s), but it's often a night of *dal bhat* (lentil soup and rice), smoke, coughing and dirt.

In this book I have used 'hotel' or 'lodge' to refer to trekkers' hotels and 'teahouse' or 'bhatti' to refer to small local-style hotels. This is really an artificial distinction, but should give you an idea of the general standard you can expect. A Nepali would probably make the distinction by calling a trekkers' lodge a big hotel and a bhatti a small hotel.

FOOD
Nepali Food
The most common meal in Nepal is dal bhat – rice (bhat) with a soup made of lentils (dal) poured over it. Hill people subsist on dal bhat and a thick paste called *dhindo*. This is coarse ground corn or millet, often mixed with a few hot chillies. In the northern regions people call this dish *tsampa* and make it from roasted and ground barley. Sherpas and other Himalayan people often mix tsampa with buttered and salted Tibetan tea.

The local diet rarely includes meat or eggs, so dal provides the primary source of protein. *Roti* (unleavened bread) or *chappati* is another frequent addition to a meal and is often substituted for rice. Of other items that may supplement a meal, the most usual is a curry made from potatoes or whatever vegetables are in season.

Trekking Food
Although some hotels in the hills can conjure up fantastic meals, the standard hotel diet is dal bhat or, at higher elevations, potatoes. Dal bhat twice a day for a month presents a boring prospect to the Western palate, though it's nutritious and healthy. On major trek routes, restaurants vary in standard from primitive to luxurious, and beer, Coke and other soft drinks are available at high prices. The menus are often attractive and extensive, but too often the menu represents the innkeeper's fantasy of what they would like

to serve, not what's available. In bhattis and small hotels the choice almost always comes down to rice, dal, potatoes, pancakes and instant noodles. If meat is on the menu, it will usually be chicken. Goat, mutton or buffalo meat is sometimes available, but never beef. In accordance with Hindu tradition, the cow is sacred in Nepal.

On the major trek routes the menus are extensive and some hotel cooks can turn out some surprisingly good Western-style meals. Apple pie appears on many menus, and most hotels can produce something resembling a pizza, but they are hindered by a limited supply of ingredients and spices, and recipes are passed along by word of mouth, often losing something in the translation. Don't get your hopes too high if you order one of the exotic dishes; moussaka, for example (often listed on a menu under Mexican food), could turn out to be anything.

Thirty years ago, Tilman observed that a person can live off the country in a sombre fashion, but Nepal was no place in which to make a gastronomic tour. It hasn't changed. In Kathmandu, a city of more than a million people, it takes a lot of imagination to provide the variety in diet that Westerners expect. In remote regions, it is almost impossible to provide this variety unless you bring the food with you. Most people can adapt to a Nepali diet, but try it for a few days at home so you know what to expect. Boiled rice with a thick split pea soup poured over it is the closest approximation to dal bhat. This experiment might help convince you to fill the remote corners of your backpack with spices, trail snacks and other goodies.

Vegetarian Food

If you're a vegetarian, you are in luck. There is very little meat available in trekking lodges, and even organised camping treks don't get a lot of meat. You will have no problem getting vegetarian food either in Kathmandu or on a trek. There is an excellent vegetarian restaurant in the back of Pilgrims Book House in Thamel. The *Naach Ghar* restaurant in the Yak & Yeti Hotel is also vegetarian.

STAN ARMINGTON

This bakery in Namche Bazaar makes good use of an abundant hydroelectricity supply to tempt trekkers with fresh-baked delicacies.

Kathmandu Restaurants

Trekkers attach great importance to their stomachs. Kathmandu's restaurants have responded by offering some of the most varied menus in Asia. In Thamel, try *KC's*, the original budget travellers' restaurant; *La Dolce Vita* for Italian food; *Northfield Cafe* for Mexican food; or walk down to Lazimpat, where *Himthai* serves Thai food. There are many other restaurants and pie shops, particularly in Thamel, that serve meals in the Rs 50 to Rs 100 range. Old stand-bys in Thamel include the *Pumper-nickel Bakery*, *Le Bistro*, *G's Terrace*, *Utse*, *Old Vienna* and *Narayan's Restaurant*. On Durbar Marg try *Hot Breads* for cakes and snacks, *Wimpys* and *Nirula's* for fast food, *Baan Thai* for Thai and *Tansen* for Indian food. On the way back to Thamel, stop at *Fire & Ice* for pizza and soft ice cream. Local expats and mountaineers gather at *Mike's Breakfast*, which is near the police headquarters, a short taxi or bicycle ride from Thamel. You can find dal bhat and momos at street-corner restaurants, but for safety, stick to the *Kathmandu Kitchen*, *Bhanchha Ghar* or the *Nanglo Pub* if you want Nepali food.

For a big splurge, head to the hotels for

good Indian, Chinese and Continental food. Indian food at the *Ghar E Kabab* in the Hotel Annapurna and *Far Pavilion* in the Everest International is expensive. The *Kabab Corner* in the Hotel Gautam is cheaper. The Soaltee Holiday Inn is a bit out of town, but has two excellent restaurants: *Bukhara* and *Al Fresco*. *Imperial Pavilion* in the Malla has Sichuan food and the *Chimney Room* in the Hotel Yak & Yeti is the last incarnation of Boris' legendary restaurant. All restaurants and bars in Kathmandu, except those in large hotels, must close at 10 pm.

DRINKS
Soft Drinks & Bottled Water

Nepal has all the international brands of soft drinks. All are made in Kathmandu and distributed in bottles, not cans. The bottle deposits are more than the cost of the drink, so leave the bottle behind when you quaff a Coke at a trailside stall. Locally produced fruit drinks are sold in cardboard cartons and many of these have made their way into the hills, offering a refreshing thirst quencher. Look for mango *frooty* and apple *appy*.

So-called mineral water is available throughout Nepal and the bottles it comes in make emergency trekking water bottles. The plastic bottles are not recyclable and there are mounds of discarded mineral water bottles throughout the hills. You can help reduce this aspect of litter by passing up the mineral water and drinking water you have treated with iodine. This may, in fact, be a safer solution than drinking mineral water. Even in Britain there was a scandal about tap water being sold in bottles; imagine what happens in Nepal, where controls and testing are nonexistent.

Alcohol

For a small country, Nepal has a thriving beer industry. The local brands, Star, Golden Tiger, Iceberg and Cheers, come in 650 ml bottles. Tuborg, Carlsberg, San Miguel and Singha also brew in Nepal, and distribute in cans if you want to carry beer on your trek. There's no need to carry it, however, because you can get bottled beer in lodges and teahouses, even in the remotest villages.

Despite the traditional Brahman abstinence, a lot of alcohol is consumed in Nepal. The local potions are chhang and rakshi, which can be quite tasty and potent, but there are also numerous Western-style liquors available. The notorious Kukhri Rum makes a fine after-trek drink on cold nights. Snow Lands Gin advertises its roots in London, Glasgow and Kathmandu. A few districts in Nepal are dry, including Jumla and the region near Royal Bardia National Park in the Terai. Local women, concerned about drunken husbands, are agitating in several more districts to enact similar legislation.

Trekking Drinks

Don't drink tap water or stream water anywhere. Instead, stick to soft drinks, bottled water, beer, or water you have purified yourself. It can be difficult to get boiled water on a trek. Ask an innkeeper if the water is boiled and they will assure you that it is, even if it has just been taken from the river. This response illustrates several unusual facets of Nepali culture and personality. Most hill people do not understand germs. They accept good-naturedly the desire of Westerners that their drinking water be boiled, but few people understand why. They often believe that Westerners like only hot water. Another consideration is that Nepalis like to please others and dislike answering any question negatively. So you get a 'yes' answer to almost every question, particularly 'Is this water boiled?'. In addition, hotels do not like to prepare boiled water because it uses fuel and takes up space on the stove – and they can't charge for the service.

There are two easy solutions which ensure that you have safe drinking water: a properly made cup of tea will be made with boiled water (though tea made with tea bags – as it sometimes is these days – may not); and treating water with iodine solves the problem in a way that does not consume scarce fuel. See the discussion of this technique in the Health & Safety chapter.

If you decide to sample chhang and rakshi,

Don't Drink Mineral Water on a Trek

A recent phenomenon in the hills is the large-scale use of bottled mineral water by trekkers. So-called mineral water is produced in both India and Nepal and is always packaged in sealed plastic bottles. Assuming you get a genuine bottle, what you are usually getting is tap water that has been filtered and passed by an ultraviolet light – a process that is supposed to purify the water. What you really get could be anything.

What happens to the bottle when you drink this litre of water? It is not recyclable, it is of no use to anyone, it does not biodegrade (ever) and it is bulky. Empty mineral-water bottles have surpassed pink Chinese toilet paper as the prime eyesore of the Nepal Himalaya.

There are many ways to obtain safe drinking water. All these are described in detail in the Health & Safety chapter of this book. If you don't like the taste of iodine, bring flavouring. Vitamin C tablets are also said to kill the iodine taste, but be sure you let the iodine do its work before you add the vitamin C or flavouring. You can also purchase bottled soft drinks wherever you find mineral water. These come in glass bottles that are valuable enough that trash collectors wander the hills collecting bottles to carry back to Kathmandu for refilling. In addition to the environmental considerations, there's also an economic incentive. A bottle of mineral water costs Rs 50 or more in the hills, and water treated with iodine is almost free. ■

remember that chhang is made from water straight from the river, not boiled water.

Throughout Nepal a cup of tea is served with a large dollop of milk and presweetened with sugar. If you want to avoid this, order 'black tea'. A cup of tea in a trekking lodge is usually served in a glass. It takes a bit of practice to drink the hot tea without burning your fingers. When the 'glass' is made of stainless steel, you'll probably have to break out your handkerchief in order to hold it.

If you want to avoid caffeine, try the herbal teas that are made in Nepal. Most hotels in the hills don't supply them, but you can buy a supply in most shops in Thamel, including Pilgrims Book House. Another good caffeine-free drink is hot lemon, which is available everywhere.

THINGS TO BUY

Bring enough money to buy whatever souvenirs, incredible bargains or art objects you may find. In Kathmandu there are Tibetan carpets (US$90 to US$150), woollen jumpers and jackets (US$5 to US$25). Some genuine Tibetan art pieces (US$20 on up to thousands of dollars) and semiprecious stones (US$15 to US$25) are also available. On the trek you may find objects from Tibet (prayer wheels, *thangka* paintings, butter lamps and bells) or Sherpa household arti-

cles (chhang bottles, boots, aprons, carpets and cups) at prices from US$1 to more than US$100.

Most Tibetan jewellery, statues and handicrafts were historically and traditionally made by Newar craftspeople in Nepal. You can often buy recently made Tibetan art that is as authentic as an antique smuggled in from Tibet. For serious art purchases there are shops in Thamel and Durbar Marg. Indigo Gallery, located upstairs at Mike's Breakfast, is a reputable dealer in fine art.

If you plan to make a major purchase in Nepal, first visit an importer at home and find out what is available at what price. Especially note the quality, so that you will have a basis for comparison in Nepal. Many pieces exported from India and Nepal may be available in your locale at prices lower than in retail shops in Kathmandu because of large-volume discounts. Tibetan carpets made in Nepal are for sale in San Francisco, for example, for less than it would cost to buy one in Nepal and ship it home.

Other bargains in Kathmandu include photo processing, extra visa photos, trekking and climbing gear, woollen socks and cotton clothing. You can also buy embroidered T-shirts in a variety of standard patterns or with your own special design or you can have your own shirt or jacket embroidered.

Locally made sandals (fake 'Tevas') and trekking gear with fake brand names are cheap and may last through a trek, but they're not a good long-term investment. Outrageous velvet top hats, wizards' hats and court jester hats are available from many shops in Thamel, including the Mad Hatter.

Trekking Information

ABOUT TREKKING IN NEPAL

A trek in Nepal is a different kind of outdoor holiday from most other mountain walks or climbs. On a trek you walk up and down steep hills through remote hill villages where farmers raise crops and herd their livestock. In most villages there is no electricity, no telephone, no airport and no hospital. Most villages do have a school, a rudimentary post office and some sort of facility that provides food and lodging for travellers.

A typical trek is one to three weeks long. Since you'll be walking for many days, you'll need food and accommodation along the way. In Nepal there are two options for this. You can rely on local facilities, or you can travel with an entourage that carries all its food and tents with it. On major trekking routes the hotel facilities are well developed and cater to basic Western standards of taste and hygiene, so it's easy and practical to rely on them. In more remote regions, the facilities are local-style bhattis that can be dirty and crowded and serve unhygienic, monotonous food. If you trek off the beaten track, you will be better off (and, in some places, required by government regulations) to trek with a full complement of tents, porters and camp staff.

A Trek is Not a Climbing Trip

Whether you begin your trek at a roadhead or fly in to a remote mountain airstrip, a large part of your trek will be in the Middle Hills region at elevations between 500m and 3000m. In this part of Nepal there are always well-developed trails through villages and across mountain passes. Even at high alti-

tudes there are intermittent settlements used during summer by shepherds, so the trails, though often indistinct, are always there. You can easily travel on any trail without the aid of ropes or mountaineering skills. There are rare occasions when there is snow on the trail, and on some high passes it might be necessary to place a safety line for your companions or porters if there is deep snow. Still, alpine techniques are almost never used on a traditional trek. Anyone who has walked extensively in the mountains has all the skills necessary for an extended trek in Nepal.

Though some treks venture near glaciers, and even cross the foot of them, most treks do not allow the fulfilment of any Himalayan mountaineering ambitions. Nepal's mountaineering regulations allow trekkers to climb 18 specified peaks with a minimum of formality, but you must still make a few advance arrangements for such climbs. Many adventure travel companies offer so-called climbing treks which include the ascent of one of these peaks as a feature of the trek. There are a few peaks that, under ideal conditions, are within the resources of individual trekkers. A climb can be arranged in Kathmandu if conditions are right, but a climb of one of the more difficult peaks should be planned well in advance. The appendix on mountaineering at the back of this book describes these processes in more detail.

A Trek Requires Physical Effort

A trek is physically demanding because of its length and the almost unbelievable changes in elevation. During the 300 km trek from Jiri to Everest base camp and return, for example, the trail gains and loses more than 9000m of elevation during many steep ascents and descents. On most treks, the daily gain is less than 800m in about 15 km, though ascents of as much as 1200m are typical of some days. You can always take plenty of time during the day to cover this distance, so the physical exertion, though quite strenuous at times, is not sustained. There is always plenty of time for rest.

Probably the only physical problem that

may make a trek impossible is a history of knee problems on descents. In Nepal the descents are long, steep and unrelenting. There is hardly a level stretch of trail in the entire country. If you are an experienced walker and often hike 15 km a day with a pack, a trek should prove no difficulty. You will be pleasantly surprised at how easy the hiking can be if you carry only a light backpack and do not have to worry about meal preparation.

Previous experience in hiking and living outdoors is, however, helpful as you make plans for your trek. The first night of a month-long trip is too late to discover that you do not like to sleep in a sleeping bag. Mountaineering skills are not necessary, but you must enjoy walking.

A Trek is Long

A short trek is three to seven days long, an average trek is two weeks, and a long trek may be 30 days or more. Every day you walk leads you one day further into the hills; unless there is an airstrip, you will also have to walk that same distance to get back to Kathmandu. It's worth making proper preparations before you start a trek so that you don't end up a week away from Kathmandu and find that you are ill-equipped, totally exhausted or unable to cope with the thought of walking all that distance back.

TYPES OF TREK

There is endless discussion among trekkers about which is the most environmentally sensitive and culturally rewarding way to trek. There are valid arguments on all sides, but in the end it will be how you, the trekker, interact with Nepal and its people that will determine the richness of your experience. Those on camping treks can learn Nepali and gain great cultural insight from the sherpas that accompany them, or they can ignore them and treat them like servants. Similarly, trekkers who stay in lodges can befriend a family that runs the lodge, or can view the kids crawling around and playing with cameras as an irritating intrusion. In the end, your choice of a trekking style will depend

The Rest Step
Of course you know how to walk; you've been doing it all your life. But walking all day in the mountains is very different from walking on city streets. One of the most important things you can learn to make your trek more pleasant is the mountaineers' rest step. If you learn to do this right, you can push on up the steepest hill without getting tired. My old (age 73) trekking partner, Bob Peirce, has mastered this technique (he says it's because he's lazy). He often falls far behind, yet he is often the first one into camp – and still has energy to walk back down to the village for a beer.

Practice this on a reasonably steep hill. Lock your downhill leg and swing the uphill leg up, placing it on the ground. Pause for an instant, being totally relaxed, with your locked downhill leg carrying all your weight. Shift the weight to your uphill leg, straighten it and lock it, and repeat the process. Move *slowly* up the hill. You will fall behind the porters at first, then pass them as they rest and you keep walking. You can go on like this for hours without stopping if you maintain the rhythm and coordinate your breathing with your walking. It's so easy that you can even carry on a conversation as you walk up a steep trail. Don't look up the trail; just concentrate on walking, and before you know it, you'll be at the top of the hill. ■

on your own personality, your ability to deal with uncertainty and bureaucracy, and the amount of time and, more importantly, money that you have available. No style of trekking is intrinsically 'better' than any other, and whatever you do, your trek will infuse money into the hill economy and provide employment for people in remote villages.

There are numerous ways to structure a trek because of two major factors. Firstly, there is inexpensive (by Western standards) professional and nonprofessional labour available to carry loads and to work as guides and camp staff. Secondly, you can almost always find supplies and accommodation locally because there are people living in even the most remote trekking areas. The traditional backpacking approach of a light pack, stove, freeze-dried food and a tent is not an appropriate way to trek in Nepal. So much food is available in hill villages that it doesn't make much sense to try to be totally self-sufficient while trekking. Similarly, with so many trekking companies in Nepal, it hardly makes sense to try to hire your own crew of sherpas and porters and try to organise a fully equipped camping trek yourself. By shopping around, you can certainly find a trekking company that will outfit your trek for a price that matches your budget.

The many possible ways of trekking can be reduced to two primary approaches: lodge treks and camping treks.

Lodge Treks

The most popular way to trek in Nepal for both Nepalis and Westerners is to use local inns for accommodation as they travel. Decent hotel accommodation for trekkers is most readily available in the Annapurna region, Langtang and the Khumbu (Mt Everest) region. In these areas you can operate with a bare minimum of equipment and rely on lodges for food and shelter. In this manner, it will cost US$3 to US$10 a day, depending on where you are and how simply you can live and eat. It becomes much more expensive at high altitudes and in very remote areas.

Bedding is not usually available at lodges, so on most treks you should carry your own sleeping bag. An exception is the Pokhara to Jomsom trek, where most Thakali inns have bedding available – usually a cotton-filled quilt. Sometimes the bedding has the added attraction of lice and other bed companions. Bring along your own sheet or sleeping bag to provide some protection against these bugs. During the busy trekking seasons in October to November and March to April, it may be difficult to find bedding every night on the Jomsom trek.

Although most trekkers' lodges in the hills are reasonably comfortable, the accommodation in some places may be a dirty, often smoky, home. Chimneys are rare, so a room on an upper floor of a house can turn into an intolerable smokehouse as soon as someone lights the cooking fire in the kitchen below – and if they're frying chillies, you'll be

driven out in a hurry. Often it is possible to sleep on the porches of houses, but your gear is then less secure. The most common complaint among trekkers who rely on local facilities is about smoky accommodation.

By arranging your food and accommodation locally, you can move at your own pace and set your own schedule. You can move faster or slower than others and make side trips not possible with a large group. You can spend a day photographing mountains, flowers or people – or you can simply lie around for a day. Lodges in the hills provide a special meeting place for trekkers from throughout the world. You are free (within the limits imposed by your trekking permit) to alter your route and change your plans to visit other out-of-the-way places as you learn about them. You will have a good opportunity to see how the people in the hills of Nepal live, work and eat and will probably develop at least a rudimentary knowledge of the Nepali language.

You are, however, dependent on facilities in villages or in heavily trekked regions. Therefore you must trek in inhabited areas and on the better known routes. You may need to alter your schedule to reach a certain lodge for lunch or dinner. You can miss a meal if there is no lodge when you need one or if the hotel you are counting on is closed. A few packets of biscuits in your backpack are good insurance against these rough spots. Most of the major routes are well documented, but they are also well travelled. A hotel can be out of food if there are many other trekkers or if you arrive late. You may have to change your planned destination for the day when you discover that the lunch you ordered at an inn will take a very long time to prepare. You will usually make this discovery only after you have already waited an hour or so. It is wise to be aware of these kinds of problems and to prepare yourself to deal with them.

If you deviate from popular routes, be prepared to fend for yourself at times. If, however, you carry food, cooking pots and a tent to use even one night, you have already escalated beyond the lodge approach into a more complex form of trekking with different problems. If you've set your sights on a high mountain destination, you might combine lodges with a bit of backpacking. Depending on the terrain and local weather conditions, villages are found up to 4000m, but above this there isn't much accommodation available except in tourist areas such as the Annapurna Sanctuary, Everest base camp and Gokyo. It is also difficult to arrange to hire porters who have the proper clothing and footwear for travelling in cold and snow. If you plan to visit these higher regions, you may wish to alter your trekking style and utilise a backpacking or mountaineering approach to reach high passes or the foot of remote glaciers.

A good solution is to have a porter carry your high-altitude gear to the highest hotel, then leave your low-altitude gear behind at a temporary 'base camp' in the care of your (hopefully trustworthy) porter or hotel keeper. You can then spend a few days carrying a reduced load of food and equipment on your own. This will provide you with the best of both worlds: an enriching cultural encounter that conforms to the standards and traditions of the country in the lowlands, and a wilderness or mountaineering experience in the high mountains.

If you undertake a lodge trek, you can hire a porter to carry your gear or perhaps hire a guide to accompany you. A guide is not particularly necessary, but if you are travelling without a companion, it's a good idea to hire someone to travel with you. A guide can be invaluable if you have an accident or become ill, and travelling with a Nepali will give you a chance to learn more of the language and culture of Nepal. Your porter and/or guide will also stay in lodges, though porters will probably find their own, cheaper facilities in a local-style bhatti.

Organised Lodge Treks A number of adventure travel companies offer escorted lodge treks, which they often call 'teahouse treks'. Most companies take over an entire lodge for their group and provide all food and accommodation as part of the package.

Porters carry your gear, and a guide travels with the group during the day and handles all the arrangements for lunch and dealings with bureaucracy. This may be a good way to arrange your trek, particularly in the busy autumn season, though the price is still much higher than arranging everything as you go.

Camping Treks

The classic style of trekking in Nepal is to camp in tents and employ porters to carry your gear and sherpas to set up camp, cook and serve meals. You carry a backpack with only a water bottle, camera and jacket. At last count there were 338 trekking companies in Nepal whose business it is to organise camping treks and provide all sherpas, porters and equipment. There are companies that cater to almost any budget, though you may have to shop for an agency that suits you. Be particularly careful in your negotiations and have a clear understanding of who is expected to pay for what; while many trekkers have had great treks, others have complained bitterly about the service they have received. On a camping trek there are numerous hidden expenses that drive up the price; if you are overly concerned about getting 'ripped off,' then you're better off doing a lodge trek and paying for everything as you go.

Several companies offer treks with fixed departure dates and advertise them on bulletin boards and signposts in Thamel and by the lakeside in Pokhara. These treks can turn out to be excellent bargains, especially if your time is limited and one of these treks happens to fit your schedule.

One measure of protection when choosing a trekking company is to verify whether it is a member of the Trekking Agents Association of Nepal (TAAN). Only 149 trekking companies are TAAN members; if you trek with one of these companies and have a problem, TAAN may be able to help you gain some redress. There are many items that the larger, more reputable companies include as a matter of course and some smaller companies add later as extra fees. Check whether the cost of your trek includes the following:

trekking permit, national park or conservation fee, porter insurance, transportation from Kathmandu to the start of the trek, transport back to Kathmandu, sleeping bags, foam pads, tents, a 'fuel surcharge' for the use of kerosene, porter insurance and advancing money on your behalf for emergency rescue.

If you want to arrange everything in advance, you can contact a trekking company in Kathmandu or Pokhara by mail or fax and ask it to make arrangements for your trek. Unless you have a good idea of what you want, it will take a huge volume of correspondence to provide you with the information you require, to determine your specific needs, to define your precise route and itinerary and to negotiate a price that both parties understand. Mail takes up to three weeks each way to and from Australia, the Americas or Europe. It's far better to communicate by fax or email. Be specific in your communications and be sure that the trekking company understands exactly who will provide what equipment. It is most embarrassing to discover on the first night that someone forgot the sleeping bags.

You can go to Nepal and simply sort out the details in an hour or two of face-to-face negotiations with a trekking company. You should be prepared to spend several days in Kathmandu settling these details and another day or so while the logistics are organised. One disadvantage of this on-the-spot approach is that you may have to wait several days for a flight booking, or perhaps wait while the trekking company collects a sherpa crew and porters for you.

Another alternative to endless correspondence with Nepal is to use the services of the overseas agent of a Nepal trekking company. These agents should have someone who can give you the information you require, and they should have a regular system of communication with Nepal. Dealing with an agent usually involves paying them a fee to make all the arrangements. This is virtually identical to the process of booking your trek through an adventure travel company, as described in the next section.

Prices for camping treks vary significantly depending on the destination, the number of days, the size of the group, and the mode of transport to the start of the trek. If you, your sherpas and porters all pile into a local bus with the luggage on the roof, you'll pay much less than if you travel separately in the relative comfort of a taxi or Land Rover. Similarly, if you arrange a trek starting from Lukla or Jomsom, you will have to pay for the staff to fly or walk there and the gear to be transported from Kathmandu. If you're a group of 10 or more, the basic cost will start at about US$20 to US$25 per day from the cheapest trekking company and US$35 per day from a more up-market company. If there are only one or two of you, expect to pay US$30 to US$60 per day or more in addition to transportation costs.

Because the food for the trek is carried by porters, a variety of meals is possible. This may include canned goods from Kathmandu and imported food bought from expeditions or other exotic sources. A skilled cook can prepare an abundant variety of tasty Western-style food. The meals a good sherpa cook can prepare in an hour over a kerosene stove would put many Western cafes to shame.

On a camping trek you sleep in a tent; this gives you a place to spread out your gear without fear that someone will pick it up, and probably means that you will have a quiet night, away from the uproar of a lodge. In addition, a tent also gives you the freedom to go to bed when you choose. You can retire immediately after dinner to read or sleep, or sit up and watch the moon rise as you discuss the day's outing. Because there are also tents for the sherpas, and often the porters, you do not need to camp near villages, and can trek comfortably to remote regions and to high altitudes.

Money and staff hassles rarely surface on a camping trek. The trek is under the control of a *sirdar*, or trail boss, who is responsible for making minor purchases along the way and ensures a full complement of porters every day. Unless you are particularly interested, or quite watchful, you may never be

A Typical Day on a Camping Trek

On a camping trek the day begins at 6 am with a call of 'tea sir'. A cup of tea or coffee soon appears through the tent flap. After you drink your tea or, as I do, spill it all over the tent, you pack your gear and emerge to a light breakfast of Darjeeling tea, coffee, porridge and eggs or pancakes. While you are eating, the sherpas take down the tents and pack up loads for the porters. The entire group is usually on the way by 7 am. The early start takes advantage of the cool morning to accomplish most of the day's hike. Even on a group trek, many trekkers find an opportunity to hike alone for much of the day. The porters are slower and the sherpas, especially the cook crew, race on ahead to have lunch waiting when you arrive.

There are many diversions on the trail. It is not unusual to find sherpas and fellow trekkers in shops or bhattis. Sometimes the entire group may stop to watch a festival or some other special event along the way. At a suitable spot, usually at about 11 am, there is a stop of an hour or two for lunch. The noon meal includes the inevitable tea, a plate of rice, potatoes or noodles, some canned or fresh meat and whatever vegetables are in season.

The afternoon trek is shorter, ending at about 3 pm when you round a bend to (hopefully) discover your tents already set up in a field near a village. The kitchen crew again prepares tea and coffee soon after arrival in camp. There is then an hour or two to nurse blisters, read, unpack and sort gear, wash or explore the surrounding area before dinner.

Trekking cooks usually serve Western food. It is tasty and plentiful, but can be pretty boring after two weeks or so. Even so, the meals will be taxing the imagination of the cooks, who will be providing a variety of foods which they never experience in their own meals. Most trekkers feel healthy and fit on this diet as the food is fresh and organic, with no preservatives.

The sun sets early during the trekking season, so it is dark by 6 pm. There is time to read by candlelight in tents or to sit around talking in the dark. To conserve firewood, there is never a campfire. Most trekkers are asleep by 8 or 9 pm. ■

---

aware that these negotiations are taking place.

Treks with an Adventure Travel Company

There are companies in the USA, Germany, the UK, Japan, Switzerland, France, Australia, New Zealand and Scandinavia that specialise in adventure travel. Almost all of these companies have a Nepal trekking programme among their offerings. Each adventure travel company works through a particular trekking company in Nepal, and some have agreements for the exclusive representation of a Nepal trekking company in their own country. The names and addresses of some of the major adventure travel companies that specialise in Nepal are listed in the Getting There & Away chapter. You can find advertisements for many other similar companies in any outdoor magazine such as *Outside* or *Sierra Club Bulletin* in the USA, *High*, *Outdoor* or *Outdoors Illustrated* in the UK, *Wild* in Australia, or *Action Asia*.

Adventure travel companies advertise group treks on specific dates. They usually provide a Western leader to act as guide, cultural interpreter, first aid practitioner and social director. Though they specialise in group treks, most companies can also make the arrangements, including a leader, for a family or a collection of friends according to their own schedule. Though most of the treks you will find advertised are fully equipped camping treks, some companies also offer escorted, prearranged lodge treks; often these are advertised as 'teahouse treks'.

There are numerous advantages to booking a trek through an adventure travel company, the most obvious one being the ability to telephone a knowledgeable person locally for assistance and advice. You should also consider booking a trek in advance if you don't have a partner to trek with; the adventure travel company advertises for companions on your behalf.

On a prearranged trek, you will be trekking with people you have not met before. Although some strong friendships may develop, there may also be some in the party you would much rather not have met. For some people, this prospect alone rules out their participation in a group trek. The major drawback, however, will probably be the cost. Group camping treks usually start at US$100 per person per day of the trek. On the positive side, by fixing the destination and schedule in advance, all members of the group will have prepared themselves for the trip and should have proper equipment and a clear understanding of the schedule and terrain. Read the brochures and other material prepared by the trip organiser to see if it is likely to attract the type of people you'd get along with.

Most adventure travel companies cater for people to whom time is more important (within limits) than money. For many, the most difficult part of planning a trek is having the time to do so. These people are willing to pay more to avoid wasting a week of their limited vacation sitting around in Kathmandu making arrangements or waiting along the way for a spare seat on a plane. Adventure travel companies try to cram as many days in the hills as possible into a given time span. They also make reservations for hotels and domestic flights well in advance. Thus, theoretically, these hassles are also eliminated.

A usual condition of a group trek is that the party must stick to its prearranged route and, within limits, must meet a specific schedule. This means that you may have to forego an appealing side trip or festival and, if you are sick, you will probably have to keep moving with the rest of the group. You also may not agree with a leader's decisions if the schedule must be adjusted because of weather, health, or political or logistical considerations.

A group camping trek follows a tradition and a routine that trekkers and mountaineers have developed and refined for more than 50 years. You can travel in much the same manner as the approach marches described in Hunt's *The Ascent of Everest*, Herzog's *Annapurna* and Ullman's *Americans on Everest*, a feature not possible with other styles. If your interest in the Himalaya was kindled through such books, you still have the opportunity to experience this delightful way to travel. There are many reasons why these expeditions went to all the trouble and expense to travel as they did.

You can have a wonderful and altogether refreshing holiday when all the camp and logistics problems are removed from your responsibility and you are free to enjoy fully the land and the people which have attracted mountaineers for a century.

PERMITS & FORMALITIES
Trekking Permits

Trekking permits are issued by the central immigration office, a branch of the Home Ministry. The procedure is similar to getting a visa extension and involves a lot of queueing and waiting. Submit your application between 10.30 am and 2 pm Sunday to Thursday or between 10.30 am and noon on Friday.

To start the process, collect an application form and a card from the reception counter in the immigration office. The card is the trekking permit, and you must fill in all the details yourself. There are separate colour-coded forms and permits for Annapurna, Everest, Langtang and Kanchenjunga. If you are trekking to some other region such as Rara Lake, Dolpo or Makalu, get the form for 'miscellaneous' areas.

Be sure you fill in the right application form and permit card, otherwise you will wait in a long queue, only to be sent back for another form if the preprinted destination is incorrect. Once you have filled in the application, waited in a queue, presented all the necessary documents and photos and paid the fee, you will be told to come back after 5 pm. After queueing again, you will receive the completed permit, which is the card you originally filled out embellished with stickers, stamps and signatures.

The preprinted forms allow all the possible routes in each region. For any 'miscellaneous' destinations, you should include on the application an extensive list of village or district names. If you are headed for an unusual locale, be careful as you write these destinations on your trekking permit, and when you get the permit back, check that nothing has been crossed out. Only the immigration offices in Kathmandu or Pokhara may alter a permit.

It is not necessary, as it once was, to have a trekking company arrange a trekking permit for you, although a trekking company can usually get a permit faster than you can. Permits for restricted areas and for Kanchenjunga are issued only to camping treks arranged by a trekking company; most other areas are open to individual trekkers.

You *must* have a trekking permit. Police checkposts are abundant on every trekking route and you will be endlessly hassled if you do not have proper documentation. Rangers at entrance stations to national parks and ACAP checkposts also conscientiously check permits and entrance fee receipts.

A trekking permit to the most popular areas (see the list below) costs US$5 per week for the first four weeks of trekking and US$10 per week thereafter. The cost of a permit for other areas is different for each region. The rationale for the exorbitant fees for restricted-area trekking permits is discussed in the chapter on restricted areas. You must have a valid visa extension for the full period of trekking before you can apply for a trekking permit.

Area	Fee
Annapurna, Mt Everest, Langtang, Gorkha, Jumla & others	first four weeks $5 per week; after four weeks $10 per week
*Kanchenjunga & Dolpo	first four weeks $10 per week; after four weeks $20 per week
*Upper Mustang & *Upper Dolpo	$700 for 10 days, then $70 per day
*Manaslu	September to November $90 per week; December to August $75 per week
*Humla	$90 for seven days, then $15 per day

Treks to those regions marked with an asterisk (*) must be fully equipped treks arranged by a trekking agency.

National Park & Conservation Fees

If you trek in the Annapurna or Makalu regions, you will enter a conservation area and must pay a conservation fee, and if your trek enters a national park, you must pay a national park fee. You can buy an entrance ticket for all national parks and conservation areas in advance at an office in the basement of the Sanchayakosh building across the road from the immigration office, or you can just pay the fee when you arrive at the park entrance station. Currently, the fee is Rs 650 (US$11) for national parks and Rs 1000 (US$18) for conservation areas. If you trek into the Shivapuri Watershed & Wildlife Reserve on the north side of the Kathmandu Valley you must pay an additional Rs 250 entry fee.

Restricted Areas

Officially there are no longer any restricted areas in Nepal. Nevertheless, there are many parts of Nepal into which the entry of foreigners such as trekkers is strictly controlled. The immigration office rules now state that 'trekkers are not allowed to trek in the notified areas previously known as restricted'. Many treks that may be suggested on a map are in such areas, and you either cannot get a trekking permit for those regions or must travel with a policeman (a liaison or 'environmental' officer) and pay for a special permit. Rather than get involved in too much semantic complication, I will continue to use the word 'restricted' to refer to places that are closed to trekkers, or open to trekkers only when accompanied by a liaison officer.

Some areas are still specifically closed to foreigners under any circumstances; these include Walunchung Gola, Limi and the route to Nangpa La in Khumbu. When planning your trek, assume that these areas will remain closed. Don't count on a last-minute change in the rules. Police checkposts are numerous in the hills and police will turn you back if you try to trek into a restricted area.

There are many reasons why the restricted areas exist. In most cases, the situation is a hangover from a time when the border with China was more sensitive than it is now. Environmental groups, particularly the Nepal Nature Conservation Society, are pressuring the government to keep some places closed for ecological reasons to avoid both cultural and environmental degradation. Because trekkers require assistance when something goes wrong (accident, illness or theft), the government restricts some areas because it doubts that it could provide the security that trekkers need. There are also political reasons for some restrictions. In the 1970s, for example, the Jomsom trek was closed because a major foreign-aided military operation had been mounted there in support of the Khampas in Tibet.

There are many influences on the decision to open or close certain parts of Nepal to foreigners. Recent political changes have liberalised both trekking and climbing, and there is considerable pressure to open more areas to trekkers. You should check with a trekking agency or the central immigration office before planning an unusual trek.

INFORMATION SOURCES
Government Departments
Mountaineering Section There is a special section of the Ministry of Tourism & Civil Aviation that handles expedition permits. Its office (☎ 217865; fax 227758) is in Singha Durbar; it maintains information files about expeditions, approach routes and other aspects of mountaineering in Nepal.

Department of National Parks & Wildlife Conservation The office of the Department of National Parks & Wildlife Conservation (☎ 220912, 227926; fax 227675) in Kathmandu is at Babar Mahal on the road to the airport. It has material available about Nepal's national parks and wildlife reserves and can provide information about current conservation efforts. There is also a national parks information office in the basement of

the Sanchayakosh building, next door to the office that collects park fees. This office is staffed by well-informed people and has information available about the park system.

Trekking Companies
In addition to normal travel agencies, Nepal has a special type of travel agency that is licensed as a trekking company. In theory, a trekking company arranges treks and does not handle air tickets or transportation, while a travel agency does handle transportation but does not arrange sherpas, porters or food for treks. In practice, either kind of company manages to furnish all the facilities that are needed for any aspect of travel and trekking.

There are more than 300 trekking agencies in Nepal, ranging from large organisations that operate in cooperation with major adventure travel companies to small operations that support a single family. The following is an arbitrary list of agencies which have a reliable history and are likely to reply to correspondence and faxes from overseas. The list includes the biggest and best trekking companies, those that have office staff and can deal with correspondence and a few small ones that have made a name for themselves. A complete list of about 350 trekking companies is available from the Department of Tourism.

A walk through the bazaars of Kathmandu will uncover many trekking company offices that are not on this list or the TAAN membership list. Many of these are reliable and easy to deal with in person once you arrive in Nepal, and some can handle enquiries by mail, fax or email. Most companies price their treks using a complicated formula based on the number of days, the number of people trekking and the destination.

You can get a lot of advice from trekking companies, but remember that they are trying to sell you their services. You will be more welcome, and get more comprehensive information, if you choose one company, work with it while planning your trek and then buy your air tickets and rent equipment through it.

Adventure Nepal Trekking
   Tridevi Marg, Thamel, PO Box 915, Kathmandu
   (☎ 412508; fax 222026)
Ama Dablam Trekking
   Lazimpat, PO Box 3035, Kathmandu (☎ 415372,
   415373; fax 416029)
Annapurna Mountaineering & Trekking
   Durbar Marg, PO Box 795, Kathmandu
   (☎ 222999; fax 226153)
Asian Trekking
   Keser Mahal, Thamel, PO Box 3022, Kathmandu
   (☎ 424249, 415506; fax 411878, email asiant@
   asian-trekking.com)
Bhrikuti Himalayan Treks
   Nag Pokhari, PO Box 2267, Kathmandu
   (☎ 417459; fax 413612)
Crystal Mountain Treks
   Naxal, Nag Pokhari, PO Box 5437, Kathmandu
   (☎ 412656; fax 412647)
Himalayan Hill Treks & River Tours
   Patan, PO Box 1066, Kathmandu (☎ 520609;
   fax 521057; email brian@hilltrek.mos.com.np)
International Trekkers
   Chabahil, PO Box 1273, Kathmandu (☎ 371397,
   371694; fax 371561)
Journeys Mountaineering & Trekking
   Kantipath, PO Box 2034, Kathmandu
   (☎ 225969, 229261; fax 229262)
Lama Excursions
   Chanddol, Maharajgunj, PO Box 2485, Kath-
   mandu (☎ 425812, 410316; fax 425813)
Malla Treks
   Lekhnath Marg, PO Box 5227, Kathmandu
   (☎ 410089; fax 423143; email trekinfo@
   mallatrk.mos.com.np)
Mountain Travel Nepal
   PO Box 170, Kathmandu (☎ 411225; fax 414075;
   email tiger@mtn.mos.com.np)
Nepal Himal Treks
   Baluwatar, PO Box 4528, Kathmandu (☎ 413305)
Sherpa Co-operative Trekking
   Durbar Marg, PO Box 1338, Kathmandu
   (☎ 224068; fax 227983)
Sherpa Society
   Chabahil, Chuchepati, PO Box 1566, Kathmandu
   (☎ 470361; fax 470153)
Sherpa Trekking Service
   Kamaladi, PO Box 500, Kathmandu (☎ 220423,
   227312; fax 227243)
Thamserku Trekking
   PO Box 3124, Kathmandu (☎ 420044, 414644;
   fax 412323)
Treks & Expedition Services
   Kamal Pokhari, PO Box 3057, Kathmandu
   (☎ 418347, 410895; fax 410488)
Venture Treks & Expeditions
   Kantipath, PO Box 3968, Kathmandu
   (☎ 221585, 225780; fax 220178)

Yeti Mountaineering & Trekking
   Ramshah Path, PO Box 1034, Kathmandu
   (☎ 410899; fax 410899)

Other Information Sources

Kathmandu Environmental Education Project (KEEP) This internationally recognised project (☎ 250646, 250070) operates an information centre, reading room and coffee shop in an alley near the entrance to Thamel. KEEP is the best source of advice and information about environmentally sensitive trekking. The centre is open from 10 am to 5 pm daily, except Saturday and holidays, and sells iodine bottles, biodegradable soap and other environmentally friendly trekking equipment. There is also a library and an excellent notice board. See the very end of this chapter for information about how you can become a member of KEEP.

Himalayan Rescue Association (HRA) The HRA (☎ 418755) has an office upstairs in the Tilicho Hotel. The office maintains a logbook with recent information about trekking conditions and provides information on altitude sickness, equipment and health considerations for trekkers. It's open Sunday to Friday from 11 am to 5 pm.

The HRA was founded in 1973 and operates aid posts staffed with volunteer doctors in Pheriche on the Everest trek and Manang on the trek around Annapurna. The aid posts charge for medical services to cover their operating costs and the salaries of Nepali staff, but otherwise the entire organisation is operated by volunteers. The HRA survives because of donations, memberships and the sale of T-shirts and emblems. This organisation deserves your support.

Nepal Mountaineering Association (NMA) This office (☎ 411525; fax 416278) is in Nag Pokhari, Naxal. It issues all permits for trekking peaks and collects reports from expeditions when they return.

Trekking Agents Association of Nepal (TAAN) The TAAN office (☎ 419245), PO Box 3612, is in Naxal, near Nag Pokhari. It can provide an up-to-date list of trekking companies in Nepal and may be able to give you information about new or changed trekking regulations.

Himalayan Explorers Club The Himalayan Explorers Club is a nonprofit organisation that provides an extensive array of travel services to its members, publishes a quarterly newsletter and offers assistance to people of the Himalaya. The clubhouse in Kathmandu is in the same office as KEEP. You can contact the club by mail at PO Box 9178, Kathmandu, by email at himexp@aol.com, or in the USA at ☎ 303-494 9656.

TREKKING ROUTES

The following quotation is one of the Tibetan 'elegant sayings' attributed either to Nagarjuna, the Indian mystic who lived in the 2nd century CE, or to the head lama of the Sakya Monastery in Tibet in 1270 CE:

The teacher can but point the Way,
The means to reach the Goal
Must vary with each Pilgrim.

In this book I have described most of the well-known trekking routes in Nepal, and also suggested some treks to remote and virtually untouched areas. These descriptions will give you some insight into the type of country and culture that you may encounter on specific treks. They should also help you to choose the area you wish to visit, because they give an indication of the difficulty of each trek and the number of days it will take to follow a particular route.

I've tried to include a general explanation of the lie of the land and cultural background, but these are not self-guiding trail descriptions. If you are not travelling with a Nepali companion, you must continually ask hoteliers or other trekkers about the correct path. If you are with a guide, he or she will be asking questions as you travel. What to us Westerners may be a major trekking route is likely to be, for the people of a village, only a path from Ram's house to Bir Bahadur's house to Dawa's house. In our minds we

string all these sections of trail together to form a major route to some place where village people may never go.

Many trekking routes either travel in an east-west direction or go to high mountain regions. Local people do not often follow these routes because most trade routes in Nepal go from south to north and avoid high elevations.

There is nothing more frustrating than wandering around the hills of Nepal looking for the correct trail. It is impossible, no matter how detailed the route description, to document every important trail junction. Also, trails change for a multitude of reasons. The descriptions that follow portray what you may expect if you follow the shortest available routes, but it will be all too easy to get lost if you try to walk through Nepal using only this as a guide. Develop the habit of talking to people and asking questions. Be sure to read the section on route-finding later in this chapter for some suggestions on how to find the correct trail.

Just as it is impossible to document every trail junction, it is also impossible to describe every possible trek. What follows is a description of the major routes, a few optional side trips and some alternative routes that avoid backtracking. You should seriously consider backtracking, however. Often the second time over a particular trail provides insights and views that you did not see or appreciate the first time.

If you're making your first trek in Nepal, it is likely that you will choose a trek to Annapurna, Everest or Langtang. These are not only the best known, but are also the most attractive. There is good reason for the fame of the Everest trek, the Jomsom trek and other famous Himalayan treks. Most of the treks I've described, except those in the restricted areas, have reasonably well-defined trails and accommodation of some sort available every night. The exceptions are those in western Nepal, the Khumbu to Hile route, Makalu base camp and Barahbise to Jiri.

You may be tempted to go somewhere else, where there won't be so many tourists, because of stories and articles you may have read about the 'freeway' to Everest. When you listen to these discussions you should place them in their proper perspective. Even in 1995, the 'overcrowded' conditions in the Everest region consisted of 14,900 trekkers over a period of a year. More people would stay in a typical US national park camping ground on a single weekend night.

No matter where you trek, there will be local people living and moving through the area. Getting to remote and unexplored areas has little meaning in Nepal unless you are prepared to tackle a Himalayan peak.

New in This Edition

I have done a lot of trekking since the last edition, walking some trails I have not travelled for many years, and finally getting to Makalu base camp where I had earlier relied on information from others. I have included information about the extensive changes to the Around Annapurna and Jiri to Everest treks. This edition also has a lot of new detail about the Pokhara to Dolpo trek and the Tarap to Phoksumdo Lake trek over the Numa La and Baga La.

Route Descriptions

The main trekking routes described in this book are summarised in the table on pages 98-9. In each section of the book there is a brief introduction outlining some of the untold other options possible in that region. There are many routes in Nepal that proceed over high passes, but I have described only three of these: Ganja La, Thorung La and Kagmara La. These pass crossings have the dangers of rock fall, avalanches and high altitude. All members of the party, including the sherpas and porters, must have good equipment before you attempt these routes. The chance of snow increases during the period from December to April, though at any time of year snow on a pass might force you to turn back.

Daily Stages

I have separated the route descriptions into daily stages. This helps to make them reada-

ble and gives a quick estimate of the number of days required for each trek. The suggested night stops are the ones most trekkers use. In all cases, wood, water, food for porters (and usually chhang for sherpas) and a place large enough to pitch four or five tents are available at each night stop. Accommodation and food are also usually available at each suggested stop for those who are relying on lodges.

When you trek these routes, either with a group or alone, you may find that you are not stopping at the places listed here. Don't panic. This is not a tour itinerary that requires you to be in Namche Bazaar on Tuesday. Your actual stopping place will depend on your fitness, whether you or someone in your party is sick on a particular day, the weather, trail conditions, arrangements with the porters and whether you find some place more interesting or attractive than the village I have described.

Porters can severely influence the speed at which you travel, as their heavy loads make them slow. Your trek should allow you the freedom to move as fast or as slowly as you wish. It's a vacation, so don't take schedules and timetables too seriously where they are not necessary.

It is easy to alter the number of days suggested here. Perhaps you can cut a day or two off the time if you walk from first light to sunset each day, but since a trek is a continual experience, not simply progress towards a particular destination, there is little point in rushing the trip only to get to some place that may not be as engrossing as where you are now. At high altitudes, in order to avoid altitude sickness, you should proceed no faster than the ascent times recommended here. You can lengthen any trek to almost any degree by side trips, rest days and further exploration of inviting-looking villages.

On most treks you can move a half-day off the night stops suggested here and avoid the largest crowds. The stages I have outlined are the traditional camping places used by both individuals and trekking groups, so hotels in between these spots are often empty at night. If you do alter your schedule, you will also help to provide much-needed income to lodges that don't get many overnight guests. In larger villages you could consider staying at some of the smaller lodges that are not mentioned here. This also puts your money into the hands of those who may need, and appreciate, it more.

Readers continually point out that they trekked either slower or faster than the 'schedules' in this book. That is the way it should be. Nobody gets a prize for completing a trek in fewer days than the route descriptions in this book, nor is there any punishment for taking longer. The suggested daily stages are simply guidelines to help you select and plan a trek and to help you understand what distances porters will agree to carry their loads each day.

Times & Distances

The route descriptions do not list approximate walking times. Any moderately fit trekker can accomplish the suggested daily stages in one day. The stages do, however, tend to become more difficult in the later days of each trek, because fitness improves as the trek progresses. Porters can accomplish each stage in a single day and will almost always agree to the stages listed here.

I did try to record walking times, but it is boring trying to keep track of when you stop, when you walk and when you rest. When I compared the times on a particular trip with the times for that same trek the last time I travelled it, I found unbelievable variations. This must have depended on other factors that I did not record, such as my mood and physical condition, the condition of the trail, the number of other people and cattle on the trail, how many photographs I took, and the weather. Because of these wide variations in my walking times, I have not attempted to project approximate times for anyone else. Most days require from five to eight hours of walking.

If you really need to know times, you can ask people on the trail. Hill people in Nepal use a unit of distance called a *kos*, the distance that a person can walk in one hour. *'Namche Bazaar kati kos laagchha?'* should

elicit a reply that approximates the number of hours to Namche Bazaar (as should *'Namche Bazaar kati gantaa laagchha?'* or 'How many hours to Namche Bazaar?'). It is more fun and rewarding to try to talk to people instead of continually looking at a book and checking it against your watch.

Another statistic that is difficult to determine is distance. It is easy to judge distances from a map, but a printed map is in two dimensions. With the many gains and losses of altitude – and all the turns and twists of the trail – a map measurement of the routes becomes virtually meaningless.

In researching a guidebook to Glacier National Park in the USA, a friend pushed a bicycle-wheel odometer over every trail in the park to get accurate distance measurements. I have neither the ambition nor the patience for such a project and, besides, it would take most of the fun out of a trek. You gain a different perspective of travelling by discussing how many days to a particular destination rather than how many kilometres. Most of the days listed here are 10 to 20 km of trekking, depending on the altitude and steepness of the terrain.

Maps

The maps in this book are based on the best available maps of each region. As with everything else, they are reasonably accurate but not perfect. To make them legible, I have omitted most villages and landmarks not mentioned in the route descriptions. In some cases, even major villages and mountains have vanished from the maps. The maps do not show elevations of villages; these are given in the route descriptions.

Instead of contour lines, the maps depict ridge lines. These show the line of the highest point on a ridge. If the trail crosses one of these brown lines, you must walk uphill. If the trail leads from a ridge line to a river, you must walk downhill. In the lowlands, where the hills are gentle, the location of ridge lines can be more arbitrary than when they cross the top of a high peak.

The maps show mountain peaks in their

Trekking Routes in this Book

	Days	Difficulty	Maximum Elevation	Trekking Permit	Other Fees
Mt Everest Region					
Jiri to Namche Bazaar	9	***	3500m	US$5 pw	Rs 650
Lukla to Everest Base Camp	15	****	5545m	US$5 pw	Rs 650
Namche Bazaar to Gokyo	9	****	5318m	US$5 pw	Rs 650
Namche Bazaar to Thami	2	***	3750m	US$5 pw	Rs 650
Barahbise to Shivalaya	6	***	3320m	US$5 pw	none
Annapurna Region					
Annapurna Panorama	7-8	**	3800m	US$5 pw	Rs 1000
Ghandruk Loop	3-4	**	3800m	US$5 pw	Rs 1000
Tatopani Loop	7-8	**	3800m	US$5 pw	Rs 1000
Jomsom Trek	9	***	3800m	US$5 pw	Rs 1000
Baglung to Tatopani	2	**	1180m	US$5 pw	Rs 1000
Annapurna Sanctuary	15	***	4095m	US$5 pw	Rs 1000
Around Annapurna	16	****	5416m	US$5 pw	Rs 1000
The Royal Trek	4	*	1730m	US$5 pw	Rs 1000
Langtang & Helambu					
Langtang Trek	10	***	4300m	US$5 pw	Rs 650
Across Ganja La	12	*****	5106m	US$5 pw	Rs 650
Helambu Circuit	7	**	3490m	US$5 pw	Rs 900
Gosainkund	7	***	4610m	US$5 pw	Rs 900
Jugal Himal	13	***	3800m	US$5 pw	Rs 650
Eastern Nepal					
Solu Khumbu to Hile	12	****	3349m	US$5 pw	Rs 1000
Makalu Base Camp	20	****	5000m	US$5 pw	Rs 1000
Kanchenjunga North	22	****	5140m	US$10 pw	Rs 1000
Kanchenjunga South	16	***	4620m	US$10 pw	Rs 1000
Kanchenjunga North Side to South Side	2-4	*****	4663m	US$10 pw	Rs 1000
Western Nepal					
Jumla to Rara Lake	6-9	***	3710m	US$5 pw	Rs 650
Jumla to Dolpo	6-12	***	3820m	US$10 pw	none
Across Kagmara La	4	****	5115m	US$10 pw	Rs 650
Dunai to Phoksumdo Lake	6	***	3660m	US$10 pw	Rs 650
Dunai to Tarap	10-14	****	5318m	US$10 pw	none
Baglung to Dolpo	13	****	4270m	US$5 pw	Rs 650
Restricted Areas					
Mustang Trek	9-14	****	4070m	US$700	Rs 1000
Around Manaslu	20	****	5100m	US$70 pw	none
Shey Gompa	5-6	***	5400m	US$700	Rs 650
Humla to Mt Kailas	20-25	****	5630m	US$90 pw	none

** = easy, ***** = hard; **pw** = per week; **N/A** = only camping treks allowed*

true position, but the position of villages may not always be shown precisely. The problem occurs because of the size of villages. Where does the dot go for a village that is three km from end to end and which has no real centre or town square? The trails and roads follow

Season	Hotels	Other Information	Page
Oct-May	very good	lots of up and down; allow 22 days to visit base camp	176
Oct-Dec	excellent	potential altitude problems; flight hassles in Lukla	187
Oct-Dec, Feb-May	good	altitude problem (easy to get too high too fast)	206
Oct-May	good	side trip from Namche; good for acclimatisation	209
Oct-May	minimal	alternative to long bus ride to Jiri	210
Oct-Apr	excellent	outstanding views from Poon Hill	219
Oct-Apr	excellent	good introduction to trekking; scenic Gurung villages	220
Oct-Apr	good	Gurung villages, apple pie & hot springs	220
Oct-May	excellent	up the deep Kali Gandaki gorge to Muktinath	221
Oct-May	good	easy route that avoids climb over Ghorapani hill	234
Oct-Nov, Mar-Apr	very good	spectacular mountains; danger of avalanches	236
Oct-Nov, Mar-Apr	mostly good	varied scenery; one high pass; probable snow	244
Oct-Apr	almost none	easy introductory trek but few facilities, so few trekkers	260
Oct-May	very good	high mountains and glaciers close to Kathmandu	264
Oct-Nov, Mar-May	none	may require technical mountaineering skills when snow	272
Oct-Apr	very	good transport from Kathmandu cheap & easy	273
Oct-Nov, Mar-Apr	acceptable	great mountain views; dangerous when there is snow	279
Oct-Nov, Mar-Apr	none	fewer trekkers than most destinations	283
Oct-Apr	primitive	hot in Arun Valley; alternate exit or approach to Khumbu	289
Oct-May	none	steep climb to Barun valley; rain or snow likely	297
Oct-May	primitive	long hot approach; remote base camp	308
Oct-May	primitive	flights to/from Taplejung; excellent mountain scenery	312
Oct-May	none	glacier crossing; possible snow	315
Mar-Oct	terrible	complicated logistics, but an outstanding trek; lots of birds	322
Mar-Oct	minimal	deep forests; interesting villages with unique culture	326
Mar-Oct	none	high, remote and potentially dangerous	335
May-Oct	only two	remote high-altitude lake; dramatic Tibetan plateau scenery	336
May-Oct	none	steep, exposed trails; Tibetan villages	338
May-Oct	none	long walk with few villages; great views of Dhaulagiri	343
May-Oct	N/A	walled city; Tibetan culture and scenery	350
Oct-May	N/A	long trek on steep trails; great views of Manaslu north face	361
May-Oct	N/A	lots of mystique surrounding 'Crystal Mountain'	373
Jul-Oct	N/A	very remote; extra expense to travel in China	374

the general direction indicated on the maps, but maps this size obviously cannot show small switchbacks and twists in the trail.

Trek Profiles

These profiles indicate the altitude changes for the major treks. The unit of scale on the horizontal axis is one day's trek; hence each profile gives an indication of the steepness of the trail and the duration of the trek. Most high and low points are marked for each day, but when there are many ups and downs in a single day, some of the smallest ascents and descents are not shown. The vertical scale is the same on each chart, so it's easy to compare treks and see the average elevation. All the profiles look rather like saw teeth because most treks in Nepal go from ridge top to river valley and back to ridge top.

Altitude Measurements

The elevations given in the route descriptions are composites based on my measure-

---

Altimeters

If you carry a properly calibrated altimeter on a trek you will find that it agrees with the elevations listed here up to an elevation of about 3500m. At higher elevations your altimeter will read lower than the elevations in this book and those shown on maps. To understand the reason for this, you will have to think back and recall a bit of high school physics.

Altimeters calculate barometric pressure by measuring the change in the volume of air in a tiny sealed container called an aneroid drum. This volume changes according to pressure – and temperature. Altimeters are calibrated to compensate for temperature change according to a standard formula. Most altimeters follow the Comité International de Navigation Arienne (CINA) standards in which the temperature is assumed to drop 0.65°C for every 100m of altitude. Using this formula, the assumed temperature at 4000m is -11°C and at 5000m is -17.5°C. On a typical day in Nepal during the trekking season the temperature is likely to be closer to +15°C, a difference of 26°C at 4000m and 32.5°C at 5000m. This causes the altimeter to read 416m low at 4000m and 650m low at 5000m. To be accurate you must record the temperature and make the necessary conversion to obtain the correct altitude. Read the book that came with your altimeter for more details. There are some altimeters on the market, such as the Avocet, that have built-in thermometers, but most of these still assume that temperature varies according to the CINA specifications and do not make the temperature correction automatically. ■

---

ments with an altimeter or GPS unit and the best available maps. Most elevations correlate with the Survey of India maps of the 1960s except where these are obviously wrong, a frequent occurrence in western Nepal. The Schneider map series used the Survey of India maps as a starting point but refined most elevations, so I have used elevations from Schneider maps in the areas they cover. Except for specific elevations shown on the Schneider maps, I have rounded all heights to the nearest 10m. The elevations of peaks are those shown on the official mountaineering regulations of Nepal except for peaks in the Everest region, where I have used the elevations as shown on the 1978 edition of the Schneider Khumbu map.

This uncertainty over precise elevations will cause no problems during a trek. The primary reason that you need to know the elevation is to learn whether the trail ahead goes uphill or downhill and whether the ascent (or descent) is a long or a short one. The elevations shown here fulfil that purpose. The idea of precise elevations becomes even more complicated because villages cover such large areas. What is the 'correct' elevation of a village such as Bung, which extends almost 500 vertical metres up a hillside?

Place Names & Terminology

The route descriptions assign many places names that do not correlate with those in other descriptions of the same route or with those on maps. The diversity occurs because there is no universally accepted form of transliterating Nepali and Tibetan names into English. Different authorities will spell the same place name in different ways. To make matters more complicated, a particular place may have several different names. Mt Everest, for example, is also known as Sagarmatha (Nepali), Chomolungma (Sherpa) and Qomolangma Feng (Chinese). The same applies for many village names.

In 1984 the government of Nepal set up a committee to assign new Nepali names to 31 peaks and three tourist places that had been known before only by English names. I have

Global Positioning System

A recent development in mapping is the Global Positioning System (GPS). This involves 24 satellites operating in six orbital planes at an altitude of 20,200 km. These birds put out coded signals that may be received by small units on earth. A GPS unit reads the signal from at least four satellites at once and solves several sets of simultaneous equations to produce readings that determine the unit's location (latitude, longitude and elevation) with surprising precision.

The satellites emit two signals. The precise positioning service (PPS) signal is coded so that it is available only to the US military. The standard positioning service (SPS) code is available to the public, but the US department of defence deliberately degrades this signal by broadcasting slightly erroneous clock and orbital data for 'security purposes'. The intentional 'noise' they put into the signals is called 'selective availability' (SA). This means that GPS readings vary every second or so. If you have a GPS unit you can see this at work: when you are standing still, the unit says that you are moving almost constantly over a distance of several hundred metres.

Even with SA, you can establish a good approximation of your location; an error of 100m or so makes no difference on the scale of most maps of Nepal, typically 1:250,000. However, this is not satisfactory for elevation measurements. If I told you that the climb from the river to the ridge was 100m, give or take 500m, this book would probably end up in the river. To further complicate matters, because of the geometry of the satellite positions, elevation is the least accurate of the GPS readings; the error in vertical position is two to five times worse than the accuracy of the horizontal position.

To overcome the SA problem, surveyors use a system called 'differential GPS' (DGPS). This involves having two GPS units, one at a fixed, known location and the other in the field, operating at precisely the same time, and using either a computer or a two-way radio to coordinate the two readings. This is obviously not a practical system to employ while trekking hundreds of km away from a base station. Without a radio link, you must store the readings and do the correction when you get back from the trek. This will give you an accurate reading of where you *have been*, but it's not much use in the field for finding out exactly where you are.

Thanks to the kind people at Trimble Navigation, there is a base station in Kathmandu, and I have hauled a Trimble GeoExplorer GPS around on several treks. Using these facilities, I have established elevations and location that should be accurate to within five to 15 metres. Most of the readings I obtained have either agreed with maps or shown mapping errors, particularly on the old Survey of India maps. A GPS naturally attracts village children, and occasionally the police, who wonder what this machine is – with all its lights, buttons and beeps. I have had to learn to be a bit surreptitious therefore, though not as secretive as the *pundits*, the explorer spies of the Survey of India. These were Indians who travelled through Nepal and Tibet in the 1860s disguised as traders or pilgrims and paced off the country, counting their steps on rosary beads, determining elevation by measuring the temperature of boiling water, and concealing their notes inside prayer wheels. With all this, we can understand how a few errors crept into their maps.

US President Clinton announced in 1995 that SA scrambling would end within 10 years. This means it could happen any time between now and 2005. In the meantime, the only way to get accurate readings is the DGPS process.

The price of GPS receivers has come down drastically; for US$250 or so, you can buy a receiver that will allow you to plot your position on a map with reasonable accuracy. Until SA is turned off, the elevations that it shows can be off by several hundred metres. If you want to do some serious elevation measurements, I suggest you investigate the higher end models that have a facility to average many readings. If you are even more serious about recording elevations in Nepal, contact me and I will try to arrange to provide you with the material from the Trimble Community Base Station to use in doing differential corrections. ∎

mentioned the new names in the text, but I have also used the old English names to avoid confusion.

Many maps produced before 1960 had very little ground control, and the village names on them had little resemblance to reality. This is particularly true of the maps prepared by the US Army Map Service that

Nepali mappers have traced and distributed as trekking maps in Kathmandu.

Throughout the text I refer to 'trekking peaks'. These are the 18 peaks that can be legally climbed by trekkers with a simple application and payment of a fee to the NMA. Although they are called 'trekking peaks', each climb is a true mountaineering challenge and should not be attempted by the unprepared.

Proper geographical usage defines the left side of a river or glacier as that which is on the left when you face downhill in the direction of flow. This terminology often confuses me when following a river uphill: in this situation the 'left side' of the river is on your right. Fortunately, most Himalayan rivers travel either north-south or east-west, so I have tried to avoid the 'proper' usage by referring to river banks by points of the compass, but in some cases it has been necessary to refer to the 'true right' bank.

Nepali & Tibetan Terms In the route reports that follow I have translated many names and descriptions, but to avoid a lot of repetition I have used several Nepali and Tibetan words throughout the text. These include names of the ethnic groups that populate Nepal's hills: Tamang, Chhetri, Brahman, Rai, Sherpa, Gurung, Limbu, Newar and Magar.

You will encounter many Buddhist monuments during a trek. A *maani* is a single stone or stone wall carved with the Tibetan Buddhist prayer *om mani padme hum*. A *chorten* is a round stone monument; a *kaani* is an arch over a trail, usually decorated with paintings on the inside; and a Tibetan Buddhist temple or monastery is called a *gompa*. A *chautaara* is a stone resting place under a tree and usually has a shelf for porter loads.

Rivers are called, in decreasing order of size: *kosi*, *khola* and *naalaa*. A very large river is called a *nadi*, but this is a Hindi word and is almost never used in Nepal. Large rivers such as the Trisuli, Narayani and Bagmati, are technically 'nadi', but all Nepalis refer to them by their proper name without any qualifier. I've skirted the issue by referring to the these rivers, such as the Trisuli, as simply 'river'. In western Nepal a river is often a *gaad*.

A mountain pass is called *la* in Tibetan and Sherpa and *bhanjyang* or *laagna* in Nepali. Lakes are *taal*, *kund* or *pokhari* and a ridge is a *daanda*, *lek* or *deorali*. A high pasture is a *yarsa* or *kharka*; during summer, herders live in a kharka in a temporary shelter called

a *goth* (pronounced like 'goat'). The flat plains of Nepal, near the Indian border, are called the Terai, and the local booze is either chhang or rakshi.

All those 'aa' words look strange, so I have lexiconically misspelt several frequently used words, including *tal*, *danda*, *mani*, *kani*, *nala*, *lagna*, dal and bhat.

As explained under Accommodation earlier in this chapter, I have used the words 'hotel' and 'lodge' to refer to a facility that caters to trekkers. These places usually have English signboards, Western-style menus and often private rooms. I have used 'bhatti' and 'teahouse' to refer to a local-style village inn that caters mostly to porters and probably does not have a signboard at all. In a teahouse your choice of food will probably be limited to dal bhat, and the sleeping facilities will be the floor or a rough bed in the family living quarters.

Changes

Access to most treks continues to change. Frequent flights of Russian helicopters have made remote airstrips far more accessible, resulting in serious overcrowding in the Everest region. The road from Dumre to Besi Sahar (at the start of the trek around Annapurna) is being repaired, and there are plans to extend it as far as Chame. If this happens, access to this trek will become far more comfortable. The Jomsom trek now starts with a drive that bypasses the old trekking haunts of Hyangja, Suikhet and Naudanda. The road provides access to Birethanti, then heads south and west to Baglung, offering a shorter approach to Jomsom and Dhorpatan. There was a major road planned up the Arun River valley to provide support for the construction of a hydroelectric scheme, but this was scuttled when the World Bank withdrew its support for the Arun III project. The road up the Indrawati valley towards Helambu is finally being repaired and put back into service, and there is a road under construction from the south that will reach Salleri, the district headquarters of the Solu Khumbu region. Kanchenjunga treks will become less cumbersome when the road from Ilam to

Taplejung is finally completed – as of 1997 much of the road is passable only by 4WD. Western Nepal is also getting roads; there is a road planned up the Karnali River to Bhajang and beyond towards Simikot.

New roads change the relative importance of villages. Lamosangu, for example, was a major roadhead from 1970 to 1981. It lost its importance and many of its facilities when Jiri became the roadhead. Dumre's importance depends very much on the state of the road; it's a minor highway stop during the dry season, when buses can ply up the Marsyangdi to Besi Sahar. Roads also bring an increase in theft. Before a road reaches a village, travel must always be on foot and nobody complains. No self-respecting Nepali will walk once a bus becomes available, but the bus fares on the new roads are expensive, and this creates a new demand for cash. For many, the only source of easy cash is theft, and the road offers a quick getaway. Be especially watchful of your possessions within a few days walk of any road.

Trail and bridge construction is also proceeding at a furious pace in the hills. Local village development committees and foreign aid programmes have reconstructed or widened many trails. The Swiss are constructing an extensive new series of bridges in the hills. Landslides and flood damage are becoming more frequent as villagers remove the forest cover and topsoil washes away. These phenomena can alter trek routes drastically as whole villages can disappear and trails can require extensive detours to cross slide areas.

The construction of lodges and the conversion of private homes into hotel facilities for trekkers is proceeding at an even more frantic pace. New hotels spring up every week on the major trek routes. They also vanish when the innkeepers get bored or discover that the costs are higher than the returns. The competition for trekker rupees is intense, so innkeepers lower their prices to attract customers, and it becomes hard to make a hotel pay its way. There are pressures for hotels to improve the way they deal with fuel usage and sanitation, particularly toilet facilities, so this may change the number and location of hotels before long. Both ACAP and the national parks administration have removed existing hotels from places that they want to preserve. The tea shop halfway up the Namche Bazaar hill suffered this fate and is now only a pile of stones, as is the settlement of Bagar at the entrance to the Annapurna Sanctuary.

Numerous rural electrification projects are in the works, and many villages have locally produced hydroelectric power. Another project is bringing telephone service to even the most remote locations; this has already increased the reliability of airline operations and rescue facilities.

I have mentioned many hotels by name. When you look for these places, you may find a hotel with a different name. There is a funny system in Nepal that allows a business to avoid tax by changing the name of the company. Often the change is minor – the Namaste Hotel, for instance, might become the New Namaste Hotel – but sometimes the new name is quite different.

A trek route may change because of the season. The routes described here work during the trekking season from October to May, though some high passes, particularly in Dolpo, are open only in October and November and again in May. If you trek during the monsoon, the trails may not bear any resemblance to those described in this book. Bridges can be washed away and trails become flooded during this season. In early October, and again in April and May, rice is growing in the terraces along most trek routes. Many camp sites that are excellent in November and December are underwater in the rice-growing season. Hotels in high places, particularly Gorak Shep, Annapurna Sanctuary and along the Ghorapani to Ghandruk route, often close in the coldest part of winter (December to February) and during the monsoon.

GUIDES & PORTERS
Guides
On the Everest, Langtang and Annapurna treks everyone knows the routes so well that

The Moral Dilemma of Porters

Many people worry about whether it is exploitive, cruel or insensitive to hire a porter. There was an extensive discussion of this subject on the Internet in 1996, and *Himal* magazine ran a conference that discussed the problems of porters. Here are a few comments that may help you understand the situation better.

Portering is not an easy job, nor is it at all prestigious. It does provide income to people who have few resources and little education. It is also the only means by which goods can be transported into many regions of Nepal. Without porters there would be villages that had no soap, candles, salt, sugar, cooking pots and other necessities.

Most of the porters in the hills are villagers who turn to portering to generate cash income. They are typically farmers who have their own houses and grow their own food. In many cases, they carry their own surplus food to markets themselves. They then return to their village carrying items they have purchased with the money they have earned. Other village people travel to roadheads and seek a portering contract with merchants who are shipping goods to hill villages. They earn a fixed rate, based on the weight of the load and the usual number of days required to carry it to its destination. It is not unusual for a porter to carry a double load, or for two porters to carry three loads between them in order to supplement their income. There are some professional porters who do nothing else, but most porters do this work only when they do not have their own domestic chores to attend to.

Some trekkers think it is immoral, insensitive or un-macho to hire a porter and think they are being independent and tougher by carrying everything themselves on a trek.

Dr Raju Tuladhar, a Nepali, takes the following view:

... taking a porter will greatly enhance your enjoyment of the trek and will help the livelihood of one man, his family, and therefore his village.

For most porters, the economic burden is heavier than the weight of the backpack that they would be carrying for the tourists. The porters, just like any Westerners, have their dignity too, and they would like to earn their livelihood by honest means. Working manual labour is not derogatory by any means. Whereas most Westerners may feel ecstatic by giving some donations (which is equivalent to giving alms), it is ironic that they feel their conscience pinched to use them as porters and pay for their labours. Using a porter is not much different than riding a cab or taxi in which we pay someone to drive for us.

By hiring a porter, the person is doing a great virtue by providing an honest means of livelihood for the porter, provided the porter gets reasonably paid (which does not have to be by the Western standard). If all the tourists start carrying their own backpack, think about how many people working as porters will lose their livelihood. In most cases, these porters are not well educated and not skilled to do other work which will give them some earnings. In absence of all the possible means of earnings, they may resort to begging or petty crimes even. Therefore, if saving the money is not a big concern for the tourist, by all means, a porter should be hired, especially if some porter is willing to do it. Let the porter share your load, in return, share his economic burden.

An American trekker, Scott Yost, suggests:

... hiring a porter is good for both of you. For one thing, it will help you understand how bizarre and western your idea of even being concerned about hiring a porter is. I will admit that it is weird at first to have a personal servant doing everything for you. But you should remember that it is a respectable occupation, often the best which is available to many Nepalis. Porters are as essential to rural Nepal as truck drivers are to America, and they are every bit as professional.

Foreigners pay much better than locals, so most porters are very happy to work for a trekker. Also, working for a foreigner gives the porter an opportunity to learn English if he chooses. This can be an essential step in upward mobility for them. Practising English is very valuable. You should remember that the English skills of most porters are negligible. If you want someone you can talk to more easily, hire a guide/porter. They know English and will help you carry things, but charge more also. Either way, the constant contact with a Nepalese person will help you get over your strange Western ideas, which are otherwise not likely to change much. You can also make a very good friend in the process. So my recommendation is to hire a guide or porter, whether you think you need to or not (I consider them to be totally unnecessary from any practical point of view, if you can carry a moderate size pack). Then go with an open mind, and try to understand how your guide/porter sees the world, and learn from him.

In many cases you do not *need* a porter; you can certainly hump all your gear yourself. But a porter can enrich your trip culturally and will make the walking more pleasant. Porters will not feel demeaned, and the salary that you pay the porter will do far more good for everyone than spending that same money on pie and beer in a tea shop. If you are crossing a high pass like Thorung La, you *must take responsibility* to ensure that the porter is equipped for cold and snow, but otherwise having a porter is usually hassle-free. You should not feel any less self-reliant because you have hired a porter. ■

you do not need a guide to help you find the way. Still, a good guide will make your trek easier (and often cheaper) by negotiating on your behalf for food and accommodation during the trek. Ideally, too, a guide will show you places of interest and short cuts that you might otherwise have overlooked. Guides can ask local people about trail conditions, find out what hotels are open, and help you learn a bit of Nepali. There are, of course, poor guides who will do nothing but complicate everything throughout the trek and make considerable money at your expense.

If you travel with a Sherpa to Khumbu there is almost always the additional benefit of an invitation to the house of your guide. Part of this introduction to the Sherpa culture will probably involve you and your guide getting drunk as a result of Sherpa hospitality. In remote regions there are fewer signs that say 'Hotel', so a traveller must find accommodation and food by asking from house to house. A guide can be indispensable in such situations.

Porters

Hiring only a single porter, or several porters, without a guide sounds like a good idea and is usually easy to arrange, but it is not always easy to control this sort of situation on the trail. While most porters are reliable, they usually have little education in the Western sense. They tend to be superstitious and are, of course, subject to fear, fatigue, uncertainty and ill health. Porters may decide that they have gone far enough and want to return home, in which case they may just vanish. If you have a sherpa guide who has hired the porters for your trek, their performance is the guide's responsibility. Thus, if a porter vanishes your sherpa may be embarrassed enough to carry the load until another porter can be found. Sherpa guides are not at all happy about carrying a load, so you can be sure that they will find a new porter in a hurry. If you have hired the porter yourself, you must either sit alongside the trail until a replacement comes along, or carry your own heavy baggage.

Trying to manage your own team of porters without a guide is complicated because you must constantly be aware of where each porter is in order to protect your possessions. Unless, of course, you have somehow managed to secure the services of people who have already proven their reliability. Even this isn't foolproof. I've had a porter, who had already been on two treks, disappear on the third trek with two duffel bags of gear. On camping treks the sirdar hires a porter leader, or *naike*, who chases up and down the trail keeping track of porters and coaxing them on to the day's destination.

The Porter-Guide – a Rare Combination

Nepal has a very structured society – a hangover from the caste system. This structure leads to people having very definite ideas, ingrained since birth, about what jobs they will and will not do. If someone considers themselves a trekking guide, they will be reluctant to carry a porter load. Porters are often reluctant to do camp chores or other duties unless they have hopes of moving up in the pecking order. If a porter agrees to do extra work, guides may discourage or even prevent this to maintain their own status. The ideal guide-porter combination is a rare phenomenon, though some do exist. If you are lucky enough to find one of these people, you can probably get away with a single employee for a trek.

Where to Hire Guides & Porters

You can hire guides through trekking companies, trekking equipment shops or referrals from other trekkers. Trekking shops are more willing to help you if you offer a fee for their advice or hire equipment from them. Many trekking companies in both Kathmandu and Pokhara will arrange a single sherpa or porter, though some will undertake only the entire arrangements for a trek.

If you hire a guide or porter through a trekking company, the company will charge you more than it pays to the person it provides. This, obviously, is how the trekking company survives, but many trekkers have written letters expressing outrage when they discover that a middleman takes a cut of a porter's wages. If this concerns you, then you should try to hire someone directly. Many restaurants and hotels, particularly in the Thamel area of Kathmandu and in Pokhara, have bulletin boards. These often have messages from trekkers who are looking for trekking companions or are recommending a reliable guide. Also check at the KEEP, Himalayan Explorers Club and HRA offices for guide, porter and companion referrals.

You can often find out-of-work sherpas outside the immigration office or in tiny momo and rakshi stalls in Asan Tole. Hiring a guide directly is a hit-or-miss situation. You might find someone brilliant or you might have endless problems. They will convince you of their ability by producing certificates and letters from past (always satisfied) customers. It is not likely that you will hit upon someone whose sole purpose is to steal from you, but such people do exist and are offering their services as guides. All embassies in Nepal suggest that you either go through a known intermediary or check references carefully before you employ a guide.

October, November, March and April are very busy trekking months. A sherpa who does not have a job during these months may be of questionable reliability. At other times, it is often possible to find excellent staff.

You can sometimes hire sherpas and porters in Lukla, Pokhara and Dhunche. Except during October and early November you will probably be successful if you fly to Lukla or drive to Dhunche and try to arrange a trek without any advance preparations. There may be porters available in Jomsom, but it's unlikely that you'll find a sherpa there.

A good trekking guide can arrange porters. Things will work much better if you tell the guide where you wish to trek and how much you are prepared to pay, after which you go off for a cup of tea to let the guide do all the negotiations on your behalf. On a long trek, an experienced guide will lay off porters as the party eats through porter-loads of food. Guides will also replace porters

when they get nervous because they are too far from their homes.

Wages

It is difficult to suggest specific rates for porters' and guides' wages. Political and social pressures in Nepal have resulted in occasional exorbitant demands for wages and benefits. Union organisers are working to improve the lot of trekking workers and are trying to establish minimum wages and other facilities. Many guides and porters, however, are operating at a subsistence level and will work for considerably less than the union scale. Consult KEEP, HRA, TAAN or a trekking company (see page 94 for contact details) for the latest guidelines.

Wages for porters will probably be between Rs 150 and Rs 350 per day for trekking; the higher rates are for porters hired in Lukla and Jomsom. Demand from big group treks and expeditions can drive prices higher. Road-building in the hills also pushes up porter wages while the construction passes through a village. Porters expect to buy their own food out of their wages, so you do not ordinarily have to carry food for them. However, unless you do provide food and shelter for porters, you will always have to camp near a village where they can buy food.

Tradition dictates that guides receive a lower salary than porters, usually Rs 150 to Rs 200 a day (in 1997), but they also receive accommodation and food. If you are staying at inns, it will amaze you how much your guide can eat and drink. Set a limit on the guide's food bill before you set out, or pay him a daily food allowance, though either must increase at higher elevations where food is more expensive. If you are really watching your pennies you could always carry a small amount of food and cook it yourself if you have a guide. This leads, however, to hiring a porter to carry the food and cooking pots because tradition also dictates that a guide does not carry a load. Suddenly your trek transmogrifies into a fully arranged camping trek with all its attendant bureaucratic hassles.

Porter Clothing & Equipment

One important point to consider when you employ porters is the provision of warm clothing and equipment for cold and snow. If you are going into snow, you must provide goggles, shoes, shelter and clothing – porters are not expendable. Also provide plastic sheets (available in Kathmandu) so that porters can protect themselves and your baggage from rain.

In Khumbu, clothing is usually not a problem because you will probably hire Sherpas who have their own shoes and warm clothing, but ask them in order to be sure. The place where most problems occur with porters is crossing Thorung La, the pass between Manang and Muktinath on the trek around Annapurna. From whatever direction you approach the pass, the route starts in low tropical country and any porters that you hire will probably be from these lowland regions. When you reach the snow, the ill-equipped lowland porters either quit and turn back, or continue foolishly without proper clothing or footwear, often resulting in frostbite, snow blindness or even death. Porters are not usually available in Manang or Muktinath, so it is really worth the extra planning and expense to buy porter equipment in Kathmandu (though occasionally such items are available in Manang) if you plan to use porters on this pass.

When you do provide equipment for porters, be sure to make it clear whether it is a loan or a gift. In reality it will be very hard to get back equipment that you have loaned unless you are very determined and thick-skinned. The porters and sherpas have special techniques to make you feel guilty and petty when you ask for the return of equipment.

Porter Insurance

Trekking rules require that trekkers insure all their sherpas and porters for Rs 100,000 (about US$2000) against accidental death. So few trekkers do this that you would surprise an insurance company if you asked them to arrange insurance. There is no system for checking on whether you actually purchase insurance, though you will certainly have a major row if there is an accident and you cannot produce an insurance certificate. If you are planning to climb one of the trekking peaks, you must insure any Nepali who go beyond base camp. There is a system for checking on insurance in this situation.

Trekking companies have a blanket policy that covers all their staff. Oriental Insurance Co and Rashtriya Bima Sansthan in Kathmandu can provide the required coverage for a fee of Rs 1100 per porter for 30 days and Rs 1500 for 60. These companies can also provide, at a higher cost, the mandatory insurance for sherpas if you are climbing a trekking peak.

Stoves for Porters

The rules for restricted areas prohibit the use of firewood for cooking, even by porters. This policy is encouraged by environmental groups in Nepal and by ACAP. To implement this, you will need to arrange stoves for the porters. This usually includes providing a cook to prepare porter food unless someone in the party is prepared to take on the role of permanent stove mechanic. As you plan the trek with your sirdar, pay special attention to how the preparation of porter food will be handled. Certain ethnic groups cannot eat food prepared by others and many porters can be unhappy about eating certain kinds of food or food prepared in a particular way. Stoves are regarded as part of the group camping gear, so it is not customary for porters to keep the stoves at the end of the trek.

It's easiest to avoid the issue entirely and camp near villages so that porters can eat in teahouses.

Other Considerations

An important consideration when you decide to trek with a guide or porters is that you place yourself in the role of an employer. This means that you may have to deal with personnel problems including medical care, insurance, strikes, requests for time off, salary increases and all the other aspects of being a boss. Be as thorough as you can when hiring people and make it clear from the beginning what the requirements and limitations are. After that, prepare yourself for some haggling – it's almost impossible to protect against it.

FOOD ON THE TREK

On treks to the most popular areas, you can rely entirely on hotels for meals and not carry any food at all. Most trekking lodges have supplies of tinned food, chocolate bars, biscuits, toilet paper and other essentials, but you may want to carry a small supply of goodies for emergencies or to relieve the boredom of dal bhat. On camping treks the trekking company sends along an extensive assortment of supplies for the cook to work with, so you don't need to worry about food at all.

If you've arranged a camping trek through a trekking company, the company will make major food purchases of canned goods, rice and other staples. All good trekking cooks can estimate how much you need for a trek, depending on the number of people, the destination and duration. You might want to accompany the cook on a shopping expedition to help make the meals conform to your likes and dislikes. There are food wholesalers that operate out of tiny shops in Asan Tole and Lazimpat that can provide amazing quantities of food in a few hours.

Kitchen Equipment

If you are on a camping trek, the trekking company will provide a portable kitchen. A kerosene pressure lantern is a useful but noisy and troublesome addition to the kitchen gear. It helps to extend the day by letting the crew prepare breakfast early and allowing you to eat your dinner after dark. If you are staying in lodges, you won't have to worry about kitchen equipment because the innkeeper will prepare all your meals over a kerosene stove or wood fire. All hotels and trekking companies provide eating utensils such as cups, spoons and plates.

Stoves & Fuel

National park rules prohibit trekkers from using firewood in all mountain national parks. The use of kerosene is also required in the Annapurna Sanctuary, even in hotels. Most responsible trekking companies now send stoves on all their treks even in places where it is not mandatory. Indian kerosene stoves are expensive and delicate, so there is usually a special stove porter who clanks up the trail. Kerosene is now for sale in many places on major trekking routes, but there will still be several kerosene porters on any camping trek.

If you are doing some high-altitude backpacking, you will probably have to rely on kerosene for cooking. Unleaded petrol (gasoline) is not available in Nepal. You can usually find butane cartridges for camp stoves and lanterns, but be sure you get new ones; these cylinders are refilled in Nepal with propane at low pressure. You can tell if a gas canister has been refilled because a special distinctive odorising agent is added to propane in Nepal to help warn local housewives of leaky gas connections. You are not allowed to carry kerosene or gas on aeroplanes, though it's sometimes possible on helicopters.

Backpacking Food

If, for some reason, you are arranging your own food, there are numerous food shops in Thamel and Asan Tole that carry a large range of staples. If you are shopping for supplementary food or trail snacks, start with Bluebird Supermarket, which has branches in the Blue Star Hotel and Lazimpat. There are many other markets that have open shelves where you can wander about and choose from a wide variety of Indian and imported foods, packaged trekkers' foods, tinned meat and fish, spices and sweets. These include Central Department Store in Khicha Pokhari, Fresh House in Joche Tole (near Freak St) and the Best Shopping Centre at the entrance to Thamel.

Most of these shops also carry a few imported medical supplies and useful chemicals such as potassium permanganate to sterilise vegetables and Lugol's solution to purify drinking water. You can often find drink powders, such as Tang, which make iodine-treated water more palatable. Check prices as you fill your shopping basket in these shops. They carry expensive imported food alongside Indian and Nepali equivalents that are much less expensive.

There are several Nepali-produced packaged foods that can add variety to meals. Two brands of muesli and granola are available, and several companies produce a large variety of biscuits. Yak cheese is available in Thamel shops and at the dairy near the Hotel Malla. The Pumpernickel Bakery in Thamel can provide natural grain bread that will last for many days on the trail. Pilgrims Book House carries a variety of herbal teas that offer a respite from caffeine-based tea and coffee. Nepali natural peanut butter will appeal to many trekkers, but be careful how you carry it because the oil tends to leak into your backpack. You can buy imported cheese and excellent locally made trekkers' salami from the Gourmet Vienna Delicatessen on Kantipath. Most supermarkets also carry the trekkers' salami.

TREKKING EQUIPMENT

I place considerable emphasis on the selection of equipment for a trek, but in fact you can get by with a minimal kit if you can handle rough conditions and do not plan to go above 4000m. The task of selecting proper gear can almost overwhelm some people, but it is not a complex or difficult undertaking. Preparing for a trek is no more complicated than equipping yourself for a weekend backpacking trip. In some ways it is simpler. There is no food to worry about and no eating utensils or cooking pots to organise. There are no tents to stow and less overall concern with weight and bulk.

I've seen people trekking with almost nothing – a jumper (sweater) and a hash pipe. When the weather is good, when hotels are not full and you have no health problems, this arrangement can work, though innkeepers and police frown on the hash pipe. But the mountains are not always kind, and you may not find warm bedding or space in a hotel. If you do head out totally unprepared,

you will be on your own. Few people, either locals or other trekkers, will give up their own clothing or sleeping bag to help you when you run into trouble.

You probably already have most of the equipment needed for the trek if you hike much in cold weather. A trek is a good place to destroy clothing that is outdated or nearly worn out. A long trek, five weeks or so, is just about the maximum useful life for some clothing items. If your clothing wears out during the trek, you can have repairs done at village tailor shops; they use hand-operated sewing machines.

If you follow my suggestions for equipment, you can have many happy hours planning the trek, sorting gear, packing and repacking. It is a fine way to spend boring evenings. If you don't have lots of time, you can probably gather most of the items you need in a single visit to an outdoor equipment shop. See the Personal Equipment appendix near the back of the book for detailed information and a checklist of clothing and other gear to take.

It is helpful to have all your gear – particularly shoes and socks – before you leave home, but some very good new and used equipment is available in Nepal (particularly useful if you're in the middle of a longer trip through Asia). Most of the gear available in Kathmandu is at lower prices than elsewhere, and you can rent almost anything. You cannot depend on getting the proper size of boots and running shoes, and socks are hard to find, but otherwise you can fully outfit yourself if you have two or three days.

If you are on a group trek, it is better to have your entire kit organised in advance, otherwise you might spend the night before the trek scouring all over Kathmandu for a particular item. If you are on a group trek, make a special effort to reduce the amount of gear you carry. Porters carry 30 kg, and it is expected that a porter will carry the luggage of two trekkers. Hence, any baggage over 15 kg is a complication. North Americans, in particular, haul huge duffel bags to Nepal; these complicate porter and flight arrangements, and much of the gear is unnecessary.

Trekking Equipment Shops

The best trekking equipment shops are in Thamel, the neighbouring area Jyatha Tole and Basantapur (Freak St). These specialise in equipment rental, but most are happy to sell used gear if you prefer. Some new trekking equipment is imported, most of it from Korea, but most of the high-quality gear that is available in Kathmandu was brought into the country by mountaineering expeditions. The other source of equipment for trekking shops is trekkers who sell off their sleeping bags and other cold-weather gear before they head off to the warmer climate of South-East Asia. Other than Korean trekking shoes, the majority of the imported gear in shops is second-hand.

Because equipment is imported in such a haphazard way, the trekking gear available in Kathmandu tends to be either high-tech mountaineering equipment or low-quality, travel-worn castoffs. For trekking, you want a middle ground. A down parka suitable for the top of Everest isn't very practical for a trek to Tatopani, and a sleeping bag that has spent a month on the beaches of Goa isn't going to do the job at Everest base camp. There is neither a reliable stock of any particular item nor a complete range of clothing sizes. In order to find what you need, you will have to spend time going from shop to shop looking for the right size, quality and price.

Nepal-Made Equipment In addition to hand-me-downs there is a wide range of locally produced trekking and climbing gear. Nepali tailors are producing tents, sleeping bags, down jackets, wind jackets, rucksacks, camera cases, gaiters and ponchos. Most items are reasonably well made and will probably last through a trek. However, the nylon fabric, thread and fittings used will not survive the beating of a mountaineering expedition. Many items are copies of high-tech brand-name equipment, right down to fake labels bearing such names as The North Face, Karrimor and Lowe Pro. The prices are right, but don't be fooled into thinking you are getting a bargain on genuine brand-name equipment. Some items, such as ponchos for

Rs 350 and small day-packs for Rs 700, are such bargains that you can almost afford to use them once and throw them away.

Common problems with locally produced gear include defective zippers, clasps that break and straps that continually slip back through the buckle. The wind jackets with the words 'Gore-Tex' emblazoned on them are certainly *not* as advertised and are not suitable for use as rainwear. Buy a locally made poncho, or an umbrella, instead.

Approximate selling prices for new Nepal-made gear with fake brand names are as follows:

Item	*Cost*
sleeping bag	Rs 5500
down jacket	Rs 5000
wind jacket	Rs 1300
pile jacket	Rs 1200 to Rs 1500
daypack	Rs 1000 to Rs 2500
expedition pack	Rs 3500
duffel bag	Rs 350 to Rs 450

Hiring Equipment

It is possible to hire everything that you need for a trek – from clothing to sleeping bags and tents. Large sizes of shoes are often difficult to find; otherwise, you can rent everything you need in Kathmandu, though it will probably take a day of shopping and negotiating.

If you plan to rent gear, remember that all shops require a deposit to ensure that you return the equipment in good condition. This can cause complications if you don't want to change money to pay the deposit. You might leave signed travellers' cheques or a passport with the shop, but neither of these is a good idea. Cash dollars can solve the problem, so carry some if you plan to rent equipment. A trekking guide whom the shopkeeper knows can occasionally make a personal guarantee that you will return the gear, thus saving the hassle of a deposit. Be sure to check the bill and receipt carefully before you leave the rental shop.

A limited supply of equipment is available for sale and rent in Pokhara, Lukla, Namche Bazaar and a few private homes in the

Everest region. Namche Bazaar has fantastic trekking equipment shops because many expeditions jettison their gear here. If you are trekking around Annapurna, you need high-altitude equipment only for the two or three days it takes to cross the pass. Some lodges have equipment for sale in Manang and Muktinath, and you might even find a jacket or sleeping bag for rent. Other than these places, you probably won't find any gear for rent or sale in the hills except by blind luck (a mountaineering expedition returning home, for example).

In 1997, depending on quality, rental rates per day were as follows:

Item	Rate
mattress	Rs 6 to Rs 10
sleeping bag	Rs 20 to Rs 40
down jacket	Rs 15 to Rs 40
pack	Rs 15 to Rs 30
tent	Rs 50 to Rs 150

ON THE TREK
Staying in a Lodge

When you arrive at a lodge for the night, reach an agreement with the innkeeper on the cost for sleeping. Look around and see what facilities the hotel provides and read the menu to decide if the food that the hotel offers is what you want. The cost of accommodation or 'sleeping charge' is nominal; you are expected to eat your meals in the same establishment where you sleep. If you eat elsewhere, the innkeeper may increase the cost of your accommodation. Therefore, choose your hotel based on the quality of both food and lodging. If you have booked a private room, you will usually receive a padlock and key. If you are staying in a dormitory, the best way to protect your 'booking' is by unrolling your sleeping bag on the bed you have selected. Experienced trekkers do this as soon as they arrive, even before having a cup of tea.

There are a few special hotels in the hills, particularly those that obtained government loans, and a few facilities in Lukla and Jomsom that cater to people who are tired of trekking. These all charge US$20 or more.

During times of heavy demand, such as during a flight back-up at Lukla or when snow on the Thorung La has caused a backlog of trekkers at Manang or Muktinath, innkeepers charge what the traffic will bear. Accommodation then becomes expensive and difficult to find. Most times, however, basic accommodation will cost Rs 20 to Rs 50 and will be found without too much trouble.

Lodges at high elevations rarely have private rooms. Instead, their dormitories have several huge beds that sleep 10 or 20 people, often in two tiers. High altitude can make people uncomfortable, sleepless, crabby and strange. In hotels there can be a lot of thrashing about and opening and closing of doors throughout the night. Earplugs are a good investment. If you value sleep and privacy, reconsider the advantages of bringing your own tent.

Since a hotel also doubles as a home, whether it has a sign that says 'Hotel' or not, you may have a difficult time sleeping until the entire household has retired. Trekkers who walk and exert themselves all day require more sleep than they normally would at home, often as much as 10 or 11 hours each night. Village people who are not exerting themselves during the day can get by with six to eight hours. This presents an immediate conflict in sleep requirements and lifestyle. The conflict escalates when the inevitable booze and card party erupts in the next room or, worse yet, in your bedroom. Another universal deterrent to sleep is the ubiquitous Radio Nepal, which does not stop broadcasting until 11 pm.

During the trekking season there is a daily rush for hotels. It's quite mad to spend your holiday in competition with other trekkers racing to get a good space or a private room at the best hotel in the next village. In the Everest region, in particular, this can be dangerous because of the elevation gain and the chance of altitude sickness. If you find yourself travelling on the same schedule as a gaggle of other trekkers, relax for half a day and try to operate a half-day behind them. As I've already suggested, traditional lunch spots are often deserted in the evening and hotels that are crowded at night can be empty at lunch time.

Meals Usually the innkeeper keeps an account of all the food and drink that you consume and collects payment for everything in the morning. Most hotels maintain an order book in which guests write their orders on separate pages. This makes the accounting reasonably simple. If there's no order book, it's worth keeping track yourself of what you eat because other trekkers' food often makes its way onto your account when a lodge gets busy. Many hotels have menus that show all their prices, including the charges for sleeping. There is rarely any bargaining and the menu really does represent a fixed, and usually fair, price. Check the prices before you order to avoid later hassles. Strangely, the places most prone to bargaining are the fancy hotels – the US$20 per night and up variety – that have lost a lot of business to smaller and cheaper facilities.

Meals typically take an hour or two to prepare unless there is stew or dal bhat already cooked, so soon after arriving you should order your meal and tell the innkeeper what time you wish to eat. There are some pretty sophisticated short-order kitchens in the hills, the best being at Namche, Lukla, Ghandruk and along the Kali Gandaki. If you patronise one of these, you may get an exotic Western-style meal. More often the choice is between dal bhat with vegetables *(tarkari)* at Rs 25 to Rs 50 and dal bhat with meat *(maasu)* for Rs 30 to Rs 50 extra. Eggs *(phul* or *andaa)*, when available, cost Rs 2 to Rs 6 each. Traditionally, you will be offered a second helping if you've ordered dal bhat. It's not an all-you-can-eat feast, but in most places the server will come around with extra dal, rice and vegetables.

Most hotels offer an extensive choice of bottled soft drinks, beer and bottled water. Tea or coffee will be made with milk and laden with sugar. If you want black tea or coffee, be sure to order it that way. Many hotels can also concoct exotic drinks with rum, local rakshi and fruit.

At high altitudes, hotels become more expensive. Tea costs Rs 2 in the lowlands, Rs 3 in places more than three or four days from the nearest road, and Rs 10 or Rs 20 in high places such as Lobuje and Annapurna base camp. When food and drink is expensive it is tempting to economise and eat and drink less. You must resist this temptation because a large liquid intake is one of the important aids for the prevention of altitude sickness. Most hotels can provide a pot or vacuum flask of tea or hot lemon drink at a saving over the cost of individual cups. Be sure to eat enough also; a low food intake can leave you weak and susceptible to hypothermia.

Daily Routine Most Nepalis do not eat breakfast and have only milk tea when they arise. They have a heavy brunch of rice and vegetables around 10 am. When staying in a local inn, you will find it faster to operate in the same manner. If you order a large breakfast early in the morning, you will probably have a late start. Sophisticated inns are usually able to deal with short orders in the morning, though it is customary to order your breakfast the evening before. You can also save time in the morning by carrying some cereal or muesli for breakfast. *Chiuraa* (beaten rice), available locally, makes a less tasty but satisfactory substitute. You should be able to move for a few hours on tea and biscuits, arriving at 9 or 10 am at a place that has dal bhat prepared.

If you want to have lunch at noon or 1 pm you will almost certainly have to wait an hour or two while the hotel keeper cooks rice specially for you. Depending on your mood and fitness this may or may not be an attractive break in the day. If you find yourself with a long wait, accept it and use the time for a good rest rather than agitate to try to get things moving faster in the kitchen. A hotel can become chaotic when 20 people order 20 different things in a dozen diverse languages. This confuses even a Western cook who uses order slips and has a complete stock of goods. In a small hotel where the innkeeper cooks everything over a single wood fire or kerosene stove with a limited supply of pots, it can get crazy. If you can adjust to the local schedule of tea for breakfast and a 10 am brunch, you will avoid a lot of waiting in kitchens. If you cannot adjust, you can still save yourself a lot of time and hunger by talking to other trekkers and combining your orders into two or three dishes. In addition to saving time, this is also the environmentally sound way to conserve scarce fuel. One quick choice for lunch is instant noodles, which are known in Nepal as *chow-chow* or by their brand names of Rara, Wai Wai and Yum Yum.

Food for Your Guide Dealing with an inn when you have a guide is another matter. Theoretically a guide is more sophisticated than a porter and should have the ability to organise an inexpensive and trouble-free trek. This sophistication also may be a mastery of ways to make money with a minimum of work. If you have a responsible guide, the easiest approach is to have your guide arrange everything and then pay the bill yourself in the morning. Sometimes the guide will leave you with a bill for several glasses of chhang, extra food and the losses at last night's card party. In such cases, one solution is to agree on a daily rate for his subsistence. Each of you can then pay for your own food and accommodation separately. It should cost Rs 80 to Rs 150 per day for a guide to live on a trek. If you add another Rs 50 for drinks and cigarettes you are providing a generous allowance.

Cultural Considerations At inns along the main trekking routes you can behave just as you would in any small hotel anywhere. In remote regions where the tea shops cater mainly to locals, you should take special care to follow the customs of the people. Staying out of the kitchen goes a long way towards this. Nepalis traditionally eat rice with their right hand and always wash their hands before and after eating. There is usually a water tap outside, or you may ask for a container of water that you can pour over your hands – outside the hotel. Many small bhattis will serve you a meal without provid-ing eating utensils, but most can find a spoon if you ask.

Staying in a Nepali Home
If you are in a particularly remote region where there are no teahouses, you can often arrange food and accommodation in private homes. You could also end up in a home if your guide has friends in a particular village, if someone is just opening a new lodge or in an emergency when you cannot make it to the next hotel. Though it may appear that you are a guest, the householder always expects that you will pay for your food and lodging. Prices are flexible in such a situation, but usually the owner of the house will quote a fair price in the morning when you depart. They will, however, be shy and you will have to ask how much.

In a private home, you will probably have to wait until everyone else decides to go to sleep before you can roll out your sleeping bag. Be sure to find out where the toilet facilities are, if they exist. Don't dispose of garbage of any kind in the cooking fire. If there is a religious statue or altar, arrange your bed so your feet do not point in that direction when you sleep. (See also the Society & Conduct section in the Facts about the Country chapter for more details about avoiding offence.)

Beware of low doorways when you enter a house. It is said that a low doorway teaches you humility, but more often it can result in a nasty bang on the head.

Coping with Guides & Porters
If you are on an organised trek, whether it's a lodge or camping trek, the sherpa sirdar's resources will include only the food, equip-ment, money and instructions that the trekking company has provided. No matter how scrupulous the arrangements and how experienced your sherpa staff, there will be some complications. A trek is structured according to a prearranged itinerary and the sherpas expect to arrive at certain points on schedule. If you are sick or slow, and do not tell this to the sherpas, you may discover that camp and dinner are waiting for you far

ahead. Be sure to communicate such problems and other desires to the staff.

Most trekking sherpas are true professionals. They will make a lot of effort to accommodate you if they understand what you want. If you do not wish to follow their daily routine, you must decide this early in the trek. A routine, once established with the sherpas, is difficult to change later.

You may buy or bring some special food – 'goodies' – that you are saving for high altitudes or an important occasion. If you hand these over to a cook at the outset of the trek, you are likely to find them (despite instructions to the contrary) cooked during the first few days of the trek or, worse yet, served to the sherpas. You should keep any special food in your luggage to prevent such mistakes.

If you are trekking with porters, their ability to cover the required distance each day will limit your progress. Porters carrying 30 kg up and down hills cannot move as fast as a trekker carrying a light backpack. Other factors such as weather, steepness of the trail, sickness and festivals can turn a schedule upside down. Beware especially of the Dasain festival in October, when porters are almost impossible to find and tend to vanish without warning.

You will rarely experience a strike, but you may find that the evening discussion of the next day's destination has turned into a delicate negotiating session. On major trails there are certain stopping places that all the porters are familiar with, and it is difficult to alter them. I once congratulated myself on having covered three 'porter days' of walking by lunch time the third day. I looked forward to covering a good distance after lunch. An embarrassed sirdar then informed me that our lunch spot would also be our camp for the night. He explained that by definition it took three full days to reach where we were, and whether it had in fact taken us that long or not was immaterial. Nothing I could say (or pay) would entice the porters to go further until the following day, when we were able to start trekking early in the morning, on schedule.

Route-Finding

It isn't easy to get totally lost in the hills, but finding the trail you want, particularly through a large village, can sometimes be a challenge. If you are on a major trekking route, most local people know where you are going. If you see children yelling and pointing, you probably have taken a wrong turn. Watch for the lug sole footprints of other trekkers and for arrows carved into the trail or marked on rocks by guides with trekking parties. It is always worthwhile to talk to local people and ask them about the trail to your next destination and discover what facilities you can expect to find on the way. If you find yourself going a long way down when the trail should be going up, if the trail vanishes, or if you suddenly find yourself alone, *stop and ask for directions.*

If you are in a less frequented area, you must ask people. Be sure to phrase the question in a way that forces them to point the way. *'Kun baato Namche Bazaar jaanchha?'* ('Which trail goes to Namche Bazaar?') will usually do the job. If you point to a trail and ask if it goes where you want to go, most Nepalis will say yes, because they like to please you. When asking directions, ask the name of the next village. Many people near Jiri have never been to Namche Bazaar, but they know the trail to Shivalaya, the next village.

In particularly remote areas, be ready for confusion about destinations and times. I've seen situations where asking directions has developed into a massive argument involving 10 people, each having an opinion on the best route and the time involved.

Police Checkposts

There are police posts throughout the country. While the trekking rules do not specifically state that you should seek out and visit every police post along a trekking route, some police officers seem to believe this to be the case. As a general rule, if there is a sign, a barrier, or a cop standing on the trail, it would be prudent to pay a call on the local constabulary. Formalities are usually as simple as writing your name in a register, but in some places they can become cumbersome with forms to fill in and endorsements on your trekking permit. In national parks, what looks like a police checkpost is usually an army post where your national park entrance receipt will be examined to make sure you've paid the park fee.

RESPONSIBLE TREKKING
Problems

The population of Nepal is growing at a furious rate. In the 22 years since this book was first published, the population has increased from 12 million to more than 21 million. The number of trekkers per year has increased from 6000 to nearly 70,000. Development is moving ahead at an even faster pace. During the 18 years from 1978 to 1996, the number of motor vehicles in the country increased from fewer than 7500 to more than 150,000, the majority of which are in the Kathmandu Valley. There are now real traffic jams in Kathmandu, and the unnecessary noise and pollution caused by these vehicles is immediately noticeable. There are now few days with clear mountain views, yet 20 years ago, towering white peaks and clear blue skies framed the Kathmandu Valley. Today you can see the smog from your plane as it approaches Kathmandu.

In the hills, this growth is manifested in many ways. Numerous groups complain loudly about garbage left by trekkers and expeditions along the Everest route. This issue pales compared to the problems of population growth, sanitation, overgrazing, deforestation, landslides and uncontrolled development of hotels for trekkers.

There is no systematic waste-disposal system in the hills, and many hill people are acquiring more and more manufactured items from Kathmandu. A look at the stream of worn-out shoes and broken toys in the streets of Namche will show that litter is not only a trekking problem. The piles of garbage and human waste at Ghorapani and on the route to Annapurna Sanctuary and the relentless clearing of rhododendron forests between Ghorapani and Ghandruk to allow even more hotel construction are, however,

related to trekkers. Yet the protection afforded by a national park can lead to greater pressures. It takes a staff of more than 100 army personnel to manage and enforce the regulations of Sagarmatha National Park, which has a local population of less than 2500 people.

It is naive to think of maintaining the ecological balance of the Himalaya in a pristine state. There are simply too many people living in the hills. To accomplish this goal it would be necessary to relocate entire villages, as was done in both Lake Rara and Royal Chitwan national parks.

The primary reason for the destruction of forests throughout the Himalayan hill region is the pressure of a population that requires natural vegetation for food, fodder, fuel and even shelter. The lack of roads and other development, combined with the lack of any local deposits of fossil fuels, allows no easy alternative. About 70% of Nepal's total domestic energy consumption is wood. The inevitable result of the destruction of forests is an increase in erosion and extensive loss of topsoil.

The most dramatic result of deforestation is huge landslides that carry away fields, houses and occasionally entire villages. As you fly or trek in Nepal you can easily spot many examples of these landslides. One solution would be a massive tree-planting campaign, but to hill people this is expensive and unrewarding because they must fence off the plantations to protect them from cattle and goats. Goats, probably more than trekkers and villagers, are highly destructive because they pull grass and shrubs out by the roots in order to eat. Fencing is expensive and the financial returns are a long way off.

Tourists, particularly trekkers, contribute to the mess. A typical hotel burns from three to eight loads (about 25 kg each) of firewood per day and a large trekking party can consume from three to five loads a day. Regulations that ban the use of firewood in national parks and restricted areas do not apply to those who use hotels, except in parts of the Annapurna region where ACAP has ensured that firewood is forbidden to every-

Pack it Out – to Where?

One of the pressing problems in Nepal is the large amount of trash that trekkers and mountaineering expeditions generate in the hills. The problem is compounded as Nepali villagers use more and more cans, bottles and plastic items in their daily lives. Environmental groups have been active in making both trekkers and villagers aware of the problem, and the hills are now much cleaner than they were a decade ago.

Part of the conservation ethos is to pack out those items that cannot be properly disposed of in villages. This is an excellent solution for recyclable items such as soft-drink and beer bottles, but you might think twice before you pack up a load of tins and plastic bottles to bring to Kathmandu. The rubbish disposal facilities in Kathmandu are poor and are rapidly running out of space. Patan's garbage ends up at the side of the Ring Road or in the Bagmati River. Kathmandu's garbage ends up in a poorly maintained landfill on the road to Sundarijal.

You should carry any bottles back to Kathmandu and see that they are recycled. The huge pile of beer bottles at Shyangboche airport is a dramatic example of why you should do this. Spent batteries are toxic waste, and you should carry these back home where there are suitable disposal facilities. You would, however, contribute more to a long-term solution to Nepal's conservation efforts if you were to encourage the use of local rubbish-disposal facilities in the hills rather than bring other forms of unrecyclable trash back to Kathmandu for disposal. Villagers should be encouraged to develop their own properly maintained rubbish dumps that both they and trekkers can use. ■

In 1953 Edmund Hillary and Tenzing Norgay Sherpa became the first people to stand on the summit of Mt Everest. Since 1961 Sir Edmund and the Himalayan Trust he founded have been building hospitals, bridges, airstrips and schools in cooperation with the Sherpas of Khumbu.

Annapurna region and 8422 for Langtang. The number of individual trekkers, as opposed to group trekkers, is an indication of how many people used trekking lodges. In Langtang the majority of the trekkers (64%) trekked on their own; in Everest 40% were individuals and in Annapurna 48% trekked without using a trekking company.

What You Can Do to Help

Everyone should agree that the hill people have a right not only to live in their traditional home sites but also to try to improve their standard of living. Their lifestyle may appear picturesque, but in many places it is a meagre, subsistence-level lifestyle that could be improved in numerous ways by many forms of development. Trekkers can contribute to this development, not only with their cash but by their example. Solutions to the energy problem, such as hydroelectric plants, biogas generators, solar energy units and the wholesale importation of fossil fuels, all take time and cost money.

As solutions are developed and implemented, they will change the trekking experience – and certainly increase costs. When attempts are made in this direction, it is reasonable to support them, even when the result is a more expensive trek. It will cost more to eat at a hotel that has a new, energy-efficient wood stove or a kerosene stove and a proper latrine, and it costs more to trek with a group that uses no firewood. It is through this sort of direct economic encouragement that you can help and teach hill people. If you are on a camping trek, be sure the toilet pits are dug deeply and are filled in completely when you leave a camp site. If your trek staff is not digging the pits deeply enough, or not filling them in properly, the time to solve that problem is on the spot. It does no good to go home and write a letter complaining about something that could have been easily solved by some simple assistance and instructions from you.

Hoteliers have become aware that clean hotels and toilets and solar heating attract more customers. Trekkers should encourage hotels that adhere to environmentally sound

one. This hotel loophole exempts individual trekkers and the porters of trekking parties from any limit on fuel consumption. During 1995, 14,902 trekking permits were issued for the Everest region, 32,655 for the practices so that hoteliers will find the means to continue their attempts. The hotel system in the hills should become something that not only turns firewood into cash, but also serves as a demonstration for all villagers of the need for, and the advantages of, limiting their dependence on the forests.

One good start is to spurn offers of hot showers unless they are solar-heated. You can talk to other trekkers and try to order the same food at the same time so a hotel can do all the cooking at once instead of keeping a fire roaring throughout the day. You can purify your water with iodine instead of ordering boiled water. The process of conserving energy will take time and effort, as old habits and traditions are hard to change.

Even in Kathmandu and Pokhara, where alternatives are readily available, many homes, hotels and restaurants rely on firewood for cooking. Hundreds, perhaps thousands of loads of wood are carried into the cities, not only by porters but also by huge Mercedes trucks.

Conditions admittedly are bad, but the situation is not totally bleak. Trekking companies and many hotels in the hills now use alternative fuel as a matter of course. Trekking sherpas dispose of trash properly and are far more concerned about their country than they were when I first started trekking. Most Nepalis now understand the magnitude of the problem. While some bureaucrats are simply waiting for a foreign aid project to provide answers, some government officials and Nepali entrepreneurs are making efforts to develop Nepal-style solutions.

An excellent way to help villagers to become involved in development activities is to carry a few *Trekkers Educational Gift Packs*. This is a collection of books in Nepali produced by Himal Association and is available in Kathmandu book shops. If you present these books to teachers and village elders in the hills, you are contributing far more to long-term progress than you would by giving a cash donation or passing out pens.

In the Khumbu region the Sagarmatha Pollution Control Committee (SPCC) has collected empty beer and soft-drink bottles and is gradually transporting them back to Kathmandu whenever there is space on an empty helicopter. One look at the mountain of bottles at Lukla and Shyangboche should make you think twice before you ask a hotel to open that tempting bottle of beer. In Kathmandu you should never patronise the blue smoke-belching *tempos* (taxi scooters); take the white, electric-powered, nonpolluting *safa tempos* whenever possible.

If you are interested in current events in Nepal's efforts towards environmental protection, subscribe to *Himal South Asia*, a magazine published in Kathmandu. An annual subscription costs US$29.50 and is available from Himal, PO Box 7251, Kathmandu, Nepal (fax 521013, email himal@ himpc.mos.com.np).

KEEP also publishes a newsletter. You can become a friend of KEEP for UK£12 or US$20 per year. Contact KEEP at PO Box 9178, Tridevi Marg, Kathmandu, or 3 Bangor Rd, Holywood, Co Down, Northern Ireland BT18 0NT, or by email at tour@ keep.wlink.com.np.

Economic & Cultural Considerations

Although Nepal has been accessible to foreigners only since 1950, there are few places in the kingdom that either trekkers, photographers, expeditions or representatives of foreign aid organisations have not visited. Foreigners, particularly light-skinned Westerners, stand out readily in Nepal. The Nepalis view foreigners according to the stereotype created by those who have preceded them. They, in turn, will contribute to the image of the next Westerners who happen to come along.

Unfortunately, the image which has predominated is one of great wealth and a superior culture which Westerners wish to share with the people of Nepal. Such traditions as passing out balloons, sweets and pens to kids are partly responsible for this, but it is on a far grander level that the real image has developed.

Mountaineering expeditions have spent seemingly limitless sums of money for

Contributing to Projects in Nepal

Many trekkers, upon returning home after what is often a life-changing experience, want to return something to the part of world that has given them so much.

There are many nongovernmental organisations that provide assistance in Nepal, the most famous being Sir Edmund Hillary's Himalayan Trust. Sir Edmund launched this endeavour to return the countryside of Nepal to the way it was before the forests were decimated to provide fuel – the way it was when he first visited. His other great campaign is to provide opportunities, through education, for the Sherpa people to have careers other than portering. You can contact the Himalayan Trust at PO Box 224, Kathmandu, Nepal.

If you wish to support the Himalayan Trust, you can do so through the American Himalayan Foundation (AHF). This is a nonprofit foundation that was established in 1979 and is dedicated to helping the people and the ecology of the Himalaya. The AHF works to improve health care and education, and preserve culture and the environment. It supports reforestation projects and helps build schools, equip clinics and provide homes for some of the neediest. Its ventures in Nepal include the dental clinic in Namche Bazaar and the operating theatre of the Hospital for Disabled Children in Banepa. The AHF publishes a newsletter, which is available from the American Himalayan Foundation, 909 Montgomery Street, Suite 400, San Francisco, CA 94133, USA (☎ 415-288 7245; fax 434 3130).

Other organisations that you could contact if you wish to offer assistance to Nepal are:

The Fred Hollows Foundation
    Suite 1, Level 2, 414 Gardeners Rd, Locked Bag 100, Rosebery NSW 2018, Australia. This group works to counteract cataract blindness in Nepal.
Child Haven
    RR1, Maxville, Ontario K0C 1T0, Canada. This organisation provides orphaned and abandoned children with homes and education.
Terres des Hommes
    PO Box 912, CH1000 Lausanne 9, Switzerland. This is the organisation that operates the Hospital for Disabled Children in Banepa, near Kathmandu.
World Neighbors
    PO Box 916, Kathmandu (☎ 412009; email sasia@neighbor.mos.com.np). World Neighbors assists local Nepali organisations to address basic needs such as drinking water, livestock improvement, management of community forests, community health and family planning. ■

porters, sherpas and equipment, including a lot of fine gear for the high-altitude sherpas. At the conclusion of an expedition, excess food and gear is usually given away rather than repacked and shipped home. This type of extravagance, though often supported by foundations and other large organisations and not by the expedition members themselves, leads many Nepalis to believe, with some justification, that Westerners have a tremendous amount of money and will simply pass it out to whoever makes the most noise.

The sherpas and hotel keepers who deal with trekkers are aware of the cost of an air ticket to Nepal from the USA, Europe or Australia. For people in a country with an annual per capita income of US$170, US$1500 for a plane ticket is an astronomical amount of money. No matter how small a trekker's budget may be, they were still able to get to Nepal. The Nepalis know this and are unwilling to accept a plea of poverty from someone who, according to their standards, has already spent enough money to build two large houses. It is impossible to explain the difference in our relative economic positions to a Nepali in the hills.

Many trekkers and expedition members in the past have given substantial tips to sherpas. Reports of tips of several hundred US dollars are not unheard-of. This type of extravagance forces wages up, resulting in higher demands on the next trekker or expedition. It also contributes to an unhealthy view of Westerners as rich, lavish and foolish. This image makes it difficult for individuals on a tight budget to convince a Nepali person that they cannot afford outrageous salaries, tips or huge amounts of food during a trek.

Well-intentioned trekkers often overreact to the needs of porters and sherpas on treks and provide an exorbitant amount of free equipment to their staff. This is certainly kind and generous, and porters do need to be equipped with warm shoes, clothing and goggles when they are travelling into the mountains. Many trekkers overdo this, however, and it is becoming increasingly common for porters to demand fancy new equipment. They then pack it away to keep it in pristine condition and later sell it. On the trek they often use their own old blankets to keep warm. Porters need protection and attention, but many trekkers have gone far beyond what is necessary. This overgenerous behaviour has created unreasonable expectations in the minds of many porters and makes it difficult and expensive to hire them, especially in the Annapurna region.

Foreign aid projects have built schools, hospitals, roads, and electricity and water projects in Nepal. These facilities are largely supported by contributions from Western organisations, although there is usually an effort to require contributions of local labour and money. Nepal needs these projects and they perform a great service, but this method of financing helps to sustain the preconception of Westerners as people with a lot of money from which they can readily be parted if they are approached with enough cleverness.

Many trekkers feel a strong affinity for villagers or sherpas they have met. Many have supported the education of local children or even provided free trips abroad for them. This practice, too, is certainly worthwhile and kind, but it does encourage Nepali people to seek such favours in their dealings with Westerners. The US Embassy has published a paper, titled *So You Want to Take Your Sherpa to America*, that points out some of the procedures and pitfalls of this process.

The problem is not confined to the hills and the efforts of some thoughtless individuals. Many nations are eager to gain a foothold in what they feel is a strategic part of the world. They spend vast sums of money on aid programmes in Nepal to strengthen their position.

The Nepal government seems to assume that foreigners have an endless supply of money and will continue to pay for the privilege of visiting, trekking and climbing in Nepal. The vast array of visa, trekking, rafting, climbing, filming, conservation, national park, entry, re-entry, import, export, hunting, liaison officer and departure fees all appear to be aimed at collecting as much money as possible from tourists under any pretext. The US$50,000 fee for climbing Mt Everest and the 1993 fine of US$100,000 for violating expedition rules seem to indicate not only a lack of appreciation for 'the freedom of the hills', but also an unrealistic evaluation of the amount of money typically impoverished Western mountaineers have at their disposal.

This is the Westerner with whom the Nepali is familiar. They may also recognise the qualities of sincerity, happiness or fun, but the primary quality they see is wealth. Many Nepalis consider it their personal obligation to separate Westerners from a share of their money. They may do this by appealing to a sense of fair play, through trickery or blackmail (a porter's strike in a remote location), through shrewdness, or even by outright thievery. Westerners retain this image, no matter what they do personally to dispel it, and an appreciation of this is very helpful in developing an understanding of local attitudes during a trek in Nepal.

Health & Safety

This chapter was written by Dr David R Shlim, Medical Director of the CIWEC Clinic Travel Medicine Centre, Kathmandu, and medical adviser to the Himalayan Rescue Association for the past 17 years.

Most people look forward to a trek in Nepal as the adventure of a lifetime. However, the very term 'adventure' suggests that there will be some inherent uncertainty, isolation and risk. In regard to health, there is a higher risk of getting ill in Nepal than if you stayed home; there may be uncertainty as to what illness you have and what to do for it; and the illness may occur in an isolated setting, far from medical care. The main health concern in Nepal is the relatively high risk of acquiring travellers' diarrhoea, a respiratory infection or a more exotic tropical infection. There are also risks associated with accidents while trekking, and altitude illness. The infectious diseases can interrupt your trip and make you feel miserable, but they are rarely fatal. Falling off trails, or having a rock fall on you as you trek, has been the number one cause of death among trekkers, but the overall death rate is low: one death for every 6500 trekkers.

As Medical Director of the CIWEC Clinic Travel Medicine Centre in Nepal, I have studied the causes of illness and accidents among trekkers for the past 15 years. The advice in this chapter reflects the fact that the various health risks in Nepal have been well defined. The risk of becoming ill, or the length of time that your trek is interrupted, can be significantly reduced by obtaining the proper immunisations, following preventive advice, and using this chapter to help diagnose and treat yourself in the event that you become ill in the absence of medical care. If you are in Kathmandu, or have to return to Kathmandu because of your illness, you are welcome to see us at the CIWEC Clinic Travel Medicine Centre. The phone number is ☎ 228531 and the phone is answered 24 hours a day. If you have specific questions while preparing for your trek that are not answered in this chapter, you may find the answer at our World Wide Web site at http://www.bena.com/ciwec. The Web site offers more in-depth discussion of certain health risks, and will provide updates on recent health concerns. If your question is still unanswered, you can contact us via e-mail at advice@ciwecpc.mos.com.np for a personal answer.

The following chapter is an attempt to share with trekkers and tourists to Nepal the specific knowledge the clinic has gained over the past 15 years. I hope it will give you the confidence to diagnose and treat your own illnesses when you are away from medical care, and to seek help appropriately when medical care is available to you. Remember, no amount of immunisation and medical preparation can be a substitute for the use of cautious good sense while you are trekking.

Preparation for a Trek

MEDICAL EXAM & PRESCRIPTIONS

Trekking is just walking around in the mountains, but due to the altitude, strenuous terrain and isolation, it is a good idea to make sure that you are as healthy as possible before starting out. It is worthwhile investigating little nagging problems or any unexplained recurrent symptoms before you go, because problems have a way of escalating under the stresses of travel. If you take medications regularly for chronic problems, such as high blood pressure, make sure you stay on your medications for the trek, and carry the medications with you when you fly, rather than carrying them in your luggage. If you have chronic medical problems, or a history of something complicated that could flare up on a trip, carry a brief outline of your problem with you, possibly written by your physician. This can be extremely useful in the event that you are forced to seek care from another physician while you are travelling.

A thorough dental examination is highly recommended because reliable dental care is difficult to obtain in Nepal. Preventable dental problems have ruined a number of treks over the years. People who wear contact lenses can have trouble with grit and dust both in Kathmandu and in the mountains. Make sure you have backup prescription glasses and sunglasses in case you can't wear your lenses at some point. Bring all the contact lens washing solution that you will need. People who have had radial keratotomy (an operation on the cornea to correct vision permanently) may experience visual difficulties on ascent to high altitude (over 4500m). The visual problems correct themselves when you descend, but the experience of not being able to see in a remote mountain area could be both frightening and dangerous. People with a history of asthma tend to have trouble in Kathmandu, but are generally OK in the mountains. Make sure that you bring a supply of appropriate asthma medication in case you experience difficulties away from medical care.

People over age 45 often worry about altitude and potential heart problems. There is no evidence that altitude is likely to bring on previously undiagnosed heart disease. If you are able to exercise to your maximum at sea level, you should not have an increased risk of heart attack while trekking at altitude. However, if you have known heart disease and your exercise is already limited by symptoms at low altitude, you may have trouble at altitude. If you have a history of heart disease, you should consult a doctor who has some knowledge of high altitude before committing yourself to a trek.

The pretrip visit for a checkup or for immunisations is an opportunity to obtain prescriptions for medications that you will want to carry with you. In Nepal, most medications are available without prescription, and are quite inexpensive. The first-aid kit list included in this chapter is based mainly on drugs that are available and reasonably reliable in Nepal. However, if you will be travelling to other countries first, or just want to be sure that you have a reliable drug that is exactly what you need, get prescriptions before you go. Crossing borders with prescription drugs occasionally causes anxiety in travellers, but customs officials in Nepal have never shown an interest in personal first-aid kits; see the end of this chapter for a suggested first-aid kit and a list of medications and their uses.

PHYSICAL CONDITIONING

Trekking in Nepal involves long stretches of steep up-and-down terrain. This can prove physically tiring, especially as the altitude increases, and can put a lot of stress on your knees. The best training is to walk up and, in particular, down hills as much as possible. If you have a busy life, with little access to hiking on weekends, you should train with exercise machines (such as 'Stairmasters'), ride a bicycle or jog. Trekking puts most of the strain on the quadriceps muscles in the front of the thigh. If you have no hills to train on, try putting a pack on your back to increase the strength training associated with walking or jogging. Take stairs whenever possible in preference to a lift (elevator). Trekking in Nepal is strenuous, and the time you put into physical training before you go will definitely be rewarded.

IMMUNISATIONS & PROPHYLAXIS

The government of Nepal does not check your vaccination records when you enter the country. However, there are several major diseases that can be prevented, or whose risks can be significantly decreased, by immunisations.

In recent years, clinics specialising in travel medicine have opened all over the world to help organise the availability of vaccines and good travel advice. Ask your doctor to refer you to a good travel clinic if he or she does not stock the vaccines that you need. The standard of travel medicine advice has improved as a result of these clinics, making it easier for travellers to achieve their goal of receiving all the appropriate vaccines and prophylaxis, and not receiving any that are not appropriate to their current travel objective. The following section discusses the individual products in detail, helping you to make an informed choice as to which vaccines and prophylaxis are right for you on this particular trip. Bring this chapter with you when you go to consult about your immunisations for Nepal.

Hepatitis A Hepatitis A is a miserable disease that can be fatal on rare occasions. It almost always ends one's trip, and can lead to months of recuperation. New vaccines against hepatitis A have made it extremely easy to avoid this disease. There are currently two regimens, which are equally effective. The original regimen consists of three shots of the single-strength vaccine at zero, one month, and six months. The second regimen consists of one double-strength injection, followed by one booster between six and 12 months later. With the single-strength regimen, you need to have the second shot before you travel. With the double-strength regimen, you should have the first shot at least three weeks before you travel. Side effects are minimal, and the protection lasts for at least 10 years, and maybe longer.

If you have to travel on very short notice – a family emergency, for example – you can still use immune serum globulin (gamma globulin) to give short-term protection against hepatitis A. Gamma globulin may also be the product of choice for those who do not plan to travel repeatedly to the developing world. Gamma globulin is not a vaccine, but a collection of antibodies purified from the blood of people who are immune to hepatitis A. (Note that there is no risk of acquiring HIV, the virus that causes AIDS, from gamma globulin, since the process of manufacturing the product is completely lethal to all viruses.) The 'borrowed' antibodies offer a high degree of short-term protection. The regimen is one millilitre (ml), often referred to as a cubic centimetre (cc), for every month of travel, plus one extra ml. Thus the dose would be two ml for one month, three ml for two months, four ml for three months, and a maximum of five ml for four months of travel. For long-term travellers and expatriates the hepatitis A vaccine is the method of choice for avoiding hepatitis A.

Hepatitis B Hepatitis B can be a much worse infection than hepatitis A, leading to chronic liver disease, cirrhosis and death in some cases. It is acquired through contact with blood or through sexual contact. Thus there is little chance of casually acquiring this infection without exposure to contaminated needles, receiving a transfusion or having unprotected sex. We have monitored hepatitis in foreigners in Nepal for 10 years and have found no casually acquired hepatitis B infections. For long-term travellers visiting many different countries, or for expatriates who plan to be abroad for several years, the hepatitis B vaccine is safe and effective with few side effects and is recommended. If you anticipate doing medical work, or being sexually active with local people, this vaccine is highly recommended. The regimen for hepatitis B immunisation is a series of three shots over a six month period.

Typhoid Fever This disease is highly prevalent in Nepal. Although almost never fatal in travellers, it makes people severely ill, and recovery may take several weeks. At present three typhoid vaccines are available. The original vaccine, consisting of killed bacteria, offers a very high level of protection, but the shot itself can make people feel mildly to moderately ill for 24 to 48 hours, and two shots a month apart are necessary for complete protection. A new oral typhoid vaccine (Vivotif) has become popular owing to its lack of side effects, but it may not be as protective as the injectable vaccine. It is available in capsule form (one pill taken every other day for three or four doses). A third vaccine, called the capsular polysaccharide typhoid vaccine (Typhim Vi), is marketed by Merieux. Good protection is offered by a single injection, which has very few side effects. None of these vaccines offer 100% protection, but typhoid fever can be treated with antibiotics. You should feel reasonably safe using any of these products.

Meningococcal Meningitis An epidemic of meningococcal meningitis occurred in the Kathmandu Valley in 1983; during the next two years six foreigners contracted the disease and two died. In March 1985, the US Center for Disease Control issued an alert to travellers to be vaccinated against meningococcal meningitis before travelling to Nepal. Since then there have still been sporadic cases of meningitis in travellers to Nepal, and the advice to be vaccinated still holds. Even though the risk of acquiring meningococcal meningitis in Nepal may be small, the disease can cause death within 24 hours if no treatment is available (that is, while trekking). The vaccine is free of serious side effects, is not painful, and gives good protection that lasts for three years or more from a single injection.

Polio The current generation in the West is no longer afraid of polio because vaccination has made it rare there. However, polio has not been eradicated from Nepal, and a booster for people who have been previously immunised is recommended before travelling to Nepal. Childhood polio immunisations wear off over time because there is no longer any boosting effect from exposure to wild polio virus. If you have been immunised in childhood, one booster as an adult (either oral or injectable) should be obtained before you travel to Asia. If you somehow grew up without getting immunised, you should have the injectable vaccine before you head out to Asia. Do not use the oral polio vaccine as an adult if you have never had polio vaccine in any form. You can use the oral vaccine as a booster if you have been previously immunised by either method.

Rabies Modern rabies vaccine is now a highly purified substance with high effectiveness and few side effects. The drawback is that it is relatively expensive. Rabies is a severe brain infection caused by a virus transmitted by animal bites, mainly from dogs. The disease is uniformly fatal once the symptoms have manifested. Therefore, every effort must be made to avoid getting the disease once you have been exposed.

There are two strategies employed with the rabies vaccine. One is called pre-exposure immunisation and consists of three shots spaced over one month. These injections prime your immune system against rabies, and if you are bitten by a suspicious animal, you just need two more shots, three days apart, as a booster. If you don't take the pre-exposure immunisation, and you are bitten by a potentially rabid animal, you will need the full post-exposure immunoprophylaxis, which consists of five injections spaced over one month and a single injection of rabies antibodies called human rabies immune globulin. The human rabies immune globulin is often very hard to obtain (in Nepal it is available only at the CIWEC Clinic Travel Medicine Centre) and is very expensive (from US$350 to US$650 for the injection, depending on your body weight).

A study that we conducted in Nepal calculated that only one out of 6000 visitors is bitten by a suspicious animal. If you are planning to come to Nepal for only one or two months, I think that the pre-exposure series is not necessary. If you are planning to travel in Asia for three months or more, and are going to remote areas where the rabies vaccine is hard to obtain (and rabies immune globulin impossible to obtain), then you should consider having the pre-exposure series. Once you have the series, a booster should be obtained every two or three years.

Tetanus & Diphtheria The vast majority of people from Western countries receive these vaccines in childhood. The tetanus and diphtheria germs are worldwide, and preparing for overseas travel is a good chance to boost your immunity. You should take a booster if it has been longer than 10 years since your last one. It is especially important to ask for a tetanus booster if you are over 50 years old, as studies have shown that this population is more likely to have let their tetanus boosters lapse.

Cholera Although cholera vaccination is no longer required to enter any country in Asia, the recent spread of cholera to South America, and the emergence of new strains in Asia, have kept that disease in the limelight. Although the disease can be devastating to local populations at times, the risk of acquiring cholera as a traveller to Nepal is close to zero, and the few cases have been indistinguishable from ordinary travellers' diarrhoea. Therefore, cholera vaccine, whether the old injectable vaccine or the new oral vaccine, is not necessary in Nepal.

Malaria There is currently no vaccine against malaria. Travellers to areas where malaria is a risk must rely on trying to prevent mosquito bites and taking prophylactic medication to try to avoid malaria infections. In Nepal, malaria transmission is limited to the lowland area adjoining India (the Terai). There is no risk of malaria in Kathmandu, Pokhara, or any of the main trekking areas. I have never known anyone to acquire malaria while trekking in Nepal, but I have seen several treks ruined by adverse reactions to antimalarial drugs that were not needed in the first place.

The risk in the Terai is very low, and travellers traversing the area for one or two days (on the way to a trekking destination) probably do not need malaria prophylaxis. Travellers who visit a jungle lodge in Nepal are at theoretical risk, but there have been only two cases of malaria acquired by foreigners in the Terai in the past 12 years.

Although resistance of *Plasmodium falciparum* malaria to chloroquine has been documented in Nepal, most of the malaria is the more sensitive *Plasmodium vivax* strain. Thus, chloroquine phosphate (Aralen) or chloroquine sulfate (Nivaquine) as a single weekly dose (500 mg) would probably be adequate in the Terai. Mefloquine (Lariam) is also a good choice, and would cover most chloroquine-resistant strains as well.

Special Note Although resistant malaria has not yet proven to be a problem to travellers in Nepal, it has become a serious problem in certain parts of India that did not have a problem only a few years ago. Thus, the advice above could change in the future. If you are planning to travel to India, make sure you take malaria prophylaxis that covers resistant *Plasmodium falciparum*. India is no longer a low-key malaria risk.

Japanese Encephalitis This disease is caused by a virus transmitted by mosquitoes, with a maximum risk during the monsoon and just afterwards. The disease exists in Nepal, mainly in the Terai, and mainly during the period from August to October. However, no foreigners have ever acquired this disease in Nepal, so it is hard to calculate the actual risk. This vaccine is not currently necessary for trekkers or for casual visitors to the Terai.

Special Note A few cases of Japanese encephalitis were noted among local people in the Kathmandu Valley in the summer of 1995. The implication of these few cases for the 300,000 tourists a year visiting Kathmandu is not yet known. Until at least one foreigner acquires the disease in Nepal, it is difficult to make a blanket recommendation that all tourists be vaccinated against Japanese encephalitis. However, if cases of Japanese encephalitis continue to be noted in Kathmandu Valley, Japanese encephalitis vaccine may become a recommendation in the future.

Yellow Fever It is a legal requirement in Nepal to have this vaccination if you are coming from an infected area, eg Africa or South America, even though vaccination records are not checked. The disease does not exist in Nepal.

Tuberculosis This disease is highly endemic in Nepal. However, because infection requires continuous close contact with an infected person, tuberculosis cases are extremely rare among travellers to Nepal. We have documented only two new cases of tuberculosis (TB) among foreign residents in Nepal, and none among travellers. Thus, although there is a perception of risk, the actual risk is very low. Those who are concerned about acquiring TB while travelling should have a skin test before travel; if the test is negative for TB antibodies, a person can be tested after travel to see if they have been exposed to TB. Although a vaccine exists that offers some protection against TB, it gives incomplete protection, and changes the skin test to positive, making it difficult to tell if a person has actually been exposed to TB or not. We do not recommend TB vaccine for travellers to Nepal.

Hygiene on the Trek

WATER PURIFICATION

As repugnant as it sounds to put it this way, the germs that cause diarrhoea, typhoid fever and hepatitis are acquired mainly from eating someone else's stool. One of the major medical advances of Western countries was to develop a sure way of keeping stool out of the water supply. This problem has not been solved in Nepal, and all water must be viewed as being potentially contaminated. Obviously, some urban water may be extremely contaminated, and some mountain water may be almost pure, but it is better to disinfect all water in Nepal before drinking it. In recent years, bottled water has become widely available in Nepal, with porters even carrying water in plastic bottles high up into trekking areas. There is no quality control over the production of bottled water in Nepal, and preliminary studies have shown that many brands of bottled water are highly contaminated with bacteria that can cause diarrhoea. Avoid drinking untreated bottled water, and do not purchase bottled water in trekking areas. Not only are you buying a false sense of security, but the empty plastic bottles have become a major pollution problem in the mountains. While there is no consensus on the best method of purifying water in all circumstances, the following section examines some of the considerations.

Boiling

All of the stool pathogens (disease producers) are killed by boiling water. Although there is some confusion as to the optimum length of time that water must be boiled to make it safe, a consensus paper by the Wilderness Medical Society in the USA has confirmed that just bringing water to the boil is sufficient to kill all potential disease-causing organisms, even at high altitude.

Iodine

As an alternative to boiling, chemicals can be added to water to kill the pathogens. Iodine preparations and chlorine preparations are equally effective in killing the germs, but iodine is a bit more reliable in the field. There are three practical ways to carry iodine on a trek: as tetraglycine hydroperiodide tablets, Lugol's solution and iodine crystals.

Tetraglycine hydroperiodide tablets are not available in Nepal, and can deteriorate in as little as six months in their original containers. Purchase bottles in your home country before travelling to Nepal. The tablets are convenient to use and not messy to carry.

One bottle contains 50 tablets, enough to purify 50 litres of water.

Lugol's solution is a water-based iodine concentrate; four to eight drops per litre of water are sufficient to make the water drinkable within 20 to 30 minutes. It is available in Kathmandu at supermarkets and most pharmacies. If you choose to use this method, it is best to bring along a small bottle with an eye dropper, as these are difficult to purchase in Nepal.

Iodine crystals have the advantage of being able to purify an almost unlimited amount of water. Four or five grams of iodine crystals in a 30 ml glass bottle will purify water for months. The crystals will only dissolve in water to a certain degree; once the water is saturated, it will not accept any more iodine. To make a saturated solution, fill the small bottle with water and wait 30 minutes. The resulting saturated solution may be added to your water bottle to purify the water for drinking: add 15 to 30 ml of the solution to your one-litre water bottle and wait for 30 minutes before drinking. Refill the glass bottle at the same time, and after 30 minutes it will be ready to use again as well. Be particularly careful not to ingest an iodine crystal as this can be fatal.

Special Note If your main objection to using iodine is the taste, this can be completely eliminated by adding a small quantity of vitamin C (ascorbic acid) after you have waited for the iodine to work. Approximately 50 mg of vitamin C when crumbled into a litre of water and shaken for a few seconds will completely neutralise the iodine flavour in the water, making the water taste like pure spring water. Some people are concerned about possible health consequences of using iodine over long periods of time or during pregnancy. However, no evidence has been presented that using iodine to purify water, even for long periods of time, causes any harm.

Water Filters

Filtering devices for field use have become popular in recent years. No filtering device can guarantee the elimination of viruses that cause diarrhoea or hepatitis, so iodine must also be used in addition to a filter in Nepal. *Cyclospora* and *Cryptosporidium* are two protozoal organisms that are not killed by iodine (see the Diarrhoea section later in this chapter). However, they are both large enough to filter easily.

The risk of both organisms seems to be limited to the late spring and early summer. If you are trekking in the spring, and boiling all your water is not practical, then the use of a filter would eliminate the risk of these two organisms. Iodine would still be necessary to kill all other pathogens. Some filters incorporate a pentaiodine resin which iodinates the water as it filters it. For the most part, water in Nepal appears clear and has good taste, so filtering for sediment and taste is not usually necessary. If you plan to use a filter, make sure it has a pore size of 0.2 microns or less.

Special Note Do not believe a manufacturer who claims that filtering without also adding iodine will eliminate viruses from water.

FOOD PREPARATION

Unfortunately, just treating your water carefully will not eliminate the chances of eating someone else's stool. Throughout Nepal there is very little use of sewers to dispose of human waste. Thus, stool is found throughout the environment, and finds its way into your food. In the spring trekking season, flies are abundant and can be a major factor in spreading stool contamination into restaurants and trekking kitchens. Lapses in kitchen hygiene, such as the preparation of raw meat on the same counters as other foods, failure to wash kitchen surfaces regularly, and cooks who do not wash their hands after going to the toilet, contribute to the risk of gastrointestinal illness in Nepal. Vegetables and fruits can also be contaminated from the soil they are grown in, or from handling along the way. The general rule is to not eat any vegetables that cannot be peeled or freshly cooked unless you are certain of the methods that have been used to soak them. Many restaurants in Kathmandu now soak their vegetables in an acceptable manner to make them safe, but if you are not sure, don't eat them. The locally brewed *chhang*, a fermented brew made from corn, rice or millet, is reconstituted with untreated water and is a frequent source of infection for unwary travellers. However, since the drinking of chhang is so tied up in social custom, many travellers are forced to put aside their judgment so as not to offend generous hosts.

Try to avoid eating foods that are cooked once early in the day, and then reheated (perhaps inadequately) when you place your order. These foods, such as lasagne and quiche, can incubate bacterial growth throughout the day. Another food item that has been found to be highly associated with diarrhoea is the popular blended fruit-and-yoghurt drink called *lassi*. The risk of illness is probably associated with not cleaning the blender between orders.

PERSONAL HYGIENE

Making a point of washing your own hands frequently can also help prevent illness. The tiny amounts of water that might cling to dishes and glasses washed in untreated water are not likely to make you sick, and drying the dishes can eliminate this problem. In general, the likelihood of getting sick is related to the amount of contamination you ingest. You should always do your best to avoid known sources of contamination, but don't worry excessively about those areas in which you have no control.

One area you can control is the disposal of toilet paper. The trails of pink and white toilet paper in popular trekking areas are disgusting and totally unnecessary. To successfully burn toilet paper after use, pull it open before lighting (put matches or a cigarette lighter in with your toilet paper). Urine-soaked paper is harder to burn; carry it in a plastic bag for later disposal. There is no excuse for leaving toilet paper exposed along the trail!

Medical Problems & Treatment

DIARRHOEA

Diarrhoea is the most common illness acquired by travellers in Nepal. Travellers' diarrhoea is simply infectious diarrhoea, acquired while travelling, usually because standards of public health and hygiene in developing countries are minimal to nonexistent. The organisms that cause diarrhoea are passed in stool, and are acquired from eating or drinking contaminated food or water. See the earlier Hygiene on the Trek section for a discussion on how to purify water and avoid contaminated food.

Travellers' diarrhoea is often described in travel books as a mild, self-limiting disorder, for which no specific treatment is required. However, antibiotic treatment for travellers' diarrhoea has been shown to be highly effective at shortening the illness, sometimes ending it within several hours. Since travellers' diarrhoea can vary in intensity from a few loose bowel motions to severe fever, cramps, vomiting and watery diarrhoea, the decision to treat should be based on the severity of illness and the need to carry on with your travel plans. The following section will discuss when and how to treat your own diarrhoeal illness.

Causes of Diarrhoea

The vast majority of cases of travellers' diarrhoea in Nepal – 85% – are caused by bacteria. This fact makes it easier to guess what might be causing your particular case of diarrhoea. Bacteria are all susceptible to antibiotics, and thus a bacterial diarrhoea can easily be shortened by antibiotic treatment. However, there are other causes of diarrhoea in travellers, and I will give an overview of these other causes before focusing on how to diagnose and treat your own diarrhoea case.

Diarrhoea in travellers can be caused by toxins, viruses, bacteria or protozoa. The toxins are waste products of certain bacteria that can grow on food and, once ingested, can cause severe intestinal symptoms, such as vomiting and diarrhoea, for six to 12 hours. This is what is known as food poisoning; no infection takes place in the intestine and treatment can only be supportive. Viruses can cause vomiting and diarrhoea, or either one alone, but account for less than 5% of diarrhoea cases at the CIWEC Clinic Travel Medicine Centre. Once again, treatment can only be supportive. As mentioned above, bacteria are the major cause of diarrhoea in travellers in Nepal. The bacteria that can cause diarrhoea include *Escherichia coli*, *Shigella*, *Campylobacter* and *Salmonella*, in decreasing order of frequency. There are several other organisms, known collectively as protozoa, that can also cause diarrhoeal disease. The most common protozoan is *Giardia lamblia*, known popularly as *Giardia*, which accounts for about 12% of diarrhoea cases. *Entamoeba histolytica* is the name of the amoeba that can cause diarrhoea, but this organism accounts for only about 1% of diarrhoea in travellers. From late spring through to midsummer, another protozoan called *Cyclospora* is a significant risk of diarrhoea, but this is outside the main tourist season. Two other protozoa, *Dientamoeba fragilis* and *Cryptosporidium*, are uncommon and more difficult to diagnose.

The most common variety of diarrhoea, bacterial diarrhoea, is characterised by the sudden onset of relatively uncomfortable diarrhoea. Protozoal diarrhoea is characterised by the gradual onset of tolerable diarrhoea. Although these two syndromes can overlap to some extent, this method of looking at the problem has proven extremely useful. 'Sudden onset' means that you can usually recall the precise time of day your illness began. Patients will also report that the diarrhoea and associated symptoms were quite bothersome right from the start. In contrast, protozoal diarrhoea usually begins with just a few loose stools, making people wonder if they are getting sick. The symptoms might be two to five loose stools per day, with mild cramping and urgency as the usual accompanying symptoms. People often wait one to two weeks before seeking treatment, whereas those with bacterial diarrhoea will seek help within one to two days.

Bacterial Diarrhoea

The sudden onset of relatively uncomfortable diarrhoea is the minimum description of bacterial diarrhoea. Additional specific symptoms can only add to the certainty of the diagnosis. Fever, vomiting or blood in the stool can all be present, and are much more often associated with bacterial diarrhoea than with protozoal diarrhoea. Sulphurous-smelling farts and burps, thought by many to be an indication of a *Giardia* infection, are also common with bacterial infections. Thus this finding is rarely helpful.

Food poisoning (caused by toxins that can be produced by bacteria growing on contaminated food) can present exactly like bacterial diarrhoea. However, the difference is that by the time the person who has food poisoning is able to seek help (that is, strong enough to leave their rooms or the immediate vicinity of a toilet), they are usually on the way to recovering rapidly. People with bacterial diarrhoea may have vomiting and fever in the first 12 hours of their illness, but these symptoms usually subside spontaneously, leaving diarrhoea and cramps as the only persistent symptoms. The distinction between food poisoning with vomiting and bacterial diarrhoea with vomiting is not critical to make in the first 12 hours, since the patient can't take an antibiotic until the vomiting has stopped anyway. If all symptoms go away rapidly, no therapy is needed; if diarrhoea persists, it is likely to be a form of bacterial diarrhoea.

Viral gastroenteritis has essentially the same symptoms as bacterial diarrhoea. However, since we know in Nepal that viruses are uncommon in comparison to pathogenic bacteria, we usually treat patients as if they presented with bacterial diarrhoea.

Bacterial diarrhoea is almost always self-limiting, but the length of time can vary from a few hours to over two weeks. However, now that effective treatment exists, it doesn't make sense to wait from two to 10 days to see if you are going to get better on your own.

Currently all pathogenic bacteria that can cause diarrhoea are susceptible to a group of antibiotics known as fluoroquinolones. The two most commonly used are norfloxacin or ciprofloxacin. Therefore, it is not necessary to know exactly which bacteria you have in order to recommend treatment.

Antibiotic treatment with a quinolone antibiotic can shorten the illness to one day, and side effects are extremely rare. Antibiotic resistance will inevitably come, but as long as the use of the antibiotic is limited to travellers, resistance will be almost impossible to induce against a background of millions of local people who are not using the drug.

The treatment for all bacterial diarrhoea is either norfloxacin (400 mg) twice a day for three days, or ciprofloxacin (500 mg) twice a day for three days. Longer treatment is not necessary, and shorter treatment is currently under study. Some studies have shown that a single dose of ciprofloxacin or norfloxacin can cure a bacterial diarrhoea. There is little difference between norfloxacin and ciprofloxacin; we prefer norfloxacin since it works very well, is less expensive, and may have slightly fewer side effects than ciprofloxacin.

Other antibiotics, such as sulfamethoxazole-trimethoprim (Bactrim), ampicillin, tetracycline or doxycycline do not have much usefulness against bacterial diarrhoea in Nepal. Bacterial resistance to these antibiotics ranges from 30% to 95%.

Protozoal Diarrhoea

Protozoa are single-celled animals which inhabit the upper intestine, just beyond the stomach. They are oval-shaped and propel themselves around with a tail when they are in the host. When they decide it's time to move to another host, they secrete a sturdy outer coating and become a nonactive cyst. These cysts are strong enough to survive in mountain streams, in dust, and to pass through the intense stomach acid of a new host. They can be killed in water by boiling or by adding iodine.

Giardiasis An infection with the *Giardia lamblia* parasite is characterised by the gradual onset of rumbly diarrhoea and increased gas. Stools are often urgent and sometimes crampy. Upper abdominal pain can occur, but vomiting is rare. There is often a daily pattern of several loose stools in the morning, followed by a relatively normal day except for the occasional urgent bowel movement. This organism is thought by tourists to be the most common cause of diarrhoea in Nepal, but this is not true. It is present in about 12% of our patients.

Once *Giardia* protozoa have been ingested, they begin causing symptoms after one or two weeks (not the next day after a suspect meal). Upper abdominal discomfort, 'churning intestines', foul-smelling burps and farts, and on-and-off diarrhoea are the main characteristics of *Giardia* infections. Often people have symptoms for a week to a month or more before deciding to seek treatment because it is not very severe each day, and they hope it will go away. Sulphurous-smelling burps and farts can be associated with *Giardia*, but are equally common in bacterial diarrhoea, and thus are not useful in helping to make the diagnosis.

The best treatment for giardiasis is tinidazole, which is available in Nepal without prescription. The dose is two grams as a single dose each day for two consecutive days. Tinidazole has the potential for side effects, which consist of mild nausea, fatigue and a metallic taste in one's mouth. Tinidazole cannot be taken with alcohol. An alternative is albenazole (400 mg) once a day for seven days. This drug has very few side effects.

Amoebiasis The term amoebiasis refers to an infection with a specific type of amoeba known as *Entamoeba histolytica* and accounts for only 1% of diarrhoea in our patient population in Nepal. This is an important figure to remember, since the local laboratories diagnose amoebiasis in almost everyone who submits a sample. The reasons for overdiagnosis of *E histolytica* infection seem to be firstly that the labs mistake macrophages for amoebas (macrophages are large white blood cells commonly seen in severe bacterial infections), and secondly that they call any amoeba *E histolytica* (a number of other, nonpathogenic amoebas are commonly encountered in stool exams). If you have had diarrhoea for only a few days, be very sceptical of a local laboratory that reports that you have amoebas, especially if they also report the presence of white blood cells. A person presenting with amoebiasis will commonly have several weeks of low-grade diarrhoea, alternating every few days with either normal stool or constipation. Very rarely, a person with *E histolytica* will present with classic amoebic dysentery: frequent passage of small amounts of bloody, mucoid stool, associated with cramps and painful bowel movements. This classic form of amoebiasis is so rare in travellers in Nepal that we see about one case per year at most. *E histolytica* infection is treated easily in Nepal with two grams of tinidazole per day for three consecutive days, followed by 500 mg of diloxanide furoate (furamide) three times a day for 10 days. However, diloxanide furoate is no longer available in Nepal except through the CIWEC Clinic Travel Medicine Centre. This regimen is highly effective and well tolerated. In the USA, tinidazole is not available, and metronidazole is used at a dose of 750 mg three times a day for 10 days.

Cyclospora This organism infects the upper intestine, causing diarrhoea, fatigue and loss of appetite. The illness lasts from two to 12 weeks, averaging six weeks. Fortunately, the illness is a risk in Nepal mainly from May to September, which is outside the main trekking seasons, so most trekkers are not at risk. It has been shown to be waterborne, and iodine is not sufficient to kill it. The organism is relatively large, and can be filtered by almost all backpacking filters. It is easily killed by boiling. The treatment for *Cyclospora* diarrhoea is sulphamethoxazole-trimethoprim (Bactrim) twice a day for 7 days. This is a sulphur drug, and cannot be taken by people allergic to sulphur.

Cryptosporidium This is another parasite of the upper intestine which causes a prolonged, low-grade diarrhoea. It is rare in Nepal, accounting for only a handful of cases per year. It can cause symptoms for one to three weeks, but eventually goes away by itself. No treatment is available at present.

Dientamoeba fragilis Because this parasite resembles an amoeba, and has no cyst form, diagnosis is difficult. It can cause low-grade symptoms for a number of weeks. When diagnosed, it can be treated with tetracycline (250 mg) four times a day for 10 days, with excellent results.

Other Causes of Diarrhoea
Tropical Sprue Tropical sprue is a syndrome of fatigue, weight loss and chronic diarrhoea. Sometimes patients can date the onset of this illness to an acute bout of diarrhoea that never quite cleared up. The cause of tropical sprue is thought to be an infection with some type of intestinal organism, but the exact cause has not been discovered. The diarrhoea is often not prominent after a while, and people present to the doctor with fatigue and weight loss. We usually look at the stools a few times to try to find a protozoan parasite, and often treat people for suspected *Giardia* or *E histolytica* infections. If we fail to find a cause for their diarrhoea, or the treatment fails to improve their symptoms, we perform a d-xylose absorption test. This test can determine whether the upper intestine is able to absorb food normally. This test is always abnormal in the presence of tropical sprue. If the d-xylose test shows poor absorption, we treat for tropical sprue, with tetracycline (500 mg) twice a day for six weeks, along with folic acid, five mg per day. Improvement is dramatic within a few days of the start of treatment.

A few travellers return from their trip to Nepal with persistent gastrointestinal symptoms that defy all efforts at diagnosis and treatment. It is possible that these travellers have developed a form of bowel discomfort referred to as 'irritable bowel syndrome'.

Treatment is symptomatic, and the condition may gradually improve over time.

Symptomatic Treatment

Drugs & Antibiotics For many years travellers have relied on antimotility drugs, such as diphenoxylate hydrochloride (Lomotil) or loperamide (Imodium), to control the symptoms of diarrhoea until the self-limited infection runs its course. These days, loperamide seems to be favoured over diphenoxylate, but both drugs are used with more caution. Prolongation of symptoms in people who have invasive bacterial diarrhoea seems to be the major risk. We see people getting distended bowel, and increased discomfort in some cases, and prolonged constipation is also common. Effective antibiotic treatment of bacterial diarrhoea can make people asymptomatic within a day, whereas untreated bacterial infections can last from several days to two weeks. I recommend that diarrhoea severe enough to make you think about an antimotility agent should be treated with an antibiotic. Loperamide should be used when travel is required before the antibiotic can bring the infection under control. What else can you do when you wake up at 5 am with severe diarrhoea and have to ride a bus for the next 12 hours?

Supportive Care Diarrhoea can result in the loss of a great deal of fluid from the body, and much of the ill feeling associated with diarrhoea (weakness, dizziness) is just from dehydration. People with diarrhoea are often reluctant to drink fluids because they feel nauseated, or the fluids cause cramping when they reach the stomach. The best approach to rehydration is to take frequent small sips of fluid (a friend can often encourage the sick person to drink). Under all circumstances fluid replacement (at least equal to the volume being lost) is the most important thing to remember. Weak black tea with a little sugar, soda water, or soft drinks allowed to go flat and diluted 50% with clean water are all good. Oral rehydration solution (ORS), a mixture of sugars and salt that is easily absorbed by the intestines, is important when vomiting is present, limiting the amount of fluid intake, and for severe diarrhoea. ORS is also very important in the care of diarrhoea in infants, who can lose proportionally more water in a shorter period of time than adults. In an emergency you can make up a solution of six teaspoons of sugar and a half-teaspoon of salt to a litre of clean water. In adults, allow the person to drink whatever fluids seem palatable at the time. ORS solutions often taste salty, and may actually limit the amount of fluid taken in if this is the only liquid allowed. Urine is the best guide to the adequacy of replacement: if you have small amounts of concentrated urine, you need to drink more.

Much has been written about specific dietary approaches to diarrhoea, but there is no scientific evidence to support any one view. Some people believe that not eating for a while will improve diarrhoea, while others suggest specific foods such as bananas, dry toast or yogurt. However, none of these ideas have been tested. I would suggest that if you are not hungry, you should not force yourself to eat, but should continue to drink fluids. If you're hungry, it is OK to eat foods that appeal to you as long as you initially avoid greasy or spicy foods.

When you have diarrhoea there is an exaggeration of the gastro-colic reflex, which means that when you put food in your stomach, it immediately causes your intestines to contract, resulting in cramps and more diarrhoea. This reflex is not harmful, nor will it make whatever caused your diarrhoea worse. Once the initial cramps or diarrhoeal episode pass, it is often possible to finish eating your meal.

VOMITING

Vomiting associated with bacterial diarrhoea is a potentially serious problem, since it adds to dehydration and hinders efforts at rehydration. We have never seen severe dehydration in adults who had diarrhoea but not vomiting. Vomiting almost always occurs at the beginning of bacterial diarrhoea, and usually lasts six to 12 hours.

Rarely, vomiting and diarrhoea persist together for four or five days, resulting in individuals who are quite dehydrated and miserable. They often have to be helicoptered out of the Himalaya in this condition.

Vomiting also prevents taking an oral antibiotic to shorten the infection. There are currently no injectable drugs known to shorten the course of bacterial diarrhoea. The only option is to try treatment with an anti-vomiting drug until the person can retain the oral antibiotic, such as norfloxacin. In our experience, however, it is almost impossible to stop the vomiting associated with bacterial diarrhoea by injecting an anti-vomiting agent. Anti-vomiting therapy appears to work most effectively if given just as the repeated, spontaneous vomiting is stopping. An injection of promethazine, or prochlorperazine, or a suppository of either drug, can eliminate the threat of further vomiting, allowing norfloxacin to be taken, which will then shorten the diarrhoeal illness dramatically. One can also try an oral anti-vomiting agent at this point, but it could come up again.

WORMS

These intestinal parasites are never the cause of diarrhoea and rarely the cause of any symptoms. They can occasionally be associated with vague mild abdominal discomfort. It takes seven weeks or so for a worm egg, once ingested, to grow into an adult worm and to start to lay eggs, which can be seen in the stool exam. Studies have shown that approximately 95% of Nepalis have worm eggs in their stool. Despite these overwhelming figures, worm infestation in foreigners is relatively rare. Even among US Peace Corps volunteers living for two years in remote villages, the rate of worm infestation was less than five per cent.

Whether it is important to take worm medicine at the end of an Asian trip is hard to say. However, the medicine is quite free from side effects, and thus it is not a major decision if you want to be sure you are not carrying worms home. The medicine is mebendazole (Wormin in Nepal): one pill twice a day for six days.

The most common worms, *Trichuris* and *Ascaris*, are acquired by eating the eggs. Hookworms are acquired by walking barefoot through areas where people defecate. The larvae burrow through the skin and make their way to the intestine through the bloodstream. Very rarely, travellers acquire tapeworms from eating undercooked meat. All of these worms have a limited life span and cannot reproduce within the intestines, so infections in travellers tend to be extremely light and would all end within two years without treatment. The only exception is the rare infection with *Strongyloides stercoralis*. The eggs of this worm can hatch in the intestine, and the larvae can burrow back into the intestine, causing a gradually increasing infection.

UPPER RESPIRATORY INFECTION
Colds

Upper respiratory infection almost always begins as a virus (the common cold). The symptoms consist of some combination of runny nose, congestion, sore throat and cough. The viruses can be picked up on aeroplanes, crowded buses and trains, in restaurants, or any place where you might encounter people with colds. Under normal circumstances the cold should last three to seven days and go away by itself. However, under the stress of travel, and particularly trekking, colds can be complicated by bacterial infection. The viruses break down the defensive barriers in the lining of your nose, throat and lungs, allowing the normal bacteria that are living there to become invasive. This can result in ear infections, sinus infections or bronchitis (chest infection). Twenty per cent of the patient visits at the CIWEC Clinic Travel Medicine Centre are for complications of colds. Severe colds can result in missed treks and missed goals on a trek. Knowing how to recognise and treat the complications of a cold appropriately can save you many days of misery, and help preserve your long-established trekking plans.

Sinus Infection (Sinusitis)

Sinus infection is the most common complication of a cold. The sinuses are hollow spaces in the bones of the face that connect to little holes in the back of the nose. Viruses can travel from the nose to the sinuses, causing inflammation which can allow bacteria to invade. Once the bacteria invade, you might feel pressure or pain in a particular portion of your face, and the mucus running from your nose might turn thick and yellow or green in colour. Finding small amounts of blood when you blow your nose is also common. As the infection goes on, you may lose your appetite and feel much more tired than usual.

There may be no clear-cut division between your initial cold symptoms and the sinus infection. Many people come to us with a 'cold' that simply hasn't gone away after two or three weeks. This is how sinus infections most commonly present. Any cold that is either not getting better, or getting worse, after seven to 10 days should be considered a possible sinus infection, and you should think about taking an appropriate antibiotic. Some of these prolonged infections will eventually clear up on their own, but an antibiotic will make them better within days. The antibiotic of choice is amoxicillin if you are not allergic to penicillin. If you are allergic to penicillin, you can try erythromycin, but it is not as sure a cure. There is a new generation of erythromycin-based antibiotics, such as azithromycin or clarithromycin, which are taken once or twice a day and have a much broader spectrum. If you are allergic to penicillin, you should ask your doctor about these new antibiotics.

Tuberculosis

Tuberculosis (TB) is a bacterial infection usually transmitted from person to person by coughing but which may be transmitted through consumption of unpasteurised milk. Milk that has been boiled is safe to drink, and the souring of milk to make yoghurt or cheese also kills the bacilli. Travellers are usually not at great risk as close household contact with the infected person is usually required before the disease is passed on.

Bronchitis & Pneumonia

Bronchitis is the second-most common complication of a cold. Bronchitis is an infection of the breathing tubes in the lungs. The symptoms are a progressively worse cough, accompanied by the production of greenish or yellowish mucus when you cough. Bronchitis is similar to sinusitis in that there may not be a clear point in time at which your viral cold becomes a bacterial bronchitis. Seven to 10 days is long enough to wait before thinking of treating a cough that is not getting any better on its own. The same drugs recommended for sinusitis are good treatment for bronchitis as well, and the two infections are often present at the same time.

A deep cough accompanied by high fever may represent a deeper infection called pneumonia (an infection of the lung tissue itself). The same antibiotics can be used, but you may be quite sick with pneumonia and should seek professional medical attention.

Inner Ear Infection

The third common complication of a cold is an inner ear infection (otitis media). This type of infection is very common in small children because their Eustachian tubes (which allow the inner ear to equalise air pressure with the outside) are small and can get blocked easily. The infection is uncommon in adults, but seems to be more common in adult travellers. A cold is almost always present for several days, and then one gets the sudden onset of severe ear pain, usually in only one ear. A doctor can make the diagnosis by looking at the ear drum through an otoscope, but if this is not available, you can treat yourself with any of the antibiotics used to treat sinusitis or bronchitis.

FEVER

Fever means an elevation in body temperature above normal, which is usually 37°C (98.6°F). Fever almost always means that you have acquired some kind of infectious disease. By itself, it does not tell you the cause, but by evaluating the associated symptoms and the travel history, one can often make a good guess, even while trekking in a remote area. Some fever-related illnesses go away without treatment (eg the flu), while others will require treatment (eg typhoid fever). The purpose of trying to guess the cause of a fever is to determine whether specific treatment will be of benefit, and whether the trek should be abandoned.

If specific symptoms are associated with a fever, the cause can usually be determined. If one has the onset of severe diarrhoea and fever, a bacterial dysentery can be suspected. If one has a thick or colourful nasal discharge and sinus pain and a fever, sinusitis may be present. Fever with a severe cough may be bronchitis or pneumonia. A large abscess in the skin also can cause a fever.

Sometimes a fever occurs with only a vague feeling of being unwell, such as headache, fatigue, loss of appetite, or nausea. In the first few days of such an illness it is difficult to determine the cause of the fever. We have found, however, that there are five main diseases which account for almost all the presentations of fever and headache and malaise in Nepal. By taking a careful history and noticing key aspects of the fever and headache, a presumptive diagnosis can often be made. The six diseases are as follows:

Viral Syndromes
The circumstances of travel bring exposure to many more viruses than one would encounter at home. The influenza viruses and others can be passed through respiratory droplets, which means they can be inhaled in aeroplanes, buses and crowded restaurants. The disease usually has an abrupt onset of fever, often very high (40°C) on the first day. A headache is often present, and is typically very motion-sensitive, which means it hurts to turn the head suddenly or to step down hard. The illness usually lasts two to four days and goes away without specific treatment. It usually ends abruptly, the fever and headache staying about the same for the duration of the illness. The key hints that you may have a virus are the abrupt onset, the

characteristic motion-sensitive headache, and the fact that it goes away just about the time that you are getting worried that it might not.

Meningococcal Meningitis
This very serious disease attacks the brain and can be fatal. There are recurring epidemics in a number of countries, including northern India and Nepal.

A fever, severe headache, sensitivity to light and neck stiffness which prevents forward bending of the head are the first symptoms. There may also be purple patches on the skin. Death may occur within a few hours, so urgent medical treatment is required.

Trekkers to rural areas of Nepal should be particularly careful as the disease is spread by close contact with people who carry it in their throats and noses, spread it through coughs and sneezes and may not be aware that they are carriers. Lodges in the hills where travellers spend the night are prime spots for the spread of infection.

Treatment is by large doses of penicillin given intravenously, or chloramphenicol injections.

Enteric Fever (Typhoid & Paratyphoid)
Enteric fever is an infection with one of two specific bacteria, *Salmonella typhi* (typhoid fever) or *Salmonella paratyphi* (paratyphoid fever). The two illnesses are identical, which is why it is convenient to refer to them as enteric fever. The bacteria are passed in the stools of infected people, and Nepal has a very high rate of enteric fever in the local population. The same precautions that one follows to prevent diarrhoea will help to prevent enteric fever. Any of the three typhoid vaccines can significantly reduce, but not eliminate, your chances of getting enteric fever. So don't think that because you took a typhoid vaccine that you can't get enteric fever.

The illness begins with the gradual onset of fever, headache and fatigue. For the first few days the fever is often low, and it is hard to tell if you are really getting sick or not. After three or four days, the fever rises to 40°C or more, and fatigue begins to be profound, although some people have milder cases. The headache is typically dull and not motion-sensitive. Loss of appetite, nausea, and even vomiting can develop as well as poor concentration. Overall, after four or five days, the patient feels very weak, moves slowly, and doesn't want to eat. The disease can be distinguished from the viral illnesses by its gradual onset, the dull character of the headache, and the fact that the person is getting worse at a time when the viral patient should be getting better.

Enteric fever is one of the treatable causes of prolonged fever. If suspected, treatment should be started while trekking, since the person will remain sick for up to a month without treatment, and complications can result. The treatment for adults is ciprofloxacin (500 mg) every 12 hours for 10 days. In children under 18, the drug of choice is amoxicillin in high doses: 50 mg per kg per day in three divided doses. For a 40 kg child, this would be 50 x 40 = 2000 mg per day divided by three, or 667 mg every eight hours. This can safely be rounded down to 500 mg every eight hours. Some cases of enteric fever will be resistant to amoxicillin, in which case the only alternative would be ciprofloxacin. This should be given to a child only under the guidance of a physician.

The response to treatment is slow but steady, with the fever persisting for another two to five days. You can tell that the treatment is working because the patient starts to feel better, and the height of the fever is a little bit lower each day until it is gone. The infected person is only contagious through his or her stool, and does not need to be isolated from the group. Since the disease produces such profound fatigue and malaise, the person almost always has to abandon his or her trek.

Hepatitis A

Hepatitis A is a viral infection of the liver which is acquired by eating something contaminated with stool from an infected person. There are three main viruses which can cause hepatitis in Nepal: hepatitis A and hepatitis E are passed in stool, while hepatitis B is only spread by blood or sexual contact. Hepatitis A can be virtually 100% prevented by the hepatitis A vaccines or by appropriate doses of immune serum globulin (gamma globulin). If you get sick with fever, headache and nausea, and you have taken either of the above measures, you can basically rule out hepatitis A as the cause. Hepatitis E is an illness very similar to hepatitis A, and there is at present no way to immunise against this virus. Very few travellers, however, get hepatitis E.

The incubation period of hepatitis is usually four weeks. Shorter periods have been noticed, but they are unusual. So if you have only been travelling in developing countries for two weeks, you can't have hepatitis. If you have travelled for a few months, and have not taken any protection against hepatitis A, then you must consider the diagnosis. Hepatitis A starts with the relatively gradual onset of fever, headache, nausea and loss of appetite. The nausea and loss of appetite are often more pronounced than in the other illnesses. The headache is slightly motion-sensitive, but is usually dull. These symptoms go on for four or five days. At that point the urine turns a dark tea colour, and the whites of the eyes appear yellow (this colour change is called jaundice). The fever ends at this point; nausea, fatigue and loss of appetite are now the main symptoms and can go on for two weeks to a month. There is no specific treatment to shorten the illness, and the trek (and usually the whole vacation) is finished at this point. The person should be encouraged to drink to prevent dehydration, and to eat and drink whatever he or she can stomach (except alcohol) to avoid profound weight loss. The bright side is that illness with hepatitis A does confer lifelong immunity to that disease.

The main clues to hepatitis A infection are at least a month of travel in developing countries; no history of immunisation or prophylaxis against hepatitis A; relatively gradual onset of fever, nausea and loss of appetite; and the abrupt end of fever when the jaundice becomes apparent.

Malaria

Malaria is a protozoan parasite which is transmitted between humans by a certain species of mosquito. There are four types of malaria, but two types, *Plasmodium falciparum* malaria and *P vivax* malaria account for 90% of all cases worldwide. *P falciparum* malaria is the most severe form of malaria, and can occasionally be rapidly fatal. It also tends to rapidly become resistant to drugs. Malaria can be prevented in most cases by taking appropriate prophylactic drugs and trying to avoid mosquito bites in endemic areas; see the Immunisations & Prophylaxis section earlier in this chapter. The risk of malaria in Nepal is extremely low, and would require spending a lot of time in the Terai. However, if you have been travelling in other malaria endemic areas before you trek, then malaria could begin while you are in a remote mountain area. This has happened a number of times among trekkers in Nepal.

The clues to a malaria infection are travel in an endemic area without prophylaxis (or in a *Plasmodium falciparum* area that might be resistant), and the abrupt onset of chills followed by high fever and sweats. The initial bout resolves in several hours, leaving the person feeling remarkably well between episodes. A return bout of the symptoms in one to two days is the clue that malaria might be present. Steady fever can also occasionally be a presentation of malaria, and a blood test might eventually be necessary to make the diagnosis. If you are ill where a blood test is available, by all means have the test before starting self-treatment.

The incubation period is usually a minimum of two weeks, but it can stretch to several months or a year or more in the case of *Plasmodium vivax* malaria, so if someone presents with malaria symptoms, check their travel history: they may have visited Africa or India the year before. The treatment of malaria is complicated by the fact that *P falciparum* can be highly resistant to the usual drugs, and it is difficult to tell which form of malaria you might have without a blood test by a highly experienced technician. If you suspect malaria, try to have a smear done at a local health post before treatment. Then begin treatment with fansidar by taking three pills all at once. If it is available, also start taking doxycycline (100 mg) twice a day for seven days; if it is not, however, fansidar should be sufficient. Bring the blood smear with you back to follow-up medical care in a reliable centre to see if the diagnosis can be confirmed. If you have *P vivax* malaria, you will need a follow-up course of primaquine as well.

Dengue Fever

Dengue fever is caused by a virus carried by a mosquito which tends to favour urban environments. It is endemic in northern India, particularly during the month of October. It is also endemic in Thailand throughout most of the year. The disease is not present in Nepal, and thus all the cases that we see in Nepal are imported from India or Thailand.

The disease has a very predictable incubation period, from three to 10 days. Thus, if the person has not been in an endemic area within the past 10 days, the disease is not possible. Exposure in transit in Delhi or Bangkok, however, can be a risk for the disease.

The disease has a very typical presentation which can allow the diagnosis to be made presumptively in most cases. The onset is very abrupt, with high fever on the first day. Headache is almost always present, centred mainly behind the eyes, with movement of the eyes exacerbating the pain. Muscle aches and backaches are more prominent than in the other diseases discussed here. The nickname for the disease is 'breakbone fever'. Nausea and vomiting can be present. A characteristic rash is almost always present, but is not seen unless looked for. The rash is a continuous faint reddening of the skin on the trunk, which resembles a light sunburn. If you press your hand flat against the stomach or back for a few seconds, and then remove it, the skin will blanch white from the pressure and preserve the imprint of the hand for a few seconds. This blanching effect lasts only a half-second or so on normal skin.

There is no treatment for the disease, but making the diagnosis allows you not to start treatment for some other disease, or to panic. The fever lasts from three to six days, then goes away suddenly, along with all the other symptoms. Most people feel weak for an additional one to two weeks, but some recover quite quickly.

ALTITUDE ILLNESS

Three trekkers on average die each year of altitude illness in Nepal despite the fact that we now know as much as we need to know to prevent every trekker from dying of altitude illness. Why is this? People who choose to trek in Nepal these days are not always hikers and mountaineers; they range from travellers who find themselves in Nepal and hear that trekking might be fun to busy business people looking for a more adventurous holiday. These people may not think of the potential hazards of their chosen holiday, and may not ask the right questions or read the right sources before heading out. This section will review the problem of high-altitude illness as it relates specifically to trekking in Nepal. The concepts are not difficult, and we look forward to a time when trekkers will no longer die needlessly from altitude illness.

Acclimatisation & Altitude Illness

Our bodies have the ability to adjust to higher altitudes if given enough time. This process of adaptation is called acclimatisation. If you were flown to the summit of Mt Everest, you would have a few minutes of consciousness before you passed out and died. However, acclimatised climbers have made it to the summit safely without using supplemental oxygen by allowing their bodies to adjust gradually to the increasing height. If a person travels up to altitude more rapidly than his or her body can adjust, symptoms develop that are called acute mountain sickness (AMS). If ignored, the symptoms can occasionally progress to more severe forms of altitude illness described in the following paragraphs.

Your body adjusts to altitude initially by increasing the rate and depth of breathing. Studies have shown that people who adapt well to altitude automatically increase their breathing more than individuals who get altitude sickness easily. This sensitivity to a change in altitude appears to be genetic. Other adaptations include an increase in heart rate and a gradual increase in red blood cells. Once you are acclimatised to a given height for a few days, you are very unlikely to get mountain sickness at that height, but you can still get ill when you travel higher.

Altitude illness occurs as the result of failure to adapt to a higher altitude. Fluid accumulates in between the cells in the body and eventually collects where, unfortunately, it can do the most harm: in the lungs and brain. As fluid collects in the lungs, you become breathless more easily while walking, and eventually more breathless at rest. A cough begins, initially dry and irritative, but progressing to the production of pink, frothy sputum in its most severe form. The person ultimately drowns in this fluid if he or she doesn't descend. This syndrome is referred to as high-altitude pulmonary edema (HAPE). When fluid collects in the brain, you develop a headache, loss of appetite, nausea and sometimes vomiting. You become increasingly tired and want to lie down and do nothing. As you progress, you develop a problem with your balance and coordination (ataxia). Eventually you lie down and slip into coma, and death is inevitable if you don't descend. This syndrome is called high-altitude cerebral edema (HACE). HAPE and HACE can occur singly or in combination.

Prevention of AMS: the Acclimatisation Line

As you prepare for your trek in Kathmandu, you are at an altitude of 1300m. You can probably move safely and rapidly up to a height of around 2800m without getting ill. This height will be slightly different for each individual. The altitude below which you will be fine, and above which you will develop AMS, is called the 'acclimatisation line'. Awareness of this line as you travel up in altitude can help you prevent illness and react appropriately if you do develop symptoms.

Although itineraries are designed to try to prevent AMS on treks, some people will be more susceptible than others, and unless one chooses a very conservative schedule, some people are likely to get AMS. The purpose of advice on altitude illness is not to prevent all people from getting AMS. The purpose is to prevent anyone from dying of AMS. In other words: it's okay to get altitude illness; it's not okay to die of altitude illness.

Try to spend your first night on trek at 2800m or lower. If you do fly in to a higher altitude, be sure to rest there for two days before trying to go higher. If you start to get symptoms of AMS, you have crossed your acclimatisation line. If you have been ascending relatively slowly (less than 300m per day), it is likely that you are only a short distance above the line, and resting at the same altitude will allow you to get over your symptoms. However, if you are ascending rapidly, it is more difficult to determine at which point you crossed your acclimatisation line, and you may be far above it. In that case, it will be necessary to descend below the line at which your symptoms began in order to get better.

For example, trekker A has slept at 2800m, then ascends to 3300m. She spends an extra day at that height to help acclimatisation, then ascend to 3700m. She feels fine when she gets there, but the following morning she awakens with a headache, loss of appetite, and fatigue. Since AMS symptoms generally take several hours to develop after arriving at a new height, her symptoms most likely began close to 3700m. By resting for a day at the same height, she will likely acclimatise and be able to continue her ascent.

On the other hand, trekker B has slept at 2800m and then ascended to 3300m the next day. The following day he climbs to 3700m and the next day to 4200m, arriving at that camp with a headache and nausea. He spends the night at 4200m, but is worse in the morning, with a severe headache, vomiting and lack of coordination. Since he has been ascending so rapidly, it is difficult to determine exactly where his symptoms began. However, a clue is the fact that the symptoms began as he was ascending to 4200m. Therefore, he crossed his acclimatisation line at least six to 12 hours earlier. Since his symptoms are now so severe, he must descend immediately and not try to wait for his body to adjust. He is too far above his acclimatisation line for further acclimatisation to take place. Most likely he will have to descend to 3700m or lower in order to improve.

These two examples show how the acclimatisation line concept can be useful in determining what course to take in regard to AMS symptoms. There are three rules which, if followed closely, should prevent anyone from dying of altitude illness:

Rule One Learn the early symptoms of mountain sickness, and be willing to recognise when you have them.

You must become familiar with the early symptoms of altitude illness, such as headache, loss of appetite, nausea and fatigue. Once you are familiar with these symptoms, you must be willing to admit that you have them. Trekkers tend to be very goal-oriented, and ambition can lead people to want to deny their symptoms. Over the years trekkers have come to me with AMS symptoms which they explain away as being due to the sun, dehydration, hitting their head on a low doorway, sleeping in smoky teahouses, medicine they have taken, bronchitis, the flu – in fact, anything except mountain sickness. If you feel ill at altitude and you are not sure why, assume it is AMS and respond accordingly. Guessing wrong can have serious consequences.

Eighty per cent of altitude-illness deaths occur in organised trekking groups, even though only 40% of people trek in an organised group. It is ironic that people who would seem to be in the safer situation of having an experienced group leader and plenty of logistical support are significantly more likely to die of altitude sickness than trekkers who are travelling on their own from teahouse to teahouse. The reasons for this apparent disparity are that people who elect to trek with organised groups have the problem of sticking to a group schedule. If they fail to acclimatise on a given day they often have to be left behind. Since people don't want to be left behind on a 'trip of a lifetime', they will often hide or minimise their symptoms. Even if their symptoms become apparent, an inexperienced trek leader may choose to minimise the importance of the symptoms to avoid the logistical complications of having to split up the group. Trekkers arranging their own treks have the luxury of being able to take an extra day at will if they don't feel well. This luxury of extra time in the schedule can be life-saving.

Rule Two Never ascend to sleep at a new altitude with *any* symptoms of AMS.

Once you recognise that you have the early symptoms of AMS, it is not necessary to descend immediately. But it is imperative that you do not ascend to sleep at a higher altitude. Virtually all fatalities from altitude illness occur in people who persist in ascending despite symptoms that should have been recognised as AMS. You may find yourself in a situation where it is necessary to ascend in order to descend – for example, when crossing a pass. If your symptoms are still mild, and you feel certain that you can get over the pass to a lower height by the end of the day, this may be all right. But it is a decision that requires some mountaineering judgment. However, if you climb to a higher altitude and spend the night, even the most mild symptom of AMS will become worse, and you will now be much higher above your acclimatisation line. This rule is the single most important point to prevent deaths from altitude illness.

Rule Three Descend if your symptoms are getting worse while resting at the same altitude.

If you are too high above your acclimati-

sation line, and your symptoms are slowly becoming worse instead of better while resting at the same height, it is imperative that you descend to a lower altitude. Once the cycle of AMS symptoms starts to get progressively worse, it will not start to improve without descent. Most of the time it is necessary to get below the height at which the symptoms began, but if what that height was is not clear, you must descend until you feel that the symptoms are starting to get better. Once they start to improve, you can generally continue to rest at that altitude until recovery is complete.

Two symptoms deserve prime attention. People with the cerebral form of altitude illness, ie headache, nausea, vomiting and fatigue, must be checked for signs of uncoordination while walking, known medically as 'ataxia'. Have the person stand up and walk a straight line while putting the heel of the front foot on the toe of the back foot (the classic 'drunk test' administered to drivers by police who are looking for signs of alcohol intoxication). If the person steps off the imaginary line, or falls altogether, they have developed severe HACE and must descend immediately. Someone with moderately severe symptoms of AMS, but who can still walk the line without imbalance, should think about descending, but if it is night time, or if descent would be logistically difficult due to weather or terrain, they can be watched closely for a while. Anyone with signs of ataxia, however, should descend immediately, regardless of the time of day. They are only hours away from unconsciousness.

The other significant symptom to watch for is breathlessness at rest. HAPE can have an insidious onset, starting out as just feeling like you can't hike as fast you think you should. Later you find that you have to rest more and more often, and don't recover your breathing rate at rest. No matter how hard you have to breathe while walking uphill at altitude, your breathing rate should return to normal after five to 10 minutes rest. If you continue to feel breathless after 10 minutes at rest, you are developing HAPE, and you should immediately descend. The problem with HAPE is that exercise makes it worse, and even exerting to descend can make things worse before the decrease in altitude starts to make things better. This can be a fine line to walk, so early recognition of the signs of HAPE is imperative. Breathlessness at rest is a serious sign of HAPE at altitude.

Once you have recovered completely from altitude illness by descending, you have the option of re-ascending slowly, watching for relapse. Many people will have had enough by then, but determined people can try to go back to altitude once they have completely recovered from all their symptoms.

Treatment of AMS

The treatment of AMS is, first, not to ascend with symptoms; and, if symptoms are more severe, to descend. Descent will always bring improvement and should not be delayed in order to try some other form of therapy in serious cases. In rare cases where descent is difficult or impossible, a portable pressure chamber (Gamow bag) is effective.

The Gamow bag is the newest form of treatment for altitude sickness but is, in a sense, a simulation of the oldest: descent. The bag has been in use at the HRA aid posts in Pheriche and Manang since 1988. It seems that one hour's treatment in the bag is very effective at improving the mild to moderate symptoms of AMS, and this improvement may persist even after coming out of the bag. Severe cases of mountain sickness (HACE and HAPE) are improved in the bag, but this improvement tends to deteriorate after coming out of the bag, requiring repeat or prolonged (four to six hours) treatment in the bag.

The Gamow bags sell for about US$2500. A similar pressurisation bag is manufactured by Certec in France. It is possible to rent pressurisation bags in Kathmandu and in other countries. You should consider carrying a pressurisation bag if you are travelling into a remote high-altitude area where descent is difficult.

Three medications have been proven useful as an adjunct to treating AMS:

Acetazolamide (Diamox) Diamox can prevent mild symptoms of AMS if taken prior to ascent. You should not routinely take Diamox for a trek in Nepal, as most people will not need it for the gradual ascents that are usually associated with trekking. However, if you know from past experience that you do not acclimatise well, and that the itinerary you are going on has an unavoidable sudden increase in altitude, Diamox taken before you ascend may prevent you from getting AMS symptoms. Diamox does not prevent the progression to severe symptoms of HAPE or HACE, so you must still watch closely for AMS symptoms and respond appropriately. Diamox prevents or improves AMS by increasing the respiratory rate and depth, mimicking the breathing of someone who is a good acclimatiser. Thus, if you feel better on Diamox, you actually are better, and Diamox does not mask the symptoms of AMS.

Diamox is useful in treating the headache and nausea associated with mild AMS, and it also can improve your sleep at altitude if you are being disturbed by the irregular breathing and breathlessness that can occur. My recommendation regarding Diamox is to carry it with you, use it to treat mild symptoms, and use it prophylactically only if you have had experience before with AMS on a certain schedule. The usual dose is 125 mg (half a tablet) every 12 hours as needed. Mild tingling of hands and feet is common after taking Diamox and is not an indication to stop its use. Diamox is a diuretic, and increased urine output can be expected when taking the drug. People with a known allergy to sulphur drugs should not take Diamox, although allergic reactions to Diamox itself are extremely rare.

Dexamethasone (Decadron) Dexamethasone is a potent steroid drug which improves the symptoms of HACE through an unknown mechanism, apparently without improving acclimatisation. It is an important drug to carry for emergency use, but it should never be taken prophylactically to prevent AMS. People with severe headache and loss of balance can be improved enough with this drug to allow them to avoid a night-time descent, or to convert them from a stretcher case to being able to walk. The improvement with dexamethasone is occasionally so dramatic that people might be tempted to continue upward while still taking the drug. However, since adaptation to altitude has not been improved, this could be dangerous. Once the drug is started, the person should refrain from going to a higher altitude while still taking it. If you are able to go off the drug for 24 hours and have no further symptoms, you may continue your ascent.

Nifedipine Nifedipine is a drug that is ordinarily used to treat heart problems and high blood pressure. However, it has been shown to reduce pressure in the main artery in the lungs, dramatically improving severe HAPE. For this reason, nifedipine should be included in trekking first-aid kits. The initial dose is 10 mg every eight hours. Treatment with nifedipine should be accompanied by immediate descent.

On a Happier Note Remember, some people are more susceptible to altitude illness than others. If you know that you get altitude illness easily (as I do), you just have to adjust your acclimatisation schedule accordingly. If you get a severe case of altitude illness, it doesn't mean that you can never go to high altitude again, but it means that you will have to be much more cautious in the future.

Awareness of altitude illness has caused some trekkers to be unnecessarily anxious as they trek. The progression of symptoms is usually gradual, and you have plenty of time to react appropriately. As long as you don't ascend with any symptoms of AMS, and you descend promptly if your symptoms appear to be worsening, you have virtually no chance of becoming an altitude illness statistic in Nepal.

FROSTBITE

Frostbite is the injury resulting from frozen skin tissue. The circulation of warm blood to the extremities can ordinarily prevent them from freezing in cold weather provided the extremities are protected enough from the environment. When hands or feet get cold they first feel cold, then numb, and then they begin to freeze. In extreme cold, touching a piece of metal or spilling petrol on your hands can induce instant freezing of skin, but in the Himalaya one almost always goes through the progression from cold to numb to frozen.

Frostbite is not a major concern on most trekking trails on most days. However, from October to April, storms can occur that dump a metre or more of snow on the high passes. The two most popular treks, to Kala Pattar

and around Annapurna, take people above an altitude of 5000m. The combination of high altitude and snow can produce frostbite very easily in unwary or unprepared trekkers.

On the Annapurna circuit, most of the walking is at low to moderate altitudes on easy trails. Therefore, the temptation is great to wear either running shoes or lightweight cloth-and-leather hiking boots. The heavy boots that would be necessary to cross the Thorung La in snow seem like too great a burden to carry for the one or two days they might be needed. If snow catches trekkers at the pass, they try to push on in their light shoes, and frostbite can result. High altitude plays a deceptive role in inducing frostbite, making tissue more susceptible to cold injury due to lack of oxygen to protect the skin cells. Several frostbitten people have told me that they were very surprised to see that they were frostbitten because they had felt colder in other settings without getting any cold injury.

Prevention of Frostbite

The key to prevention is to notice when your feet or hands have gone numb and to stop *immediately* to warm them up. Once they have gone numb, you have no control over whether they are starting to freeze, since you can't feel it. To warm up numb feet you must stop walking, get out of the wind, avoid sitting directly on the snow if possible, take off your boots, and place your feet against someone's abdomen or under their arms. The return of feeling is often painful for a short time. Put on dry socks if your socks are wet. Be prepared to stop and warm your feet every time they go numb. If your whole body is cold, it's important to increase your clothing layers, add a hat, get out of the wind, and drink hot drinks where possible.

Response to Frostbite

If you are not vigilant enough, you may notice that the skin on your toes or fingers has frozen. The digits will be numb and feel hard and waxy, with a whitish appearance. The one acceptable way to warm up frozen extremities is by a process of rapid rewarming, which may be hard to perform if you are not carrying stoves and large pots. The technique is to heat enough water to submerge the frozen extremity. The water should be at a temperature of around 34°C to 37°C (91°F to 97°F). The extremity is placed in the water until it rewarms and a red flush of circulation returns. This process can be very painful. Blisters may form, and the foot will then have to be protected from further trauma.

Most of the time the frostbite is not noticed until the person reaches their next destination, and the foot has already rewarmed during the descent. The people take off their shoes and notice that blisters have formed. If a disaster has occurred, such as getting lost on a pass and spending one or two nights out, the toes may appear blackened and shrivelled, without the formation of blisters. This is a sign of freezing, thawing and refreezing, and means that deeper damage has taken place.

There is no way to undo the damage that has been done once frostbite has occurred. Further treatment is aimed at preventing the situation from getting worse by avoiding trauma to the affected areas and preventing infection. It is not necessary to start taking antibiotics. If there are blisters or open skin, the involved area should be washed in a sterile fashion, and a sterile dressing applied. If there are only deep blisters, with hard skin over them, or blackened skin, dressings may not be necessary. Walking should be abandoned or kept to a minimum. Evacuation by horse, yak or helicopter may be necessary depending on the degree of injury.

Only a handful of people get frostbite injuries each year but, like altitude sickness, these injuries are all preventable. Even relatively minor frostbite ends the trip and forces a return to one's home country, since healing can take several months. If you are going above 4000m, be prepared for walking in snow.

TRAUMATIC INJURIES

Trauma is the most common cause of death among trekkers in Nepal, and a major cause of evacuation. Trauma results most often from falling off a trail, or having something fall on you while trekking. Nepal features a wide variety of trails, ranging from smooth valley bottoms to exposed rock traverses that make even hardened mountaineers queasy. Many accidents take place during a momentary lapse in judgment: scrambling up or down for a photo, not paying attention to your feet, or trying to climb between trails on steep terrain after taking a wrong turn. Ironically, one activity associated with serious trauma among trekkers is getting up at night to go to the toilet. I have seen a dislocated hip and badly broken arms, legs and ribs from misjudging where the toilet was, or simply walking off a wall or cliff in the dark. Review your night-time toilet route before going to bed!

We found in our studies of trekking accidents that sometimes it was the more experienced trekkers who got hurt. This seemed to be due to the fact that they were going into harder terrain on less-travelled routes. It is important to concentrate when you are walking, and to concentrate even harder towards the end of the day when your legs and mind are both tired. We tend to see more ankle injuries towards the end of the day, when people are tired and can't control their foot placement so well. It is also important to look up and try to assess the risk of rock or snowfall from above. Some gullies are obvious chutes for rock fall or avalanche. Look for signs of recent rock fall or falling ice, and don't linger in these areas. If you are crossing an obvious landslide or large rockfall area, rest before you start across, and then don't stop in the middle. This simple advice once saved my life in the Everest region, when I forced myself to push on across an unstable area near a river even though I was out of breath at 4200m. Thirty seconds later the area where I had wanted to rest was swept by a huge rock fall.

Initial Assessment

Trauma usually occurs in a very sudden and unexpected manner, leaving bystanders momentarily stunned. Scrambling to reach someone who has fallen, you may forget some basic rules of safety. Make sure that other members of the group are out of danger, and then be careful to take a route to the victim that doesn't expose that person to further rock fall. If the situation is still very unstable, with continued rock or ice fall, you may have to move the person out of danger before making a complete assessment.

When you and the victim are in a safe spot, you have to make an initial assessment of his or her condition. This can be done quite quickly, and the process of doing this helps you to organise your thoughts and begin to come up with a plan. It is important to approach the person with a set of priorities in mind, rather than be forced to react emotionally as each injury is uncovered. The rule of 'ABC' has proved very useful to help a rescuer move from an overall emotional reaction to a plan of action. ABC stands for 'Airway, Breathing and Circulation'. If the person is conscious and talking, then obviously the airway and breathing are all right. If the person is unconscious, however, it is necessary to check immediately to see if their breathing is obstructed, and if not, whether they are breathing at all. You can then check for signs of circulation by feeling for a pulse. In a traumatic fall, if the victim has no respiration or pulse when you reach them, they are dead. Cardiopulmonary resuscitation (CPR) is futile in this situation.

If the person is still alive but is not conscious, or is confused and combative, then they have a head injury. Make note of that, but keep on with your initial assessment. Inspect the head, look for signs of scalp laceration (feel the back of the head), and then feel all the rest of the bones in the body briefly, looking for swelling or deformity that might indicate a fracture. If the person is awake, they can generally tell you where they hurt, but do a complete assessment anyway; the person may be unaware of a large cut on their back, for example. Once you have done an initial assessment, you will be aware of their level of consciousness, any large bleeding cuts or bruises, and any signs of broken bones. The next step is to begin to stabilise all these injuries.

Bleeding

Most cuts will stop bleeding on their own, but relatively large arteries may keep pumping blood for a long time, particularly from scalp wounds. Put direct pressure with a cloth or dressing over the area that is bleeding, and press relatively hard. Don't keep pulling off the dressing and looking to see if the bleeding has stopped. Apply pressure for five full minutes (use your watch) before you look to see if the bleeding has stopped. You can then tie a dressing over the wound and hopefully move on to assessing other injuries. If you move the patient around, you may restart the bleeding, so make sure you check the dressing as needed. Large wounds may benefit from cleaning and suturing, even in the field, but this can wait until all other aspects of the situation have been stabilised. It is not necessary to elevate a limb to stop bleeding, and it is almost never necessary to use a tourniquet on a limb to stop bleeding. Large lacerations can be cleaned and sutured even several days later, so don't feel a great urgency to do a repair unless you are trained to do so and have the appropriate equipment. If you do know how to repair lacerations, I recommend doing so, since the infection rate in my experience has been very low, and the comfort and ease of caring for a wound that has been closed makes it worthwhile to take the risk of closing a wound in a field situation.

Fractures

Broken bones hurt. A conscious person can usually direct your attention to an area of concern. If a limb appears deformed, a fracture is likely. If the bone is broken, but not bent out of place, the person may just have pain in that specific area. There is relatively little urgency to trying to fix a broken bone, since healing will take many weeks at best. Suspected non-displaced fractures should be splinted to protect them from further injury. Obviously displaced fractures should be splinted after some attempt is made to straighten out the deformity by pulling gently in a straight line on the hand or foot until the arm or leg straightens out. Have someone else stabilise the joint just above the fracture so you have something to pull against. This will work well on the arm and lower leg, but it will be impossible to hold a broken thigh bone (femur) straight without a special splint. In the case of a broken femur, try to straighten the leg gently, and then tie the injured leg to the good leg to try to hold it in place. A good splint will keep the broken bone ends from moving around inside, will decrease internal bleeding, and will make the patient much more comfortable. Pad the inside of the splint to protect the skin, and check frequently to make sure that the splint is not cutting off circulation to the hand or foot.

If the broken bone is associated with a laceration of the skin, the fracture is said to be 'compound', which means that the normal problems of the fracture have been 'compounded' by the risk of infection due to the exposure to the outside environment. Compound fractures require much more urgency than non-compound ('simple') fractures. Most compound fractures need to be taken to an operating room and thoroughly cleansed as soon as possible. Until then, put a sterile dressing soaked in povidone iodine (Betadine) or other disinfectant over the wound, and splint as usual. If you have antibiotics, you should start them immediately. The best choice would be cephalexin (500 mg) four times per day. This drug should not be taken by people who may be allergic to penicillin.

Internal Injuries

Bleeding from the skin is obvious and can be controlled by direct pressure. Internal bleeding may not be obvious at first, and there is no way to stop this bleeding in the field. You can suspect internal bleeding if the person shows signs of a rapid pulse and pale, cool skin after you have otherwise stabilised them. A tender or gradually distending abdomen can mean internal bleeding in the abdomen, usually from the spleen or liver. Bleeding in the chest can be from major arteries, and there is little that you can do to stop it. 'Shock' is a very specific medical

term that is often misused by the general public. It refers specifically to the inability of a person to maintain an adequate circulating blood volume. It does not refer to the emotional reaction to an injury. If a person is truly in shock, then evacuation to a hospital is your only hope. Since evacuation in Nepal can take 24 hours, some people will die before they can be rescued.

Head Injury

The terms 'unconscious' and 'coma' are vague generalisations. These two terms can describe a wide range of reactions, ranging from temporary amnesia following a blow to the head through to complete unresponsiveness to deep pain. An altered mental state following a blow to the head is due to direct trauma to the brain. Most often this is just a bruise, and the person will improve steadily. However, if a blood vessel is actually torn, blood may accumulate in the closed space of the skull, gradually squishing the brain. Thus, it is important to note whether a head-injured person is getting better or worse with time.

Most cases of brief unconsciousness lasting less than a minute are not associated with any serious internal injury to the brain. The person may be confused, combative, or have trouble remembering what is happening to them, but they improve steadily over a number of hours. The medical term for this condition is 'concussion', which simply means a blow to the brain severe enough to cause a brief change in consciousness. A more seriously injured person may not respond to spoken commands, but might be making spontaneous movements, or push your hand away when you touch them. The most seriously injured person will not respond in any way to your touching them or talking to them. Try to note just how an unconscious person is responding when you first see them, and then keep track of whether they appear to be getting worse or better. If they are slowly getting better, you usually can be reassured that they will recover. If they are getting worse, there is very little you can do except to try to get them to advanced medical care, and to be sure that they are in a position that allows them to breathe freely.

OTHER MEDICAL PROBLEMS
Animal Bites (Rabies)

All mammals are thought to be capable of carrying and passing on rabies. Dogs are the most common transmitter of rabies virus to humans, but the virus has been passed by cats, monkeys, cows, horses, raccoons, foxes, bats and skunks among others. Although rodents are generally thought not to become rabid, it is not certain that they cannot transmit rabies. Nepal is considered to be highly endemic for rabies, mainly in the street dog population. There are numerous monkeys around certain temples in Kathmandu, and since they have constant contact with the dogs, they are thought to be capable of transmitting rabies as well. Tourists are occasionally bitten by rodents while staying in local houses. Although rodent bites are thought to be low risk, we recommend rabies treatment for rodent bites acquired in Nepal.

Dogs infected with rabies may not show any signs of illness at the time you are bitten. However, all infected dogs who had rabies virus in their saliva at the time they bit you will go on to show signs of brain infections within seven to 10 days. The bottom line is that if you receive a bite or a scratch from an animal in Nepal, and the animal is not a closely observable pet, you will need to seek post-exposure rabies immunoprophylaxis. One should try to obtain these shots as soon as possible after the incident, but it is not necessary to try to find a doctor in the middle of the night. In practice, tourists in Nepal have been able to get to a doctor within three days, and people who were trekking have got back to medical care within five days. This figure compares favourably to the average delay in treatment in the USA, which is five days.

We have noted, over the years, that we have never treated anyone twice for a possible rabies exposure. This suggests that either it is rare to get bitten (which it is), or that people who have been bitten modify their behaviour towards animals such that they avoid future incidents. It is sensible to be aware of animals around you in the street. Don't step around blind corners, or step into courtyards without looking first to see if you will surprise a sleeping dog, or a dog with puppies. Be aware that the monkeys around temples are extremely aggressive, and are used to humans having food in their hands or in their backpacks. Don't walk around eating, and don't try to feed the monkeys. A little awareness can save you hundreds of dollars in treatment, many hours of worry, and weeks of having to arrange your schedule around a series of rabies shots; for more information, see the Immunisations & Prophylaxis section earlier in this chapter.

Conjunctivitis

Conjunctivitis is a bacterial or viral infection of the pink lining around the eye (the conjunctivae). One often awakens with a slightly swollen eye with increased redness in the pink areas, and occasionally some redness in the white part of the eye. Usually there is some sticky material around the eye that you can wash away in the morning. Although it can be painful, it is more of a nuisance than anything else. Antibiotic eye drops can clear up bacterial infections within a day or so. Viral infections will clear themselves in a few days as well. Most of the infections seem to be bacterial, so using antibiotic eye drops makes sense. The infection almost always starts in one eye, but can spread to the other eye. Use the drops frequently on the first day, every two to three hours. As the infection improves, you can use the drops less often, and then stop as soon as the eye seems normal (usually two to three days).

If the eye is severely painful, or the white part of the eye is very red, or your vision is impaired, seek medical help from an eye specialist. There are a few eye conditions which travellers occasionally get that require specialised diagnosis and treatment, such as uveitis, or herpes virus infections of the cornea.

Gastritis

The stomach and upper intestine are usually quite resistant to the normal stomach acid that aids in digestion. However, raw areas in the stomach lining or intestinal lining can develop, and these raw areas are very sensitive to acid, much as an abrasion on your skin would be more sensitive to acid than your intact skin would be. If these raw areas are in your stomach, we call the illness 'gastritis'. If the raw area is in the intestine beyond the stomach we more often call it an 'ulcer'. The main symptoms of gastritis or an ulcer are burning pain in the upper part of the stomach. In the beginning it can be intermittent, either when your stomach is quite empty, or sometimes right after you eat. If you develop a consistent pattern of burning upper abdominal pain while trekking, you can treat it either with antacid pills or liquid, which soak up the acid in your stomach, or more effectively, with an acid-blocking medication which stops the stomach from making acid. The two most commonly used acid-blocking medications are cimetidine and ranitidine. If you have any history of ulcer or gastritis, it would be a good idea to carry some of these medicines with you on a trek, just in case your symptoms are stirred up by the combination of new organisms, stress and diet.

Haemorrhoids

The veins of the lower intestine form loops around the anus. Under conditions of strain (either constipation or diarrhoea), a loop of vein can become distended and form a blood clot, which is initially quite painful. The veins are called the haemorrhoidal vessels, and a clotted, distended vein is called a haemorrhoid. If the swollen, tender vein is on the outside of the anus, it is called an 'external haemorrhoid', and if the vein is on the inside, popping out occasionally, it is called an 'internal haemorrhoid'. External haemorrhoids can occasionally be cut open and the pain relieved, but this procedure is fairly painful, even with a local anaesthetic, and difficult to perform in the field. Soaking the haemorrhoid in hot water will quickly reduce inflammation and swelling, and within a few days the crisis will have passed.

Internal haemorrhoids require special treatment from a physician. However, external haemorrhoids are much more common among trekkers. The various creams that exist to treat haemorrhoids offer marginal benefit at best.

Kidney Stone

Over a period of time, chemicals from the urine can begin to harden and form small stones in the collecting system of the kidney. Occasionally these stones dislodge and become wedged in the narrow channel of the ureter (the tube from the kidney to the bladder). The pain associated with a stone in the ureter is excruciating. The pain usually starts rather abruptly in the back under the lowest ribs and spreads around to the groin in front. The pain is always on one side or the other, not both. Victims usually are very restless; unable to find a comfortable position; they often pace around or lean over a table or chair. Severe abdominal pain from some other cause usually causes people to want to lie still, so someone with severe pain on one side who wants to keep moving around probably has a kidney stone. The person may vomit from the severe pain. Blood is usually not visible in the urine, but can be found on microscopic examination.

Fortunately, 95% of kidney stones eventually work their way down the ureter into the bladder, at which point the pain is completely relieved. The stone is later urinated out without further difficulty. All one can do is try to control the pain, with injectable narcotics, if available, or whatever is at hand. Most of the time we allow three days or so for the stone to pass on its own, as long as there is no fever. The presence of a kidney stone and a fever may mean that the kidney is infected, and this is a medical emergency since the infection cannot be cleared until the stone is removed. Evacuation is usually necessary for a kidney stone that doesn't pass within one day, as the person usually cannot tolerate the pain. If the pain subsides and stays away for 12 hours or so, the stone has probably passed, and the trek can continue.

Skin Diseases

Skin problems are common in travellers. Travellers generally are bothered by one of four major problems: allergic reactions, bacterial skin infections, fungal infections and skin mites (scabies).

A generalised rash due to an allergic reaction can consist of raised red spots in a variety of locations, often with a symmetrical distribution (equal on both sides of the body). One can also experience slightly raised flat red lesions that come and go relatively rapidly over a period of time (urticaria, or 'hives'). Either rash is usually caused by a new medicine, a new vaccine, or a new food. However, in many instances, it is impossible to figure out just what triggered the rash. Travellers are often taking new medications for the first time and may discover that they have an allergy to one of these new drugs. In general, a rash scattered over most of the body is due to something taken internally, and not to something that you touched with your skin. The rash can be treated with antihistamines in mild cases, or corticosteroids in more severe cases.

A painful, red swelling that keeps getting worse over the hours is probably a bacterial skin infection. Staphylococcal infections that cause boils are common in travellers and account for about two-thirds of the skin problems in our clinic. If the boil is tense and painful, it may need to be opened and drained by a physician. Antibiotics are necessary to get rid of the infection. Cephalexin is the best choice (if you are not allergic to penicillin).

A round red patch, clearing in the centre and advancing at its edges, is usually a fungus and can be treated with an anti-fungal cream. These lesions can also occur in the groin and in the armpits. They are not painful, and do not cause swelling of the skin around the lesion.

Small, very itchy red spots, usually seen in clusters or in small straight lines, suggest an infestation with a tiny skin mite, causing a disease called 'scabies'. This is relatively common in travellers, and is treated by a skin cream rubbed onto the whole body and left on for one day.

Many other skin conditions can arise, but we can't list them all here. Just remember that skin conditions (such as psoriasis, eczema and allergic dermatitis) that could have occurred at home can coincidentally occur while travelling. You need to consider, when you have a new skin problem, whether it is travel-related or not.

Snow Blindness

Snow blindness is a temporary painful condition resulting from a sunburn of the clear surface of the eye (the cornea). It results from heavy exposure to ultraviolet radiation, almost exclusively in situations where someone is walking on snow without sunglasses. Snow blindness is almost unheard-of where there is no snow on the ground to reflect additional light rays into your eyes. In Nepal it can affect people who don't carry sunglasses, someone who has an accident on snow and loses their sunglasses, and porters, who generally don't own sunglasses, or sell the ones they have been given. If you are in a party of trekkers attempting to cross a high pass that is covered with snow, try to make sure that everyone has something to protect their eyes as they go.

The treatment is simply to try to relieve the pain. Cold cloths held against the outside of the eyelids help relieve the pain and swelling. Antibiotic eye drops are not necessary, and anaesthetic drops should be avoided as they slow down the healing and make the eyes vulnerable to other injuries. The cornea will be completely repaired within a few days. There are no long-term consequences of this injury.

Trekker's Knee

Trekking in Nepal invariably involves multiple long ascents and descents. If your legs have not been gradually accustomed to walking uphill and downhill through training, there is a chance that you will develop some degree of knee soreness after a long descent. The pain generally comes from mild trauma repeated thousands of times on the descent. The two areas that are most involved are the outer side of the knee, and the area under the kneecap. The pain can make it difficult to walk, and you may have to rest for a few days before continuing. Anti-inflammatory pills are helpful, as are ski poles or a walking stick. The pain can take several weeks to go away completely, but there are no long-term consequences.

Blisters

Blisters on the feet result from repeated rubbing of the skin against a hard surface (the inside of your shoe or boot). The superficial surface of the skin eventually gets lifted off its base, and fluid collects in the resulting bubble. Blisters can usually be avoided by conscientious attention to your feet as you hike. Any sore spot on your foot while walking should be investigated immediately, and some form of additional protection should be put over the area that is being rubbed. There are many commercial products on the market to protect the feet from blisters in specific areas. Moleskin is the most popular item, but adhesive tape can also work well. Newer products, utilising soft gels, have recently been added to the mix of products. Using a thin inner sock inside a thicker sock can provide a sliding layer that can reduce the friction on the foot. Try not to begin a trek in brand-new shoes or boots.

Blisters are not infected when they first form, but after the bubble breaks, bacterial infection can develop. Try to wash the area and keep it clean. If swelling and redness develop, you will need to take oral antibiotics.

Psychological Issues

Stress Even at the best of times, travel involves a level of stress that is higher than we usually deal with at home. Trekking in Nepal involves jet lag, loss of contact with familiar support systems, bombardment of sights and sounds, beggars, and uncertainty as to whether you are strong enough to complete your itinerary. Even trying to absorb a particularly beautiful or moving event can be a form of stress. Trying to accomplish simple tasks, such as finding a decent room, buying a bus ticket or obtaining a visa can lead to

hours of frustration and uncertainty. If you are headed to remote areas, you can have a sense of being too far removed from familiar surroundings. You may suddenly realise that you are two weeks walk from a strange and terrifying capital city, which is still 36 hours of flying time away from your home environment.

Most of us try hard to avoid the unexpected, to exert control over our surroundings, to expect things to go a certain way. When things don't go as we think they should, we expect someone to be able to account for it, to take responsibility. When one shifts to an environment and culture half way around the world, these rules can change as well. Michael Palin, while trying to travel around the world in 80 days without flying, summed it up nicely: 'What in Europe had been problems to solve, in Asia became limitations to accept'. One of the most difficult things for travellers to adjust to is the loss of their sense of control. They may fall quite ill despite all their efforts to avoid it. Their trip of a lifetime might be scrubbed by three days in a row of bad weather that prevents the flight in. Since we are used to being in control, not having to handle situations beyond our control, our stress levels can reach astronomic proportions. However, in adventure travel, events may truly be beyond anyone's control. The successful travellers are the ones who can learn to accept the limitations and work within the new systems as they are encountered.

Personal Physical Goals Adventure travellers often add an artificial stress to their journeys: the question of whether they will 'make it' or not. Trekking is often very goal-oriented: the viewpoint of Kala Pattar near Mt Everest, or crossing the Thorung La. Setting out to do something that you are not sure you can do is part of the adventure. But linking the attainment of this goal with a psychological sense of worth can be dangerous. I have seen so many neurotically anxious people heading out for routine adventures, heedless of the needs of their travelling companions, oblivious of the local culture, compulsively monitoring their own health, all with the goal of standing on some patch of ground that they have read about.

People who are planning adventurous journeys should think about the psychological aspects, of finding a balance. They should train physically to gain confidence in themselves and have more fun. They should realise that it is truly the journey, not the goal, that will be their adventure.

Decompensation Sometimes travellers are simply overwhelmed by the sights and sounds and lack of coherence of their environment. The exposure to what appears to be abject poverty is taken personally, as if they have to do something themselves to fix it. The food is perceived as different, unappealing and unsafe. The rooms are dirty and noisy. Usually, people gradually adapt, but occasionally they go home within a few days, feeling personally defeated. If you encounter someone in this condition, a gentle approach can be helpful. You can point out that they don't have to feel responsible for the unpleasant things that they are seeing. You can try to get them to question whether the people they are seeing, who are quite poor, are actually suffering or unhappy. You can point out that they chose to travel to see and experience new things, including unfamiliar food and accommodation. If they can't recover their composure within a few days, they should either go home, or – less defeating – travel to a less formidable part of Asia (eg Thailand).

Panic Attacks 'Panic attack' is the term that is used to describe a terrifying sense of being unable to breathe and about to die. Such attacks can be associated with chest pain, weakness, dizziness and overbreathing (hyperventilation). A panic attack usually leads to abandoning a trek, occasionally a helicopter rescue, and then a series of unsatisfying encounters with doctors who may not recognise the true diagnosis. The point to remember is that an overwhelming sense of dread is part of this syndrome, and the patients are often certain that they are dying.

The combination of symptoms present at the same time in an otherwise healthy person is the key to the diagnosis. In people who have never experienced panic attacks before, reassurance and an explanation of the diagnosis works well. The cause of panic attacks is not known, and they may not be a purely psychological condition.

SEXUALLY TRANSMITTED DISEASES

Most of the STDs that we used to worry about have become minor concerns in the face of the very real threat of acquiring HIV infections (AIDS) from casual sexual contact.

Travellers often behave as if the time that they spend travelling is not part of their 'real' life. Those looking for adventure may be looser with their sexual behaviour than when they are at home. They may be lonely after prolonged travel, or just in search of new thrills. The new sexual partner might be another traveller, a local man or woman, or a prostitute. Any of these people could be a source of an STD. I have seen several cases of women who contracted genital herpes from one or two nights spent with a casual partner (another traveller) who failed to warn them that they had this disease. Male travellers may recently have been with prostitutes (especially in Thailand), and could also be harbouring gonorrhoea, syphilis or HIV. Apart from abstinence, the only sure way of minimising the chances of contracting STDs is to use condoms.

Sores, blisters or rashes around the genitals, discharges or pain when urinating are common symptoms of gonorrhoea, herpes and syphilis. In some STDs, such as wart virus or chlamydia, symptoms may be less marked or not observed at all in women. Syphilis symptoms eventually disappear completely but the disease continues and can cause severe problems in later years.

AIDS can also be spread by infected needles and by blood transfusion. Insist on brand-new disposable needles and syringes for injections. These can be purchased from local pharmacies. Blood screening for AIDS has been introduced in most Asian countries, but can't always be done in an emergency. Try to avoid a blood transfusion unless it seems certain that you will die without it.

Women's Health

VAGINITIS

Women face a few medical problems that men don't have to be concerned about. One fairly common condition is yeast vaginitis, often known as thrush, an uncomfortable irritation and itching of the vagina due to an overgrowth of yeast. There is often an increased vaginal discharge. Taking antibiotics can sometimes initiate a yeast infection. The risk of developing vaginitis while trekking is large enough that all women should carry with them an appropriate treatment. Definitive treatment is with an antifungal cream or lozenge, such as miconazole or clotrimazole, inserted nightly for seven days. A new oral medication, taken as a single dose, is also available, but can have side effects. If the symptoms don't clear up promptly, you may have acquired another vaginal infection, and you should try to see a doctor if you can.

AMENORRHEA

Some women travellers note that their periods stop for a while, or become irregular. This may be associated somehow with the stress of travel. Your periods will return to normal after a while. Pregnancy is the other main reason that travellers might stop having periods, so be sure to check for this possibility if you have been sexually active.

URINARY TRACT INFECTION

The urinary tract is usually free from bacteria. In women, the short tube from the bladder to the outside (the urethra) can allow bacteria to invade from the vagina. An infection called 'cystitis' (inflammation of the bladder) can result. The symptoms are burning on urination and having to urinate frequently and urgently. Blood can sometimes be seen in the urine. Fever is usually not present unless the infection has spread to the kidneys. Sexual activity with a new partner, or with an old partner who has been away for a while, can trigger an infection, probably from the trauma of sexual intercourse. Symptoms of cystitis should be treated with an antibiotic because a simple infection can spread up the ureters to the kidneys, causing a more severe illness. The best choice of antibiotic is either norfloxacin (400 mg) or ciprofloxacin (500 mg), taken twice a day for three days. Commonly used antibiotics for urinary infections, such as Bactrim and Amoxicillin, are not as effective in Nepal due to widespread resistance to these two antibiotics. However, if they are all you have, certainly try them.

PREGNANCY

Although little is known about the possible adverse effects of altitude on a developing foetus, almost all authorities recommend not travelling above 3650m while pregnant. In addition to altitude, there is the constant risk of getting ill, and not being free to take most medications to relieve either the symptoms or the disease. There is no evidence that travel increases the risk of miscarriage, but one in five pregnancies ends in miscarriage in any case, sometimes accompanied by profound bleeding which might require an emergency dilatation and curettage, or put you at risk of requiring a blood transfusion.

Even normal pregnancies can make a woman feel nauseated and tired for the first three months, and have food repulsions or cravings that can't be satisfied by the diet available on a trek. During the second trimester, the general feelings improve, but fatigue can still be a constant factor. In the third trimester, the size of the baby can make walking difficult or uncomfortable.

Most vaccinations can be given safely during pregnancy, but the actual effects of all immunisations during pregnancy are not known.

One can certainly find examples of successful travel while pregnant. But since the outcome of pregnancy is always in doubt, one should be careful about exposures to altitude, infectious diseases or trauma while pregnant. Travelling to Nepal while pregnant should not be undertaken lightly, and if you are uncertain about how you will feel, it might be better to wait and come trekking with your child; see the section on Trekking with Children in the Facts for the Trekker chapter.

Rescue

If you walk into the mountains for two weeks from Kathmandu, you are two weeks walk from Kathmandu. This fact often does not impress itself on trekkers until they become sick or injured on the trail and need to return to Kathmandu. Communication from the mountains to Kathmandu is still primitive, although telephones are now showing up in some trekking areas. The police and the army staff radio posts throughout the country, and most rescue requests are passed through these stations. There are a few reliable medical posts in the hills (the HRA aid posts at Pheriche and Manang, and the Khunde Hospital, are all staffed by Western doctors), but most of the time your accident or illness will occur in the absence of reliable medical care. If you find yourself ill or injured in the mountains, here are the steps to take to get rescued.

First of all, don't panic. If someone falls, take some time to assess the situation: suspected broken bones may only be bruises; a dazed person may wake up and be quite all right in an hour or two. If the problem is severe diarrhoea, try to follow the guidelines in the diarrhoea section. If it is severe mountain sickness, descend with the victim; do not wait for help. If the illness is severe, but not diagnosable, evaluate your options. In most areas of Nepal, some kind of animal will be available to help transport a sick or injured trekker. In western Nepal, ponies are common; in the mountains, yaks are usually available. As extraordinary as it may seem, many Nepalis are both willing and capable of carrying Westerners on their backs for

long distances. An Australian woman who broke her leg by slipping on some ice on Poon Hill above Ghorapani was carried for three days by a series of porters. She later became tearful as she recalled how kind and thoughtful they had been, demonstrating concern for her comfort while they were struggling under a 60 kg load.

Sometimes either the seriousness of the injuries or the urgency of getting care will make land evacuation impractical. If you happen to be near one of the airfields in the hills, you may be able to arrange a seat on a scheduled flight. By negotiation, space can usually be found for a seriously injured or ill trekker, or a charter flight might be arranged, but airport officials are quite unsympathetic to trekkers who are merely demoralised by the unexpected hardships of trail life and hope to jump the queue in order to get out sooner. If there is no nearby airfield, or if you have missed the available flights, then the only alternative is to request a helicopter rescue flight.

HELICOPTER RESCUE

Since this chapter was first written, the number of helicopters available for rescues in Nepal has jumped from six to over 30. There are several private airlines that operate scheduled helicopter passenger service, and whose helicopters can also be chartered for rescue. Initial requests for rescue should still go first to the army; if it can't provide help, then you should look to the private companies. The main contact number for the army helicopter wing to request a helicopter rescue is ☎ 471653; additional numbers are ☎ 473297, ☎ 473290 and ☎ 474953. These numbers are answered between 6 am and 5 pm.

Helicopter rescues involve three important steps that you need to understand:

• *Getting the message from the mountains to Kathmandu* Invariably, local people will know where the nearest radio post or telephone is. These radios will usually be within four to eight hours walk. If you can send a reliable Westerner, it may improve the chances of passing an accurate message, but if you need to send a Nepali, you can write the message out carefully, using only capital letters. The message will probably go first to the police or army radios in Kathmandu, who will then phone either your trekking agency (if you have one) or your embassy.

- *Getting a guarantee of payment in Kathmandu* Helicopters will rarely fly on a rescue mission without someone having guaranteed the payment in Kathmandu by making either a cash deposit or a promise in writing. If you are trekking with an agency, they will usually arrange the rescue. If you have no agency, you will have to depend on your embassy to guarantee payment. Register with your embassy in Kathmandu before starting your trek. This greatly facilitates arranging a rescue for you if you later require it.

- *Availability of helicopters, pilots, and adequate weather* With so many helicopters and pilots in the country now, lack of equipment is rarely a limiting factor. However, mountain weather can restrict flying at any time. Usually the weather is less windy early in the morning, so most mountain rescues take place the morning after the message is received. Most afternoons are too windy to attempt the tricky high-altitude flying involved.

The victim is entirely responsible for the cost of the rescue flight. Nepal is much too poor a country to guarantee free rescue for comparatively wealthy tourists. The cost is from US$850 to US$1100 per hour of flight time. In most instances, a rescue will cost between US$1300 and US$3000.

Facilitating Rescue

There are three steps you can take in advance to facilitate helicopter rescue:

- If you are trekking without a trekking agency, register with your embassy. This greatly facilitates the embassy's ability to organise a helicopter rescue for you.
- If you are trekking with an agency, ask it for written instructions that you can carry with you in case you need to organise a helicopter rescue from the mountains. It is always possible that you may have been left behind by the group at some point, and then find that you require rescue. If you are unsure of your agency's ability to organise a rescue, register with your embassy as well.
- If you are not with an agency and your country does not have an embassy or honorary consul in Kathmandu, you should try to identify someone in Kathmandu who would be willing to help organise a rescue for you if you required it.

Trekking First-Aid Kit

The following is a suggested list of supplies and medications that would be useful for a group of four people travelling for two weeks or more on trek in Nepal. It is based on the experience of what happens most often to people on trek. The list should be modified to adjust for individual preferences and allergies, and for the remoteness and difficulty of the particular trek. Refer to the boxed aside Description of Medications & Their Use on the following pages in making your selection.

Supplies

- [ ] thermometer
- [ ] scissors
- [ ] tweezers
- [ ] 2.5 cm adhesive or paper tape (1 roll)
- [ ] sewing needle
- [ ] 10 cm x 10 cm gauze pads (x 10)
- [ ] large sterile dressing
- [ ] 10 cm rolled cotton bandages (x 2)
- [ ] 7.5 cm rolled cotton bandage
- [ ] 2.5 cm Band-aids or similar plasters (x 20)
- [ ] moleskin
- [ ] muslin triangular bandage for sling
- [ ] Betadine antiseptic
- [ ] 10 cm elastic bandage
- [ ] Steri-strips

Medications

- [ ] paracetamol (acetaminophen) 500 mg (x 20)
- [ ] Actifed (x 20)
- [ ] azithromycin 250 mg (x 12) (for penicillin-allergic people)
- [ ] bisacodyl pills (x 10)
- [ ] cephalexin 500 mg (x 40)
- [ ] codeine phosphate 15 mg (x 60)
- [ ] diphenhydramine 50 mg (x 15)
- [ ] hydrocortisone 1% cream (1 tube)
- [ ] ibuprofen 600 mg (x 40)
- [ ] loperamide (Imodium) (x 20)
- [ ] metoclopramide 10 mg (x 10)
- [ ] clotrimazole 1% cream (1 tube)
- [ ] mycostatin vaginal tablets (x 14)
- [ ] norfloxacin 400 mg (x 24)
- [ ] promethazine suppositories 50 mg (x 4)
- [ ] ranitidine 150 mg (x 10)
- [ ] rehydration salts (3 packets)
- [ ] sodium sulamide 10% eye drops (1 bottle)
- [ ] throat lozenges, eg Strepsils (x 20)
- [ ] tinidazole 500 mg (x 16)

Description of Medications & Their Use

Modern medicines have great value in fighting disease and relieving suffering, but all medications are potentially harmful. Some have very rare but serious side effects (eg penicillin), while others have very common but not serious side effects (eg tinidazole). Every decision to use a medication must weigh the risk (usually small) versus the benefit (usually great). The medications included in this kit are generally safe to use *provided you have no history of allergy to the particular medication*. If you have a history of drug allergy, you must adjust the list so that it will be of use to you in the field.

In general, there are two reasons for using medications: symptomatic (to relieve the ill effects of a disease without treating the cause) and therapeutic (to treat the underlying cause of the disease and thereby relieve the symptoms). Symptomatic drugs can be used as needed. Therapeutic drugs should be given as a complete course. The table states which kind of medicine each one is and what it is used for, potential side effects and the usual doses. The problem of brand names versus generic chemical names remains confusing. Brand names are marked with an asterisk (*).

Drug	Type	Description	Potential Side Effects	Dose
Actifed*	symptomatic	decongestant for relief of discomfort due to colds, sinus infection or internal ear infection	jitteriness, sedation	1 tablet every 8 hrs as needed
azithromycin 250 mg	therapeutic	erythromycin-related antibiotic with the advantage of being a 5 day course of one dose per day; can be used to treat a wide variety of infections, including ear, sinus and urinary tract infections, bronchitis and pneumonia. Necessary for penicillin-allergic people, azithromycin may be preferred as well by others who prefer to take less medication.	rare	2 pills together on the first day; then 1 pill each day for 4 more days
bisacodyl 10 mg	symptomatic	can work overnight to induce a bowel movement if constipation becomes a problem on the trail, but can occasionally cause diarrhoea	abdominal cramps, diarrhoea	1 tablet every 12 hrs until relief
cephalexin 500 mg	therapeutic	penicillin-related antibiotic that can be used to treat a wide variety of infections, including inner ear, sinusitis, bronchitis, pneumonia, urinary tract infection and skin abscesses. Note: must not be used in people allergic to penicillin.	none in non-allergic individuals	1 tablet every 6 hrs for 10 days
clotrimazole 1% cream	therapeutic	anti-fungal skin preparation for suspected fungal infections	rare	apply 3-4 times a day until rash goes
codeine phosphate 15 mg	symptomatic	narcotic pain-reliever which also serves as a cough suppressant to allow sleep and a constipating agent to allow bus travel and relieve intestinal cramps; often supplied in combination with paracetamol	nausea, vomiting, stomach pain, rash	1 or 2 tablets every 4 hrs for cough or diarrhoea; up to 4 tablets every 4 hrs for severe pain
diphenhydramine (Benadryl*) 50 mg	symptomatic	antihistamine for the relief of severe itching due to insect bites or allergic reactions; can also be used as a mild sedative for sleeping	sedation	1 tablet every 6 hrs as needed
hydrocortisone 1% cream	symptomatic & therapeutic	steroid skin cream for the relief of itching insect bites or allergic rashes	essentially none if not used indefinitely (for more than a month)	apply to lesions every 2-4 hrs as needed

Drug	Type	Description	Potential Side Effects	Dose
ibuprofen 600 mg	symptomatic & therapeutic	anti-inflammatory drug with pain-relieving properties; can be used for 'trekker's knee' and other muscular aches and pains; should always be taken with food, never on an empty stomach	can cause allergy if allergic to aspirin; stomach pain (can cause an ulcer). Stop taking if stomach pain develops.	1 tablet every 6 hrs as needed
Imodium* (loperamide) 2 mg	symptomatic	narcotic-derived drug which para-lyses the bowel for symptomatic relief of diarrhoea; should not be used casually, but can be useful for bus or air travel. Note: paralysing the bowel can allow infections to worsen and prolong the illness. Do not use in the presence of fever or bloody stool unless also taking the appropriate antibiotic.	constipation	2 tablets to start, then 1 after each loose stool until relief, then 1 every 6 hrs to maintain; not to exceed 8 in 24 hrs
metoclopramide 10 mg	symptomatic	for relief of nausea and vomiting. Vomiting can be difficult to stop with oral medication, but this can be useful in the recovery period of a severe gastroenteritis.	rarely, uncontrolled muscle contractions of face and neck	1 tablet every 6 hrs as needed
mycostatin vaginal tablets	therapeutic	for the treatment of yeast vaginitis, which can develop relatively suddenly, especially after the use of some oral antibiotics	rare	insert 1 tablet in vagina at night for 7 days
norfloxacin 400 mg		antibiotic with a broad range of activity; most useful in suspected bacterial dysentery, or urinary tract infection. Note: cannot be used in children under 18 years; use ciprofloxacin instead.	nausea, rash	1 tablet every 12 hrs for 2-3 days for dysentery, 3 days for simple urinary tract infection
paracetamol (acetaminophen) 500 mg	symptomatic	for relief of mild pain and to help reduce a high fever	none	2 tablets every 4 hrs as needed
promethazine suppositories	symptomatic	anti-nausea medication for the symptomatic relief of nausea and vomiting; can be used while unable to keep down anything taken orally	sedation	1 inserted in rectum every 8 hrs as needed
rehydration salts	symptomatic & therapeutic	salts and sugar in a packet designed to be mixed with one litre of boiled water; allows faster uptake of water from the intestinal tract, and replaces chemicals and fluid lost through vomiting and diarrhoea	none	should be encouraged in anyone suspected of becoming dehydrated
sodium sulamide eye drops	therapeutic	antibiotic solution for the treatment of bacterial conjunctivitis	possible local allergy	1-2 drops every 3 hrs for 3-5 days
throat lozenges	symptomatic	for soothing inflamed throats; quite useful in high-altitude travel	none	1 every half-hour as needed.
tinidazole 500mg	therapeutic	antibiotic effective against Giardia and amoebas; can be used to treat a suspected infection	fatigue, a queasy feeling, a metallic taste in the mouth	4 tablets taken together each day for 2 consecutive days for Giardia, or for 3 days for suspected amoebic infection

Rescue Requests & a New Rescue Code

Flying on rescue flights has made me familiar with the difficulties involved. One of the most important pitfalls is the rescue request itself. Most helicopter rescue requests describe the victim's condition as follows: 'Very sick'. One such message actually read, 'No arms, no legs'. The embassies, trekking agencies and pilots will be trying to assess what degree of risk the rescuers should take, based on the perceived urgency of the medical condition. Since messages are often written down, carried by an illiterate porter to an uninterested radio operator, and translated from English into Nepali and back into English, it is difficult to obtain a true picture of the situation. I would like to introduce a code into the rescue request system that might help rescuers get a better understanding of rescue requests. Use of the code would require an honest assessment of the situation. The code would be as follows:

Level One
> Incapacitated by injury or illness and unable to proceed on foot. Not in severe pain, and not in danger of dying. Eg sprained ankle; knee injury; recovering from a severe illness; frostbite.

Level Two
> Needs urgent medical attention, but is not in danger of dying. Eg compound fracture; severe pain (for any reason); a severe undiagnosed illness.

Level Three
> Severe injuries or illness with a chance of dying within a day. Eg severe trauma with suspected internal bleeding, or severe head injury; suspected heart attack; severe infectious disease such as meningitis.

In a level one request, the helicopter would be dispatched when the time of day and weather permitted, minimising the risk to the pilots. For a level two request, the pilots would try to come as soon as possible, again taking into account the factors that increase the risk for the pilots. In a known level three request, the pilots might attempt a rescue in less-than-ideal conditions and might have to abort the flight and return the next day (thus increasing the expense).

On the basis of your rescue request alone, the pilots and the doctors involved will have to decide whether to take a chance and fly through bad weather or wait for the usually better weather in the morning. The army pilots do not receive extra pay for rescue flights, and are often forced to take unusual chances while trying to perform rescues. Don't risk other lives needlessly with unnecessary flights or inadequate information.

Once a request is sent, stay put for at least two days, or make it clear in the message where and how you will be travelling. If you see the helicopter, make an effort to signal it. It is very difficult to pick out people on the ground from a helicopter moving at 145 km/h, especially if you are unsure where to look. Try to locate a field large enough to land a helicopter safely, but do not mark the centre of the field with cloth, as this can fly up and wreck the rotors on landing. If you are a trekker who has not sent for a helicopter, *do not wave at a low-flying helicopter!* We have made a number of unnecessary and occasionally dangerous landings only to find that the people were not involved with a rescue and were just waving.

In the last few years there has been a disturbing trend for tired and disillusioned trekkers to try to charter helicopters out of the mountains. With the increased availability of charter helicopters, trekkers now have the expensive option of aborting their trek for rather minimal reasons. Please make sure that any such request comes as a request for a charter, and not as a rescue request, so it can be given the lack of priority that such a request deserves.

While helicopters can fly as high as 6000m, they are unable to land and take off above 5500m as the air is too thin to give the rotors sufficient lift. Therefore, there is at present no way to expect to be rescued from trekking or mountaineering peaks.

Insurance which specifically covers rescue is available at low cost in your home country, and a rescue insurance policy has recently been introduced in Nepal, although its effectiveness remains untested; see Travel Insurance in the Facts for the Trekker chapter for more information.

Treating Nepalis

Almost every trekker will encounter a situation where they are asked to give some kind of medical treatment to a sick Nepali in the hills. The potential patient may just have a headache, or may be covered with severe burns from which he or she will most likely die. The moral dilemma that the trekker is occasionally faced with can remain with them long after the trek. There is no simple answer, but I will offer some guidelines to help you think about the problem before you encounter it.

The government of Nepal is attempting to establish and maintain health posts in remote areas. So far, this has not brought medical care to the majority of the people. The local people often have their own healers, beliefs and practices regarding health. When these prove ineffective, or out of growing curiosity, the local people may consult passing trekkers, whether they are doctors or not. In many areas there is no understanding at all of the basis of Western medical practice. Ideas that we take for granted, such as the relationship of germs to infection, have no meaning to these villagers. A pill can be seen as a form of magic, the shape, size, and colour often having more meaning than an attempted explanation that the medicine will kill the germs.

Thus, some of the medical interactions are based on villagers' desire to get closer to a form of Western magic. This has created a form of medical 'begging', whereby it is not clear whether the person is indeed ill at the time of the encounter. It is fair and advisable under these circumstances to say that you have no medicine. Otherwise the pills are indiscriminately given out at later times, possibly doing someone some harm.

A Nepali person who is clearly suffering from a problem presents another level of dilemma. If you have the expertise to recognise the problem and know that your treatment will be effective, and have a way of explaining this to the people involved, there is no reason to withhold this treatment from someone who can clearly benefit. If you do not know what is going on, or are not sure of the right treatment, don't try to give medical treatment due to misguided compassion. You may do more harm than good, or the treatment failure may lead the villagers away from seeking appropriate Western medical care at a health post in the future.

The fact that you are trekking through at that moment does not mean that you suddenly have to take on the continuing and insoluble problems of remote village life. The feelings of compassion and wanting to help are natural, but if you see that you truly can't offer anything that is likely to improve the situation, don't feel obligated to 'do something'. The fact that there are many people in the world who can't call an ambulance and be rushed to a hospital with serious illness is a reality that catches many a Western trekker emotionally unprepared. The discovery of these feelings and the processing of your reactions are among the reasons to trek. Perhaps when you get home you might donate money to one of the aid agencies working to solve these very problems.

In summary, the problem remains a difficult one. Try to refer to local health posts whenever possible (the Khunde Hospital in the Khumbu is a good example). If this is not possible, determine whether you can definitively help someone and then do so if your resources allow. If you are not sure what to do, you can express your concern but admit that you don't have anything to offer. Nepalis can usually accept this gracefully.

Getting There & Away

AIR

Airports & Airlines

The only international airport in Nepal is Tribhuvan airport in Kathmandu. The combination of altitude and runway length means that fully loaded 747s cannot take off. Aviation fuel is expensive and has to be trucked from India, and Nepal is really not on the way to anywhere. As a consequence, Nepal is very much a sideline on the routes of the carriers that serve it. The big airlines that serve Kathmandu are Thai International, Singapore Airlines, Aeroflot and Pakistan International. The rest are regional carriers: Indian Airlines, Bangladesh Biman, China Southwest, Druk Air and Qatar Airlines. Royal Nepal Airlines Corporation (RNAC), the national carrier, operates flights to both Europe and Japan as well as regional destinations. Nepal has declared 1998 'Visit Nepal Year' and has announced plans to greatly expand air services, including allowing Nepal's private airlines to operate overseas.

Asia

The most reasonable connections to Kathmandu are via Bangkok, Hong Kong and Singapore. Bangkok flights are often overbooked in the high season, but it's sometimes worth hanging around the airport looking for a stand-by seat to Kathmandu. The one-way reduced inclusive tour (IT) fare from Bangkok costs from US$180 to US$190.

From India the fares are high, flights are fully booked – usually by Indian tourists – and reservation procedures are chaotic. The only concession fares are for students. There are flights to Kathmandu from Delhi, Mumbai (Bombay), Calcutta and Varanasi. The one-hour Delhi to Kathmandu flight costs US$142.

Kathmandu has some other interesting connections. China Southwest Airlines operates a flight from Lhasa to Kathmandu on Saturday and Tuesday. This spectacular one-hour flight costs US$190 and is supposed to operate from April to December. You can also fly from Paro in Bhutan on Druk Air, or from Dhaka (Bangladesh).

Europe & the Middle East

RNAC operates flights into and out of London and Paris via Dubai and Frankfurt. Contact its agency in London or Frankfurt for cheap excursion fares. Lufthansa cancelled its Kathmandu service in April 1997, but there are rumours that British Airways and several charter companies might start operations to Nepal.

Pakistan International, Bangladesh Biman and Aeroflot have one-airline service from Europe to Kathmandu, though they require a connection in Karachi, Dhaka or Moscow. Also try charter companies; LTU operates a weekly flight from Germany to Kathmandu during winter.

North America

North America is halfway around the world from Nepal, so you have a choice of crossing either the Atlantic or the Pacific Ocean. If you are flying via India, be sure your baggage gets rechecked to Kathmandu, as the transit procedures at Delhi airport are complex. Pacific routes usually require an overnight stay in Bangkok or Hong Kong, but there are frequent flights and most airlines have APEX fares of about US$600 one way from the west coast to Kathmandu. RNAC's Osaka flight makes good connections with North American flights.

Australia & New Zealand

Look for routes via Singapore, Hong Kong or Bangkok. Typical fares are around A$1600 return. Kathmandu is not on any airline routes for 'round-the-world' (RTW) tickets, and is usually charged as an extra segment on the Australia to London route. If you are travelling to the UK, you might find a cheap fare on RNAC from either Bangkok or Singapore, via Kathmandu, to London.

LAND

There are only eight entry points into Nepal by land that foreigners can use: six from India and two from Tibet.

A steady trickle of people still drive their own motorbikes or vehicles overland from Europe; there are some interesting, though difficult, new routes to the subcontinent through Eastern Europe and the republics that were once a part of the USSR. An international carnet is required. If you want to abandon your transport in Nepal, you must either pay a prohibitive import duty or surrender it to customs. It is not possible to import cars more than five years old.

India

The crossing points from India are Mahendranagar, Dhangadhi and Nepalgunj in the west, Sunauli (near Bhairawa, south of Pokhara), Birganj (south of Kathmandu) and Kakarbhitta (near Siliguri and Darjeeling in the far east).

Through Tickets Many travellers have complained about scams involving ticket packages from Nepal to India. The package usually involves coordination between at least three different companies so the potential for an honest cock-up is at least as high as the potential for a deliberate rip-off.

Two long-standing and reliable companies in Kathmandu that handle through tickets are Student Travels & Tours (☎ 01-225452; fax 226348) in Thamel; and Yeti Travels (☎ 01-221234; fax 226152) on Durbar Marg. Bear in mind, however, that everyone has to change buses at the border whether they book a through ticket or not, and that, despite claims to the contrary, there are no 'tourist' buses on either side of the border. A through ticket to Varanasi by bus costs from Rs 500, and to Darjeeling Rs 650. Bus/train packages to Agra or Delhi cost Rs 2250 including an air-con sleeper on the train, or Rs 950 in 2nd class.

Delhi To travel to or from New Delhi or elsewhere in western India the route through Sunauli, just south of Bhairawa, is the most convenient. You can also enter at Mahendranagar, Dhangadhi or Nepalgunj in the west of Nepal, but these are not served by good long-haul public transport.

Via Sunauli The first leg, from Delhi to Gorakhpur, involves an overnight rail journey. From Gorakhpur, frequent buses make the three hour run to Nautanwa, the Indian town across the border from Sunauli. It's then a short rickshaw ride to Bhairawa, which is also known as Siddharthanagar.

Buses from Bhairawa to Kathmandu or Pokhara travel via Mugling and take around nine hours.

Via Mahendranagar The Mahendra Highway from the border to the Karnali river is still under construction. Until it's completed, this route is a dry-season-only proposition, and strictly for the hardy.

There are daily buses from New Delhi to Banbassa, the nearest Indian village to the border (11 hours). It's a one km walk (or rickshaw ride) from Banbassa to the Indian border post, then a further km to the Nepali post and another bus ride to Mahendranagar.

There are direct buses from Mahendranagar to Kathmandu (at 2 pm), but they take a gruelling 25 hours. You can break the journey at Nepalgunj or one of the jungle camps in Royal Bardia National Park.

Varanasi Once again, the Sunauli/Bhairawa crossing is the most convenient. There are direct buses from Varanasi for Indian Rs 81 to Rs 100, depending on the degree of luxury, and the journey takes about nine hours.

Catch a bus to Sunauli, stay overnight in Bhairawa, then catch a Nepali bus the next morning. From Bhairawa it's another nine hours to Kathmandu or Pokhara.

Calcutta & Patna The Birganj entry point is the most convenient option in the east of India. All buses from Birganj to Kathmandu or Pokhara travel via Narayanghat and

Mugling rather than the slower, though more scenic, Tribhuvan Highway via Daman.

Calcutta to Patna takes about 10 hours, and you can do this by overnight train. It's then a five hour journey from Patna to Raxaul Bazaar (the Indian border town opposite Birganj in Nepal). Both towns are dirty, unattractive transit points strung along the highway and are full of heavy traffic. The border is open from 7 am to 7 pm every day.

Direct buses between Birganj and Kathmandu take around 11 hours; the trip between Birganj and Pokhara is marginally shorter.

Darjeeling Kakarbhitta is at the eastern end of Nepal's east-west Mahendra Highway. A number of companies handle bookings between Darjeeling and Kathmandu, though with all of them you have to change buses at the border and again at Siliguri.

It's almost as easy to get from Darjeeling to Kathmandu on your own, though this involves four changes – a bus from Darjeeling to Siliguri, then a minibus from Siliguri to Raniganj at the border, a rickshaw across the border to Kakarbhitta and a bus from Kakarbhitta to Kathmandu.

Tibet

The route from Nepal into Tibet via Kodari is sometimes closed to individual travellers, but if you are travelling in the other direction, from Tibet, you can cross the border into Nepal without problems.

The road is regularly closed by landslides during the monsoon and it's often necessary to walk for several kilometres in Tibet and again in Nepal. Political problems in Tibet are frequent and are usually followed by restrictions on travellers. If you intend to enter or leave Nepal via Tibet you should come prepared with alternative plans in case travel along this route proves impossible.

The final land option is to walk from Taklakot (Tibet) to Simikot in far northwestern Nepal. This option is only open to group trekkers who have made special arrangements. See the Humla to Mt Kailas section in the Restricted Areas chapter for details of this route.

ORGANISED TREKS

If you arrange a trek through an adventure travel company, it should be able to either recommend a group flight or arrange air transportation, hopefully at a reasonable rate, on space that it has prebooked. In October, early November and late December these may be the only seats available to Nepal.

Adventure Travel Companies

Adventure travel companies specialise in organising treks and getting you to Nepal. They normally operate group treks, usually escorted by a leader, though many of them can also organise private trips.

If you book a trek through an adventure travel company, be aware that various organisers of treks provide different equipment and facilities. Be sure to read the material that the company provides. It may supply some of the equipment (such as sleeping bags) or services that I have suggested you arrange yourself.

It becomes difficult to prepare an up-to-date list of all adventure travel companies throughout the world because new ones spring up (and others disappear) every season. The following list includes a number of established companies that have specialised in trekking in Nepal for many years. It makes no pretence of being a complete list of every adventure travel company in the world. You can find numerous other companies by looking in outdoor magazines or searching the Internet for adventure travel companies.

The huge number of agents now selling trekking trips makes it difficult to make any judgment about the quality of service you may expect. From each company you should be able to get any additional information you need about Nepal and trekking; most have staff who have trekked in Nepal. All the companies listed here offer a variety of treks and several choices of dates.

Australia & New Zealand

Footprints Tours
Box 7027, Nelson, NZ (☎ 03-548 0145; fax 546 6179; email diane@greenkiwi.co.nz)
Peregrine Adventures
258 Lonsdale St, Melbourne, Vic 3000 (☎ 03-9663 8611; fax 9663 8618)
Sydney Adventure Centre
Level 7, Dymocks Bldg, 428 George St, Sydney, NSW 2000 (☎ 02-9221 8555; fax 9223 7261)
World Expeditions
3rd floor, 441 Kent St, Sydney, NSW 2000 (☎ 02-9264 3366, 1800-803 688; fax 9261 1974)

USA & Canada

Adventure Center
1311 63rd St, Suite 200, Emeryville, CA 94608 (☎ 800-227 8747; fax 510-654 4200; email tripinfo@adventure-center.com)
Geographic Expeditions
2627 Lombard St, San Francisco, CA 94123 (☎ 415-922 0448; fax 346 5535; email info@geoex.com)
Himalayan Travel
112 Prospect St, Stamford, CT 06901 (☎ 800-225 2380; fax 622 0084)
Himalayan Treasures & Travel
3596 Ponderosa Trail, Pinole, CA 94564 (☎ 800-223 1813) – Peter Owens Asian Treks and a good source of air tickets to Nepal
Ibex Expeditions
2657 West 28th Ave, Eugene, OR 97405 (☎ 503-345 1289; fax 343 9002)
Journeys International
4011 Jackson Rd, Ann Arbor, MI 48103 (☎ 313-663 4407; fax 665 2945; email journeysmi@aol.com)
Mountain Travel Sobek
6420 Fairmount Ave, El Cerrito, CA 94530 (☎ 800-227 2384; fax 510-525 7710; email info@mtsobek.com)
Nature Expeditions International
6400 E El Dorado Circle, Suite 210, Tucson, AZ 85715 (☎ 520-721 6712; fax 721 6719)
Vajra Travel
13 Belton St, Arlington, MA 02174 (☎ 617-648 3020; fax 641 4744; email vajrat@aol.com)
Wilderness Travel
801 Allston Way, Berkeley, CA 94710 (☎ 800-368 2794; fax 415-548 0347; email info@wildernesstravel.com)

UK

Abercombie & Kent
Sloane Square House, Holbein Place, London SW1W 8NS (fax 0171-730 9376)

Exodus Expeditions
9 Weir Rd, London SW12-OLT (☎ 0181-673 0859)
Explore Worldwide
1 Frederick St, Aldershot, Hants GU11 1LK (☎ 01252-344161)
Specialist Trekking Co-op
Chapel House, Low Cotehill, Carlisle, Cumbria CA4 0EL (☎ 01228-562358) – Doug Scott's community support treks
WEXAS International
45 Brompton Rd, Knightsbridge, London SW3 1DE (fax 0171-589 8418)
World Expeditions
4 Northfields Prospect, Putney Bridge Rd, London SW18 1PE (☎ 0181-870 2600; fax 870 2615; email worldex@dircon.co.uk)

France

Explorator
16 Place de la Madeleine, 75008 Paris (fax 01 42 66 53 89)

Germany

Dav Berg-und-Skischule
Am Perlacher Forst 186, D-81545 München (☎ 089-651 0720; fax 651 0727)
Hauser Exkursionen
Marienstrasse – 17, D-80331 München (☎ 089-235006-47; fax 2913714)

Other European Countries

ARTOU
8 Rue de Rive, CH-1204 Genève, Switzerland (☎ 022-818 0202; fax 781 2058; email group@artou.ch)
Intertrek
Nollisweid 16, CH-9050 Appenzell, Switzerland (fax 071-872-423)
Trekking International
Via Giafrancesco Re, 78-10146 Torino, Italy

Asia

Himalaya Kanko Kaihatsu
5F Kaikei Building, 3-26-3, Shimbashi, Minato-ku, Tokyo
World Expeditions Consultants
4F Pine Building, 6-20-4 Shimbashi, Minato-ku, Tokyo 105 (fax 03-3437 8849)

LEAVING NEPAL
Reconfirming Reservations

Airline reservations out of Kathmandu are difficult to get at any time, but are particularly hard to obtain during the trekking

Reconfirm

The importance of reconfirming international flights is a standard piece of travellers' lore; in Kathmandu from October to January it can be vital. At that time of year flights are often packed out, and 72 hours before the flight is due to depart anybody who has not reconfirmed that they intend to fly will be scrubbed off the passenger list and end up at the tail of what can be a very long waiting list.

It happened to Maureen and me a few years ago, and we only scrambled back on the flight after a great deal of messing around and pulling of strings. We had come to Kathmandu after a two week visit to Bhutan, and our stay in Nepal was only 48 hours, so officially we didn't need to reconfirm at all. Furthermore, our Kathmandu-Bangkok flight was a totally separate one-way ticket, not the continuation of another flight or part of a return ticket, so once again reconfirmation was not officially necessary. Big deal! We hadn't reconfirmed, and 72 hours before our flight departed and 24 hours before we even arrived in Nepal, we were dumped.

In retrospect, what we should have done was get a friend in Nepal to reconfirm for us, or try to reconfirm in Bangkok before we flew to Bhutan. The message, however, was loud and clear: reconfirm, reconfirm, reconfirm.

Tony Wheeler

season in Nepal. You must always reconfirm reservations or the airline will cancel them. This is not an idle threat; it often happens. Take the time before your trek to reconfirm your flight out of Nepal.

A bit of planning can save a last-minute drama at the airport. If you don't have a reservation, make a booking before you start your trek. By booking three to five weeks ahead, you may get a seat. If you wait until you finish your trek to book a seat, you will certainly have to wait a week or two for a flight. Be sure to allow a three or four day

buffer if you are flying out of Lukla or Jomsom.

Departure Taxes

The airport tax on departure is Rs 600 to nearby countries that are members of SAARC (see Glossary), Rs 700 to other destinations. Other airport taxes in the region are:

From	Tax
Bangkok, Thailand	250 baht
Dhaka, Bangladesh	Tk 300
Hong Kong	HK$150
India	I Rs 150 to Nepal, I Rs 300 to places outside the Indian subcontinent
Karachi, Pakistan	Rs 200
Lhasa, Tibet	yuan 60
Singapore	S$15

WARNING

The information in this chapter is particularly vulnerable to change: prices for international travel are volatile, routes are introduced and cancelled, schedules change, special deals come and go, and rules and visa requirements are amended. Airlines and governments seem to take a perverse pleasure in making price structures and regulations as complicated as possible. You should check directly with the airline or a travel agent to make sure you understand how a fare (and ticket you may buy) works. In addition, the travel industry is highly competitive and there are many lurks and perks.

The upshot of this is that you should get opinions, quotes and advice from as many airlines and travel agents as possible before you part with your hard-earned cash. The details given in this chapter should be regarded as pointers and are not a substitute for your own careful, up-to-date research.

Getting Around

AIR

Nepal's domestic network includes some of the most remote and spectacular airstrips in the world. The approaches to these airstrips are difficult. Many are on mountain sides surrounded by high peaks. Therefore, if there are clouds or high winds, the pilot cannot land. The classic remark by one captain explains the picture perfectly: 'We don't fly through clouds because in Nepal the clouds have rocks in them'. Domestic service in Nepal is famous for delayed or cancelled flights to remote regions because of bad weather.

If your trek involves a flight into or out of a remote airstrip, you will probably experience a delay of several hours or, more often, several days. Delays are the price you pay for the convenience of flights in Nepal and the time they save. Pack a good book into your hand luggage to make the inevitable waiting at airports a little more tolerable.

There are now a number of private companies operating alongside the long-running, government-owned Royal Nepal Airlines Corporation (RNAC). The new companies charge the same prices as RNAC, although RNAC offers a 25% discount to students under 26 with valid ID. Several private airlines operate huge Russian MI-17 helicopters that carry up to 21 passengers plus baggage and are capable of operating to high-altitude airstrips. These choppers were originally built for the Soviet army, not for civilian service. Nepal's Department of Civil Aviation has questioned their suitability as passenger aircraft, and the Russian leasing companies are seeking international certification. The result is that these helicopters may or may not be allowed to carry passengers at any time.

Domestic Airlines

RNAC RNAC (☎ 220757; fax 225348) still operates the most comprehensive range of scheduled flights around the country using short take-off and landing (STOL) Twin Otters. It serves all domestic airports in Nepal except Shyangboche. Destinations of interest to trekkers that are served by RNAC include Biratnagar, Dolpo, Jomsom, Jumla, Lamidanda, Lukla, Manang, Nepalgunj, Phaphlu, Pokhara, Simikot, Taplejung and Tumlingtar. Many of these airports are served only by RNAC. Its offices are on the corner of Kantipath and New Rd.

Everest Air Everest Air (☎ 222290, 228392; fax 228266) flies German Dornier 228 planes with good-sized windows that offer excellent viewing for mountain flights. It has scheduled flights to Bhairawa, Bharatpur, Biratnagar, Jomsom, Jumla, Lamidanda, Pokhara, Ramechhap and Rumjatar. The airport in Lukla is too rough for the Dorniers, so Everest Air only operates helicopters to Lukla. The sales office is on Durbar Marg.

Nepal Airways Nepal Airways (☎ 412388, 410052; fax 420585) has Yak-12s, Chinese-made Twin Otter-type aircraft, and Avros. It operates flights to Bhairawa, Bharatpur, Biratnagar, Jomsom, Lukla, Nepalgunj, Pokhara and Tumlingtar. It also has a subsidiary that operates helicopters. Nepal Airways' office is in Hattisar.

Necon Air Necon Air (☎ 472542; fax 471679) operates 44-passenger Avros to Bhairawa, Biratnagar, Janakpur, Nepalgunj and Pokhara. Necon's offices are on Putali Sadak.

Dynasty Aviation Dynasty (☎ 414626; fax 414627) is basically a charter operator and operates small helicopters. Helicopter charter service is available up to an altitude of 4875m (16,000 feet) at a cost of US$1000 per flying hour. The office is in Lazimpat.

Asian Airlines Helicopter Asian Airlines (☎ 423273, 416116; fax 423315) is a Sherpa-run company that was the first to operate the Russian MI-17 helicopters. It operates scheduled helicopter flights to the trekking destinations of Lukla, Shyangboche, Jomsom, Manang, Taplejung, Phaphlu and Tumlingtar. Its office is on Tridevi Marg, near the immigration office, PO Box 4695.

Gorkha Air Another operator of MI-17 helicopters is Gorkha Air (☎ 423137, 414039; fax 471136), operating daily scheduled flights to Lukla and other destinations. Its office is in Hatisar, on the way to Kamal Pokhari.

Manakamana Airways The newest of Nepal's airlines, Manakamana Airways (☎ & fax 482187), operates MI-17 and Bell Jet Ranger helicopters for both charter and scheduled flights. Its office is in New Baneswor, on the road to the airport.

Reservations

It may seem a bit silly to describe how to buy an air ticket, but RNAC has so many complicated and strange rules and regulations that it's worth some discussion.

It is advisable to book domestic flights at least two weeks in advance for Lukla, and a week in advance for other destinations. Just as for flights out of Nepal, the most important rule is to reconfirm and reconfirm again. Names can easily 'fall off' the passenger list, particularly where there is pressure for seats.

In Kathmandu It is best to book domestic flights in person because the airline will confirm seats only after you pay the fare and it has actually issued the ticket. You must pay for tickets in foreign currency. RNAC doesn't take credit cards, so bring cash or travellers' cheques – and exact change, if possible. If you are using a trekking company or travel agency, it can make the flight booking for you and expedite the payment process. Local people pay a lower fare than foreigners on most flights.

There are many obstacles to booking a seat on a domestic flight, but the most common problem is 'no seats'. Local travel

agents in Nepal book seats to Lukla, Jomsom and Pokhara up to two years in advance for their groups. There is a lot of seat swapping among local agencies in Kathmandu, so when the airlines have no seats you may still find one by checking with a few travel agencies or trekking companies. Seats can also mysteriously become available at the last minute, so it's always worth a trip to the RNAC office to ask for a reservation. It's more complicated now with so many airlines; this is where a resourceful trekking company or travel agent can be helpful.

In the Hills There are no airline computers or telexes in the hills. Each airline operates a manual system with handwritten reservation lists for outlying stations. Once the reservation list leaves Kathmandu, only the outlying station can confirm a seat. The Kathmandu office usually sends the list a week ahead of the flight, but the time varies for each destination.

If you are planning to fly out from Lukla, it would be prudent to confirm your flight back to Kathmandu before starting the trek. The trouble is that you must then buy a ticket. If your flight does not operate and you decide to walk or chopper out, you can only obtain a refund for the ticket in Kathmandu.

Reservation Cancellations On domestic flights there is always a cancellation charge. If you do not fly, be sure to cancel your reservation on time and have it recorded on your ticket as proof. If you cancel a reservation more than 24 hours before the flight there is a 10% cancellation charge. If you cancel less than 24 hours before the flight, the charge is 33% of the ticket cost. For 'no shows' there is no refund at all. An interesting loophole is that if a flight is delayed by more than one hour, there is no cancellation charge if you decide not to fly.

Flight Check-In

Once you have a ticket and a confirmed seat, the fun is just beginning. If you are lucky, your flight will exist when you get to the airport, your name will still be on the seating chart, your baggage will be accepted, the flight will depart and it will land at the destination. This sometimes happens, but often something goes wrong. Bad weather or other complications frequently force the delay or cancellation of flights.

Check-in for domestic flights begins an hour before the flight. It is wise to be in line when the counter opens in case of some snag. In the morning, there are often Sherpa business people at the airport trying to send cargo to Lukla and other remote destinations. These people often offer to assist you with checking in so that they can use your unused baggage allowance. It's usually safe to accept their offer and also let them try to solve any glitches that occur.

If you have a lot of trekking gear, try to have someone with you who can send it later if it is off-loaded from the flight. The allowance on Lukla flights is nominally 25 kg, but sometimes this limit is arbitrarily reduced. On other domestic flights the limit is 15 kg. Sometimes space is at such a premium that extra baggage cannot be carried even if you pay an excess charge.

Both checked luggage and hand luggage are subject to a security check. Be sure you put your pocket knife in your checked baggage so that airport security does not confiscate it. Theoretically you will get the knife back on arrival, but it's one more delay.

Flight Cancellations

When these happen, start again. Having a confirmed seat on a flight that did not operate usually does not gain you any priority for the next flight. In Lukla you will go from having a boarding pass in hand to the bottom of the waiting list. If you are lucky, and your plane does come, you will go ahead of those who may have been waiting a week or more. In Kathmandu there is no such system, but RNAC operates a complex programme of 'delayed schedule', 'nonscheduled' and 'charter' flights. You can often find a seat if you are willing to spend some time at the RNAC office, but it's almost like starting from the beginning again. An agent can be helpful in such situations.

BUS

The public bus service in Nepal is very much designed to accommodate the Nepali people. The buses are rickety, slow, tremendously crowded and noisy; the seats are narrow and closely spaced; and the roads are dreadful. Tickets are written only in Nepali script and departure announcements are made only in Nepali.

If you are going to Pokhara or to Chitwan, there are more comfortable tourist buses which operate more like a Western bus service. Check with travel agencies in Thamel or the Tourist Bus Association, which has offices at Sundhara, near the post office in Kathmandu (☎ 240274, 240019, 240324), and at the lakeside in Pokhara (☎ 22920, 23224). Student Travels, Memoire Travels, Arun Travels and the famous Swiss Bus all provide more comfortable seats than their competitors at a cost of Rs 200. The other advantage of the tourist buses is that they are allowed to depart from central Kathmandu. This saves an early-morning taxi ride to the bus terminal, and endless delays as the driver looks for extra passengers along the Ring Road as the bus winds its way out of the valley.

In 1993 a new bus terminal opened at Gongabu on the Ring Road about five km north of the Kathmandu city centre. Nearly all buses for destinations outside the Kathmandu Valley depart from this facility, known to Nepalis as the 'bus park'. The exceptions are the buses to Jiri, which leave from the old bus station in the centre of Kathmandu, and the tourist buses. Tickets are sold from a row of counters, each labelled (in Nepali only) with a number and a destination. Several companies operate on each route so tickets are sold on a rotating system. For this reason, it's fairly arbitrary which company's bus you will travel on, though this probably doesn't make much difference. Seats are assigned when you purchase a ticket; if possible try to get a front seat, or a seat near the door, as these have a bit of legroom.

Tickets go on sale the day before departure, so if you make two trips out to the bus

Ticket Windows at the Kathmandu Bus Station

Window Number	Destination	Travellers' Information
1, 2	Kakarbhitta	Darjeeling, India
3	Ilam	far eastern Nepal
5	Dharan, Hile & Dhankuta	Eastern Nepal treks
6	Biratnagar & Ilam	far eastern Nepal
10	Janakpur,	Terai
13	Nepalgunj, Mahendranagar, Surkhet, Dhangadi, Hetauda, Tadi Bazaar (Chitwan), Narayanghat, Birganj & Janakpur	
14	Trisuli & Dhunche	Langtang treks
15, 16	Birganj	Indian border
17	Pokhara	
18	Gorkha, Besi Sahar & Pokhara	
23, 24	government buses (Sajha Yatayat) to Palpa, Bhairawa, Nepalgunj, Tadi Bazaar, Bharatpur, Rajbiraj, Dang, Surkhet, Birganj, Pokhara & Trisuli	

station, you might have a choice of seats. Otherwise it's fairly safe to assume that you can arrive a few hours before departure and get a seat on one of the many buses that operate to each destination. A notable exception to this is during the Dasain holiday in the autumn, when bus seats are at a premium.

There is a long row of ticket windows. When tickets go on sale for a particular route, a temporary sign with a number and destination, both in Nepali, is hung above the window. The numbers are not necessarily in order. To make matters more confusing, the numbers on the ticket windows do not correspond to the entirely separate numbers that are used to label the departure bays.

There is an enquiries counter at the bus terminal, and many Nepalis speak enough English to point you in the right direction. As you wait, watch your fellow passengers for sudden movement. One common announcement interspersed with the blaring music on the loudspeaker is something like 'Bus No 2153 is broken, so please come to the window and exchange your tickets for seats on bus 1535'.

To help get you started, see the table showing ticket window numbers for some important trekking and tourist destinations.

When budgeting your expenses, include the extra charges for luggage. Large pieces of baggage go on the roof. You must either drag them up the ladder on the back of the bus or pay a rupee or two to have someone do it for you. The baggage charge is often negotiable with the conductor and is higher for the so-called express and deluxe services. If you have a lot of gear, the baggage costs can add up to more than the cost of the bus seat. There are frequent reports of thefts of luggage placed on the roof of local buses, especially on the road to Jiri. Buses stop frequently and there is always someone climbing up and down to the roof, so it's impossible to watch your gear all the time. Some people suggest padlocking your bag to the top of the bus.

An 'express' bus is anything but express, but it certainly beats a local bus. Local buses can take twice (or more) as long as an express. An express bus, in turn, takes about twice as long as a private vehicle.

Unlike aeroplanes, which depart with a minimum of ceremony, buses in Nepal make a great drama out of their departure. Honking horns, racing engines, last-minute baggage loading and an attempt to cram a few extra passengers, chickens and goats on board make for a huge production that can often delay departures. Bring a book to read.

Occasionally it is possible to sit on the roof of the bus after it leaves Kathmandu. This is often an attractive spot if the weather is warm and it gets you out of the smoke-filled bus. The roof is either a more or a less dangerous place to be in case of an accident, depending on the circumstances. Buses have a nasty habit of rolling over, driving off steep embankments or colliding head-on. One place on the bus is probably as safe as another.

Buses stop for a multitude of reasons – breakdowns (mostly), police checkposts, road tolls, tea breaks, meal stops and chats with the drivers of other buses.

CAR & 4WD

It's expensive to hire a car or Land Rover to get to the start of a trek, but it's much more comfortable and can save a lot of time compared to public transport.

You can rent a car in Nepal, but even Hertz and Avis usually supply a driver – free. Traffic is chaotic, everyone ignores the rules, and an accident puts the driver in jail until the situation is resolved, so it's not a good idea to drive in Nepal unless you are familiar with the country and are used to dodging the cows, chickens, kids, bicycles and rickshaws that pop up out of nowhere. Traffic is supposed to stay on the left side of the road, though this is not obvious when you watch vehicle movements.

Land Rovers that will undertake either long or short-distance trips can be found in front of the Mt Makalu Hotel, near New Rd. Rates are negotiable.

TAXI

Most travel agencies can arrange cars for long-distance travel, or you can negotiate with one of the private taxis that are available through the Nepal Tourist Service booking office (☎ 241507) in a lane just off Durbar Marg behind the Hotel Sherpa. Taxis can reach the starting points for many treks, including Pokhara, Jiri and Dhunche, and are much cheaper to hire than a Land Rover. Remember, however, that most Kathmandu taxi drivers are not experienced in driving on mountain roads.

Road Building

From Kathmandu, narrow mountain roads run north to China and south to India to connect the valley to the outside world. Nepal is undertaking a major road-building programme, however, and extensive construction is under way everywhere. The east-west highway that runs near the Indian border is nearing completion, and many roads now wind their way a long distance into the hills.

Roads planned for the 1990s include one from Surkhet to Jumla in western Nepal and on to Mugu and Humla. If this road is built, these regions, at present inaccessible, will become more popular trekking destinations. A road from the Terai that heads north to Okhaldunga and Salleri should be completed by 1998. This will change the character of the entire Everest region. The road to Taplejung is also nearing completion, but it's still a long, rough drive from Ilam. There is a plan to build a tunnel to bring drinking water from the upper Helambu Valley to Kathmandu, and a road is being constructed up the Malemchi Khola to support this project.

Another road on the drawing board is a major east-west road in the Middle Hills, connecting Dipayal and Silgadi in the far west to Jajakot and Musikot, then to Beni and Pokhara. The eastern part of the route leaves the Jiri road and heads south to Ramechhap, then heads east to Okhaldunga, Bhojpur and Taplejung. The new trekking opportunities that this road presents are endless.

When trekking in the Annapurna region, you will use the new road from Pokhara to the Kali Gandaki valley. The master plan is for this Chinese-financed road to extend all the way to Lo Manthang in Mustang and on to Tibet. Depending on your outlook, this may either enhance or destroy the trek to Jomsom.

Roads are subject to landslides, washouts and damage from outrageously overloaded trucks and buses. The road out of Kathmandu Valley is in terrible condition. Despite almost constant repair, travelling on this road is one of the worst journeys on earth. But all roads eventually end, and once they do, all travel is on a system of trails that climb the steep hills of Nepal as no road ever could. ■

HITCHING

Hitching is unheard-of in Nepal. Even the poorest Nepali pays for a ride in a bus or truck, so you will almost certainly be expected to pay for any ride you get unless you are picked up by a kindly expatriate.

LOCAL TRANSPORT

The Airport

Taxis are usually available at the Tribhuvan airport, but fares vary according to demand. Drivers should use a meter, but often do not. There is a limousine service with a booking counter inside the airport where you can arrange a private car for Rs 200. Taxis usually charge the same as the limousine service. When taxis are in short supply, drivers cover their meters with a dirty rag and prices double or triple. There are blue public buses that operate on a fixed route to several hotels, including those at Thamel, for Rs 15.

Bus

Blue Isuzu and Mitsubishi buses and private minibuses cover the entire Kathmandu Valley on various routes. During rush hours they resemble sardine cans, but at other times Rs 1 or Rs 2 gets you around in relative comfort.

Taxi

Metered taxis are inexpensive and abundant in Kathmandu during the day. However, they are hard to find after 8 pm, and those that are available will quote you their own 'take it or leave it' rates. If you are stuck out late without a taxi, try a large hotel or call the night-taxi service on ☎ 224374. Surya Taxi Service operates radio-dispatched cabs (☎ 414018, 417978). In 1996 hundreds of new taxis were imported and all have electronic meters that usually work. Many of the drivers of new taxis recently graduated from

rickshaws, so a ride can be a bit hair-raising. Many of these drivers don't have experience on mountain roads, so if you are negotiating with a taxi for a long-distance trip, look for an older, more experienced driver.

Three-wheeled scooters are also metered and are slightly cheaper than taxis, but a ride in one of these is a bone-rattling adventure.

Rickshaw

Bicycle rickshaws are available in some parts of the city. They can be fun, but be sure to negotiate the price beforehand.

Motorbike & Bicycle

It costs Rs 40 per day to rent a Chinese or Indian single-speed bicycle. Mountain bikes are available in Thamel for Rs 100 to Rs 125 per day. Be careful of cars when you are on a bicycle, especially vehicles making non-stop left turns at red lights.

With a driving licence, you can rent motorbikes for Rs 60 per hour or Rs 300 per day.

Tempo

There is a system of jitneys that operates on fixed routes throughout Kathmandu using blue three-wheeled Indian scooters called *tempos*. These are powered by inefficient engines originally designed for use in water pumps and are one of the major contributors to Kathmandu's air pollution. They carry loads of up to nine Nepalis, but will handle only four or five large Westerners. Part of the tempo fleet has been converted to electric-powered *safa tempos* ('clean tempos'). The conversion project is supported by Nepali environmental groups and USAID. It's an excellent start to resolving Nepal's problems with noise and air quality; safa tempos are painted white.

Mt Everest Region

The Mt Everest or Solu Khumbu region is the second-most popular trekking area in Nepal. It would probably be the most popular destination, but it is more expensive and difficult to get to Solu Khumbu than to the Annapurna area. To get near Everest, you must either walk for a week or fly to Lukla, a remote mountain airstrip where flights are notoriously unreliable.

Solu Khumbu is justifiably famous, not only for its proximity to the world's highest mountain (8848m), but also for its Sherpa villages and monasteries. The nominal goal of an Everest trek is the Everest base camp at an elevation of about 5340m. You cannot see Everest from the base camp, so most trekkers climb Kala Pattar, a 5545m bump on the southern flank of Pumori (7145m). From Kala Pattar there is a dramatic view of Everest.

Other than the problem of access, the other major complication to an Everest trek is the high likelihood of Acute Mountain Sickness (AMS). This potentially deadly disease, commonly known as altitude sickness, is caused by climbing too quickly to a high elevation. Be sure to read the Altitude Illness section in the Health & Safety chapter if you are planning an Everest trek. If you suffer symptoms of altitude sickness and cannot go to base camp, you can still make a worthwhile trek to less ambitious destinations such as Namche Bazaar, the administrative headquarters of the Khumbu region; Khumjung or Thami, which are more typical Sherpa villages; or Tengpoche monastery. From Tengpoche you will have an excellent view of Everest and its more spectacular neighbour Ama Dablam (6856m).

An Everest trek involves a tremendous amount of up-and-down walking. A glance at the map will show the reason why. All the rivers in this part of Nepal flow south from Himalayan glaciers, but the trek route proceeds east. Therefore the trail must climb to the ridge that separates two rivers, descend

to the river itself, and ascend the next ridge. Even though the trek begins at an elevation of 1860m, on the sixth day it crosses the Dudh Kosi at only 1500m – after considerable uphill (and downhill) walking. If you total all the uphill climbing, it will come to almost 9000m of elevation gain from Jiri to Everest base camp. The Jiri road saves almost 4000m of uphill walking over the old approach from Lamosangu, but this is still a long, hard trek with a lot of uphill walking.

INFORMATION
Fees & Permits
All the treks described in this chapter require payment of the Rs 650 entrance fee to Sagarmatha National Park. There are no other specific fees for treks in the Everest region, but you should make a donation to any monasteries and *gompas* that you visit.

Foreigners are not allowed to trek north of Thami towards the Nangpa La, the pass leading to Tibet.

Maps
The Everest area has been mapped to death; there are more detailed maps of this area than of any other part of Nepal. The entire region is covered in detail at 1:50,000 by the Schneider maps: *Khumbu Himal* (which covers Namche Bazaar to Mt Everest); *Shorong/Hinku* (Solu and the Hongu valley); *Dudh Kosi* (Lamidanda to Lukla); *Tamba Kosi/Likhu Khola* (Jiri to Junbesi); *Rolwaling Himal* (Rolwaling and Gauri Shankar); and *Lepchi Kang* (Barahbise and Kodari).

A map titled *Mount Everest Region*, published in the UK, covers about the same region as the map of the same name in this book. There is an eight-colour 1975 version for UK£5 and a six-colour 1964 version; add UK£2 for postage to the price. Both are available by mail from the Royal Geographical Society, 1 Kensington Gore, London SW7.

The November 1988 issue of *National*

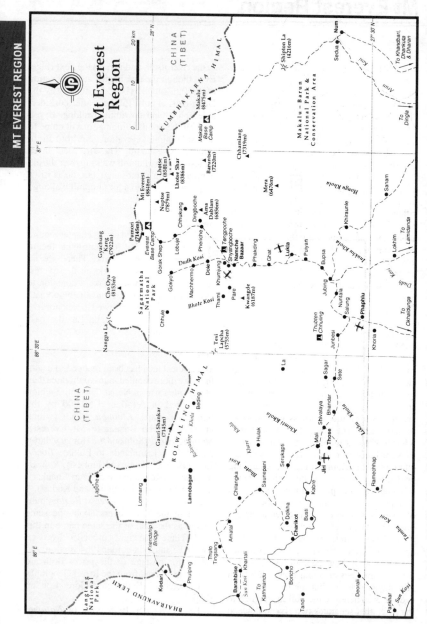

Geographic contained a 1:50,000 computer-enhanced topographic map of the Everest area. This map does not cover much of the trekking route, but is a fascinating document to study. Copies are available in Kathmandu bookshops.

The US Army Map Service sheet, 45-2 *Mount Everest*, isn't worth carrying because there are so many better maps of the region. Many locally produced maps are available in Kathmandu. The *Nepal-Khumbu* map produced by Nepa Maps is available in Kathmandu, as are numerous blueprinted maps that vary in detail and quality. For fun, there's also a reprint of the map that was produced by the 1920 Everest expedition.

Books

There is almost too much information available about Everest. In addition to the books I have listed, there are at least 100 more books and thousands of magazine articles about the Sherpas and Mt Everest. Whether your interest is in mountaineering, Buddhism, anthropology, natural history or environmental preservation, you will be able to find literature about the Everest region that you can relate to.

Sagarmatha, Mother of the Universe, by Margaret Jefferies, is a detailed description of the Sagarmatha National Park.

The Sherpas of Nepal, by C Von Fürer Haimendorf, is a rather dry anthropological study of the Sherpas of the Solu Khumbu region. This book is out of print and unavailable, except in libraries; the author has written a sequel titled *The Sherpas Transformed*.

Sherpas – Reflections on Change in Himalayan Nepal, by James F Fisher, is an account of changes in Sherpa culture and practices as a result of schools and tourism.

High in the Thin Cold Air, by Edmund Hillary & Desmond Doig, describes many of the projects undertaken by the Himalayan Trust. It also contains the story of the scientific examination of the Khumjung yeti skull.

Schoolhouse in the Clouds, by Edmund Hillary, describes the construction of Khumjung school and other projects in Khumbu.

This provides good background information on where all those bridges, hospitals and schools came from.

Mani Rimdu, Nepal, by Mario Fantini, contains colour photos and descriptions of the dances of the Mani Rimdu festival at Tengpoche monastery.

Forerunners to Everest, by Rene Dittert, Gabriel Chevalley & Raymond Lambert, translated by Malcolm Barnes, is a description of the two Swiss expeditions to Everest in 1952. It includes a fine description of the old expedition approach march.

Faces of Everest, by Major HPS Ahluwalia, is an illustrated history of Everest by a summiter from the 1965 Indian expedition.

Everest, by Walt Unsworth, gives a detailed history of mountaineering on Everest.

Place Names

Maps and route descriptions for the Everest trek become confusing because of conflicting names for the same place. There are both Sherpa names and Nepali names for many villages. I have used the Nepali names because these are on all official maps and records. The Sherpa names for villages along the route appear in parenthesis after the more common Nepali name.

Festivals

In addition to the February celebration of the Tibetan New Year, or Losar, there are two uniquely Sherpa festivals that you may encounter in Solu Khumbu.

Mani Rimdu This festival is celebrated at the monasteries of Tengpoche, Thami and Chiwang. The monks wear elaborate masks and costumes and, through a series of ritualistic dances, dramatise the triumph of Buddhism over Bon, the ancient animistic religion of Tibet. The first day of Mani Rimdu involves prayers by the lamas in the monastery courtyard. The second day is the colourful lama dancing, when lamas wear brocade gowns and wonderfully painted papier-mâché masks. Hundreds of Sherpas from all over

MT EVEREST REGION

Mt Everest Region – Flora & Fauna

Trees The chir pine and blue pine are the only two species of pine found in Nepal, so they are easy to identify. The **chir pine** (also known as the long-leafed pine) is a tall, straight conifer that appears on sunny slopes in the subtropical zone. It has long, often bright green, needles in bundles of three, and medium-sized, oval cones.

The **blue pine** is generally found higher than the chir pine, growing at altitudes up to 4000m. Blue pines have shorter needles that are bluish green and come in bundles of five. Look for the long, dangling cones that distinguish this pine from the other.

Junipers are found in a dwarfed form in the subalpine region at altitudes over 4000m. Their distinctive foliage should be unmistakable. Junipers in tree form are found around Thami. Look for the fleshy, berry-like fruit in both of these varieties. **Hemlock** and **silver fir** are also well represented in this area. See the boxed aside 'Around Annapurna – Flora & Fauna', in the Annapurna Region chapter, for help in identifying these trees.

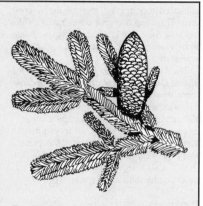

The silver fir has the shape and appearance of a Christmas tree. Its needles are silvery underneath and its cones ooze resin.

Birds The **golden eagle** is the most common of the resident *Aquila* eagles. This soaring bird can be distinguished from the griffon and lammergeier, not only by its smaller size, but by its broad wings, indented at the base, and its wide-open 'V' profile in flight. These tawny brown birds are often seen in their juvenile plumage, which shows white markings in the wings and the base of the tail. Look for hunting pairs in the upper Khumbu region.

Another smaller but noticeable raptor is the **Eurasian kestrel**, a long-winged, long-tailed falcon that often hovers. The male has a cinnamon-coloured back that contrasts with the grey, black-banded tail, and is mostly pale from the front. Also look for the **goshawk**, the largest of the *Accipiter* species, which can be seen poaching snow pigeons in this area.

The bold, playful flocks of black birds you often see are **red-billed** and **yellow-billed choughs** from the crow family. These birds are fearless and can usually be seen quite closely without the aid of binoculars. The yellow-billed choughs often pesters trekkers and mountaineers while they are eating, and is so unafraid of humans that it can virtually be snatched from the air.

Another species observed in large, muted flocks is the **snow pigeon**. Its sooty back provides camouflage while it forages in fallow fields, but the white undersides are exposed when it takes flight. Pheasants are probably the most spectacular birds seen on the ground in the Himalaya. The males tend to be regal in bright, rich colours, while the females are drab-coloured and may even seem to be a different species to the undiscerning eye. The religious sanctuary around the Tengpoche monastery in the Khumbu area creates ample opportunities to observe pheasant species such as the blood pheasant and the impeyan pheasant, the national bird of Nepal. The male **impeyan pheasant** (or Himalayan monal), which appears almost black in poor light, gleams radiantly in sunlight to reveal an iridescent, multicoloured plumage. You cannot mistake this bird for anything else. It is frequently seen

Khumbu attend the performance; it is an important social occasion as well as an entertaining spectacle. Along with the serious and intricate dances the lamas also dramatise two absurd comic sequences that make the entire performance a grand and amusing event. On the final evening of Mani Rimdu the villagers join in an all-night Sherpa dance.

The Tengpoche celebration of Mani Rimdu usually takes place at the November-December full moon. As large crowds of Westerners attend this ceremony, both hotel and tent space is hard to come by. Prices creep up in accordance with the capitalist tradition of charging what the traffic will bear. The monastery charges for entrance digging for tubers in the stark winter fields of Khumbu. The **blood pheasant** is a finely streaked bird with a red and green tinge. Look for the reddish legs in both sexes.

It is also possible to spot the **crimson-horned pheasant** in this same region. Considered by some to be the most beautiful of the family, this bird is more secretive and prefers the cover of forests.

Look for **Tibetan snow cocks** above the tree line on scree slopes or among dwarf juniper. These grey birds have white underparts with black streaks and are often heard before seen, though they are quite visible in the Gorak Shep area. Also look for the large (hawk-sized) **raven** that, while on the ground, 'croaks' as it hops and swaggers. This bird prefers the high, dry trans-Himalayan areas.

Blood pheasants move together through undergrowth gathering berries and other food. Their usual call is a repetitive 'chuck' sound.

Mammals Contrary to what one might think, the Himalaya is mostly devoid of deer species. This is not necessarily because of hunting or environmental degradation, but because most of Nepal's deer species prefer the lowland jungles. The *muntjac*, or **barking deer**, a small, reddish mammal with short antlers, found at altitudes up to 2400m in temperate forests, has a sharp, single-note alarm call, or 'bark', and is often heard rather than seen.

An even smaller, more unusual 'deer' (about 50 cm tall at the shoulders) is the **musk deer**, a beast taxonomically stranded between deer and antelopes. The male is not only hornless, but has oversized canine teeth that protrude from the mouth. The male's musk gland is found in the abdomen; its value to humankind has accelerated the demise of the species. This diminutive deer is very secretive and prefers forest cover near the tree line. Look for this species in the area from Phortse to Tengpoche.

The **Himalayan tahr** is another creature that's difficult to classify, though its niche is that of a 'mountain goat'. Except during the winter rutting season, these animals are found in two different kinds of herds. The females, young, and inferior males form one group and the older, more dominant males form the other. The dominant males are sometimes also seen alone and have a long, flowing ruff and coat and short, curved horns. Tahr are quite visible in Gokyo and on the high trail from Khumjung through Phortse to Pangboche. ■

The male Himalayan tahr with its flowing mane is sometimes seen alone on grassy slopes in inner Himalayan valleys.

tickets, with a hefty surcharge for movie cameras.

A spring celebration of the Mani Rimdu festival is held on the day of the full moon closest to the middle of May each year in Thami. Mani Rimdu at Thami tends to be a little more spirited (literally) than the festival in autumn at Tengpoche because the weather is warmer in spring and the *rimpoche*, or reincarnate lama, at Thami is more liberal than the Tengpoche lama.

Mani Rimdu is also held in autumn at Chiwang gompa in the Solu region, usually on the same day as Tengpoche's Mani Rimdu. This monastery is set high on a ridge overlooking Phaphlu and Salleri. The Chiwang gompa celebration may be the more authentic version because it is presided over by the head lama of Thubten Chhuling, who is the reincarnate lama of Rongbuk, where the festival had its origins.

Dumje Dumje is a celebration of the birth of Guru Rimpoche (Padmasambhava). It is a six day celebration that takes place in June when few tourists are in the Khumbu. Eight families sponsor the event each year. It is a heavy financial burden, so this responsibility is rotated in turn among the villagers. Separate celebrations take place in the villages of Namche Bazaar, Khumjung and Thami.

Accommodation & Supplies

There are lodges of varying degrees of sophistication all the way from Jiri to Everest base camp, and there are few places where you will walk more than an hour without finding some kind of facility. In Lukla and beyond, the competition among lodges is intense and the facilities are better than those on the walk from Jiri. Almost all the lodges on the entire route have both private rooms and dormitory accommodation. There is a lot of variety in price and facilities, so you can walk on to the next place if you cannot find something that suits you.

Above Namche Bazaar most lodges have only dormitory facilities consisting of huge bunks that sleep eight to 10 people. One common phenomenon at high altitude is very strange dreams and even nightmares. These occurrences lend a bit of entertainment to a night in a crowded lodge on the way to Everest.

During the trekking season, hotels fill up quickly. You will probably get involved in a daily race with other trekkers to get the best, and sometimes the only, accommodation. This can be dangerous at high elevations because altitude sickness is encouraged by overexertion and a fast ascent. At Pheriche and Lobuje, particularly, you must be a bit aggressive in dealing with the crowds.

The *Hotel Everest View*, above Namche Bazaar, is a Japanese project that caters to the blue-rinse set. The hotel was closed from 1982 until 1989, but it has been renovated and is now open – and expensive. All 12 rooms have private bathrooms with Western toilets. Rates start at US$135 per person per night; meals are extra. The Everest View operates flights to Shyangboche airstrip and offers charter flights in Pilatus Porter aircraft for US$740 per hour. Book through its Kathmandu office on Durbar Marg (☎ 224854, 223871; fax 227289).

Hotel Sagarmatha in Lukla offers package deals with flights, hotel accommodation and short treks. Prebook with its Kathmandu office, PO Box 500, Kathmandu (☎ 220423, 222489; fax 227243).

Fuel

The use of kerosene as a fuel is required in the Sagarmatha National Park and is encouraged elsewhere. The Lukla Himalayan Club has convinced villagers not to sell firewood to trekking groups. Kerosene is expensive because it must be carried by porters or helicopter; it costs Rs 50 per litre in Lukla and Rs 60 in Namche, compared to Rs 9.50 in Kathmandu.

Electricity

Many villages between Jiri and Namche Bazaar have public or privately supplied electricity of varying standard that usually operates during the evening hours only. Electricity is expensive, so many private homes cannot afford it, but most lodges have electricity for lighting. Most electricity schemes do not have enough capacity for cooking, so lodges still rely on firewood or kerosene. Among the villages on the Everest trek that have electricity are Jiri, Kenja, Junbesi, Salari, Manidingma, Khari Khola, Lukla and Tengpoche.

The Austrian-financed 630 kW hydro plant at Thami is operated by the Khumbu Bijuli (electricity) Company and provides a reliable, abundant power supply 24 hours a day to Thami, Namche, Khumjung, Khunde and the Hotel Everest View. Many homes, lodges and bakeries use this power for cooking, so the consumption of wood in the region has decreased. All the wiring within villages is underground. The electricity project is part of an effort to conserve energy and reduce environmental degradation in Khumbu.

GETTING THERE & AWAY

You can either fly or walk to the Everest region. Those who fly to Lukla miss out on the historic and culturally fascinating route followed by the Everest expeditions of the 1950s and 60s, although the trek has changed a lot in the past 40 years. If you can possibly find the time and energy to walk from Jiri, you will have a more rewarding trip and will be in much better physical shape to tackle the high mountain region of upper Khumbu.

Air

If you fly to one of the mountain airstrips near Everest, do not attempt a quick visit to the base camp because you won't have had time to acclimatise. Allow at least eight or nine days to reach the base camp region if you fly to Lukla. You can return from the base camp to Lukla in as few as four or five days, so it takes an absolute minimum of two weeks for a safe trek to the base camp. Precise scheduling is complicated because flights to Lukla often do not take off as planned. Allow a few spare days for both the flight in and the flight out.

Lukla At 2800m, this airstrip is served by Royal Nepal's 19-passenger Twin Otter aircraft that carry (due to the high elevation) only 14 or 15 passengers to, or from, Lukla. It's also served by several companies that operate Russian MI-17 helicopters. If you truly have a limited amount of time, you can fly to Lukla and spend as little as five days to visit Namche Bazaar and Tengpoche, then trek back to Lukla for a flight back to Kathmandu, but beware of flight delays.

Lukla is unique. A Hillary team built the airstrip as part of the Khunde Hospital project in 1965, envisioning it as a makeshift strip to handle emergencies at the hospital. RNAC expanded the strip in 1977 and the Department of Civil Aviation added a control tower in 1983. It is now the third-busiest

airport in Nepal. The flight approach path is totally visual; there are no instruments or navigational aids of any kind. If it's cloudy, planes cannot make the approach, though helicopters can often sneak in.

High on the side of a mountain, the grass strip is built on a slant so that there is an elevation difference of about 60m between the ends of the runway. This slope slows planes and helps them stop before they run into the mountain peak that rises from the eastern end of the 450m-long runway.

RNAC's service to Lukla has decreased as the helicopter service has increased. In the season there are frequent chopper flights and it's usually easy to get a seat from Lukla to Kathmandu with RNAC or one of five helicopter companies. You can often roll in to Lukla, check which company has space, and have a good chance of being able to jump aboard. If the Russian helicopters cannot carry passengers, Lukla will be a bottleneck with too many trekkers and too few aircraft.

Check with Asian Airlines, next door to the immigration office in Kathmandu, for seats on a Lukla-bound helicopter. Since so many companies run both charter and scheduled flights to Lukla, it is easiest to contact a travel agent or trekking company and have them search for seats by telephone. If you want to run around yourself, try the helicopter sections of Everest Air, Nepal Airways, Gorkha Air and Manakamana Airways.

Shyangboche This tiny airstrip, above Namche Bazaar at an elevation of 3730m, is served by a single six-passenger, single-engine Pilatus Porter aircraft and by occasional helicopter flights. It was built to accommodate guests at the Hotel Everest View, but is now used for major cargo shipments to Khumbu. You can sometimes get a seat on the Everest View's Pilatus Porter plane. A ticket costs US$145, but priority is given to hotel guests, so you may have to spend a night there to gain a place in the queue. Asian Airlines, a helicopter company, has an office at the airstrip (☎ 038-21115).

In 1995 and 1996 there were daily passenger helicopter flights between Shyangboche

Flight Cancellations at Lukla

When Lukla flights are cancelled, those who have planned to fly to Kathmandu must wait. A backlog of people soon builds up, each person convinced that he or she must fly on the next available aircraft. The situation often becomes ludicrous, but provides a great opportunity to develop patience and to become acquainted with trekkers from all over the world as you wait together. You can now witness overcrowding in the Everest area first-hand. In previous years, before large-scale helicopter operations began, 350 or more people would get stranded here, especially in late October and early November. It can still happen. The problem usually solves itself within a week, but it's important to prepare yourself for a delay on any flight to or from Lukla. It's also possible to depart from Lukla exactly on schedule.

Occasionally the pile-up of people at Lukla becomes unmanageable. Imagine 350 people vying for seats on planes that carry just 15 passengers. Many people, having completed a great trek, make themselves miserable by fighting for seats out of Lukla. It's a helpless feeling to be in a place where no amount of influence or money can make the planes come, but this is a developing country. If you expect things to operate on time (or, sometimes, to operate at all), you should head for the mountains of Switzerland.

Unbelievable things happen when people flip out at Lukla. I've seen the station manager chased around the airport by a tourist brandishing an ice axe. I've seen chanting mobs outside the airline office. I've seen rock fights on the airstrip. Twice I've seen planeloads of police arrive in Lukla to get things under control, and I've heard endless tales of woe from people who had to be at work the following day (they didn't make it). If it gets like this – usually in late October and early November, and occasionally at other unpredictable times – the only way to maintain your composure is to be sure your name is somewhere on the reservation list. Assign one of your sherpas (or better yet, your innkeeper or the Lukla representative of your trekking company) to ensure that other names are not slipped in ahead of yours, then retire to a kettle or two of chhang to consider your alternatives.

You can wait. It might be a day (I've seen 14 flights to Lukla in a single day), or as long as two weeks. You can walk to Jiri. At a normal pace, it's six days to Jiri, where you can get a bus to Kathmandu. If you walk 10 to 12 hours a day (you save days in Nepal by walking a longer time each day, not by walking faster), you could reach Jiri in four days, perhaps even three. You can walk to the airstrip at Phaphlu, two long days (or three comfortable days) from Lukla. It is an appealing walk, but it's uncertain that it will hasten your return to Kathmandu. There are only six flights a week and seats are in heavy demand for government officials stationed in nearby Salleri.

You can walk from Phaphlu south to Janakpur in six days. The 10-day trek from Solu Khumbu to Hile described in this book is also a route to escape from Lukla. Another alternative is to walk to Lamidanda, an airstrip five days to the south. The important thing is not to make yourself, and everyone else, miserable by fighting and bemoaning your fate. Do something positive instead. You can always go back to Namche Bazaar for a few days and wait for things to clear up, or you can climb the ridge behind Lukla, where there are some wonderful high meadows and a good view of Kariolung Peak. ■

and Kathmandu. The flights cost US$120, and many trekkers chose to fly out of here to avoid the walk back to Lukla. The Sherpas of Lukla and other villages in the Dudh Kosi valley lost a lot of business, so they protested (by herding their yaks onto the runway) and forced an agreement that prohibits foreign trekkers from flying from Shyangboche. Since January 1997, Shyangboche helicopters have carried only cargo and Nepali passengers.

Many expeditions fly their cargo in on choppers, so there is often lots of empty space back to Kathmandu at the start of the climbing season. The chopper companies are anxious to sell this unused capacity, and are pushing for a new agreement with the Lukla people. A change is not likely, however, so you should plan on walking back to Lukla for a flight back to Kathmandu.

If passenger flights are restarted, remember that it's fine to fly out of Shyangboche, but *it's dangerous to fly in to Shyangboche* because of the high risk of altitude problems.

Phaphlu It's a four day walk from Lukla, or six days from Namche Bazaar, to Phaphlu (2364m). If you have an extra few days, this may be a viable alternative for flights both to and from the Everest region. Phaphlu airstrip was extended in 1986 to accommodate Twin Otter aircraft. Few tourist groups use the airstrip, so you might find a seat at the last minute. RNAC operates four flights a week, Everest Air serves Phaphlu with two flights weekly and there are many helicopter flights, both scheduled and chartered.

Lamidanda This airport is about five days walk south of Lukla. It is a largely unknown alternative as either an approach to or exit from the Everest region. From Lamidanda there are RNAC and Everest Air flights to Kathmandu and Biratnagar. Lamidanda used to be a good alternative to Lukla before the helicopter service began, but now there are many helicopter seats available from Lukla. This is the alternative airport for Lukla, so sometimes planes and helicopters land here for a while to wait out a spell of bad weather at Lukla.

Airfares The following are one-way fares between the main mountain airstrips and Kathmandu airport:

Kathmandu-Lukla	US$83
Kathmandu-Phaphlu	US$77
Kathmandu-Lamidanda	US$66

Flight Delays RNAC schedules three or four flights a day to Lukla. In reality there are usually either more or less than four flights because of cancellations, extra flights, charters or delayed flights. The huge helicopters arrive and depart in seemingly random patterns, and it takes a bit of research to find out which airline's chopper is coming next. Tickets are not interchangeable between any of the airlines, so it becomes an amusing lottery as you try to get onto the next available flight. But the situation is much improved over years past when there were crowds of more than 350 people waiting for periods of up to 10 days. Weather, operational difficulties, strikes or some other factor could cause the problem to recur, so it's important to prepare yourself for a possible long delay for any flight to or from Lukla. It's also possible to depart from Lukla exactly on schedule.

Bus & Taxi

Jiri Jiri is 188 km from Kathmandu and is the starting point for 'walk to Everest' treks. You should plan on one week to trek from the roadhead at Jiri to Namche Bazaar. If you take the time to walk from Jiri, the hike will help to acclimatise and condition you to visit Everest base camp and climb Kala Pattar. You can then fly out from Lukla or walk back by an alternative route to Kathmandu. There are at least four buses daily to Jiri, and they depart from the old bus terminal across from Ratna Park in central Kathmandu. The first bus leaves at 6 am and tickets cost Rs 120. The buses that serve Jiri are dilapidated, crowded and slow (one trekker described the trip as 'hell on earth'). There are also frequent reports of theft from rucksacks on the roof of Jiri buses during the 10 to 12 hour trip. If you have the wherewithal, and a group of two or three people, you might consider hiring a taxi for Rs 5000 or so.

Barahbise Five km beyond Lamosangu and 85 km from Kathmandu is the starting point of an extended Everest walk-in trek. There is no express bus service to Barahbise, so you must take a funky local bus from the old bus park in the centre of Kathmandu. It takes five to six hours, but it's cheap – only Rs 41. You can make the trip by private car or taxi in about 2½ hours for Rs 1400.

Lamosangu Lamosangu was the starting point for Everest treks before the road to Jiri was completed. It is still shown on many trekking maps, but it is now simply a transit point for buses headed to Barahbise and Jiri.

Dharan & Dhankuta These villages in south-eastern Nepal can be used as starting or ending points for an Everest trek. See the details of how to get to these villages in the Eastern Nepal chapter.

Jiri to Namche Bazaar

Duration 9 days
Difficulty Medium
Maximum elevation 3500m
Permit cost US$5 per week plus Rs 650
Season October to May
Accommodation Very good
Summary Follows the classic Everest expedition route through hill villages. Lots of climbing as the route crosses several ridges, then descends to cross a river. An excellent trek that offers a good chance to acclimatise before heading to Everest base camp.

This section details the first seven days of a 19 day trek from Jiri to the Everest base camp. This is the best way to do an Everest trek, but I have broken it into two sections because most people fly to Lukla and only trek the high-altitude portion of the route. This means that the portion of the trek from Jiri to Lukla is often uncrowded, and therefore excellent trekking country. From Namche you can follow the route from Lukla to Everest base camp described in the following section and fly out. You can also make an excellent 30 day trek by walking on to Hile instead of flying from Lukla. The description of the Solu Khumbu to Hile route is in the Eastern Nepal chapter. You can also start an Everest trek by walking much of the route that is traversed by the Jiri road; see the Barahbise to Shivalaya trek at the end of this chapter.

Access

It's an uncomfortable all-day drive to Jiri from Kathmandu. The first part of the drive is via the Arniko Rajmarg or Kodari Highway, the Chinese-constructed road that links Nepal with Tibet. The road follows the Chinese trolleybus route to Bhaktapur, then passes smoke-belching brick factories, finally leaving the Kathmandu Valley and passing by the old Newar towns of Banepa and Dhulikhel. If it is clear as you pass Dhulikhel, you should have an excellent panoramic view of the eastern Himalaya, including Ganesh Himal, Langtang Lirung and Dorje Lakpa.

The road descends to Panchkal, the starting point for Helambu treks, then follows the Indrawati downstream to Dolalghat at Km 57. It crosses the river on a large bridge just upstream of its confluence with the Sun Kosi. The Sun Kosi ('gold river') is one of Nepal's major rivers; it is possible to make a week-long rafting expedition from Dolalghat all the way to the Terai. The road climbs over a ridge behind Dolalghat, passing the junction of the road to Chautaara and the trek to Jugal Himal (see the Langtang & Helambu chapter). The road descends from the ridge and follows the Sun Kosi north through Balephi to Lamosangu, a clutter of restaurants and shops 37 km south of the Tibetan border. Just north of Lamosangu is a hydro-electric power plant built with Chinese aid.

At Lamosangu the road crosses the Sun

The Road to Jiri

By bus it takes a full day to cover the 188 km from Kathmandu to Jiri. The development of roads has been a characteristic of this trek since the first Everest expedition in Nepal. In 1953 the British Everest expedition started from Bhadgaon in the Kathmandu Valley. By 1963 the US expedition could begin from Banepa, saving a day of walking over the British expedition. The Kodari road allowed the trek to begin from Dolalghat in 1967 and from Lamosangu in 1970. The Jiri road reached Kirantichhap in 1980, and by 1984 it was finally possible to drive all the way to Jiri. There is talk of continuing the road further, perhaps to Phaphlu or even to Namche Bazaar, but in 1997 this is still only a dream and no firm plans exist.

The Swiss Association for Technical Assistance (SATA) built the Jiri road as part of the Integrated Hill Development Project, a large programme of agricultural development in this region. It employed labourers to build the road instead of using machines. This was intended to have a beneficial economic impact by employing hundreds of workers. A direct effect of this approach to road building is that it raises porter wages and creates a porter shortage. ∎

RICHARD I'ANSON

STAN ARMINGTON

Mt Everest Region
Top: Pumori (right) and, in front of it, the dark shape of Kala Pattar, which many trekkers
ascend from Gorak Shep for the view of Mt Everest
Bottom: Mt Everest from Kala Pattar

GLENN TEMPEST/OPEN SPACES PHOTOGRAPHY

BRIAN K WEIRUM

RICHARD I'ANSON

Mt Everest Region
Top Left: The spectacular Lukla airport, at an altitude of 2800m, the third-busiest in Nepal
Top Right: Kantega, the saddle-shaped mountain, from Khumjung village
Bottom: Looking down the Ngozumpa Glacier from above Gokyo

Kosi and joins the Swiss road to Jiri. A new series of kilometre posts starts here. The bridge is Km 0 and Jiri is Km 110. After some initial switchbacks as the road leaves the Sun Kosi valley, the road turns east and heads up a canyon towards the top of the 2500m ridge that forms the watershed between the Sun Kosi drainage to the west and the Tamba Kosi drainage to the east. The first large settlement along the road is the Tamang village of **Pakhar** (1980m). From Pakhar the road climbs along the top of a ridge towards the pass. There is little mineral wealth in Nepal, but about 15 km beyond Pakhar there is an economically viable source of magnesite, a mineral that refractories use. Nepal Orind Magnesite Corporation has a huge open pit mining operation and exports magnesite to India and other countries using a cable ropeway that stretches down to Lamosangu. Buses often stop at either Bhote or at **Muldi** (3540m) for tea or lunch at one of several *bhattis*.

After crossing a pass at 2440m the road makes a long sweep around the head of the valley, finally reaching the large village of **Charikot** at the road junction for **Dolkha** at Km 53.

Dolkha is a large bazaar 3.5 km to the north, and is the departure point for treks to Rolwaling (see the Other Trekking Areas chapter). There are several lodges in Charikot and it might be prudent to grab a snack at the *Sagan Guest House* or the *Laxmi Lodge* if the wait is particularly long, as the police often decide to check trekking permits and record all comings and goings of vehicles and foreigners. Though buses are often late because of breakdowns, road problems or an excess of bureaucratic formalities, you rarely need to spend a night in a hotel along the road. The buses continue their trip at night, no matter how late. The Swiss project has published a pamphlet, titled *Dolkha*, that describes several short treks and excursions in the region near Charikot.

The road descends from Charikot through a region of heavy settlement to Kirantichhap (1300m) at Km 64. It makes a circuitous descent from Kirantichhap into the Tamba

Kosi valley. This is a fertile area, containing a good deal of terraced land for irrigated paddy cultivation. The population is mainly Brahman and Chhetri, but there are also Tamangs and a few Newars. Just before the road crosses the river on a large steel bridge at 800m, there is a junction with a road leading to the large bazaar of Ramechhap, 56 km to the south. The Jiri road makes a steep ascent to a large school at Namdu, then to its neighbouring village, Kabre. Reforestation and agricultural projects, part of the Swiss development scheme, are operating in both villages.

The road climbs above Kabre, then past the road project station at Mina Pokhari to Hanumante Pass, the top of a forested ridge at 2555m. It remains high and contours around the head of the valley in forests above Thulo Chaur. The road descends along the top of a ridge above Jiri to Jiri Bazaar (2100m), where there are a few bhattis and lodges and a weekly Saturday market. It is a short descent to Jiri (1890m), where the road ends at a bus stop beyond a cluster of shops and hotels. The *Sherpa Guide Lodge*, the *Cherdung Lodge* and the *Sagarmatha Hotel* are all along the road, which attracts a collection of buses that start blowing their horns much too early in the morning.

The people of Jiri and the surrounding area are Jirels, a subgroup of the Sunwars whose language is related to that of the Sherpas.

Day 1: Jiri to Bhandar

You have a few choices to make as you plan your first few days of trekking. On your own, you can reach Deorali or Bhandar on the first day (it is a long, hard day) and Sete on the second day, in accordance with the schedule here. If you have porters, or are not in good shape, you may have trouble reaching Bhandar the first day. You will probably have to settle for Shivalaya on the first day and Bhandar on the second day. Whichever way you schedule it, plan on spending a night at either Sete or Sagar to break the long climb to Lamjura Bhanjyang into two stages. The

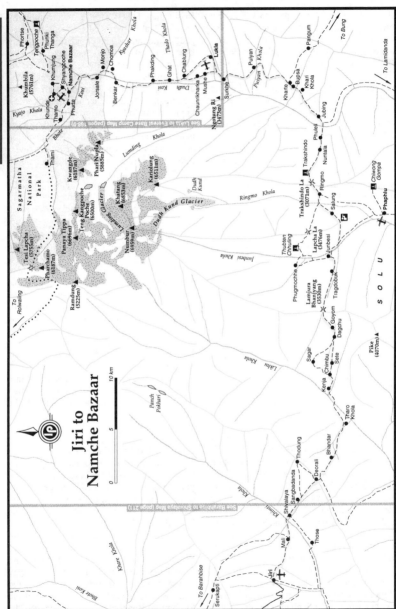

Jiri to
Namche Bazaar

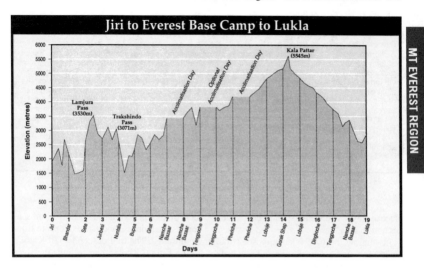

elevation gain from the river to the pass is almost 2000m – a fairly difficult climb to make in a single day unless you are in outstanding condition.

The walking starts at the end of the road, beyond the bus stop. It's a short, level walk through deep forests, then the trail starts uphill to the tiny settlement of Bharkur. Contour for a bit, then climb again to Rato-·mati and through pastures to a few bhattis at Chitre, and the *Solu Khumbu Lodge* a short distance beyond.

Keep climbing to the ridge at 2370m and begin the descent into the Khimti Khola valley. Trek through **Mali**, a sparsely populated Sherpa settlement at 2240m, then down a steep eroded trail to the *Passang Sherpa Lodge*. Drop to the stream, follow above it for a while, then cross it on a steel suspension bridge at 1790m. After a short walk down the river bank the trail emerges into the main valley and the *Shivalaya Tourist Lodge & Restaurant*. A suspension bridge leads to **Shivalaya**, a small bazaar and police checkpost at 1750m. There's decent food and accommodation available in the *Trekking Guide Hotel*, the *Mt Sagarmatha Trek Guide Lodge* and *Good Sherpa Lodge*. The speciality in Shivalaya is banana pie. At night you may hear the howls of *shyaal* (jackals) that roam the nearby hills.

From Shivalaya the route crosses a stream, then starts a steep ascent towards the next pass. Climb to a schoolhouse at **Sangbadanda** (2150m), and the funky *Sushila Lodge*. The trail climbs less steeply past several isolated, but large and prosperous, houses. There are a few bhattis at Kosaribas (2500m), then the trail becomes reasonably level, and even descends a bit, as it goes towards the head of the canyon.

Crossing a stream on a wooden bridge, the trail ascends steeply in forests to another tea shop at Mabir, crosses another stream, this time on two logs, then makes a final climb through forests. On the pass at 2705m is an impressive array of long *mani* walls, signifying that the trek is now entering an area dominated by Tibetan culture. There is a sweeping view of the Likhu Khola valley and Bhandar (Chyangma), a large Sherpa settlement, far below in a hanging valley. The settlement on the pass is called **Deorali**; there are several good lodges here, including the *Lama Guest House*, the *Mt Gaurishankar View* and the *Namaste Lodge*. This is a good

---

Chortens

A *chorten* is literally a receptacle for offerings, and most chortens do have religious relics or the ashes of lamas inside them. Each of the elements of a chorten has a symbolic meaning. The square or rectangular base symbolises the solid earth. On the base is a hemispherical dome, symbolising water. On top of the dome is a rectangular tower, the four sides of which are painted with a pair of eyes, the all-seeing eyes of Buddha. What appears to be a nose is actually the Sanskrit character for the number one, symbolising the absoluteness of Buddha. Above the rectangular tower is a conical or pyramidal spire (symbolising fire) with 13 step-like segments, symbolising the 13 steps leading to Buddhahood. On top of the 13 steps is an ornament shaped like a crescent moon, symbolising air, and a vertical spike, symbolising ether or the sacred light of Buddha.

There are chortens in most villages and on mountain passes in regions of Buddhist influence. A special type of chorten is a *kani*, which is an arch-like monument erected on the trail. A large chorten is called a *stupa*; there are stupas at Boudhanath and Swayambhunath in Kathmandu. ∎

---

place to stay if you want to postpone the long descent to Bhandar.

Just below the pass is an important trail junction. After a one or two-minute walk from the pass, take the left-hand trail towards Bhandar. By continuing straight you would stay high on the ridge, descend to the valley far south of the established trek route, and eventually end up crossing a pass south of Lamjura into the Solu region. Few foreigners ever use this route.

After an initially steep descent on stone steps, the trail reaches the outskirts of **Bhandar** and descends gradually through fields and pastures to a gompa and two imposing *chortens* at 2150m. One has a pyramidal spire and the other has a conical spire. They are painted frequently and are well preserved. There's an excellent camping spot in a large meadow about 15 minutes walk below. Several lodges surround the flagstone-paved village square and several others are just below these; try the *Ang Dawa Lodge*, the *Buddha Lodge* or *Shobha Hotel*. There is a police checkpost just below the square that maintains a logbook with all the comings and goings of trekkers.

Alternative Route via Those The old trail went via **Those** (pronounced 'toe-say') and provides an alternative to the newer, direct route. To reach Those (Maksin) from Jiri, follow a trail downstream along the eastern side of the Jiri Khola. The trail climbs in forests, then drops to join the old route from Lamosangu. The trail descends past Kattike to the Khimti Khola, then follows the river upstream to Those at 1750m. A good camp site is just beyond the suspension bridge. There are several lodges in the village itself. Beware of rooms above smoky kitchens here. Those is a large, pleasant bazaar with a cobblestone street and whitewashed houses. Once the largest market on the trail between Lamosangu and Namche Bazaar, it has diminished greatly in importance now that the Jiri road is complete, and many of the Newar shopkeepers have closed or abandoned their shops and hotels. It's possible to buy items manufactured locally from the nearby sources of low-grade iron ore. Rooster lamps are a speciality. From Those, the trail leads upstream to Shivalaya, where it joins the route from Jiri.

Side Trip: Thodung Cheese Factory You can make a side trip to **Thodung** either by climbing north for about 1¼ hours from the pass at Deorali, or by detouring from the main trail just beyond Sangbadanda. Thodung (3090m) is the site of Nepal's first cheese factory, which was built by the Swiss in the 1950s and is now operated by the Dairy Development Corporation. Your reward for the long, hard climb to the factory is a feast of cheese, yoghurt and yak (actually nak) milk. Cheese is available year round, but other fresh dairy products are available only during autumn. From Thodung you can trek down the ridge and rejoin the main trail at the top of the pass, then descend to Bhandar. Good food and accommodation are available in Thodung if you have the courage to seek out the manager in the presence of several huge Tibetan mastiff dogs.

Day 2: Bhandar to Sete

From the village square at Bhandar the trail descends through the lower fields of the village past the *Downhill Lodge* and *Monsoon Lodge*, then follows a small stream. It crosses the stream on a covered wooden bridge at Deokarba (1980m) and descends through deep forests. Leaving the forests, the trail drops into a canyon, passing Baranda, where the local kids sell walking sticks to help you out on the steep descent. The rough trail finally meets the stream, crossing it at Tharo Khola (1480m). There are a few bhattis near the bridge, but better food is available in Kenja, about 1½ hours away. The route turns north, following the Likhu Khola and crossing it on a high suspension bridge at 1490m. This bridge replaces an ancient chain-link bridge that collapsed under a load of 12 porters during the approach march for the US Everest expedition in 1963. You can see the remains of the abutments for the old bridge just downstream of the new one.

As you follow the trail up the east bank of the river to Kenja, watch for grey langur monkeys in the forests. Continue along the east bank of the river, climbing over a spur, through Namang Gaon, to a small suspension bridge at **Kenja** (1570m), a small village inhabited by Newars and Magars. When I first came here in 1969, Kenja was a single dingy shop. Now there are 15 shops and at least 10 lodges operated by Sherpas who have migrated from Kyama, several km to the north. The *New Everest Guest House*, *Shanker Hotel*, *Sonam Lodge* and others line the flagstone-paved trail. The large *Sherpa Guest House* at the far end of the village has accommodation for more than 40 people. There is a weekly market in Kenja on

Sunday, and a speciality is instant tailoring performed on hand-operated sewing machines. There's also a police checkpost and a video parlour.

Leaving Kenja, the ascent towards the high Lamjura Bhanjyang begins. The first part of the ascent is very steep, then it becomes less severe as you gain elevation. It's a hot walk in the sun, but numerous bhattis along the way offer both shade and refreshment.

After about two hours of climbing, you reach **Chimbu** and the *Top Himalayan Guest House* at 2140m. This is a trail junction. If you are trekking on your own, take the right-hand fork. This is the trail to **Sete** (2575m), a small, defunct monastery where there are several lodges and a camping ground. *Hotel Sunrise*, at the foot of the village, is the newest; the *Sherpa Guide Lodge* and the *Solu Khumbu New Green View Blue Sky Lodge & Restaurant* are near the gompa.

The left fork leads to the north and climbs around the hillside to the Sherpa settlement of Sagar (Chandra) at 2440m, a large village with two-storey stone houses and an ancient village gompa. It is possible to camp in the yard of the school in Sagar, one of the projects of the Himalayan Trust (headed by Sir Edmund Hillary). There are no true hotels here, but this is a Sherpa village, so many people are willing to take guests into their homes. The trek is now completely in Sherpa country. With the exception of Jubing, all the remaining villages from here to Namche Bazaar are inhabited by Sherpas.

Day 3: Sete to Junbesi

It is a long, but fairly gradual, climb – although in spots it gets steep – from Sete to the top of the 3530m Lamjura Bhanjyang. The way is scenic and varied, and this is one of the few parts of the trek where there are no villages. The trek gets into moist mountain forest with huge, gnarled, moss-covered rhododendron, magnolia, maple and birch trees. There is often snow on the trail, and the mornings are usually frosty throughout the trekking season. On very rare occasions snow blocks the pass for a few days, but the crossing usually presents no difficulties.

In spring the ridge is alive with blooming rhododendrons – the white, pink and red blossoms cover the entire hillside. The flowering occurs in a band of a few hundred metres that moves up the hill along with the spring weather. The first blooms start at lower elevations in mid-February and the last ones reach the pass in mid to late April. This day is also a delight for the bird lover. Nepal has more than 800 species of birds and some of the most colourful ones are found in this zone – sunbirds, minavets, flycatchers, tits, laughing thrushes and many others.

About an hour above Sete the trail from Sagar rejoins the route at **Dagchu**, a settlement of several simple lodges near two small ponds at 2880m. The forest changes from pines to rhododendrons, and the trail continues to climb to **Goyom** – several lodges in three different settlements at 3300m. The trail climbs steeply up the ridge to the *Lamijura Sherpa Rest House*, finally reaching a mani wall at 3400m. The trail leaves the ridge and begins to contour northward towards the pass; this section is always muddy and often covered with snow or ice.

After a stretch deep in a forest of large silver birches, the trail reaches open country and a *kharka* (common pasture) at 3430m. This was once strictly a summer settlement used only by herders, but there are now four substantial lodges around a flagstone-paved courtyard. This is a good place to stop for lunch.

Since you will probably be crossing the pass about noon or early afternoon, it will be cloudy, cold and windy. There is no view of Himalayan peaks from the pass, though there are glimpses of the top of some snow peaks on the way up. If you're crossing in the early morning, you will undoubtedly see planes flying over the pass en route to Lukla. The deforestation on the upper portion of this route is shocking; it has all happened in the past 15 years.

It's a half-hour climb from the tea shops to Lamjura Bhanjyang. At 3530m, this is the highest point on the trek between Jiri and

Namche Bazaar. It is marked by a tangle of stones, twigs and prayer flags erected by devout travellers. On the eastern side of the pass the route descends steeply for about 400m through fragrant fir and hemlock forests to a stream and a small wooden hotel. The trail enters open, grassy country and makes a long, gentle descent through fields and pastures to the small settlement of **Tragdobuk** (2860m). There are lodges here, but many close on Saturday when the owners go to the market in Salleri, about three hours walk to the south. The trail climbs to a huge, painted mani stone at the head of the valley, then climbs over the ridge to a vantage point overlooking Junbesi (Jun), a splendid Sherpa village amidst beautiful surroundings at 2675m. Away to the north, Numbur (6959m), known in Sherpa as Shorong Yul Lha ('god of the Solu'), towers over the large, green valley.

Junbesi is the northern end of the Sherpa region known as Solu (Shorong in Sherpa). Before the advent of large-scale tourism, the Sherpas of Solu were economically better off than their cousins in Khumbu because the fertile Solu Valley is at a lower elevation and they can thus grow a wide variety of crops. In recent years employment with expeditions and trekking parties has done much to improve the lot of both the Solu and Khumbu Sherpas.

You can take a short diversion to Serlo monastery at the top of Junbesi village by staying on the upper trail. To reach **Junbesi**, stay on the main trail, which slopes gently down to the village. There is an abundance of accommodation in Junbesi so it is worth doing a bit of investigation before settling in. Several lodges offer hot showers and other enticements. The *Ang Domi Lodge* is the first hotel you reach; in the village square are the large *Junbesi Guest House* (which offers satellite TV) and the very clean *Ang Chopa Lodge*. Pass the telephone office to more lodges near the *kani* (archway) and police post at the foot of the village. Trekking groups camp either behind the *Everest Trekkers Lodge* or below the village on the banks of the river. The Junbesi school is one of the largest and most active of the 28 Hillary schools and has more than 300 pupils attending classes from primary through to high school.

The region near Junbesi is well worth exploring, and a day spent here can offer a variety of alternatives. The yellow-roofed gompa is the oldest in the region. To the north of Junbesi, about two hours away, is **Phugmochhe** (3100m), where you can visit a Traditional Sherpa Art Centre.

Side Trip: Thubten Chhuling En route to Phugmochhe, a short diversion will allow a visit to Thubten Chhuling, a huge Tibetan Buddhist monastery about 1¼ hours walk from Junbesi.

The trail to Thubten Chhuling starts in front of the gompa and follows the Junbesi Khola upstream past a large chorten and a health post. It crosses the river near the Junbesi powerhouse at Mopung, then makes the final climb to the monastery at 3000m. There are big dogs in the monastery courtyard; be sure that you announce yourself so that a monk can restrain them when you pass. The central gompa is large and impressive and often has more than 100 monks and 200 nuns chanting both inside and outside. The monastery expects an offering from any visitor, whether foreign or Sherpa. There is no accommodation or food available here. There are small cells all over the hillside that are the residences of monks and nuns. You won't be welcome at these because many of the inhabitants are on extended meditation programmes. The monastery was founded in the late 1960s by Tushi Rimpoche, who travelled to Nepal with many monks from Rongbuk monastery in Tibet. There are several relics from the original gompa at Rongbuk preserved inside the Thubten Chhuling gompa. This is a large, impressive and active religious community living in exile.

It is possible to rejoin the main trail without returning to Junbesi. To do this, follow a yak trail that climbs from Thubten Chhuling to the Lapcha La (3476m), a pass marked by a large chorten and many prayer flags. The Schneider map does not show this trail, but it shows Thubten Chhuling incorrectly as Mopung. The trail is steep, tiring and confusing, so a guide is almost essential. From the monastery, continue up the hill, cross a stream and angle steeply up the side of the ridge. As you near the ridge there is a maze of trails but you should proceed generally south-east and always up. The trail down from the Lapcha La is a herders' trail that drops steeply to the Ringmo Khola, passing through the yards and fields of several houses. It requires about three hours of tough walking to reach Ringmo from Thubten Chhuling.

Day 4: Junbesi to Nuntala
Below Junbesi the trail crosses the Junbesi Khola on a wooden bridge at 2610m. Just beyond the bridge there is a trail junction. The right-hand or downhill trail leads to Phaphlu, the site of an airstrip and a hospital that is operated by the Himalayan Trust. If you are looking for a bit of luxury, walk to Phaphlu and spend a night at the *Hostelrie de Sherpa* (☎ 038-20166) near the airport. South of Phaphlu is Salleri, the administrative centre for the Solu Khumbu district. The route to Khumbu follows the left-hand trail that leads steeply uphill in the trees. The trail contours above some houses to the end of the ridge, looping in and out of side valleys. After it has climbed high on the ridge, to nearly 2980m at Khurtang, there is an excellent view of Everest, Thamserku (6608m), Kantega (6779m), Kusum Kangru (6367m) and Mera Peak. This is the first view of Everest on the trek, and the peak seems dwarfed by its much lower neighbours. The *Everest View Sherpa Lodge* can provide you with a cup of tea, yak cheese, apples and a comfortable seat from which to contemplate the scene.

The trail turns north, still climbing, then descends past three simple lodges in **Salung** (2980m) to a suspension bridge over the Ringmo Khola at 2570m. This is one of the last opportunities to wash clothes and bathe in a large river, as the next, the Dudh Kosi, is too cold for all but the most determined.

From the river the trail ascends to **Ringmo**, where Dorje Passang, an enterprising (and very patient) Sherpa, has succeeded in raising a large orchard of apples, peaches and apricots. The fruit has become so abundant that many fruit products – including delicious apple *rakshi*, apple cider, dried apples and even apple pickles – are available at reasonable prices from the *Apple House*. There are a few other lodges, including the *Paradise* and *Quiet View*, along the wide trail that passes through Ringmo.

At Ringmo the trail joins the 'road' from Okhaldunga to Namche Bazaar rebuilt by several aid programmes between 1980 and 1984. Labourers widened and levelled the trail and rebuilt many bridges all the way to Namche. The aid programmes paid for the work with food instead of cash. The result will probably never be a motorable road, but you can now walk side by side with your friends on the wide trail and the route avoids many steep ascents and descents that had characterised the old expedition route.

Just beyond Ringmo the trail passes two mani walls. The second wall hides another unexpected opportunity to get lost. After you pass to the left of the mani wall, make a U-turn and head uphill near the rustic wooden *Clean Restaurant*. The straight trail heads north through unpopulated country (with not even a single house), eventually reaching Ghat in the Khumbu Valley after five days. It is not a practical trekking route; several porters perished on this trail during the approach march for the 1952 Swiss Everest expedition.

Assuming you are on the correct trail, it is a short ascent from Ringmo to **Trakshindo La** (3071m), marked by a large chorten. A little above Ringmo is a sign advertising a 15 minute walk to the Trakshindo cheese factory; in 1996 this factory was closed and there was no food or accommodation available there. There is food available at the pass itself in three tea shops.

A few minutes below the pass, on the eastern side, the trail passes the isolated monastery of **Trakshindo**, a superb example of Sherpa monastic architecture at 2900m

elevation. The monastery is certainly the most imposing building seen so far on the trek. Two lodges are outside the monastery grounds. The trail descends through a conifer and rhododendron forest alive with birds. There are a few shepherds' huts alongside the trail, but the route is mostly in dense forest. The trail crosses several picturesque streams on wooden bridges just before it reaches **Nuntala** (Manidingma) at 2250m. There is a huge choice of facilities here. The *Quiet View* and the smaller *Khumbu Guest House* are on the outskirts of town. Pass the paper factory and powerhouse and enter the main part of town, where there are stone-walled compounds enclosing shops and numerous lodges ranging in quality from pretty good to crummy. Facilities include the large *Shangri La Guest House*, *Naulekh View* and *Sherpa Land*; there are some unnamed tea shops along the main street, but these are patronised mostly by porters.

Day 5: Nuntala to Bupsa

From Nuntala the descent continues to the Dudh Kosi ('milk river') – the largest river crossed since the Sun Kosi. Most of the trail is well graded, though it sometimes passes through terraced fields, the yards of houses and the *Neejam Hotel* in Phuleli. The trail descends steeply through scrub forests to the *Rai Tea Shop* and the *Kirant Hotel*. It's a short walk to a new 109m-long suspension bridge across the Dudh Kosi at 1480m. The trek has concluded its trip eastward and now turns north up the Dudh Kosi valley.

Beware of *sisnu* (stinging nettles) between here and Chaunrikharka (see Day 6). Local people use nettles as cattle fodder, as a vegetable (they pick them with bamboo tongs) and to make rough cloth. The nettles inflict a painful rash the instant you touch them. At the end of the bridge, turn left and climb steeply out of the river valley through fields of barley, wheat and corn to the sprawling village of **Jubing** (Dorakbuk) and the *Gurkhali Lodge* at 1680m. The people of this village are Rais. Look for signs of Rai culture in this area – the garlands of marigolds that decorate the Dudh Kosi bridge and the traditional bamboo pipes instead of plastic hose for the village water supply.

The trail stays below the village, climbing past the *Green Garden Hotel* to the *Amar Hotel* and the post office at its northern edge at an elevation of 1800m. Beyond Jubing there is a short climb across a side valley, then another climb to two lodges at Choka. Stay on the highest trail and make a long, steep climb to the top of a spur at 2100m. From this ridge you can see Khari Khola (Khati Thenga) below you and the peak of Khumbila (5761m) at the northern end of the Dudh Kosi valley. Descend a bit on a sandy trail, then it's a long but pleasant walk into Khari Khola at 2070m. This is predominantly a Sherpa village, though it also has a small Magar community. It is a large village, and there are numerous lodges spread out throughout it and competition is intense. The first establishment you come to is the *Sagarmatha Lodge*, which offers free lodging if you eat there. Other hotels at the western end of town are the *Trekkers Inn* and the *Namaste Hotel*. In the noisy and congested bazaar in the centre of town at 1960m are shops, including a tailor shop, and the *Blue Haven*, *River View*, *Five Star* and *Nuru* hotels.

From Khari Khola you can see your next destination: a cluster of buildings high above on the ridge in Bupsa. You can add a day to your programme and have a more leisurely trek by staying in Khari Khola and spending the following nights in Surkhe and Phakding before continuing to Namche.

The trail descends from the village and crosses the Khari Khola on a suspension bridge near some water-driven mills at 1930m, then makes a steep climb to **Bupsa** (Bumshing) at 2300m. There is a tea shop halfway up the ridge and a big hotel complex on the ridge that includes the *Everest Guest House*, *Hotel Yellow Top* and *LT Sherpa Guide Lodge*. There are some less fancy lodges in Kharte, about 20 minutes up the trail. The tiny Bupsa gompa is said to be 50 years old and is in pretty poor condition. The lama is seeking donations in the hope of renovating it and will be happy to show you around.

Day 6: Bupsa to Ghat

From Bupsa the trail climbs steadily, but gently, through forests inhabited by monkeys. The Dudh Kosi canyon is extremely steep, and in many places you can see all the way to the river, 1000m below. Climb past several tea shops to a mani wall on the ridge, where there are views of Khumbila and Cho Oyu (8153m). Keep climbing up to a cleft in the rock, then into another canyon before reaching a bamboo tea shop on the ridge at 2840m overlooking Puiyan (Chitok), a Sherpa settlement of about 10 houses completely surrounded by forests at 2720m. Much of the forest near this village was cut down in the 1970s to make charcoal which many hotels and villagers used for fuel in the Khumbu region before kerosene became easily available.

From the ridge, the trail turns almost due east as it descends into the deep canyon of the Puiyan Khola. This portion of the trail was built during the 1984 renovation; in many places it is narrow and exposed, especially where it was blasted out of a vertical rock wall. At one point there is a collection of logs and shrubbery to give you a false sense of security as the trail crosses a rock face above a precipice. After crossing a large slide area, the trail climbs on a stone staircase. Be careful; at least two trekkers have fallen on this portion of the trail.

After crossing a stream on a wooden bridge, you reach the Puiyan Khola, where an extensive bhatti for porters has been built into a cave formed by a large, overhanging rock. A few minutes beyond the bridge are a hotel complex and a camp site. The *Hotel Mountain View* and the *New Kala Patar* are probably the best bets among the eight lodges in this very jungly village. There are a few less substantial lodges scattered along the trail as you walk through the forests that surround Puiyan.

The trail climbs up and down for about an hour after Puiyan to several tea shops that make up the hamlet of Chewabas, then to a tea shop on a ridge at 2750m. Traverse and climb to another ridge that offers a good view of the Khumbu region. You will easily pick out Lukla from here by its airstrip and multitude of large buildings. You might also be able to spot the remains of one of the planes that crashed there. The trail descends to a tea shop, then makes a long, 500m drop to **Surkhe** (Buwa) at 2290m on the Surkhe Khola, a small tributary of the Dudh Kosi. The fancy *Yak and Yeti Home* offers the best accommodation. There are a few tea shops near the bridge, but some of these cater to the porters who serve the Namche market. Beware of Friday and Saturday nights in Surkhe and adjoining villages. The porters to and from the market start to travel at first light – if there is a full moon, this can be at 2 am – causing an uproar in every hotel.

From Surkhe the trail climbs for about 15 minutes to a junction where a stone staircase leads off to the right. This is the trail to Lukla; it requires about an hour of steep climbing to reach the airstrip. It is not necessary to go to Lukla at this point unless you want to make a reservation for a flight back to Kathmandu, though all you will usually accomplish is to get yourself put on a waiting list. To get to Lukla, climb the stone steps and follow the trail up a gully, then onto a ridge. The trail passes several small valleys, through a forest that has been severely denuded by woodcutters, then comes to a stream. Cross the stream on a wooden bridge near two houses and climb to the ridge. The trail switchbacks through rocks to the foot of the airstrip. You can head up either side of the runway; there are trails just outside the barbed-wire fence. Both routes pass the litter of propellers, wheels, wings and other pieces of crashed planes. Since you don't know whether planes are coming, it's not a good idea to walk up the runway itself.

The Khumbu trail goes north up the steep canyon on a route that a Sherpa contractor blasted out of the rock. The trail crosses the large stream that comes from Lukla, then climbs steeply up some wobbly stone steps past several caves to another stream where there is a small bhatti. It's a half-hour walk uphill through a jumble of boulders past several stone houses to a series of mani walls in **Mushe** (Nangbug). There are more mani stones and walls as you trek along the wide stone trail through Mushe. Unlike the houses along the rest of the trek, very few of the houses in Mushe have been converted into tea shops. Mushe blends almost imperceptibly into Chaunrikharka (Dungde), a large village at 2630m.

The region from Khari Khola to Jorsale is called Pharak. The Sherpas in this area have slightly different traditions from their neighbours in Solu and Khumbu and have better agricultural opportunities due to the gentler climate in the Dudh Kosi valley. Pharak villagers raise large crops of corn (maize) and potatoes in summer. They grow wheat, turnips, cauliflower and cabbage in winter and raise herds of cows and yak crossbreeds, as well as sheep and goats.

The first hotel in **Chaunrikharka** is the *Namaste Lodge* on the right of the trail just after the short, steep climb from Mushe. The better lodges are beyond the stone kani over the trail. Around the corner, near a large chorten, are a small shop, the *Tourist Lodge & Restaurant* and the *Buddha Lodge*. There are three more chortens, a gompa and some wonderful mani walls, then the trail climbs, gently through fields at first, then steeply, to a small ridge at the beginning of Chablung (Lomdza).

The trail from Lukla now joins the route and the character of the trek changes abruptly. When flights are able to operate, more than 100 trekkers fly into Lukla every day. If you have walked from Jiri, you will immediately recognise those who have stepped straight off the plane – their clothes are cleaner than yours and they don't smell. From here on, accommodation becomes more frequent, crowded and expensive. Between 1990 and 1997 more than 150 new lodges have been built between here and Namche Bazaar.

For the rest of the day, follow the route described in Day 1 of the Lukla to Everest Base Camp trek to reach **Ghat**. This is a longish day; there are plenty of places to stay in Chaunrikharka and Chablung if you don't feel like pushing on, and you can still easily reach Namche the following day.

Day 7: Ghat to Namche Bazaar

This is described as part of Day 1 and all of Day 2 of the Lukla to Everest Base Camp trek. You will enjoy the climb to Namche more than those who flew to Lukla because you'll be in good physical condition and have a better understanding of your surroundings.

Lukla to Everest Base Camp

Duration 15 days
Difficulty Medium to hard
Maximum elevation 5545m
Permit cost US$5 per week plus Rs 650
Season October to December
Hotels Excellent
Summary Fly in by plane or helicopter and walk to the Sherpa village of Namche Bazaar, the monastery at Tengpoche and on to Everest base camp. It is important to allow enough time on this trek for acclimatisation. Can be very crowded in the high season.

Season

It's possible to trek in the Khumbu year round. Helicopters operate to Lukla during the monsoon, and the summer is a lovely time to visit Khumbu. The best weather is in autumn, but it can be frightfully crowded. There can be clouds and rain during spring, but the weather is warmer and the days are longer than in autumn. It can be bitterly cold in winter as soon as the sun drops behind the mountains at about 3.30 pm, but the days are comfortable. At some time during the season from October to March there is certain to be a snowstorm or two that will blanket the countryside with snow. Depending on the depth, it will either vanish immediately or, as it did after the blizzard of 1995, remain on the ground until April.

Warning

Be sure to read the section on altitude illness in the Health & Safety chapter before you start this trek, and be sure to seek help if you exhibit severe symptoms. There are several rest days suggested in the following trail description. They are very important for acclimatisation, and will allow you to see much more of the Khumbu region than you'd see if you rushed to base camp.

Access

After a long wait at the Kathmandu airport and an exciting landing at Lukla, you'll emerge from the plane to a throng of sherpas, porters and trekking company representatives clamouring for your attention. Nearby will be a group of trekkers clutching their boarding passes waiting to board your plane for the return flight to Kathmandu. Behind a barbed-wire fence will be the mournful faces of those who did not get a seat on this flight. If you arrived by helicopter, hide behind a building when it takes off or you'll get a real dust bath.

If you are trekking with a group, your sirdar should magically appear and hustle you off for tea while the sherpas organise things for the trek. Most trekking companies do not make the final preparations for the trek until they actually see the trekkers get off the plane. If you are on your own, you can retire to one of Lukla's numerous hotels to plan your next move.

Day 1: Lukla to Phakding

The trail from Lukla, elevation 2800m, leads north from the airstrip past lodges, *carom* game parlours, airline offices and shops to the edge of the Lukla plateau. The trail drops steeply for a bit, then descends gently past the Chaunrikharka school to the intersection of the Jiri trail at Chablung, elevation 2660m.

In **Chablung** try the *Kwange Hotel & Lodge* or the *Himalayan Guest House* with its glass-enclosed dining room overlooking the trail. The gompa, high on the hill under a cliff, is being renovated and is worth a visit. From Chablung the trail crosses a stream, makes a detour around a large mani stone, passes a few lodges, then heads north through a brief stretch of forest. The trail descends steeply to the Thado Khola (also

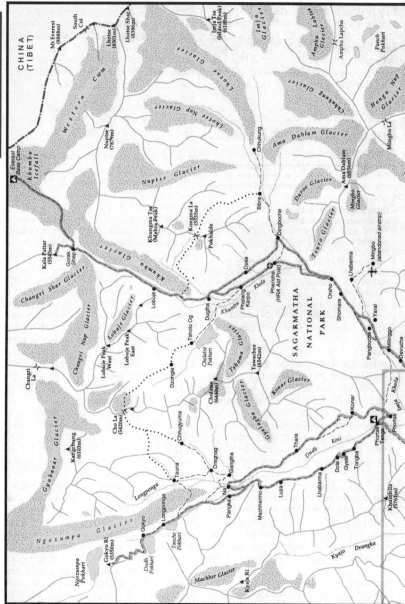

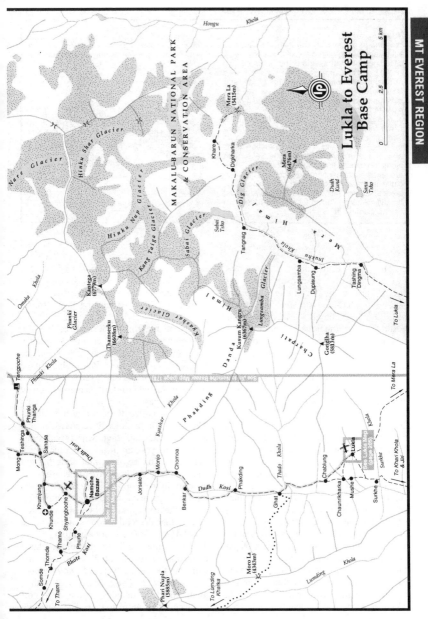

Lukla to Everest
Base Camp

Yaks

We tend to oversimplify the many manifestations of the yak into this single word, yet it is only the full-blooded, long-haired bull of the species *Bos grunniens* that truly has the name yak. The female is called *nak* by Sherpas and *dri* by Tibetans.

Yaks and naks are crossbred with local cows or Tibetan bulls, which the Sherpas call *lang* and Nepalis call *khirkoo*. A nak-lang or yak-cow crossbreed is a *dzopkyo* if it is male and a *dzum* if it is female.

A dzum is prized for its butterfat-rich milk, which Sherpas use to make cheese and butter. The male crossbreed, the infertile dzopkyo, is (relatively) docile and is used to transport loads and as a draft animal. Most of the 'yaks' seen along the trails of Khumbu are dzopkyos. There are numerous other names for crosses between cattle and for second-generation cross-breeds, but yak, nak, dzum and dzopkyo should be sufficiently confusing for this short lesson in yak husbandry. ■

known as the Kusum Kangru Khola), crossing it on a local-style suspension bridge. Just past the bridge are the *Saino Lodge* and Passang Temba's *Tawa Lodge*. The peak at the head of the valley is Kusum Kangru, the most difficult of the trekking peaks.

Soon you will probably meet your first yaks, wonderful shaggy beasts that create lumbering mobile roadblocks on the trail. Technically, the animals you will meet are mostly *dzopkyos*, male crossbreeds of yaks and cows, but 'yak' is easier to remember and pronounce. Though yaks are uncomfortable at low elevations, Sherpas use them to transport trekking gear between Lukla and Everest base camp. They are relatively tame and well controlled, but beware of waving horns or an out-of-control yak roaring down a steep hill. Yaks are all-purpose animals. In addition to their role as load carriers, their wool is woven into blankets and ropes, dung is burned as fuel and female yaks give high-quality milk. Since yaks are relatives of the cow, their slaughter is prohibited in Nepal, but when one of these sure-footed animals 'falls off the trail', the tasty meat makes its way into yak steaks and yakburgers in restaurants throughout Khumbu. Since 1992 the yaks have been joined by teams of mules that

carry loads for both trekkers and the Namche market. Yaks, mules, porters, Sherpas, trekkers, army and government officials all crowd the trail, often causing severe traffic jams.

Beyond the Kusum Kangru bridge, the trail climbs a bit, then contours around a ridge to **Ghat** (Lhawa), at 2530m, on the banks of the Dudh Kosi. Part of this village and much of the old trail were washed away by floods in 1997 (described below). A new trail climbs past several smaller lodges to the large *Lama Lodge* at the top of the village. The owner, Dorje Lama, has a private gompa and has marked the prayer wheels with signs instructing you to turn them clockwise. People sleep on the funny platforms that you can see in the fields in order to chase bears away from the crops. Cross a ridge marked with painted mani stones and climb a bit above the river, passing several scattered houses, then descend a stone staircase to the *Hotel Alpine Trekkers* and a camping place. The trail climbs again to **Phakding**, a huge collection of lodges at 2800m. You first come to the well-advertised *International Trekkers Guest House* (quiet, and with a good view from its beds), and after a short distance seven more lodges. The big *Kala*

Sagarmatha National Park – Rules & Requirements

At the entrance station to Sagarmatha National Park in Monjo, the rangers check your trekking permit. The rules printed on the back of the entrance ticket are:

Children below 12 years of age shall pay half the entry fee. This permit is nontransferable and good for one entry only. You enter the park on your own risk. His Majesty's Government shall bear no liability for damage, loss, injury or death. Trekking is an acceptable challenge, but please do not:

- litter (dispose it properly)
- remove anything from the park
- disturb wildlife
- carry arms and explosives
- scale any mountain without proper permission
- scale any sacred peaks of any elevation

Please keep all the time to the main trek routes. Please be self sufficient in your fuel supply before entering the park. Buying fuel wood from local people or removing any wood materials from the forest is illegal. This will apply to your guides, cooks and porters also.

Park personnel are entitled to arrest any person in charge of having violated park regulations or search his belongings.

For further information visit Park headquarter or ask any park personnel.

National Parks Family Wishes Your Trip Pleasant.

Local people are not required to use firewood to cook food for trekkers. If you are staying in hotels and wish to minimise your impact, you should patronise only those few hotels that cook exclusively on electricity, gas or kerosene. Hotels do this in the Annapurna region, but because there are no firm rules, many hotels in Khumbu still rely on huge piles of firewood. In theory, the national park rules will eventually prohibit this.

It is not difficult to buy kerosene for fuel, but it's almost impossible to find petrol or cooking gas. Kerosene is usually available in Namche at the Saturday market in 16-litre tins that are carried by porters from the roadhead south of Okhaldunga. The price is negotiable depending on demand. Lesser quantities are available from shopkeepers in Namche throughout the week. If you plan to use kerosene, bring along a filter. Dirt and water can mess up stoves, and both are present in most of the locally available kerosene.

Lukla general store operates a kerosene depot out of the Yeti Lodge near the RNAC check-in counter in Lukla. It supplies kerosene and stocks stoves, jerry cans, lanterns and repair parts – available for either sale or rent. It maintains a smaller supply in Namche Bazaar, but Lukla is the main source of kerosene in Khumbu. Kerosene is an unpleasant load for porters. It sloshes around and throws people off balance, and plastic jerry cans and tins always leak and cause chemical burns and irritate the skin of the porters. The Lukla kerosene depot transports kerosene to Lukla by plane and helicopter and has been quite successful in maintaining a reliable supply. The price is high because of the exorbitant cost of the flights. In 1996 the cost was Rs 50 per litre in Lukla and Rs 60 per litre at the Namche depot compared to the official rate of Rs 9.50 per litre in Kathmandu. The price is not unreasonable, however, because it costs Rs 3 to Rs 4 per litre per day to carry kerosene from Jiri by porter. ■

Patar Lodge caters to organised teahouse treks; the other up-market hotel is the *Tashi Taki Lodge*. The trail crosses a stream to another bunch of lodges, including the *Namaste Lodge* and several other smaller facilities.

In September 1977 an avalanche from Ama Dablam fell into a lake near the base of the peak. This created a wave of water 10m high that raced down the Dudh Kosi and washed away large parts of the trail, seven bridges and part of Jorsale, killing three villagers. The drama was repeated in 1985

when a glacial lake above Thami broke loose. There is another glacial lake building up near Chhukung, above Dingboche. When the moraine that created this lake breaks there will be yet another flood here, so be prepared for changes in this part of the route.

Just beyond the cluster of lodges at Phakding, the first signs of this devastation become apparent. Beyond the *Riverside Lodge* cross the suspension bridge to the *Five Star Hotel* and some group camping grounds. Below the camp, near the river, are the stone cottages of the defunct *Khumbu Alpine Camp*. You can climb to the gompa in Gumila, high on the hill above Phakding, for views of the high peaks. The icy winds from Khumbu combine with the river dampness to make Phakding a particularly chilly spot.

Day 2: Phakding to Namche Bazaar

From Phakding the trail continues north up the Dudh Kosi valley, staying 100m or so above the river on its west bank as it passes several new hotels in Zamphuti. The trail crosses a small stream where a tiny lodge sits on the opposite side of the wooden bridge. Take the route straight up the hill and do not follow the old level trail that leads to the right. Climb through fields past a few lodges to a waterfall. A short distance beyond the waterfall there is an excellent view to the east of the peak of Thamserku. Climb steeply over a rocky ridge, then traverse high above the river to **Benkar** at 2700m. There are several hotels here; the largest are the *River View* on the ridge just as you enter the village and the *Thamserku View Lodge* just below. Beyond Benkar the trail crosses the Dudh Kosi to its east bank on a new suspension bridge.

The trail follows a pleasant route along-side the river, then climbs to **Chomoa**, the site of an agricultural project that was set up to serve the Hotel Everest View. The largest facility is the *Hatago Lodge*, a creation of eccentric Mr Hagayuki, who lived here for almost 10 years without a visa before being deported. He was one of the most colourful of Nepal's many strange characters. All along this part of the trail, villages are interspersed with magnificent forests of rhododendron, magnolia and giant firs. In both the early autumn and late spring, the flowers on this portion of the trek make it a beautiful walk. On the cliffs above the river it is possible to see musk deer and Himalayan tahr. If you sit quietly beside the Dudh Kosi you may see water rats swimming in the fast current. When I first heard of these, I assumed they must be related to the legendary yeti, but they actually do exist in the river here and further upstream towards Thami.

From the lodge at Chomoa, the trail climbs a bit to another hotel (there are more than 300 inns and lodges in Khumbu) and a camp site, then descends steeply into a big valley below Thamserku. The trail crosses the Kyashar Khola and climbs out of the valley to **Monjo**. The *Mount Kailas Lodge* with its solar electricity is up a little rise at the northern end of the settlement of only three or four houses at 2800m elevation. The small Uche Chholing monastery is on a hill above the village; if you wish to contribute to this monastery, there is a convenient donation box just beside the trail.

Just beyond Monjo the trek enters the Sagarmatha (Everest) National Park. There is an entrance station where rangers check your entrance permit to be sure you have paid the Rs 650 fee.

Beyond the entrance station, the trail makes a steep rocky descent to a large farm. The trail turns left at the cluster of buildings at the bottom of the hill, crosses the Dudh Kosi on a high 120m-long Swiss-built suspension bridge and follows the west bank. A short distance up the river is **Jorsale** (Thumbug) at 2810m. Several lodges are packed together along the main street of Jorsale, and you usually have to detour around cows and crowds of porters hanging around the village. The trail follows the river for a while, then recrosses the Dudh Kosi, follows along the river bank, then makes a steep climb near the confluence of two rivers – the Bhote Kosi from the west and the Dudh Kosi from the east. The trail crosses the Dudh Kosi on a suspension bridge that's at a dizzying height above the river. The approach to the bridge on the north end is up a set of steep concrete stairs; it's prudent to choose a time when there are no yaks on the bridge – or the stairs – to make your crossing.

The climb to Namche is long and takes you from a 'safe' altitude to one in which altitude sickness is a real danger. One important aid to acclimatisation is to avoid getting exhausted; therefore, it is important to *walk slowly on this hill*. Many fit trekkers have spoiled their trek by racing up this hill and becoming exhausted or worse. After a long climb up switchbacks there is a view of

Mt Everest peeking over the ridge of Nuptse. Because clouds usually obscure the peaks in the afternoon, Everest will probably not be visible when you reach this point. Leaving the ridge, the trail climbs less steeply, but still steadily, through pine forests to a national park forest nursery and some tea shops at Mishulung. Just beyond is a small spring and a hydraulic ram system that – when it works – pumps water to the national park and army offices on the hill. When the trail turns into a stream, take the right, upper trail to reach the main street of Namche. The

left-hand trail leads to the lower pastures of the village.

Namche Bazaar (Nauche), at 3440m, is the administrative centre for the Khumbu region and has a police checkpost, the headquarters for Sagarmatha National Park, numerous shops selling items of every description and a proliferation of hotels and restaurants among its 100-odd houses. One of the first places you reach as you enter Namche is *Hermann Helmer's Bäckerei und Conditorei*, which uses the village's abundant electricity supply to bake pizzas, sticky

MT EVEREST REGION

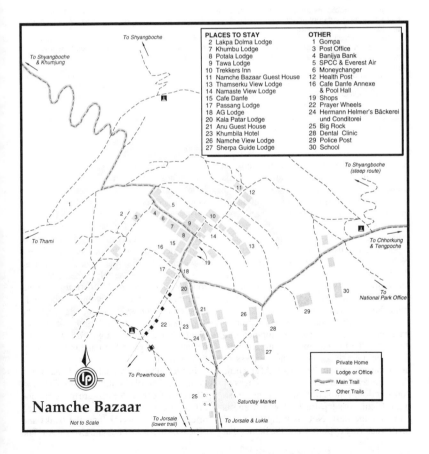

PLACES TO STAY
2 Lakpa Dolma Lodge
7 Khumbu Lodge
8 Potala Lodge
9 Tawa Lodge
10 Trekkers Inn
11 Namche Bazaar Guest House
13 Thamserku View Lodge
14 Namaste View Lodge
15 Cafe Danfe
17 Passang Lodge
18 AG Lodge
20 Kala Patar Lodge
21 Anu Guest House
23 Khumbila Hotel
26 Namche View Lodge
27 Sherpa Guide Lodge

OTHER
1 Gompa
3 Post Office
4 Banijya Bank
5 SPCC & Everest Air
6 Moneychanger
12 Health Post
16 Cafe Danfe Annexe & Pool Hall
19 Shops
22 Prayer Wheels
24 Hermann Helmer's Bäckerei und Conditorei
25 Big Rock
28 Dental Clinic
29 Police Post
30 School

To Shyangboche
To Shyangboche & Khumjung
To Thami
To Shyangboche (steep route)
To Chhorkung & Tengpoche
To National Park Office
To Powerhouse
To Jorsale (lower trail)
Saturday Market
To Jorsale & Lukla

Private Home
Lodge or Office
Main Trail
Other Trails

Namche Bazaar

Not to Scale

Sagarmatha Pollution Control Committee

The Sagarmatha Pollution Control Committee (SPCC) was founded in 1991 with the help of the World Wildlife Fund and the Nepal Department of National Parks and Wildlife Conservation. It is in the process of changing its name to the Khumbu Environmental Conservation Committee.

The organisation is based in the Khumbu region with local inhabitants staffing it. Villagers also serve as elected members of the committee, chaired by the rimpoche of Tengpoche monastery. It undertakes a wide variety of activities, with its main concerns being the environment, cultural conservation, community services and the sustainable development of tourism.

The committee receives funding from the Ministry of Tourism and Civil Aviation, which is making an effort to plough back some of the revenue from peak fees into conservation in Khumbu. The committee's mandate includes:

- preservation of cultural heritage
- preservation of natural heritage
- litter removal
- education

In addition to public awareness campaigns, SPCC has organised lodge owner training, emphasising fuel efficiency, food conservation and hygiene. Conservation education programmes have also been established in local schools.

SPCC maintains visitor information centres in Namche and Lukla where you can learn about their activities and get information on trekking. These visitor centres are equipped with telephones. There is also a radio-telephone at Tengpoche, where a trained member of staff runs a first aid and rescue post.

Trails and bridges are maintained on the main trekking routes. Support has been given for village trail maintenance and the congested market place at Namche has been enlarged. Other community service projects have included providing water supplies, maintaining Namche's water prayer wheels, and health education schemes. ■

buns, bread and other delicacies to tempt you as you walk into town. You can stock up on food, film, postcards and souvenirs. You can also buy or rent any trekking or climbing gear that you need. If you discover that your jacket or sleeping bag is not warm enough, you can rent one here. Several trekkers have reported that postcards they sent from the Namche post office actually reached their destinations. On the hill is a dental clinic, sponsored by the American Himalayan Foundation, that is staffed by two Canadian-trained dental therapists.

It is probably futile trying to keep up to date on the latest tourist developments in Namche. The flow of money into Khumbu from trekkers has encouraged excessive hotel construction in the village. At any time there are several hotels in various stages of construction, renovation and expansion, so it's difficult to keep track of which one is currently the best. Not counting the small bhattis catering to porters and the homes that

offer food and accommodation but do not have hotel signs, there are at least 11 major hotels here. The most popular is Lakpa Dorje's *Trekkers Inn*, which churns out yak steaks by the hundred. One of the largest is Passang Kami's *Khumbu Lodge*, which offers private rooms including the 'Jimmy Carter slept here' suite. At the *Tawa Lodge* you can sit in the sun and watch the village activity as you eat freshly baked cinnamon rolls. *Namche Bazaar Guest House* also has a camping ground and features Friday night slide shows. Other popular lodges are the *Thamserku View*, *Kala Pattar* and *Sherpa Guide*. Nima Nuru's large *Cafe Danfe* has private rooms, good food and the only pool hall in town.

In the centre of Namche the Sagarmatha Pollution Control Committee (SPCC) has an information centre. Nearby are the telephone office, bank and moneychanger (which offers speedier service than the bank) and offices of Asian Airlines and Everest Air. The

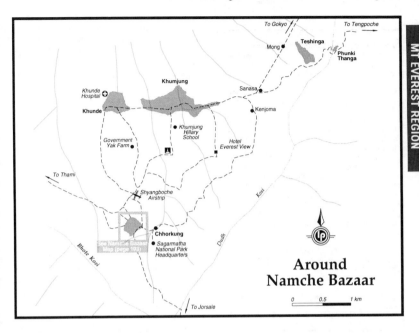

To Gokyo / To Tengpoche
Mong ● Teshinga
Phunki
Thanga

Khumjung
Sanasa
Khunde ✚
Hospital
Khunde
Kenjoma
Khumjung
Hillary
School
Government
Yak Farm ● Hotel
Everest View

To Thami
Shyangboche
Airstrip

Kosi

See Namche Bazaar
Map (page 193)

Chhorkung
● Sagarmatha
National Park
Headquarters

Bhote Kosi

Dudh

To Jorsale

**Around
Namche Bazaar**

0   0.5   1 km

large area fenced in by stones above Namche is a forest plantation. Sometimes tahr come into the upper part of Namche and eat the potatoes in the fields. There are three competing clocks in the village. The bank, police and army all sound the hour, day and night, by striking an empty oxygen cylinder.

Historically, Sherpas were herders and traders. Namche Bazaar was the staging point for expeditions over the Nangpa La into Tibet with loads of manufactured goods from India. On the return trip they brought wool, yaks and salt. Today, Sherpas raise barley, potatoes and a few vegetables in the barren fields of Khumbu, but their economy has always relied on trading. As you walk through Khumbu you will see women excavating potatoes from the deep pits in which they store them during winter to keep them from freezing. Trekking has provided the people of Khumbu with the income to remain here despite the limited indigenous food supply.

Day 3: Acclimatisation Day in Namche

Acclimatisation is important before proceeding higher. This is the first of two specific 'acclimatisation days' that everyone should build into their trek schedule. You can spend the day by taking a day hike to Thami (see the Namche Bazaar to Thami section later in this chapter), by visiting Khunde or Khumjung, or by relaxing and exploring Namche Bazaar. Many hotels in Namche offer slide shows at night.

One formality that you must complete before you spend the day gorging yourself on apple pie or getting sloshed on rakshi is registration with the police. The police checkpost is on the hill to the east of Namche near the school. The police officials endorse your trekking permit and enter the details into a register. Sometimes there is a form to fill in and often the police require that trekkers sign the register. If so, you will have to go personally to the police checkpost, but often a trekking guide can take your permit

MT EVEREST REGION

The Saturday Market in Namche

Each Saturday in Namche there is an important weekly *haat* or market. Lowland people come to sell corn, rice, eggs, vegetables and other items not grown in Khumbu. During the trekking season, butchers usually slaughter two or more buffaloes each week, so meat is available on Saturday and Sunday.

Porters carry their loads to Namche Bazaar from villages six to 10 days away (the buffaloes walk themselves) and sell their wares directly. It is an important social event, as well as the focus for the region's trade. Sherpas from all the neighbouring villages come to purchase food and socialise, and the bazaar becomes a crowded rumpus of Sherpas, government officials, porters and sightseers. It is a cash market, in which Sherpas exchange money they have received from trekking or mountaineering parties for the goods they require. The market starts early and is usually finished by noon.

The fun-loving Sherpas often tell the Rais and other people who carry goods to the market that the money comes from Mt Everest, and it is not uncommon to find an unsuspecting lowland porter shivering with cold as he accompanies a trekking party to Everest base camp in search of the free money that tumbles from the highest peak on earth. ■

---

and undertake the formalities for you. Bring both your trekking permit and national park entrance ticket for police to examine.

Above the police checkpost, at the top of the hill, is the Sagarmatha National Park headquarters (☎ 038-21114). The visitor centre is well worth a visit. It has displays about the people, forests, wildlife, mountaineering and the impact of tourism.

The name of the region above Namche, but below the national park headquarters, is **Chhorkung**. This suburb of Namche has grown a lot, and now has several lodges and camping grounds. By far the largest is Lhakpa Sonam's *Hotel Sherwi Khangba*, which has private rooms, a museum, library, photo gallery (the owner is a photographer), cultural centre and its own chorten. It's quieter and less dusty here; other facilities include the *Passang Lodge* and *Tengpoche Lodge*.

Some of Namche's strangest visitors are the runners in the Everest Marathon, held in late November of odd-numbered years. The run follows a route from Gorak Shep to Tengpoche, then to Namche and a loop out to Thamo before returning to the finishing line in Namche. Runners complete the 42 km (26 mile) run in a respectable 4½ to five hours, but remember that they made a slow ascent in order to acclimatise.

You may also encounter Tibetan refugees who have crossed the Nangpa La and are headed for Dharamsala in India, the home of the Dalai Lama and the Tibet Government in Exile.

Day 4: Namche Bazaar to Tengpoche

There is a direct, reasonably level, route from Namche Bazaar to Tengpoche that starts at Chhorkung, winds around the hill to the tea and souvenir shops of Kenjoma, and joins the trail from Khumjung just before Sanasa. Look for tahr on the hillside below the trail in the early morning.

A more varied, slightly longer route visits Khumjung, the largest village in Khumbu, at the foot of the sacred peak of Khumbila. From Namche Bazaar it is a steep one-hour climb to the Shyangboche airstrip, which serves the Hotel Everest View. In the early morning you might see the spectacular landing (or the more spectacular takeoff) of a Pilatus Porter STOL plane or a big Russian helicopter at Shyangboche.

There are a few tea shops near the airstrip that cater to helicopter passengers. From the airstrip it is a 20-minute walk to the hotel, which provides excellent views of Everest and Ama Dablam. The hotel was closed for many years, but was refurbished in 1990. You can get a cup of coffee or tea or an extravagant meal here. Breakfast is US$7, lunch US$12 and dinner US$16, plus tax. Rooms are US$135 per person per night with an extra charge for oxygen or a pressurised room. Just outside the door of the posh hotel is a bhatti that offers cheaper food and lodging.

A trail descends from the hotel to **Khumjung** village (3790m), or you can walk from the airstrip directly to Khumjung. To take the direct trail from the airport, head for the chorten at the top of the hill and follow the trail down through the forest. In the morning, just follow the schoolchildren from Namche to Khumjung.

The Khumjung gompa possesses what is said to be the skull of a yeti, or abominable snowman. Sir Edmund Hillary, village headman Khunjo Chumbi, Desmond Doig and Marlin Perkins took this relic to the USA in 1960 to be examined by scientists. The scientists said the scalp was made from the skin of a serow, a member of the antelope family, but the yeti legend still continues.

Also in Khumjung is the original Hillary school, which has succeeded in providing an excellent primary education for many of the children of Khumbu. In 1983 the Himalayan Trust expanded the facility to include a high school. Sherpa children no longer have to go to boarding school at Salleri, a week away, to complete their education. It is only a short detour from Khumjung to **Khunde**, the site of the Khunde Hospital, built in 1966 and still maintained by the Himalayan Trust. The *Nima Lodge* is below the gompa in Khumjung, and there are several other lodges in lower Khumjung near the school. The *Everest Bakery* uses electric ovens to produce bread and rolls and sells them from the attached restaurant and coffee shop.

From Khumjung the trail goes eastwards down the valley, continuously passing picturesque mani walls and chortens. After a short descent it meets the main Namche Bazaar to Tengpoche trail. Beyond a few mani stones is another group of tea stalls. This settlement, called **Sanasa** by the locals and 'schlockmeister junction' by trek leaders, is inhabited primarily by Tibetans. There is always an extensive display of Tibetan (and made-in-Kathmandu) souvenirs to tempt you. Bargaining is very much in order. The trail descends gradually to Labisyasa, just at the foot of **Teshinga**, where there are a few tea shops. The trail drops steeply on a dusty trail to **Phunki Thanga**, a small settlement with three small lodges and several water-driven prayer

wheels on the banks of the Dudh Kosi at 3250m. The army post is part of the national park administration.

It is a two-hour climb from Phunki Thanga to **Tengpoche**. The trail climbs steeply at first, then makes a gradual ascent through forests and around mani stones as it follows the side of a hill up to the saddle on which the monastery sits at 3870m, in a clearing surrounded by dwarf firs and rhododendrons. The view from this spot, seen to best advantage in the morning, is rightly deemed to be one of the most magnificent in the world. Kwangde (6187m), Tawachee (6542m), Everest, Nuptse (7879m), Lhotse (8501m), Ama Dablam, Kantega and Thamserku provide an inspiring panorama of Himalayan giants. Kantega means 'horse saddle', and from Tengpoche it's clear how this peak got its name.

The following sign used to appear near the monastery guesthouse:

I am happy to welcome you to Tengpoche. This is the religious centre of the whole 'Sherpa-land', in fact the entire Solu-Khumbu area.

A very modest rest house has been built on the far end of the meadow facing Chomolungma (Mt Everest).

It has been erected with the funds collected from friends and visitors who have come to this sacred and beautiful place. If you wish, you may contribute to our meagre funds to enable us to make it more comfortable when you come again, for we hope you will. Anything you wish to give will be gratefully accepted.

While you are a guest at Tengpoche, whether you stay in the rest house or in your own tents, I wish to request you to observe the few rules in observance of the Divine Dharma. Please do not kill or cause to kill any living creature in the area of this holy place. This includes domestic fowls and animals, as also wild game.

Please remember that this holy place is devoted to the worship of the Perfect One, and that nothing should be done within these sacred precincts which will offend or cause to hurt those who live here in humility and serenity. May you journey in peace and walk in delight, and may the blessings of the Perfect One be always with you.

Nawang Tenzing Zang-Po
The Reincarnate of Tengpoche

The sign has long since disappeared and has been replaced by a fancy carved sign that directs visitors to the New Zealand-built *Tengpoche Trekkers Lodge*, a part of the Sagarmatha National Park development. The lodge is operated on contract and has dormitory accommodation and a small kitchen. It's warm and comfortable, but can also be noisy and crowded.

There are few other facilities at Tengpoche. The gompa-owned *Tengpoche Guest House*, north of the monastery grounds, has dormitory accommodation. The *Tashi Delek Lodge* across the field from the gompa is small and usually full, but Passang Thongdup is a personable and helpful hotelier. The *Himalayan View* sometimes has rooms available, but it's often taken over by trekking groups. There is another unnamed tea shop nearby, but it caters primarily to porters.

If you have visited Tengpoche in years past and remember the raucous evenings at the Gompa Lodge, you'll be disappointed; it is no more. The gompa charges a fee for each tent erected at Tengpoche and a monk comes around with a receipt book to be sure that you pay. It is one of the few sources of revenue for the monastery, which supports about 50 or 60 monks, so it isn't reasonable to argue about this charge. Several trekking companies donate money to the monastery each year and in return receive the use of certain camp sites. The monks won't let you camp in these places. The small *Lhotse Lodge* is 15 minutes walk north of Tengpoche.

There are also a camping place and two lodges at Devuche, about a 20 minute walk from Tengpoche. Ang Kanchi's *Everest Rhododendron Lodge* is more unassuming than Pemba Dorje's large, green-roofed *Ama Dablam Garden Lodge*. A bit further on, near the nunnery, is the *Anny Gompa Lodge*. These may be better choices when Tengpoche is filled to capacity – or at any time, some would argue, to relieve the pressure on Tengpoche's limited water supply and general environment.

Day 5: Optional Acclimatisation Day in Tengpoche

You will do much better in the high country if you spend another day acclimatising. You can make a day hike to Pangboche, climb up the hill behind Tengpoche for good mountain views or explore the monastery itself.

Tengpoche (many older maps spell it Thyangboche, but the preferred, phonetic spelling is Tengpoche) was founded by Lama Gulu, a monk from Khumjung, on the instructions of the abbot of Rongbuk monastery. Construction of the main temple building was completed in 1919. An earthquake destroyed the gompa in 1934, killing Lama Gulu. The temple was rebuilt a few years later and the remains of the founding lama were buried inside the gompa. On 19 January 1989 a fire devastated the monastery. Many items of the monastery's extensive collection of books, paintings and religious relics were saved, but the entire gompa building was destroyed. The Sherpa people of Khumbu, with help from many international organisations, have raised funds for the reconstruction of the gompa building. Construction began in April 1990 and the new gompa was consecrated in September 1993. The statues in the gompa are of Pawa Chenrizig (Avalokitesvara) and Guru Rimpoche (Padmasambhava). The chapel is dominated by a statue of Sakyamuni (Buddha) that is almost four metres tall.

Tengpoche is the largest and most active monastery in Khumbu, but it is not the oldest. Sherpas believe that Buddhism was introduced into Khumbu towards the end of the 17th century by Lama Sange Dorje, the fifth of the reincarnate lamas of the Rongbuk (or Rong-phu) monastery in Tibet, to the north of Mt Everest. According to legend, Lama Sange Dorje flew over the Himalaya and landed on rocks at Pangboche and Tengpoche, leaving his footprints. He is thought to have been responsible for the founding of the first gompas in Khumbu, at Pangboche and Thami.

The gompas of Khumjung and Namche Bazaar are of a later date. None of these were monasteries. Their priests were married lamas and there was no monastic community with a formal organisation and discipline. The first monasteries were established at Tengpoche and Thami (at about the same time) as offshoots of the Nyingmapa (Red Hat) sect monastery of Rongbuk in Tibet, and young monks were sent there to study. Tengpoche's charter bears the seal of the abbot of Rongbuk. A nunnery was later founded at Devuche, just north of Tengpoche. Trakshindo was established in 1946 by a lama from Tengpoche.

A library and cultural centre behind the gompa was designed by the abbot to cater to both Tibetan scholars and trekkers. The plan is to develop an extensive library of books on religion, culture and history in several languages. A school building adjoining the gompa provides facilities for about 30 young monks to pursue their religious education. Technically, only the abbot of the monastery is called a lama; the Sherpa word for a monk is *tawa*.

Day 6: Tengpoche to Pheriche

From Tengpoche it's a short, steep and muddy descent to Devuche through a forest of birches, conifers and rhododendrons. Because of the ban on hunting at Tengpoche, you can often see almost tame blood pheasants and Nepal's national bird, the Himalayan monal or impeyan pheasant, which lives only at high altitudes. Only the male is colourful, with a reddish tail, shiny blue back and a metallic green tinge and pure white under its wings. It appears almost iridescent when seen in sunlight. Another common bird in this region is the snow pigeon, which swoops in great flocks above the villages of Khumjung, Namche and Pangboche. The crow-like birds that scavenge any food that you might drop (I have even seen them fly away with a full packet of biscuits that they have stolen) are red-billed choughs and occasionally ravens. The Sherpas call both birds *goraks*. Near Gorak Shep you are likely to see Tibetan snow cocks racing happily down the hillside. High above you may see goshawks, Himalayan griffons, golden eagles and lammergeiers circling on the updraughts from the mountains. In the early morning and just before dusk you may see musk deer, especially in the forests below Tengpoche, leaping like kangaroos.

The few houses and the gompa of the tiny village of **Devuche** are off in the trees to the west, and the nunnery is up the hill to the east. From Devuche the level trail passes many mani walls in a deep rhododendron forest. Watch the leaves curl up in the cold and open in the morning when the sun strikes them. After crossing the Imja Khola on a steel bridge, swaying a terrifying distance above the river at a spot where the river rushes through a narrow cleft, the route climbs past some magnificently carved mani stones to **Pangboche** at 3860m. Just before the village are two chortens, a *kani* (archway) and a resting place. East of the chortens is a monument where you can see the footprint of the patron saint Lama Sange Dorje preserved in stone.

Pangboche is the highest year-round settlement in the valley. The Pangboche gompa is the oldest in Khumbu and once had relics that were said to be the skull and hand of a yeti. These items were stolen in 1991, so another chapter of the yeti legend continues unsolved. Pangboche is actually two villages, an upper and a lower village. On the way to the Everest base camp the lower route is best, but on the return trip, use the upper trail and visit the gompa, 120m above the lower village. There are three lodges in lower Pangboche, one at each end of the village and one in the centre – good choices for lunch.

Beyond Pangboche the route enters alpine meadows above the tree line. Most of the vegetation is scrub juniper and tundra. During the summer the hillside is covered with wild flowers, including edelweiss. At Shomare there is a tea shop, then the trail passes several yak herders' *goths* (huts) as it ascends on a shelf above the river to Orsho, where there is a small lodge. Beyond Orsho the trail divides. The lower, more important-looking trail leads to Dingboche while the trail to Pheriche goes up to the left, through the front yards of a few herders' huts, over a stone wall and climbs a small ridge before descending to the Khumbu Khola, crossing it on a wooden bridge. From the bridge it is a 10 minute walk, usually in the wind, to **Pheriche** at 4240m. Pheriche is windier, and

Yetis

The yeti is a large human-like mammal, though taller than humans, that walks with a lumbering gait. It often stands upright, but usually moves on all fours. Its body is covered with thick black or brown fur and its feet are big. Its diet consists of fruit, vegetables and small mammals. It lives in caves and forests near the snow line in Nepal and Tibet, is very elusive and probably hibernates during the winter as bears do. It has a high, piercing yell and its body gives off a garlic-like smell. Its hair covers its eyes, it has no tail and the female has long, pendulous breasts. No yeti has been photographed at close range, but it has been seen by several people. Its tracks and spoor have been seen and photographed. It has a close relative that lives in the forests of north-western USA.

The word yeti is derived from the Tibetan *yeh*, 'snow valley', and *teh*, 'man'. The concept of an elusive human-like animal that lives in the high country is reflected in the various names that have been applied by people from many different cultures. Tibetans call it *ye-teh*, *mah-teh* or *mehton kangmi*, the last of which translates as 'abominable snowman'. In the USA it is known as 'sasquatch' or 'bigfoot'.

Before you dismiss all this as fiction, consider some of the sources.

The first recorded sighting of a yeti by a Westerner was in 1889 when Major LA Wassell saw footprints in north-eastern Sikkim. Since that time yeti footprints have been found by many mountaineering expeditions in Nepal and Tibet. The most famous footprint was the one found by Eric Shipton during the Everest reconnaissance in 1951. Both Lord Hunt and HW Tilman found yeti tracks on the Zemu Glacier in Sikkim in 1937. The late Tenzing Norgay once saw a yeti. Tim McCartney-Snape and Greg Mortimer found unexplained tracks near the summit of Everest in 1984. Don Whillans saw a yeti on Everest in 1970 and Reinhold Messner claims to have encountered a yeti in Tibet in 1986.

Several expeditions have set out to find the yeti, including three expeditions in the 1950s sponsored by the late Tom Slick, a Texas millionaire. The Himalayan Scientific & Mountaineering Expedition during 1960-61 included yeti hunting as part of its objective. It was this expedition that arranged for Sir Edmund Hillary to carry a yeti skull to the USA for examination and study.

Of course, all this evidence is inconclusive, and the mountaineering and scientific communities include a large number of unbelievers. In *High in the Thin Cold Air,* Hillary expresses his scepticism of Sherpa sightings of yetis: 'We found it quite impossible to divorce the yeti from the supernatural. To a Sherpa, the ability of a yeti to make himself invisible at will is just as important a part of his description as his probable shape and size.'

Be on the lookout for yetis in the high country of Nepal and Tibet, particularly in Khumbu, Gokyo and the upper Hongu. In 1992 the people of Mustang reported a herd of yetis in Tibet, just north of Mustang, and produced yeti hair that was collected by Peter Matthiessen. In 1993 two Tibetans told me that they had seen yetis near Mt Kailas, so this may be another place to search for them. If you do spot one, or want more information, contact the Bigfoot Information Center (☎ 1-800 BIGFOOT) in the USA. ■

hence feels colder, than most places in Khumbu. Be sure that you carry your warmest clothing on this day.

A trekkers' aid post operates at Pheriche, supported by the Himalayan Rescue Association (HRA) and Tokyo Medical College. A Western physician is usually in attendance during the trekking season. This establishment, and the doctors who operate it,

specialise in the study and treatment of altitude sickness and strive to educate trekkers in the dangers of too fast an ascent to high altitudes. The doctors give lectures every day, normally at 3.30 pm. The aid post also lends books and sells HRA emblems, T-shirts and mani stones to raise money. Visit the clinic if you have even the slightest problem with altitude. Even though the doctors are volunteers, the HRA has considerable expenses, so there is a charge for consultation and treatment.

Pheriche is a labyrinth of walls and pastures. There are five lodges, including the *National Park Lodge*, which is an on-off affair depending on who has the contract to operate it. The biggest facility is Nima Tsering's *Himalayan Hotel*, a two storey place with a tin roof. Other lodges are semi-permanent buildings which have evolved from mud huts with a tarp on the roof into more substantial structures that are forever expanding.

Be careful when you sit down in these crowded places – that comfortable-looking cushion in the corner is likely to be a baby wrapped up in blankets. The *Snow View Hotel* has a mountaineering equipment shop. The usual jumble of new and used climbing equipment is for sale and there is often an unlikely collection of expedition food available, such as Bulgarian stews, Russian borshch, French snails or American granola bars – depending on which country recently mounted an Everest expedition.

Day 7: Acclimatisation Day in Pheriche

The most important key to acclimatisation to high altitudes is a slow ascent. Therefore it is imperative that you spend an additional night at Pheriche to aid the acclimatisation process. This is the second of the mandatory acclimatisation days on this trek.

You can spend the day in many ways. You may wish to declare a rest day and relax in camp or you may wish to do some strenuous exploring. It is a short hike to the small Nangkartshang gompa, a climb of about 400m above the village. From this vantage point there is a good view to the east of Makalu; at 8463m it is the fifth-highest mountain in the world.

A more strenuous trip is to climb the hill to Dingboche, then hike up the Imja Khola valley past Bibre to **Chhukung**, a small summer settlement at 4730m. The views from Chhukung and further up the valley on the moraines towards Island Peak (6189m)

are tremendous. The great south face of Lhotse towers above to the north, while Amphu Lapcha (a 5780m pass) and the immense fluted ice walls that flank it dominate the horizon to the south.

To the south-west, the eastern face of Ama Dablam provides an unusual view of this picturesque peak. This hike is one of the highlights of the trek. It is a fast trip back down the valley to Pheriche for the night. There are lodges in both Chhukung and Dingboche that can provide lunch.

Day 8: Pheriche to Lobuje

The trail ascends the broad, gently sloping valley from Pheriche to **Phalang Karpo** at 4340m. In many places the trail crosses small streams on boulders. Look back down the valley from Phalang Karpo to see how much elevation you have gained. The views of Tawachee and Cholatse (6440m) are particularly good from this portion of the trail, which passes through country reported to be the habitat of the snow leopard and yeti. Ama Dablam is seen from a different aspect and is hardly recognisable. The true top of Kantega is visible far to the left of the prominent saddle seen from Tengpoche. Beyond Phalang Karpo the trail climbs steeply onto the terminal moraine of the Khumbu Glacier, then contours down to a stream, crossing it on a bridge just before **Duglha** (4620m). There is a tea shop near the stream and two others a bit higher that specialise in lunch.

From Duglha the trail climbs higher on the moraine to a row of stone monuments in memory of six Sherpas who died in an avalanche during the 1970 Japanese skiing expedition on Everest. There are many other monuments to climbers, mostly Sherpas, who have perished since then. The trail drops a bit and follows the western side of the valley to **Lobuje**, a summer village that boasts several lodges at 4930m. The New Zealanders who helped set up Sagarmatha National Park built a lodge at Lobuje that has 24 bed spaces and is run on contract by Karma Sherpa. The *Above the Clouds Lodge* accommodates 18 and the *Kala Pattar* and

Sherpa hotels provide a few more beds. The sherpas and porters that accompany trekking groups further crowd the hotels when they come in for tea or rakshi (which can have a dramatic effect at this elevation).

Everything is expensive in Lobuje. Prices are at least double those in Namche, but there is still a lot of variety thanks to expeditions that have jettisoned their supplies. If you are travelling with a group, the sherpas will race ahead to stake out a good camp site and get the use of one of the two herders' huts as a kitchen. You can almost always rely on finding food and accommodation (though it may be crowded) at Lobuje, but you will certainly need a warm sleeping bag – there is usually no bedding available and only a limited supply of mattresses. The toilet facilities are minimal and the mess that this has caused is truly horrible. In contrast, the sunset on Nuptse, seen from Lobuje, is a memorable sight.

Day 9: Lobuje to Gorak Shep

The first section of the trail from Lobuje follows the western side of the broad Khumbu Valley and ascends gently through meadows beside the glacial moraine. A pyramid-shaped Italian research station that looks like an invading spaceship is in the first side valley beyond Lobuje. Fortunately, you cannot see it from the trail. The station is open from March until mid-November and has communications facilities that can be used to contact Kathmandu in an emergency.

The ascent becomes steeper and rougher as it crosses several side moraines, although the trail is usually well defined. In places, however, an active glacier is under the moraine, so the trail is constantly changing. Routefinding techniques include looking for stone cairns as markers and watching for traces of yak dung – a sure sign of the correct trail.

After rounding a bend in the trail, the conical peak of Pumori comes into view. On the lower slopes of this mountain a ridge extending to the south terminates in a small peak. This peak, Kala Pattar, meaning 'black rock', is 5545m high and provides the best

vantage point for viewing Mt Everest. Kala Pattar is actually a Hindi name. Legend has it that the late Dawa Tenzing accidentally named the peak when he accompanied the first foreigner, Jimmy Roberts, to the top. Roberts and Dawa Tenzing communicated in Hindi, not Nepali. You can easily make the ascent of Kala Pattar from Gorak Shep in the afternoon or the following morning.

The trail makes a short descent onto the sandy, flat expanse of **Gorak Shep** (5160m). This was the base camp for the 1952 Swiss Everest expedition. In 1953 the British Everest expedition called this 'lake camp'. Gorak Shep has a small lake that is usually frozen and several monuments to climbers who have died during various Everest expeditions. The carved stone in memory of Jake Breitenbach of the 1963 US expedition and the monument for Indian ambassador H Dayal, who died during a visit to base camp after the 1965 Indian expedition, are northeast of the lake.

Most people reach Gorak Shep by lunch time and spend the remainder of the day resting, but if you are not tired by the altitude, you can climb Kala Pattar or go to the base camp in the afternoon. There are two herders' huts at Gorak Shep near the lake, but they are small and dirty and are only emergency shelter. The *Yeti Tea Shop*, run by Ang Lamu Sherpani, has a few bunks in its one-room building. Ang Lamu often shuts up shop during the coldest months from December to February and returns to Khumjung, so it is best to enquire at Lobuje before counting on this facility during winter. It should be possible to find food and shelter at most other times during the trekking season. The best plan of all is to start early in the morning and go from Lobuje to Kala Pattar via Gorak Shep and return to Lobuje for the night, avoiding the necessity of staying at Gorak Shep.

Day 10: Gorak Shep to Lobuje

It is impossible to explain the discomfort of high altitude to someone who hasn't actually experienced it. Most people have an uncomfortable, often sleepless, night at both Gorak

Shep and Lobuje, despite the extra time taken for acclimatisation. By descending 300m to Lobuje, or better yet, by descending further, to Pheriche, most people experience an immediate improvement, so it is really not worth spending an additional night at 5160m.

Mornings are usually sparkling clear, and the climb of Kala Pattar is one of the most rewarding parts of the trip. It is a steep ascent up the grassy slopes west of Gorak Shep to a shelf at the foot of Pumori. Even from this low vantage point the entire Everest south face is visible as well as the Lho La (the pass between Nepal and Tibet, from which George Leigh Mallory looked into Nepal in 1921 and named the Western Cwm), Changtse (the northern peak of Everest) and most of the West Ridge route climbed by Unsoeld and Hornbein in 1963. Those familiar with the accounts of expeditions to the Tibetan side of Everest will be able to spot the North Ridge and the first and second steps, prominent obstacles during the attempts on the mountain in the 1920s and 30s. As you near the top of Kala Pattar, more of the peak of Everest itself comes into view, and a short walk north from the summit of Kala Pattar on the ridge towards Pumori will allow an unobstructed view all the way to the South Col.

The walk to base camp from Gorak Shep is about a six hour return trip, possibly more unless an expedition in progress has kept the ever-changing trail in good condition. The route follows the Khumbu Glacier, sometimes on the moraine and sometimes on the glacier itself. The walk is especially intriguing for the views it has of the 15m-high seracs of ice, a feature peculiar to Himalayan glaciers.

Everest base camp is not actually a specific site. Various expeditions have selected different locations for a semipermanent camp during their assault on the mountain. Some of the sites that expeditions have used as base camps are identifiable from debris on the glacier at 5360m or more. The trip to base camp, while fascinating, is not as spectacular as the ascent of Kala Pattar because there is no view of Everest itself from base camp.

It is difficult to go to both base camp and Kala Pattar in a single day. If you wish to do both, use the afternoon of the day at Gorak Shep for one trip and the next morning for the other. The exhaustion and lethargy caused by the altitude limit many people to only one of the possible options. The descent to **Lobuje** is easy, but seems endless because of the many uphill climbs from Gorak Shep. The night, however, will be much more comfortable than the previous one.

Day 11: Lobuje to Dingboche

To go to Dingboche, retrace your steps back to Duglha, then go straight up the hill from the bridge to reach an upper trail, staying high above the valley floor, past the yak pastures at Dusa to a chorten at the head of the Imja Khola valley. The views are great – you can easily recognise Island Peak because its name is an apt description. Makalu is the greenish-grey peak visible in the distance over the pass to the right of Island Peak. Descend from the chorten to **Dingboche** at 4410m, following the trail as it traverses east into the valley. The high pastures in this region are sometimes referred to as 'summer villages'. Sherpas with homes lower in the valley own small stone huts in the higher regions and occupy them in summer while their herds of yaks graze in the surrounding pastures. A few crops, especially barley, are also grown in these high fields. Dingboche is a more pleasant place than Pheriche, and the mountain views are outstanding, so many tourist facilities have recently been developed here. There are four large lodges, including Sona Hishi's *Sonam Friendship Lodge* that – according to Bob Peirce – plays Vivaldi as wake-up music. Dingboche, incidentally, is the only place in Khumbu where barley is grown. There are also two small lodges in Chhukung, several hours up the valley.

Day 12: Dingboche to Tengpoche

The route from Dingboche descends the Imja Khola valley, then crosses the Khumbu Khola on a wooden bridge and climbs to rejoin the upward trail at some stone huts near Orsho. Following the trail downhill, it is easy to make a detour and visit the upper part of Pangboche and the village gompa, then continue to Tengpoche for the night. If you want to avoid the crowds below, you can choose from four lodges in upper Pangboche. While ascents at high altitudes must be slow, you may safely descend as fast as you wish.

Day 13: Tengpoche to Namche Bazaar

The route descends to Phunki Thanga, then ascends the ridge towards Namche Bazaar. The direct route to Namche turns south just above Sanasa, passes Kenjoma and traverses along the side of the ridge. This avoids a lot of climbing, but it's a long walk in and out of side valleys. An alternative route through Khumjung allows a visit to either the Hotel Everest View or Sherpa villages before the steep descent to Namche, but involves climbing an extra 200m. In Namche Bazaar you will have a last opportunity to buy (mostly) fake Tibetan jewellery from Tibetan merchants who spread their wares alongside the trail through the village.

Day 14: Namche Bazaar to Lukla

It's a long walk from Namche to Lukla, but you are probably in good shape by now. If not, break the trip into two days with a night at Chomoa or Phakding.

From Namche, the steep descent back to the Dudh Kosi at Jorsale is a bit rough on the knees, but the warmer climate offers a good opportunity to finally shed down-filled jackets and woollen jumpers. Don't lose your national park permit or pack it away; you must check out of the park at Jorsale and show the permit to prove that you duly paid for the use of the national park facilities. You must be at the airport at Lukla the night before your flight to reconfirm reservations if you have these – your seats will vanish if you do not reconfirm reservations. The trail from Jorsale to Lukla follows the upward route as far as Chablung, then turns off above Chaunrikharka towards Lukla.

There are signs beyond the stream at Chablung pointing you in the direction of Lukla. The broad trail leading uphill to the left climbs steadily past a few bhattis and the school, then through scrub forests above the school and houses of Chaunrikharka. After a steep final climb there is a collection of houses and bhattis in Tamang Tole, a new settlement a short distance from the airport. As you approach the airstrip the houses and hotels rapidly proliferate.

Lukla, 2800m, has a good choice of accommodation. The up-market *Trekkers Cabin* halfway down the airstrip offers rooms for about US$10 a night. The hotel's Tibetan-style dining room is the centre of Lukla's social life and is also the source of all the rumours about flight operations. *Sagarmatha Resort* near the airport check-in building is the newest, fanciest and most expensive at US$25 per night. *Buddha Lodge* and *Paradise Lodge*, both near the airport, also have private rooms, hot showers and reasonably efficient short-order kitchens. There are many other lodges in the village that offer both private rooms and dormitories and have extensive menus.

The RNAC office is open for an hour in the evening – usually from 5 to 6 pm, but sometimes from 6 to 7 pm. There is usually a sign announcing the office hours. You can reconfirm flights only during this period. If you are not present the night before the flight you probably will lose your seat. The radio message telling the RNAC staff how many flights are scheduled for the following day usually doesn't come until after the office closes. This adds an atmosphere of mystery and intrigue to the proceedings. In fact, the airline does not prepare the actual flight schedule for each day until about 7 pm, when they know where each plane ended up for the night. Check-in begins early and can be chaotic. If your innkeeper or a trekking company representative offers to check you in for the flight, take advantage of this. There isn't much to do at Lukla other than wait for planes or talk about when they will come.

Day 15: Lukla to Kathmandu

The trek to Hile (see the Eastern Nepal chapter) becomes attractive because it

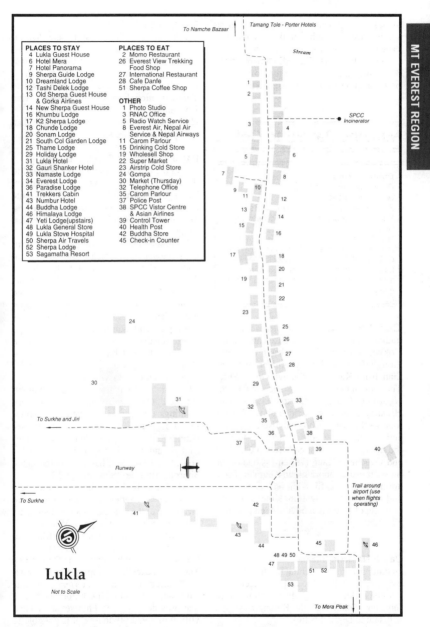

PLACES TO STAY
4 Lukla Guest House
6 Hotel Mera
7 Hotel Panorama
9 Sherpa Guide Lodge
10 Dreamland Lodge
12 Tashi Delek Lodge
13 Old Sherpa Guest House
     & Gorka Airlines
14 New Sherpa Guest House
16 Khumbu Lodge
17 K2 Sherpa Lodge
18 Chunde Lodge
20 Sonam Lodge
21 South Col Garden Lodge
25 Thame Lodge
29 Holiday Lodge
31 Lukla Hotel
32 Gauri Shanker Hotel
33 Namaste Lodge
34 Everest Lodge
36 Paradise Lodge
41 Trekkers Cabin
43 Numbur Hotel
44 Buddha Lodge
46 Himalaya Lodge
47 Yeti Lodge(upstairs)
48 Lukla General Store
49 Lukla Stove Hospital
50 Sherpa Air Travels
52 Sherpa Lodge
53 Sagamatha Resort

PLACES TO EAT
2 Momo Restaurant
26 Everest View Trekking
     Food Shop
27 International Restaurant
28 Cafe Danfe
51 Sherpa Coffee Shop

OTHER
1 Photo Studio
3 RNAC Office
5 Radio Watch Service
8 Everest Air, Nepal Air
     Service & Nepal Airways
11 Carom Parlour
15 Drinking Cold Store
19 Wholesell Shop
22 Super Market
23 Airstrip Cold Store
24 Gompa
30 Market (Thursday)
32 Telephone Office
35 Carom Parlour
37 Police Post
38 SPCC Vistor Centre
     & Asian Airlines
39 Control Tower
40 Health Post
42 Buddha Store
45 Check-in Counter

To Namche Bazaar

Tamang Tole - Porter Hotels

Stream

SPCC
Incinerator

To Surkhe and Jiri

To Surkhe

Runway

Trail around
airport (use
when flights
operating)

Lukla

Not to Scale

To Mera Peak

avoids the confusion of Lukla and explores some unusual country unlike any that you have seen on the first portion of the trek.

The flight from Lukla to Kathmandu takes 35 minutes and is a jarring return to the noise, pollution, confusion and rush of a large city.

Namche Bazaar to Gokyo

Duration 9 days
Difficulty Medium to hard
Maximum elevation 5318m
Permit cost US$5 per week plus Rs 650
Season October to December, February to May
Hotels Good
Summary A high-altitude trek to a valley east of Everest base camp. Excellent views of Everest, small lodges on the entire route and usually less crowded than the base camp trek.

The trek to Gokyo offers an alternative to the traditional trek to Everest base camp. From Gokyo, more of Everest itself is visible, though from a slightly greater distance, than from Kala Pattar above Gorak Shep. The mountains are more spectacular, the Ngozumpa Glacier is the largest in the Nepal Himalaya, and from a ridge above Gokyo, four 8000m peaks (Cho Oyu, Everest, Lhotse and Makalu) are visible at once. The view of the tremendous ice ridge between Cho Oyu and Gyachung Kang (7922m) is one of the most dramatic panoramas in Khumbu. There are many options for additional exploration and high-altitude walking, including the crossing of Cho La, a 5420m-high pass into Khumbu.

Day 1: Namche Bazaar
Acclimatisation is essential for this trek. It is easy to get too high too fast and succumb to altitude sickness. Only after a minimum of three days in the Namche-Khumjung region is it safe to begin this trek.

Day 2: Namche Bazaar
Don't rush. The Himalayan Rescue Association doctors have determined that you must acclimatise before you begin the Gokyo trek. There are lots of things to do here. Take a hike to Thami (see the Namche Bazaar to Thami section later in this chapter), visit Khumjung or eat apple pie in Namche. Hiking will help acclimatisation more than the apple pie, however.

Day 3: Namche to Phortse Thanga
Climb the hill to Khumjung and descend to the east of the village down the broad valley leading to the Dudh Kosi. The Gokyo route turns north, climbing above the more frequented route to Tengpoche and Everest base camp.

There is a choice of routes in the beginning: the yak trail, which climbs gently, but traverses a long distance around the ridge; or the steep, staircase-like trail made of rocks embedded in a narrow cleft in a large boulder. The Sherpas claim that the steeper trail is better – for exercise. The two trails soon join and continue towards a large chorten on the ridge top at 3973m. This ridge descends from Khumbila (5761m), the abode of the patron god of the Khumbu region. Khumbila (or, more correctly, Khumbu Yul Lha) translates as 'Khumbu area god'. On *thangkas* and other monastery paintings this god is depicted as a white-faced figure riding on a white horse. Numbur, the mountain that towers over Junbesi and the Solu region, is the protector god of that area and has the Sherpa name Shorong Yul Lha ('Solu area god').

At **Mong** (Mohang) there are three tea-houses and a chorten. This is said to be the birthplace of the saint Lama Sange Dorje, the reincarnate lama of Rongbuk Monastery in Tibet who introduced Buddhism to Khumbu. The trail descends in a series of steep switchbacks down a sandy slope to the Dudh Kosi. There is an excellent camping spot at **Phortse Thanga**, near the river *(thanga* means 'riverside') at 3500m, just before the bridge that provides access to Phortse, an isolated village of about 60 houses. It is possible to

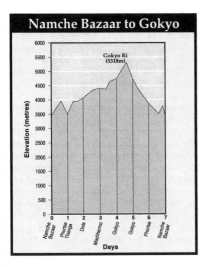

Khumbila and Tawachee are tremendous throughout the day, and it is possible to climb a ridge behind Dole for an even broader view up and down the valley.

Day 5: Dole to Machhermo
The trail is steep in most places as it climbs through scrub junipers to **Lhabarma** at 4220m. There are kharkas wherever there is a flat spot and the slightest hint of water. In winter, many of these villages have no nearby water source, so there are no lodges and you cannot camp at them.

Luza at 4360m is a good camping place and supports two lodges because it is on the banks of a large stream and has a year-round water supply. All the kharkas on this side of the valley are owned by people from Khumjung. Families have houses in several settlements and move their herds from place to place as the grass becomes overgrazed and the snows melt.

The trail continues to climb along the side of the valley, high above the river, crossing sandy spurs to **Machhermo** at 4410m. It was in Machhermo in 1974 that a yeti killed three yaks and attacked a Sherpa woman. This is the most credible yeti incident ever reported in Khumbu, so be watchful as you visit this region. There are three lodges and good mountain views in Machhermo.

Day 6: Machhermo to Gokyo
Beyond Machhermo the trail climbs a ridge for an excellent view both down the valley to Kantega and up towards Cho Oyu. Beyond the ridge, the valley widens as the trail passes through **Pangka** at 4390m. An entire trekking group was killed here by an avalanche in November 1995. The trail descends to the river bank before beginning the climb on to the terminal moraine of the Ngozumpa Glacier.

It is a steep climb up the moraine, switchbacking alongside the stream to the first small lake at 4650m, where a family of Brahminy ducks has resided for many years. The trail now becomes almost level as it follows the valley past a second lake, known as Longponga, at 4690m and finally up a

go much further in a single day from Khumjung – as far as Tongba or Gyele – but it can be dangerous because of the rapid increase in elevation. There are two basic lodges and a national park army post nearby. The army may require you to dig your trekking permit out of your luggage so they can examine it.

Day 4: Phortse Thanga to Dole
You should make this another short day to aid your acclimatisation to the altitude. The trail climbs steeply out of the valley through rhododendron forests which give way to fragrant stands of juniper and large conifers as the elevation increases. This portion of the trek is especially beautiful in spring when the rhododendrons are blooming (late April and early May at this elevation).

The trail passes through many kharkas, summer settlements used when sherpas bring herds of yaks to graze in these high pastures. Some of the villages in this valley are occupied as late as December by people grazing their herds.

The route passes through the settlements of Tongba (3950m) and Gyele (3960m) to **Dole** (pronounced 'doe-lay'), at 4200m, where there are two lodges. The views of boulder-strewn path to **Gokyo** at 4750m. Gokyo is a collection of stone houses and walled pastures on the shores of a large lake. The setting is reminiscent of an abandoned summer resort. There are five lodges at Gokyo; the *Gokyo Resort*, built by the 1991 Australian ballooning expedition, boasts a sun room.

Day 7: Gokyo

The views in the Gokyo region are tremendous. For the best view, climb Gokyo Ri, the small peak above the lake. This peak of 5350m is sometimes called Kala Pattar (not to be confused with the Kala Pattar above Gorak Shep, though the views are similar). It is a two hour climb to the top of the peak, providing a panoramic view of Cho Oyu, Gyachung Kang, Everest, Lhotse, Makalu, Cholatse and Tawachee.

Those with more time and energy can make a trip up the valley to another lake, marked with the name Ngozumpa on the maps, or even beyond to a fifth lake. There are several small peaks in this region that offer vantage points for the surrounding peaks and views of the Nangpa La, the old trade route into Tibet.

Day 8: Gokyo to Phortse

You can descend to Phortse in a single long day, or you can spend the night at Thare or Konar to make the day less strenuous. Rather than retrace the upward route, follow the eastern side of the valley to gain different views of Khumbila. You will also enjoy somewhat warmer weather, because the sun stays on these slopes longer in the late afternoon.

The route to Phortse retraces the upward journey back to Pangka, then turns east and climbs across the terminal moraine of the Ngozumpa Glacier to **Na** (4400m), the only year-round settlement in the valley. There are two scruffy tea shops, but nothing resembling the quality of the lodges in the rest of Gokyo. The descent from Na along the eastern side of the Dudh Kosi valley is straightforward, passing through Thare and Konar, making a few ups and downs where

landslides and streams have carved side valleys. The trail enters **Phortse** at its upper end. There are camping places in the potato fields of this large village. The *Khumbu Lodge* is near the top of Phortse village and the *Namaste Lodge* is lower down.

Alternative Route via Cho La If you have mountaineering experience and are well equipped, you can make a challenging side trip across the Cho La to the Khumbu Valley. About halfway between the first and second lakes a trail leads off across the moraine to the east. This is the route to the 5420m Cho La (or Chhugyuma Pass) into the Everest region. The pass is not difficult, but it is steep and involves a glacier crossing on the eastern side. Allow three days from Gokyo to Pheriche on this high-altitude route. An ice axe, crampons and a rope are often necessary for negotiating the small icefall at the foot of the glacier on the other side of the pass, although in ideal conditions there are no technical problems and there is a trail of sorts in the rocks beside the icefall.

The western approach to the pass varies in difficulty depending on the amount of snow. Sometimes it is a rough scramble up a scree (gravel) slope, and other times it's an impossible technical ice climb. The best conditions are when there is snow soft enough for kicking steps up the slope. The pass is not possible for yaks and sometimes not suitable for heavily laden porters, but you can send the porters and yaks around the mountain via Phortse and they can meet you in Lobuje or Pheriche three days later. If you plan to cross the pass, spend a night at Chhugyuma and the following night at Dzongla on the other side. There is no teahouse or shelter in Chhugyuma, but there is a small lodge in Dzongla.

Day 9: Phortse to Namche Bazaar

A slippery trail descends from Phortse to the bridge at Phortse Thanga and rejoins the original route from Khumjung. It is easy to reach Namche Bazaar, or even go beyond to Jorsale, for the night.

An alternative route from Phortse leads

STAN ARMINGTON

STAN ARMINGTON

Mt Everest Region
Top: A chorten is part of the Sherpa cultural centre at Hotel Sherwi Khangba in
   Chhorkung, above Namche Bazaar.
Bottom: The Saturday market in Namche Bazaar.

SARA JANE CLELAND

GLENN BEANLAND

GREG ELMS

Annapurna Region

Top: Looking up the Manang Valley towards Tilicho Peak on the Around Annapurna trek
Middle: Early morning light on Dhaulagiri from Poon Hill, above Ghorapani
Bottom: Trekkers on a valley-floor trail

from the village gompa up a steep, exposed trail with spectacular views to upper Pangboche, where it joins the trail to the Everest region. There is an offshoot of this trail that descends steeply to the Imja Khola and climbs through forests to Tengpoche.

Namche Bazaar to Thami

Duration 2 days
Difficulty Medium
Maximum elevation 3750m
Permit cost US$5 per week plus Rs 650
Season October to May
Hotels Good
Summary A short side trip to a more traditional Sherpa village. Excellent mountain views.

Thami lies at an elevation of 3750m, near the foot of a large valley to the west of Namche Bazaar. This is the departure point for crossing Tesi Lapcha, the 5755m pass into the Rolwaling Valley. Only experienced, well-equipped and well-informed parties should attempt Tesi Lapcha because frequent rock falls near the pass present a very dangerous complication.

If you are in good shape and well acclimatised, it is possible to make the trip to Thami and back to Namche Bazaar in a single day, but it's a long, hard day, so it's better to spend a night in Thami to see the peaks in the clear morning. This side trip provides a good acclimatisation day before proceeding to higher elevations.

The trail to Thami leaves the Khumjung trail near the Namche gompa and leads west past a large array of prayer flags, mani stones and a chorten. The carved mani stones all the way to Thami are some of the most complex and picturesque in Khumbu. Contouring around the hill on a wide and almost level trail, the route passes through forests to **Phurte**, at 3390m, where there is a forest nursery that was established by the Himalayan Trust. You can see Laudo gompa high on

the hill above. A few Westerners study and meditate here under the tutelage of an English-speaking lama.

Cross a ridge marked by a chorten and trek into another side valley, crossing under power lines to the large village of **Thamo**, at 3440m, where the *Kwangde View* and *Everest* restaurants offer lunch. Thamo is the headquarters of the electricity project; the original powerhouse was built below Thamo, but the site was destroyed in the 1985 flood, so the generating plant was moved far upstream to Thami itself.

Climb past Khari monastery at the top of Thamo and trek above the fields of Thomde to a few tea shops at Somde (3580m). The scenery becomes even more dramatic, and there is a good view towards Tesi Lapcha and the peak of Pharchamo (6187m) above it.

From Somde the trail traverses high along the side of the valley, then makes a sharp descent to a bridge high above the river. The paintings on the rock cliff are of Guru Rimpoche and Green Tara. Cross the bridge and make a steep ascent beside a stream to **Thami**, a total trek of about three hours from Namche Bazaar. The *Thami Lodge* is at the foot of the village, and there is an unnamed lodge in the centre of the village that gets the first sun in the morning.

Thami is in a large valley with good views of the snow peaks of Teng Kangpoche (6500m) and Kwangde to the south. To the north of the village is a police checkpost that doesn't allow trekkers to travel further north on the trade route between Nepal and Tibet. That trail leads to Nangpa La, the 5741m pass crossed by trains of yaks carrying goods between the two countries. The pass is still a major crossing point for Tibetan refugees, and is also used by both Sherpas and Tibetans for the trade of yaks, wool and Chinese goods.

About 150m above Thami is the **Thami gompa**, a picturesque monastery set among the many homes of lamas and lay people. It's perched high on the side of a hill overlooking the valley. As you climb through juniper forests towards the gompa, stay left; it's a one-way trail that makes a long detour around mani walls. The reincarnate lama operates the *Tashi Delik Lodge* below the gompa, and several monks sell paintings alongside the trail. The gompa is not in good condition and is scheduled for a major renovation effort. This is the site for the spring celebration of the Mani Rimdu festival, held about the middle of May each year. During Mani Rimdu many Sherpas set up temporary restaurants near the gompa and offer *momos* (meat-filled dumplings), *thukpa* (noodles) and endless quantities of tea, *chhang* and rakshi.

Barahbise to Shivalaya

Duration 6 days
Difficulty Medium
Maximum elevation 3320m
Permit cost US$5 per week
Season October to May
Hotels Minimal
Summary An off-the-beaten-track route through both highland and lowland villages that bypasses the road to Jiri. Very few lodges, so you'll need to arrange a camping trek.

It takes a bit of the continuity out of the Everest trek when you drive all the way to Jiri. The following route from Barahbise to Shivalaya avoids the Jiri road entirely, passing through country that trekkers rarely visit. Few people, including locals, follow the route I have described here, so villagers will probably not be able to point you in the right direction. A guide (or a basic knowledge of Nepali) is almost essential for this trek. There are so many trails leading in every direction that it is impossible to document all the junctions and alternatives. This description is only a suggestion. You can modify it in many ways once you are on the trail.

Accommodation

There are some bhattis on this route, but they are local style and don't often cater to West-

erners, and there are none of any kind from Biguti to Mali, so you will be more comfortable if you arrange this as a camping trek.

Access

Barahbise is a 10-minute drive beyond Lamosangu on the east bank of the Bhote Kosi. Just south of Barahbise, a small branch of the Sun Kosi joins the Bhote Kosi ('river from Tibet') to form the much larger Sun Kosi.

Day 1: Barahbise to Khartali

Barahbise is a crowded bazaar at 820m, inhabited mostly by Newars and Chhetris. The route begins on an unpretentious set of stone steps between two shops – the start of what will eventually, when you reach the ridge above Mali, be more than 2400m of uphill walking. Passing through a few scattered Gurung villages, the route soon enters country inhabited mostly by Tamangs. Most of the route is in open, cultivated country with a few pipal trees, surrounded by stone chautaaras, providing welcome shade on hot days. The trail climbs steeply to Parati at 1300m, then becomes less steep, and even has a few level stretches, as it continues through heavily cultivated country to the large Tamang village of Khartali at 1680m.

Day 2: Khartali to Thulo Tingsang

Beyond Khartali the trail continues to traverse eastward along the ridge, high above the Sun Kosi. Most of the travellers on this trail are porters carrying rice, wood and slate for roofing down to Barahbise. The trail climbs a ridge to a small bhatti and a rushing stream at 2290m. After the ridge, the trail enters deep rhododendron forests and makes some short climbs and descents as it weaves in and out of wooded side valleys. Below the trail and across the valley there are houses splashed across the hillside, but above the trail there is mostly forest. Rounding a ridge, the trail offers a view of the large, spread-out Sherpa village of Dolangsa. From the ridge, the trail enters another side canyon (watch for stinging nettles) and crosses a stream on a bridge hewn from a huge tree – a reminder of what the forests of this region must have been like before a rising population forced the cutting of large amounts for firewood. A short distance beyond the bridge, take the left trail which makes a steep uphill climb to **Dolangsa**, at 2380m, with clean white-washed houses, each surrounded by fields of corn, potatoes, wheat and barley. High above the village is a gompa.

Beyond Dolangsa the trail climbs through rhododendron forests past a few kharkas used during summer as pastures for herds of cattle. The pastures are uninhabited during the trekking season and make excellent camp sites if you have a tent. The trail makes a steep climb to the Tingsang La, crossing the pass at 3320m. At the pass there are good views in every direction. On a clear day Gauri Shankar (7145m) dominates the horizon to the north-east and peaks are visible from Chhoba-Bhamare (6108m), a rock spire in the west, all the way to Pigpherago (6730m) and Numbur in the east.

A short distance below the pass is **Thulo Tingsang**, a large kharka at 3260m. The views from this camp are as good as those from the pass. During summer, many people live in this high pasture and there are even a small shop and a teahouse. In the winter, people remove the roofs from the stone huts and carry their household effects to lower permanent settlements. During the trekking season there is no food or accommodation here.

Day 3: Thulo Tingsang to Amatal
From Thulo Tingsang ('big Tingsang') the trail descends through conifer and rhododendron forests to Sano Tingsang ('small Tingsang'), another kharka at 3000m. The trail continues a gradual descent (a very pleasant walk – most descents in Nepal are steep and rough) through forests and past small kharkas to a stream at 2230m. There is a small paper factory here, and you'll see frames with Nepali paper drying in the sun.

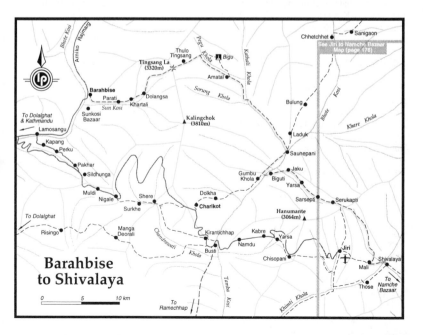

Barahbise to Shivalaya

A few minutes below is another stream crossed by a covered bridge at an elevation of 2100m. From this point a rough, steep trail climbs 400m to Bigu at 2500m. Bigu is a Sherpa village with a large gompa and a nunnery. It is a strenuous side trip that involves a steep descent to rejoin the main trail. The direct route continues down the river valley through Tamang, Chhetri and Kami (blacksmith caste) villages with slate-paved courtyards, to **Amatal** at 1680m.

Day 4: Amatal to Saunepani
It is a long but pleasant walk along the lower reaches of the Pegu Khola to its confluence with the Tamba Kosi (here called the Bhote Kosi). Stay on the south bank of the river at first, passing through Kopai and a few other small villages. Much of the route is in pine forest. Villagers have cut off the lower branches of most trees for firewood – a traditional method of avoiding total deforestation. The trail ascends and descends over ridges and spurs, finally making a steep descent to the Sangawa Khola and crossing it at 1220m. The route then follows the north bank of the river, making a few ups and downs, but generally staying level and passing a few side streams, two of which flow from beautiful tropical waterfalls. Not only is the trail level, but the route is almost totally uninhabited during the afternoon's walk – two very unusual things in Nepal. Finally the route reaches the Tamba Kosi at **Saunepani** (Sigaati) at 1000m. The village has a few houses and a small shop.

Day 5: Saunepani to Serukapti
Walk south for about an hour along the west bank of the Tamba Kosi. (This trail, if followed in the opposite direction, leads to the Rolwaling Valley after a week of walking.) The trail is level as it follows the river south to **Biguti**, across the Tamba Kosi on the east bank at 950m. About five minutes south of the bridge on the west bank is a new trading centre, **Gumbu Khola**. The ground floor of every house is either a shop or a restaurant.

Once you are on the east side of the river

at Biguti, turn north and cross a small stream, then climb the ridge to the north-east. The trail climbs a bit and turns east as it passes through the Tamang villages of Jaku (1460m) and Yarsa. Unlike the brief walk along the Tamba Kosi, which is a main trade thoroughfare, this is a rarely used route that climbs through forests and small villages towards the head of the valley. Because this is an out-of-the-way trail, there are places where it is steep and narrow. Routefinding is also a problem. Ask for the trail to Serukapti when you reach a dead end in someone's front yard. The trail becomes better and more clearly defined as it passes through Sarsepti, a large Tamang village at 1760m, then continues to climb through beautiful forests of oak and rhododendron with an abundance of ferns and orchids. After more climbing, you will reach the Sherpa village of **Serukapti** at 2300m.

Day 6: Serukapti to Shivalaya
From Serukapti the trail continues up into forests. A trail junction is about 15 minutes beyond the village. The lower (right-hand) trail goes to Jiri, and the upper (left-hand) trail crosses Hanumante Danda, bypassing Jiri. Since one of the purposes of all this uphill climbing is to avoid the motor road, there is no good reason at this point to go to Jiri, so continue up the valley to a beautiful high-altitude meadow surrounded by big trees, at 2300m. Climbing through a forest of large, moss-covered pines, the trail finally emerges at the top of the ridge at 2900m, high above Jiri. There are many trails here. One trail descends to a cheese factory, then climbs back to the ridge above Mali. The most direct trail runs along the ridge to the east for a while, then drops slowly below the ridge top, making another easy descent past a few slate mines before reaching the Patashe Danda and descending on a broad trail (stay on the ridge) to Mali, a Sherpa village at 2200m. The route now joins the trail from Jiri (see the Jiri to Namche Bazaar section earlier in this chapter) and continues to **Shivalaya** and Bhandar.

Annapurna Region

Central Nepal is dominated by the Annapurna Himal and the town of Pokhara. There are three major trekking routes in this region: to Jomsom, to the Annapurna Sanctuary and a circuit of the entire Annapurna massif. Pokhara is also a good starting place for a number of short treks of one to four days duration, including the 'Royal Trek', which I describe in this chapter. Mustang is also geographically a part of the Annapurna region, but because treks to Mustang are subject to special restrictions, I describe it in the separate chapter on restricted area treks.

About two-thirds of the trekkers in Nepal visit the Annapurna region. The area is easily accessible, hotels in the hills are plentiful and treks here offer good scenery of both high mountains and lowland villages.

No matter where you trek in the Annapurna region, you will eventually pass through Pokhara, the main city in central Nepal. The trek to Jomsom begins a short journey by bus from Pokhara and the Around Annapurna trek ends at the same point.

The town is known for its lake, Phewa Tal, and its large collection of inexpensive hotels and restaurants along the lakeside. A spectacular panorama of Nepal's central Himalaya, the Annapurnas, Machhapuchhare and Manaslu, dominates the skyline. Pokhara, being at a lower elevation, is warmer than Kathmandu. The telephone dialling code for Pokhara is ☎ 061.

CLIMATE

The climate in the Pokhara area is unique because there is no formidable barrier directly to the south to obstruct the spring and monsoon rain clouds. Consequently, it is subject to abnormally high rainfall, almost double that of Kathmandu. This accounts for the large glaciers at relatively low elevations in the Annapurna Sanctuary. Always be prepared for rain when you trek in central Nepal.

INFORMATION
Fees & Permits

No matter where you trek in the Annapurna region you come under the jurisdiction of the Annapurna Conservation Area Project (ACAP) and must pay the Rs 1000 conservation charge in addition to the normal trekking permit fee. Your guide and porters must each pay Rs 10 to enter the conservation area. You can get a visa extension or trekking permit for the Annapurna region at the Pokhara immigration office (☎ 21167), which is about 150m north of the Tragopan Hotel.

Maps

There is a 1:100,000 Schneider topographic map entitled *Annapurna* that is similar to the Schneider maps of Everest and Langtang; it was produced in 1993 and shows the Pokhara to Baglung road accurately. ACAP has produced a contour map entitled *Annapurna Conservation Area* with trekking advice on the back. These maps are available in bookshops in Kathmandu and Pokhara for Rs 300 each. Cartoconsult (Austria) has produced an expensive (Rs 400) 1:250,000 colour map titled *Annapurna Satellite Image Trekking Map* that shows the major trek routes. The US army maps that cover the region are NH 44-16 *Pokhara* and NH 45-13 *Jongkha Dzong*, but these are so out of date that they are useless. The Leomann Map 1:200,000 series sheet 4 covers the Annapurna region and, like this book, shows ridge lines instead of contour lines.

There are many locally produced maps available in Nepal, some printed and some blueprints; most are titled *Around Annapurna*. The best of the lot is the 1:150:000 Mandala map. The new 1:250,000 Nepa *Trekking Around Annapurna* map is also good; don't buy the old 1:320,000 version.

Books

The Moated Mountain, by Showell Styles, is a very readable book about an expedition to

213

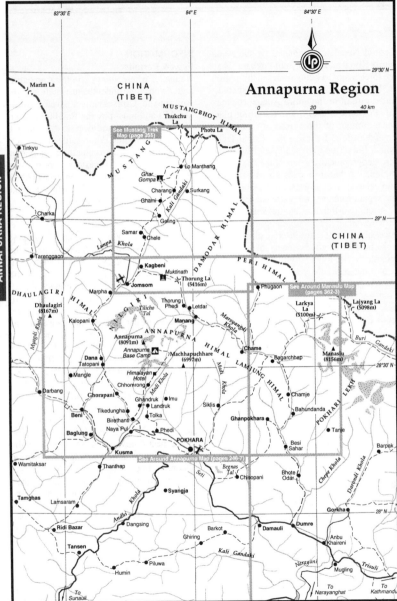

83°30' E   84° E   84°30' E

29°30' N

29° N

28°30' N

28° N

Annapurna Region

0   20   40 km

ANNAPURNA REGION

Marim La

CHINA
(TIBET)

MUSTANGBHOT HIMAL

Thukchu La

Photu La

See Mustang Trek Map (page 355)

Tinkyu

MUSTANG

Ghar Gompa

Lo Manthang

Charang   Surkang

Ghami

Charka

Goling

DAMODAR HIMAL

Tarenggaon

Samar

Chele

Lumpa Khola

Kagbeni

Muktinath

PERI HIMAL

CHINA
(TIBET)

DHAULAGIRI

Marpha

Jomsom

Thorung La (5416m)

Phugaon

See Around Manaslu Map (pages 362-3)

Dhaulagiri (8167m)

Kalopani

Thorung Phedi

Letdar

Larkya La (5100m)

Lajyang La (5098m)

NILGIRI HIMAL

Tilicho Tal

Manang

Marsyangdi Khola

Buri Gandaki

Annapurna (8091m)

ANNAPURNA HIMAL

Chame

Manaslu (8156m)

Dana

Tatopani

Annapurna Base Camp

Machhapuchhare (6992m)

Bagarchhap

LAMJUNG HIMAL

Mangle

Himalayan Hotel

Chhomrong

Madi Khola

Chamje

POKHARI LEKH

Darbang

Ghorapani

Ghandruk

Imu

Landruk

Siklis

Bahundanda

Beni

Tikedhunga

Tolka

Ghanpokhara

Tanje

Baglung

Birethanti

Naya Pul

Phedi

POKHARA

Besi Sahar

Barpak

Kusma

See Around Annapurna Map (pages 246-7)

Wamitaksar

Thanthap

Seti

Begnas Tal

Chisopani

Bhote Odar

Chepe Khola

Daraudi Khola

Syangja

Tamghas

Lamsaram

Andhi Khola

Dangsing

Ghiring

Barkot

Damauli

Dumre

Gorkha

Ridi Bazar

Kali Gandaki

Anbu Khaireni

Tansen

Piluwa

Humin

Mugling

Trisuli

To Sunauli

To Narayanghat

Narayani

To Kathmandu

The ACAP Minimum Impact Code

Please assist in our efforts to maintain the natural and cultural equilibrium along the trekking route by following our 'minimum impact' code during your Himalayan sojourns:

- Avoid the use of non-biodegradable items, especially plastic mineral water bottles. Iodine drops are available at any ACAP office or drug store.
- Dispose of your trash responsibly. Use ACAP recycling and compost bins wherever available, take your used batteries home to your country, and incinerate all other wastes.
- Use ACAP toilets en route. If your trekking agency carries its own portable toilet tent, make sure the pit is covered on departure. Please encourage your porters to use toilet facilities as well.
- Insist on using kerosene for cooking and heating purposes. This should apply to your porters as well. If possible, avoid lodges and tea shops that use wood for fuel, and only take hot showers with solar-heated water.
- Trek gently. Do not trample or collect the flora of the region. It is illegal to hunt in the area or buy items made from endangered species. Please do not remove any religious artefacts from the area.
- Respect the culture by wearing modest clothing, asking permission before taking photographs, avoiding public displays of affection, behaving appropriately while at religious sites, and respecting local customs in your dress and behaviour.
- Encourage young Nepalis to be proud of their culture.

Baudha Peak. Styles records poignant cultural observations as he makes the trek to the mountain.

Annapurna, by Maurice Herzog, is a mountaineering classic (more than 10 million copies) that describes the first conquest of an 8000m peak. There is a good description of the Annapurna region, including Manang, and a visit to the Rana court of Kathmandu in 1950.

Annapurna South Face, by Chris Bonington, describes the beginning of a new standard of mountaineering in Nepal and provides an excellent description of the problems of organising an expedition.

Eco-Trekking in the Southern Annapurna

Himal, by Hum Bahadur Gurung and Barry Arthur, is a guide to environmentally sensitive trekking in the Annapurna region. It is for sale in Kathmandu at bookshops and at the KEEP office.

A Popular Guide to the Birds & Mammals of the Annapurna Conservation Area, by Carol Inskipp, is an excellent field guide to the natural history of the region.

Annapurna Conservation Area Project (ACAP)

ACAP was established in 1986 under the guidance of the King Mahendra Trust for Nature Conservation. The project encompasses the entire Annapurna range, an area of 7683 sq km. In an innovative approach to environmental protection, it was declared a 'conservation area' instead of a national park. Traditional national park practices dictate that few, if any, people reside within park boundaries. A new system of conservation management was necessary because a large number of people live within the region that ACAP protects. ACAP's programmes rely on the participation of local people and emphasise environmental education and 'conservation for development'.

Projects include the training of lodge owners, with an emphasis on sanitation, avoidance of deforestation, and cultural pride. They have trained trekking lodge operators and encouraged hoteliers to charge a fair price for food and accommodation. ACAP encourages the use of kerosene for cooking throughout the region, and requires its use in hotels above Chhomrong in the Annapurna Sanctuary and on the route between Ghandruk and Ghorapani. ACAP is supported by a 'conservation fee' of Rs 1000 that is collected from all trekkers who obtain trekking permits for the Annapurna region.

ACAP has encouraged the construction of toilets throughout the area; use them no matter how disgusting they are. ACAP has also made provision for the supply of kerosene throughout the region.

In Pokhara, visit ACAP's Trekkers Information & Environmental Centre (☎ 21102).

ANNAPURNA REGION

It's in an alley in the section of Pokhara known as Mahendra Pul. In addition to providing information, the centre sells iodine, solar battery chargers and other products that can help you to protect the environment while you are trekking. There is also a 'trekkers' meeting board' and a battery drop-off centre. There are ACAP checkposts and visitor centres throughout the region.

Accommodation & Supplies

Pokhara Accommodation in Pokhara includes the peaceful lakeside *Fish Tail Lodge* (☎ 20071). The Western-style *Hotel New Crystal* (☎ 20035) and the Tibetan *Hotel Mt Annapurna* (☎ 20037) are across from the airport. The *Tragopan* (☎ 21708), *Dragon* (☎ 20391) and *Tibet Resort* (☎ 20853) are all a short distance south of the airport in the part of town known as damside. The range of hotels along the lakeside is enormous. The *Base Camp Lodge* (☎ 21226; fax 20903), *Kantipur* (☎ 20886), *Baba Lodge, New Pokhara Lodge* (☎ 20875) and the *Pumori Hotel* (☎ 21462), which is air-conditioned, are all at the eastern end of the lake. There are dozens of other cheaper hotels and a government camping ground to the west along the shore of Phewa Tal. New large luxury resort hotels include the *Shangri La Village* (☎ 22122, 23676) and the *Fulbari Resort* (☎ 21675; email fulbari@fulbari .wlink.com.np), which is a long taxi ride out of town and has an office in Kathmandu (☎ 01-527588; fax 523149).

Among the lakeside restaurants, try *Baba Lodge,* the *Hungry Eye*, *Billy Bunter*, *Le Bistro*, *Lhasa Tibetan* and *Beam Beam.*

Gorkha Gorkha is an alternative starting point for the trek around Annapurna. If you find yourself benighted, try the fancy *Hotel Gorkha Bisauni*, about half a km from the bus stop, or the *Hotel Thakali* at the bus stop itself. A few km before Gorkha, on a ridge with good mountain views, is the up-market *Gorkha Hill Resort.*

Trekking Lodges There are numerous trekkers' hotels throughout the region; most

are adequate and some are outstanding. You can assume that you will be able to find a room and food wherever you go on the main routes in the Annapurna region. During the busy October and November season most lodges are crammed beyond their capacity; at this time it might be prudent to bring a mattress in case everything is full and you are forced to sleep on a floor. Bedding is often available, but you should not rely on this at high elevations, especially on a trek to Thorung La or Annapurna Sanctuary.

The *Lakshmi Lodge* (☎ 410740 in Kathmandu) in Birethanti will take advance bookings. *Ker & Downey* operates a deluxe chain of lodges in Dhampus, Ghandruk and Birethanti (☎ 416751, 410355; fax 410407 in Kathmandu). All three lodges feature private rooms with attached baths. Food is prepared using gas, hot water is provided by solar power and electricity by generator. You can prebook an all-inclusive trek with them starting at US$70 per day.

The hotels and lodges throughout the Annapurna region have formed local committees to fix prices. They have prepared printed menus for each locale – with increasing prices the further you go from Pokhara. This is a positive move because trekkers used to bargain and stay in the cheapest hotel. Now everyone quotes the same rate, so you choose a hotel according to quality, not price. The prices increase dramatically in the Annapurna Sanctuary and near Thorung La. The menu tends to be a bit boring, but each lodge has its own specialities and hotel-keepers are very resourceful at producing things like pies and cakes over a roaring kerosene stove. A speciality in this region is 'Mustang coffee', sweetened milk coffee with a large shot of local *rakshi*.

Fuel

If you are camping you will need kerosene for cooking. Environmentally aware trekkers use alternative fuels wherever they trek whether required to or not, but kerosene makes a cumbersome and difficult porter load. The use of kerosene is made easier by depots in the most heavily trekked parts of

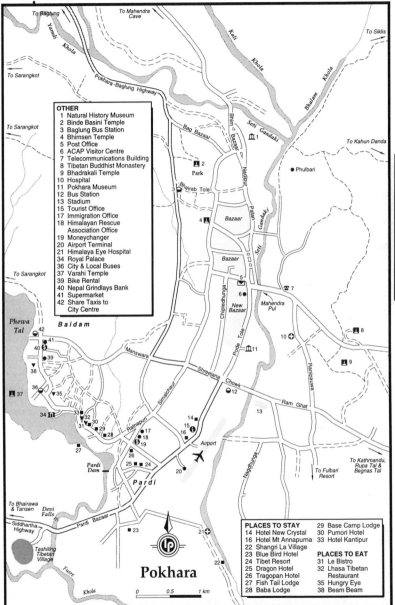

OTHER
1 Natural History Museum
2 Binde Basini Temple
3 Baglung Bus Station
4 Bhimsen Temple
5 Post Office
6 ACAP Visitor Centre
7 Telecommunications Building
8 Tibetan Buddhist Monastery
9 Bhadrakali Temple
10 Hospital
11 Pokhara Museum
12 Bus Station
13 Stadium
15 Tourist Office
17 Immigration Office
18 Himalayan Rescue
   Association Office
19 Moneychanger
20 Airport Terminal
21 Himalaya Eye Hospital
34 Royal Palace
36 City & Local Buses
37 Varahi Temple
39 Bike Rental
40 Nepal Grindlays Bank
41 Supermarket
42 Share Taxis to
   City Centre

PLACES TO STAY
14 Hotel New Crystal
16 Hotel Mt Annapurna
22 Shangri La Village
23 Blue Bird Hotel
24 Tibet Resort
25 Dragon Hotel
26 Tragopan Hotel
27 Fish Tail Lodge
28 Baba Lodge
29 Base Camp Lodge
30 Pumori Hotel
33 Hotel Kantipur

PLACES TO EAT
31 Le Bistro
32 Lhasa Tibetan
   Restaurant
35 Hungry Eye
38 Beam Beam

Pokhara

0   0.5   1 km

the Annapurna region. Kerosene costs Rs 9.50 per litre in Kathmandu. The locations of depots and the price for a litre of kerosene are:

Chhomrong	Rs 16
Ghandruk	Rs 13
Ghorapani	Rs 14.50
Jomsom	Rs 24
Kagbeni	Rs 28
Manang	Rs 37
Muktinath	Rs 25
Naya Pul	Rs 10
Tal	Rs 15.25
Tikedungha	Rs 12

Electricity
There is locally produced electricity in most villages in the region.

Warnings
The Annapurna Sanctuary trek is subject to deadly avalanches. Be sure to read – and heed – the avalanche information in that section, particularly if there has been recent heavy rainfall.

Thorung La is a high pass and crossing it is potentially dangerous. See Safety on Thorung La in the Around Annapurna Trek section later in this chapter.

GETTING THERE & AWAY
Air
Pokhara Pokhara is a 30-minute flight from Kathmandu (US$61). Most domestic airlines operate a Pokhara-based network that serves Jomsom and Manang with early-morning flights. All the domestic airlines serve Pokhara with daily flights.

Jomsom Jomsom is in the upper Kali Gandaki valley and is served by frequent flights from Pokhara (US$50) and occasional flights from Kathmandu (US$83). Don't fly to Jomsom; if your time is limited, walk up the spectacular Kali Gandaki valley to Jomsom, trek up to Muktinath, then fly from Jomsom back to Pokhara.

Flights between Kathmandu and Jomsom are notoriously unreliable because the wind

in Jomsom makes flying impossible after 10 or 11 am. Because Kathmandu is often fog-bound until 10 am during the winter, flight departures can be delayed until it is too late to land in Jomsom. Everest Air schedules two flights per week from Kathmandu to Pokhara; RNAC and Nepal Airways operate Jomsom flights only from Pokhara.

Pokhara to Jomsom flights are far more reliable because there is no fog problem in Pokhara. Though the morning check-in at Pokhara airport is particularly chaotic, it's easier to get to Jomsom from Pokhara than from Kathmandu. RNAC operates one daily 'tourist flight' to Jomsom on which even local people must pay the full tourist fare, and a second, regular flight that carries Nepali passengers at a subsidised rate. Because the fare is significantly higher on tourist flights, there is less competition for seats from locals.

Several helicopter companies also operate flights from Pokhara to Jomsom. The heavy Russian choppers can operate in the afternoon winds of the Kali Gandaki, so they often make several flights a day. If you get stuck while trying to fly out of Jomsom it is possible to walk to Pokhara in four days or less.

Manang At the upper end of the Marsyangdi valley is Manang, just across the pass from Jomsom. There is a severe risk of altitude sickness if you fly to Manang and try to cross Thorung La. You should view Manang as an emergency airport; it is not a sensible starting point for an Annapurna trek. RNAC is the only airline that serves Manang. The flight from Pokhara to Manang costs US$50.

Bus, Truck & Taxi
Pokhara There is frequent service by both day and night buses from Kathmandu to Pokhara. The fare is Rs 82, Rs 200 for a more comfortable 'tourist bus' and Rs 3500 for a private car. The road is often washed out by monsoon floods; when it's in good condition the 200 km drive takes five or six hours. The special tourist buses that operate between Kathmandu and Pokhara, including the

famous 'Swiss Bus', are more expensive, but more comfortable and faster, than the rattle-trap public buses.

Baglung A new Chinese-built road was completed .in 1994 between Pokhara and Baglung, a village on the Kali Gandaki. Buses depart frequently from a separate Baglung bus terminal near Bhairab Tole in the north-western part of Pokhara. Naya Pul is at Km 42, at the foot of the hill below Khare; if you get off here it's only a 20 minute trek upstream to Birethanti. If you are trekking to Jomsom and want to head directly to Tatopani, continue on to the end of the road at Baglung. The master plan is to extend the road all the way to Jomsom, through Lo Manthang and into Tibet, but the people of Jomsom have announced that they don't need, and don't want, a road. Now that the road to Baglung exists, there's little point in walking the first few days of the old trek route through Naudanda, Khare, Lumle and Chandrakot.

Dumre Dumre is 135 km from Kathmandu and is the starting place for the trek around Annapurna. There is no service that specifically serves Dumre, so you should take a Pokhara bus and jump ship at Km 135. A taxi from Kathmandu costs Rs 2200.

Besi Sahar A 43 km road links Dumre to Besi Sahar (also called Lamjung), the headquarters of the Lamjung district. The road is not paved, it fords several streams and is poorly – if ever – maintained. The trip is reasonable, though bumpy, in late autumn when the weather is dry. The road is rutted and often impassable when it rains, especially during, or just after, the monsoon. When the road is impassable, and sometimes when the bus driver is tired, you will get dumped at Bhote Odar or earlier.

There is a daily minibus from Dumre to Besi Sahar, a four to five hour trip in good conditions. Another bus takes the unusual route from Narayanghat in the Terai to Besi Sahar for a fare of Rs 48. When it is muddy you can ride in a tractor or 4WD truck. A bumpy, dusty ride in a decrepit, breakdown-prone ex-army truck costs Rs 100 to Rs 200, plus an extra charge for luggage; trucks leave from Dumre only when they have a full load of passengers and baggage. The road dries out in early November, allowing larger Indian Tata trucks to get through, so there is a better selection of vehicles later in the trekking season. In the dry season there are also buses from Kathmandu; a minibus costs Rs 165 and the slower local bus costs Rs 115.

Gorkha An alternative starting point for the trek around Annapurna is Gorkha. The 24-km-long Gorkha road starts at Anbu Khaireni, seven km from Mugling, and provides access to a route that avoids part of the dusty Besi Sahar road, joining the trek in the Marsyangdi valley near Tarkughat. Gorkha is served by two buses daily; the cost is Rs 55 for the seven hour bus ride, or Rs 2400 for a taxi from Kathmandu. There is no night bus service.

Short Treks near Pokhara

Most of the treks described in this book last several weeks. One of the attractions of the Pokhara region is the opportunity to make a short trek ranging from a few hours to a week. If you don't have time for one of the longer treks, or don't think you are ready for one, you can cobble together an interesting trek from parts of longer treks. Many fine short treks begin and end near Pokhara. You can reach the starting point of these treks with a short journey by bus or taxi. Try one of the following.

ANNAPURNA PANORAMA
After a stiff climb to Ghorapani for great views of Dhaulagiri and Annapurna, this trek returns through Ghandruk, a large Gurung village and headquarters of ACAP.

ANNAPURNA REGION

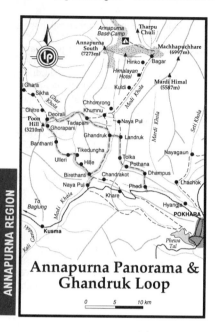

Annapurna Panorama & Ghandruk Loop

0   5   10 km

Days 1-2: Naya Pul to Ghorapani

Start from Naya Pul, about an hour's drive from Pokhara, and trek to Tikedungha and Ghorapani, following days 1 and 2 of the Jomsom trek.

Days 3-4: Ghorapani to Landruk

Follow the Ghorapani to Ghandruk description which follows at the end of the Annapurna Sanctuary trek later in this chapter, then descend to the Modi Khola and climb to Landruk.

Days 5-6: Landruk to Phedi

Follow the first 1½ days of the Annapurna Sanctuary description in reverse, overnighting in Deorali or Pothana.

GHANDRUK LOOP

The shortest trek in this book, this offers good mountain views, forests, birds and glimpses of traditional village life.

Days 1-2: Phedi to Ghandruk

Follow the Annapurna Sanctuary description to Landruk, then drop on a stone staircase to the Modi Khola and the *Beehive View Guest House* at 1310m. It's a long climb up a rough stone staircase – with high steps – to the tiny settlement of Yumle. There is a tea shop here, and there are a few more as you climb to Ghandruk at 1970m.

Day 3: Ghandruk to Naya Pul

Follow the clearly defined trail south from Ghandruk to Birethanti. See Day 11 of the Annapurna Sanctuary trek for details of this route. Walk out to the road at Naya Pul and catch transport back to Pokhara.

TATOPANI LOOP

This loop features Gurung villages, mountain views from Ghorapani and a long descent to the Mexican restaurants and pie shops of Tatopani. It finishes with two days of walking through villages that see more Nepali pilgrims than foreign tourists.

Days 1-2: Phedi to Ghandruk

Same as the first two days of the Ghandruk Loop.

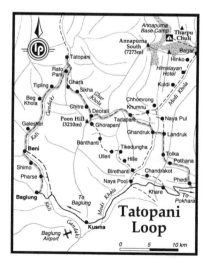

Tatopani Loop

0   5   10 km

Days 3-4: Ghandruk to Ghorapani

Follow the Ghorapani to Ghandruk description in reverse. It will probably take you two days because the trail is generally uphill.

Day 5: Ghorapani to Tatopani

Make a long, steep descent to Tatopani. See Day 3 of the Jomsom trek for details.

Days 6-7: Tatopani to Baglung

Follow the Baglung to Tatopani description later in this chapter in reverse and take a bus or taxi from Baglung back to Pokhara.

Jomsom Trek

> **Duration** 9 days
> **Difficulty** Medium
> **Maximum elevation** 3800m
> **Permit cost** US$5 per week plus Rs 1000
> **Season** October to May
> **Hotels** Excellent
> **Summary** The classic lodge trek starts with a long climb to Ghorapani, then drops into the world's deepest gorge. Crosses the main Himalayan range to Tibet-like country in Jomsom.

This trek boasts some spectacular mountain views, and the route actually crosses to the other side of the main Himalayan range for views of the northern flanks. From the Kali Gandaki valley, you can make excursions to either the 1950 French Annapurna base camp or the base camp for Dhaulagiri, though there are no hotels on either of these side trips and the first one, in particular, is a difficult undertaking.

If you don't go to Muktinath you can remain below 3000m and still have a trek that is strenuous enough to be stimulating (see the route profile in this section). This is a good trek if you wish to avoid high altitudes.

Accommodation

The trek to Jomsom is the classic teahouse trek and boasts some of the best trekking hotels in Nepal. You can trek to Jomsom and

back in 14 days, and you will share the trail with trains of burros and ponies travelling to Mustang and other areas in the far north of Nepal. This is a major trade and trekking route, so there are frequent facilities for trekkers all along the way. Many of these are surprisingly well equipped hotels operated by Thakalis, people who inhabit the valley between Annapurna and Dhaulagiri.

Access

From the lakeside or the airport in Pokhara, you can take a taxi (for about Rs 40) to the Baglung/Kusma bus station at the northern end of Pokhara. You can also walk through the Pokhara bazaar, but it is a long uphill walk on a paved road full of noisy traffic. There are buses throughout the day to Baglung; you should buy a ticket as far as Naya Pul.

The road passes the Tibetan camp, where there is a carpet factory, a monastery and a few hotels, then continues to Hyangja at 1070m. In the morning, there is often a good view up the valley to Machhapuchhare. The road emerges into the broad Yamdi Khola valley at Suikhet and goes on to Phedi at the foot of the Dhampus hill, then switchbacks up to **Naudanda** on the top of the ridge at 1430m. Naudanda is a large village with a police checkpost, school and lodges. The correct name of this village is Nagdanda, but local people, and most maps, call it Naudanda.

The road zigzags up to a few tea shops on the ridge at Khare and then winds down past the British Agricultural project at Lumle where they record one of the highest amounts of rainfall in the world. The road snakes its way into the Modi Khola valley, reaching **Naya Pul**, a small collection of roadside shacks, just beyond Km 42, where you can leave the road, drop down the embankment to the trail and start walking. If you want to avoid the long climb over the Ghorapani hill, stay on the bus and go on to the end of the road at Baglung. From there you can reach Tatopani in two days of fairly level walking; for details, see the Baglung to Tatopani section later in this chapter.

ANNAPURNA REGION

Day 1: Naya Pul to Tikedungha

To get to Birethanti, go upstream behind a ridge and walk about 20 minutes on a level trail to the *Fishtail Lodge* and a steel bridge. On the opposite bank of the Modi Khola is **Birethanti**, elevation 1065m, a large and prosperous town with a winding street paved with large stones. Birethanti boasts many well-stocked shops, hotels, sidewalk cafes, a bank, a shop that stocks medical supplies, a bakery and a police checkpost. The *Lakshmi Lodge* is expensive, but is also interesting and comfortable; one trekker described it as a real throwback to the days of the raj. Other options include the nearby *Riverside* and *River View* lodges. At the far end of the village is a newer collection of hotels, including the *Gurkha Lodge*, *Uttam Lodge* and *Hotel Ever Green View*.

A trail up the Modi Khola to Ghandruk begins at Birethanti, starting alongside the river and then heading uphill on a rocky trail that leaves the river bank just beyond a small shrine. See Day 11 of the Annapurna Sanctuary trek for a description of that trail.

The hotels in Birethanti are excellent, but if you spend a night here, it is a long, 1700m climb the next day to Ghorapani. It is more comfortable to break the climb into two stages by continuing to Hille or Tikedungha for the night. (If you are coming from Jomsom and doing the trail in reverse, then Ghorapani to Birethanti is an easy, though long and knee-cracking, descent and Birethanti makes a good stopping place.) The trail follows the main street of Birethanti, going through bamboo forests and past a large waterfall and swimming hole. A small tea shop provides cold drinks after your swim. The trail stays on the north bank of the Bhurungdi Khola to Baajgara, so don't cross the large and inviting-looking suspension bridge.

Beyond a pasture used by pony caravans, the trail reaches Sudami, then climbs steadily up the side of the valley, reaching **Hille** at 1495m. There are several hotels alongside the wide stone trail and others in **Tikedungha**, about 15 minutes (and 30m in elevation) above Hille. There is a large camp

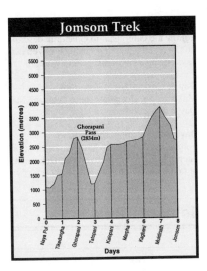

site just beyond Tikedungha near two suspension bridges. If you started from Birethanti, this will be a short day. If you arrive early, you can easily trek on up the endless stone staircase to Ulleri.

Day 2: Tikedungha to Ghorapani

The trail crosses a stream on a suspension bridge near the camp site at Tikedungha, then drops and crosses the Bhurungdi Khola itself on a large bridge at 1410m. The trail climbs very steeply on a stone staircase; there are no tourist hotels from the bridge to Ulleri, just a few *bhattis* that have tea and cold drinks. As you climb, the tops of Annapurna South (7273m) and Hiunchuli (6441m) begin to emerge from behind the hills. The climb continues steeply to the large Magar village of **Ulleri** at 2070m. There are hotels in the centre of the village, and others above the village where the trail climbs gently through pastures and cultivated fields. The fields soon give way to deep forests as the trail climbs to **Banthanti**, a settlement of hotels in a forest clearing at 2250m.

Beyond Banthanti, there are magnificent oak and rhododendron forests. The trail crosses two sparkling clear streams, a small ridge and another stream before making a short, final climb to **Nangathanti**, a hotel complex in a forest clearing at 2460m. *Thanti* is a Magar word meaning 'rest house' or 'dharamsala'. In the winter the trail can be covered with snow, and in many places it is sloppy mud, so all sorts of short detours are necessary in this section.

Ghorapani is about an hour past Nangathanti, at 2775m. There are several hotels in Ghorapani, but most people continue to the pass and village of **Deorali** (which means 'pass'), at 2834m, about 10 minutes beyond Ghorapani. There is a large collection of hotels, shops and camping places, plus the requisite police checkpost, in Deorali.

There is a big map on a signboard in the village that shows the location of 11 lodges; the *Annapurna Hotel* and the *Snow View Hotel* are among the largest. The *Super View* is said to be the best. All the hotel-keepers have standardised their prices, so it's a waste of time to look for the cheapest food and accommodation. It is worth staying at the pass to see the spectacular panorama of Dhaulagiri I, Tukuche, Nilgiri, Annapurna I, Annapurna South, Hiunchuli and Tarke Kang (formerly known as Glacier Dome). An early-morning excursion to **Poon Hill** (3210m), about an hour's climb, provides an even better, unobstructed view of the high Himalaya.

Ghorapani means 'horse water', and it is no doubt a welcome watering stop for the teams of horses, mules and ponies that carry loads between Pokhara and Jomsom. The exotic horse caravans, with melodious bells that echo over great distances and wondrous plumes and headdresses on the lead horses, are reminiscent of ancient Tibet. Herded by Tibetan men who shout up and down the trail, they lend a unique touch to the Jomsom trek. The ponies also grind the trail into dust and slippery mud with their tiny, sharp hooves and career downhill, frightening trekkers into jumping into the bushes, but the colourful photographic possibilities and the harmonious tinkle of bells almost make it worth the trouble.

Some people, almost overcome by the ammoniacal stench of horse urine on the trail, suggest a different derivation of the name Ghorapani. On a typical day, you will encounter 200 to 300 pack animals, travelling in large trains and ranging in size from huge mules to tiny burros no bigger than a large dog.

Day 3: Ghorapani to Tatopani

From the pass at Deorali, the trail makes a muddy, steep descent through rhododendron and magnolia forests, interspersed with a few shepherds' *goths* (huts), bhattis and pastures, to **Chitre** at 2390m. The *New Annapurna* is the dominant lodge here. There are several trail junctions along this part of the trip. The correct trail almost invariably leads downhill. The country opens up into a region of extensive terracing. At one point the trail crosses a huge landslide. Observe the way the slick mica soil has slid off the underlying rock.

The trail descends towards **Sikha**, a large and prosperous Magar village at 1980m with many shops and hotels. *Shanti View* is near the top of the village, above the British army training centre. From Sikha, the trail makes a gentle descent across another slide area to

STAN ARMINGTON

Porters on a snow-covered track at Ghorapani with Dhaulagiri in the background

ANNAPURNA REGION

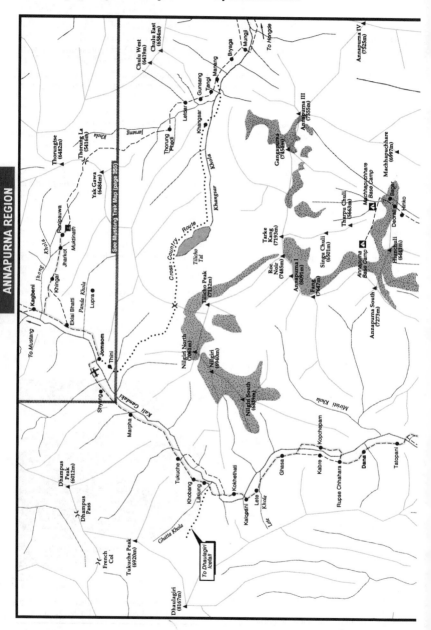

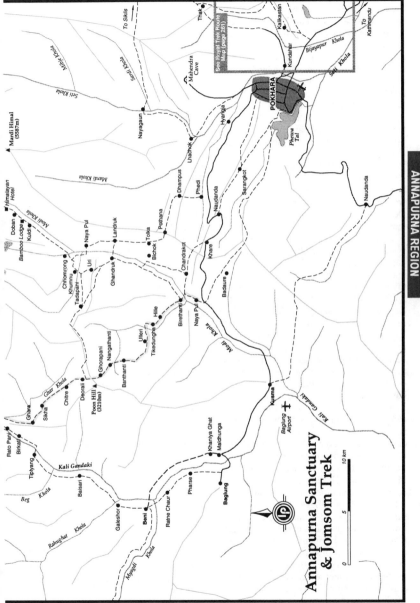

Annapurna Sanctuary & Jomsom Trek

ANNAPURNA REGION

Ghara at 1705m, then climbs to some bhattis on the top of a rocky spur. The trail makes a steep descent of about 500m to the Ghar Khola, crossing it on a suspension bridge near Ghar Khola village. It then makes a short climb above the Kali Gandaki and crosses the river on a large suspension bridge at 1180m. The peak to the north is Nilgiri South (6839m). On the opposite side of the river, the trail turns north; it is a short distance upstream to **Tatopani**. Just south of the village is a police checkpost where you must register.

Tatopani means 'hot water' in Nepali; the village gains its name from the hot springs near the river below the village. There are two cement pools on the banks of the river. Don't pollute these pools by using soap in them.

Tatopani is the epitome of the Thakali inn system; the extensive choice of hotels and garden restaurants rivals Thamel in Kathmandu and the lakeside in Pokhara. The town is supplied with electricity, but some hotels have installed bio-gas (which the Nepalis call *gobar*) generators to produce fuel for cooking. It is intriguing to see these facilities in daily use and indicates good progress in the alternative energy field. Many people who are making only a short trek come from Pokhara and spend their time relaxing in the hot springs and enjoying the hospitality of Tatopani.

A monsoon flood in the late 1980s washed away a number of lodges and bathing pools, and the remainder of the village sits precariously on a shelf above the river. Most of the lodges have garden restaurants and specialise in exotics such as steaks, pizzas and Mexican food. The *Evergreen Lodge*, *Trekkers Lodge* and *Tatopani Lodge* are at the south end of the village. The *Kamala* and *Namaste* lodges are at the northern end of town. The food at *Dhaulagiri Lodge* gets rave reviews. Tatopani's other facilities include many shops, a bank, blacksmith, tailor, shoemaker, bookshops, barber, lending library and several jewellers. This is citrus fruit country, so you can stock up on small mandarin oranges.

From the mid-1970s until 1985 the Kali Gandaki valley was the focus of the US Resource Conservation & Utilisation Project (RCUP), and a vast amount of money was spent on an integrated approach to rural development. The primary legacy of this effort is a collection of Western-style buildings, both offices and residences, that you will encounter on your journey up the valley. When you see a facility that looks totally out of place on this trek, it's probably an RCUP leftover.

Day 4: Tatopani to Kalopani

The trek now starts up the Kali Gandaki gorge, said to be the deepest in the world. The rationale for this is that between the top of Annapurna I and the top of Dhaulagiri I (both above 8000m and only 38 km apart) the terrain drops to below 2200m. From Tatopani, the route ascends gently, passing through a small tunnel carved out of the rocky hillside, then along a cliffside trail. On the opposite side of the river is the power plant that generates electricity for this area. Cross the Bhalu Khola on a high suspension bridge to reach **Dana** at 1400m. Dana consists of three separate settlements. At the southern end of the village are the post office, houses and the *Kabin Guest House*. The *Gauchan* and *Dana Riverside* hotels are in the centre of Dana, on the banks of the Ghatta Khola. On the opposite side of the stream (which you might have to wade across if there is no bridge) is the old part of Dana where the houses of wealthy traders have elaborately carved windows and balconies. The *Raju Lodge* is in this part of town, and the *Annapurna Lodge* is a bit to the north. Most of the people of Dana are Magars, though there are also a few Brahmans and Thakalis. The large peak across the valley is Annapurna South (7273m); the large village high on the hillside across the valley is Nerchang.

Beyond Dana is the hamlet of **Rupse Chhahara** ('beautiful waterfall') at 1550m. The *Rupse Lodge* is in the village; it's a short distance to the high waterfall after which the village was named. The falls tumble into a

Jomsom Trek – Flora & Fauna

Trees The **schima** and **chestnut** are the two dominant species of the wet subtropical forest (1000m to 2000m) and are easily distinguished from each other. The schima is called *chilanune* ('itchy') in Nepali due to the irritant nature of its bark. It is a medium-sized tree of the tea family with evergreen leathery leaves and fragrant white flowers that appear in late spring. Look for its small, round, woody fruit in the fall. The chestnut is a larger tree and is a member of the oak family. Its leaves are large and elliptical with serrated edges. This species has small white flowers on spikes and a distinctive prickly seed capsule that often litters the trail.

The **evergreen oaks** are found in the temperate zones, from 1700m to 3000m. They either form their own extensive forests or grow with conifers and rhododendrons. Unless acorns are present they may be difficult to identify because the several varieties of oaks come in an assortment of sizes and leaf types. One common species of oak, the brown oak (*khasru* in Nepali), has young leaves that are spiny like holly, while older leaves have smooth-edged margins. Oaks also tend to appear in many unusual shapes due to the extensive pruning by hill tribes for fuel and fodder.

There are more than 30 species of **rhododendron** (in both shrub and tree form) in the temperate and subalpine zones of Nepal. Rhododendrons are readily recognised when they burst into magnificent blooms in spring and summer. The main tree variety, and national flower (*lali gurans* in Nepali), has funnel-shaped flowers clustered at the ends of the branches in a wide variety of colours such as white, pink, mauve and red. When no flower is present, look for tapering leaves that can be silvery or rust-coloured on the undersides and for the loose, pale salmon-coloured bark.

Birds In the skies the raptors, or birds of prey, are the birds most likely to catch one's eye. Of particular note are the large, soaring raptors that ride the thermals effortlessly for hours, such as the **Himalayan griffon** and **lammergeier**. These huge, graceful vultures are often mistaken for eagles, but are much more common than eagles and substantially larger with long, broad wings. The former is striking with white under-wing coverts that contrast with the black flight feathers, a stubby tail, and a wing span of about two metres. Although the lammergeier has a wing span of nearly three metres, its body is slighter and its plumage gold and brown-coloured. Look for the long, wedge-shaped tail, which differentiates it from anything else of this size. Both of these birds can be seen frequently across the high Himalaya.

Lammergeier

Mammals The two species of monkey found in Nepal are the **rhesus macaque** and **common langur** both of which are protected for religious reasons. There should be little confusion distinguishing these two monkeys from each other. The former is small and stout with a pink face, brown fur and short tail, while the langur is large and lanky with a black face, greyish-white coat and long tail. The common langur is also found at higher altitudes than the rhesus, up to the tree line at 3700m. Occasionally, while on all fours in the shadows of a tree, this monkey can be mistaken for a leopard. Both of these species range from the Terai to the temperate zones across the Himalaya.

Common langur

There are several smaller carnivores found in the Himalaya, which include the mustelids, or weasels and martens. They feed on various smaller mammals, birds, eggs and even insects. The **yellow-throated marten** is found in the subtropical and temperate forests and displays great agility when cavorting amongst treetops, where it is most visible. The **Himalayan weasel** inhabits the realm above the tree line, where it can be seen stalking prey and following scent trails, occasionally stopping to stand on its hind legs for a look around. ■

Annapurna North Base Camp

Just beyond Dana, a bridge provides access to a trail on the eastern side of the Kali Gandaki. After several days of rough climbing in bamboo jungle above the Miristi Khola, this trail reaches the base camp used by Maurice Herzog's Annapurna expedition in 1950. At the time of this first ascent, Annapurna I (8091m) was the highest mountain ever climbed. The base camp is also accessible by an equally difficult trail from Lete. Herzog's book *Annapurna* provides essential background reading for the trek up the Kali Gandaki. The route up the Miristi Khola is poorly defined, long and difficult, and is used only by shepherds and mountaineering expeditions. There are no villages or hotels along it. ■

---

series of cataracts after passing through some water-driven mills. The millstone is turned by a wooden turbine; these home-made mills are found throughout Nepal and are a very unusual design. A restaurant overlooking the waterfall displays a large supply of cakes and pies; a sign suggests: 'eat dessert first, life is uncertain'.

The next stretch of trail is through the steepest and narrowest part of the Kali Gandaki gorge; much the way is cut through solid rock and is subject to frequent landslides. The route used to stay on the western side of the river, but landslides destroyed that trail, so now the east-bank trail is the preferred route. Just beyond Rupse Chhahara the trail crosses a bridge as the river roars through a narrow chasm below. Climb a stone staircase over a ridge, then descend and follow alongside the river for a short distance before climbing to Kopchepani and the *New Namaste Lodge*. Trek a short distance to some teahouses and make a steep, rocky climb to the top of a large landslide. The route passes several tea shops and an ACAP sign that marks the boundary of the Mustang district, then descends to the small *New Bimala Hilton* at Pairotapla. The trail climbs again over a ridge, and finally drops to the river on a rocky cliffside trail. The route crosses back to the western side of the Kali Gandaki on a suspension bridge at 1935m.

There is a short climb to **Ghasa** (2080m), which has three separate settlements. This is the first Thakali village on the trek and the southernmost limit of Tibetan Buddhism in the valley. The *Eagle's Nest Guest House* at the southern end of the village is said to be the best and has a trailside garden. Other good facilities are in middle Ghasa; these include the *Kali Gandaki* and *Mustang* guesthouses. There are fine *kanis* (archways) in upper Ghasa, and there is a large locally supported reforestation project behind the school. At the north end of Ghasa is the *Sugat Guest House* and the comfortable new *Flowrida Guest House*. The vegetation changes from subtropical trees and shrubs, including stinging nettles and cannabis, to mountain types such as pine and birch. You might spot grey langur monkeys in this area.

The trail crosses a ridge, descends to a stream, then travels through forests to the *Bimala Hotel* in Kaiku at 2250m. There are several small ups and downs, and a few bhattis; finally the trail drops into a side valley where a long, high suspension bridge crosses the Lete Khola. There are more bhattis and the *Namaste Lodge* near the bridge. The trail climbs 100m on a rough rocky trail to a cold drink shop, then is level to **Lete**, a spread-out town at 2470m. It's a long walk through town on a trail that varies from well-crafted flagstone paving to a muddy wallow through piles of nettle-infested rocks. There are several bhattis and lodges here, including the large *Lete Guest House*. The *New Horizon* is across from the police checkpost, near the Mustang English School.

It's not clear exactly when you leave Lete and enter **Kalopani**, elevation 2560m. Passing the *See You Lodge*, you reach the high school, the *Kalopani Guest House* (with western toilets) and the huge Dhaulagiri Technical School at the north end of Kalopani. Several trekkers have complained about unfriendly service and poor food at the hotels in this village. There is a 360° panorama of peaks: Dhaulagiri, the three Nilgiris, Fang and Annapurna I.

Day 5: Kalopani to Marpha

A short distance beyond Kalopani the trail crosses the Kali Gandaki at 2560m where the river rushes through a narrow gorge. On the east bank of the river a stone-paved trail leads past a few houses and tea shops, then through past the old picturesque houses of Dhampu. There is a short alternative route across the gravel bars of the river that avoids the village. Climb on a stone staircase to a wooded ridge, then descend to the *Earth Home* in Kokhethati. Climb a steep rocky trail to another ridge, then descend through fir, juniper and cypress forests to a high suspension bridge over the Kali Gandaki at 2600m. Trek through forests past a bhatti and over a ridge to the Ghatta Khola. There's a good bridge a long distance upstream, but most local people just wade through the icy

waters of the river. The trail makes several ups and downs before a steep climb over a ridge. Descend and make a short walk across gravel bars to **Larjung** (2560m). At the southern end of Larjung are two hotels; the *Larjung Lodge* is the better of the two and may be able to offer information about the trip to Dhaulagiri icefall.

Trek through the small village of Larjung past the school, cross a stream and trek for 10 minutes to **Khobang** at 2560m, an architecturally exotic town with narrow alleyways and tunnels connecting houses that are built around enclosed courtyards. This complex and picturesque system provides protection from the winds of the Kali Gandaki gorge. Pass the *Sunrise Guest House* and *Peaceful Lodge* as you enter the village, then follow the trail along a narrow alleyway as it passes under several houses. You can make a side trip to the Kanti gompa on a hill just above Khobang. There are good views of Dhaulagiri (8167m) and Nilgiri North (7061m) along this part of the trail. In 1972 the French adventurer Michel Peissel

ANNAPURNA REGION

Dhaulagiri Icefall

A two day side trip up the side of the Kali Gandaki valley will take you to the foot of the Dhaulagiri Icefall and give you great views of Dhaulagiri I and the Annapurna range. It's a 1200 metre climb, so it's a bit rough to climb up and back in a single day. There is no accommodation on this route, so you need camping arrangements in order to spend the night.

There are a few potential dangers to this trip: if it's cloudy, route-finding is a problem; there is a danger of altitude sickness, especially if you have just started your trek from Baglung or Birethanti; and there are avalanches in, and sometimes near, the icefall itself.

The mountaineering route up the icefall is a hazardous climb. Herzog's expedition explored this approach in 1950 and abandoned it because it was too dangerous. In 1969 an avalanche in the icefall killed seven members of the US Dhaulagiri expedition.

The route starts just south of Larjung village on the main trail between Kalopani and Marpha, at the Ghatta Khola with its wide gravel bed. Look for a small trail up through the forest on the south bank of the river. Make a short, steep ascent in trees to some overgrown fields. Follow a small trail through these fields, then alongside a stream to reach a small lake. There is a clearing above the lake suitable for a camp site.

Find the trail at the other end of the clearing and follow this into the trees. Turn right in about 10 minutes and climb through forests to a small hut, about an hour above the clearing. The path is now well defined, but extremely steep, in grasslands. You should reach a cairn in another hour and a small basin with yak pastures in a further 30 minutes. There are great views of the Kali Gandaki below and the Nilgiris and Annapurna I across the valley. Cross the basin, keep slightly to the right and climb up to reach some large boulders in a further 45 minutes. The glacier is now immediately below with the icefall beyond.

The return route is the same, though there are a few short cuts. Descend to the Ghatta Khola and continue down to the main valley-bottom trail. ■

Trade in the Kali Gandaki

The Kali Gandaki/Thak Khola valley has been a major trade route for centuries. Until 1959, traders exchanged salt collected from salt lakes in Tibet for rice and barley from the Middle Hills of Nepal. They also traded wool, livestock and butter for sugar, tea, spices, tobacco and manufactured goods from India, but the salt-for-grain trade dominated the economy. This trade has diminished, not only because of the political and economic changes in Tibet, but also because Indian salt is now available throughout Nepal at a much lower price than Tibetan salt.

Indian salt, from the sea, contains iodine. Many people in Nepal once suffered from goitres because of the total absence of iodine from their diet. Indian aid programmes distributed sea salt in a successful programme to prevent goitres, but the Tibetan salt trade suffered because of the artificially low prices of Indian salt. The Thakali people of the Kali Gandaki valley had a monopoly on the salt trade of this region. They are now turning to agriculture, tourism and other forms of trade for their livelihood. ∎

travelled up the Kali Gandaki in a hovercraft and managed to get this far before he was forced to abandon the project. Beyond Khobang the trail makes numerous climbs up and down on a cliffside trail to Tukuche, sometimes making short cuts across riverside gravel bars.

In its upper reaches, people call the Kali Gandaki the Thak Khola, thus the name Thakali for those who live in this region. At 2590m, **Tukuche** was once the most important Thakali village. Tukuche (*tuk*, 'grain', and *che*, 'flat place') was the meeting place where traders coming with salt and wool from Tibet and the upper Thak Khola valley bartered with traders carrying grain from the south. The hotels in Tukuche are in beautiful old Thakali homes with carved wooden windows, doorways and balconies. The *Himali*, *Laxmi* and *Sunil* guesthouses are along the stone-paved main street and offer garden restaurants. The *Tukuche Guest House* has an extensive display of maps and charts showing estimated walking times

between villages. At the northern end of town the *Yak Hotel* advertises a 'real yak on display inside' – it's worth a look.

Tourism has not totally offset the economic effect of the loss of the grain trade, so many people have moved from Tukuche to Pokhara, Kathmandu and the Terai. A walk along the backstreets of the village, particularly close to the river, will reveal many abandoned and crumbling buildings behind the prosperous facade of the main street.

A dramatic change in the vegetation, from pine and conifer forests to dry, desert-like country, takes place during this stretch of trail. The flow of air between the peaks of Annapurna and Dhaulagiri creates strong winds that howl up the valley. The breezes blow gently from the north during the early hours of the day, then shift to powerful gusts from the south throughout the late morning and afternoon. From here to Jomsom, these strong winds will be blowing dust and sand at your back after about 11 am.

The trail heads north through desert-like country, passing some large boulders. Across the river is Chhairo, a Tibetan refugee settlement with a carpet factory. Traders from Chhairo often sit along this part of the trail selling their wares. There are two bridges, so you can cross the river, visit Chhairo and then rejoin the west-bank trail. Pause a minute along this part of the trail and look at the scenery – high snow peaks, brown and yellow cliffs, splashes of bright green irrigated fields, and flat-roofed mud houses clustered here and there.

As the trail proceeds north, it passes the large stone buildings and orchards of an agricultural project set up in 1966 to introduce new types of produce into the region. The motivating force behind this project was Passang Khambache Sherpa, who accompanied David Snellgrove during his studies throughout Nepal. It may be possible to purchase fresh fruits, vegetables and almonds here. Local apple cider and fruit preserves are available in Marpha and Tukuche, and there is also, of course, excellent apple, apricot and peach rakshi. Try the bottled Tukuche Brandy and then try to pronounce the official name of this establishment: His Majesty's Government of Nepal National Temperate Horticulture Research Station.

Between the agricultural project and Marpha is *Om's Home Marpha*, a very clean hotel that has excellent food and a range of accommodation from dorms to rooms with private baths. **Marpha** (2665m) is huddled behind a ridge for protection from the wind and dust. This large Thakali village exhibits the typical Thak Khola architecture of flat roofs and narrow paved alleys and passageways. The low rainfall in this region makes these flat roofs practical; they also serve as a drying place for grains and vegetables.

In Marpha, the Thakali inn system has reached its highest level of development. Hotels have private rooms, menus, room service and indoor toilets. An extensive drainage system flows under the flagstone-paved street of this clean and pleasant village. There is a library (open from 5 to 7 pm) and impressive kanis mark both ends of town.

There are 16 hotels in Marpha and a surprising number of souvenir shops. Near the southern end are the *Hungry Eye Restaurant*, the *Neeru Guest House* and the *Paradise Guest House*. Central Marpha hotels include *Dhaulagiri Lodge* and *Baba's Lodge*. Both have elaborately carved windows, comfortable inner courtyards and good toilet facilities; the *Miami* has a solar-heated shower. A small signboard identifies *Bhakti Guest House*; the proprietor, Bhakti Hirachan, is an excellent source of information and assistance. Alongside a flagstone-paved trail just north of Marpha is the up-market *Hotel Trans Himalaya*, which has rooms with attached bathrooms (and sit-down loos) for Rs 350. Opposite the hotel is a solar drying facility that processes apples, apricots and vegetables.

Marpha's large, impressive gompa was renovated and enlarged in 1996. An efficient system allows you to deposit your rucksack in a storage room before climbing the steps to visit. This is a Nyingmapa Buddhist gompa; as in Tengpoche, the Mani Rimdu festival is celebrated in the autumn here. The

gompa, as are all the buildings in Marpha, is painted with a whitewash that is produced from a special local stone.

Marpha is a much better choice than Jomsom for a night stop because the hotels are better and there is less wind. It's a bit far, but not unreasonably so, to reach Muktinath in a single day from Marpha, but it's more interesting to take an extra day and break the trip up with a stop at Kagbeni.

Day 6: Marpha to Kagbeni

From Marpha, the trail continues along the side of the valley, climbing imperceptibly past a few tea shops, to **Shyang**, where the only facility is the *Hotel Pratichchya*. The route passes a few houses and trailside trinket vendors before climbing over a low ridge to **Jomsom** (more correctly Dzongsam, or 'new fort'). Jomsom is the administrative headquarters for the region and straddles the Kali Gandaki at an elevation of 2713m. The major inhabitants are government officials, army and merchants engaged in the distribution of goods brought in by plane and pony caravans. From Jomsom, you can make an easy side trip to the gompa at Thini, about an hour from Jomsom on the east bank of the Kali Gandaki.

Jomsom has three distinct parts. You enter the town from the south, near the *Dancing Yak Lodge*. Just beyond is the airport, where there are large hotels, restaurants, the RNAC office (open from 11 am to 4 pm) and offices of Everest Air and Nepal Airways. The hotel *Lali Guras*, the *Trekkers Inn, Hotel Mona Lisa* and the *Alka Marco Polo* are all near the airport. Each has a central courtyard surrounded by rooms, and meals are often served at a *kodatsu,* a Japanese-style table covered with a blanket to warm your legs with the heat from a charcoal brazier. There is a bakery at the *Magic Bean Coffee Shop* and there are numerous well-stocked shops.

The up-market *Om's Home* has rooms with private tiled baths and electric hotwater heaters at prices starting from Rs 350. Also near the airport is the mandatory police checkpost. It is important to obtain a stamp from this checkpost on your trekking permit, because all police posts from here on will want to see it. The arrival of the morning flight from Pokhara is the highlight of the day in Jomsom. In addition to most of the townspeople, there is also a collection of fruit and vegetable vendors in front of the airport in the morning.

North of the airport, on the west side of the Kali Gandaki, are shops, bhattis, a shoe repair shop and a large army camp that houses the High Altitude Mountain Warfare Wing of the Nepal army. You can often see the army practising rock climbing on the cliffs above. There are two bridges over the Kali Gandaki; just across the southernmost bridge is the telecommunications office. The section of town on the east bank of the river is the main part of Jomsom, with dwellings, bhattis, shops, the large *Dhaulagiri Guest House*, *Thak Khola Lodge & Jimi Hendrix Restaurant*, bank, German bakery, ACAP kerosene depot and post office. The military people jogging in the mornings are a bit incongruous in this remote location.

Follow the narrow main street past several hotels to the school and a statue of King Birendra at the northern end of town. The trail follows the broad river valley, sometimes above the river, but mostly along the rocky bank of the river itself as it passes beneath vertical rock cliffs. The trail passes a stream (which you may have to wade if the water is high) and a side trail that leads to Lupra, a Thakali village and a Bon-po gompa. Pass a walled tree plantation and climb over a small ridge to Chhancha Lhumba, better known as **Eklai Bhatti** ('alone hotel'), at 2730m. Despite its name, it is a substantial outpost where the *Hotel Hill Ton*, *Hotel Monal* and *Holiday Inn* offer you a chance to get out of the wind. In the *Kagbeni Lodge* you can shop for 'all kinds of Tibetan something' and eat woldrop salad or a potato coo cooat. The direct route to Muktinath leads straight up the hill behind the village.

Unless you are in a tremendous rush, you should follow the trail along the river from Eklai Bhatti to **Kagbeni**, a green oasis at 2810m at the junction of the Jhong Khola

and the Kali Gandaki. Kagbeni looks like a town out of the medieval past, with closely packed mud houses, dark tunnels and alleyways, imposing *chortens* and a large, ochre-coloured gompa perched above the town. Many people still dress in typical Tibetan clothing, though the children have, even in this faraway village, learned to beg, rather insistently, for sweets.

The large *Nilgiri View Lodge* at the southern entrance to the town is at the trail junction for the route to Muktinath. There are other hotels throughout the town, with the *Red House, Muktinath View* and *New Annapurna* lodges clustered around the town's main square. The ACAP office that administers upper Mustang is in Kagbeni.

Kagbeni is the northernmost village in this valley that foreigners may visit on a normal trekking permit. The police checkpost at the northern end of the village fastidiously prevents tourists from proceeding towards Lo Manthang, the walled city of Mustang, without the proper documentation.

Alternative Route: Direct to Muktinath
The direct route to Muktinath climbs from Eklai Bhatti along a windswept slope to a plateau above the Kali Gandaki, then turns east up the Jhong Khola valley. The trail ascends to **Khingar** through country that is arid and desert-like, in the same geographical and climatic zone as Tibet. The striking yellows of the bare hillsides contrast dramatically with the blue sky, white peaks and splashes of green where streams allow cultivation. The views of Dhaulagiri and Nilgiri are tremendous.

Day 7: Kagbeni to Muktinath
The trail to Muktinath starts at the southern end of Kagbeni, behind the Nilgiri View Lodge. It makes a steep climb up the Jhong Khola valley, passing the windmills that sometimes provide electric power for Kagbeni, and joins the direct trail to Muktinath below Khingar. Along the way you will see hundreds of small piles of rocks erected by pilgrims to honour their departed ancestors.

Vishnu in Stone
The Tibetan traders of the Kali Gandaki valley are unrelenting in their efforts to convince you to buy their wares. One item that is unique to this region is the *saligram*. These are black stones that, when broken open, reveal the fossilised remains of prehistoric ammonites, formed about 130 million years ago. You might find some saligram yourself between here and Jomsom, though you can always buy them, at inflated prices, from the traders – and then curse yourself all the way back to Pokhara for carrying a backpack full of rocks. The gold specks that appear on many saligram are pyrite (fool's gold). Hindu pilgrims purchase these ammonites because they represent the god Vishnu. ■

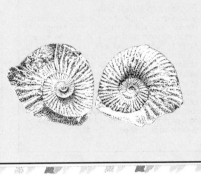

ANNAPURNA REGION

The walk from Khingar at 3200m to Jharkot is a delightful one amongst meadows, streams and poplar and fruit trees. There are often flocks of cranes in the area. The trail is high above the Jhong Khola as it climbs to **Jharkot**, an impressive fortress-like village at 3500m. The *New Plaza Hotel* and *Hotel Sonam* are in the centre of town, and just above the village is the *Himali Hotel*, which offers solar-heated rooms. Jharkot, with its picturesque kani and large gompa, is well worth exploring, and many people suggest staying here instead of Muktinath. There are some peach trees nearby; people press the peach seeds to make oil. Across the valley you can see the ruins of Dzong, the ancient capital of this region, and the smaller villages of Purang and Changur.

Climb over some walls, then trek past the village mule stables and up a steep, barren hillside on a wide trail. The first part of Muktinath that you reach, at 3710m, is known as **Ranipauwa** and is the site of a large rest house for pilgrims and a host of hotels, bhattis and camping places. This area is often crowded with both pilgrims and foreign tourists. The *Shree Muktinath Hotel* and *Mona Lisa* are good, but the *North Pole Lodge* is reported to have the best food in town. More mediocre choices include the *Hotel Pole Star*, the *Nilgiri View*, the *Lali Guras Lodge* and *Hotel Mona Lisa*. The *Hotel Dhaulagiri View & Bob Marley Restaurant* also has a good reputation – if you like reggae. It's wise to avoid the smaller, local-style hotels that cater to Hindu pilgrims. In the middle of the settlement are a police checkpost and a poorly maintained government camping ground.

There is a municipal hot shower in Ranipauwa that heats water with the excess electricity from the local hydroelectric project. A five minute shower costs Rs 25 and the money goes to the school. Beware of exposed wiring.

The temple and the religious shrines of **Muktinath** are about 90m in elevation above Ranipauwa. There are no hotels, and the temple committee does not allow camping. Muktinath is an important pilgrimage place for both Hindus and Buddhists. The holy shrines at Muktinath are in a grove of trees, and include a Buddhist gompa and the pagoda-style temple of **Vishnu Mandir**, containing an image of Vishnu. Around the temple is a wall from which 108 waterspouts, cast in the shape of cows' heads, pour forth sacred water. Even more sacred is the water that issues from a rock inside the ancient Tibetan-style **Jwala Mai** temple a short distance below the pagoda. Inside this gompa, behind a tattered curtain, are small natural gas jets that produce a perpetual holy flame alongside a spring that is the source of the

Pilgrims to Muktinath

Muktinath is an important pilgrimage place for Hindus. You will encounter many Nepali and Indian pilgrims on the trail. Well-to-do Indians fly in to Jomsom and walk or ride horses to Muktinath. The most colourful pilgrims to Muktinath are the ascetic *sadhus*, whom you must have already seen many times. They travel in various stages of undress, smear themselves with ash and often carry a three-pronged spear called a *trill*. A rupee or two donation to these holy men is not out of place. They are Shaivite mystics on a pilgrimage that, more often than not, began in the heat of southern India. ■

sacred water. This auspicious combination of earth, fire and water is responsible for the religious importance of Muktinath. It is often possible to see Tibetan women, with elaborate turquoise-embedded headdresses, engaged in devotions at these shrines.

The most charming description of Muktinath is the one on the signboard erected by the Ministry of Tourism at Jomsom:

Muktinath is beautiful, calm and quiet,
great and mysterious for pilgrims,
decorated with god and goddess.
Although you are kindly requested not to snap them.

Day 8: Muktinath to Jomsom

It's an easy walk back to Jomsom, though it becomes tedious if there is a strong wind. This is not the time to decide that you are going to cross Thorung La and trek around Annapurna. If you have come in this direction from Pokhara, you probably do not have the warm clothing and boots necessary for crossing the pass. It is also a long, hard climb of 1600m from Muktinath to the pass.

Day 9: Jomsom to Kathmandu

From Jomsom it's easiest to fly to Pokhara first and then travel on to Kathmandu. In the early morning, Jomsom airport is the social centre of the town with tourists and locals alike vying for the limited number of seats.

BAGLUNG TO TATOPANI

Duration 2 days
Difficulty Easy to medium
Maximum elevation 1180m
Permit cost US$5 per week plus Rs 1000
Season October to May
Hotels Good
Summary A short cut to avoid the 1600m climb over Ghorapani hill. A long walk up a valley that narrows as you walk north. Trekking lodges are pretty basic.

You can avoid the long climb over the Ghorapani hill on the Jomsom trek by travelling by bus to the trailhead at Baglung and following the Kali Gandaki valley to Tatopani. This can be a particularly attractive prospect if you have trekked around Annapurna and decide you don't want to cope with the 1650m climb from Tatopani to Ghorapani. The Baglung trek has no significant climbs and takes only a day and a half of walking, so it's reasonable to plan on two days for the trip between Pokhara and Tatopani in either direction. The facilities along the route are more local in style than those north of Tatopani, but they do have English menus and are reasonably clean.

Access

It is 73 km from Pokhara to Baglung on a good, but winding, road. The trip takes less than three hours by bus from the Baglung bus station in the north of Pokhara. A taxi takes two hours and costs Rs 1600 to Rs 2000, depending on demand. See the description of the road as far as Naya Pul, the jumping-off place for Birethanti, in the Jomsom trek section. From Naya Pul the road follows the Modi Khola south to Patichaur, then crosses the river and starts climbing up the side of the ridge to **Kusma** (Km 58), perched at the end of the ridge between the Kali Gandaki and the Modi Khola. There are some trekkers' hotels left over from the time when the road ended at Kusma. The road drops into the Kali Gandaki valley passing Armadi, then reaches **Maldhunga** (Km 68), a few shops at the bridge over the Kali Gandaki, elevation 720m. The road crosses the bridge and continues up the ridge to the bazaar at Baglung.

There is a road under construction up the east side of the Kali Gandaki from Maldhunga towards Beni. In 1996 only a small portion of the work on this road had been completed, but it may be open by the time you read this. If so, you can save some walking by getting off at the squalid settlement of Maldhunga and taking whatever transport is available as far as possible on the road.

Day 1: Baglung to Beni
On leaving Baglung the trail descends through forests into the Kali Gandaki valley. It's level for a while to **Pharse**, at 760m, where there are several tea shops. A suspension bridge leads across the river to the unfinished road on the east bank. Stay on the west bank and trek across several landslides through heavily farmed country and the villages of Belbot Dodane, Saremre, Shimo, Lamoghara and Ratne Chaur, crossing many small landslides. The trail passes the Beni jail, climbs over a ridge and a landslide, then crosses the Myagdi Khola and enters Beni.

Beni, on a plateau above the river at 820m, is a large village with a long main street that has interesting facilities such as photo studios and barbers as well as the usual shops and bhattis. The trail to Dhorpatan and Dolpo starts at the southern end of Beni; see the Western Nepal chapter for details. Mule trains follow this route up the Myagdi Khola towards Dhorpatan. The *Hotel Dolphin* (☎ 069-20107), which does very heavy advertising along the trail, is in the centre of town. A better choice is the *Hotel Yeti* or the *Namaste Lodge*, which caters to trekkers and is below the Beni plateau at the north end of the village. If you arrive early, continue an hour on to Galeshor, which is a more pleasant place to stay.

Day 2: Beni to Tatopani
Follow the west bank of the river, crossing several landslides, to **Galeshor**, also known as Rahughat, just above the Rahughat Khola at 870m. Near the river is the seedy *Riverside Guest House*; at the south end of the village is the pleasant *Paradise Guest House*. In late November each year there's a large fair *(mela)* in Galeshor. Cross a suspension bridge over the Rahughat Khola to Ranipauwa at 920m. The Kali Gandaki now starts to close in and the rolling terraced hills disappear.

The route crosses numerous landslides before reaching **Baisari**, a small settlement at 960m that includes the *Annapurna* and *Lete* guesthouses. A bit beyond are a cluster of tea shops and the *Super View Lodge*. The route is now mostly in forests as the trail makes numerous ups and downs crossing more landslides. After crossing the Beg Khola on a suspension bridge you will find yourself in a three-sided tunnel blasted out of the side of the cliff. The next stretch of trail is a particularly dramatic construction along the steep valley. There are numerous ups and downs, but they are all less than 100m, so the trekking, while tedious, is not exhausting. Trek out of the tunnel, then through forests and corn fields to two small lodges in the village of **Tiplyang**. The *Mustang Restaurant*, *Star Lodge* and *Sherchan Lodge* are in the centre of the village; a bit beyond are the *Hill View Lodge* and *Ama Lodge*. Despite the English signboards, all of these would probably be best described as tea shops because they mostly cater to Indian and Nepali travellers and pilgrims.

At Tiplyang the route crosses a long suspension bridge to the east bank of the Kali Gandaki and the Magar village of Dorsale. Trek through rice fields to the *Stream Memorial Restaurant* in Mahabhir, then climb broad stone steps inside a three-sided cliffhanging tunnel. The route gets a bit complex as it uses footholds cut into a large boulder to cross a landslide, then drops steeply to a tiny tea shop at Birkati on the banks of the river.

Climb a long set of stone stairs to another vertigo-inducing, cliffhanging trail, then descend to the Brahman village of **Rato Pani**, the *Nilgiri View Hotel* and *Hema Hot*

Spring Lodge at 1150m. Trek on for another 20 minutes to the Ghar Khola, where the route meets the trail that descends from Ghorapani, then cross the Ghar Khola and finally the high suspension bridge over the Kali Gandaki into **Tatopani**.

Annapurna Sanctuary

> **Duration** 15 days
> **Difficulty** Medium
> **Maximum elevation** 4095m
> **Permit cost** US$5 per week plus Rs 1000
> **Season** October to November, March to April
> **Hotels** Very good
> **Summary** Walk through villages, then climb through forests into the Annapurna Sanctuary, a valley surrounded by high Himalayan peaks. A great opportunity to get into the mountains without the altitude problems of the Mt Everest region.

The route to Annapurna Sanctuary (Annapurna Deuthali in Nepali), the site of the Annapurna south face base camp, is a spectacular short trek. Though it has some steep climbs, the trek is not difficult.

The trek to the Annapurna Sanctuary traverses a variety of terrain, from lowland villages and rice terraces to glaciers, and offers outstanding high mountain views. This is a fine opportunity to surround yourself with Himalayan peaks in a short time, without having to contend with the altitude and flight problems of the Everest region.

You can make the trek from Pokhara to Annapurna base camp and back in as few as 10 or 11 days, but it is best to allow two weeks to fully appreciate the high altitude scenery. A diversion to Ghorapani on the return route provides a view of Dhaulagiri from Poon Hill.

This trek appears on the Annapurna Sanctuary & Jomsom Trek map on pages 224-5.

Season

The major problem with this trek is that it can become impassable because of snow and avalanches in winter and early spring. It is the only major trekking route in Nepal that has significant avalanche danger, so you must enquire locally whether the trail is safe. Some trekkers have died because of avalanches, and others have been stranded in the sanctuary for days.

Accommodation

There are frequent tea shops along the entire trek, sometimes five or 10 minutes apart, and you will rarely walk for as long as an hour without finding some source of refreshment. The lodges extend all the way into the Annapurna Sanctuary, except in winter when the hotel-keepers retreat to their homes in Chhomrong.

Access

Take a taxi or bus from Pokhara to the couple of shacks known as Phedi, then continue a few hundred metres along the road to a taxi stand. Here you will find the *Dhampus Mailee Hotel*, a small cluster of local-style hotels and a mineral-water bottling plant. The start of the trail is obvious, heading up the hill on a set of steps to the west of the car park in front of the hotel.

Day 1: Phedi to Tolka

The entire region from Phedi, on the valley floor, to the top of the hill is commonly known as Dhampus, but the main part of Dhampus village is on the top of the ridge, more than 500m above. The area is inhabited by Brahmans, Chhetris and a few Gurungs. Starting at an elevation of 1180m, in a forest that is so overgrazed that it looks like a manicured municipal park, the trail climbs steeply for about 45 minutes to the tiny *Mina Lodge*. It becomes less steep as it follows a stone staircase through fields past scattered houses, then it climbs over a wall to a small temple. Here a sign directs you to the steep uphill trail to Dhampus. Trek past the *Evergreen Restaurant* and more houses to another trail junction where a steep uphill trail leads to the main part of **Dhampus**, on top of the ridge at 1750m. You are rewarded

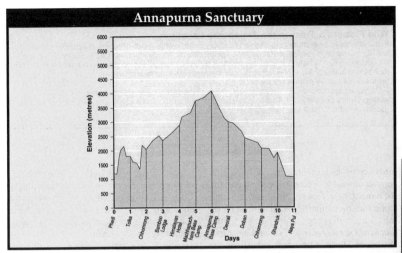

Annapurna Sanctuary

with great views of the mountains that continue to improve as you ascend along the ridge. There are a few hotels at this end of Dhampus, including the *Lali Guras Restaurant* and the Ker & Downey *Basanta Lodge*. Follow along the ridge to a small lake, camp site, hotel complex, police checkpost and the up-market *Dhaulagiri View Hotel*, perched atop a hillock.

Dhampus is the centre of the theft racket in central Nepal. Thieves often cut the tents of trekkers and remove valuable items during the night, so it is not a good idea to camp alone here. Trekking groups pitch their tents in a circle like an old-time wagon train and post a guard with a lighted lantern throughout the night. If you stay in a hotel, be sure that you know who is sharing the room with you, and lock the door whenever you go out – even for a moment. The thieves watch everyone in order to decide who has something worth taking or is likely to be careless. They will wait patiently all night to make their move if necessary.

The trail climbs to a small tea shop that announces itself as the ending point of Dhampus. The route enters a damp rhododendron forest and follows a trail paved with

stones. There are no hotels for about an hour as the trail makes a steep climb to **Pothana**, a large collection of hotels at 1990m. Just before Pothana is an inconspicuous trail junction; this is a trail that leads to the 'Australian Camp' and a route back to the Baglung road at Khare. The view of Machhapuchhare, the 'fish tail' mountain (from *machha*, 'fish', and *puchhare*, 'tail'), is excellent from Pothana, except that from this angle it looks more like the Matterhorn than a fish tail. To see the mountain in its proper perspective you wait several days until you get into the Annapurna Sanctuary. You can spend the night in the *Annapurna Lodge*, *Heaven's Gate* or one of Pothana's other hotels to get a good view in the morning from the tower atop a hotel. Most hotels from here on boast large billboard-style maps of the region that portray the route to the sanctuary with varying degrees of accuracy and provide their own version of estimated walking times throughout the area.

The trail climbs on a stone-paved trail through forests to two lodges at Deurali, atop a hill at 2150m, where there are views of Annapurna South and Hiunchuli. Make a steep descent through forests alive with

---

Wild Flowers & Trees in the Annapurna Sanctuary

In the Annapurna Sanctuary region a wide variety of wild flowers linger in bloom long after the monsoon, thanks to the high rainfall of this area. Look for **luculia** (a pink mallow that is often mistaken for rhododendron), a variety of **impatiens** and **composites** (asters, daisies etc) and the **pleone orchids** that bloom in trees. Along the wet rock walls between Ghorapani and Ghandruk, near Banthanti, the profusion of mauve **primulas** cannot be missed.

In upper approaches to the sanctuary, the leafless **birch** trees are also readily recognisable in winter. These trees usually denote the upper limit of the tree line and are easy to identify with their reddish or whitish bark that tends to peel in sheets. ■

---

birds, ferns and orchids into a huge side canyon of the Modi Khola. Descend past the *Archana Guest House* and down a rough stone trail to another lodge in a forest clearing. The trail keeps going down to the *Sundara Guest House* and several large teahouses at **Bheri Kharka**, a suburb of the large Gurung village of Bichok, which is far below. Descend to the head of the canyon and cross a stream at 1790m. The trail climbs gently out of the side canyon on flagstone steps. Climb further to some tea shops on a ridge where the trail emerges into the main Modi Khola valley. A short distance below is the *Namaste Tourist Guest House* in the first of several clusters of hotels that comprise **Tolka**, a small settlement at 1810m. The trail descends through the village, passing the *Hilltop Ram Lodge*, the school and the camp site, then down to the *Hira Lodge*, *Babu Lodge* and the *International Guest House*.

Day 2: Tolka to Chhomrong

The trail descends a long stone staircase to a suspension bridge across a stream at 1720m, then climbs through forests to a ridge. It's then an easy walk, past streams, fields and some unusual oval-shaped houses. You can see the Modi Khola far below and the houses of Jhinu Danda halfway up the hill far ahead. Pass the school, cross a stream on a suspension bridge and you will be in the hotel complex at the top of **Landruk**, a Gurung village at 1620m. There is a large choice of hotels here; the best ones are above the village and include the *Footrest*, *Lali Guras* and *Hungry Eye*, all in whitewashed stone

buildings. Along the trail you will probably meet people collecting money for schools. They will produce a ledger book showing the donations of other trekkers and enter your contribution into their records. The donations may be legitimate, but it is an adult version of the creative forms of begging that tourists have encouraged.

Descend the stone staircase through the paved courtyards of Landruk past the *Mount View Hotel* to the small *Hotel Himalaya*, 10 minutes below the village at 1550m. The trail to the sanctuary leads to the right, just behind the hotel. There may be a signpost pointing the way north to Chhomrong and down the hill to Ghandruk.

The downhill trail leads to the river and then climbs to Ghandruk. You can see Ghandruk high above you on the opposite side of the river.

The narrow trail to the sanctuary turns north up the Modi Khola valley, passing alongside rice terraces, then through forests, to the rustic *Namaste Lodge*. A short walk up the river bed leads to **Naya Pul** (New Bridge), also known as Shiuli, at 1340m. There are several substantial hotels here on both sides of the suspension bridge that was built in about 1985. The trail climbs steeply to Samrung, then crosses a stream at 1430m on a cement bridge. This is the lower part of the Khumnu Khola, but here it is known as the Kladi Khola.

A stiff climb leads to **Jhinu Danda**, where there are several hotels on a ridge at 1750m. There is a hot spring with cement bathing pools about 15 minutes downhill (and a half-hour back up) on a side trail; ask a lodge owner about them. You can see houses on the top of the ridge far above; this is your next destination. It is a long, steep climb, broken only by a few teahouses, to a cluster of tea shops at **Taglung**, atop the treeless ridge at 2180m. The trek now joins the Ghandruk to Chhomrong route, so the trail is wider and better from here to Chhomrong.

A short distance from Taglung is the isolated *Himalayan View Lodge*, then the trail rounds a bend and enters the upper part of **Chhomrong**. This Gurung village has evolved into two separate parts. New Chhomrong is the upper part, at an elevation of 2040m, with resort hotels, the school and a helicopter pad. Old Chhomrong, at 2060m, is the main part of the village with shops, offices and lodges. The fancy hotels in New Chhomrong have slate patios, private rooms and dining rooms with picture windows.

Down a long staircase in the centre of the village are a kerosene depot, the ACAP office and several shops. *Captain's Lodge* is Chhomrong's most popular inn, though the captain himself has a strong personality. The *Chhomrong Guest House* is also near the centre of town. All the hotels have provision shops at which you can stock up on food for the trip into the sanctuary. Some hotels also rent equipment like gaiters, gloves, sleeping bags and down jackets; be sure you have warm clothing before you go on. The ACAP regulations prohibit the use of firewood beyond Ghandruk, so all trekkers and hotels must cook with gas or kerosene. If you are camping, you can buy fuel and rent Indian pressure stoves and plastic jerry cans here. If you are staying in hotels, the hotelier will take care of the fuel problem. Beyond Chhomrong, camping is restricted to certain ACAP-designated camp sites and hotel construction is strictly controlled.

The houses and hotels in old Chhomrong once had electric lights thanks to Mr Hayashi, popularly known as Bijuli Japani, the 'electric Japanese', who installed a small hydroelectric plant and equipped the houses with miniature light bulbs. The system has broken down and the villagers are negotiating with

ACAP over plans to build a new generating facility.

This is the highest permanent settlement in the valley, but herders take sheep and goats to upper pastures in the sanctuary during the summer. There is a tremendous view of Annapurna South, which seems to tower above the village, and there are good views of Machhapuchhare, the 'fish tail' mountain, across the valley. It is from this point onwards that the reason for the name of this peak becomes apparent. In 1957 Wilfred Noyce and David Cox climbed Machhapuchhare (6997m) to within 50m of its summit. After this attempt, the government prohibited further climbing on the mountain, so technically the peak remains unclimbed. A lower peak to the south, Mardi Himal (5587m), is open to trekking parties.

Day 3: Chhomrong to Bamboo Lodge

Leaving Chhomrong, the trail descends on a stone staircase and crosses the Chhomrong Khola on a swaying suspension bridge, then climbs out of the side valley. High above the Modi Khola on its west bank, the trail passes through the tiny settlement of Tilche in forests of bamboo, rhododendron and oak. Climbing further on a rocky trail (beware of the stinging nettles) you reach three hotels at **Sinuwa**, at 2350m.

Climb in rhododendron forests to **Kuldi**, at 2520m. This was once a British sheep-breeding project; now the stone houses are an ACAP visitor centre and checkpost. In winter, it's common to find snow anywhere from this point on. Descend a long, steep stone staircase into deep bamboo and rhododendron forests. It is then a short distance on a muddy trail to **Bamboo Lodge** (2340m), a collection of four hotels, none of which is built of bamboo. In early autumn and late spring, this part of the trail is crawling with leeches.

Day 4: Bamboo Lodge to Himalayan Hotel

The trail climbs steeply through stands of bamboo, then through rhododendron forest up the side of the canyon. Occasionally the

ANNAPURNA REGION

trail drops slightly to cross tributary streams, but it ascends continuously overall. When there is snow this stretch of trail is particularly difficult because the bamboo lying on the trail, hidden beneath the snow, provides an excellent start to a slide downhill. Local people hack down the dense bamboo forests beyond Kuldi to make mats for floors and roofs, and for *dokos*, the baskets that porters carry.

The trail passes an abandoned hotel at old Doban, about two hours beyond Kuldi, then traverses several avalanche chutes. At **Doban** (2630m) there is the *Tiptop Lodge* and the *Annapurna Approach Lodge*. Beyond Doban the trail is muddy. It traverses high above the river, but this is no problem for those who suffer vertigo, because thick stands of bamboo block the view of the rushing river and waterfall. Cross a landslide and another avalanche track to reach the **Himalayan Hotel** at 2900m. Just before the hotel you can see the debris left from an avalanche that killed a Sherpa kitchen crew in the spring of 1989. If you arrive early, it is worth trekking on to Deorali to make the following day easier.

Day 5: Himalayan Hotel to Machhapuchhare Base Camp

From Himalayan Hotel it's about an hour's walk, first on a rocky trail through forests, then up a steep ravine, to **Hinko** at 3160m. This is called Hinko Cave because a huge overhanging rock provides some protection against rain and avalanches. There used to be a funny hotel built into the cave, but ACAP closed this facility, so the only accommodation is at Deorali, a half-hour further on.

The trail crosses a ravine and a major avalanche track just beyond Hinko, then climbs through large boulders to **Deorali**, at 3230m, where the better of two hotels is the *Panorama Guest House*. Above Deorali, the valley widens and becomes less steep, and you can see the 'gates' to the sanctuary. After heavy snowfall, avalanches from Hiunchuli and Annapurna South, peaks which are above this point but not visible from it, come

crashing into the valley with frightening speed and frequency.

As the trail continues into the sanctuary, it crosses two wide avalanche tracks on a narrow trail that huddles up against the cliffs. The trail descends to meet the Modi Khola and follows the river to **Bagar**, a meadow and some abandoned hotels at 3310m. The normal trail follows the left side of the valley, but when an avalanche has blocked the trail it may be necessary to take an alternative route. There is a trail that crosses the river, climbs along the eastern side of the river and then recrosses on a log bridge just before Bagar. The lodge owners in Deorali can tell you when it's necessary to take this diversion, and sometimes there is a sign on the trail to direct you. The normal trail will probably be open in October and November and late spring.

From Bagar, climb across more avalanche paths, cross a moraine and a stream, then climb towards a two storey building. This is a German meteorological project office. There is a hotel here, and there are two others five minutes beyond in an area known as **Machhapuchhare base camp**, elevation 3720m. These hotels, the *Fish Tail* and the *Gurung Co-op*, may or may not be open, depending on whether the innkeeper – and the supplies – have been able to reach the hotel through the avalanche area. Most of the inns in the sanctuary close during the winter. All are operated by people from Ghandruk or Chhomrong, so you can easily find out in advance which, if any, are open.

The mountain views are stupendous; the panorama includes Hiunchuli, Annapurna I (8091m), Annapurna III (7555m), Gangapurna (7454m) and Machhapuchhare.

Day 6: Machhapuchhare Base Camp to Annapurna Base Camp

The climb to Annapurna base camp – four hotels on a knoll at 4095m – takes about two hours. Start early: clouds often come in before noon and can make the trail hard to find. The route passes a few roofless shepherds' huts alongside a moraine, then climbs to the base camp. In the high trekking

Annapurna Region
Top: Hiunchuli is one of the more difficult trekking peaks, and avalanches from it often
  come crashing down onto the route to the Annapurna Sanctuary.
Bottom: Spectacular mountain scenery in the Manang district.

GREG ELMS

STAN ARMINGTON

GREG ELMS

MARGARET JUNG

Annapurna Region
Top Left: Gurung woman and child
Top Right: Lodges and restaurants in Manang village
Bottom Left: Hillside town
Bottom Right: Preparing lunch at a teahouse

season the hotels here are ridiculously crowded. The *Snow Land* and *Paradise Hotel* are the up-market establishments with high-altitude apple pie and pizza. The area is cold, windy and often snowbound. When I was here one April the snow reached the roofs of the hotels.

There are tremendous views of the near-vertical south face of Annapurna that towers above the sanctuary to the north-west. The ascent of this face in 1970 by an expedition led by Chris Bonington still remains one of the most spectacular of an 8000m peak.

Several peaks that are accessible from the sanctuary are on the trekking peak list. Tharpu Chuli (formerly Tent Peak; 5663m) offers a commanding 360° view of the entire sanctuary. Its higher neighbour to the north is Singu Chuli (Fluted Peak; 6501m). To the south is Hiunchuli, which is also open to trekking parties. All three of these peaks present significant mountaineering challenges and require skill, equipment and planning. A less challenging but worthwhile objective is Rakshi Peak, an outcrop on the southern ridge of Tent Peak.

There are few birds in the sanctuary, but there are tahr, Himalayan weasels and pika.

Day 7: Annapurna Base Camp to Deorali
It's much easier going down. You should have no problem reaching Deorali in a single day from Annapurna base camp.

Day 8: Deorali to Doban
Retrace your steps through Himalayan Hotel to Doban or beyond.

Day 9: Doban to Chhomrong
Trek back down to apple pie country.

Day 10: Chhomrong to Ghandruk
You can return to Pokhara from Chhomrong by a variety of routes. The fastest way is to trek back to Ghandruk and down the Modi Khola to Birethanti and Naya Pul, where you can find transport back to Pokhara. A more interesting alternative is to leave this day's route at Khumnu and trek to Ghorapani, as

described on page 243. From Ghorapani you can either head north to Jomsom and Muktinath, or head back to Pokhara via Birethanti or via Tatopani and Baglung; these alternatives are described in the Jomsom Trek and Baglung to Tatopani sections earlier in this chapter.

To reach Ghandruk from Chhomrong, return to the junction of the trail from Landruk and Naya Pul near the tea shops at Taglung. Stay on the wide main trail, walking west above the prosperous-looking houses and potato and wheat fields of Taglung, then descend gently through forests to a single tea shop, the *Hilcross Lodge* at 2150m. From here, the trail drops steeply on switchbacks to **Khumnu** (also called Kimrong) village, above the Khumnu Khola at 1780m. There are hotels in the village, and a very funky tea shop near the bridge.

At Khumnu, cross the suspension bridge and stay on the main trail as it climbs out of the Khumnu valley. The trail makes a steep climb to some teahouses at **Uri**, on a pass at 2220m. The trail descends through huge boulders to a small creek and drops gently into the maze of trails in Ghandruk.

Ghandruk, a huge Gurung village at 1970m, is the second-largest Gurung settlement in Nepal (the largest is Siklis), and is a confusing cluster of closely spaced, slate-roofed houses. There are neatly terraced fields both above and below the town. Older maps spell the village name 'Ghandrung', but Ghandruk is the currently accepted spelling. Ghandruk is the Nepali name, but the village's real Gurung name is Kond.

It is wonderfully easy to get lost in the network of narrow alleyways while trying to trek through Ghandruk. The hotels are scattered throughout the village and are quite far apart, both in distance and elevation. There are little signboards at most trail junctions directing you to various hotels that are '1 minute away'; the times on these signs are very optimistic.

Ghandruk has an extensive water supply with tanks, pipes and taps throughout the village. Electricity is supplied by a 50 kW hydroelectric plant that is managed by the

PLACES TO STAY
1 Shangri La Guest House
2 Excellent View Lodge
4 Eco Camping
5 Snow View Lodge
7 Gangapurna Lodge
9 Himalaya Lodge
10 Hilltop Lodge
11 Ghandruk Guest House
12 Open Guest House
17 Saktar Guest House
19 Annapurna Lodge
20 Peaceful Lodge
21 Milan Hotel
23 Mountain Lodge
24 Manisha Hotel
25 Trekkers Inn
26 Sakura Hotel
29 Namaste Lodge

OTHER
3 Ama Carpet Centre
6 Pioneer Academy
8 Snow Land
13 Carpet Shop
14 School
15 ACAP Visitor Centre
16 Health Post
18 Traditional Gurung
   Museum & Restaurant;
   Gurung Cultural Centre
22 Telephone Office
27 Post Office; Youth
   Eco Trekking Centre;
   Kerosene Sale Depot
28 Power House
30 Bishal Restaurant

Ghandruk

ANNAPURNA REGION

village. The views of Annapurna South (Annapurna Dakshin in Nepali) from here are outstanding. Machhapuchhare, seen in its 'fish tail' aspect, peeps over a forested ridge. ACAP has a visitor centre and an office in Ghandruk and provides information about its activities and demonstrations of some of its innovations. The *Traditional Gurung Museum & Restaurant* was established by a woman from Ghandruk and offers a variety of dishes and drinks that are unique to this region. If you are on a spending spree, try one of the carpet shops or visit the handicraft shop in the *Local Youth Eco Trekking Centre*, which also provides local guides and offers cultural and nature tours. Wander around the village before you decide on a hotel; there are a lot to choose from. The *Trekkers Inn* won a 'lodge of the year' award from ACAP. Its neighbour, the *Milan*, is also excellent and, like most lodges in Ghandruk, uses kerosene and gas exclusively and has a proper septic tank to handle toilet waste. Both the *Mountain Lodge* and *Manisha Hotel* have several rooms with private bathrooms.

Day 11: Ghandruk to Naya Pul

Turn south at the foot of Ghandruk and start the long descent to the Modi Khola. The trail drops at first on a staircase, then traverses high above the river on a wide stone-paved trail. There's a large landslide and a stream to cross just before Chane at 1700m, where there is a small tea shop. There is a trail to Tikedungha that starts from here; it's a five hour walk with few facilities along the way. Pass a few tea shops at Kimchi, elevation 1650m, and keep heading downhill to Kehone Danda, then to the *River View Lodge* at Kliu, at 1300m, and on to a suspension bridge over the Sadhu Khola, finally arriving alongside the Modi Khola at the *Shikhar Guest House* in **Shauli Bazaar**, elevation 1140m.

The trail is now on the bottom of the river valley, passing through a lovely birch forest, then following alongside the river on a rough trail to the extensive rice terraces of Kimrong. Continue to Lamakhet, past the Ker & Downey *Sanctuary Lodge*. It's another half-hour to Birethanti at 1030m. The last stretch of trail is rough and rocky, down a dry stream bed to a shrine by the Modi Khola. There are often people chanting and worshipping here; the shrine owes its importance to some white squiggles on a rock. See Day 1 of the Jomsom trek for a description of the facilities in Birethanti.

You can stay in Birethanti or head into Pokhara. It's a 20 minute walk on the rough trail to **Naya Pul**, then you have to climb steeply up the hill to the road. Taxis and buses to Pokhara are available at Naya Pul well into the night. Taxis charge Rs 500 to Rs 1000 and the ride takes less than an hour; a bus ride costs Rs 50.

KHUMNU TO GHORAPANI

To reach Ghorapani from Khumnu, cross the river on a suspension bridge and then walk about 20m upstream to the site of the defunct old bridge. A faint, hard-to-find trail leads steeply uphill. Don't risk getting on the wrong trail; ask the people in the teahouse near the bridge for directions. The trail becomes more distinct as it switchbacks up

through wheat fields to the Brahman village of **Melanche** at 2050m. Above the village, the trail becomes less steep, but still climbs steadily through rhododendron forests to **Tadapani** at 2540m. Here the route joins the main Ghorapani to Ghandruk trail. It's a long trek to make in a single day; you will be happier if you break it into two days and spend the night at Tadapani.

Alternative Route: Via Chuele

There's also a shorter trail that crosses the head of the valley, but it's even harder to find. It leaves the Chhomrong trail and heads westward up the valley, eventually dropping and crossing the Khumnu Khola. It then climbs through Chuele village and meets the Ghandruk trail at Tadapani. It is said that there are two small lodges on the route. An approximation of this route is shown on both the Schneider and ACAP maps.

GHORAPANI TO GHANDRUK
Warning

There have been several incidents of violent crime in the forests between Ghorapani and Ghandruk. Several trekkers, all of whom were trekking alone, were attacked and robbed in the autumn of 1996.

The Trek

It is a long day from Ghorapani to Ghandruk; it's not a difficult one, though (except when the trail is snow-covered), because the trail heads generally downhill. If you are trekking from Ghandruk to Ghorapani, on the other hand, it's a long, hard day. Few local people use this trail, but it is becoming an increasingly important trekking route, and there has been overwhelming and uncontrolled development of the area in the past 10 years. Villagers have chopped down large parts of what was once an unbroken forest of rhododendron to build hotels. In 1993 ACAP, in collaboration with local village development committees, wisely banned the use of firewood between Ghorapani and Ghandruk, so all lodges should be using bottled gas or kerosene for cooking. Unfortunately the ban does not yet apply to Ghorapani.

From the Ghorapani pass, known as Deorali, the trail climbs east on a muddy path through deep forests. It finally emerges on a grassy knoll which offers good mountain views, including a view of Machhapuchhare (not visible from the Ghorapani pass), and a panorama all the way south to the plains of India. This is a similar view to the one from Poon Hill. Keep climbing along the ridge in pine and rhododendron forests to a crest at 3030m, then descend to two inns at a second pass, also called Deorali, at 2960m.

There is a trail junction with a route that leads down to Chitre and Tatopani. The Ghandruk trail descends to the *Lali Guras Lodge* in a rhododendron forest, then follows a dry stream bed. A ridge hides the mountains as the trail makes a steep, sometimes treacherous, descent on a narrow path alongside the stream, which becomes larger as the descent continues. The stream has some clear pools alongside the trail (remember the Nepali disapproval of skinny-dipping) and finally becomes a series of waterfalls over a jumble of boulders and logs that were washed down when this harmless-looking stream ran amok during the monsoon rains.

The steep descent becomes more gentle as the route reaches **Banthanti**, six hotels in the shadow of a huge rock face. The tables and benches outside the lodges present a scene reminiscent of a ski lodge – especially when there is snow. (This is not the same Banthanti that is between Ulleri and Ghorapani.) Follow the stream down to a bridge, where a tiny trail leads off to a rock quarry; porters carry slabs of slate from here to make roofs for homes in Ghandruk and Melanche.

The trail starts climbing, leaving the moist, high mountain forests and entering a field of cane, making some ups and downs past the *Tranquillity Lodge*, to a vantage point that offers a brief view of the mountains. The trail descends steeply to a stream before climbing again through forests to **Tadapani**, a jumble of hotels with a dramatic view at 2540m. Not content with the view from ground level, one hotel has built a stone lookout tower. Tadapani means 'far water'. The village water supply is a long distance

below the village. Before the water pipe was constructed it took porters more than half an hour to fetch a load of water.

From Tadapani, there is a trail to the left that descends through forests, then through terraced fields, to the Khumnu Khola. This direct route to the Annapurna Sanctuary is described, in reverse, in the previous Khumnu to Ghorapani section.

The Ghandruk trail descends steeply through forests to a clearing with two hotels. This is yet another spot called Deorali. A short, steep descent among rocks leads to a stream crossing, then the descent continues gently past other streams, finally leading out on a ridge towards Ghandruk.

The trail reaches the top of Ghandruk near the Pioneer Boarding School and the *Snow View Lodge*, then passes the *Annapurna Lodge* and descends on stone steps into the maze of the village itself. The hotels in **Ghandruk** are spread throughout the village; see Day 10 of the Annapurna Sanctuary trek for more information about Ghandruk and a map showing the hotels.

Around Annapurna Trek

Duration 16 days
Difficulty Medium to hard
Maximum elevation 5416m
Permit cost US$5 per week plus Rs 1000
Season October to November, March to April
Hotels Mostly good
Summary Walk completely around the Annapurna massif. Trek through lowland villages to the remote Manang region, and down the Kali Gandaki. Cross a 5416m pass – probably the highest you'll ever get without climbing a mountain.

It takes a minimum of 16 days to trek around the entire Annapurna massif, visiting the Tibet-like country on the northern slopes of the Himalaya and the dramatic Kali Gandaki gorge. Nepal opened Manang to trekkers in April 1977, although a few expeditions and scientific parties visited the region in the 1950s. The last seven days of this trek are the reverse of the popular trek from Pokhara to Jomsom, which is described earlier in this chapter.

Permits & Formalities

In autumn 1996 there were 16 checkposts on the trek around Annapurna. Those in the Marsyangdi valley are more numerous and more bureaucratic than those in most other parts of Nepal and laboriously copy all the numbers on your trekking permit into ledger books. The checkposts also require an excessive amount of information from guides, so if you have a guide, it's easiest to give them your trekking permit and let them handle all the formalities for you. Each checkpost stamps your trekking permit, and there are stories of people being sent back for the previous stamp if one was missing, so be sure to stop everywhere that looks official.

Clothing & Equipment

Proper gear for porters must be a prime consideration if you are taking them over the 5416m Thorung La. Many lowland porters from Dumre have suffered frostbite or snow blindness on this pass because trekkers (and/or their sherpas) have not provided the proper footwear, clothing and sunglasses for the pass. Porters from near-tropical villages like Dumre have no idea what to expect on a snow-covered pass, or they hope that the pass crossing will be in warm weather, and they join a trekking party clad only in cotton clothing. If you employ porters for a crossing of Thorung La, you incur both a moral and a legal obligation for their safety and well-being. See the Guides & Porters section in the Facts for the Trekker chapter for more information.

Safety on Thorung La

It is easiest and safest to cross Thorung La from east to west, as in this route description. The reason is that if you travel from west to east, there are no camping spots or water sources on the west side of the pass from a meadow above Muktinath, at 4100m, to a

spot two to three hours beyond the pass on the Manang side, at 4510m. This means that you have to make a 1300m climb, plus at least a 900m descent, in a single day. This is an impossible feat for many people, especially those who have not yet acclimatised to high elevation. The trails are less steep on the Manang side of the pass and, in the event of a problem, rescue facilities are better in Manang.

From Manang to Muktinath, the pass is not difficult, but it is still a long trek at high elevation. You might have to return to Dumre if it is impossible or dangerous to cross Thorung La because of snow or altitude sickness. There are years when the weather allows it to stay open, but Thorung La is usually snowbound and closed from mid-December to mid-April. Be sure to read the section on altitude sickness so that you are aware of the symptoms. Trekkers have died on Thorung La because of altitude sickness, exposure, cold and avalanches.

Accommodation

There are frequent tea shops and lodges all along the route from Dumre to Pokhara, except on Thorung La between Thorung Phedi and Muktinath. The lodges on this trek tend to be clustered in villages. Between Besi Sahar and Manang there are many places where you will walk for an hour or more without seeing a hotel or tea shop. Once you reach Muktinath and the Kali Gandaki valley the facilities are much more frequent.

Food and lodging become more expensive as you trek further from the road. Some representative prices are:

	milk tea	dal bhat
Bhulbule	Rs 6	Rs 45
Dharapani	Rs 10	Rs 75
Pisang	Rs 14	Rs 75
Manang	Rs 18	Rs 130
Thorung Phedi	Rs 22	Rs 90

In most lodges the facilities are reasonably good, with private rooms as well as dormitory accommodation. A strange common feature of lodges in the Marsyangdi valley is

ANNAPURNA REGION

ANNAPURNA REGION

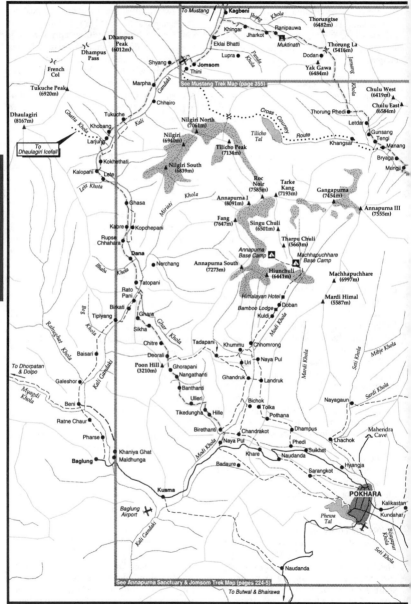

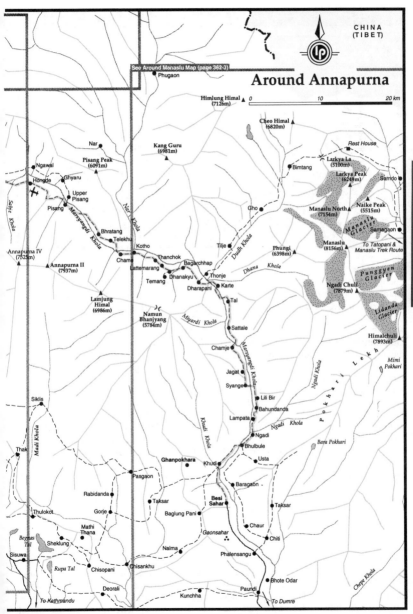

Around Annapurna

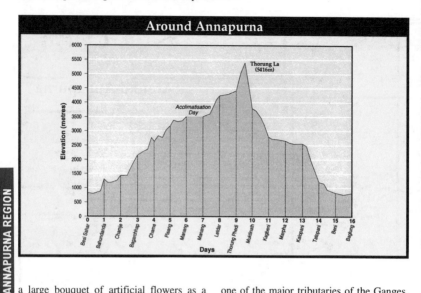

Around Annapurna

a large bouquet of artificial flowers as a centrepiece on the dining table. There are telephones in most villages up to Chame.

Access

Kathmandu to Dumre An express bus takes about five hours from Kathmandu to Dumre. The local buses are rough; you will be much happier if you book a seat on a tourist bus to Pokhara and get off at Dumre. Leaving the Kathmandu Valley, the road descends from the Chandragiri Pass on a wild series of steep switchbacks along the narrow Indian-built Tribhuvan Rajmarg, which is in a dreadful state of repair. It then continues south through cultivated fields to Naubise, 26 km from Kathmandu. Naubise is the beginning of the Prithvi Rajmarg, completed in 1971 with Chinese aid. The Tribhuvan Rajmarg continues south from this point and winds its way to the Indian border at Birganj. The Prithvi Rajmarg heads west along the Mahesh Khola to its confluence with the Trisuli. It then follows the Trisuli valley to **Mugling**, elevation 220m, at the confluence of the Trisuli and the Marsyangdi Khola, 110 km from Kathmandu. The large river thus formed flows south to become the Narayani,

one of the major tributaries of the Ganges. Many rafting companies operate trips on these rivers, often emerging in the Terai and entering Royal Chitwan National Park. A road follows the Narayani valley south from Mugling to join the east-west Mahendra Rajmarg at Narayanghat in the Terai.

Beyond Mugling, the road follows the Marsyangdi Khola, passing the huge Marsyangdi power project, actually crossing the dam in front of the powerhouse, and passing the junction of the road to Gorkha at Anbu Khaireni. **Dumre** is 25 km beyond Mugling at an elevation of 440m. This village was settled in the 1970s by Newars from the nearby town of Bandipur after the completion of the road from Kathmandu to Pokhara. Most of Dumre consists of warehouses, shops and bhattis that serve the porters who carry loads from the roadhead to remote villages. There are also a few lodges, including the *Annapurna* and the *Dhaulagiri*, that cater to trekkers.

Dumre to Besi Sahar The hotel facilities along the road above Dumre are mediocre because most trekkers bypass them and drive to Besi Sahar. The following is a brief

Around Annapurna – Flora & Fauna

Trees Two conifer species of the high temperate forest are hemlock and silver fir. The **hemlock** is a graceful pyramidal tree with outspread, sweeping branches. Be on the lookout for its short, delicate needles and small cones. The **silver fir** is a robust, symmetrical tree characterised by stiff, flattened needles with silvery undersides that appear in whorls around its branches. This species should be readily recognised for its Christmas tree-like appearance. The erect, dark purple cones oozing with resin are also keys to identification.

Hemlock

Birds There are many small birds found along the watercourses of the Himalaya that are striking despite their size. The thrushes are especially well represented. Perhaps one of the more common species is the **white-capped river chat**, a handsome red and black bird with a white crown and nape. Another species typically sighted is the **plumbeous redstart**, a slaty-blue bird with a red tail. The female, though, is completely different, appearing drab grey with a white rump and black tail. The latter is sometimes confused with the **little forktail**, another thrush found near water. The other forktails are larger with long, black-and-white tail feathers and seem clad in tuxedos. The whistling thrush may appear as a plain black bird in the shadows, but is actually dark blue with pearly-white specks. The long, lilting song of this bird carries delightfully over the din of the rushing torrents at dawn and dusk.

Plumbeous redstart

Other birds that make their niche near water are the kingfishers. On the bigger rivers look for the **large pied kingfisher**, which is black and white with a large crest, and higher up along smaller streams look for the iridescent turquoise of the **white-breasted kingfisher** and the smaller **Eurasian kingfisher**.

Still another species of the waterways to look for is the **brown dipper**, a plump, chocolate-coloured bird that appears to do deep knee-bends on the stones at the water's edge. This bird jumps into the torrents and forages on the stream bottoms. Look for the **white-breasted dipper** west of the Kali Gandaki. ∎

description of the Besi Sahar road in case you have to walk, and to provide you with some clues as to your progress if you are bouncing around in a bus or truck. The road fords the Chudi Khola at Dumre, then passes through terraced rice fields and small villages inhabited by Newars, Brahmans and Chhetris, to Bhansar, where there is the first of numerous police checkposts, at 530m. It then follows the west bank of the Marsyangdi upstream through a region dotted with gigantic banyan and pipal trees.

A short distance on, from the town of **Chambas** at 500m, there are good views of the high Himalaya, especially Baudha (6674m) and Himalchuli (7893m). The road passes through the upper part of Turture at 530m; most of this large village is below the road. Across the river you can see Palangtar, the site of Gorkha's defunct Palangtar airport. Gorkha is the major town in the central hills and is the site of the ancient palace of King Prithvi Narayan Shah, the founder of modern Nepal; the airport is no longer served by any flights because the road to Gorkha has made flying unnecessary.

The road stays on the west bank of the river through fairly level country, passing through Baisjan Ghar. It fords a stream and climbs past some teahouses at Paundi to **Bhote Odar**, at 550m, where some buses and trucks end their trip. There is a police checkpost in Bhote Odar, and the *Star Hotel* and *Hotel Thakali* offer accommodation. The road climbs over a ridge at 730m and descends to the Thakali bazaar of **Phalensangu**, which is below the road at 670m.

The road makes a few small ascents and descents and fords a lot of small streams before reaching **Besi Sahar**, on a plateau at 820m. There are several bhattis and two trekkers' hotels at the bus stop at the southern end of the town. If you are planning to spend the night in Besi Sahar, patronise the *Hotel Mountain View*, *Hotel Everest*, *Himalayan Hotel* or *Hotel Tukuche Peak* (☎ 066-20111), the last of which advertises that it is able to supply porters. There are also several bhattis; one of them offers '24 hours service in a running sour'.

The road continues for about 500m to the disagreeable bazaar of Besi Sahar, a km-long collection of shops and noisy bhattis. There are a police checkpost, radio and watch-repair facilities, shops selling Chinese and Japanese goods, a bank and several hotels.

Above and to the south-west of Besi is Gaonsahar, elevation 1370m, where there are the remains of an old fortress and palace. From the 15th to the 18th century, this region was a collection of independent kingdoms that continually waged war on each other. In 1782 the kingdom of Gorkha absorbed Lamjung, the principality that was ruled from Gaonsahar palace.

Side Trip: Bara Pokhari At Phalensangu, there is a bridge perched high above a narrow wooded gorge. If you cross the Marsyangdi on this bridge, you can make a side trip to Bara Pokhari. This is a high-altitude lake (elevation 3100m) that offers outstanding views of Manaslu, Himalchuli and Baudha. The trip involves a long, steep climb, but you can make a trek to Bara Pokhari in as few as three days, leaving the road at Phalensangu and rejoining the trail to Manang below Usta on Day 1.

Alternative Route: Phalensangu to Bhulbule The bridge at Phalensangu also gives access to an alternative route that avoids the motor road. From the east side of the bridge, a trail climbs to Chiti, then follows the river valley north. The trail passes through sal forests and rice terraces to Chaur at an elevation of 760m, then enters a sugar-cane growing region. From Chaur (also called Simbachaur), the trail stays near the river, crosses the Bhachok Khola, and climbs through Baragaon, elevation 910m, and over a ridge before descending to Bhulbule, where it rejoins the main route to Manang.

Alternative Route: Gorkha to Phalensangu Another way to avoid part of the Besi Sahar road is to start the trek from **Gorkha**. It is a three-day walk from Gorkha to **Tarkughat**, a fair-sized bazaar on the east bank of the Marsyangdi at 490m elevation. You can stay on the eastern side of the river and join the normal trekking route at Phalensangu or Bhulbule. There are basic tea shops but no trekkers' hotels on this route, and parts of the trek are in lowland country where you must wade several streams.

Day 1: Besi Sahar to Bahundanda
The first stretch of the trek is along the unfinished road that is being constructed to aid construction of a hydroelectric plant at Ngadi. Throughout the trek you will share the trail with mule caravans that transport supplies to remote villages. Mules travel from Besi Sahar to Manang village, though they only travel as far as Chame when there is snow in the higher regions of the Manang Valley.

After a long walk through the Besi Sahar bazaar, the trail drops to a stream on a rough rock staircase. Climb onto the roadbed and trek to the Bhalam Khola, where there may be a bamboo bridge, or you may have to rock-hop across. It is a long walk with several ups and downs, across rice paddies and subtropical forests, past a Danish educational project to **Khudi**, at 790m elevation, a mixture of tin and thatch-roofed houses, hotels and shops clustered around the anchors of a long, sagging suspension bridge across the Khudi Khola. The old bridge is precarious, but there is a new one about 10 minutes upstream next to a collection of government offices.

Khudi is the first Gurung village on the trek. Most of the people in the wide river valley below Khudi are Brahmans and Chhetris, although there are a few Gurung villages in the side valleys and slopes above the river. Here you also enter the Annapurna Conservation Area. Pass the *Kemix Guest House*, the Khudi school and a forest nursery, then follow the road northward up the Marsyangdi valley. Himalchuli and Ngadi Chuli (also known as Manaslu II and formerly known as Peak 29), at 7879m, dominate the horizon.

At **Bhulbule**, elevation 830m, the trail crosses the Marsyangdi Khola on a long suspension bridge. The *Thorung La Guest House*, which was said to be the best in town, was destroyed by a landslide in August 1996, but is being rebuilt near its original location on the west side of the bridge. Across the bridge is the *Heaven Guest House* and the *Hotel Arjun*; there are other hotels, bhattis and even a tailor in the centre of the village just above the bridge.

You must register at the ACAP checkpost next to the *Hotel Manang*. Beyond Bhulbule the trail travels up the east bank of the river, past a majestic waterfall 60m high that is surrounded by a tropical tree called a pandanus, or screw pine. The path wanders through small villages scattered amongst extensive rice terraces with continuing views of Manaslu (8156m) and Ngadi Chuli. There are a few trail junctions between Bhulbule and Lampata; in each case take the trail to the left. The right-hand trails lead on to ridges above the Marsyangdi. The Ministry of Tourism has erected orange signs saying 'Manang' at several confusing trail junctions along the route, so it is almost impossible to get lost.

The mountain views disappear as you near the small settlement of **Ngadi**. This used to be only a winter settlement before trekkers proliferated, but now there are several hotels run by Manangis near a defunct bridge. The *Hikers Restaurant & Lodge* is at the southern end of town, the *Himalaya Lodge* offers 'variable food clean and cosy room shower and toilet', and the *Marsyangdi Lodge* is the biggest establishment in town. There are also shops, porter hotels and a camp site. Several trekkers have suggested that Ngadi is a more pleasant and cleaner place to stay than Bahundanda.

Cross a stream beyond the tourist Ngadi to reach a Tibetan settlement and porter stop on the east side of a long suspension bridge that crosses the Ngadi Khola at 880m. There are excellent camp sites beside the river on both sides of the bridge.

It is fascinating to see the extensive public works programme in the hills of Nepal. To build this bridge, porters had to carry the steel cables and towers for several days. There are thousands of bridges throughout the country in unbelievably remote locations that have required huge expenditures of time and money for their construction. It is all too easy to see only the undeveloped aspect of Nepal and ignore the extensive expenditure of labour and money over the last 40 years that has developed an extensive network of trails and bridges. There are plans to build a power plant at the confluence of the Marsyangdi and the Ngadi Khola, but this project is proceeding very slowly. This is the end of the access road, so from here on you will be walking only on trails. The power poles along this part of the valley are not part of the new project; they bring electricity from the power station near Anbu Khaireni to this region.

On the hills above the Ngadi Khola is Usta; the trail from Bara Pokhari passes through Usta, then drops to the river and rejoins the route to Manang.

The trail moves gently upwards through scrub forests for about half an hour, then climbs to some bhattis and cold drink stalls opposite the rice terraces of **Lampata**. The trail winds around to the small *Manaslu Lodge* and a police checkpost, then makes a short, steep climb to **Bahundanda**, an attractive village in the saddle of a long ridge at 1310m. The school nestles in a grove of bamboo, and there are a few shops and bhattis, several hotels and a telephone office in the town square. The *Tibetan Hotel & Vegetrain Restaurant* is north of the square, and the *Mountain View Hotel* is on the ridge to the west. Bahundanda ('hill of the Brahmans') is the northernmost Brahman settlement in the Marsyangdi valley. If you are camping, try the school; the school yard is an excellent camping ground with decent toilet facilities. In addition to a camping fee, you are expected to leave a donation to the school.

Day 2: Bahundanda to Chamje

Descend on a steep, slippery trail past amphitheatre-shaped rice terraces. The flocks of birds in the rice fields are slaty-headed parakeets. Contour across terraces and eventually drop to a log bridge across a stream at the foot of a waterfall. Climb to the *Eagle's Nest Restaurant* at **Lili Bir**, where you can get directions to a small hot spring nearby. The trail traverses high above the river to the pleasant village of **Kanigaon**, at 1180m, where there is a Chinese restaurant. A short distance on is **Ghermu Phant**, then the trail drops to cross the Marsyangdi on a long, rattling suspension bridge at **Syange**, 1190m. This is the last of the rolling Middle Hills. Beyond Syange the valley narrows and becomes a steep canyon.

Shops, the *New Thakuri Guest House* and the *Hotel Sonam* line the stone street of Syange on the west bank of the river. One of the best trekking camps on the trip is under the eastern end of the bridge.

A half-hour beyond Syange is the *New Asia Hotel* at **Shree Chaur**. There is a hot spring across the river and the hotel-keeper pipes the water across when the river is low. Beyond Shree Chaur the trail climbs quite high on an exposed trail carved into nearly vertical cliffs, which are forested with rhododendron and pine and garnished with healthy crops of stinging nettles and marijuana. Because of the steep terrain, the villages in this region are small and infrequent. When Tilman visited Manang in 1950, this portion of the trail did not exist. Instead, the route followed a series of wooden galleries tied to the face of the rock cliffs alongside the river. As you near Jagat, there is a steep 200m climb to a trail blasted out of the rock face. The next stretch of trail is a bit exposed, but the trail is wide and safe.

It's a short descent past a small waterfall to **Jagat** at 1250m, inhabited, as are most villages in this region, by people of Tibetan heritage. Jagat means 'toll station'; this was once the site of a tax-collecting post for the Tibetan salt trade of the Marsyangdi valley. The stone village has a medieval atmosphere and the shops and hotels are packed closely together. The *Tibetan Pemba Lodge*, *Everest Hotel* and *Sushima Lodge* are near a bunch of bamboo shacks at the southern end of town; the *Manaslu Lodge* with its 'sentimental atmosphere' is at the northern end. There is a hot spring 15 minutes below the village.

From Jagat, the trail descends to the Marsyangdi and follows along the river bank, makes a long climb through forests past two bhattis to a waterfall, then slides gently into **Chamje** at 1430m. Pass through a turnstile into the venerable *Tibetan Hotel*, which has bins of roasted soybeans, *chiuraa* (beaten rice) and popcorn, and is a good place to load up on trail snacks. A bit below are the *Potala Guest House* and the three-storey *Lhasa Guest House*. Just across the suspension bridge on the east side of the river there is a place to camp.

Day 3: Chamje to Bagarchhap

Cross the Marsyangdi to the east bank and follow the trail along the river embankment on rocks and exposed wire. These wire cages filled with rocks are called *gabions*. They are used extensively throughout Nepal to stabilise river banks and road cuttings. The trail passes under an overhanging rock, then climbs a rocky trail and a steep stone staircase to a bhatti in Sattale, at an elevation of 1430m.

Climb past fields, then through stands of bamboo and rhododendron to an exposed trail that traverses high above the steep river bank. The trail makes a short descent to **Tal Besi**, three bhattis at 1580m, then a steep climb beside the Marsyangdi, which has become an underground waterfall beneath huge boulders. The trail crests a ridge and the valley suddenly opens into a large plateau. In this dramatic setting, at the foot of a large waterfall, is **Tal**, at 1675m. There are many shops and lodges in Tal, arranged so they look like an old American pony express outpost. The *Annapurna Hotel* and *Lhasa Hotel* are in the centre of the town; the *Tibetan Hotel* is at the northern end. Don't get your hopes up when you spot the sign on Jog Maya Gurung's *Manaslu Guest House* offering 'Fosters on tap'. There is another ACAP checkpost that needs to see your trekking permit. ACAP also has a kerosene sales depot and a visitor centre here. Just north of Tal is the large *Hotel Paradise*.

Tal is the southernmost village in Manang and is in a region called Gyasumdo, one of three distinct divisions within Manang. Gyasumdo was once highly dependent on trade with Tibet. Since the disruption of this trade in 1959, herding and agriculture have assumed greater importance. Corn, barley, wheat, buckwheat and potatoes are grown in Gyasumdo, which has enough warm weather and rainfall to produce two crops a year. The people of Gyasumdo used to hunt musk deer, and the sale of musk was once an important source of income and trade. Unlike other Buddhists, who have strict taboos against taking life, the people throughout Manang slaughter animals and hunt in the nearby hills. The Buddhist influence is apparent from the small white chorten on a nearby hill; the trek has now entered the Manang district.

The trail crosses the broad, flat valley that was once a lake (*tal* means 'lake'), through fields of corn, barley and potatoes, then crosses a small stream on a wooden bridge near two tea shops. There is a short climb, then the trail makes its way along a cliff and along the riverbed to Shirental. A short distance beyond, it climbs to a 60m-long suspension bridge across the Marsyangdi at 1850m.

This portion of the trail was constructed in the 1980s to replace a trail on the eastern side of the river that was destroyed by landslides. Climb past several bhattis in Ningala. Follow a trail that has been blasted out of the side of the cliff past two waterfalls to the *Manaslu Lodge* at Khokro. Descend past a bhatti in the forest to a long, high suspension bridge that leads to the east bank of the river and **Karte**. Don't expect too much from the town's only hotel, the *Dorchester*.

Follow the ACAP sign that leads you up a stone staircase and over a ridge behind Kharte, then drop to a suspension bridge that leads back to the west side of the Marsyangdi. Just after the bridge is a tiny, dirty hot spring that flows from a fissure near the trail; you need a cup to collect the hot water.

The trail climbs from the bridge to a stone kani that marks the entrance to **Dharapani**, at 1920m. All the old villages from here to Kagbeni have entrance chortens at both ends of the village; the kanis get more elaborate and picturesque as the Tibetan influence becomes stronger in each successive village.

There are two parts to this village. In lower Dharapani you will find the *Hotel Manaslu*, *Annapurna Guest House*, *Muktinath Lodge*, the *Ganga Jamuna Hotel*, telephone office, shops and a police checkpost. The *Hotel Himlung* and *Trekkers Hotel* are just north of the town, and about 10 minutes beyond are the *Tibetan Hotel* and the funkier *Dharapani Hotel & Lodge* at 2050m.

There's a long suspension bridge across the Marsyangdi that leads to Thonje, an important village at the junction of the Marsyangdi and the Dudh Khola. It's not necessary to go to Thonje en route to Manang. The police checkpost in Thonje controls the route up the valley that leads to the Larkya La. If you have trekked around Manaslu, you will emerge here and can either continue to trek around Annapurna or

ANNAPURNA REGION

trek south to Besi Sahar and Dumre. The building with the huge tin roof in Thonje is the regional high school.

Beyond Dharapani, the trail passes a school and climbs over a spur before descending to Bagarchhap. The trek enters the east-west Manang Valley in a forest of blue pine, spruce, hemlock, maple and oak. The jay-like bird that you see is the nutcracker; it eats the seeds from the blue pine cones.

Bagarchhap, at 2160m, is the first village on the trek with typical Tibetan architecture: closely spaced stone houses, with flat roofs piled high with firewood. During the same storm in November 1995 that produced avalanches in eastern Nepal, a landslide roared through Bagarchhap and destroyed much of the village, including two lodges. At the entrance to the town is a memorial to those killed. The village is slowly rebuilding, but the destruction is still very apparent. The only lodge operating at the time of writing was the *Marsyangdi Hotel*, but there was frantic construction under way. The well-maintained, whitewashed Diki gompa in Bagarchhap survived; it contains many Tibetan Buddhist paintings and statues. At the west end of the village, beyond all the destruction, is the large, new *Buddha Lodge*. The trail now travels west up the Manang Valley with the high Himalayan peaks to the south; there are occasional glimpses of Lamjung Himal (6986m) and Annapurna II (7937m) through the trees. To the east, some of the peaks of Manaslu Himal provide a dramatic backdrop at the foot of the tree-filled valley.

Day 4: Bagarchhap to Chame
Much of the Manang Valley is virgin forest of pine and fir, but construction of new houses and hotels and the constant requirement for firewood are causing people to cut down many of these fine trees. The trail climbs through forests to **Dhanakyu**, also called Syal Khola, 'the river of jackals', a settlement at 2290m with several hotels run by people from Bagarchhap. Just beyond an apple orchard (apples and peaches are avail-

able everywhere in the region during the autumn) are the *Dorje Hotel* and the larger *Trekkers Hotel*. A trail to the south of this village leads to Temang, at 2600m, and eventually climbs over Namun Bhanjyang (5784m) en route to Ghanpokhara in the south. This was the old route to Manang; few people, other than herders, use it now. Namun Bhanjyang is a difficult pass because there is often snow, and there is no food or shelter for four days.

A broad, level stretch of trail leads through forests to a wooden bridge near a spectacular waterfall, then traverses a rock ledge. Climb over a ridge on a steep, rocky trail and descend to the tiny settlement of Temang Besi. The route crosses several landslides and works its way uphill through forests to **Lattemarang** at 2360m. There are a few small but comfortable hotels here, including the *Tatopani Lodge* and *Tibetan Hotel*. There is a tiny hot spring across the river, but it is hard to get to.

The track climbs over three steep forested ridges, and crosses a large stream before descending to Thanchok and the *Hotel Marsyangdi*. Trek across another ridge to the entrance chorten of **Kotho** (2590m), also known as Kyupar, in a meadow surrounded by huge pine and spruce trees. The *Karme Cheten Hotel*, *Annapurna Lodge* and *New Chhesang Hotel* are at the south end of town; the *Hotel Manaslu* and the small *Mustang Lodge* are about 10 minutes beyond.

The police checkpost here controls access to the Nar-Phu Valley to the north. That remote valley, populated by only 850 people, is one of the three regions of Manang. It has a heritage and traditions different from that of other parts of the district. The restricted area regulations prohibit foreigners from the entire Nar-Phu Valley.

It's an easy half-hour walk to **Chame** (2630m), the administrative headquarters for the Manang district. At the entrance to the village is a long wall with many prayer wheels, typical of many villages in Manang. Be sure to walk to the left and spin the wheels clockwise. The large *Holiday Hotel* is at the south end of town, but the better hotels are across the river. Among the closely spaced stone dwellings are a telephone office, a school, many well-stocked shops, a health post, post office, bank and several hotels. The Chame police checkpost, amazingly, is not interested in seeing your trekking permit. Across the river there are two small hot springs, but they're not big enough for swimming. On the opposite side of the river is the *Sangso Guest House*. Downstream from the bridge on the way to the hot spring are the excellent, large *New Tibet Hotel* and the confusingly named *New Tibetan Hotel*, which offers 'systematised toilets'. Throughout the day there are views of Lamjung Himal, Annapurna II and Annapurna IV (7525m).

Day 5: Chame to Pisang

Trekking west from the bridge you pass an older part of Chame and the kani that marks the entrance to the village. Climb past *mani* walls to a huge walled-in field of buckwheat and the *Namaste Lodge* in Telekhu at 2775m. There's a long, pleasant, mostly level walk in forests, with one short landslide crossing, to a huge apple orchard surrounded by a stone wall. At 2840m is the rough village of **Bhratang**, where the *Hotel Beauty*, *Raju Hotel* and *Maya Hotel* offer accommodation. Just beyond this collection of lodges is a bridge leading to the old part of Bhratang, which used to be a Khampa settlement, though it is now largely abandoned. The Khampas had installed a gate on the bridge, thus controlling the traffic up and down the Manang Valley. Across the bridge there is a small stone memorial to a Japanese climber who died in an avalanche while trekking across the Thorung La – a grisly reminder to wait several days after any heavy snowstorm before trying to cross the pass. Don't cross the bridge; stay on the northern side of the river and follow a new trail that has been blasted out of the side of the cliff.

The valley is steep and narrow, and the trail goes through deep forests. When the trail rounds a bend, there is the first view of the dramatic Paungda Danda rock face, a tremendous curved slab of rock rising more than 1500m from the river. There are also views of Annapurna II to the south and Pisang Peak (6091m) to the north-east and back down the valley to Himalchuli and Ngadi Chuli. Cross to the south bank of the Marsyangdi on a suspension bridge at 3040m, make a long climb over a ridge, then descend to the large *Marsyangdi Guest House* at Dhukure Pokhari, named after a tiny lake nearby. The trek is then reasonably level as it heads into the upper part of the Manang Valley, eventually reaching the *Himali* and *Peace* guesthouses at the entrance to **Pisang**.

The lower portion of Pisang, a cluster of houses and a long mani wall with prayer wheels, is at an elevation of 3190m. Note the wooden canals for water to drive the two mills in this village. There are many facilities bunched together here, including the *Karma Beauty Hotel*, the *Hotel Maya Tibetan Guest House* and Ghalung Gurung's *Pisang Peak Hotel*. The hotels all offer guide, porter and horse riding services if you decide you want to change your style of travel. The main village of Pisang is across the river and 100m uphill, but the hotels in that part of the village are more rustic than those near the river. There are excellent camping places in the forest on the south bank of the river.

Day 6: Pisang to Manang

The trek is now in the region known as Nyesyang, the upper portion of the Manang district, which has about 5000 inhabitants in six major villages. The region is much drier than the Gyasumdo region in the lower reaches of the Marsyangdi valley. There is only a small amount of rainfall here during the monsoon because the Annapurna range to the south alters the climate significantly from that of the rest of Nepal south of the Himalaya. The people of Nyesyang raise wheat, barley, buckwheat, potatoes and beans; the cold, almost arid, climate limits them to a single crop annually. They keep herds of yaks, goats, cows and horses. Horses are an important means of transport in the relatively flat upper portion of the Manang Valley. People often ride horses, or use them as pack animals, over Thorung La between Manang and Jomsom.

Many people in Nyesyang villages speak fluent English and dress in trendy Western clothing they have bought during overseas trading excursions. This presents an incongruous picture as they herd yaks and plough the fields of these remote villages. Their exposure to the West also makes them shrewd and eager business people, so the traders and shops of Manang all charge high prices. There are few bargains to be had here. If you travelled to Kathmandu from Hong Kong or Bangkok, perhaps you were aware of the Tibetan-looking people all dressed in identical jackets or jogging suits and carrying identical luggage; these were Manangis returning from a shopping expedition.

Still on the south side of the Marsyangdi, cross a stream and climb past a memorial to a group of German climbers who died on nearby Pisang Peak. The trail makes a long climb over a ridge that extends across the valley. At the top of this spur, elevation 3380m, is an excellent view of the Manang Valley, with Tilicho Peak (7134m) at its head. A man from Pisang often sets up shop here to sell tea, Coke and souvenirs. After a short descent, the trail reaches the broad, forested valley floor. Most of the valley is used as grazing land for sheep, goats, horses and yaks. Across the river, high on the northern bank, is Ghyaru.

The trail follows along the valley floor to Manang's airstrip at **Hongde**, elevation 3325m. The largest facility here is the *Marsyangdi Lodge*; others are the *Airport Hotel* and *Maya Lodge*. Several curio shops nearby sell 'real Tibetan things' made in India, Hong Kong and Kathmandu. If you want a yak's head, this is the place to buy one. The trail passes a long mani wall with an astonishing number of brass prayer wheels, then a gompa with a huge prayer wheel. Just north of the *Jullu Lodge* is another police checkpost.

There are scheduled flights from Hongde to Pokhara, and occasional direct flights to Kathmandu. They are usually booked by rich Manangis en route to and from trading excursions, so there is little chance of obtaining a seat except in an emergency.

Half an hour beyond the airport is the huge Sabje Khola valley, with Annapurna III and IV at the head. Just south of the trail, in this spectacular setting, is a mountaineering school which was built in 1979 with a grant from the Yugoslav Mountaineering Federation. It's now operated by the Nepal Mountaineering Association in cooperation with the Union of International Alpine Associations (UIAA). It offers a six week course for climbers from Nepal and neighbouring countries during August each year.

The trail crosses to the north bank of the Marsyangdi on a wooden bridge near **Mungji** at 3360m. The snow peak at the head of the valley is Tilicho Peak; to the north of it is a black rock spire named Khangsar (5977m). The route climbs past fields of barley over a low ridge to **Bryaga** at 3475m. The largest part of this Tibetan-style village of about 200 houses hides behind a large rock outcrop. The houses are stacked one atop the other, each with an open veranda formed by a neighbour's rooftop. The gompa, perched on a high crag overlooking the village, is the largest in the district and has an outstanding display of statues, *thangkas* (ornate Tibetan religious aintings) and manuscripts estimated to be 400 to 500 years old. Take a torch (flashlight) and visit the gallery that runs behind the main altar. The kani near the trail that marks the entrance to Bryaga is particularly impressive.

There is a good place to camp in the meadow below the village. The large *New Yak Hotel* near the trail gets excellent reviews; it is now receiving competition from the nearby *Bryaga Bakery & Super Restaurant*. There are many more hotels half an hour away in Manang. Be careful when you enter Bryaga, especially at night: the dogs are vicious. In the spring there are archery contests in Pisang, Bryaga and Manang. It's a colourful spectacle with lots of drums and dancing, but be a bit careful of standing close to the target after the booze starts flowing.

The country is very arid, dominated by

weird cliffs of yellow rock, eroded into dramatic pillars alongside the trail, and by the towering heights of the Himalaya across the valley to the south. It is only a short walk, past mani walls and across a stream where several mills grind wheat and barley, to the plateau of **Manang** village at 3500m. The best hotels are at the south end of the village adjoining the fields. Near the entrance kani are the *Annapurna Hotel* and the *Manang Hotel*. The *Tilicho Hotel* is said to be the best in town, closely followed by the popular *Yak Lodge*. Other facilities here include the *Marsyangdi Hotel* and *Gangapurna Lodge*. Manang villagers have a very Western outlook; hot showers and videos are the local speciality, and Manangi youths travel up and down the valley by mountain bike. The hotel menus include hamburgers and steaks in addition to the normal trekking fare. The demand for electricity is greater than the power plant can satisfy, so there is frequent load shedding. The shops have figured out exactly what trekkers want. You can find film, sunglasses, socks, sweaters, scarves, Mars bars, shampoo, sun cream, film, batteries of all sizes, super glue, walking sticks and medical supplies. If you or your porters do not have warm socks, hats, gloves, or sunglasses, this is the time and place to buy them.

The Himalayan Rescue Association operates an aid post here, with a doctor in attendance throughout the trekking season. The HRA post occupies a new building to the north of the trail as you enter the village and offers free daily lectures on altitude sickness, usually at 3 pm. The doctors are available for consultation and treatment. Their services are not free; ask to see the schedule of charges before you request a diagnosis.

The village itself is a compact collection of 500 flat-roofed houses separated by narrow alleyways. To reach a doorway you must ascend a steep log notched with steps. The setting of the village is most dramatic, with the summits of Annapurna and Gangapurna less than eight km away, and a huge icefall rumbling and crashing on the flanks of the peaks. You can expect snow in Manang at any time from late November through February.

Alternative Route: Upper Pisang to Manang There is a high route via Ghyaru and Ngawal along the north bank of the river. The trail is steep and takes about three hours longer than the direct route along the south bank, but provides spectacular views of the Annapurna range to the south, and is a worthwhile side trip. It passes an interesting gompa in Ghyaru and a gompa in Ngawal that was built in 1990. The people of Ghyaru are happy to welcome trekkers and there are a few tea shops that offer basic facilities. This is also the start of the climbing routes to Pisang Peak, Chulu East (6584m) and Chulu West (6419m), all of which are visible from the trail. You can also make a diversion to Ser gompa on a plateau high above the river on the northern side. The high route rejoins the direct route at Mungji.

Day 7: Acclimatisation Day in Manang

You should spend the day in Manang village and the vicinity to acclimatise to the higher elevations you will encounter towards Thorung La. There are many opportunities for both easy and strenuous day excursions from Manang. It is possible to climb the ridge to the north of the village for excellent views of Annapurna IV, Annapurna II and Tarke Kang (7193m); or to descend from the village to the glacial lake at the foot of the huge icefall that drops from the northern slopes of Gangapurna (7454m).

From **Khangsar**, the last settlement in the valley en route to Tilicho Tal, there are splendid views of the 'Great Barrier', a name given by Herzog to the high ridge between Roc Noir and Nilgiri North. Another choice would be a walk to visit the **Bhojo gompa**, the red edifice perched on the ridge between Bryaga and Manang, and the most active monastery in the region. The gompa at the western end of the village is also worth visiting; it's open from 10 to 11 am and 4 to 5 pm. Check with the ACAP office or the Yak Hotel to see if they are offering an evening lecture or video show.

Modern Manang

Before the first trekkers came to Manang in 1977, the region saw few foreigners. The only traders were the people of Manang themselves, and the population was intolerant of outsiders. There was little need for inns and other facilities. In 1950 Maurice Herzog came to Manang village in a futile search for food for his mountaineering party, only to return nearly starving to his camp at Tilicho Tal. With the advent of tourism, however, there has been extensive hotel construction, and the Manangis warmly welcome tourists – particularly those with lots of rupees. The resourceful Manangbhot people have been quick to adapt to this new source of income, selling semiprecious stones (from Tibet, they claim, but more likely from Bangkok), foodstuffs, Tibetan jewellery and other items of interest to tourists. An alternative to a day hike is a bargaining session with these skilful traders. ∎

Day 8: Manang to Letdar

The trek now begins an ascent of almost 2000m to Thorung La. Local traders ride horses from Manang to Muktinath in a single day, but the large elevation gain, the need for acclimatisation, and the high altitudes all make it imperative to take at least three days to do the trip on foot. It's possible to reach Thorung Phedi in a single day from Manang, but you must spend a night at either Yak Kharka or Letdar in order to acclimatise. If you have any symptoms of altitude sickness, you should descend to Manang, or lower, to recover.

From Manang village, the trail crosses a stream, climbs to **Tengi**, 120m above Manang, then continues to climb out of the Marsyangdi valley, turning north-west up the valley of the Jarsang Khola. The trail follows this valley north, passing a few goths as it steadily gains elevation. You have left the large trees below; the vegetation now consists of scrub juniper and alpine grasses.

The trail climbs to the small village of **Gunsang**, a cluster of flat mud roofs just below the trail at 3930m. There is an irrigation and hydroelectric project under construction along this portion of the trail

that will hopefully solve Manang's electricity problem. The *Marsyangdi Hotel & Lodge* is alongside the trail and specialises in Tibetan bread and *chhang*.

The route passes through sparse forests of juniper, rose and barberry and a few meadows where horses and yaks graze. After crossing a large stream that flows from the peaks of Chulu West and Gundang, the trail passes an ancient mani wall in a pleasant meadow at 3990m.

Beyond is **Yak Kharka**, also known as Koche (4090m). The lodges are better than in Letdar; try the *Yak Hotel & Lodge*, the funny *Yak Kharka Hotel* or the *Gangapurna Hotel* operated by Maya Gurung (who specialises in pies and cakes). A large herd of yaks grazes in the fields nearby, and you can visit the yak herders' camp. Villagers from Manang collect firewood from the slopes above, which also support herds of blue sheep. An hour further, at 4250m, is **Letdar**, the next-to-last shelter before the pass. The first hotel, the *Pema Hotel*, is said to be the best; others are *Jimmy's Hotel* and the *Churi Lattar Lodge*.

Day 9: Letdar to Thorung Phedi

From Letdar (some spell it Lathar) the trail continues to climb along the east bank of the Jarsang Khola, then descends and crosses the stream on a wooden bridge at 4310m. Make a short ascent on a good trail to a tea shop. The route then follows a narrow trail across a high, unstable scree slope and descends to **Thorung Phedi**, a rock-strewn meadow surrounded by vertical cliffs at 4420m. You can stay at the *Marsyangdi Hotel* in the valley or avoid the descent and follow a small trail that leads across a scree slope and climbs to a shelf above the river and the *Thorung Base Camp Hotel*. There are camp sites by the river or at the main camp site on a shelf about 10 minutes above the hotel. The police checkpost behind the hotel requires your trekking permit in order to record your departure from the Manang Valley.

These hotels can be very, very crowded, especially if there is snow. The upper hotel can accommodate and feed up to 200 trekkers and is a maze of double rooms, dormitories and outhouses. Somehow they manage to produce decent food and get all the orders reasonably correct. Some trekkers have suggested boycotting the bread and rolls that they bake because the oven is fuelled by firewood.

Nights can be miserable because of the 3 am departure that many people schedule. It really isn't necessary to start that early. In fact, it can be dangerous because it is quite cold until the sun rises and this can lead to hypothermia and frostbite. A reasonable departure time is just at daybreak, at 5 or 6 am. Because people leave early in the morning, the hotel insists that you settle your bill at night. The hotel often has a horse available that you can ride over the pass for an exorbitant price (the most recent quotation was Rs 1500) if you are not well. Blue sheep, and even snow leopards, sometimes magically appear in this valley; the crow-like birds are choughs, and the large birds that circle overhead are lammergeiers and Himalayan griffons, not eagles. Be sure to boil or treat water here; the sanitation in Thorung Phedi and Letdar is poor, and giardiasis is rampant.

Day 10: Thorung Phedi to Muktinath

Phedi, which means 'foot of the hill', is a common Nepali name for any settlement at the bottom of a long climb. The trail becomes steep immediately after leaving Thorung Phedi, switchbacking up moraines and following rocky ridges as it ascends to the pass. Local people have used this trail for hundreds of years to bring herds of sheep and yaks in and out of Manang. Thus the trail, while often steep, is well defined and easy to follow.

The only complications to the crossing are the high elevation and the chance of snow. The pass is usually snowbound in late December and during January. Snow can also block the pass at any time of year if there is an unseasonable storm.

When there is deep new snow, the crossing becomes difficult – often impossible. It then becomes necessary to retreat back to Dumre, or to wait until the snow has consolidated and local people have forged a trail. The only shelter between here and Muktinath are a tiny seasonal tea shop at 5030m, a small stone hut on the pass, and a lodge at 4100m, far down the other side. An overnight stop in the snow, unless well planned in advance, can be treacherous and deadly, especially for porters.The trail climbs and climbs, traversing in and out of many canyons formed by interminable moraines. It is a reasonably good trail unless there is snow, in which case the route may traverse scree slopes and ascend through steep snow. It takes from four to six hours from Thorung Phedi to the pass, but the many false summits make the climb seem to go on forever.

Thorung La, with its traditional chorten, prayer flags and stone cairn, is at an elevation of 5416m. The views from the trail, and from the pass itself, are outstanding high Himalayan scenes. You can see the long ridge of high mountains that Herzog called the 'Great Barrier'. This separates the drier, Tibet-like region of Manang from the rest of Nepal. You can also see (to the south) the Annapurnas, Gangapurna and Yak Gawa (6484m), a heavily glaciated peak. The barren Kali Gandaki valley is far below to the west, and the rock peak of Thorungtse (6482m) lies to the north.

The descent is steep and rough on the knees – a loss of more than 1600m in about four hours. The descent often begins in snow, which soon gives way to switchbacks down another series of moraines. Sometimes the correct route is not obvious; just remember that you are headed downhill and that Muktinath is on the south side of the valley. During the descent there are excellent views of Dhaulagiri standing alone in the distance across the valley. Eventually the moraines yield to grassy slopes and the final descent to Muktinath is a pleasant walk along the upper part of the Jhong Khola valley.

There is a hotel at **Chabarbu** (4100m), where the grassy slopes begin. It's run by a Tibetan man from Jharkot, and offers drinks, food and even souvenirs during the trekking season. It is better to rely on this hotel only for refreshment, not for accommodation, though you could stay here if you were crossing the pass in the opposite direction. It is also possible to camp if the tiny stream nearby is flowing. If, for some reason, you are following this route in reverse, Chabarbu is about 1½ hours from Muktinath.

The trail crosses meadows, drops into a deep ravine that is the start of the Jhong Khola, climbs out of the ravine and follows a wide trail into **Muktinath** (3800m), near the temple. There is no accommodation here, but it is only a five to 10 minute walk to Ranipauwa, where there is a large choice of accommodation and a police checkpost. See the description of Muktinath on Day 7 of the Jomsom trek for suggestions on where to stay in Ranipauwa.

Days 11-16: Muktinath to Pokhara

The route to Pokhara follows the Jomsom trek described earlier, but you must read this part in reverse. Kagbeni is worth a visit, as is the Dhaulagiri Icefall above Larjung, so schedule an extra three days for side trips. The winds in the Kali Gandaki are powerful and can drive sand and dust into your face. A scarf and sunglasses provide good protection as you trek down the valley.

When you reach Tatopani you have a choice of routes. You can either follow the old trail up to Ghorapani and back down to Birethanti, or you can take a more level route that follows the Kali Gandaki to Baglung; see the Baglung to Tatopani route description. You can also make a side trip to Ghandruk, Landruk or the Annapurna Sanctuary. All these possibilities are described earlier in this chapter.

The Royal Trek

Duration 4 days
Difficulty Easy
Maximum elevation 1730m
Permit cost US$5 per week plus Rs 1000
Season October to April
Hotels Almost none
Summary A short trek with good mountain views and less uphill walking than most treks. Many camping groups use this route, but not many individual trekkers.

This is an easy, short trek that starts near Pokhara and offers good mountain views. It gained its name because Prince Charles and an entourage of 90 guests, camp followers and staff trekked here. The trek has also seen the likes of such luminaries as Mick Jagger. The route is not a popular one, so you will see few other trekkers, but this also means that the lodge facilities are mediocre.

Access

It is about five km (a 20 minute drive by taxi) to the Bijayapur army camp just east of the Bijayapur Khola. The starting point for the trek is not obvious or marked, but it's about 100m past the army camp.

Chautaaras

A chautaara is a stone resting place under a large banyan or pipal tree. These trees were planted centuries ago, and have broad leaves and branches that extend outwards for a long distance in mushroom fashion, offering welcome shade to travellers. People have built walls and chautaaras (stone benches) in the shade of these trees for porters to rest their loads upon as they pause during the hot, steep climbs. Many people build a chautaara in the name of a deceased relative. Both the banyan and the pipal tree are members of the fig family; you can tell them apart by the long roots that droop down from the limbs of the banyan. Sometimes one of each variety is planted, symbolising a male-female relationship. It was under a banyan tree (also called a bodhi tree) that Buddha attained enlightenment in India over 2000 years ago. ■

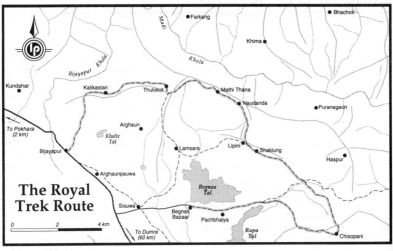

The Royal
Trek Route

0   2   4 km

Day 1: Bijayapur to Kalikastan

A broad trail starts in rice fields near the army camp, then ascends through Rakhigaun to a *chautaara*, a resting place under a large p͟pal tree.

The trail climbs gently along a ridge top through Brahman and Chhetri villages towards Kalikastan at 1370m. The children along this part of the trail are particularly persistent about asking for money, balloons or pens. Depending on the time that you start walking, you can camp either before or after Kalikastan. Both camp sites are on ridge tops with good mountain views, including of Machhapuchhare and Annapurna.

Day 2: Kalikastan to Shaklung

The trail follows along the forested ridge top through Thulokot to Mathi Thana, where there are a few tea shops. There is a short climb, then the trek reaches Naudanda. Continue along the ridge to a school at Lipini village, then make a steep but short climb through forests to the Gurung village of Shaklung at 1730m.

Day 3: Shaklung to Chisopani

The Himalayan skyline continues to change as the route comes abreast of Annapurna II, Lamjung Himal, Manaslu and Himalchuli. From Shaklung, the trail drops steeply down the south side of the hill to a large tree, a chautaara, several tea shops and a police checkpost. This is a trail junction; trails lead west to Begnas Tal and east to the Marsyangdi Khola. The Royal Trek route climbs towards Chisopani, winding around the back of the hill to the village. A short distance above Chisopani is a high knoll where there is a small temple. This is Chisopani Danda (*danda* means 'ridge top'), and there is a camp here with splendid mountain views.

Day 4: Chisopani to Begnas Bazaar

From Chisopani Danda, descend along the ridge for an hour or so, then descend steeply on the stone steps, into a small valley and a stream that feeds Rupa Tal. Continue for a short distance through the rice fields, then make a final ascent to the ridge that separates Begnas Tal and Rupa Tal, on a wide path that you will share with many local people. From the ridge, descend into the Pokhara Valley, joining the road at the crowded, dirty and noisy Begnas Bazaar. Take a taxi or a bus for the 12 km, 30 minute drive back to Pokhara.

Langtang & Helambu

The region north of Kathmandu offers a multitude of trekking destinations, all accessible without flights. The three major areas are Langtang, Gosainkund and Helambu, which can be combined in many different ways to make treks from seven to 16 days long.

Langtang is a narrow valley that lies just south of the Tibetan border. It is sandwiched between the main Himalayan range to the north and a slightly lower range of snowy peaks to the south. Langtang Lirung (7246m) dominates the valley to the north; Gang Chhenpo (6388m) and Naya Kangri (5846m) lie to the south; and Dorje Lakpa (6966m) protects the east end of the valley. The area was designated Nepal's first Himalayan national park in 1971.

This high and isolated region is inhabited by Tamangs whose religious practices, language and dress are much more similar to those of Tibet than to the traditions of their cousins in the Middle Hills. A visit to the Langtang Valley offers an opportunity to explore villages, to climb small peaks and to visit glaciers at a comfortably low elevation. According to legend, a lama following a runaway yak discovered the valley. Hence the name – *lang* is Tibetan for 'yak' and *teng* (more correctly *dhang*) means 'to follow'. Yaks still live in the valley, but they now share it with trekkers who make a seven to 11 day round trip from Kathmandu. Because there are good opportunities for moderate climbing excursions here, you should allow a few extra days for exploration of the extensive glacier system.

You can vary the trek to Langtang by returning to Kathmandu via the holy lakes of Gosainkund at 4300m, or you can make a short trek from Dhunche to Gosainkund. Thousands of Hindu pilgrims visit the lakes during a full-moon festival in August. The lake is also sacred to Buddhists.

Helambu, about 75 km north of Kathmandu, is an area inhabited by Sherpas. You can include Helambu in a Langtang trek, either via Gosainkund or across the 5106m Ganja La. In winter, both of the high routes from Langtang are usually snow-covered and dangerous, difficult or impossible. There are two versions of the Helambu trek. You can make a loop from the edge of the Kathmandu Valley at Sundarijal, over the Shivapuri ridge and down to Talamarang, then trek to Tarke Gyang and back down the ridge through Sermathang to the road. This loop is popular because it is short and is feasible all winter. The route described here, via Tharepati, is sometimes snowbound in winter, but is still a good short trek that avoids high elevations. Helambu treks are easy to organise because transport from Kathmandu to Sundarijal, the starting point of the trek, is readily available and inexpensive. It takes eight days to trek from Kathmandu to Helambu and back, or 12 to 14 days to include both Langtang and Helambu in a single trek.

The language, culture and dress of the Helambu Sherpas are very different from those of the Solu Khumbu Sherpas. The accessibility of Helambu has created an influx of tourists who have encouraged begging, the sale of 'genuine antiques' aged over the family fireplace, and several incidents of thievery.

INFORMATION
Fees & Permits

One regular trekking permit covers both Langtang and Helambu. Wherever you trek in the region, you will enter the Langtang National Park. The army is particularly conscientious about collecting the Rs 650 park entrance fee. There are entrance stations and park checkposts throughout the region that hassle endlessly about permits. The road to Dhunche passes through a portion of the park, so you must pay the park fee even if you only drive to Dhunche.

If you start or end your trek at Sundarijal, you will enter the Shivapuri Watershed & Wildlife Reserve and must pay a Rs 250 entry fee.

LANGTANG & HELAMBU

Maps

The best maps of Langtang and Helambu are the German *Helambu-Langtang* 1:100,000 map (1987) and the more detailed 1:50,000 east and west sheets titled *Langtang Himal* (1990). The Mandala *Helambu-Langtang, Gosainkund* 1:100,000 map is a Nepali version of the more expensive German map. The Hotel Langtang View in Dhunche has produced a good trekking map with route profiles and up-to-date information on tea stalls and other facilities.

The US Army Map Service maps of the region are sheets 45-1, *Kathmandu*; 45-13, *Jongka Dzong*; and 45-2, *Mount Everest*. All are based on the Survey of India maps that were published in the early 1960s, so all show the trails as they existed then – not now. Be especially wary of the area from Dhunche to Langtang village as shown on any of these maps.

Accommodation

There are trekkers' lodges throughout both Langtang and Helambu. The facilities are not as well developed as those on the Everest and Annapurna trek routes, but they are certainly adequate.

Trekking Season

The season for Langtang and Helambu is generally the same as in the rest of Nepal, but snow in the winter, or from a freak storm in the autumn, can close upper Langtang Valley, Ganja La and the route through Gosainkund. The trek through Gosainkund is particularly treacherous when there is a lot of snow on the trail.

Langtang Valley is covered in flowers during the summer, and is therefore a good monsoon trek, though there are hordes of leeches in the lower part of the valley.

Fuel

Use of firewood is prohibited throughout the Langtang National Park, so you must carry stoves and fuel if you are not staying in lodges.

GETTING THERE & AWAY
Air

Langtang The airstrip is about an hour beyond Kyanjin gompa, but has no scheduled service. Charter flights are irregular, and are only in six-passenger Pilatus Porter aircraft or helicopters, so don't count on finding a seat back to Kathmandu unless you have made prior arrangements. The airstrip is notorious for becoming snowbound in December, January and February. Some helicopter companies run sightseeing excursions to Langtang, so there is a chance of a seat in or out of here in an emergency.

Bus

Dhunche The starting place for Langtang treks is Dhunche (pronounced 'doon-chay'), 117 km from Kathmandu. Buses to Dhunche leave from the bus terminal north of Kathmandu. The first bus leaves at 7 am, costs Rs 64 and takes all day to reach Dhunche. You can also take a bus to Trisuli Bazaar and walk to Dhunche, but the trail is steep and has nothing to offer except physical exertion. It is better to take a bus all the way to Dhunche and let the bus do all the initial climbing.

The bus from Dhunche to Kathmandu leaves at 7.30 am. Make reservations the day before at the Thakali Hotel in Dhunche.

Sundarijal At 1350m, Sundarijal is the best place to start a Helambu trek. You can get to Sundarijal by minibus, or even a taxi (Rs 650), on an unpaved road seven km from Boudhanath. You can also begin the trek from Boudhanath, taking a few hours to walk to Sundarijal along the level roadway.

Panchkal This is an alternative starting point for a trek to Helambu. Panchkal (the name of the settlement where the trail meets the road is actually Lamidanda) is on the road to the Tibetan border. Take a bus to Barahbise or Lamosangu, bang on the roof of the bus just after the army camp and jump off.

The Helambu road joins the Kathmandu to Kodari road just beyond Lamidanda; you can catch one of the rickety local buses that ply between Barahbise and Kathmandu.

Indrawati Valley You can finish the Helambu trek by flagging down a jeep, truck or bus on the road in the Indrawati valley. Minibuses are available in Sipa Ghat or Malemchi, and seats are negotiable on vehicles even further up the valley. The bus fare from Kathmandu to Malemchi Pul Bazaar is Rs 50, and a taxi costs between Rs 2500 and Rs 3000.

Langtang Trek

> **Duration** 10 days
> **Difficulty** Medium
> **Maximum elevation** 4300m
> **Permit cost** US$5 per week plus Rs 650
> **Season** October to May
> **Hotels** Very good
> **Summary** Close to Kathmandu, so transportation is inexpensive. Trek through forests to an alpine valley just south of the Tibetan border. Good alpine views and interesting Tibetan-style villages.

This section suggests a five day approach to the heart of the Langtang Valley. From Langtang village or Kyanjin gompa there are several alternatives for returning to Kathmandu. It is possible to make the trek back to Dhunche in only three days from Langtang village because much of it is downhill. If you have basic mountaineering skills and good weather, you can cross by the high route over the Ganja La into Helambu. A third alternative is to trek back to Syabru from Langtang, then cross into Helambu via Gosainkund.

Access

It is about a four hour drive from Kathmandu (six hours by local bus) on a rough, deteriorating paved highway that twists and climbs over ridges to the Trisuli valley. Passing Balaju and Nagarjun, the road leaves the Kathmandu Valley at Kakani (2145m), where there are excellent views of Annapurna II, Manaslu and Ganesh Himal, and descends into the broad Trisuli valley. The bus usually makes a tea stop at Ranipauwa, the only large village on the route, at Km 27. This region is the radish capital of Nepal; you can see huge piles of long, freshly washed radishes (*mula* in Nepali) alongside the road awaiting transport to the markets of Kathmandu.

After a long descent through terraced fields, the road crosses the Tadi Khola at Km 60, then climbs onto a plateau and passes fields of mustard, corn and rice planted in bright red soil. There is a police checkpost two km before Trisuli where the police sometimes examine trekking permits. The road then passes an army camp and rolls into Trisuli Bazaar at 548m, 72 km from Kathmandu.

Trisuli is the site of a dam and hydroelectric project built by the Indian Technical Mission. A large bridge dominates the town; most shops are before the bridge, and most restaurants are on the opposite side, near the hydroelectric plant. Hotel facilities are spartan and the restaurants are pretty grim. Try the *Ranjit Lodge* for dal bhat. If you must spend the night here, take a look at the *Pratistha Lodge*, near the power plant, or the *Shakyar Lodge*, near the beginning of the Betrawati road. Otherwise, continue eight

km to Betrawati for a slightly better selection of hotels.

The unpaved road to Betrawati and Dhunche is a Nepal army project. It took almost 10 years to build the 105 km road that goes all the way to Somdang, at the foot of Ganesh Himal, where there are lead and zinc mines.

The Dhunche road starts at a petrol station in Trisuli Bazaar just before the bridge and follows the east bank of the Trisuli River. The road passes two bridges carrying massive pipes that feed the hydroelectric project and climbs slightly to **Betrawati** at 620m. Betrawati is at the junction of the Trisuli and the Phalangu Khola, at the foot of a steep ridge that rises towards Langtang and Gosainkund. It's 47 km of steep switchbacks on a wild road to Dhunche; at some points it hangs on to a steep cliff 1000m above the river. The road is subject to continual landslides – especially when it rains – so a bus trip to Dhunche can be an adventure.

At Betrawati the road crosses the Phalangu Khola, then switchbacks at the end of the ridge for 15 km, through Brahman and Chhetri villages, to **Kalikhastan** at 1390m. This is the entrance to Langtang National Park; the police examine trekking permits here. The villages now become more spread out, and as the elevation increases, the intense cultivation of the lowland rice-growing country gives way to herding, and small fields of corn, millet and vegetables. The road reaches its high point on the ridge at 1980m, then makes a long contour, with a few ups and downs through oak and rhododendron forests, passing above Ramche at Km 33, and then through Thare at Km 37. The road finally reaches **Dhunche**, the administrative headquarters of the region, at 1950m, three to four hours drive from Betrawati.

Just before Dhunche is the national park headquarters, where park personnel collect the park fee. There is a small visitor centre here, and if you ask, a brochure describing the park may be available. Keep the receipt for the park fee safely with your trekking permit since everyone from here on will

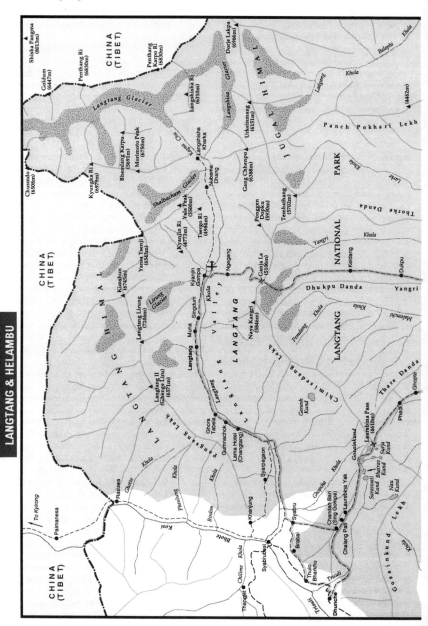

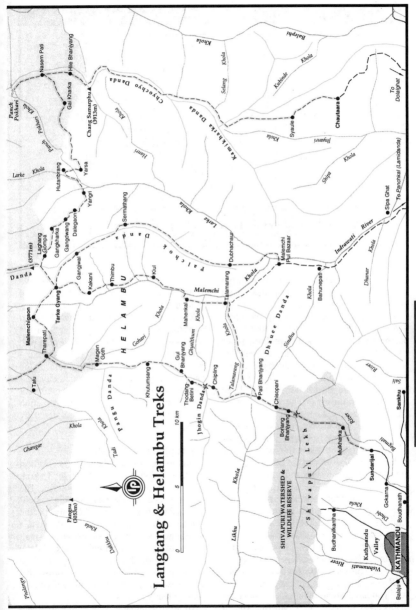

Langtang & Helambu Treks

LANGTANG & HELAMBU

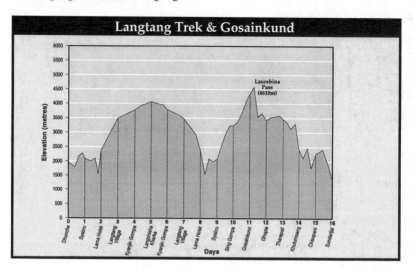

Langtang Trek & Gosainkund

want to see this document. Drive 50m further to another barrier, where the police record the vehicle information, and then a few hundred metres more to an army checkpost – your first chance to show off your newly purchased national park receipt. Formalities completed, you enter Dhunche. The bus stop is in upper Dhunche, where there are several lodges and a camping ground. Dhunche is a picturesque village with narrow streets lined with stone buildings. The main part of Dhunche is below the road, but there are no lodges there; you are better off staying near the bus stop. There is a large army installation in a compound above the road.

The *Hotel Thakali* and the *Langtang View* are the up-market establishments, but there are several less fancy operations nearby. The Langtang National Park administration has prepared a fixed menu and price list and requires lodges throughout the park to follow it, so choose a hotel based on looks and service because the prices are (or should be) the same. The camping charge is a larcenous Rs 50 per tent and Rs 100 for use of a kitchen shelter. A room in a lodge costs only Rs 20, so if you have a tent, save it for the next day or hike 1½ hours on to Thulo Bharkhu. If you have your own vehicle, it is preferable to drive the few km to Thulo Bharkhu and camp there.

You can also continue driving 15 km to **Syabrubesi**, an interesting village on the banks of the Bhote Kosi at 1420m. From Syabrubesi you can begin the trek to Langtang and save a day of walking, joining the route described here on its second day near the *Landslide Lodge* at 1550m. The 20 MW Chilimi power plant is under construction nearby; it is expected to be completed by 1998.

Day 1: Dhunche to Syabru

From the bus stop at Dhunche, take a short cut down a ravine next to the Hotel Thakali through the main part of the village. The short cut saves a long walk on a big switchback and rejoins the road at the bottom of the village. Follow the road downhill, past a government agriculture station and a small army post, to a left-hand switchback. Nearby is the start of the direct (steep) trail to Chandan Bari and Sing gompa; follow this trail eastward up the Trisuli valley if you are going directly to Gosainkund.

To go to Langtang, stay on the road and

cross a new cement bridge over the Trisuli River, which is much smaller here in its upper reaches. Take a moment to reflect on the power of Himalayan streams as you pass the remnants of a twisted steel bridge that once spanned the stream. Alongside the first waterfall beyond the bridge is an alternative trail to Sing gompa – straight up an almost vertical cleft in the rock beside the stream.

The Trisuli flows from Gosainkund, where, according to legend, Shiva released the waters of the holy lakes with his *trisul* (trident). The trail north, up the main valley, was once a major trade route with Tibet and is still used by a fair amount of traffic. The route to Tibet via the border town of Rasuwa and the Tibetan village of Kyirong may eventually be opened for trekking if the present trend of allowing cross-border trekking continues. The upper part of the river is named Bhote Kosi ('river from Tibet'), as are most of the rivers that cross the Himalaya into Nepal. When a Nepali river joins it, the Bhote Kosi assumes the name of its smaller tributary. Thus the larger fork of the Trisuli bears the name Bhote Kosi above Dhunche.

The route to Langtang follows the road up to a ridge at 1800m, then continues for a short distance to the Tamang village of **Thulo Bharkhu**, at 1860m, which has a few rough *bhattis*. About 100m from the village, the road crosses a small stream with some water-driven mills. Leave the road and climb steeply to the schoolhouse, then continue up a stone staircase. The walk eventually becomes a delightful – and occasionally level – hike through pine and rhododendron forests to Dau Danda, a single tea shop in the forest at 1980m. At the Tamang village of **Brabal** (2200m) there is a wooden bhatti near the trail. Most of the village and its potato and corn fields are hidden behind a ridge.

After a short climb, the trail reaches a ridge crest at 2300m, where the trek finally enters the Langtang Valley. There are views northward of snow peaks in Tibet, west to Ganesh Himal and east to Naya Kangri, the 5846m peak above Ganja La. A short, steep descent through bamboo forests leads to Syabru at 2100m.

Syabru is a pleasant village of about 70 houses, many with elaborately carved wooden windows, strung out along a ridge. There are numerous lodges at the upper end of the village where the trail enters it. There is no need for me to suggest a place to stay here; a bevy of very aggressive English-speaking Tamang women will accost you as you enter the village to extol the virtues of their establishments. Before you settle in for the night, consider the implications of the sign at the camp site before the village that advertises 'no dogs here'. There are good places to camp before Syabru and also in corn and millet fields far below the village.

Day 2: Syabru to Lama Hotel

The trail to Langtang descends along the ridge on Syabru's main street, then drops to the Ghopcha Khola, first through terraced fields, then through forests of oak, maple, alder and finally bamboo. The trail crosses the stream on a stone and cement bridge, then begins a climb across a ridge dotted with a few bhattis. The route descends on a steep, slippery path to the foot of a huge landslide at 1550m, where a trail junction is marked with signs painted on a rock directing you either to Langtang or back to the road at Syabrubesi. Just beyond the slide, the *Landslide Lodge* provides a chance for a short rest before you climb back along the southern banks of the Langtang Khola as the trail very quickly gains elevation.

For the rest of this day and the following morning, there are few settlements, but the forest abounds with birds. There is also a variety of wildlife in these forests: yellow-throated martin, wild boar, langur monkey, red panda and Himalayan black bear. The trail climbs to *Bamboo Lodge*, a jungly lodge at 1850m that is not quite as exotic as its name implies. This region specialises in the sale of colourful woollen socks and belts. The ascent continues to a steel suspension bridge at 2000m; there is a small bhatti on the south (shady) side and the *Hotel Bridge Side* sits on the opposite bank in the sun.

The route crosses to the north bank of the Langtang Khola, then climbs alongside a

LANGTANG & HELAMBU

Langtang & Helambu – Flora & Fauna

Trees The **larch** of the Langtang area and western Nepal is unusual among conifers in that it is deciduous. When this species displays its yellow colours in autumn it will not be mistaken for anything else.

Wild Flowers In order to really experience the wild flowers in their profusion, you must endure the monsoon rains or trek to the remote rain-shadow areas of the west during summer. There are, however, some species that bloom during many times of the year, such as the sky-blue **gentians** of the dry subalpine and alpine regions and the lavender primulas, or **primroses**, of moist areas. The varieties of **epiphytic orchids** which adorn the wet forests also flower at various times of the year.

Gentians

Birds In Langtang watch for hawks or **buzzards**, medium-sized raptors with broad wings and rounded tails, often fanned. Though there are only three species to look for, their highly variable plumage makes identification difficult. These birds are highly visible during winter and are likely to be seen in pairs, mostly below 3000m.

A much smaller but very distinctive bird seen on the open ground is the **hoopoe**, which has orange plumage and black wings with broad white stripes. This species also features a retractable crest that is flared when it alights and a long, slender, decurved bill that is used for probing the ground.

In order to identify the birds of the forest, you will need a keen eye and some tenacity. The ability to recognise birds by their calls will greatly facilitate identification in this habitat. This becomes especially advantageous when dealing with species that for the most part remain hidden when they call, and/or are nocturnal. Particular examples are the usually drab-coloured **cuckoos**, which call most often in spring and summer, the plump green, fruit-eating **barbets**, and at nightfall the various **owls** and owlets and the **nightjars**, which are similar to the North American nighthawks.

The **laughing thrushes** are another group of birds that usually betray their presence with characteristic calls before they are spotted. These diverse, animated birds are more easily seen as they often congregate in large, raucous foraging parties. Related to these species are the **black-capped sibias,** gregarious bronze-and-black birds typical of the oak forests with a persistent ringing call. Look also for the **red-billed** and **yellow-billed magpies** as they follow each other through the trees with long, trailing, white-tipped tails.

Two more species of the forest canopy stand out. The male **minivet** is bright red with black, and the female yellow on black, which is quite striking when they burst into flight together. The **slaty-headed parakeet,** the only parakeet to venture into the hills, has a long, yellow-tipped tail and is quite vocal in its feeding flocks. ∎

series of waterfalls. The forest is sparser and drier on this side of the river, consisting mainly of scrub oak, as opposed to the damp forest of large pines on the shady southern bank. Climb steeply to a landslide and the *Langtang View & Lodge* at **Rimche**, 2250m. The *Namaste Tibetan Lodge* is a bit higher at 2330m, and the *Tibetan Lodge* is 10 minutes beyond. There is a trail junction that connects to a high route back to Syarpagaon and Syabrubesi; this was the old trail to Langtang before the bridge was built across the Langtang Khola. You have now finished most of the day's climbing; descend gently

to Changtang, popularly known as **Lama Hotel**, at 2380m. There are at least five lodges here, including the *Lama Hotel* itself, and a few camping spots. The next accommodation is about 1½ hours beyond at *Riverside Lodge*.

Day 3: Lama Hotel to Langtang Village

The day starts with a gentle climb, but it soon becomes steeper, climbing high above the Langtang Khola. In places it is so steep that the trail is on logs anchored to the valley wall. Tantalising glimpses of Langtang Lirung (7246m) appear through the trees. At

Gumnachok is the *Riverside Lodge*, on the banks of the river; there is another *Riverside Lodge* in a clearing known as Chhunama, 15 minutes beyond. The trail crosses a stream on a log bridge, then climbs through meadows to **Ghora Tabela** at 3000m. Once a Tibetan resettlement project, this is now a Nepal army and national park post and has no permanent inhabitants.

The national park lodge is operated on contract and is now named *Lovely Lodge*. There is another police checkpost where they check, yet again, to be sure that you paid the national park entrance fee. If you somehow slipped past the station at Dhunche, they will collect the fee – and possibly a fine – here. The trail ascends gradually, as the valley becomes wider and wider, past yak pastures, *Thangshyap Lodge*, some *mani* stones and scattered Tamang villages to the *Langtang Gompa Hotel*. You can see the village gompa just above the hotel; if you want to visit the temple, ask the hotel owner for information and assistance. The trail descends into a valley to cross a stream and climbs past several water-driven mills and prayer wheels to the large settlement of **Langtang** at 3500m.

This village is the headquarters for Langtang National Park; the park buildings are those with green metal roofs below the village. The best lodge is the *Village View Lodge* at the entrance to the town; most other lodges in Langtang are rooms in private homes, which are heated and scented by yak-dung fires. The park administration allows an increase in prices at Langtang village and above, so everything suddenly becomes more costly. The houses of Langtang and the neighbouring communities have Tibetan-style flat roofs and are surrounded by stone walls enclosing fields of buckwheat, potatoes, wheat, turnips and barley. The villagers keep herds of yaks and cattle here and in pastures above the village.

It is easy to go beyond Langtang, but not a good idea from the point of view of acclimatisation. You may not have noticed it because the trail has climbed gently, but you have ascended more than 1000m today.

Trekkers have fallen ill, and some have died, in this region because of altitude problems. Don't go beyond Langtang village if you have come from Lama Hotel, and descend immediately if you suffer a severe headache or vomiting.

Day 4: Langtang to Kyanjin Gompa
The trail winds through the village and climbs onto a ridge dominated by a large, square *chorten* and a long row of mani walls. It then climbs gradually past the small village of Muna to Singdum, where there is a small lodge. Continuing through yak pastures as the valley becomes broader, the path crosses a wooden cantilever bridge, then climbs a moraine where you can finally see Kyanjin gompa. It is a short descent to lodges, and a cheese factory and an almost defunct gompa. The Swiss Association for Technical Assistance started the cheese factory in 1955. It now produces about 7000 kg of cheese annually, all of it hauled by porters to the dairy in Kathmandu. It is easy to reach Kyanjin gompa, elevation 3800m, before lunch, allowing time to acclimatise and explore the surroundings. The best place in town is the *Hotel Yala Peak*. The National Park Lodge, with its fancy solar heating, has been leased by a local person and has gone to seed – probably because of the park's price controls.

Days 5-6: Langtang Valley
Spend the first day hiking up the moraine north of Kyanjin gompa to an elevation of 4300m or more. From the moraine, there is a spectacular view of Langtang Lirung and the foot of one of its major glaciers.

There are two good viewpoints in the area that you can climb. The peak to the north of Kyanjin gompa is Kyanjin Ri (4773m) – about a two hour climb. Do not head directly up the ridge behind the gompa; follow the indistinct trail that starts on the opposite side of a stream beyond the national park lodge. The views are superb.

A longer excursion is to Tsergo Ri ('Tserko' on the German map), at 4984m, a four hour climb from Kyanjin gompa. Both of these peaks are visible from Kyanjin gompa and prayer flags mark their tops.

There are also two possible climbing projects: 5500m Yala Peak (not to be confused with Yala Kharka on Tsergo Ri), and 5749m Tsergo Peak (which is different from Tsergo Ri). Both are two-day expeditions that involve glacier climbing and a high camp on a saddle above the trail near Nubama Dhang.

It's also worthwhile taking an extra day or two to continue further up the Langtang Valley to **Langshisha Kharka** for views of Langshisha Ri (6310m), Gang Chhenpo (6388m), Urkeinmang (6151m), and Penthang Karpo Ri (6830m). There are no facilities beyond Kyanjin gompa, but you can make a day trip and return to Kyanjin gompa for the night. If you have a tent and food, you can camp at Langshisha Kharka at 4080m or another of the summer pastures high in the valley.

Kyanjin Gompa to Kathmandu
You can return to Kathmandu by the same route, or you might be lucky enough to find a plane at the Langtang airstrip, above Kyanjin gompa at 3960m.

It is possible to return to Kathmandu either over Ganja La or via Gosainkund when conditions are suitable on these high routes.

Across Ganja La

Duration 12 days
Difficulty Hard
Maximum elevation 5106m
Permit cost US$5 per week plus Rs 650
Season October to November, March to May
Hotels None
Summary The pass crossing from Langtang into Helambu is steep and exposed and often closed by snow. There's no accommodation for several days.

The route from Kyanjin gompa in Langtang to Tarke Gyang in Helambu requires crossing the 5106m-high Ganja La.

Warning
A guide who knows the trail, plus a tent, food and fuel are essential for crossing the Ganja La. The pass is difficult and dangerous when covered by snow, so for a safe crossing, local inquiries about its condition, good equipment and some mountaineering experience are necessary. You can assume the pass will be open from April to November, though unusual weather can alter its condition at any time.

Days 1-5: Dhunche to Kyanjin Gompa
For the first four days, follow the Langtang trek route described in the preceding section. An extra day in Langtang Valley for acclimatisation is essential before beginning the ascent to Ganja La.

Day 6: Kyanjin Gompa to Ngegang
This is a short day from Kyanjin gompa, but Ngegang is the last good place to camp before beginning the final climb to the pass, and you should minimise the elevation gain to aid acclimatisation. Crossing the Langtang Khola below Kyanjin gompa, the trail makes a steep climb along the ridge on the south side of the valley through a forest of rhododendron and juniper. Finally becoming more gentle, the trail reaches the yak pasture of Ngegang at about 4000m. There are *goths* (stone huts) here and on the other side of the pass, but they have no roofs during the winter, so a tent is very handy on this trek. During the monsoon, herders carry bamboo mats to provide roofs for the huts here, and live the entire summer in high meadows with herds of yaks and goats.

Day 7: Ngegang to Keldang
The trail continues south, following streams and moraines and climbing steeply towards the pass. As the trail climbs higher, and comes under the shadow of the 5800m peaks to the south, you will find more and more snow. Turning south-west, the trail makes the final steep ascent to the pass at 5106m. The last 100m of the climb is a tricky balancing act on a snow slope above some steep rocks.

STAN ARMINGTON

RICHARD I'ANSON

Langtang & Helambu
Top: Shiva is said to have created holy Gosainkund Lake with his trident, and its waters
    are believed to disappear underground and resurface in Kumbeshwar pool, in Patan.
Bottom: Cattle graze and stone walls surround fields in Langtang village.

RICHARD I'ANSON

STAN ARMINGTON

STAN ARMINGTON

Eastern Nepal
Top Left: Older suspension bridges such as this are gradually being replaced.
Top Right: Treks to Kanchenjunga offer views of Kyabru and its icefall.
Bottom: Makalu south face from the hill above Shersong.

Ganja La itself is flanked by pinnacles that mountaineers call gendarmes and is topped by prayer flags and a large cairn of rocks. The views to the north from the pass, of Langtang Lirung and the snow peaks in Tibet, including Shisha Pangma at 8013m, are outstanding. On a clear day there are also views of many ranges of hills to the south. West of the pass is 5846m Naya Kangri, previously named Ganja La Chuli. This is one of the trekking peaks that you can climb with a permit from the Nepal Mountaineering Association. A base camp in this region makes a good starting point for this reasonably easy climb.

The descent from the pass is steep and dangerous as it follows a loose scree slope for about 200m before emerging onto a snow slope. Somehow, the descent from Ganja La, like most mountain descents, seems more treacherous than the ascent, no matter which direction one crosses the pass. However, Ganja La is one of the steeper and more difficult of the major passes in Nepal. After the initial steep drop, the trail descends gradually in a huge basin surrounded by glaciated peaks.

The route descends through the basin along an indistinct trail, marked occasionally by rock cairns, to a small stream at 4400m. If you are travelling in the reverse direction, from Helambu to Langtang, it will require a full day to reach this point from Keldang, and you should schedule two days from Keldang to the pass.

The trail enters the steep Yangri Khola valley and drops quickly down a rough scree slope to the stream. Following the stream for some distance through grassy meadows, the trail reaches a few goths (again without roofs) at **Keldang**, at about 4270m elevation.

Day 8: Keldang to Dukpu

This is a long and tiring day as the trail descends along a ridge, making many ups and downs. In winter, there is no water from Keldang to the bottom of the ridge, near Phedi, so you should plan food accordingly for this stretch of the trail. In October and November, there is usually no water problem because the monsoon rains leave an ample ground water supply in several small springs.

The route heads down the valley, but stays high above the river, finally meeting the ridge itself, then follows the ridge line to the small summer settlement of Dukpu at 4080m.

Day 9: Dukpu to Tarke Gyang

From Dukpu, the trail descends further along the ridge, then makes a 180m climb to a pass at 4020m. The pass offers a commanding view of the Himalaya, from Dorje Lakpa east almost to Everest, and a panorama of the first part of the Everest trek, as far as the peak of Numbur in Khumbu. From the pass, the trail descends through pine and rhododendron forests past tiny herders' settlements to a ridge high above Tarke Gyang. It then drops steeply to Gekye gompa at 3020m, a small monastic community and the first permanent settlement since Kyanjin gompa. The trail continues its steep plunge to the large Sherpa village of Tarke Gyang at 2560m.

Days 10-12: Tarke Gyang to Kathmandu

For the return to Kathmandu, use one of the routes described below. You can travel in either direction, following days 5, 6 and 7 of the Helambu circuit or days 4, 3, 2 and 1 in reverse.

Helambu Circuit

> **Duration** 7 days
> **Difficulty** Easy to medium
> **Maximum elevation** 3490m
> **Permit cost** US$5 per week plus Rs 900
> **Season** October to April
> **Hotels** Very good
> **Summary** The closest trek to Kathmandu offers an easy loop through villages of varied ethnic makeup.

This is the description of a seven day trek that makes a circuit of the Helambu region. The easiest starting point for this trek is Sundarijal because of its proximity to Kathmandu. You can make the trek in either direction, because it closes a loop from Pati Bhanjyang, the first night stop of the trek. The preferred route is clockwise as I have described here; first visiting the high ridge to the west of Helambu Valley, then heading to Tarke Gyang and descending the Malemchi Khola before climbing back to Pati Bhanjyang. There are all kinds of other possible variations, including a direct route to Tarke Gyang from Pati Bhanjyang, then down the ridge through Sermathang, ending at Panchkal.

For a map of this trek, refer to the Langtang & Helambu Treks map on pages 266-7.

Season
Helambu is a good trekking destination throughout the normal October to May trekking season, though it tends to be very hot in the Indrawati valley in late spring. The trek remains at reasonably low elevations, so there is little chance of altitude problems, but you should be prepared for cold and possible snow at Tharepati during the winter. There are fewer trekkers here than in either the Mt Everest or Annapurna regions, and good lodges are abundant and uncrowded.

Access
The Helambu trek is an easy trek to organise. Transport to and from the starting point of the trek is fast and cheap. The unpaved road to Sundarijal starts beyond Boudhanath and travels seven km to the foot of the hills at the northern edge of the Kathmandu Valley.

Day 1: Sundarijal to Pati Bhanjyang
At Sundarijal (1350m) there is a large water project that supplies much of Kathmandu's drinking water via an immense pipe. The unpaved road from Boudhanath turns into a trail near a small hydroelectric plant and starts up concrete steps alongside the water pipe. Beyond Sundarijal the trail climbs continuously through forests (still following the water pipe) to a medieval-looking reservoir, dam and waterworks. Crossing the dam, the trail leaves the water supply system and

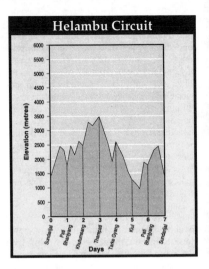

climbs steeply to a road at 1550m. Cross the road and continue the climb to the top of the Shivapuri ridge.

The road is an unfinished project that will eventually lead from Budhanilkantha to Chisopani and beyond, on the north side of the Shivapuri ridge.

The first village on the trail is the sprawling Tamang settlement of **Mulkharka**, at 1895m. There are a few small tea shops here, where you can sit and enjoy a spectacular panoramic view of the Kathmandu Valley and watch planes taking off from Tribhuvan airport. If you start the trek early in the morning, you will meet hundreds of people walking uphill to gather wood that will be used as fuel in Kathmandu.

The trail has now entered the Shivapuri Watershed & Wildlife Reserve, a 112 sq km walled area. Portions of the trail are almost level, but much of the climb is steep in deeply eroded chasms. After passing through an army camp where your Shivapuri entrance permit is checked, you can see the remnants of the village of Chaurabas. Climb further on a heavily eroded trail to the pass at Borlang Bhanjyang, elevation 2440m. Most of the Shivapuri ridge which the reserve protects is a dense forest of pine, oak and rhododendron trees.

Just below the ridge on the north side are a few tea shops. The mountain views from the ridge, or from Chisopani (45 minutes further), are excellent, but are best seen in the early morning. The sunrise on the Himalaya, from Annapurna to Everest, is particularly outstanding from this point. The route heads down the ridge through a forest of oak and rhododendron to **Chisopani** at 2300m. There is an unfinished tourist resort and several lodges here, and you can see the ongoing construction of the road you crossed early the same morning. Chisopani is a rather grubby little place, more like a truck stop (though without the trucks!) than a Himalayan village. Take care of your possessions here as theft can be problem. The *Himalayan Guest House* and the *Gauri Shankar Guest House* are both in Chisopani.

The trail continues to drop from Chisopani on a good, sometimes level, trail that crosses meadows and fields. The final descent to Pati Bhanjyang is on a trail that has eroded into a steep slippery slide.

Pati Bhanjyang is on a saddle at the bottom of the ridge at 1770m. This is a Brahman and Chhetri village with a few shops, teahouses and a police checkpost, though the police are usually not interested in trekking permits. There is a big lodge here, the *New Shivapuri Lodge*, plus the *Pati Lodge* and the *Himal Lodge*. On the Kathmandu edge of the village, the old woman who runs the down-market *Sewa Sadan Lodge* insisted in a very friendly way that I really should spend the night at her establishment. I didn't, so I cannot vouch for anything except the carda-mom-flavoured tea that she prepared.

Day 2: Pati Bhanjyang to Khutumsang

The trail heads north out of Pati Bhanjyang. If you want to do the Helambu circuit in reverse, turn east and climb the ridge, then descend into the Malemchi Khola valley. To go to Langtang, or to make the normal Helambu circuit, bear left and follow a long stretch of level trail to some lodges at the foot

of a hill. Make a very steep ascent on switch-backs to **Chipling** at 2170m. There are a few tea shops in shacks at the entrance to the village, but Chipling does not have much else to offer. At the upper end of the village the trail makes another steep, 200m climb on a stone staircase to the top of the Jhogin Danda ridge at 2470m. There are good mountain views along this stretch of trail. From the ridge the trail descends through forests to **Thodang Betini**, a long, strung-out village at 2250m. Places to stay include the *Himalayan Yogi Lodge*, *Tasi Lodge*, the *Thotung Lodge* (offering 'fooding & lodging', as do many other places along this route) and the *Thotong Sherpa Lodge*.

Continuing along the forested ridge, the trail descends to a large chorten overlooking the Tamang village of **Gul Bhanjyang** at 2140m. This is a delightful, classic hill village with a pleasant main street, several shops and a number of places to stay, includ-ing the *Shree Ganesh Lodge* on the southern side of the village, the *Gosai Kunda Lodge*, *Gol Phubhanjyang Lodge* and the *Deepak Lodge*.

The trail climbs the ridge from Gul Bhan-jyang to another pass at 2620m. From a grassy meadow you can look back over Gul Bhanjyang to the big chorten you walked past earlier. The meadow makes a good camping spot, and there's also the *Dragon Lodge*. It's downhill to **Khutumsang** at 2470m, in a saddle atop the ridge.

This village has completely adapted itself to trekkers; almost every house in town is a lodge or shop. You can stay at the *Helambu View Lodge*, *Shree Sherpa Lodge*, *Karna Lama Lodge*, *Gosainkunda Lodge*, *Dimlana Lodge*, *Dame Sherpa Lodge* or *Dolma Lodge*. The national park office is at the far side of the village. Show your park entry permit or pay Rs 650 if you started at Sun-darijal; show your permit yet again if you are headed in the opposite direction.

Day 3: Khutumsang to Tharepati

The trek proceeds due north up the Yurin Danda ridge and affords views of the peaks above Langtang and of the Gosainkund peaks. The trail climbs above Khutumsang on a steep, eroded trail, mostly through fir and rhododendron forests where there are no permanent settlements, although there are a few small shepherds' huts. There are two bhattis at **Pambu**, then the route climbs to a large cairn at the top of the Panghu Danda (3285m). This is herding country, and there are many goths along the way; in season you may be able to buy milk or curd from the herders.

The trail descends to **Magen Goth** at 3150m. There are two lodges and a fancy-looking army checkpost – again they check your national park entry ticket. Continuing to climb, steeply at first, then more gradually, the trail makes some ups and downs passing through forests, across flower-strewn meadows and crossing streams.

It finally reaches **Tharepati**, which consists of a few goths and hotels at 3490m. The very prettily situated *Himaliya Lodge* is on the Khutumsang side of the pass. The *Sumche Lodge* is just below the pass while the *Top Lodge* is right at the top. It can get very chilly here at night.

The trail to Gosainkund turns north-west from this point while the trail that completes the Helambu circuit turns east and drops steeply down from the Top Lodge. The region is now truly alpine, with meadows and shrubs typical of high elevations. If you are continuing on the Helambu circuit it is worth walking for half an hour or so up along the Gosainkund route for the fine views. The site of the 1992 Thai Airbus crash is far up the ridge to the north-west.

It was north of this section of trail that James Scott, an Australian medical student, was lost in 1991.

Day 4: Tharepati to Tarke Gyang

Turn east from the northern end of the settlement and descend steeply down a ravine. The vegetation changes to large firs, then to oaks and rhododendrons, as you rapidly lose all the altitude you gained during the last two days. Crossing a stream on a suspension bridge, the trail makes a short final climb to reach the prosperous Sherpa village of **Malemchigaon** at 2530m.

The Sherpas of Helambu are very different from their cousins in Solu Khumbu. Instead of the Tibetan-style black dress and colourful apron, the Sherpa women of Helambu wear a dress of red printed cotton. Their language is also quite distinct from the Sherpa language of Solu Khumbu. There are grammatical differences and, in addition, Helambu Sherpas speak much more rapidly than other Sherpas. Helambu women have a reputation for being very beautiful, and many Helambu Sherpa girls were once employed in aristocratic Rana households in Kathmandu during the Rana regime. Many of their benefactors gave gifts of land to these girls, so many Helambu families now own large tracts of farmland in the river valley far below.

Malemchigaon has a very glossy gompa with a line of prayer flags at the front and brightly painted walls and statues. If it's locked up, enquire at one of the nearby lodges about the key. You can stay at the *Tashi Dhalek Lodge* right by the gompa, the *Sun Lodge* or the *Green View Lodge* on the Tharepati side of the village, or the comfortable-looking *Yangrima Lodge* overlooking the village from the top end. Electricity supply lines snake down the hill from Malemchigaon, connecting it with Tarke Gyang up the other side of the valley.

From Malemchigaon, the trail continues to descend to the *River Side Lodge* and the Malemchi Khola, which is crossed on a sturdy suspension bridge at 1890m. Once across the river, the trail immediately begins the ascent towards Tarke Gyang. Sometimes hoteliers from Tarke Gyang come all the way down to the river to try to induce you to patronise their establishments. It is a long climb to this picturesque village on a shelf high above the river at 2600m.

Tarke Gyang is the largest village in Helambu and the destination for most trekkers in this region. The stone houses are close together with narrow alleyways separating them. Inside, the homes are large,

Lost in the Himalayas

In late December 1991, James Scott, a young Australian medical student, left Phedi to cross the Laurebina Pass to the Gosainkund lakes. When snow started to fall, visibility became limited and the trail indistinct, and he and his partner disagreed on the best course of action. Eventually his partner decided to press on alone to try to find a way over the pass while James opted to make his way back to Phedi. In the bad conditions he wandered off the track and followed a creek down until he became trapped below the ridge line which the trail follows from Tharepati through Ghopte to Phedi. Uncertain of his location, and with movement made difficult by the snow and his weakening condition, he soon gave up hope of walking out and waited to be rescued. Remarkably, he was rescued, but not for 43 days, by which time he was nearly dead from starvation. A huge search effort involving numerous people at ground level and in the air eventually spotted him from a helicopter.

James was very lucky to be found and the whole story reads like an object lesson of what not to do, but in similar conditions many trekkers could quickly find themselves in an equally difficult situation. His mistakes included making a difficult trek at a tricky time of year – he was attempting to cross a 4600m pass late in the season when snowfalls can be sudden and dangerous. He was not trekking with a familiar and reliable partner – the friend he had set out with had turned back due to an injury and he had only met his new partner a couple of days before he was lost. Close friends with more of a commitment to each other would have been less liable to split up at a dangerous time. He became lost by following a creek, an easy trap for the unwary: trails in Nepal generally follow ridges, and following a creek will usually bring you to a waterfall or some other dead end. When he was lost, his problem was compounded by having only limited food supplies – the famous single bar of chocolate – although he had originally set out from Kathmandu intending to make the easier Helambu circuit, where there are frequent villages so emergency rations are not necessary at all.

James was lost between Ghopte and Talu and trekking maps of the region indicate the two settlements are only about 2.5 km apart. Trekkers in Nepal soon realise that distance is of less importance than altitude and the 1000m altitude difference between Talu at 2500m and Ghopte at 3500m is probably more important than the distance. You can read the tale of his ordeal, told by James Scott and by his sister, Joanne Robertson, who was in Kathmandu during the search effort, in their book *Lost in the Himalayas*. ∎

clean and often elaborately furnished with elegant brassware and traditional Tibetan carpets on highly polished wooden floors. The gompa has a huge brass prayer wheel.

The people of Helambu do a lot of trading in India during the winter. Many of the people are quite well-to-do, and own cultivated fields in the lower Malemchi Khola valley. A special racket among the people of Helambu is the sale of antiques, usually manufactured in Kathmandu and aged over smoky fires in the homes of Tarke Gyang. Beware of any such bargain here. It is illegal to export any item over 100 years old from Nepal, so you would do better to purchase well-made handicrafts in Kathmandu or Patan, rather than try to beat the system by purchasing a fake antique in the hills.

The *Mount View Hotel* is on the Malemchigaon edge of the village. Right by the village's large gompa is the *Lama Lodge*, while the *Tara Lodge* and the *Helambu Lodge* are further back in the village. At the far side of the village the trail crosses a stream past a water-driven prayer wheel and then a long mani wall beside the entrance to the rambling *Tarkegyang Guest House*. Trekking groups often camp in the garden here.

Tarke Gyang is a good place to take a rest day, and there's the option of making a half-day climb to the peak (3771m) directly north of the village. From the chorten on the summit there are superb views of the mountains to the north. This ascent is the first part of the route to the Ganja La pass, described in reverse earlier in this chapter, which leads to the Langtang region.

From Tarke Gyang, there is a choice of trails back to Kathmandu. A description of the alternative route along the ridge through Sermathang and down to Malemchi Pul Bazaar, then to Panchkal on the Kodari road, follows the Day 7 description.

LANGTANG & HELAMBU

Day 5: Tarke Gyang to Kiul

The circuit route back to Sundarijal leaves Tarke Gyang past the guesthouse and mani wall (walk to the left), then drops off the west side of the ridge in a rhododendron forest, along a broad, well-travelled path. The trail passes several chortens, mani walls and *kanis*. Passing through the Sherpa villages of **Kakani** at 2070m and **Thimbu** at 1580m, the trail enters the hot, rice-growing country of the Malemchi and Indrawati valleys, and leaves the highland ethnic groups for the Brahman, Chhetri and Newar people who inhabit the lower regions.

The steep descent continues to **Kiul** (1280m), strung out on terraces above the Malemchi Khola. The trail is now in semi-tropical banana-and-monkey country at an elevation below that of Kathmandu.

Day 6: Kiul to Pati Bhanjyang

There is a large road under construction in this portion of the valley in preparation for the development of a tunnel that will take water from here to the Kathmandu Valley. The route is likely to be confused and dusty while construction is under way. From Kiul, the trail follows the river, descending slightly, then crosses the river on a suspension bridge at 1190m. A short distance beyond the bridge, the trail reaches Mahenkal (1130m) and joins the road. As the road descends the valley, it passes through Gheltum, the site of an imposing two-storey schoolhouse and a post office. You can follow a trail that cuts across some large road switchbacks as you descend into **Talamarang**, a pleasant village on the banks of the river at 940m. There are some small shops here, and you can probably find a jeep or truck if you decide to get a ride back to Kathmandu.

Crossing the Talamarang Khola on a long, rather precarious suspension bridge, the trail leaves the road and proceeds west along the south bank of the stream through rice terraces and fields. The trail soon deteriorates into a boulder-strewn route up the river valley. The same monsoon flood that destroyed the road at Talamarang also destroyed this portion

of the trail, and washed many fertile fields downstream in the process. After following the stream for a long distance, the trail starts climbing. This trail is hard to find, and is not used by many locals, so be sure to ask someone for directions. It's a steep climb towards the top of the ridge on a wide, well-constructed trail. From the uninhabited valley floor, the trail soon enters a densely populated region, passing through Batache en route to the top of the ridge, which it reaches near Thakani at 1890m. Following the ridge through meadows and terraced fields, the trail crosses over to its south side and descends to **Pati Bhanjyang** at 1770m, completing the circuit through Helambu.

Day 7: Pati Bhanjyang to Kathmandu

Retrace the route back to Sundarijal, as described in the opposite direction on the first day of the trek. From Sundarijal it is easy to find cheap transport back to Kathmandu.

TARKE GYANG TO KATHMANDU VIA PANCHKAL

There is an excellent alternative route from Tarke Gyang that goes to the Kodari road at Panchkal and gets you back to Kathmandu in three easy days. The trail heads south along the ridge through Sermathang, down to the river at Malemchi, and along the road to Panchkal. The first part of the trail, along the ridge through forests and Sherpa villages, is quite delightful. Although the later part of the route, on the dusty road along the Indrawati River, is boring, you can get a ride in one of the buses or trucks that ply this stretch of road or with the regular minibus service from Malemchi Pul Bazaar. The route meets the Chinese road at Panchkal, and from there it's a three hour ride back to Kathmandu. You might want to stop at Dhulikhel, before the Kathmandu Valley.

Day 1: Tarke Gyang to Sermathang

From Tarke Gyang the trail leaves the village near the big guesthouse and follows the electricity supply line around the hillside to Parachin. The trail makes a sweep around the wide valley end between Parachin and the pretty village of **Gangjwal** at around 2500m. At the end of the village the *Dolma Lodge* sells cold beer and soft drinks and from its position on the edge of the ridge has views right across to Sermathang.

The trail drops down from the edge of the ridge but then continues at around the same altitude along the side of the ridge, crossing a number of streams and waterfalls and picking its way over the debris from a huge landslide. Finally it passes a gompa at the edge of the large village of **Sermathang** (2620m). There is a Langtang National Park office in the village where you must pay the park entrance fee if you are coming from the opposite direction.

Sermathang has a number of places to stay, including the *Mountain View Lodge*, the *Tara Lodge* and the very comfortable-looking *Yangri Lodge* and *Hotel Snowfall*. If you are staying at lodges you might want to make a short day of it and stop here as there are not so many accommodation possibilities further down the ridge before Malemchi.

Day 2: Sermathang to Malemchi Pul Bazaar

From Sermathang the trail follows the ridge all the way down to Malemchi Pul Bazaar, making a drop of 1790m. After passing a large gompa at the southern end of the village the trail undulates along the west side of the ridge, passing chorten after chorten before dropping down to Kakani at around 1900m. Don't confuse this Kakani with the one, just south of Tarke Gyang, which you pass through on Day 5 of the regular Helambu circuit route.

A chorten marks the saddle at the northern end of Kakani and there is a gompa at the top of the hill overlooking the village, but at this point you are in the transition zone from the Buddhist regions to the Hindu lowlands. The fairly primitive-looking *View Lodge* and a couple of tea shops can be found near the chorten.

From Kakani the trail drops steeply past a small village and down to the attractive larger village of **Dubhachaur** at 1500m. A very Australian-looking eucalyptus tree makes a shady lunch stop in the village. The trail

descends even more steeply right down the ridge to the junction of the Larke Khola and the Malemchi Khola, where they form the Indrawati River. A suspension bridge takes you over the Larke Khola, just before the junction, and after a short walk along the river bank a larger and grander suspension bridge crosses the Indrawati into **Malemchi Pul Bazaar** at 830m. A plaque on the bridge proclaims that it was made by John Henderson & Co Ltd, Engineers of Aberdeen, Scotland. The village has a collection of shops and teahouses and numerous lodges including the *Indrawati, Helambu, Shanti* and the quite luxurious-looking *Lama Lodge*.

Day 3: Malemchi Pul Bazaar to Kathmandu

Transport (including buses) runs reasonably frequently along the road (known as the Helambu Highway) from Malemchi via Bahunepati and Sipa Ghat to Panchkal on the Kodari road.

Gosainkund

Duration 7 days
Difficulty Medium
Maximum elevation 4610m
Permit cost US$5 per week plus Rs 900
Season October to November, March to April
Hotels Acceptable
Summary An alpine lake that is a major pilgrimage site. Several days of remote back-country walking with very rough accommodation. Snowbound in winter.

You can make the trek through Gosainkund in either direction combined with a trek to Helambu or Langtang. It is also a worthwhile seven or eight day trek in its own right. There is a strict ban on the use of firewood in Gosainkund, so if you are camping, be sure to bring kerosene for fuel. The route I have described is from Dhunche or Syabru to Tharepati. From Tharepati, you can either continue to Helambu or go directly back to

Kathmandu. See page 268 for a profile of the Gosainkund trek.

Accommodation

There are lodges all along the route, but they close during the winter (late December to early March).

Warning

You can also trek in the opposite direction, starting from Sundarijal or Helambu and travelling to Langtang via Gosainkund. If you do this, beware of the route from Laurebina Yak to Ghora Tabela. Many maps show a trail here, but it does not exist. Many trekkers have been lost, and one has died, trying to follow this trail after it deteriorates into landslides near the river. Take the longer route from Laurebina Yak to Syabru and then join the main Langtang trail.

Day 1: Syabru or Dhunche to Sing Gompa

From Dhunche From Dhunche, at 1950m, follow the road to the first switchback. There is a sign marking a level trail that follows the south bank of the Trisuli River through fields and pastures to a few houses. Cross the river on a wooden bridge just before the valley narrows and becomes steeper. The trail follows the north side of the river for a short while, then begins the steep climb towards the ridge. After the initial climb, the trail levels a bit, passes through a village, then continues up to the ridge. Climb through a forest of firs and rhododendrons for about an hour to a small clearing, then another hour to a very basic teahouse where there are views back down the valley. The trail continues to climb to the ridge and a trail junction. Turn right and continue up past an army camp, then up through scrub and oaks to **Sing gompa**, near the top of the ridge in an area of dead trees. Do not take the inviting-looking trail that descends steeply to an apple farm.

From Syabru There are at least three routes from Syabru to Gosainkund. Two of these

bypass Sing gompa and head directly to two tea shops at Chalang Pati. The route described here is a more circuitous trail via Sing gompa. This trail is easier to follow and breaks the climb into more manageable segments.

The direct route from Chalang Pati to Syabru is a good choice if you are coming down from Gosainkund because the trail is easy to see from above, but it's a bad choice if you are headed uphill because it's not an obvious route. A guide who knows the way will be very helpful, perhaps essential, if you plan to climb up this route, otherwise you will probably follow a lot of useless yak trails.

Once you evade the pushy Syabru hoteliers, climb past the gompa, school and army post, and switchback up the steep hill above the village. There are a few houses and potato fields, but always take the upper, steep trail and you will eventually find yourself at two pleasant tea shops in **Dursagang** at 2550m. The trail continues less steeply, now mostly in forests, past an old chorten to the top of the ridge and two shoddy tea shops at 3000m.

This is also a trail junction; the right-hand trail leads downhill to Brabal and the Dhunche road, and the left trail is a short cut to Chalang Pati. The Sing gompa trail climbs, then cuts across the ridge top, staying fairly level in forests as it crosses the head of a valley. Take the uphill trail at each junction and cross another forested ridge. There is a view of Dhunche far below in the valley. The trail continues across the head of a second valley, then reaches a final ridge at 3260m. Sing gompa is about 100m along the trail to the left.

Sing gompa is the main attraction at Chandan Bari, elevation 3250m, which also has several lodges and a small cheese factory. The gompa, which houses a statue of the Green Tara, is not well cared for; the caretaker will unlock it for you for a small fee. The hillside near Chandan Bari is bare and scorched through a combination of logging, fire and wind storms.

Day 2: Sing Gompa to Gosainkund

The trail climbs steeply up the ridge, at several points on top of the ridge itself. The ridge is a transition zone between rich, moist mountain forests on the northern slopes and dry scrub vegetation on the slopes that face south. The trail crosses behind the ridge and stays in deep forests for a while, then emerges onto a saddle at **Chalang Pati** (3380m), where the *Chalang Pati Hotel* offers a welcome cup of tea. When you start walking again, you will see a sign in Nepali. It says that you are now entering the Gosainkund protected area, where the killing of animals, lighting of wood fires and grazing of goats are prohibited.

As the trail ascends, there are outstanding views across Langtang Valley to Langtang Lirung. There are a few goths along the way to the tea shops at Laurebina, elevation 3930m, known locally as **Laurebina Yak**. There are three lodges here; one advertises 'astounding mountain views' as you eat 'breakfast on top of the world'. The views are truly magnificent – you can see the Annapurnas, Manaslu (8156m), Ganesh Himal (7406m), some unnamed peaks in Tibet and finally Langtang Lirung.

The trail ascends, now in alpine country, up the ridge to a pair of small stone pillars that say 'Welcome to Gosainkund' – but you still have a lot more climbing to do. Continue to the ridge at 4100m and climb further for a view of the first of the lakes, **Saraswati Kund**, in a valley several hundred metres below. The trail leaves the ridge and follows a trail high above the Trisuli valley. This is not a trail for acrophobics; fortunately it is on the sunny side of the hill, so the snow melts quickly. The trail is spooky and dangerous if it is snow-covered. Indeed, if there has been a lot of snow, it may not be possible to cross into Gosainkund. People have perished floundering in the deep snow in this region, so return to Dhunche if conditions are not good.

After the trail crosses a spur, the second lake in the chain, **Bhairav Kund**, comes into view. The trail climbs gently but continuously to a ridge and drops about 20m to the third and largest lake, **Gosainkund**, at an elevation of 4380m. There are two small tea shops, a shrine and several small stone shelters for pilgrims on the north-western side of the lake. Hundreds of people come here to worship and bathe in the lake during the full-moon festival each August.

Gosainkund lake has a black rock in the middle, said to be the head of Shiva. There is also a legend about a white rock under the water that is the remnant of an ancient shrine of Shiva. According to legend, Shiva himself created this high-altitude lake when he pierced a glacier with his trident to obtain water to quench his thirst after consuming some poison. It is also said that the water from this lake disappears underground via a subterranean channel and surfaces in Kumbeshwar pool, next to the five-storey Shiva Temple in Patan, more than 60 km away.

Day 3: Gosainkund to Ghopte

The trail passes the northern side of Gosainkund lake and climbs further through rugged country towards Laurebina Pass. The trail is rough and crosses moraines, but it is well marked with rock cairns. Passing three more small lakes, the trail finally reaches the pass at 4610m. A small hillock above the trail offers good views in both directions.

From the pass, the trail descends alongside a stream through alpine country to a single hut at 4100m. Here, at **Bhera Goth**, there is a choice of trails. The upper trail is a new direct route to Tharepati. It is very dangerous when there is any snow at all on the trail, and there is no accommodation or food between here and Tharepati. Get advice from other trekkers or from the man who lives at Bhera Goth before you take this trail. The lower, safer trail descends along the middle of the valley to Phedi (3500m), which comprises two funky tea shops (the *Taj Mel* is one) by a stream and a wooden bridge.

Across the valley, you can see a ridge with a steep trail across its face at an angle of almost 45°. Yes, this is where you are going. The route continues across the head of the valley on an extremely rough trail, across moraines and past two goths that have

LANGTANG & HELAMBU

A Question of Perspective

I climbed this trail, which looks so forbidding from Phedi, in the snow, following steps that the trek cook had cut with his kitchen knife. Another sherpa led the way, tossing gravel onto the snow and into the steps to provide a footing on the hard and slippery surface. As I sat at the top of the ridge taking photographs, I was wondering how to describe this particular stretch of trail. Was it dangerous or impassable in winter? My musing was interrupted by a *sadhu* in bare feet and loincloth who carried only a blanket, a brass bowl and an iron trisul. He was on his way to Gosainkund for a day and would return two days hence. Off he went down the trail, closely followed by a Nepali in gumboots who strode along listening to a football match on a radio – the only item he was carrying. These apparitions add a bit of perspective to the trail. Just be careful, go slowly and travel with reliable companions. ■

---

minimal hotel facilities – just tea and Pepsi – to the bottom of the 160m climb to the ridge. The ascent is just as steep as it looks, but it is not as exposed (and therefore not as frightening) as it looked from across the valley; see the boxed aside.

From the top of this infamous ridge, the trail descends through forests, climbing in and out of ravines across the head of the valley. Giant cliffs tower far above, forming the top of the Thare Danda. On one of the ridges there are some prayer flags; just beyond these flags is **Ghopte** at 3430m. There are two tea shops and a cave that offers some shelter. This is a long and rough day of trekking. The lodges of Tharepati are visible on the far ridge; at night you can see the lights of Trisuli Bazaar far below and the glow of Kathmandu to the south-west.

Day 4: Ghopte to Tharepati

Descending from the ridge at Ghopte, the trail continues up ravines and across the boulders of old moraines below the wreckage of a plane that crashed in 1992, then makes a final ascent to **Tharepati**, on the ridge at 3490m. There are several lodges below the ridge, and two more on the ridge itself. Take a moment to climb the hill to the east of the ridge for views of Dorje Lakpa, Shisha Pangma and peaks all the way to Khumbu. Here, the trail joins the Helambu circuit (see Day 3 of the circuit description earlier in this chapter). You can travel for two hours downhill to Malemchigaon and on to

Tarke Gyang, or go directly down the ridge to Kathmandu via Pati Bhanjyang.

The 'new' high trail from Bhera Goth rejoins the trail here. If you are walking from Sundarijal to Gosainkund, be sure to ask the people of Tharepati if this trail is safe. The dangerous snow-covered parts of this high trail are on the north-west slopes, and not visible from this point.

This is a short day; you can hang out and take in the view, head down the hill to Helambu, or start back to Kathmandu, perhaps saving a day of walking. If you want to return directly to Kathmandu, the days work out as follows:

Day 5: Tharepati to Khutumsang

See Day 3 of the earlier Helambu circuit description.

Day 6: Khutumsang to Chisopani

You might be able to get all the way to Kathmandu from Khutumsang, but the view of the Himalaya from Chisopani is spectacular enough to justify a night here. Beware of thieves in Chisopani, especially if you are camping.

Day 7: Chisopani to Kathmandu

Follow Day 1 of the Helambu circuit in reverse, back to Borlang Bhanjyang, then down the Shivapuri ridge to the road at Sundarijal. You can get a taxi or bus back to Kathmandu.

Jugal Himal

> **Duration** 13 days
> **Difficulty** Medium
> **Maximum elevation** 3800m
> **Permit cost** US$5 per week plus Rs 650
> **Season** October to November, March to April
> **Hotels** None
> **Summary** An off-the-beaten-track trek close to Kathmandu. Climb through forests to high alpine lakes. No food or accommodation.

To the north-east of Kathmandu lies a chain of peaks called Jugal Himal, which includes Dorje Lakpa (6966m), Madiya (6257m) and Phurbi Chhyachu (6637m). From the south it is an easily accessible region, although it requires a long uphill climb. Just above Dolalghat on the Kodari road there is a road to the large bazaar of Chautaara (1410m). The trek described here climbs from Chautaara to a ridge, which it then follows north to Panch Pokhari ('five lakes') at 3600m. From Panch Pokhari, trails lead to Tarke Gyang in Helambu and then back down the ridge through Sermathang to Panchkal on the Kodari road. Several other routes described in this chapter also lead back to Kathmandu from Tarke Gyang.

Another trail from Chautaara descends to the Balephi Khola, then follows a ridge to Bhairav Kund, a holy lake at 3500m. You can return from there to Tatopani on the Kodari road or make a circuit around the head of the Balephi Khola valley to Panch Pokhari and join the route described here.

This is a remote and unfrequented region, despite its proximity to Kathmandu. Treks in this area involve a lot of climbing on narrow trails. There are few villages and no hotels on this route and water is very scarce on the ridge.

Access

Chautaara is 25 km from the Kodari road. There are local buses, or you can take a taxi from Kathmandu for about Rs 3000.

Day 1: Chautaara to Syaule

Chautaara is a large village with a police post and many well-stocked shops. There is a large clinic operated by Save the Children, UK. The main trail climbs through pleasant hill villages to Syaule.

Day 2: Syaule to Kamikharka Danda

From Syaule the trail rises steadily to **Okrin Danda** at 2300m. Continue steeply up toward the forested **Kamikharka Danda** ridge. One hour beyond Okrin Danda is an unusual double mani wall where there are fine camp sites; there may be water in the autumn, but there is no water during the spring. From this point the route ascends steeply through forests full of woodcutters to the ridge crest. Camp in a grassy area surrounded by forest. The water supply is 30 minutes' walk down the western slopes of the ridge.

Day 3: Kamikharka Danda to Chyochyo Danda

The route along the Kamikharka Danda is an excellent trail through beautiful oak and rhododendron forest with magnificent views. Water is scarce for much of the way.

The trail follows the ridge crest, rising to a large chorten at 3160m, then traverses pasture across the western slopes of **Chyochyo Danda** where there are many summer pasture shelters. After another descent the trail passes a ruined stone house and a well-used camp site with a good spring a short distance down the western slope. This is the first free water on the ridge and the site is an excellent one in pleasant forest.

Day 4: Chyochyo Danda to Hile Bhanjyang

The trail ascends steeply and steadily across stony, grassy pastures to cross the ridge near some cairns at 3750m. From the ridge the route descends through forest, crossing gullies with water to reach another crest at Chang Samarphu (3913m). The final descent to **Hile Bhanjyang** is steep. In spring this can be in deep snow with difficult icy sections in the gullies. At Hile Bhanjyang there is a camp site with water at 3800m.

Day 5: Hile Bhanjyang to Nasem Pati
The trail climbs steeply to a hillock at 3980m, then traverses open ground along a flagstone trail to another crest. The views are wonderful in clear weather. There is a stone house above **Nasem Pati** (3800m) and well-trodden trails that lead off the ridge crest to both east and west. There is no running water here in the spring. Under good walking conditions Days 4 and 5 could be combined into one day of about six hours walking.

Day 6: Nasem Pati to Panch Pokhari
It's about a four hour climb on a well-defined trail to Panch Pokhari, five holy lakes at 4050m. There are two metal-roofed huts, a sheet metal-enclosed shrine to Shiva and a pile of cast-iron tridents. During the June/July full moon thousands of Nepalis come to worship. You should not wash in the holy stream near the temples.

There is often snow on this ridge, making the trek more difficult. You can make a day trip to Panch Pokhari from Nasem Pati and avoid camping in the snow.

Day 7: Panch Pokhari to Gai Kharka
Return to Nasem Pati and descend west on a good trail, past several ravines with water but no camping, to a good camp site at Gai Kharka (2530m).

Day 8: Gai Kharka to Yangri
The descent continues through forest on a track that is sometimes steep and rough, crossing two major watercourses. Pass a few substantial villages, including Yarsa, then descend a small and very steep trail directly to the bridge over the Panch Pokhari Khola. Climb to Hutanbrang, then descend and follow the Larke Khola downstream to the first of the two bridges below Yangri village,

where there is a pleasant camp site on the east bank at 1360m.

Day 9: Yangri to Laghang Gompa
The trail crosses bridges over the Larke and Yangri kholas, and passes through Yangri village climbing rapidly to the west and north. There are lateral trails everywhere. At the stream crossing below and south-west of Dalegaon there is a beautiful lunch or camping site with fine water and big shade trees.

The trail continues, often steeply, up through country dotted with villages and fields, scrub hillsides and pleasant forest. The large village between Dalegaon and Gangkharka is called **Gangdwang**. From Gangkharka a large trail leads into the next side valley, where camping is possible, then the trail climbs relentlessly for 900m to **Laghang gompa**. This is a beautiful forested area and a lovely, quiet camp site at an elevation of 2800m.

Day 10: Laghang Gompa to Tarke Gyang
It takes just over three hours from Laghang gompa to Tarke Gyang. The trail climbs through beautiful forest, then enters an area of small pastures, stone houses, scrub growth and cow trails. Be sure to backtrack if you find yourself headed south on the ridge trail to Sermathang. The trail down to Tarke Gyang is very steep, rough and eroded.

Days 11-13: Tarke Gyang to Kathmandu
You can finish this trek via Tharepati, Khutumsang, Pati Bhanjyang and Sundarijal in another four days. You can also connect to the ridge route south via Sermathang or extend the trek to Gosainkund and Langtang.

The easiest way back to Kathmandu is to follow the Tarke Gyang to Kathmandu via Panchkal route described earlier in this chapter. This would make Day 11 from Tarke Gyang to Sermathang; Day 12 from Sermathang to Malemchi; and Day 13 from Malemchi to Kathmandu.

Eastern Nepal

Trekking goals in eastern Nepal include an eastern approach to Everest, the remote base camp of Makalu, and the area near Kanchenjunga. There is endless variety in this part of the country. Most ethnic groups are represented and many villages, such as Dhankuta, Khandbari and Bhojpur, are large, prosperous and clean. The area has hot, rice-growing districts and also encompasses the cooler tea-growing region of Ilam. The heavily populated Middle Hills are gouged by the mighty Arun Kosi, which has cut through them at an elevation of less than 400m. The Arun is flanked by the major mountain massifs of Kanchenjunga and Makalu.

Treks here tend to be expensive, since you and your gear must travel to eastern Nepal by bus or plane. The treks are also long because it requires two weeks to travel from most trailheads to the high mountains.

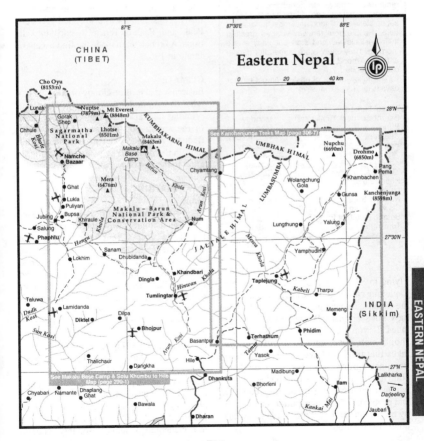

Bazaars in Eastern Nepal

One of the unique cultural institutions of eastern Nepal is the weekly market or *haat bazaar*. Almost every village from the Dudh Kosi eastward to the border of Sikkim is within a day's walk of a large weekly market. In each place the haat bazaar is held on a specific day of the week in a space that the village has set aside for the market. The schedule is coordinated throughout the region so that traders can sell their wares. Itinerant bangle sellers, tailors, barbers, cloth vendors, fortune-tellers, and con artists travel throughout the week, often with a retinue of porters, between various eastern Nepal bazaars and sell their wares. Local people bring their own goods, usually meat, grain or baskets woven from bamboo. Shopkeepers, hoteliers and village entrepreneurs set up stalls to sell food and, most importantly, drink. People from faraway villages dress in their best clothes and start out early in the morning. They often return home after dark in a festive mood, burdened with newly purchased goods.

The following list of eastern Nepal bazaar days is far from exhaustive:

Aiselukharka	Saturday
Barahbise (near Tumlingtar)	Monday
Bung	Monday
Chainpur	Wednesday
Hile	Thursday
Jiri	Saturday
Kenja	Sunday
Khandbari	Saturday
Khari Khola	Wednesday
Lukla	Thursday
Namche Bazaar	Saturday
Siswa Bazaar	Wednesday
Sotang (south of Bung)	Friday
Tumlingtar	Friday

Flying to STOL airstrips at Tumlingtar and Taplejung can shorten the time, but increases the expense. Inhabitants of this part of Nepal have not seen many Westerners in their villages. If you travel in eastern Nepal, you should take great care to avoid the mistakes that trekkers have made in the more popular regions – mistakes which have contributed to theft, over-reliance on the whims of tourists to support the economy, and problems of garbage, pollution, begging by both adults and children and unnecessary hotel construction.

Kanchenjunga, at 8598m, is the world's third-highest mountain. The peak is on the border of Nepal and Sikkim (India) and has several distinct summits. It is visible – and accessible – from Darjeeling, so many expeditions explored this region and tried to climb the mountain during British rule in India. A British team led by Charles Evans made the first ascent of Kanchenjunga in 1956. They trekked from the Terai and climbed the south face of the peak.

One of the most spectacular peaks in the region is Jannu, at 7710m. The Nepalis renamed this peak Khumbakarna in 1984 when a committee 'nepalised' the names of many peaks. Jannu was also called 'Mystery Peak' and 'Peak of Terror' by early expeditions. A French team made the first ascent of Jannu in 1962.

CLIMATE

Eastern Nepal is often cloudy or rainy. That's why the rhododendrons, magnolias and primulas (and also tea plants) grow so well. In the spring you can expect clouds and frequent rain, and even in autumn it often rains in the Arun valley when the weather is good in the rest of Nepal.

INFORMATION

Maps

The British colonial names of several peaks near Kanchenjunga were changed during the nepalising process. Tent Peak became Kirat Chuli, the Twins became Givigela Chula, White Wave is now Andesh Chuli, Wedge Peak was renamed Chang Himal and Pyramid Peak became Pathi Bhara. As most of the literature about Kanchenjunga refers to Jannu and uses other anglicised names, I have used these names throughout the text. Newer maps that are published in Kathmandu all use the Nepali names.

US Army Map Service sheets NG 45-3 *Kanchenjunga*, and NG 45-2 *Mount Everest* cover eastern Nepal, as do Mandala Maps' *Kanchenjunga* and *Arun Valley*. The *Kanchenjunga* map produced in Nepal by Nepa Maps covers the entire region from Makalu to Kanchenjunga and is reasonably accurate except for trails along the Arun valley and the fictitious trail from Helok to Torontan.

Books

Eastern Nepal has not received the attention that has been lavished on the Everest and Annapurna areas, so information about this part of the country is sparse.

The Arun, by Edward W Cronin Jr, is a natural history of the Arun Kosi valley. *Round Kanchenjunga*, by Douglas W Freshfield, is a reprint of the most definitive book about the Kanchenjunga region. Originally published in 1903, it describes a circuit of the mountain in 1899. *The Kanchenjunga Adventure*, by FS Smythe, is another account of the early exploration of eastern Nepal. *The Kulunge Rai*, by Charles McDougal, is an anthropological study of the Rais in the Hongu valley, especially the village of Bung.

Accommodation

Because eastern Nepal is not swarming with trekkers, there is not the abundance of trekking lodges that there is in central Nepal. The region is, however, well served by local *bhattis* (tea shops) that cater to the unbelievably large number of porters carrying goods to remote villages. The facilities tend to be primitive and unsanitary, and the food dreadful, but if you can handle this, you can make your way through much of eastern Nepal using local accommodation.

GETTING THERE & AWAY
Air

Biratnagar This airport is the centre of RNAC's eastern Nepal hub. There are morning flights from Biratnagar to Taplejung (US$50), Tumlingtar (US$33), Bhojpur, Rumjatar and Lamidanda. Biratnagar airport is a fancy facility built by a South Korean contractor in the 1980s when there was a vague plan to promote Biratnagar as Nepal's second international airport, but it is now dirty and run-down. The airport is quite a distance from the city and the most reliable transport into town is by rickshaw.

Unlike Lukla, the flights to Biratnagar are regular because there is rarely a weather problem. There are instrument-landing facilities and a paved runway, so airlines can use larger planes that have enough capacity to meet the demand for flights. A flight from Kathmandu takes 50 minutes and costs US$77. In clear weather, it provides excellent views of the Himalaya from Kanchenjunga to Langtang. All of Nepal's domestic airlines serve Biratnagar with daily flights, so air travel is easy to arrange. At an elevation of only 70m, Biratnagar is a typical Terai town, with noisy bazaars, inhabited mainly by people from the plains. There is nothing of interest for the trekker in Biratnagar and the chaos of rickshaws and trucks makes it pointless to spend time there sightseeing. Biratnagar is Nepal's second-largest city and the kingdom's industrial centre. The largest factories process jute into carpets, bags and rope. There are also many smaller factories making matches, cigarettes, tinned fruit, jam and other items. For trekkers, Biratnagar is best used only as a transit point because the hotels are poor. If possible, move on immediately to Hile or Basantpur. If you do stay overnight in Biratnagar, try the *Hotel Swagatam* (☎ 021-24450) or the *Hotel Himalaya Kingdoms* (☎ 021-27172), which has air-conditioned rooms for US$18 a double.

Taplejung This is the focal point for Kanchenjunga treks. There is a road from Ilam to Taplejung that is nearing completion. It's a long and rough trip: 78 km from the east-west highway to Ilam, then another 150 km to Taplejung. People who have done it say that it's easiest to walk the last portion of the route from the Tamur Kosi up to Taplejung village rather than take a jeep up the rough, steep, dusty switchbacks. There is a weekly direct flight from Taplejung to Kathmandu (US$110) and several services each week to Biratnagar. The airport is in Suketar, a village high on a hill about a 1½ hour walk above Taplejung; reservations are controlled from the city office, not at the airport. Taplejung flights are often cancelled because of clouds and fog at the airport.

EASTERN NEPAL

Tumlingtar This airport is on a flat plateau in the Arun valley and provides access for treks to Makalu, and an early bail-out from the Lukla to Hile trek. The runway is long and will accommodate 44-seat Avro aircraft, so seats to Tumlingtar may be available when all other destinations are fully booked. For some strange reason, the airfare from Kathmandu to Tumlingtar is one of the lowest in Nepal (US$44).

Bhojpur On a ridge above the west bank of the Arun Kosi is Bhojpur. It is a possible emergency airstrip if you are walking from Khumbu to Hile. Flights to Kathmandu cost US$77.

Lukla Read about Lukla in the Mt Everest Region chapter. Avoid this airport if you can.

Bus, Truck & Taxi

Biratnagar Night buses from Kathmandu to Biratnagar cost Rs 225 for the 540 km, 13 hour journey. Day buses are cheaper at Rs 180.

Dharan This town is north of Biratnagar at the foot of the hills. Dharan is 540 km from Kathmandu and is served by night buses for Rs 225, and day buses for Rs 180. The night bus takes about 14 hours. You can also reach Dharan from Biratnagar and from Itahari on the east-west Mahendra Highway. Much of Dharan's bazaar was severely damaged by an earthquake in 1988.

A good road connects Biratnagar and Dharan, passing through villages and cultivated fields for most of the distance. Originally this was all jungle and fine sal forest, but over the years logging and development have drastically reduced the extent of the forest. There is little to remind one now of the extensive malarial jungle that once blanketed this region – although there are still glimpses of it in Royal Chitwan National Park and the Terai of western Nepal. The 44 km drive takes about an hour.

You can return to Kathmandu by night bus directly from Dharan. A more costly but less tedious route is by bus to Biratnagar, then a flight back to Kathmandu.

Hile This is the starting point for treks up the Arun valley. A road connects Dharan with Hile and Basantpur, starting places for treks to Kanchenjunga and the Arun valley. Many buses from Dharan or Biratnagar go only as far as the large village of Dhankuta, 11 km before Hile. To avoid this walk, be sure you get a bus that goes on to Hile or Basantpur. There's a direct bus from Hile to Kathmandu, departing at 1 pm and arriving in Kathmandu the following morning, 604 km later, at a cost of Rs 253. You can also get to Dhankuta or Hile on a local bus from Dharan; it costs Rs 35 to Rs 40 for the three hour, 50 km trip. There is a good hotel in Dhankuta and there are several comfortable Tibetan-operated hotels in Hile.

Basantpur About two hours drive beyond Dhankuta on 48 km of rough gravel road is Basantpur, a starting point for treks to Kanchenjunga. The bus service to Basantpur is irregular, but there are usually several buses each day from Dharan. If you have trouble, hire your own vehicle or try to buy a ride in a truck from Dhankuta or Dharan.

Ilam Another possible starting point for Kanchenjunga treks is Ilam. There is a bus service from Kathmandu to Ilam, but it's a long, hard journey in a rattletrap vehicle. The new road to Taplejung starts in Ilam, so you can change to a Taplejung bus and make a marathon 24 hour journey.

To India When you finish a trek in eastern Nepal, you can go on to India instead of returning to Kathmandu. Take a bus from Hile to Itahari, connect to another bus to Kakarbhitta, cross into India and take a taxi to Siliguri. From Siliguri, it is about a three hour drive by taxi (or a seven hour ride on the famous 'toy train') to Darjeeling, a pleasant Indian hill station.

Solu Khumbu to Hile

Duration 12 days
Difficulty Medium to hard
Maximum elevation 3349m
Permit cost US$5 per week plus Rs 1000
Season October to April
Hotels Primitive
Summary The original route of the Everest explorers. Climb over several ridges through Sherpa and Rai villages to the Arun valley at 300m elevation. Basic food and accommodation available.

This section describes an alternative to the Jiri to Everest base camp trek. Though I have shown it as a route from Solu Khumbu (the Mt Everest region) to Hile, you can also begin at Hile and use it as an approach route to the Everest region. HW Tilman, the first foreign visitor to Everest base camp, used this route in 1950 and described it in some detail in *Nepal Himalaya*.

By walking from Jiri to Everest, and then walking to Hile, you can make a rewarding 32 day trek. Walking to Hile avoids the flight complications at Lukla and lends a sense of continuity to the trek that you will not feel if you fly back from Lukla.

Though it's possible to make this walk as a lodge trek, the facilities do not resemble those of the Everest region. The first six days, from Lukla to Phedi, are through country that sees few foreign travellers, so the hotels are small and the stocks of beer, Coke and other goodies are meagre. In the Irkhuwa and Arun valleys the teahouses cater primarily to locals, and the food is limited to dal bhat and biscuits.

Fees & Permits

Much of this trek passes through the Makalu-Barun Conservation Area, so you must pay a Rs 1000 conservation fee and refrain from using firewood. The permit is checked at Bung.

Access

Lukla See the Mt Everest Region chapter for information about Lukla, the starting point for this trek.

Hile Assuming you are ending the trek in Hile, you can easily find transport back to Kathmandu. There is one direct bus daily from Hile to Kathmandu, or you can travel via Dharan or Biratnagar. Bus service is frequent, but many buses are only short haul, so take whatever there is as long as it's going in the right direction and you'll eventually get where you want to go. There's no need to wait all day in Hile for a bus to Kathmandu, for example.

From Hile the road descends a spur to **Dhankuta**, at 1220m. The road does not pass through Dhankuta itself, but the town is worth a visit. It is a Rai, Newar and Limbu town – large, attractive and clean, with whitewashed houses and winding streets paved with stone. There is a police station flanked by two polished brass cannon, a hospital, a cold-storage facility, bank, bakery, telegraph office and hundreds of shops.

The road descends from Dhankuta and crosses the Tamur Kosi at Mulghat. The Tamur Kosi flows west to join the Arun at the same point where the Sun Kosi joins it after its long trip eastward across Nepal. Together these rivers form the Saat Kosi ('seven rivers') that flows to the Ganges containing the waters of the Sun Kosi, Bhote Kosi, Tamba Kosi, Dudh Kosi, Arun Kosi, Likhu Kosi and Tamur Kosi.

The road turns south, following a side valley of the Tamur Kosi until it reaches the Churia Hills, the last range of hills before the plains. In India this range is called the Siwalik Hills. The road climbs to **Bhedetar**, a pass at 1460m. From some places on this ridge, there are views of Kanchenjunga (8598m) and its prominent neighbour Jannu (7710m), on the eastern border of Nepal.

The view from the pass is a most dramatic sight – to the south are nothing but plains. After weeks in the hills, it is unusual to see

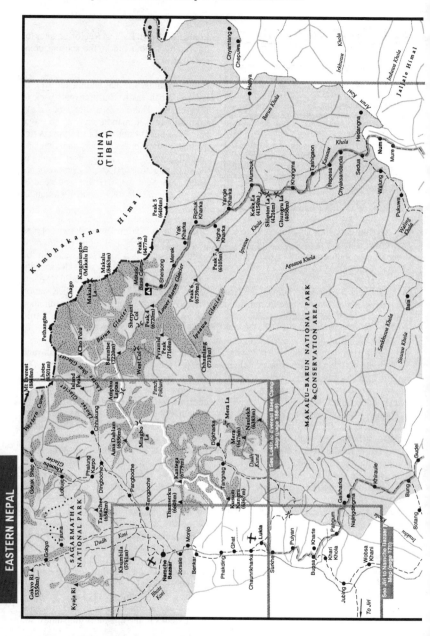

See Lukla to Everest Base Camp Map (page 186-9)

See Jiri to Namche Bazaar Map (page 178)

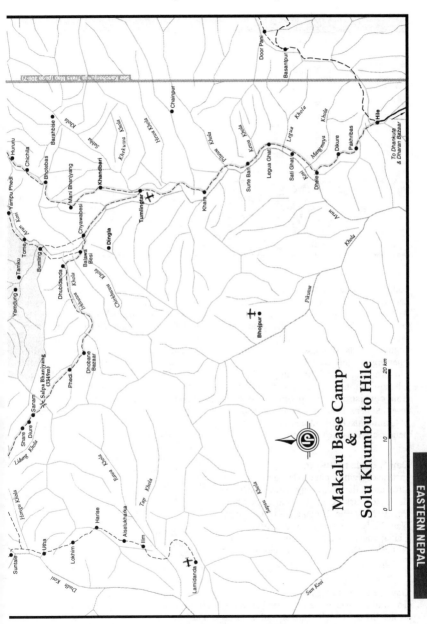

Makalu Base Camp
&
Solu Khumbu to Hile

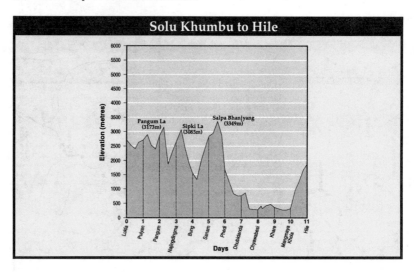

Solu Khumbu to Hile

country that is absolutely flat as far as the eye can see. The road descends to Dharan at 370m. Dharan used to be the major trading centre serving the eastern hills region, and was the site of a British Gurkha recruiting centre, but its role has changed with the opening of the Dhankuta road and the closure of the British camp. Although Dharan is in the plains, most of the population consists of hill people who have resettled here. Dharan is also a major centre of Communist Party influence, so strikes and demonstrations are common.

Day 1: Lukla to Puiyan

Instead of flying from Lukla, take a leisurely stroll down the 550m-long runway, continue down to Surkhe, then climb back up to Puiyan at 2730m. If you are travelling from Namche Bazaar it is not necessary to go to Lukla; you can walk from Jorsale to Chaunrikharka, then from Chaunrikharka to Puiyan.

Day 2: Puiyan to Pangum

The trail follows the same route (in reverse) as the Jiri to Namche Bazaar trail as far as Kharte, just above Bupsa, then heads into new trekking country. There is an inconspicuous trail junction in Kharte, just beyond the small *Gauri Shanker Hotel* in the forests above Bupsa. Ask people for the trail to Pangum (pronounced 'Pankoma' locally): *'kun baarto Pankoma jaanchha?'* The trail climbs to the ridge near a large, white house at the top of Kharte, then turns south-east up the broad Khari Khola valley.

There are some ups and downs as the trail gradually gains elevation in the forested valley, passing isolated Sherpa houses and small streams. Though the trail is not steep, it gains a lot of elevation, so it is a laborious climb to **Pangum**, at 2850m. Here is yet another Hillary school (there are 26 such schools in the region), a gompa and a paper factory. The Nepali paper produced is used for all official government transactions and is carried to Kathmandu in huge loads by porters. We call it rice paper, but actually it contains no rice; it is made from the inner bark of the daphne bush, known in Nepali as *lokta*. As you enter the town, stay on the largest trail, bearing left, to reach the *Himalayan Trekest Lodge* [sic] at the foot of Pangum.

Day 3: Pangum to Najingdingma

It is a short climb to the 3173m **Pangum La** (also called the Satu La), the pass between the catchments of the Dudh Kosi and the Inukhu Khola. At the pass there is a great view, not only of the Khumbu Himalaya, but also of the peaks at the head of the Inukhu (also called Hinku) valley, including Mera (6476m), one of the easiest but least accessible of Nepal's trekking peaks. The trail contours to the north and descends gradually through a burned rhododendron forest to **Chatuk**, a small Sherpa settlement on a ridge. This unpretentious village has a multitude of names; it is also known as Shibuche and as Basme. At the top of the village is a small gompa; keep descending to the *Namaste Hotel* and a well-stocked shop. Stay on the ridge, descending past houses and fields to the foot of the village. The trail drops almost vertically down a steep rocky face with a few trees clinging to it to the river at 1855m, then crosses an exciting bridge suspended high above the river on steel cables.

A Himalayan Trust team built a bridge here in 1971 and replaced it with a spectacular new 62m-long structure in 1993. When I asked one of the volunteers about the fantastic engineering that must be required for the construction of a bridge in such a remote location, he replied: 'We don't engineer them, we just build 'em'.

The trail ascends the side of the wild, sparsely inhabited Inukhu valley to the extensive potato fields of the Sherpa hamlet of **Gaikharka** ('cow pasture'), at about 2300m. Although the only permanent settlements in this valley are those of Sherpas, the neighbouring Rais graze their cattle here. Gurungs who live far to the south also graze large herds of sheep during the summer. There are no hotels in Gaikharka, so climb an hour further to **Najingdingma**, where several very basic lodges adjoin a large meadow at 2650m. When I first came here in 1971, this was an empty pasture with no permanent residents and Chatuk on the opposite side of the valley had only a few houses. The migration of people into the Inukhu valley is a good illustration of the pressures of population growth in Nepal.

Day 4: Najingdingma to Bung

The route crosses pastures, then makes a steep ascent in forests towards Sipki (or Surkie) Pass, a steep notch at 3085m. Beyond the pass, the trail descends a short distance through forests that were devastated by a fire in April 1992. The entire upper Hongu valley burned for six weeks as a result, they say, of a fire that started in Najingdingma. Near a tin-roofed rest house is a trail junction. Turn right (south) to reach Bung. The trail that heads straight downhill leads to Cheskam and other villages in the upper Hongu valley; the trail that leads uphill to the north goes to Panch Pokhari and eventually reaches Mera. As you descend, the valley suddenly opens up above the Sherpa village of **Khiraule**, about 2400m. Far below you can see Boksum gompa surrounded by a large circle of juniper trees that were brought from Darjeeling. It is particularly sacred, but has fallen into disuse and disrepair. There are many crisscrossing trails used by the people of Bung when they collect wood, so it is easy to get lost; aim south and a bit east to the ridge above the gompa.

The trek is now in the great Hongu valley, one of the most fertile regions of Nepal. Much of the rice for the Namche Bazaar market comes from this area and is carried across three ridges to Khumbu. Except for some Sherpas living at higher elevations, and some Chhetris and Brahmans downstream near Sotang, the Hongu valley population is exclusively Rai.

The trail descends a ridge crest to the large village of **Bung**, spread out over the hillside from about 1900m down to 1400m. The most direct route through the village follows a ravine downhill, but soon gets lost wandering among the houses, fields and bamboo groves in the lower part of the village. There are six lodges in lower Bung; the *Solu Khumbu Lodge* and the better *Sagarmatha Lodge* are both in Sherpa-style houses that look out of place among all the typical Rai dwellings. This is the entrance to the Makalu-Barun

EASTERN NEPAL

Conservation Area, so you need to present your permit to the office here. The people of Bung are a bit unhappy about trekking groups camping in the village, so it's best to continue downhill and camp in fields below the village near the river. You are almost certain to hear the drum of a *dhami*, a local shaman, in the Hongu valley.

Day 5: Bung to Sanam

From Bung, there is a steep descent through bamboo forests to the Hongu Khola, which is crossed by a large suspension bridge at 1316m, followed by an equally steep climb to **Gudel**, another large Rai village, at 2000m. It was this long, frustrating descent and ascent that Tilman, travelling in the opposite direction to that described here, described poetically in *Nepal Himalaya*:

For dreadfulness, naught can excel
The prospect of Bung from Gudel;
And words die away on the tongue
When we look back on Gudel from Bung.

There are some rudimentary tea shops and the *Alp Lodge* near the Gudel school; if you are camping, the schoolmaster will allow you to camp – for a fee. The first stretch from Gudel is steep, much of it on a stone staircase. Eventually the ascent along the side of the Lidung Khola, a tributary valley of the Hongu, becomes more gradual. It is a long and tiring climb, past a major wood-cutting operation that is devastating the rhododendron forests, to **Share**, where there are several Sherpa houses, a gompa and shop. The climb becomes more gentle as it passes through fields to a small schoolhouse and a waterfall. It then climbs on to **Diure**, at 2470m, where there is a good camp site near a house that doubles as a hotel. Descend to a stream, then climb a bit more to **Sanam** at 2850m.

Rai villages in the valley have a maximum elevation of about 2400m. Sherpas exploit different resources from Rais, so there is little economic competition between the two groups. Sanam is a compact settlement of houses arranged in a single row. The villag-

ers maintain large herds of cattle, so milk, yoghurt and excellent cottage cheese (ask for *serkum*) and dry cheese *(churpi)* are usually available. The *Sherpa Hotel* is reported to have good cheese, but is not good for sleeping. The *Gumpa Lodge* and *Salpa View Lodge* are said to be better.

Day 6: Sanam to Phedi

The route now climbs through a totally uninhabited area. The trail drops slightly to the floor of the canyon that it has been ascending, crosses the Lidung Khola, which at this point is only a stream, and makes a final steep climb to the Salpa Bhanjyang, the 3349m pass between the Hongu and Arun catchments. It is a long climb; the total height gain from the Hongu Khola is 2033m. The pass is often snowed in during winter; if you trek between December and February, ask the people in Sanam whether the route is open.

This area is covered by thick hemlock and fir forest that abounds with bird and animal life, including Himalayan black bear, barking deer and the lesser panda, a smaller, red-coloured relative of its more famous namesake. A large *chorten* marks the pass and is the final sign of the influence of Sherpa culture on the route. The first available water is about an hour beyond the pass, making the lunch stop on this day quite late.

Descend from the pass through rhododendron forests to Guranse, a meadow at 2880m. Two rough bhattis cater to porters carrying goods to and from Gudel. If you are trekking up from Phedi, this is a good place to spend the night on the way to the pass. Descend past a small, dirty lake and some shepherds' *goths* onto a rocky spur that separates the Irkhuwa Khola and the Sanu Khola. On this portion of the trail there is ample evidence of forest fires which occur in the dry season each spring. They are caused by fires in villages, lightning and shepherds burning the underbrush to allow new grass to grow.

Follow the trail through birch and rhododendron forests until it reaches a large stone overlooking the Irkhuwa Khola valley. The trail drops almost vertically through bamboo forests into the Rai village of Phedi. There are many opportunities to get lost on the ridge; stay as high as possible and keep going east. Several shepherds' trails lead down from the ridge to the north and south. You should stay on the ridge to its eastern end, where the trail to Phedi starts its steep descent. In Thulo Fokte there is a teahouse, and 15 minutes below in Jau Bhari ('barley field') there are two trekkers' hotels. Descend on a rock staircase to **Phedi** at 1680m.

The best camp is below the village, near a shop and a paper factory on the banks of the Irkhuwa Khola. You can also stay in the village at the *Sherpa Lodge*. This is one of the longest days and the longest downhill walk of the trek. The local *rakshi* in Phedi is terrible, but is preferable to a bottle of the rotgut pineapple wine or Everest Special Madira that is portered in from Dharan.

Alternative Route via Bhojpur From Salpa Bhanjyang, it is possible to follow the ridge to the south and take a different route to the one described. This route passes through Bhojpur, a large hill bazaar famous for its excellent *kukhris*, the curved Nepali knives. There are flights from Bhojpur to both Kathmandu and Biratnagar, or you can keep walking to the Arun, cross it near Sati Ghat, and rejoin the main trail on Day 10. This is the route that Tilman followed in 1949 when he was the first trekker to visit Khumbu.

Day 7: Phedi to Dhubidanda
The trek has now emerged into the fertile rice-growing Arun Kosi valley. Follow the Irkhuwa Khola, a tributary of the Arun, crossing and recrossing the stream on a series of bamboo bridges. Some of these are substantial and some very flimsy, but all are picturesque. After the continuous ups and downs of the last week, this is a particularly relaxing day. The trail loses elevation almost imperceptibly, yet by the end of the day you will have lost almost 900m. There are many pools large enough for swimming, and the water temperature – especially in comparison with streams higher up – is comfortable.

A few hours below Phedi is **Dhobane Bazaar**, which has shops and some ethnic

restaurants. There is even a tailor shop that can outfit you with a new set of clothes while you wait. Continue through Nunkwa Besi, then cross a ridge to reach a cantilever bridge over a side stream just before Gote Bazaar. There is a good camping place on the banks of the Irkhuwa Khola near **Dhubidanda**, at an elevation of about 760m.

The predominant ethnic groups in this part of the Arun basin are the Rais, Chhetris and Brahmans. Before the Gurkha conquest, about 200 years ago, the population of the Middle Hills region between the Dudh Kosi and Arun Kosi was almost entirely Rai. Following the conquest, when the Rais were defeated by the Gurkha army, considerable numbers of Hindus settled here, especially in the more fertile regions.

Day 8: Dhubidanda to Chyawabesi
The trail makes a final crossing to the south bank of the Irkhuwa Khola. Bridges get washed away frequently here, so you may cross the river on a fancy new suspension bridge or perhaps a wobbly bamboo affair. The trail soon begins to climb over a spur separating the Arun Kosi from the Irkhuwa Khola. This trail may be hard to follow; if you have a guide who knows the way or can ask local people, you can follow a circuitous course through the fields and back yards of villages as it doubles back on itself and traverses small irrigation canals and rice terraces. Ask people for the trail to Balawa Besi or Tumlingtar. If you are travelling in the reverse direction, ask for Dhobane, Phedi or Salpa Bhanjyang. As you cross the ridge, you can finally see the mighty Arun Kosi to the north. This river, with its headwaters in Tibet, is one of the major rivers flowing into the Ganges in India.

The trek turns south and descends to a small tributary of the Arun, the Chirkhuwa Khola, where there are a few small shops and bhattis. This village, called **Balawa Besi**, makes an excellent spot to stop for lunch, though it is usually hot.

Trek for a short distance through rice fields to Kartike Pul, where the route crosses the Arun Kosi on a long suspension bridge at

EASTERN NEPAL

an elevation of only 300m. There used to be a dugout canoe ferry here, but in 1984 the bridge replaced this exciting ride. From the bridge, the trail follows the eastern side of the river southward for about half an hour to a good camp at **Chyawabesi**, at 280m elevation. Along the Arun valley there are frequent bhattis, so finding food is no longer a problem, though both the quality and sanitation are marginal.

Day 9: Chyawabesi to Khare

The trail follows the Arun as it flows south, sometimes climbing high above the river and sometimes traversing the sandy river bed. The climate, even during the winter, is hot and tropical. Houses sit atop stilts for ventilation and the people are darker-skinned than those seen so far on the trek. You will probably want to change your schedule and do most of the walking in the very early morning to avoid the heat. Many of the settlements along the bottom of the Arun valley are inhabited only during the planting and harvesting seasons by people who own fertile farmlands in the valley, but live higher up in the hills.

It is a short climb to a huge plateau that provides almost six km of completely level trail to **Tumlingtar**, a small village with an airport served by regular flights. Many of the inhabitants of Tumlingtar are of the Kuhmale (potter) caste, and earn their livelihood from the manufacture of earthenware pots from the red clay of this region. There is very little water on the plateau, so you must continue a long distance in the morning before lunch. There are several hotels near the airport. For more ethnic fare, a cup of tea, some oranges or bananas, stop at the big shop under the banyan tree at the southern end of Tumlingtar. Unless you are walking in the very early morning, you will need some refreshment to help you keep moving under the hot sun.

The trek gets more pleasant immediately after the short descent from the plateau when the trail crosses the Sabha Khola, a tributary of the Arun. There is an excellent lunch spot here beside a fine swimming hole in the warmest and most delightful stream along

the entire trek route. The afternoon is short, involving a climb of only 100m to a few bhattis at Gande Pani, then a descent to **Khare**, a tropical village on the banks of the Arun. There are two bamboo hotels for trekkers at the southern end of town and a number of open-air facilities for porters.

Day 10: Khare to Mangmaya Khola

The route continues south along the east bank of the Arun. There are many porters on the trail from here to Hile. These men and boys carry goods from warehouses in Hile, Dhankuta and Dharan to the bazaars of Khandbari, Bhojpur, Dingla and Chainpur. On the return trip porters carry big loads of *rudaraksha*, the holy seeds that are used for yogi beads, from a source near Dingla. They often walk at night with small kerosene lamps tied to their *dokos* (the bamboo baskets in which they carry their loads).

In another of his classic anecdotes, Tilman imagined these porters nose-to-doko along the trail. Each porter carries a T-shaped stick that he places under his doko whenever (and wherever) he wishes to rest, usually when he is standing in the middle of the trail. Tilman imagined the entire trail backing up in a long line of porters as each one waited until the man ahead of him finished his rest. It presents a ludicrous picture, but one not totally removed from reality on this part of the trail. Beware of quick stops. A porter can shove his stick under his load and make an abrupt stop with amazing speed and agility. You risk a collision if you follow too closely.

An excursion into the villages will often uncover such appealing items as papayas *(mewa)*, peanuts *(badam)* and pineapples *(bhui katahar)*. You may find fish from the Arun Kosi for sale. This region is also famous for its wonderful oranges *(suntala)*.

Climb 100m above the river on a ledge, then descend to the Piluwa Khola. The trail along this part of the Arun varies depending on water levels. At the Piluwa Khola there is a bridge upstream, but it's far away. If the water is low, everyone wades this warm side stream of the Arun. Continue across the sandy river bank to **Surte Bari**, two settlements with tea shops about an hour apart. In some places the trail climbs above the river and in other spots it is on the river bank, passing scattered bhattis before reaching a schoolhouse at Chanawa. At **Legua Ghat** a long suspension bridge leads across the Arun toward Bhojpur. There are teahouses along the way that offer soft drinks and beer and are attempting to prepare food that will appeal to trekkers.

The route passes under a cable that supports a river-gauging station just before a small village named Sati Ghat, the site of a dugout canoe ferry. Herds of goats and sheep have devoured much of the vegetation along this part of the river. These animals, more than humans, are responsible for the extensive deforestation in Nepal, because they prevent new saplings from growing into trees. After a short distance the trail comes to a large pipal tree and *chautaara* overlooking a huge side valley of the Arun. At the foot of this valley flows the **Mangmaya Khola**; the grassy banks of this stream, beyond the village of Mangmaya at 200m, afford an excellent camp site.

Day 11: Mangmaya Khola to Hile

The trail crosses the broad valley, then climbs through hot tropical forests to **Dhele**, which has two tea shops on a small village square, at approximately 700m elevation. The upper portion of this town has several large shops. The trail continues to climb through villages inhabited by Limbus, relatives of the Rais, to Baise, at 1250m. It's a long hot climb to Panche Chautaara, a settlement at 960m that supports several porters' hotels and a huge family of pigs. The trail finally gains the ridge near **Dikure**, where there's a fine view of Makalu (8463m) and Chhamlang (7319m) almost 150 km away.

Gradually ascend the waterless ridge to **Pakhribas** at 1640m. Continue through the village and keep climbing to an English medium school and the British Agricultural Project. This fantastic development presents a real contrast to the small gardens that surround every home throughout the trek. At Pakhribas, there are huge rows of vegetables,

all neatly labelled with signs; there are walls, roads and irrigation canals, paved with stone and cement. There are buildings of every description carefully labelled according to their function. Princess Diana choppered up to visit the Pakhribas project during her 1993 visit to Nepal.

The trail climbs a ridge crest past many bhattis to the roadhead at **Hile**. This is a pleasant roadside town high on a hill at 1850m; the elevation and cool breezes provide welcome relief from the heat of the Arun valley. Many of the people who inhabit this village are Tibetans who have resettled here. They came from Tibet and other parts of eastern Nepal, particularly from Walunchung Gola, when the Chinese occupation disrupted trade with Tibet in 1959. There is often genuine Tibetan jewellery for sale here, and many Chinese goods are available at prices below those in Kathmandu. The village is also famous for its ample supply of *tongba* (a fermented millet drink) available at the *Hotel Milan*, *Doma Hotel* or the *Gajut*, all of which have little curtained-off cabins so you can get sloshed in private. The *Hotel Himali* is reported to have good food. There is telephone service and electricity in Hile; the weekly bazaar day is Thursday.

Makalu Base Camp

> **Duration** 20 days
> **Difficulty** Medium to hard
> **Maximum elevation** 5000m
> **Permit cost** US$5 per week plus Rs 1000
> **Season** October to May
> **Hotels** None
> **Summary** Make a long trek up the Arun Kosi, then climb over a high pass into the remote Barun valley, protected as Nepal's newest national park. A rough trail leads past yak pastures and glaciers to the foot of Makalu.

You can make an outstanding trek in eastern Nepal from either Hile or Tumlingtar by walking north up the Arun Kosi to Sedua and Num, then crossing Shipton La (4216m) into the upper Barun Khola valley for a close look at Makalu and Chhamlang. See the Warning on this page regarding the altitude gain on some sections of this trek. The trek to Makalu base camp visits one of the most remote and unfrequented areas of Nepal. The Barun valley is part of a huge international protected area under an agreement between Nepal and China.

A major dam project on the upper reaches of the Arun Kosi threatened to change the character of this region forever. Economic and environmental considerations convinced the World Bank to withdraw its support from this project in 1995, so the Arun valley is no longer threatened and Nepal is looking at other rivers to exploit for much-needed hydroelectric power.

Some groups have attempted an even wilder trek by crossing Sherpani Col and West Col into the upper Hongu basin. This high-altitude route requires extensive mountaineering experience and equipment and has proved itself difficult and potentially very dangerous. It's better to travel from Lukla if you want to go into the upper Hongu basin and the Panch Pokhari ('five lakes') there.

Makalu-Barun National Park

The Makalu-Barun National Park was established in 1992 as Nepal's eighth national park. The 2330 sq km park is bordered by the Arun Kosi in the east and the Sagarmatha National Park on the west. To the south the park is bordered by an 830 sq km conservation area.

Fees & Permits

The Makalu-Barun National Park is subject to all the rules relating to national parks, including an entrance fee and restrictions on firewood use. Since a trek to Makalu enters both a national park and a conservation area, you are theoretically subject to two fees, but in 1997 the government was giving trekkers a break and collecting only the Rs 1000 conservation fee.

Park personnel check your trekking permit and national park ticket at the entrance station in Sedua. The park headquarters is in Khandbari.

The region north of Num is a restricted area, and foreigners are not allowed to trek in the upper Arun valley, even with a liaison officer.

Season

I have trekked to Makalu three times, twice in the spring and once in the autumn, and it has always been raining when I was in Tashigaon and Khongma. In the spring of 1993 Khongma was buried under three metres of snow. The weather in the Arun valley is usually wetter than that in the Everest region, though it's often clear in the upper Barun valley. The general consensus is that mid-October is the best time to make this trek. The route down the Arun Kosi is particularly difficult in early October, before the harvest, because all possible camp sites are planted with rice.

Warning

There are two days on this trek – Tashigaon to Khongma and Yangle Kharka to Merek – when the altitude gain exceeds the recommended daily maximum at high elevation. There is little room for varying your programme, however, because of the national park camping restrictions. Be very wary of altitude problems when you trek here.

Access

It is a one hour flight by Twin Otter (45 minutes by Avro) from Kathmandu to Tumlingtar, on a 360m plateau just above the Arun Kosi. If you want to walk, it is a three or four day trek from Hile to Tumlingtar. See the last few days of the Solu Khumbu to Hile route description for details.

Day 1: Tumlingtar to Khandbari

If all goes well, your flight should arrive at Tumlingtar by noon. Have lunch at one of the airport hotels – *Hotel Makalu* (☎ 029-69057) or the *Kanchenjunga* (☎ 029-69120) – both of which have refrigerators full of cold drinks. In Kuhmalgaon, 100m north of the airport, are the *Hotel Manakamana, Arun*

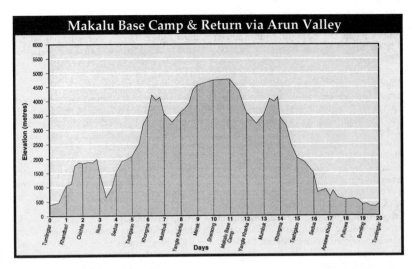

Makalu Base Camp & Return via Arun Valley

Lodge and numerous shops. Kuhmalgaon is named after the potter caste (Kuhmale) who make their living manufacturing earthenware items from the red clay of this plateau. If you are camping, follow the signs that read 'way to if you need place for camping' behind the Kanchenjunga hotel. The extensive plateau of Tumlingtar has several settlements, each surrounded by fields of rice and corn. Be prepared to dodge bicycles that schoolchildren race recklessly down the narrow paths. Tumlingtar is on a major trade route, so you will encounter many porters and local people on the first few days of the trek.

It's about a three hour climb to Khandbari. From the Tumlingtar airstrip, walk to Kuhmalgaon and immediately turn right and follow the trail that passes to the east of the small lake and temple. This leads onto a ridge, passes the school and begins an ascent between the Arun Kosi and the Sabha Khola. It's a long ridge walk with numerous teahouses and tree-shaded chautaaras. There are views of the huge massif of Chhamlang in the distance.

At Dhunge Dhara the climb leaves the ridge and becomes less steep as it contours

to the outskirts of **Khandbari** at 1030m. The police checkpost is on a hill to the south of town near the microwave antenna. They expect a visit from all passing trekkers. Continue past shops and turn left into the large village square paved with flagstones that is the site of the Saturday market. Nearby are the Makalu-Barun project office, the *Rajeeb Hotel* (☎ 029-60185), *Arati Hotel* and *Barun Hotel & Bar* (☎ 029-60182); the last offers 'modern toilets and showers'. Continue north up the shop-lined street to the bank, school, many small hotels and restaurants, carom parlours and government offices. If you have time, continue trekking for an hour to a good camp site near Mani Bhanjyang.

Day 2: Khandbari to Chichila
The trail finally emerges between shops onto a ridge, climbs to Naya Bazaar, then remains fairly level to **Mani Bhanjyang** at 1100m. The *Padma Hotel & Lodge* offers accommodation, or you can camp in a grassy meadow alongside the village. The electric power lines now end and the countryside becomes much more rural. There are two routes between here and Bhotebas. The better one turns left near the school at the northern end

EASTERN NEPAL

of Mani Bhanjyang, climbs in bamboo forests along the ridge to Arun Than at 1280m, then traverses across the hillside, still climbing through fields, bamboo groves and big rocks to Sheka at 1350m. Keep climbing to the Tamang village of **Bhotebas**, a few tea stalls at 1740m. Beyond the village the cultivated fields disappear as the trail climbs through trees to a pass at 1860m that offers a spectacular view of Chhamlang, Makalu and Jaljale Himal. Descend a bit to the next ridge, then follow the crest as it makes some ups and downs through a deep damp forest of rhododendrons and ferns for 1½ hours to **Chichila**, a tea shop and a few houses inhabited by Gurungs at 1830m. One crop grown in this region is cardamom; the official-looking building in Chichila is a government cardamom-collecting facility.

Day 3: Chichila to Num

Follow along the ridge in forests past the small Sherpa settlements of Baisake and Kuwa Pani at 1870m, then to some mani walls at Sakuranti Majuwa, 1860m. There are a few tea shops at **Hururu**, 1960m; the main part of the village is just below the ridge. The route climbs 100m and then drops into deep oak forests and follows alongside a stream for a short distance. Climb again along the ridge line to a large expanse of forest that has been burned to make fields to support the ever-growing population of the nearby villages. Continue along the ridge past a small stream to a single house, a tea shop and the *Sherpa Cold Store*, which offers the first soft drinks and beer since Khandbari. This is **Mure**, a spread-out village at 1990m that is inhabited by both Sherpas and Rais.

Below Mure the trail passes many tracts of burned trees where more fields are under development. The route cuts across a ridge, then makes a tedious descent on a rocky eroded trail to some stone steps and a final walk to **Num** at 1500m. Num is on the ridge above an S-shaped bend in the Arun Kosi. It was once planned that the intake pipes for the huge Arun power plant would be in tunnels through this ridge. There is a primary

school and a few shops and teahouses in the town square. On the opposite side of the Arun is Sedua; behind Sedua the peaks that flank Shipton La should be visible.

Day 4: Num to Sedua

The trail descends steeply from the western end of the Num ridge through the corn fields of Lumbang. The locals often use an even steeper trail that drops off the south side of the Num ridge and bypasses the village. Below Lumbang the trail becomes exceptionally steep as it drops on slippery rocks through jungle to a suspension bridge over the Arun Kosi at 630m. From the bridge the trail climbs steeply to a primitive tea shop at 820m, then through rice, corn and buckwheat fields. The country is particularly rocky; tiny terraces planted with corn and barley dot the slope as you make a long, steep, rough climb to **Sedua** at 1510m. As you enter the village there is an excellent, large camping ground operated by the conservation project. There are two tea shops and a school on a saddle that separates the Arun valley from the side valley of the Kasuwa Khola. Bureaucracy catches up with you here and you must register with both the police in the village and the national park office near the camping ground.

Day 5: Sedua to Tashigaon

Climb along the ridge from Sedua past the national park forest nursery project and then climb gently northwards through rice fields to Manigaon on the next ridge. There are several streams to cross that may (or may not) have bridges. From Manigaon the trail turns west and makes a gradual climb high above the Kasuwa Khola to a mani wall at 1890m. This is **Chyaksadanda**, and there are a school, a small shop and a camping ground here. It is now a gentle walk through terraced fields and forested areas to Hindrungma village, and on to **Ropesa**, where a monk usually sits beside the trail collecting donations for the small gompa nearby.

The route crosses meadows and several streams, then reaches the Tashigaon school. There's another stream and a small ridge to climb before you reach the foot of the Sherpa village of **Tashigaon**, the last permanent settlement in the valley. It's a long climb on a stone staircase from the bottom of the village past houses and corn fields to the top of town at 2070m. The village has a camping ground, shop and kerosene supply depot; you can rent stoves and porter blankets at the shop. A bit higher are two more camp sites and a rough hotel run by Norbu Lama. There is an emergency radio in the Department of Hydrology research station above Norbu's hotel and there is a helipad in case a rescue is called for. Many of the houses in the village are on stilts topped with round stone or wooden barriers to keep out mice.

This is a shorter day than most because there is no camping allowed between here and Khongma. The Makalu-Barun National Park allows camping only in the following designated places: Khongma, Mumbuk, Yangle Kharka, Nghe Kharka, Merek, Shersong and Makalu Base Camp.

Day 6: Tashigaon to Khongma

This is a tough day, with an elevation gain of almost 1400m on a steep trail. Climb over the ridge behind the hotel and ascend through forests to a stream, then onto a ridge where there is a small herder's hut. The trail levels out, then climbs to a shepherd's hut called Chipla atop another ridge at 2520m. Climb past two small streams and an overhanging rock that forms a cave. The route now becomes steeper, switchbacking on rocks up the ridge in forests to a kharka at 2900m and up further to the national park boundary at Unshisha, a tiny soggy meadow at 3180m elevation. The trail joins the ridge that separates the Ipsuwa and Kasuwa drainages. The slope gets even steeper and becomes a series of rough stone stairs ascending to the top of the ridge. Continue a short distance through sparse forests along the ridge and descend a bit to **Khongma** at 3560m. There are no buildings and many of the tent sites are on the sloping hillside in this rather poor, often muddy, camp site. There is a very limited water supply – often only a dirty spring. On the Kasuwa Khola side there

are primitive bivouac caves – which are good emergency accommodation for porters. If you climb to the ridge you can see the outline of Kanchenjunga far to the east.

Day 7: Khongma to Mumbuk

Climb on steep switchbacks for a while to the top of the ridge, at 3850m, where there is a stone chorten adorned with prayer flags. There is a superb view of Chhamlang, Peak 6 (6739m) and Peak 7 (6105m), whose snows feed the headwaters of the Ipsuwa Khola, and Makalu in the distance.

Follow along the ridge through rhododendrons for a while, then ascend a stone staircase. After a few false summits the trail climbs over a side ridge. This is the Ghungru La (also known as Tutu La), 4050m, the first of the three passes you must cross to reach the Barun Khola. Descend to a small lake at 3990m, then climb steeply up a shallow rocky gully to the Shipton La at 4216m; the national park sign on the pass says 4500m, but this is incorrect. This pass was named when Eric Shipton and Hillary used this route to trek out to Dharan after their 1952 reconnaissance of Everest.

Descend from the pass to two lakes at 4030m, then ascend through large boulders to the Keke La, 4150m. On the other side of the pass the route enters a valley filled with rhododendron forests, a carpet of brilliant flowers in the springtime. About 100m below the pass is a meadow called Dobato, but camping is not allowed here except in an emergency. The route traverses through huge rhododendrons, finally making a steep descent through a forest of firs to **Mumbuk**, a camp site in the trees at 3550m. Mumbuk is on a steep hillside; there are only about 15 or 20 rough tent platforms carved into the hill. This presents problems if there are several groups planning to camp here.

Day 8: Mumbuk to Yangle Kharka

From Mumbuk, descend 300m down a steep, rocky gully that turns into a stream when it's raining. At the bottom the trail turns westwards along the bottom of the Barun valley, still in fir forests. Pass a small cave under an

EASTERN NEPAL

overhanging rock at 3250m, then traverse up and down in the mud among huge, gnarled rhododendron roots until you reach an open area. This is an active landslide, and rocks still bounce down the hill. It's a rough, ill-defined trail just above the Barun Khola, with lots of boulder hopping and streams to jump across. Beyond the worst of the slide area the route traverses alpine meadows with good views of Peak 7.

The trees are now birch and scrub rhododendron, and the valley widens. Cross several streams, then cross the Barun on a wooden bridge to **Yangle Kharka**, a large meadow at 3600m. There is a rough tea shop that offers shelter to porters here. This often has beer; in 1996 the price was Rs 200. The building that looks like something out of an American Western movie is a gompa that was built in 1991. Huge rock cliffs dominate the view on the opposite side of river.

Day 9: Yangle Kharka to Merek

The climb starts out gently from Yangle Kharka, passing **Nghe Kharka**, a large, open, grassy plain at an elevation of 3750m on the opposite side of the Barun Khola. Beyond Nghe Kharka, follow the Barun valley past Riphuk Kharka, 3930m, as the river makes a huge S-shaped curve and the walls rise almost vertically 1500m to 2000m above the river. Climb alongside a waterfall, then on to a swampy meadow and a stream. The trail turns westward and makes a short climb to the potato fields and a single house at **Jhak Kharka**, 4210m. Yet another climb brings you to the meadows of **Yak Kharka** (Lamgmale), 4400m, where there are a rough hotel and a well-equipped shop. The hotel-keeper, Passang Ongchhu, is hoping that this spot will soon be authorised as a camp site by the national park. It is a far better camp than Merek, and camping here would conform to the recommendations for safe acclimatisation to altitude.

Beyond Yak Kharka the trail climbs over a ridge and ascends alongside a moraine formed by the Barun Glacier. There are excellent views of Peak 4 (6720m), Chhamlang, Peak 3 (6477m) and Peak 5 (6404m),

but Makalu is not yet visible. **Merek** is at 4570m and is an inhospitable site with some danger from avalanches and rock fall. It's about 1½ hours from Merek to Shersong, so if you arrive early, you could push on.

Day 10: Merek to Shersong

The trail from Merek climbs in sand and scree beside a stream alongside the moraine. As you pass a ridge, the valley turns slightly north. You enter an alluvial valley and Makalu pops into view just before Shersong. Stay towards the eastern side of the valley; don't follow the well-defined trail that leads northwards up the west side. Head north up the valley over a low ridge to Shersong at 4650m elevation. There is a small stone hut here, and there are some good camp sites in yak pastures. Shersong is somewhat sheltered, but is still a very cold spot. If the clouds have not formed by the time you arrive here, a walk up the valley towards base camp, or up the ridge, is worthwhile.

Day 11: Shersong to Makalu Base Camp

From Shersong, stay to the right in a gully on the east side of the valley. It's a gradual climb to a minor pass about 100m above Makalu base camp. You then descend to a stream and cross on boulders to the base camp on the west bank of the river. There are terrific views of the south face of Makalu. The large buttress of the south face rises across from base camp. An ascent of this buttress yields views of Peak 6, Peak 7 and Baruntse (7220m). Everest and Lhotse complete the panorama. There are no huts, shelters or vegetation at the base camp, which is at an elevation of about 5000m. The so-called Hillary Base Camp and the French Base Camp are far up the glacier, past Barun Pokhari.

You can make this a day trip and return to Shersong for the night. Or you can forgo the base camp and climb the ridge north-east of Shersong. It is a spectacular climb up grassy slopes to the top of the ridge. Keep climbing northwards towards the foot of Makalu. At a height of about 5250m there is an outstanding view of Everest, Lhotse and Lhotse Shar.

You can see both the south-east and north ridges of Everest, along with the Kangshung Face and the South Col. Makalu looms above the ridge to the north.

Day 12: Makalu Base Camp to Yangle Kharka

Retrace your steps down the Barun valley to the pleasant camp of Yangle Kharka.

Day 13: Yangle Kharka to Mumbuk

Continue descending through the rock-fall area and then climb up the rocky gully to the trees of Mumbuk.

Day 14: Mumbuk to Khongma

Trek across the Shipton La and descend to Khongma. It's possible to continue all the way down to Tashigaon, but that makes it an extremely long and hard day.

Day 15: Khongma to Tashigaon

Make a long steep descent back to civilisation. Norbu's hotel at Tashigaon usually has a good stock of beer and Kukhri rum to help you recover from the high altitude.

Day 16: Tashigaon to Num

Day 17: Num to Chichila

Day 18: Chichila to Mani Bhanjyang

Day 19: Mani Bhanjyang to Tumlingtar

Alternative Route down the Arun Valley

You can return to Tumlingtar the same way you came (Days 16-19 above), but for variety you can follow a direct route down the Arun Kosi from Sedua. Be prepared: it's hot along the bottom of the Arun valley no matter what the season.

This route is not used frequently by local people, so it is poorly maintained and often overgrown with vegetation. Much of the route is in forests, but where there is suitable land, there are extensive tracts of rice terraces. Finding camp sites is a serious problem in autumn and late spring, when rice is growing. During the rice growing season,

there is no place to camp between Mulgaon (a settlement 20 minutes down the Arun valley from Sedua) and the Apsawa Khola. It's pretty difficult to reach the Apsawa Khola camp in a single day from Tashigaon, so you should plan to reach Sedua on Day 16 and spend the night there. During the winter, you can camp in Balung, which is within easy reach of Tashigaon.

The trail is steep and narrow in many places; where there are rice terraces, the trail often passes along the top of narrow dykes or beside irrigation canals. Often the route is not obvious, so a guide who knows the way can save a lot of problems. Villages are small and sparsely inhabited, and the only facilities on the route are tiny shops in Pukuwa and Bumling. Several of the places I've mentioned are far above the trail, so you may not even notice that you are passing near a village.

Day 17: Sedua to Apsawa Khola From Sedua, follow a trail that starts out traversing high above the Arun Kosi, first through forests, then large boulders and rice terraces. The trail descends gently to the pleasant Rai village of Mulgaon at 1410m. Below the village school it drops steeply on large rocks through fields of rice, corn and barley to the Ipsuwa Khola, crossing it on a suspension bridge at 780m elevation.

The trek has now entered the hot bottom lands of the Arun valley. Most of the settlements in this area are temporary houses used by Rai and Chhetri farmers who live in villages high on the hillside above. They live here in rough bamboo and wooden shelters while they tend their crops. The trail makes many steep, but short, ascents and descents as it climbs in forests over ridges and descends into side valleys. The trail makes more ups and downs through rocky fields to the bamboo huts of Balung at 860m.

Continue through temporary farming settlements to the spread-out Rai village of **Walung** at 900m. If the rice fields are empty, this is a good place to camp. The route descends to the **Apsawa Khola**, crossing it on a suspension bridge at 630m. It's possible to camp on the sand banks alongside the river. A flood washed away part of the trail here, so you may have to climb over a rocky ridge on a temporary trail on the south side of the bridge.

Day 18: Apsawa Khola to Pukuwa Make a long, steep climb from the river to Chhoyang, a pleasant Rai village with an extensive bamboo-pipe water supply at 860m elevation. A long, reasonably level stretch through forests and rice terraces and past a few scattered houses follows, then the trail drops steeply through trees. When I trekked in 1996, one section of this trail had fallen away and there was a 15 metre descent down some steps chopped into a couple of trees.

The trail traverses into a side valley, crossing a stream at 610m, then makes some ups and downs to Parangbu, an excellent camping spot (assuming that the rice has been harvested) in rice fields on the banks of the Arun Kosi at 540m. Continue in forests past several small streams, then through rice fields to **Pukuwa**, where there are a house and a very basic tea shop.

Day 19: Pukuwa to Bumling Start the day trekking through a huge expanse of rice terraces, then over a ridge to a suspension bridge high above the Waling Khola at 550m. Climb to another ridge at 570m, pass a few houses and trek in forests alternating with rice paddies. Across the Arun are a large mine and a collection of administrative buildings; the mine has been closed and the buildings unused for several years. The large village of Yamphu is high on the hillside above. Climb past the rice paddies and planters' shelters of Yamphu Phedi, then traverse above the river on a narrow cliffside trail. Much of the trail is very overgrown with brush and there are many small streams running across it. Cross a large landslide and traverse above rice terraces to another stream with a wooden cantilever bridge. The route enters a region of intense valley-bottom cultivation, crosses another stream and passes through some more scrub jungle before descending to Tome, a collection of planters' huts among rice fields at 520m.

Below Tome the Arun valley becomes wider and more U-shaped. The trail crosses a stream, then climbs a steep, narrow stairway of rock steps. There are some flimsy bamboo handrails to help you feel secure on this high and exposed route. At the top of the ridge, at 570m, the trail traverses in the forest, then descends to a delightful camp at 360m on the banks of the Sankhuwa Khola at the Chhetri village of Bumling. This part of the trek is through country that tends to be hot, even in the winter. There is a great swimming hole under the suspension bridge that crosses the Sankhuwa Khola. This is the southern boundary of the Makalu-Barun Conservation Area. A trail up the north bank of the river leads to numerous large Rai villages in the extensive Sankhuwa valley.

Day 20: Bumling to Tumlingtar The trail passes through the fields of lower Bumling. The most direct route climbs over a ridge, but you need to ask directions to find it. The most obvious trail passes a small temple and follows the banks of the river to a large suspension bridge over the Arun. The trail on the opposite side is reported to be not good, so stay on the west bank. Follow a circuitous route through rice terraces, finally rejoining the higher trail near some huge, rounded rocks.

Climb a bit out of the Arun valley, cross a low ridge and descend to the Irkhuwa Khola, crossing it on a new steel bridge at 360m. The trail follows the river downstream for a while, then climbs to a ridge at Majuwa Besi, where there is a small shop. Follow around the top of a rice-filled valley through Kartaki village, then descend into the small bazaar of Balawa Besi on the banks of the Chirkhuwa Khola. Cross the river to the *Arun Valley Hotel & Lodge* and trek alongside rice paddies to the small settlement of Kartaki Pul. In the middle of the village, opposite the shabby *Arun Hotel & Lodge*, turn eastwards, pay a Rs 2 toll to an old woman sitting by the trail, and cross the Arun on a long suspension bridge at 300m.

Now following the east bank of the Arun, the route passes through **Chyawabesi**, where there are a few rough lodges. The trail makes some ups and downs alongside the river, passes two bamboo bhattis at Bhangale, then traverses the sandy river bank. Climb over a low ridge to Sati Ghat, where there is a wooden ferry, then make a short climb back to the Tumlingtar plateau and yet another *Arun Hotel & Lodge*. It is a few km of completely level walking to the **Tumlingtar** airstrip at 360m. If you want to walk all the way to Hile, see the last few days of the Solu Khumbu to Hile description.

Kanchenjunga Treks

Nepal opened the Kanchenjunga area to trekkers in 1988, though people had trekked in the area in connection with mountaineering expeditions since the turn of the century. Kanchenjunga is a long way from Kathmandu, and the nearest roads and airports are a long way from the mountain. You can trek either to the north or south Kanchenjunga base camp, but it takes luck, determination and a lot of time to visit both sides of the peak. The northern side is particularly remote; it takes almost two weeks of walking to get to the base camp at Pang Pema.

Kanchenjunga is on the border of Nepal and the Indian state of Sikkim, so a circuit of the mountain is politically impossible. The next best alternative is to visit both the north and south sides of the mountain from the Nepal side; you need to be equipped for a high pass crossing and have a minimum of four weeks to spare. If for any reason you cannot cross the pass, it's a long way around.

It's difficult to cross either the Lapsang La or Mirgin La. Bad weather and snow are often to blame, but more often it is simply a lack of time. Unless you have at least four weeks to spare, and preferably five, you should plan to visit either the north or south base camp, not both. If you can get to Taplejung by either road or air, the trek can be shortened by several days, making it a bit more reasonable.

The lowland portion of this region is culturally intriguing, but there are few good mountain views. The two treks that I have described will probably need to be extended by a few days because of porter problems, weather, or the need for a rest day.

The Kanchenjunga region is the home of the Limbus. Relatives of the Rais, Limbus dominate the region east of the Arun Kosi and few live elsewhere. Limbu men wear a distinctive, tall *topi*, a Nepali cap that is much more colourful than that worn by other Nepalis.

A noteworthy contribution of Limbu culture is the drink tongba. A wooden pot is filled with fermented millet seeds and boiling water. You sip the dangerously potent mixture through a special bamboo straw, with tiny filters to keep the seeds out of the drink, as the hotelier merrily adds more hot water. It is often served in a large plastic mug, but ethnically correct hotels serve it in a special wooden tongba pot, which has brass rings and a wooden cap with a hole for the straw. Tongba goes down easily, as you might do yourself when you arise after a lengthy tongba session. Watch for this speciality anywhere north of Dharan.

Fees & Permits

The immigration office will issue trekking permits for the Kanchenjunga region only to groups, not to individual trekkers. The Kanchenjunga region remains technically restricted, and you can trek here only if you arrange your trek through a trekking company and get a special US$10 per week trekking permit. The region was made a conservation area in June 1997 and is also subject to a Rs 1000 conservation fee.

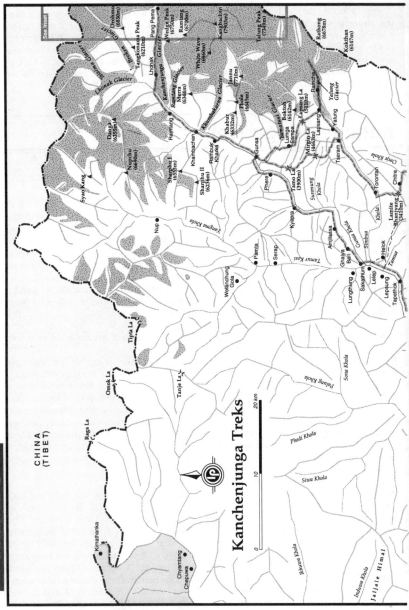

Kanchenjunga Treks

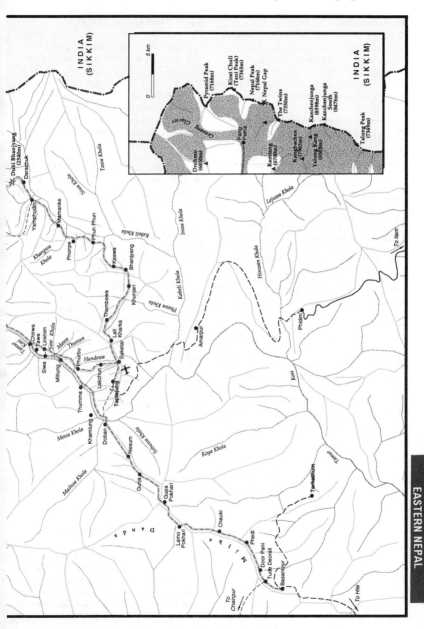

Accommodation
There are a few teahouses in the lowlands, but in the high country you must have food and a tent. If you are planning to take porters across the Lapsang La or Mirgin La, you will need to provide shoes, clothing and snow goggles for them.

Basantpur to Kanchenjunga North

Duration 22 days
Difficulty Medium to hard
Maximum elevation 5140m
Permit cost US$10 per week plus Rs 1000
Season October to May
Hotels Primitive
Summary A long walk in the lowlands eventually leads to spectacular high-altitude scenery on the north side of Kanchenjunga, third-highest mountain in the world.

Access
This trek is best started from Basantpur, which is accessible by an unpaved road. You can save some driving by flying to the Terai city of Biratnagar and hiring a vehicle there. Try to get a morning flight to Biratnagar. The flight takes about 50 minutes, so if you have arranged for vehicles to meet you in Biratnagar, there may be time to drive to the trailhead at Basantpur before dark. If you are travelling by bus, take the direct night bus to Dharan or Hile, then a local bus to Basantpur.

From Dharan, the road climbs over the Siwalik Hills to Dhankuta, then to Hile, a Tibetan settlement at 1850m. The paved road ends here, but a gravel road wends its way to **Basantpur**, a large bazaar at 2200m on a ridge above the Tanmaya Khola, with a view of the entire Kanchenjunga massif. There are lots of shops and local-style teahouses here, but it's a dirty, noisy roadhead town; the first bus leaves at 3 am and starts blowing its horn at 2.30. It's more pleasant to walk about a kilometre up the trail and camp in a meadow beyond the village.

Day 1: Basantpur to Chauki
The trek starts with a slow ascent on a wide trail through mossy rhododendron forests, with super views off both sides to the Arun Kosi and Tamur Kosi drainages and north to Makalu. This is a major trade route to Chainpur and the Arun valley, as well as to Taplejung and the upper Tamur valley, so you will travel in the company of droves of porters. At **Tude Deorali** the Chainpur trail turns off, so the horde of porters diminishes a bit as you approach Door Pani at 2780m. It's uphill to a tea shop at Panch Pokhari, then the trail drops gently to Tinjuri Danda and climbs through Phedi to a good camp site at **Chauki**, elevation 2700m.

Day 2: Chauki to Gupa Pokhari
Most of the day's hike is along the the Milke Danda ridge, through pretty meadows with views of Chhamlang, Mera, Makalu and Kanchenjunga. After some ups and downs through Manglebare, Srimani and Balukop, the trek reaches two small lakes at Lamo Pokhari. Then it's generally downhill past the bamboo huts at Koranghatar to more lakes at **Gupa Pokhari**, at an elevation of 2930m.

Gupa Pokhari has several lodges and lots of places to buy food, biscuits, beer, rum and *chhang*. The shopkeepers are Tibetans who say they settled here two generations ago. Industrious women weave scarves and carpets alongside the trail. A large pond behind the village has a Buddhist shrine beside it and prayer flags in the trees surrounding it. The murky waters of the lakes are heavily polluted; boil or chemically treat the water here. The area is subject to violent windstorms.

Day 3: Gupa Pokhari to Nesum
The route leaves the Milke Danda and heads out onto a ridge above the Tamur Kosi. The trail wanders uphill along the ridge through rhododendron forests to Akhar Deorali at 3200m, then makes some ups and downs en route to Buje Deorali, down to a *kharka*, up again to Mul Pokhari, then down through

hazel and chestnut forests to **Gurja** at 2000m. Keep going down through cultivated country to Chatrapati, and then to **Nesum** at 1620m. There is a tea shop in Chatrapati and two bhattis in Gurja.

Day 4: Nesum to Thumma

Make a long, zigzagging descent past scattered houses and the village of Banjoghjara to the Maihwa Khola. Deal with formalities at the police checkpost and cross the suspension bridge into **Doban** at 640m.

The trail now meets the Tamur Kosi. There are trails up both sides of the river. Both are lousy and subject to landslides; it seems to make little difference which side of the river you start out on. There are frequent bridges across the Tamur Kosi in various stages of technological advancement and repair. Inquire locally and change your route to suit the current situation, though you need to end up on the east bank by the time you reach Siwa.

At Doban, you can cross the Tamur Kosi and climb almost 1200m up to Taplejung. It is a long ascent and the village is not particularly lively, so there is no point in making a

side trip unless you are trying to confirm flight reservations. Once the road is completed from Ilam to Taplejung it will be possible to drive to this point to begin the trek.

The population of the Tamur valley is primarily made up of Limbus, with a few Chhetris in the lower regions and Sherpas at higher elevations. Doban is a small, grubby Newar bazaar town with shops selling soap, toothpaste, cloth, thread, sandals, beer and rum. Many Tibetans live in flimsy bamboo shelters alongside the bazaar here, and sell tongba and weave woollen scarves and aprons.

If you cross the Tamur Kosi on the suspension bridge at Doban and follow the east-bank trail, you will travel up the Tamur in tropical forests, sometimes climbing above the river and sometimes on the river bank itself. **Thumma** is on the west side of the river about two hours beyond Doban. If you stay on the west bank you will pass through Khamlung, then reach Thumma about two hours beyond Doban where you can cross to the east side on a reasonably safe suspension bridge.

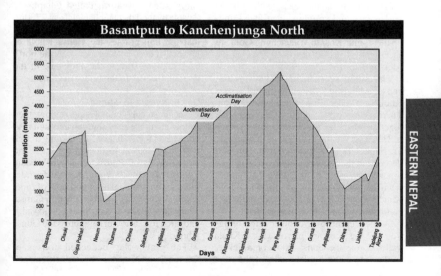

EASTERN NEPAL

Day 5: Thumma to Chirwa

Stay on the east bank as the trail undulates along the riverside through rocky fields and across landslides to the Chhetri bazaar of Mitlung, elevation 800m, then climb over a ridge to Sisnu. A trail crosses the river on a bamboo bridge here and follows the west bank for about 45 minutes before crossing back to the east side. This diversion may not be necessary if the trail on the east side is in good condition. Pass the settlements of **Siwa**, Tawa and Porke. At Porke there is a flimsy bamboo and wire bridge which, fortunately, you do not have to cross. The valley narrows and the trail becomes worse as it climbs across landslides and boulder-strewn river deposits to **Chirwa**, a pleasant bazaar with a few bhattis and shops at 1190m. Take a look at the village water-supply system. It's an elaborate setup of bamboo chutes, pipes and channels that Rube Goldberg or Heath Robinson would have been proud of – if it has not yet been replaced with plastic pipe.

Day 6: Chirwa to Sakathum

Continue up the Tamur across big boulders, passing below the Chhetri village of **Tapethok**. Beyond Tapethok, there is a bridge across the Tamur that leads to the Sherpa settlements of Lepsung, Lelep and Lungthung. Don't go this way. Lelep and the route up the Tamur Kosi to Walunchung Gola are specifically listed as restricted areas on the back of your trekking permit.

The trail makes more ups and downs, traverses a landslide, then crosses the Tamua Khola on a suspension bridge below **Helok**. There is a tongba and tea shop near the junction where the trail to the Limbu village of Helok leaves the main Tamur Kosi route. To bypass Helok, climb over a spur and descend to the Simbua Khola, crossing it on a new suspension bridge. This river comes from the Yalung Glacier on the south side of Kanchenjunga; if you trek to the south base camp, you will reach its headwaters.

A short climb over another ridge brings you into the steep and narrow Gunsa Khola valley. Cross the Gunsa Khola on a rickety bridge and camp by the banks of the river near the Tibetan village of **Sakathum** at 1640m. There is a helipad, tea shop and vegetable garden here. If it's clear, you will have your first good close-up views of Jannu up the Gunsa Khola valley.

Day 7: Sakathum to Amjilassa

The hike is along a steep, narrow trail up the north bank of the Gunsa Khola. Climb steeply for 100m, then drop back to the river and follow its bed for about a kilometre. The trail then begins a sustained climb on stone steps to a waterfall and Ghaiya Bari. The ascent becomes gentler, following an exhilarating, exposed and potentially dangerous trail through arid country to a crest at 2530m, then descends a bit to the Tibetan settlement of **Amjilassa** at 2490m.

Day 8: Amjilassa to Kyapra

Ascend for 100m, then level off and round a bend of the river into lush bamboo, oak and rhododendron forests, with views of the south-western part of the Kanchenjunga massif. The trail makes many short climbs and descents and passes several waterfalls and pastures. Beyond a large waterfall in the Gunsa Khola itself, start a steep climb to a camp site at **Kyapra**, called Chapla or Gyabla by the Tibetan inhabitants, at 2730m.

One edition of the Mandala map shows that the trail crosses the Gunsa Khola at Kyapra; it does not. Kyapra is on the north bank and you stay on the north side of the river all the way to the bridge at Gunsa.

Day 9: Kyapra to Gunsa

Descend steeply into a side ravine, then follow along the river through a fir and rhododendron forest. It takes all morning to trek past Killa and on to the yak pastures and potato fields of **Phere**. Both are Tibetan villages with pleasant gompas and friendly monks; you may find a better supply of food, especially potatoes, in Phere than in Gunsa. The valley widens as you trek through fields and larch forests to a bridge across the Gunsa Khola.

The prayer-flag bedecked houses of **Gunsa** (which means 'winter settlement') are on the south side of the river at 3430m. The police checkpost in Gunsa takes itself very seriously; be sure your permit is in order before you pay them a visit. The high route to the south Kanchenjunga base camp via the Lapsang La begins here. Gunsa is slowly developing into a trekking village and has a teahouse and a few shops.

Day 10: Acclimatisation Day at Gunsa
The trek is now getting into high country; since you have been traipsing about in the lowlands for almost two weeks, you need to spend some time to allow your body to acclimatise to high altitude. You can use the day to reconnoitre the route over the Lapsang La by trekking to a small lake at the foot of the Yamatari Glacier, south of Gunsa. The people of Gunsa move their yaks over the Mirgin La to the high country south of Kanchenjunga in the summer, and take them down to Phere in the winter.

Day 11: Gunsa to Khambachen
The trail makes a gradual ascent along the south bank of the Gunsa Khola, then crosses a boulder-strewn flood plain and crosses back to Rambuk Kharka on the north side of the river. Once on the opposite side, the trail passes a waterfall then makes a short, steep ascent to a very unstable scree slope. It's a dangerous 250m passage across the slide, with loose footing, a steep fall to the river and lots of tumbling football-sized rocks. Beyond the slide, the trail drops to the single locked hut at Lakep, then traverses to **Khambachen**, a Tibetan settlement of about a dozen houses at 4040m.

Day 12: Acclimatisation Day in Khambachen
It's again time to stop and acclimatise. There are views of the high peaks near Kanchenjunga: Khabur (6332m), Phole (6645m), Nango Ma and Jannu. Climb a ridge above the village for more views, or take a day hike to the Jannu base camp. You might come across blue sheep grazing in the valley or on the slopes above.

Day 13: Khambachen to Lhonak
The trail climbs gradually through open rocky fields to Ramtang at 4240m, then across moraines north-west of the Kanchenjunga Glacier. Lhonak, at 4790m, is near a dry lake bed on an open, sandy plain; water is scarce here. There are no houses, but you can camp among the large boulders to get out of the wind. Terrific mountain views abound in all directions.

Day 14: Lhonak to Pang Pema
You cannot see the main Kanchenjunga peak from Lhonak; for a view of this peak you must go on to the base camp at Pang Pema, elevation 5140m. You could make a day trip from Lhonak, but clouds often obscure the peak after about 9 am, and you could find yourself in Pang Pema without a view. It's really worth camping in Pang Pema in hopes of a cloudless vista just before sunset or in the early morning.

From Lhonak, the trail ascends gradually across the plain, then gets a bit steeper as it follows the moraine. You can drop off the moraine and follow the bottom of the valley to avoid the steeper section. The views are dramatic, but you cannot see Kanchenjunga or Wedge Peak until you are near Pang Pema. The spectacular main peak of Kanchenjunga, and a panorama of other peaks that make up one of the largest mountain masses in the world, tower over the single roofless hut at Pang Pema.

Day 15: Pang Pema to Khambachen
Take a morning hike up the ridge north of Pang Pema. A climb of 200m to 300m leads to a vantage point with views of Kanchenjunga, Wedge Peak (6750m), the Twins (7350m), Pyramid Peak (7168m) and Tent Peak (7365m). As usual, the descent goes faster, so you can easily get back to Khambachen in a single day.

Day 16: Khambachen to Gunsa

Day 17: Gunsa to Amjilassa

Day 18: Amjilassa to Chirwa

Descend to Helok. If your destination is Taplejung, retrace your steps through the lower part of Helok and meander back down the Tamur Kosi to Chirwa.

If you are headed for the south side of Kanchenjunga, start climbing the stone stairs in Helok to the ridge. A local guide will probably save you a lot of energy on this route, because the trails are used primarily by woodcutters and herders, not by trekkers.

The Mandala map shows a trail from Helok up the Simbua Khola towards Tseram. This trail, where it exists at all, is strictly for monkeys. There is a way through, but it is not a trail, it's a steep, slippery climb through thick bamboo forests up the side of the Deorali Danda. I came down this once; it was great fun, but it's not a sensible route. Everyone seems to agree that it's more practical to take an extra day and follow the woodcutters' trail up the ridge from Helok to Yamphudin, then climb to the Lamite Bhanjyang from the south and re-enter the Simbua valley.

Day 19: Chirwa to Linkhim

It's a straight shot down the Tamur Kosi to Taplejung. You can, however, avoid the steep climb from Doban by contouring up the side of the valley instead. From Chirwa, start uphill, passing through **Diwa** village. Climb over a landslide and keep going up steeply, staying above Tawa. The trail drops into a large side canyon, then climbs back to the ridge before reaching **Linkhim**.

Day 20: Linkhim to Suketar

Trek in and out of side canyons through the small Limbu villages of Helate, Pumbur and Phurbu to a ridge overlooking a monstrous slide area. Climb above the slide area to the Sherpa villages of Bung Kulung and Lakchun and you can get directly to the airport without going into Taplejung. If you plan to take a flight, stay in **Suketar**; see the end of the Taplejung to Kanchenjunga South trek for details.

Day 21: Fly to Kathmandu

Taplejung to Kanchenjunga South

Duration 16 days
Difficulty Medium
Maximum elevation 4620m
Permit cost US$10 per week plus Rs 1000
Season October to May
Hotels Primitive
Summary Several days of walking through Limbu villages lead to a glacial valley south of Kanchenjunga.

There are lots of ways to make this trek, but the way I have described is the easiest – if you can arrange a flight in to Taplejung or are prepared to take a long, difficult bus ride. Take a look at the route profile for this trek; there is an incredible amount of up-and-down walking. When I trekked this route, I calculated that we climbed – and descended – more than 15,000m during two weeks of walking. Be sure you are ready for this kind of effort before you set out: there are no escape routes if you get sick, tired or bored.

Access

A flight to Taplejung takes half an hour from Biratnagar and 1½ hours from Kathmandu. To avoid clouds and wind, Taplejung flights operate early in the morning, so you can probably accomplish a few hours of walking on the day you fly in. The airport is on the top of a ridge in **Suketar** village, above Taplejung. Unless you need to confirm a flight back to Kathmandu or load up on supplies, it's not worth the long walk into Taplejung and the tedious, very steep climb back to Suketar. If the road is open, you will probably spend a night in a hotel in Taplejung, then start the trek to the south base camp with a climb up the ridge to the airport.

Day 1: Taplejung to Thembewa

From Taplejung airport in Suketar village, elevation 2300m, the trail climbs gradually along a rhododendron-covered ridge. The trail crosses the ridge and contours past the

Deorali Khola and four more streams to a pass at 2570m. Descend through forests to Lali Kharka, two houses at 2220m, then through fields to the substantial Limbu village of Thembewa at 1880m.

Day 2: Thembewa to Keswa

From Thembewa, the trail ascends to a ridge, then drops steeply through Shimu and Pokara villages to a suspension bridge across the Phawa Khola at 1430m. There is a good swimming hole here, and a possible camp site near the river. Climb steeply to **Khunjari**, a Limbu village at 1700m. Turn left just beyond the school and climb through wheat fields to a saddle. From here, the trail makes a long, looping traverse to **Bhanjyang**, a Gurung settlement with several bhattis, on a pass at 2120m. From Bhanjyang there are views of Kanchenjunga and Kyabru.

The trek has now entered the Kabeli Khola valley, but you will spend the next two days climbing up and down, in and out of ravines and over ridges, only to end up in Yamphudin at the bottom of the valley. Turn left from Bhanjyang and head north just below the top of the ridge, descending to the scattered village of **Keswa** at 1960m.

Day 3: Keswa to Mamanke

Pass below waterfalls and cross several streams and a landslide to reach Phun Phun, which is shown on some maps with the fanciful spelling 'Fun Fun'. Cross a saddle, where a stately pipal tree offers a rest in the shade, and traverse to Yangpang, then head generally upwards through forests past a large waterfall. Descend through a series of side valleys to two shops on a ridge at 1850m, then drop a bit to **Phonpe** village at 1780m. Descend steeply through rice terraces into a side canyon, cross a stream on a long suspension bridge at 1540m, then climb back to **Mamanke**, a prosperous Limbu village with bhattis, shops and a large school at 1810m.

Day 4: Mamanke to Yamphudin

Climb to a ridge and then descend gradually to the Tenguwa Khola. Forgo the decrepit bridge; cross the stream by jumping from stone to stone. Switchback steeply up to another ridge marked by a chorten and prayer flags, then descend across rubble and rock slides and cross another stream. This portion of the valley is steep, and parts of the trail are on cliffs high above the river as it

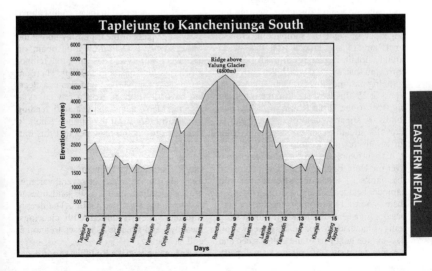

Taplejung to Kanchenjunga South

makes its way down to the Kabeli Khola at 1640m. There is a lot of flood damage here, so it becomes a rock-hopping exercise, over boulders, tree roots and intersecting stream channels, as you head upstream. Stay on the west side of the Kabeli Khola, climbing gently to **Yamphudin** (1690m) at the junction of the Omje Khola and the Kabeli Khola.

Yamphudin is a mixed community of Sherpas, Limbus, Rais and Gurungs. Among the corn and rice fields of the village there are a police post, a school, and some shops with minimal supplies. The 1989 monsoon produced floods that washed away parts of the village and many fields. A goat trail leads from Yamphudin up the ridge to the west, to Helok and the Tamur Kosi valley. See Day 19 of the Basantpur to Kanchenjunga North route description for more information about this rough and difficult trail.

Day 5: Yamphudin to Omje Khola
Beyond Yamphudin, you should plan to carry your own food and shelter. The only facility from here on is a teahouse in upper Omje Khola which is only open when the proprietor is in the mood.

Cross the Omje Khola on a couple of bamboo poles and follow the Kabeli Khola upstream for a short distance, ignoring the suspension bridge. After you pass behind a ridge out of sight of Yamphudin, cross a small stream and take a trail that heads straight uphill. Zigzag up through fields of corn and barley to Darachuk, and keep climbing past meadows to Dubi Bhanjyang, a pass at 2540m. Descend through ferns and big trees to the **Omje Khola** at 2340m and follow the stream uphill for a short distance. Cross the stream on a log bridge, and go a bit further upstream to a camp site.

It's a bit depressing to make the long climb over the Dubi Bhanjyang only to end up on the banks of the same stream that you camped beside last night. Unfortunately, there is no trail that follows the stream bed; besides, most Nepalis do not fret about steep trails as much as we do. This is a pretty short day, but the next part of the trek is steep and has few camp sites. If you are a small party

you might keep going on to Chitre, but there isn't space there for a large camp.

Day 6: Omje Khola to Torontan
From the stream, the trail makes a steep climb through bamboo to a kharka at Chitre (2920m) and continues up to a notch. After a short descent, the ascent to a clearing is less strenuous, and then the trail passes through a forest of pines and rhododendrons to a pond at Lamite Bhanjyang, 3410m elevation. This is not a good place to camp. There is a water shortage in the spring and it is muddy in the autumn. On a clear day this ridge provides views of Jannu and of the Taplejung road far to the south.

From the ridge, you can see a trail across a huge landslide scar; a better route is to stay on the ridge and follow it east along its top until you are well beyond the landslide, then follow a steep set of switchbacks leading downhill. Once the initial steep descent is finished, the trail becomes more gentle. The trail is generally level and wide, though it is muddy in the autumn and there are a few short, steep descents. It passes through damp, orchid-filled forests, crossing streams and isolated clearings used by herders and woodcutters.

The trail emerges into the open just above the Simbua Khola. A 1987 flood washed away large parts of the trail. Stay above the white, silty river and follow it upstream, on a series of ascents and descents, to a temporary bridge built of stones and logs. There are camp sites near the river, and also in a clearing beyond Torontan, near a few caves at 2990m. Many maps show a trail leading from **Torontan** down the Simbua Khola to Helok; I can find no evidence that this trail really exists.

Day 7: Torontan to Tseram
The hike starts in forests of several varieties of rhododendron, then crosses landslides to Tsento Kang, a goth at 3360m. The deeply forested valley is dotted with clearings, meadows and streams as it rises to another goth at Watha.

An hour beyond is a Buddhist shrine decorated with rock cairns, prayer flags and three-pronged iron trisuls. The shrine is in a cave that has a streak of dark stone along it, which is thought to be the image of a snake. This shrine marks the boundary of a sacred part of the valley, beyond which killing animals is prohibited. Peaks begin to appear in the distance as you climb further. There is a short stretch along the gravel bottom of the stream bed, then a climb to **Tseram**, a large, flat meadow with a single house at 3870m. The settlements in this valley are goths used by yak and cow herders from Gunsa who cross the Mirgin La to graze their animals during the summer.

Day 8: Tseram to Ramche
Climb through forests to a landslide area; the junction with the trail to the Mirgin La is nearby, but the trail is hard to find. Stumble across a stream on a loose, rocky path and climb to some *mani* walls and a stone house near the tree line at 4040m. The peaks of Rathong and Kabru loom at the head of the valley; it's hard to believe they are both less than 6700m high. The trail climbs into the valley alongside the moraine of the Yalung Glacier. The valley opens up as you approach Yalung, a pasture full of yaks at 4260m.

Climb alongside the moraine through scrub junipers up a stream to a lake at **Lapsang**, 4430m. You can see the start of the route to the Lapsang La as it heads off over the moraines in a valley to the north. Keep climbing to another lake and a big meadow at Ramche, elevation 4620m. There are two well-built stone houses here; one of them thinks it is a hotel, but the owner spends so much time away that it rarely fulfils its ambitions. The view is dominated by the spectacular peak of Rathong (6678m), which straddles the Nepal-India border to the east. Herds of blue sheep live on the cliffs above.

Day 9: Day Trip to Yalung Glacier
To make a day trip to the Yalung Glacier, follow a stream alongside the moraine for a long distance, then bear right to climb onto the moraine itself. From a chorten at 4800m elevation there is a fine view of the south face of Kanchenjunga. A short distance beyond the chorten is a view of Jannu. This is a good place to turn around. To go further, you must climb down the rough moraine onto the Yalung Glacier and pick your way through the boulder-strewn glacier towards Kanchenjunga. It's a one or two day project to reach the base camp itself.

Day 10: Ramche to Tseram

Day 11: Tseram to Lamite Bhanjyang

Day 12: Lamite Bhanjyang to Yamphudin

Day 13: Yamphudin to Phonpe

Day 14: Phonpe to Khunjari

Day 15: Khunjari to Suketar
There are a few tea shops at the airport that have rooms for rent. If you are camping, set up your tents near the airfield and hope for clear weather for the flight in the morning. The hotel specialises in tongba, so you will have something to amuse you if the plane does not come.

Day 16: Fly to Kathmandu
Fly to Biratnagar or, if you are lucky, directly to Kathmandu.

Kanchenjunga North Side to South Side

Duration 2 to 4 days
Difficulty Hard
Maximum elevation 4663m
Permit cost US$10 per week plus Rs 1000
Season October to May
Hotels Primitive
Summary A rough yak trail leading across several high passes allows you to make a trek to both the north and south sides of Kanchenjunga.

There are two routes between Gunsa, on the northern route to Kanchenjunga, and the upper Simbua Khola, on the southern route.

EASTERN NEPAL

The higher route crosses the Lapsang La, elevation 5110m, which is often snow-covered and may be difficult and dangerous for both trekkers and porters. This is a very remote area where help is a long way off and evacuation is almost impossible. You will need to make a choice whether to cross the Lapsang La or the lower and safer Mirgin La, or whether to retreat down the Tamur Kosi valley. Either of the high routes takes three days, with high camps on either side of the pass. The most critical factor on the high passes is snow. There is no regular traffic on these routes; if there is snow, you will have to break the trail yourself without any rock cairns or other landmarks to guide you.

The Mirgin La route actually crosses five passes: the Tamo La, 3900m; an unnamed, 4115m pass; the Mirgin La, 4663m; Sinion La, 4660m; and a final, unnamed pass of 4724m elevation. It then makes a long, steep 1000m descent to the Simbua Khola. The route enters the Simbua Khola valley above Tseram, at 3900m, and you can probably make it on to Ramche the same day.

The Lapsang La route starts at Gunsa and climbs across the foot of the Yamatari Glacier to a goth at Lumga Sampa. Cross the Lapsang La and make your way down through the large boulders of a moraine to a camp below the glacier. Descend further into the valley and meet the Simbua Khola trail at Lapsang, elevation 4430m. Then it's a short distance up the valley to Ramche at 4620m.

Western Nepal

Many people describe western Nepal as 'unexplored', but Westerners have a bad habit of assuming that what is unknown to them is unknown to everyone. Western Nepal was once the centre of a large empire that extended into Tibet and India and it now has a large population of both Hindus and Buddhists. It is remote and unknown from the Western viewpoint because of its relative inaccessibility and its distance from Kathmandu. Regular flights to Jumla, Simikot, Dolpo and other airstrips in the west reduce this remoteness somewhat, but they add considerably to the cost of trekking.

Another factor that discourages trekkers in western Nepal is that many of the culturally and scenically exotic regions are in restricted areas with high permit fees. Many of the trails in the west continue to the northern side of the Himalayan ranges of Nampa, Saipal and Kanjiroba, making it easy for trekkers to zip up trails along river valleys and into Tibet – a practice that the governments of both Nepal and China would like to discourage. Some of these treks, including Shey gompa to the north of Phoksumdo Lake and Humla, the district to the north-west of Jumla, are described in the Restricted Areas chapter.

The history and anthropology of western Nepal is complex and fascinating. The region is predominantly Hindu. Tibetans make up only a small part of the population, yet they have had a significant influence on the area through trading. Most of the homes – even of people not of Tibetan ancestry – are built in Tibetan style. Their flat roofs covered with packed earth are well suited to the semi-arid conditions of the region behind Dhaulagiri. In many villages the houses are packed closely together one atop another, climbing up the hillside and sharing common roofs. There are few stairs inside the dwellings; instead, people climb from one level to another on carved log ladders outside the house.

Cultural roots extend north into Tibet and west to Kumaon in India. Until Jumla was conquered by the army of Bahadur Shah in 1788, the people of western Nepal had very little reliance on Kathmandu. The Chhetris of western Nepal are categorised into three groups: Thakuris, who are the aristocracy; normal Chhetris as found throughout Nepal; and Matwali Chhetris, 'those who drink liquor'. The status of Matwali Chhetris is fascinating because many of them are Tibetan immigrants who long ago masqueraded as Chhetris. For many generations they have evolved their own peculiar combination of Hinduism and Buddhism.

INFORMATION
Fees & Permits
You must pay the standard park entrance fee of Rs 650 to enter Rara Lake and Shey Phoksumdo national parks and the Dhorpatan Hunting Reserve. The Dolpo trek requires a special US$10 per week trekking permit, but this is easy to obtain, even for individual trekkers. Parts of western Nepal, including Shey gompa and the trek from Simikot towards the Tibetan border, are governed by the restricted area regulations and are subject to high permit fees. The rules for these two treks are described in the Restricted Areas chapter.

Maps
The US Army Map Service sheets 44-11 *Jumla*, 44-12 *Mustang* and 44-16 *Pokhara*, and Mandala Maps' *Jomsom to Jumla & Surkhet*, *Dhaulagiri Himal* and *Api, Nampa & Saipal* cover western Nepal. The US army Mustang sheet 44-12, edition 1-AMS, contains a large amount of fantasy. Phoksumdo Lake, Shey gompa and many other features on this map are totally misplaced more than 12 km to the south of where they actually are. A 1:30,000 map titled *Dolpa* by Paolo Gondoni details much of Dolpo; it is published

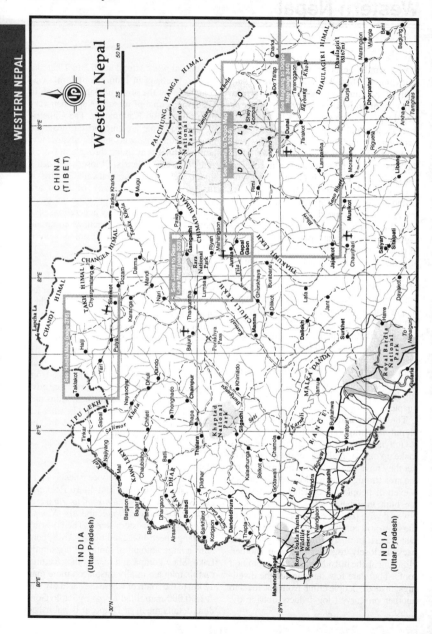

by Nepa Maps and is available in Kathmandu.

Elevations are difficult to confirm in this region. All the available maps were derived from the Survey of India maps which had little ground control in remote western Nepal. Most elevations I have indicated are based on GPS or altimeter readings related to the known elevations of Jumla and Dolpo airports, and to the Royal Geographical Society's *Kanjiroba Himal* map of 1967.

Books

Karnali under Stress, by Barry C Bishop, is a study of western Nepal's geography and trading patterns. *Dolpo: The World Behind the Himalayas*, by Karna Sakya, is an early account of a Nepali naturalist's trip to Dolpo. *Stones of Silence*, by George B Schaller, is another naturalist's view of travels in Dolpo. *The Snow Leopard*, by Peter Matthiessen, is a personal account of the same trip to Dolpo that George Schaller made.

Tales of the Turquoise: A Pilgrimage in Dolpo, by Corneille Jest, is a collection of legends and stories collected by an authority on Dolpo.

Language & Place Names

The people of western Nepal speak their own version of Nepali. When local people speak among themselves, Kathmandu Nepalis can barely understand them. One porter told me that the hike to the next village was an easy one by saying that the trail was *sasto*, which translates as 'inexpensive'. He also said that one trail was *ek bhat* shorter than another; this translates as 'one rice' or 'one meal' – a charming way to say half a day. This charm, of course, can lead to complications.

West Nepali lingo also pervades place names. The name for a river is *gaad*, a high meadow is a *patan*, a pasture or camping place is a *chaur* and a pass is a *lagna*.

Accommodation & Supplies

Nepalgunj Nepalgunj is the jumping-off place for flights and buses throughout western Nepal. It is in the Terai near the Indian border.

Nepalgunj is not an exciting place, but because it is the largest city in a region that has a considerable number of development projects, it boasts some moderately good hotels. The *Sneha* and the *Batika* are both on the main road, three km from the main bazaar, three km from the Indian border and about 10 km from the airport. Costs are in the Rs 1000 range for a room with an air cooler and Rs 2500 for a double room with air-con. Another possibility is the *Rapti Hotel*, near the hospital. In the bazaar, at Birendra Chowk, the *Shanti Sakya* and *Punjabi* hotels offer low-end accommodation. The Punjabi is said to have excellent Indian food, otherwise the fare is basic *dal bhat*. You can also stay at a rough hotel adjoining the airport.

Accommodation on the Trek One of the largest ethnic groups in the region is the Thakuris, a Chhetri caste that has the highest social, political and ritual status. Westerners, who are considered low caste by high-caste Hindus, are traditionally not welcome in Thakuri homes. For this reason tea shops are scarce and cater mainly to locals. Consequently, it is quite difficult to trek in much of western Nepal using teahouses for food and accommodation.

Buying Food Despite extensive cultivation of red rice near Jumla, and the Nepalgunj to Jumla shuttle flights that carry in white rice and other staples to supply the army and government officials, it is difficult to purchase enough food for a trek in Jumla Bazaar. It is better to carry all your food from Kathmandu – if you can get it onto the plane.

Merchants fly white rice to Jumla and then transport it to more remote regions using trains of horses, mules, sheep and goats. The goat 'trucks' of western Nepal are fascinating. Traders equip herds of 100 or more sheep and goats with tiny woollen panniers that carry 10 kg of rice, then herd the animals through the countryside. Hundreds of kilos of rice and sugar are delivered throughout western Nepal in this manner.

Porters

There are a few porters available in Jumla, but they are expensive, they don't speak English, and they are not particularly eager to leave their homes. That being said, I was lucky enough in Jumla to hire two teams of excellent porters who, unlike porters in other parts of Nepal, were willing to carry loads long distances each day.

Trekking Season

Most of western Nepal is either outside the monsoon's influence or in the rain shadow of Dhaulagiri Himal. Summers tend to be drier here than in the rest of Nepal and there are few leeches. The best time for trekking is from late August to September when the wild flowers are in bloom. Winters are cold and there is a considerable amount of snow – so much, in fact, that there is some potential for skiing in parts of western Nepal. The trekking season, therefore, is from late spring and throughout the summer until late October. One problem with summer treks in the west is the inordinate number of flies that gather on food and inside tents.

Warning

There is an amazing amount of marijuana in western Nepal, both wild and cultivated. The locals do sometimes smoke it, but it is cultivated because the seeds are used to make cooking oil. The police and national park officials have been known to arrest trekkers who transport dope in their luggage.

In many places you may walk through, or camp in, a cannabis plantation. If this happens, it's worth giving your boots and gear a good scrubbing before you head home so that your luggage doesn't attract the attention of the airport sniffer dogs when you arrive.

GETTING THERE & AWAY

Air

Nepalgunj RNAC, Nepal Airways and most helicopter companies operate a western Nepal hub here with frequent flights to Jumla (US$44), Dolpo (US$77), Simikot (US$88)

and many other destinations (some fascinating and others dreary) in western Nepal.

The daily 1½-hour Nepalgunj RNAC flight is reasonably reliable because it operates in the afternoons when there is less demand for aeroplanes. Necon operates Avro flights to Nepalgunj via Pokhara (US$67 from Pokhara) and both Nepal Airways and Everest Air have a regular service (US$99).

Transport from Nepalgunj airport into town is difficult to arrange. There are no taxis or buses; the only motorised transport is three-wheel rattletrap *tempos*. It's a half-hour ride in a horse-drawn *tonga* or one hour by bicycle rickshaw. If you call before you leave Kathmandu, the Sneha Hotel (☎ 081-20119) will send a jeep to collect you for Rs 500.

Jumla, Dolpo and Simikot flights are scheduled to depart at dawn. Transport from Nepalgunj to the airport is also difficult to arrange, so be sure you have a firm commitment on this the night before.

Beware of baggage charges on Jumla and Dolpo flights. The free allowance is a miserly 15 kg. The rate for excess baggage from Nepalgunj to Jumla is Rs 24 per kg. Many cargo charter flights are operated by business people sending rice and other goods, so if you are having trouble sending all your gear, you may be able to freight it on one of these flights.

Jumla Everest Air operates two flights per week from Kathmandu to Jumla, but seats are very difficult to get. The day before the reservation chart is opened, Jumli people camp in front of the airline office to be first in line to get seats. The most reliable, though expensive, way to get to Jumla is to fly via Nepalgunj (US$99 plus US$44). There are often seats available on Russian helicopters from Nepalgunj to Jumla.

The flight from Nepalgunj to Jumla (US$44) takes 35 minutes, climbing from the plains over many sets of hills and into the huge Tila valley. Jumla airport is one of the best of Nepal's remote airstrips – 900m long and an easy approach – so flights operate more regularly than at places such as Lukla.

Upon arrival at Jumla airstrip you must register with the police. An official sits in the security check booth and writes down the names of all passengers, both Nepali and foreign, who arrive by air.

Jumla Bazaar is a 10-minute walk from the airport. There are shops, pharmacies, a bank, camps for both army and police, and a few restaurants along the stone-paved main street. Jumla has electricity, and a few houses sport television satellite dishes. Accommodation is available at the *Rara Hotel* near the airport and also at the *Himalaya Trekking Hotel* in the western part of the bazaar, near the police post. The hotels are basic, food is limited to dal bhat and potatoes, and many goods are in short supply or are totally unavailable. There is a small supply of canned goods, jam and other packaged items, but you probably will not find speciality foods such as muesli. Local regulations have declared Jumla a dry district, so no alcohol is available.

Jumla, on the banks of the Tila Khola at 2370m, is one of the highest rice-growing areas in the world. The entire Tila valley is covered with paddy fields growing a unique red rice that is more tasty than white rice but scorned by most Nepalis.

Dolpo The airport for the Dolpo region is in Juphal village, on a hill about three hours walk from Dunai. There are regular scheduled flights and also lots of charter flights by both plane and chopper that carry food into the region. Flying in is difficult because of heavy passenger and cargo traffic, but flying out is often easy, even without advance planning, because the cargo charters carry passengers on the return trip. There is no direct service from Kathmandu to Dolpo. All Dolpo flights originate in Nepalgunj and cost US$72 by plane and US$110 by helicopter.

Chaurjhari This airport is three days south of Dunai on the Bheri River. A good trail from Chaurjhari to Dunai involves almost no climbing. It is an alternative to Dolpo airport when winds or snow delay flights.

Bajura Named after the Bajura district, the airport is actually in Kolti. It is two days hard walking south of Simikot and could be used in an emergency if Simikot is snowed in. RNAC operates several flights a week between Nepalgunj and Bajura.

Simikot Perhaps the most remote airstrip in Nepal, Simikot is the jumping-off place for treks to Humla, the restricted area trek to Mt Kailas and, if it is opened, Mugu. Sometimes snowed in during the winter, Simikot is served by RNAC, Everest Air and Nepal Airways, all of which operate flights from Nepalgunj (US$88). A seat on a chopper, when available, costs US$120. There is no direct service between Simikot and Kathmandu.

Bus

Nepalgunj Night buses from Kathmandu to Nepalgunj charge Rs 225 for the 16-hour, 530-km trip. Day buses are cheaper (Rs 180), but take longer.

Surkhet A night bus from Kathmandu goes to Surkhet (renamed Birendranagar), a roadhead in the hills north of Nepalgunj. It costs Rs 265 for the 600-km, 15-hour trip. It takes eight or nine days to walk from Surkhet to Jumla with porters, and there are no trekkers' hotels along the way. Local traders in Jumla bring most of their goods by horse or mule caravan from Surkhet.

Salyan This roadhead south of Chaurjhari is a four to five-day walk from Dunai. There is no direct bus service from Kathmandu. Take a bus to Tulsipur or Nepalgunj, then a local bus to Salyan. Porters from Salyan and other villages in this region will probably refuse to go beyond Dunai.

Baglung The trek from Baglung, near Pokhara, to Dolpo takes 13 days, or you can make a long trek from Baglung all the way to Jumla via Dolpo.

WESTERN NEPAL

Jumla to Rara Lake

> **Duration** 6 to 9 days
> **Difficulty** Medium
> **Maximum elevation** 3710m
> **Permit cost** US$5 per week plus Rs 650
> **Season** March to October
> **Accommodation** Terrible
> **Summary** Lots of up-and-down walking through forests and isolated villages leads to a high-altitude lake surrounded by trees. A good choice if you are a bird-watcher or desire something close to a wilderness experience.

Rara Lake (2980m) is the focal point of Rara National Park and is a good destination for a trek in western Nepal. The route is very much 'off the beaten track' and affords glimpses of cultures and scenery very different from those in the rest of Nepal. Rara is a clear, high-altitude lake ringed with pine, spruce and juniper forests and snowcapped Himalayan peaks. In winter there is often snow on the ridges surrounding the lake. Except for the army personnel assigned to the park, nobody lives at the lake because the government resettled all the people of Rara and Chapra villages when the area was declared a national park.

Accommodation & Supplies

The trek to Rara is somewhat strenuous and tends to be expensive because both food and labour are scarce and overpriced in this part of Nepal. If you are looking for wilderness solitude, and can overcome the logistical complications of the region, this trek is a good choice.

Access

The best way to begin this trek is to fly to Jumla via Nepalgunj, though you could walk to Jumla all the way from Surkhet.

Day 1: Jumla to Danphe Lagna

There are two routes to Danphe Lagna. When there is snow, take the longer, lower route.

High Trail This route crosses a pass that is closed when there is heavy snow. Follow the main street of Jumla north up the Jugad Khola valley past the red-roofed hospital. The wide, level trail leads past college buildings to a settlement known as Campus. As the trail slowly gains elevation it passes a collection of Western-style houses. These are the residences of teachers and administrators from the Karnali Technical Institute, a vocational school at **Ghumurti**, a short distance above. The school is a collection of more than 40 buildings at 2550m. It is operated by the United Mission to Nepal and has about 150 students studying agriculture, engineering and health.

After a long climb past the school, the trail passes through Sisnamul, at 2830m, then enters a forest of big trees that soon gives way to meadows. **Chere**, at 3010m, is a large horse and sheep pasture with a few open herders' huts. Beyond Chere the trail becomes steeper and climbs through meadows to a pass at 3600m that offers views of Patrasi Himal (6860m) and Jagdula Himal (5785m) to the east. The trail descends gently through forests of spruce, birch and rhododendron to **Danphe Lagna** at 3130m. A single house stands in an attractive meadow beside a clear stream. It is often possible to spot the Himalayan monal (or impeyan pheasant), the colourful national bird of Nepal, in the nearby forests.

Low Trail From Jumla the lower trail to Rara follows the north bank of the Tila Khola, then turns north up the Chaudhabise Khola. The Jumla Valley disappears behind a ridge as the trail follows the river, keeping fairly level and passing through fields and pine forests. The trek heads in the direction of Uthugaon (2530m), then begins an ascent up the Dusni Khola valley, beginning gently but becoming steeper as the climb continues. There is a good camp site near the school, across the river from the village.

From Uthugaon the trail begins an ascent up the Dusni Khola valley, gently at first but becoming steep as the climb continues. The canyon becomes very narrow with vertical

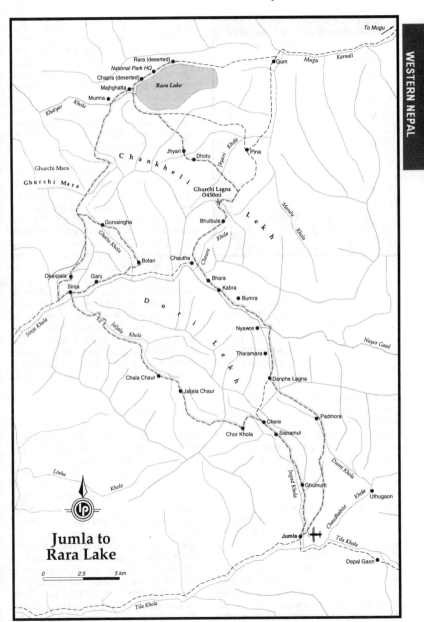

To Mugu

Rara (deserted)
National Park HQ
Chapra (deserted)
Majhghatta
Murma
Khatyar
Khola

Rara Lake

Gum
Mugu
Karnali
Mugu

C h a n k h e l i

Jhyari
Dhotu
Pina
Jhyari Khola

Ghurchi Mara

Ghurchi Mara

Ghurchi Lagna
(3450m)

L e k h

Mandu Khola

Gorosingha

Chatta Khola

Bhulbule

Chaura Khola

Botan
Chautha
Chaura

Okarpata
Ganj
Sinja

Sinja Khola

D o r i

Bhara
Kabra
Bumra

Nyawre

Nayor Gaad

Jaljala Khola

Tharamara

L e k h

Chala Chaur

Jaljala Chaur

Danphe Lagna

Padmora

Chere
Chor Khola
Sisnamul

Dusni Khola

Linba
Khola

Isgad Khola

Ghumurti

Chaudhabise Khola

Uthugaon

Jumla

Tila Khola

Depal Gaon

**Jumla to
Rara Lake**

0   2.5   5 km

Tila Khola

WESTERN NEPAL

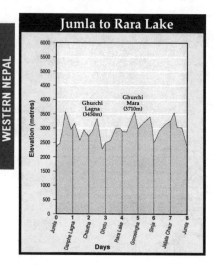

Jumla to Rara Lake

Elevation (metres) — Ghurchi Lagna (3450m), Ghurchi Mara (3710m)

Days: Jumla, Danphe Lagna, Chautha, Dhotu, Rara Lake, Gorosgogna, Sinja, Jaljala Chaur, Jumla

cliffs on both sides as the trail ascends through a deep forest of pines, spruces and firs. The large Chhetri town of **Padmora** is the last village in the valley, at 2900m. The climb continues in forests over a pass at 3400m and down to **Danphe Lagna** on the opposite side. This route takes half a day longer than the high trail.

Day 2: Danphe Lagna to Chautha

The trail descends gently alongside the stream to two *bhattis* at Tharamara (3280m). The descent becomes steep, through forests of fir, birch, walnut and bamboo, to a single house at Hiran Duski (2840m). After a short level stretch the trail zigzags down to the Sinja Khola, crossing it on a log bridge at 2680m. Follow the river downstream to some tea shops at **Nyawre** (2660m), then through potato and wheat fields near the riverbed. The big trail which climbs steeply up the ridge is longer and more difficult than the riverbed route.

The trail leaves the river and starts a serious climb, passing through marijuana fields below Bumra village, then over a ridge into a side valley, dropping to cross a stream near some water-driven mills. A steep, nasty

set of switchbacks leads to **Kabra**, where, crammed under a huge overhanging rock, there is a ludicrous hotel and dirty health post. The health post specialises in natural Ayurvedic medicines. The rock is a source of *silaji*, a mineral that has such amazing properties that it is carried to Jumla, then flown to Nepalgunj and exported to India. I bought some in Kathmandu and the literature claimed that ' … there is hardly any curable disease which cannot be controlled or cured with the aid of Silaji'.

The steep climb continues for a while, then levels out before **Bhara**, also known as Bhadgaon (2920m). This is a classic Tibetan-style village surrounded by splendid fields of wheat. Beyond this large village the trail makes a turn into a big valley then descends to the Chaura Khola. Just across this stream are two shops and a school in the tiny village of **Chautha** (2770m). The *Bhandari Hotel* offers rough accommodation. If you are camping, try the fields before the village or else continue an hour or more up the valley and make a camp in the forest alongside the stream. The trail that exits the village to the south follows the Sinja Khola to Sinja. The Rara Lake trail heads north up the Chaura Khola. Local folklore says that Chautha is the halfway point between Jumla and Rara Lake.

Day 3: Chautha to Dhotu

A rocky trail follows the stream uphill, crossing the stream as the wooded valley becomes narrower. About half an hour beyond Chautha the valley widens, and there is a single house and some fields at Chante Chaur (2940m). The climb continues to **Bhulbule**, the Rara Lake National Park entrance station at 3130m. Show your entry ticket or pay Rs 650, and then have a cup of tea at a bhatti five minutes beyond the entrance station. Above Bhulbule the trail emerges into an immense treeless meadow, and climbs gently but steadily to an assortment of *chortens*, cairns and prayer flags atop the Ghurchi Lagna, a 3450m pass. From the pass there are views of the Mugu Karnali river and snow peaks bordering Tibet.

The trail follows the trade route to Mugu through the Mandu Khola valley. From the pass the route descends gently on a broad path to a hut, then drops precipitously down a rough trail through spruce forests. The trail levels out at around 2900m elevation, 45 minutes below the pass. Watch for a trail junction. It may still be marked with a wooden post with 'Rara' painted in red. The inconspicuous trail to the left (west) is the direct route to Rara Lake. The broad trail that goes straight on is the trade route that leads to Pina (2400m), and then on to Mugu. Follow the direct trail to Rara Lake which stays more or less level through pine forests, then descends to the Jhyari Khola at 2400m. Another stretch of easy walking leads to the small settlement of **Dhotu**, an army camp and helipad. Stay level and left; do not descend and cross the river.

Day 4: Dhotu to Rara Lake

Cross a stream and make a steep climb to the squalid Thakuri village of **Jhyari** at 2630m, in a picturesque grove of giant cedars. Continue climbing through cedar forests to a huge meadow atop a 3050m ridge with a great view of **Rara Lake**. Don't follow any of the trails that lead along the top of the ridge; descend a short distance to the lake. There are no camping spots along the southern shore. The national park headquarters and camping ground are on the northern side of the lake. It will take two hours or more to walk around the lake to the camping ground. The ban on the use of firewood is strictly enforced, so your trek crew will cook on kerosene stoves.

Day 5: Rara Lake

Rara Lake (3062m) is the largest lake in Nepal. It is almost 13 km around the lake, and a day devoted to making this circuit is well spent. Designated a national park in 1975, the region offers a remoteness and wilderness experience unlike any other in Nepal. There are a few park wardens' houses, and the remnants of the now deserted villages of Rara and Chapra on the northern side of the lake, but otherwise it is an isolated

region where birds, flowers and wildlife thrive. Among the mammals in the region are Himalayan bear, Himalayan tahr, serow, goral, musk deer, red panda and both rhesus and langur monkeys. The 170m-deep lake has otters and fish and is an important resting place for migrating water fowl.

Day 6: Rara Lake to Gorosingha

Although you can return to Jumla via the same route, it is more rewarding to make a circuit via a different trail. From the bridge at the western end of Rara Lake the trail follows the Khatyar Khola (called the Nisa Khola in its upper reaches) to a small hotel in **Majhghatta**, about 15 minutes from the bridge. A trail ascends from here to Murma, but you do not have to go through Murma on the way back to Jumla. Take a lower trail that descends gradually to the river, cross the river on a log bridge, and then cross another stream beside a decrepit mill that grinds away merrily. A small trail leads straight up the hill, climbing first through an area reforested with pine, then through spruce and rhododendron forests.

The ascent gets less steep through forests of pine and birch, then across meadows to a ridge at 3660m. There are views of Rara Lake far below as the trail skirts the head of a huge valley to the crest of the Ghurchi Mara at 3710m. If the weather is clear, there is an excellent view of the western Himalaya from the top of this ridge.

There are two choices of route from here to Sinja, the long route and the short, steep route. Both will allow you to reach Sinja in one more day, as described in Day 7 below.

To go by the longer route, follow the main trail as it drops into the Ghatta Khola valley, then heads towards **Gorosingha**. The local people call Gorosingha 'the poster', referring to the army post there. From above, the army 'poster' looks like a classic Hollywood western ranch in a beautiful grassy vale. There are several excellent camping places along the Ghatta Khola, both above and below Gorosingha.

To go the shorter, steeper way to Sinja, watch for an inconspicuous trail junction at

3000m, about an hour below the crest of the Ghurchi Mara and just before the main trail reaches the Ghatta Khola. Don't descend into the valley towards Gorosingha. Stay high on the side of the treeless Ghatta Khola valley and follow the trail until it descends to a small camping place by a stream.

Day 7: Gorosingha to Sinja

The Long Way This route heads down the Ghatta Khola valley from Gorosingha, then follows the Sinja Khola downstream to Sinja. After working your way down the Ghatta Khola past Botan you will meet the Sinja Khola. It is then a short walk down the fertile valley, on a newly renovated trail, through a heavily populated region to Sinja itself.

The Short (Steep) Way From the stream, the trail climbs a big gully to a ridge at 3450m. It's easy to get lost between here and Sinja, so you'll be much better off with a local guide if you can find one. From the ridge, follow the left trail and stay as high as possible on the ridge, looping in and out of side valleys and descending gradually to **Okarpata** at 3070m. This is a big village of whitewashed, flat-roofed houses, with huge fields of wheat and barley and extensive apple orchards. The trail descends to a stream and then goes steeply down the ridge on a rough, rocky trail to the Brahman and Chhetri village of **Sinja**, on the banks of the Sinja Khola at 2440m.

From the 12th to the 14th century, western Nepal was ruled by a Malla dynasty that was different from the that of the Malla rulers in Kathmandu. Sinja was the capital of the western Malla kingdom. The ruins of the palace can be seen across the river. The large temple at the top of a promontory is the Bhagwati Than, a temple dedicated to Bhagwati, the goddess of justice who rides atop a tiger. The big buildings across the river from the village are government offices and a school.

Day 8: Sinja to Jaljala Chaur

It is very difficult to reach Jumla in a single day from Sinja, so it's best to break the trek with a night in the high meadows near the ridge. From Sinja, the trail crosses the Sinja Khola on a wooden cantilever bridge, then begins a long trip up the Jaljala Khola. After passing a few small villages and the trail to the temple, the trail crosses back and forth across the river on a series of quaint log bridges. Most of the trek is through forests of pine, birch and oak, though there are a few scattered houses and fields of barley and corn. From Chala Chaur, a meadow with a few herders' huts at 2900m, the trail makes a steep climb to Jaljala Chaur, a gigantic meadow full of horses at 3270m.

Day 9: Jaljala Chaur to Jumla

Keep climbing through forests to yet another meadow, just below the ridge at 3510m, then descend to a few houses at Chor Khola (3090m). Cross a stream and contour around the head of the valley, staying high, eventually crossing another ridge to rejoin the upward 'high trail' at **Chere** (3010m). The final descent to Jumla is the reverse of Day 1, through Sisnamul, past the school at Ghumurti, then from Campus village to **Jumla**.

Jumla to Dolpo

Duration 6 to 12 days	
Difficulty Medium	
Maximum elevation 3820m	
Permit cost US$10 per week	
Season March to October	
Hotels Minimal	
Summary Walk through Nepal's 'wild west' with its strange mixture of ethnic groups. No high Himalayan peaks, but lots of good high-altitude scenery.	

Dolpo is a remote region, most of which is now protected by Shey Phoksumdo National Park. It is bounded in the east and south by the Dhaulagiri and Churen Himal ranges and in the west by the Jumla district. The district headquarters is in Dunai, in the south of the region. Dolpo has been bypassed by development and, until recently, by tourism. Although a few anthropologists and geographers had explored the region, the entire district was closed to trekkers until 1989 when the southern part of Dolpo was opened to organised trekking groups. In 1990, individual trekkers were allowed into the region if they obtained a special trekking permit (US$10 per week) and did a bit of a bureaucratic run-around.

There are no teahouses along the route to Dolpo. I met a couple of trekkers who had trekked here on their own and bought food in villages, but they'd had a rough time. You would be far better off in Dolpo with a fully equipped trek.

You can reach Dolpo from Jumla (six days), Dhorpatan (10 to 12 days), Surkhet (nine days), Salyan (five days) and Jomsom (11 days, but subject to a US$700 permit fee). The Dolpo airport in Juphal is half a day from the district headquarters in Dunai.

Isolated from the rest of Nepal by high passes to the south, Dolpo is also known as Ba-Yul, or the Hidden Land. Peter Matthiessen's *The Snow Leopard* and Snellgrove's *Himalayan Pilgrimage* have contributed to the mystique and attraction of Dolpo. Both writers visited Shey gompa to the north of Phoksumdo Lake. See the separate section on Shey in the Restricted Areas chapter.

There are Tibetan-style 'Inner Dolpo' villages in Tarap and at Phoksumdo Lake. Much of Dolpo remains culturally and religiously linked with Tibet and the people continue to trade with Tibet on the ancient 'grain for salt' trade routes, but the southern part of Dolpo is a region of Hindu influence.

The following sections describe the trek from Jumla to Dunai, side trips to Phoksumdo Lake and Tarap, and an alternative high route over the Kagmara La to the Dolpo district. There's also a full description of a trek from Baglung, near Pokhara, to Dolpo. All these trips could be combined into one long trek of 25 to 30 days, from Baglung to Jumla via Dolpo.

Accommodation & Supplies
The facilities on this route are very sparse. There are a few shops and teahouses, but nothing that resembles a trekkers' lodge, between Jumla and Dunai. You would do well to bring a tent for your porters so that they don't have to hunt for accommodation in Thakuri homes where they may not be welcome.

Access
It's best to fly into Jumla and then spend the rest of the day hiring porters, buying last-minute provisions and sorting loads. If you fly into Jumla and start walking the same day, you will probably have to alter the stopping places I have suggested, because it takes a full day to reach Gothi Chaur.

See the Jumla to Rara Lake section for information about flights to Jumla.

JUMLA TO DUNAI
Day 1: Jumla to Gothi Chaur
From Jumla (2370m) the trail leads past the airport to the eastern end of the runway, past several water-driven mills, then drops to the confluence of the Tila Khola and the Chaudhabise Khola (also known locally as the Juwa Nadi) at 2330m. Cross both rivers on cantilever bridges that look like they are held together by giant clothes pegs. A major logging operation is taking place on the upper reaches of the Chaudhabise. Loggers upstream dump logs into the river. They float down to this point where they are snared and cut into timbers for use in Jumla and neighbouring villages. Unlike most rivers in Nepal, which are filled with silt, the Tila and the Chaudhabise are clear because they are not glacier fed.

The trail climbs gently in a fertile valley of rice terraces along the southern side of the Tila to Depal Gaon. It crisscrosses irrigation canals to Jharjwala, then leaves the Tila Khola and climbs a ridge to the small villages of Bhajkati, Dugri Lagnu and finally **Dochal Ghara** at 2530m. Do not follow the steep trail that leads uphill here. Instead, take the lower trail that follows a stream through a forest of maple and walnut to a meadow at

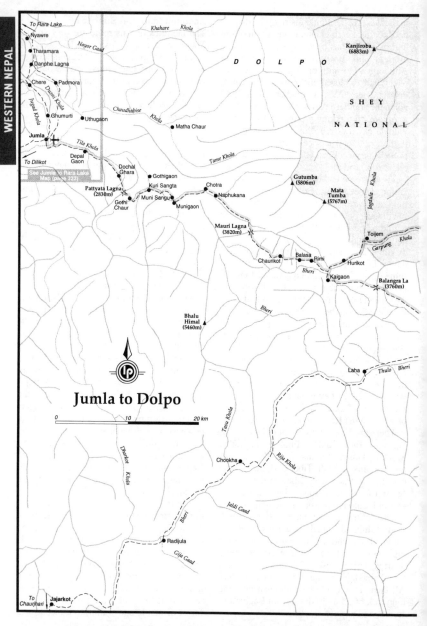

Jumla to Dolpo

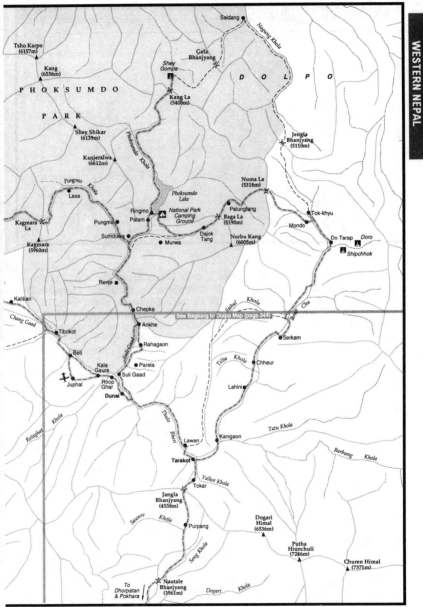

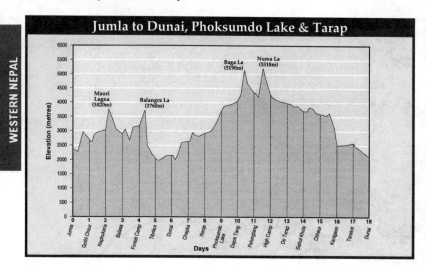

Jumla to Dunai, Phoksumdo Lake & Tarap

2830m. In season the wild flowers include cinquefoils, louseworts, scrophs, terrestrial orchids, forget-me-nots, geraniums, asters, mints, buttercups, impatiens, edelweiss, primulas and gentians.

Beyond the meadow the trail climbs to a rock cairn at Pattyata Lagna pass (2830m), then descends into a magnificent alpine amphitheatre. Hidden behind a ridge is a huge government sheep-breeding research project, but there are no villages in this isolated valley. The trail descends past the project buildings at **Gothi Chaur**, to a stream at the bottom of the valley. There are some 13th century Malla dynasty stone carvings at the spring here.

Day 2: Gothi Chaur to Naphukana

There is another trail junction at Gothi Chaur. Do not take the trail that leads uphill out of the Gothi Chaur valley. Instead, walk downstream through forests to a series of mills at **Kuri Sangta**. There is a good camp site a short distance beyond where the Kuri Sangta Khola joins the Tila Khola.

The route has now re-entered the Tila valley and over the next day you will follow the river to its source. Here the Tila is known

as the Bapila Khola. The largish villages of Gothigaon and Khudigaon are visible high on the opposite side of the river. The trail crosses to the northern side of the Tila and passes corn and potato fields, then climbs through fields of buckwheat and barley and attractive meadows full of grazing horses and cows.

The river forks at Munigaon, a village with a complex mixture of Chhetri, Thakali and Tibetan inhabitants. There are several houses and a rudimentary hotel at the trail junction, **Muni Sangu**. Look both above and behind the houses for some peculiar carved wooden faces. You will see these effigies throughout Dolpo. They are called *dok-pa* and are supposed to offer protection from evil. The cops at the Muni Sangu police checkpost will probably want to see your trekking permit.

The route follows the left fork of the Tila Khola which has again changed its name and is now the Churta Khola. The valley narrows and enters a forest of oaks, spruce, poplars and maples. The trail stays on the southern side of the river, so don't cross any of the several bridges that you pass. A short distance beyond Changrikot (a series of four

Dolpo – Flora & Fauna

Mammals The **blue sheep** is not, strictly speaking, a true sheep, nor is the **Himalayan tahr** a mountain goat. The tahr is considered a primitive member of the goat/antelope family, while the blue sheep is lost, in an evolutionary sense, somewhere between sheep and goats. Both of these ungulates can be found in the same locale, generally high above the tree line. The tahr, though, prefers habitats in the vicinity of precipitous cliffs, while the blue sheep likes scree slopes and plateaus of high desert. The blue sheep has horns like a sheep, except that they are not as long, curved or swept back. This beast is referred to as 'blue' due to the slaty blue and grey colour of its winter coat. Look for these animals in the rain shadow areas of not only Dolpo, where they are common, but also Manang and Mustang. The tahr, though known to the Dolpo area, is more readily seen in Khumbu and the Annapurna Sanctuary.

The **jackal**, found up to 3700m, is another carnivore that you may come across, or at least hear. This member of the dog family, often a timid scavenger, has a sustained, macabre howl that is heard after dark. The **wolf**, a larger canine than the jackal, has a thick coat and bushy tail and is known to roam up to 6000m. Its movements generally follow those of wandering game and grazing herds, but it will also prey on domestic livestock, particularly from the high summer settlements.

The **spotted leopard** is found up to the tree line and the **snow leopard** is usually found beyond, more often in the trans-Himalayan areas. Deforestation has severely encroached on the habitat of both the spotted leopard and its prey species. This, compounded by its secretive habits, makes the likelihood of seeing a spotted leopard quite remote. If you happen to come across one of these cats, it's difficult to say whether human or beast will be the more surprised.

The snow leopard, which has distinctly

Blue sheep

Himalayan tahr

Snow leopard

paler coloration than the spotted leopard, is often placed in another genus due to its different skull shape, broad paws and long, thick tail. It competes for virtually the same space as the wolf and consequently, when the two encounter each other, one is usually displaced. As wolves have a tendency to be more sociable and to hunt in packs, they will outnumber the cat, which generally must depart. Your chance of sighting a snow leopard is better in sparsely populated Dolpo and other remote areas of western Nepal. Realistically, though, you are about as likely to see a snow leopard as you are to catch a glimpse of a yeti. ■

houses built into the hillside on the opposite side of the river at an elevation of 2900m) the trail finally crosses the river and climbs

to the grey stone houses of **Chotra** at 3010m. The inhabitants of Chotra are Khampas, people from eastern Tibet who are Buddhists by tradition. The village has the typical Tibetan *mani* walls and a *kani* arching over the trail. Despite their background, these villagers long ago adopted Hindu names, dress and traditions in an effort to integrate themselves into mainstream Nepali society. Anthropologists categorise these people as Matwali Chhetris and trace their heritage to Kumaon in India. Their religious practices have very little to do with Hinduism. Their rites are conducted by shamans known as *dhamis* or *jhankris* and their major deity is the god Mastha. There are shrines to Mastha in Tibrikot and Rahagaon.

A short distance beyond is the Tibetan settlement of **Naphukana** at 3080m. The large *gompa* above the village is Urgen Sanga Chorling, where Tulku Tsewang Dorji Lama was recently installed as *rimpoche* (reincarnate lama). The villagers of Naphukana keep large herds of yaks and horses. There are camp sites near the village, but better camping places are an hour further on, in a meadow at 3200m.

Day 3: Naphukana to Balasa

The trail becomes steeper as it climbs past the rocky fields of Rapati Chaur to forests of oak and birch trees tangled with Spanish moss. After crossing a side stream, the trail crosses the Churta/Bapila/Tila Khola and starts a serious climb through birch, oak and rhododendron forests to **Mauri Lagna** ('honey pass') at 3820m. When trekking in spring, the final approach to the pass is through meadows alive with blue lilies and stands of blooming azaleas and rhododendrons. In winter the trail is hidden under deep snow. From the pass there are views of the snow peaks of Gutumba (5608m) and Mata Tumba (5767m) to the north-east and Bhalu Himal (5460m) to the south.

From the pass the trail descends a bit, then makes a long traverse across a potentially dangerous area. A Tibetan porter told me a tale of 20 yaks tumbling down this slope in an avalanche a few winters ago. At the end of the traverse, marked by cairns of stones, the trail starts a steep descent into a forest of pines and oaks, passing a few herders' huts

before reaching a stream at 3110m. Staying in forests, the trail makes a few ups and downs, then climbs again to a ridge at 3140m. The trail turns into the Bheri valley, keeping high on the side of the ridge, making short excursions in and out of side valleys past scattered houses and fields of corn and potatoes en route to **Chaurikot** at 3060m. There is no possible camp and no hotel – or even a shop – in this large Khampa village, but the children are already trained in the ritual of asking for pens.

From Chaurikot the trail drops to a stream at 2940m then climbs right back up again to an inviting-looking notch on the ridge at 3080m. This would be an excellent camp except that there is no water. About 30 minutes beyond the ridge is **Balasa**. There are several possible camp sites alongside the trail, and others further on in the fields of Jyakot or Rimi. You can see Kagmara Peak on the horizon and Balangra La, the next obstacle on the route to Dolpo.

Day 4: Balasa to Forest Camp

The trail descends to a stream, then climbs to the ridge in a forest of walnut trees. Walnuts will be constant companions throughout the rest of the trek to Dolpo. Although the local people occasionally eat them, their primary value is as a source of cooking oil. The trail contours past the corn and potato fields and apple orchards of Jyakot then descends to **Rimi** at 2890m, where the amusing faces of more dok-pa peek from the tops of houses. The trail

Mixed Ancestry

I met a man in Chaurikot who was 67 years old and insisted that his grandfather's grandfather settled here from Kham in eastern Tibet. He had the unlikely name of Pemba (a Tibetan first name) Budhathoki (a pure Hindu surname) and, like many men in this part of Nepal, wore an Afghan-style turban. Many Matwali Chhetris, like Pemba, are of Tibetan ancestry and have names and traditions that encompass both Hindu and Tibetan traditions. ∎

Flexible Feasts

The shopkeeper in Kaigaon told me a peculiar story about religious practices in Kaigaon, Chaurikot and Hurikot. The Hindu Chhetri people in these villages practise Tibetan Buddhism, hence the prayer flags that festoon the houses. The complication is that they also celebrate Hindu festivals, including Dasain, during which each house sacrifices an animal. It's all very complex and strange, especially when combined with Pemba Budhathoki's tale of the Chaurikot Khampa heritage. ■

---

descends, steeply in places, through walnut groves to the closely spaced stone houses of **Majagaon**, then down a rocky trail to the Bheri River. A police checkpost and a large school and hostel complex dominate the bank of the Bheri at 2610m.

Just across the bridge is **Kaigaon**, which boasts a veterinary station for cattle, a bhatti and the first real shop since Jumla. Stock up on the items for sale here – biscuits and cigarettes and, if you are lucky, beer.

Kaigaon is the departure point for a crossing of the Kagmara La. See the description of this crossing later in this chapter.

From Kaigaon the route climbs through pastures, then into a forest of birch and wild rose. Near the top of the ridge the climb rates the maximum scale for steepness. There are no stone steps, so you must either walk sideways in a crab-like fashion or walk uphill on your toes. It's so steep that your heel cannot reach the ground unless you are double jointed. The trail crests at an elevation of 3230m, then levels out in a forest of rhododendron and oaks, the home of a band of black langur monkeys. A trail heads south from the pass and this is a route to Jajarkot and Chaurjhari. The Dolpo trail continues east, and descends gently along the side of a large valley to a few small camp sites in forests of pine draped with Spanish moss.

Day 5: Forest Camp to Tibrikot

The trail makes many ups and downs as it contours out onto a ridge. Soon the downs become shorter and the ups longer, ending in a long climb to a false summit at 3660m. There is yet another false summit before the **Balangra La** itself, marked with cairns and prayer flags at 3760m. If it's clear, you'll see Dhaulagiri Himal to the east. You will also probably see herds of yaks grazing high on the grassy slopes above the pass.

There are two trails off the pass. The old trail heads straight down into forests while a new trail contours around the ridge to the left. Both end at a government yak farm in a forest at 3160m. One trekker commented on the profusion of health facilities for animals along this trek, in contrast with the total lack of health care for people. Keep this in mind as you put together your medical supplies for a Dolpo trip.

From the yak farm, the trail heads out onto a ridge high above the Chang Gaad. There are a few camp sites along the route and there's even a bhatti at Ghora Khola. Stay on the upper trail and beware of any steep drop towards the river. Beyond Bungtari, cross a stream and climb to **Kaliban**. Drop to a stream in a large side valley, then climb again to Dagin at 2930m. After passing Para and a few other small villages, the route reaches a treeless, waterless, uninhabited ridge, then makes a miserable 500m descent on a clutter of loose rocks to a stream just below **Tibrikot** at 2100m. You can make a good camp by the stream.

Day 6: Tibrikot to Dunai

From the stream, the trail climbs slightly to Tibrikot, a picturesque village on a promontory overlooking the Thulo Bheri ('big Bheri') valley. This is an old fortress town and the police checkpost commands a view up and down the river. The houses have carved wooden windows and a large shrine and temple is dedicated to the goddess Tripura Sundari Devi. From the shrine, the trail descends past extensive rice terraces to a long suspension bridge at 2050m.

For the rest of the day, you will follow the large, fast-flowing, dark grey Thulo Bheri, through arid country on the new trail that follows the Bheri all the way from Chaurjhari. Because of heavy silting, water from the Thulo Bheri is unfit to drink, so settlements in the valley occur only where there is a side stream. Passing the tiny settlement of Su Pani, the route passes over a low ridge and drops to Beti, several houses beside a small stream.

The trail to Dolpo airport, above Juphal village, starts at Beti; see the following section for details. If you want to confirm a flight, take the upper route that climbs 450m to the airport and rejoins the river trail at Kala Gaura. The lower trail passes far below the airport. The stream leading from Juphal village creates a green oasis atmosphere in contrast to the barrenness of the valley. After more desolate country you will reach a few tea shops at Kala Gaura where the airport trail rejoins the route. The trail climbs a little over two ridges, then drops to a large side stream and three small bhattis at **Roop Ghar**. This is an excellent place to camp if you want to avoid staying in Dunai village. You can see the start of the trail to Phoksumdo Lake high on the opposite river bank.

From Roop Ghar the trail remains level, passing the national park and army offices that are on the opposite side of the river at the confluence of the Suli Gaad and the Thulo Bheri. A few twists and turns of the trail lead to a view of **Dunai** and a large new hospital complex across the river. The trail enters the village through a fancy gate near the health post, then passes through the old bazaar along a stone pavement. There are a few teahouses and shops in this part of the town, but these cater mostly to porters and traders. The larger facilities are at the eastern end of the village, past government offices, the police post and a statue of King Mahendra.

At the eastern end of the village is the *Rigmo Restaurant* and the comfortable and friendly *Blue Sheep Trekkers Inn*, which has private bedrooms and a separate restaurant facility. The large complex with turrets across the river is the district jail. From Dunai you can trek to Phoksumdo Lake (see the description of this route later in this chapter). From the lake you either return to Dunai, continue on to Shey gompa (see the

Restricted Areas chapter) or make a high altitude circuit via Tarap.

Dunai has a single telephone; connected in 1996, it was the last district headquarters in Nepal to receive the telephone service. Despite its remoteness, it is a progressive village. The Dunai boarding school is providing an excellent education to local kids. The school has established an environmental education programme called DESERT (Dolpo Educational, Social & Environmental Reservation Team).

DUNAI TO JUPHAL (DOLPO AIRPORT)

Dolpo flights always arrive and depart early in the morning. This is because high winds in the Thulo Bheri valley begin around 10 am, making later flights impossible. It takes at least three hours to walk from Dunai to the airport in Juphal village, so the only reasonable solution is to spend a night at the airport.

To get to the airport, follow the south bank of the Bheri past the Suli Gaad confluence and on to Roop Ghar, a tea shop and camp site at 2050m on the banks of a side stream. Continue along the river bank to some tea shops at **Kala Gaura** (2030m). Take the trail that leads uphill and climb steeply through meadows to the houses of Dangi Banda. Stay high and climb less steeply around the head of the valley towards Juphal. As the village comes into view take the left-hand trail to traverse above the village and climb to the large school. There is a maze of trails, but keep heading up and eventually you will emerge at **Juphal**, a collection of houses, offices and crummy hotels adjoining the airport at 2490m. There are some basic shops in a complex of flat-roofed, mud buildings beside the airport. The *Mt Puthajup Hotel* has funky accommodation and camping; you may be able to camp on the rooftops of teahouses or shops.

You should reconfirm your seats in person with the airline the day before the flight. The best way to find the airline station manager is to ask the police near the control tower.

Take a walk down the runway, one of the most unusual airports in Nepal. With a length of 490m, the runway is the minimum length required for Twin Otter landings at this elevation. To make matters even more frightening, the runway is on a slope and has a depression in the middle, which makes a takeoff reminiscent of a roller-coaster ride. Also, there is a huge rock just at the end. Fares are high at US$77 (US$120 by helicopter) for a 35 minute flight to Nepalgunj. Weight limits are strictly enforced on planes and excess baggage is expensive. The RNAC staff have been known to enforce a 10 kg free baggage allowance and leave extra baggage behind, but the chopper operators are more liberal. A helicopter may be a more practical option if you have lots of luggage. There is a lot of cargo traffic in and out of Dolpo. If you were a crate of apples you could fly at a subsidised rate of Rs 1.50 per kg.

Across the Kagmara La

Duration 4 days
Difficulty Medium to hard
Maximum elevation 5115m
Permit cost US$10 per week plus Rs 650
Season March to October
Hotels None
Summary A high pass crossing offers a variation on the route from Jumla to Dolpo and a short cut to Phoksumdo Lake.

A high route to Dolpo leads across the 5115m Kagmara La. It is not a difficult crossing, but you may have trouble finding porters willing to make the trip. The pass is snowbound, and potentially dangerous or impassable, from November to early May. A reasonable crossing takes four days from Kaigaon to Sumduwa. Kagmara translates as 'crow killer'; the high pass on the eastern edge of Dolpo is Cheelmara, 'eagle killer'.

Day 1: Kaigaon to Toijem
From the school at Kaigaon (see Day 4 of the Jumla to Dolpo trek), stay on the west bank of the Bheri, passing Hurikot, to a sign proclaiming the entrance to Shey Phoksumdo

National Park. The trail stays high above the river to the confluence where the Jagdula and Garpung rivers join to form the Bheri. Drop to the Jagdula Khola, crossing it on stones, and camp near the army post at Toijem (2920m).

Day 2: Toijem to Kagmara Phedi
Follow the trail up the western side of the Garpung Khola to about 3650m, then cross to the eastern side and continue upstream. The valley narrows and the river becomes a series of waterfalls as the trail climbs to a moraine at 3900m. Make a high camp in boulders at an elevation of about 4000m. The panoramic views of the peaks are sensational. Wild flowers are of the more hardy alpine species, including blue poppy, buttercup, mint, gentian and puffball. Among the birds you may sight are snow pigeons, redstarts, ravens and griffons. This is also an excellent place to sight blue sheep.

Day 3: Kagmara Phedi to Lasa
Start early and climb alongside the Kagmara Glacier to the Kagmara La at 5115m, then descend about 900m alongside a stream to a camp on pastures in the Pungmo Khola valley. On this side of the pass there are sweeping scree slopes and massive rock formations in stacked layers which contrast with the vertical uplifts and thrusts of the southern side. Descend to a shepherd's camp called Lasa.

Day 4: Lasa to Sumduwa
The trail stays high above the stream, which eventually becomes the Pungmo Khola (incorrectly named the Dorjam Khola on the Survey of India maps). The route enters birch and juniper forests which give way to blue pine as the trail crosses the river on a wooden bridge. There are views up side valleys of Kanjeralwa (6612m) in the stretch before the barley fields of **Pungmo**, a fortress-like village. Continue downstream to the national park headquarters at Sumduwa.

The following day, follow the trail up the Phoksumdo Khola to Phoksumdo Lake.

Dunai to Phoksumdo Lake

Duration 6 days
Difficulty Medium
Maximum elevation 3660m
Permit cost US$10 per week plus Rs 650
Season May to October
Hotels Only two
Summary New trail provides easy access to Nepal's highest waterfall and the dramatically clear waters of Phoksumdo Lake.

The trek to Phoksumdo Lake has been made much more practical since the construction of a new trail up the Suli Gaad from its confluence with the Thulo Bheri. There are not a lot of camping places, and there are lodges only in Chepka and Ringmo, but the trek has some lovely forest walks, Phoksumdo Lake is dramatic, and the region contains a tiny pocket of the unusual Bon-po culture.

The lake is within Shey Phoksumdo National Park, which was established in 1981. The national park literature uses the spelling Phoksumdo, but local informants believe that the correct transliteration is *Phok, sum* (three), *do* (stones), relating to the three arms of the lake. The park is said to abound in wildlife, though the most spectacular inhabitants – snow leopards and herds of blue sheep – are found primarily in the restricted regions of the park near Shey gompa. The lake and trail are snowbound from mid-November to mid-May. Almost all the inhabitants of Ringmo village move to lower elevations at this time.

See page 330 for a profile of this trek.

Fuel

National park restrictions prohibit the use of firewood, so you must carry kerosene in addition to food. This requires some advance planning because there is no reliable kerosene supply in Jumla, though there is often kerosene in Dunai.

Access

There are numerous ways to get to Dunai on foot or by air. You can walk from Jumla (see the description of the trek from Jumla to Dunai) or fly to Juphal and walk down to Dunai. See the Jumla to Dunai description for information about Dunai village.

Day 1: Dunai to Chepka

From the King Mahendra statue in Dunai, cross the big steel suspension bridge and turn west, following the trail past the hospital, then it's a level walk along the bank of the Thulo Bheri to its confluence with the Suli Gaad at 2070m. There is a large army post on the opposite side of the Suli Gaad. Follow the new trail north up the west bank of the Suli Gaad to a collection of tea shops run by wives of army personnel. Another hour of walking takes you to Kala Rupi and then on to **Raktang** at 2260m, where there is an excellent camp site just south of the bridge over the Suli Gaad.

Cross to the west bank and trek past numerous *goths* and horse pastures to the small village of Celas, a wintering spot for the people of Ringmo. Keep walking upstream to another bridge, cross it, and make your way past some crude tea shops at Sankta to a bridge over a side stream, the Ankhe Khola, at 2460m. The trail climbs through grass and ferns to a trail junction. Take the left fork; the right fork is the old trail that leads to the army and national park post at Ankhe, and on to the old trail that passes the villages of Rahagaon and Parela, high on the ridge above. These three villages have a strange name connection: Parela (*parela* means eyelash), Rahagaon (*raha* means eyebrow) and Ankhe (*ankha* is eye). This region produces a lotus-like plant called *chuk* that is used to make vinegar and medicines. It is dried and flown from Dolpo to Nepalgunj and exported to India.

The Phoksumdo Lake trail climbs over a ridge at 2710m, then descends to **Chepka**, at 2670m, which is inhabited by three brothers and consists of a collection of interconnected shops, *rakshi* stalls and lodges. The *Karma Fancy & Kirana Stores* offers beer, Coke,

RICHARD l'ANSON

STAN ARMINGTON

STAN ARMINGTON

Eastern Nepal
Top: Trekkers' camp at Pang Pema, on the northern side of Kanchenjunga
Bottom Left: A house in the Arun Kosi valley
Bottom Right: Rai boy carrying water in traditional bamboo containers

Western Nepal

Top: Chorten at Ringmo village, beside Phoksumdo Lake.
Middle: The deep turquoise waters of Phoksumdo Lake contain no aquatic life.
Bottom: Danphe Lagna, en route to Rara Lake.

Fanta, noodles, batteries and other items brought on cargo helicopters to Juphal. You can find another good camp site beside a huge rock in a walnut grove about 20 minutes beyond Chepka.

Day 2: Chepka to Renje

The new trail should be completed, so you should be able to stay near the river, crossing to the west side to avoid a large ridge, then returning to the east side. If the new trail is in disrepair, you may have to follow the old route, which makes several ups and downs on a dusty trail, then climbs in a forest of big cedars to Shirak, a tea shop in a tent at 3010m. The old route then traverses a grassy slope in and out of side valleys, continues through birches to a ridge at 2940m, then descends steeply through a fir forest to the riverbank where it rejoins the new trail.

Alongside the river at 2900m, the trail becomes a collection of rocks and sticks that form a dyke along the river bank. If the water is high and covers the trail, this can be a treacherous, or impossible, place to traverse. The trail makes several more ups and downs as it continues upstream to a bridge that leads to nine houses comprising the village of **Renje** on the opposite side of the river at 3010m. There is a good camp here and another is about five minutes further on.

Day 3: Renje to Phoksumdo Lake

The Suli Gaad valley turns eastwards and becomes even steeper and narrower. The trail continues its ups and downs along the valley floor to the confluence of the Suli Gaad with the Pungmo Khola. North of this point the Suli Gaad is known as the Phoksumdo Khola and is spectacularly clear. You can cross to the western side of the Phoksumdo Khola on a wooden bridge and climb to the park headquarters at Sumduwa or take a lower trail that heads upstream. This is a major trail junction. The route to Kagmara La leads up the Pungmo Khola; the trail to Tarap leads up the east bank of the Phoksumdo Khola; and the trail to Phoksumdo Lake and Shey gompa follows the west bank of the river. The

village name reflects this. In Tibetan, *sum* means 'three' and *duwa* is 'trail'.

Follow the trail up the western side of the river through forests to another bridge. Stay on the western side. There is a trail up the eastern side of the river, but it goes to Murwa and eventually to Tarap, not to Phoksumdo Lake. The Phoksumdo trail climbs though a forest of big cedars to a good camp site and then on to **Palam** (3340m), a winter settlement used by the people of Ringmo village. The houses are almost buried in the sandy soil. The entrance station for Shey Phoksumdo National Park is at the south end of the village. After your park entrance ticket is examined, you may be subjected to a baggage inspection – ostensibly for drugs and stolen art objects. It's a very peculiar formality in this remote locale.

The route switchbacks steeply on a sandy trail through open country to an elevation of 3480m, then starts up a steep set of switchbacks to a ridge at 3760m. From the ridge there are distant views of Phoksumdo Lake and a close view of a spectacular 330m-high waterfall, the highest in Nepal. This is the source of the river that you have been following for several days. The trail makes a steep descent in birch forests to the upper reaches of the brilliantly clear, rushing waters of the Phoksumdo Khola, then climbs gently to **Ringmo** village, a picturesque settlement with lots of mud-plastered chortens and mani walls. Ringmo has a few shops selling basic supplies at high prices that reflect the remoteness of the village. You can usually find locally made blankets and yak hair belts for sale and there are a few private gompas and some interesting chortens along the narrow lanes. There are a few houses that advertise themselves as lodges. They can supply a basic meal, but you'll have to pitch your tent on their roof; no other accommodation is available.

Just below Ringmo, cross a bridge and follow a trail north to the ranger station at **Phoksumdo Lake**. Continue to the shores of the lake near the point where the Phoksumdo Khola flows out of the lake. The national park's camping ground is south-east of the lake. Park rules prohibit camping in other places, except perhaps on rooftops in Ringmo.

A trail along the lake's western side leads to Shey gompa. However, access to this route is restricted to those with a special US$700 permit, so you may not be allowed to go beyond the first wooden bridge on this trail. The large snow peak above the ridge on the western side of the lake is Kanjeralwa (6612m), also known as Kanchen Ruwa.

The lake is spectacular. It is 4.8 km long, 1.8 km wide and is said to be 650m deep. It is known for its aquamarine colour – a greenish blue similar to a special Tibetan turquoise. There is no aquatic life in the lake, which helps to make the waters brilliantly clear. If you toss a rock in, you can watch it for a long time as it sinks to the bottom. According to legend, Phoksumdo Lake was formed by a spiteful female demon. In *Buddhist Himalaya* David Snellgrove recounts how the demon was fleeing from the saint Padmasambhava and gave the village people a turquoise after they promised not to tell that she had passed by. Padmasambhava turned the turquoise into a lump of dung, which upset the local people so much that they revealed the demon's whereabouts. She, in return, caused the flood. It is said that you can see the remains of a village below the surface of the lake.

This is Bon-po country, where people practise a shamanistic religion that predates Tibetan Buddhism. Much of Bon-po symbolism is the opposite of Buddhist practice. You should walk to the right of the ancient mud chortens which are inscribed with swastikas that have their arms pointing in the opposite direction to the Buddhist version. Instead of the Buddhist chant of *'om mani padme hum'*, the Bon-pos chant *'om ma tri mu ye sa le du'*, which Snellgrove found untranslatable except that *sa le du* in Tibetan means 'in clarity unite'.

A trail leads from the lakeside through juniper trees to the white Pal Sentan Thasoon Chholing gompa, an ancient ramshackle gompa that overlooks the lake. This is a Bon-po gompa said to have been built 60

generations ago. There are five other private gompas in various houses of the small monastic community near the lake. The insides of the temples contain dusty Buddhist paintings and statues, but the trappings also reflect the animistic elements of the Bon-po religion, so some of the chapels are reminiscent of an ancient witch's cavern. A donation to the ragtag collection of dirty monks will gain you entrance to the gompas; if you're travelling with sherpas they will be as fascinated as you by the strange iconography and practices of the Bon-po religion.

From Phoksumdo Lake you can make a loop via Baga La and Numa La to Tarap, following the Tarap route description backwards.

Dunai to Tarap

Duration 10 to 14 days
Difficulty Medium to hard
Maximum elevation 5318m
Permit cost US$10 per week
Season May to October
Hotels None
Summary A long walk up a steep, uninhabited river valley leads to a high, isolated valley that is an enclave of Tibetan tradition. Continue from Tarap to Phoksumdo Lake by crossing two high passes and traversing remote country that is the home of snow leopards.

Tarap is a remote valley of pure Tibetan influence east of Phoksumdo Lake and south of Shey gompa. You can visit Tarap by making a loop from Dunai up the Thulo Bheri to the Tarap Chu, across two high passes to Phoksumdo Lake and back to Dunai. You can also make the trek in the reverse direction, starting from Dunai or even from Jumla.

Access
You can start from Dunai, or you can follow the Pokhara to Dolpo route and join the Tarap route at the Yalkot Khola bridge, just below Tarakot.

To get to Tarap it's best to take the river route along the Tarap Chu. This trail was rebuilt between 1992 and 1995 after a flood washed out all the bridges. There is a high route up the ridge opposite Tarakot village. This trail is particularly scenic, but the first day is incredibly steep. Local folklore, reported by Norbu, the Tibetan from Jumla, says that the trail is so steep that when you climb up you hit your nose on the trail ahead of you.

Day 1: Dunai to Tarakot

Follow the trail eastwards out of Dunai along the south bank of the Thulo Bheri. A short distance beyond Dunai the route crosses to the north bank, then back to the south bank at **Lawan**. There's a police checkpost near the bridge, then the trail passes below the fields of Tarakot to a camp site near the Yalkot Khola at 2520m, just below the fortress of **Tarakot** village.

Day 2: Tarakot to Kanigaon

Above Tarakot the Bheri is known as the Barbung Khola. There is a new trail that climbs over a ridge on the west bank of the river to a village, then stays high above the river and, after a few ups and downs, crosses it on a 2560m. Just above the bridge the Tarap Chu (*chu* is Tibetan for river) joins the Barbung Khola. It's a short distance along the Tarap Chu to the Kanigaon police post. When I made this trek in the spring of 1995, the Barbung Khola was low and the locals led us to a place where we crossed the river on a combination of log bridges and broad jumps, then led us alongside the river on a goat trail to the lower fields of Kanigaon, then to the police post – all to avoid climbing over the ridge. I recommend the new ridge trail; there was almost as much uphill on the so-called short cut.

At 2540m there is a place to camp on the banks of the Tarap Chu in a lovely cedar grove near the police post, just north of their volleyball court. **Kanigaon** village is on the hillside above, and there is a small gompa across the Tarap Chu that you can visit if you

feel secure crossing a rushing stream on a single log. The police post is your last contact with officialdom for several days, but they make up for it with attentiveness to detail. Be sure that your permits are in order for Tarap.

Day 3: Kanigaon to Chheur

In 1989 a glacial lake burst and caused an enormous flood that wiped out the entire trail and made it impassable for several years. It has now been rebuilt thanks to a Netherlands volunteer (SNV) project. For most of the trek up the Tarap Chu the trail stays on the west side of the river (river right), though in the upper part of the valley there are several points where it crosses to the east bank for short distances.

From the Kanigaon police post, trek through cedar forest and fields of cannabis as the trail climbs over the tops of some spectacular landslides. The new trail is excellent, with wide stone steps and three-sided tunnels blasted out of the rock through the steepest part of the gorge. The river drops steeply alongside the trail – 600m in only three km. Finally the gorge begins to widen at **Lahini**, a meadow at 3160m. There is no village or house here; Lahini was a camp used by the trail construction crew and is now abandoned. The trail follows the riverbank for a while to another meadow, then climbs a rock cleft to cross a ridge as the gorge narrows again. The trail switchbacks and climbs stairs to a crest at 3540m, then makes a long high traverse on an exposed but wide and safe trail – with the usual ups and downs – to another crest at 3600m. The trail stays high for a while before descending to a rushing side stream, the Tilba Khola, at 3570m. Climb one more ridge and descend to **Chheur**, also known as Dolom, a small camp site beside a stream at 3610m. A rough stone house under a rock offers cave-like accommodation for porters, but there is no other shelter here. There are large rose shrubs, yellow poppies, magenta-blooming legumes and bicoloured impatiens along the route. Crag martins fly above the gorge and wall creepers probe fissures in rock faces as

WESTERN NEPAL

they chase insects. The total uphill today is about 1300m.

Day 4: Chheur to Sishul Khola

The trail now climbs a scree slope to cross a ridge, but if the Tarap Chu is low and the bridge is not washed out, you can cross the river here, walk 10 minutes upstream, and cross back to the west bank to avoid the climb. The trail continues along the river bank for a while, then crosses two rocky ridges with a small camp site between them. The local slate-like rock is excellent for building bridges and stair steps for the trail. The old trail is on the east bank of the river, but the new trail stays on the west bank, making some short climbs before reaching Nawor Pani, a trail-crew shelter at 2620m. What forest remains – mostly spruce, fir, juniper and cypress – is high on cliffs and inaccessible to humans.

The valley turns a bit to the west as the trail makes its way to a grassy meadow and passes several potential camp sites. Then the trail crosses and recrosses the Tarap Chu on a series of log and stone bridges past Tar Tar at 3660m and Tol Tol at 3680m. The trail switchbacks up a steep slope to a ridge at 3710m and descends back to the riverside, following the river to Gyam Gyar at 3740m. Norbu collected the names for all these uninhabited spots from a trail crew during a tea stop at Nawor Pani; I think they are correct, though it's hard to check.

The route crosses the Tarap Chu on a very short bridge where the river emerges from a narrow, steep gorge. Climb on the east bank through a true trans-Himalayan landscape to a chorten on a ridge at 3870m. This is **Serkam**, an abandoned border post that was the checkpoint between Nepal and Tibet in the 19th century. This is blue-sheep country; there are numerous herds that live among the yellow rocks and cliffs. Be sure to look for the white-breasted dippers, only found in western Nepal, along the river. Descend from Serkam and cross back to the west bank on a crooked wooden bridge high above the Tarap Chu. A kilometre or so of walking brings you to the **Sishul Khola**, where

there's a grassy camp site with good caves for porters at 3770m. The high trail back to Dunai via Cherka Dingla and Lawan heads west and climbs high before making a spectacular drop to the Thulo Bheri north of Tarakot. It's only about four hours to Do Tarap from here, so you could push on if your porters agree.

Day 5: Sishul Khola to Do Tarap

Climb gently to two weatherworn chortens atop a ridge, then descend to the river where there is a flat place that could be used as a camp site. The trail is rocky as it traverses beneath cliffs to a bridge at 3890m. Cross to the east bank where a huge side valley enters the Tarap Chu valley. There is a trail up this canyon along the Lang Chu to the remote village of Lang. The Tarap trail heads north up the Tarap Chu, climbing slowly alongside the river; before long you can see the white Ribo Bhumpa gompa ahead in Do Tarap. Climb to a line of ancient chortens at 4010m; it's then an easy level walk through fields of 'naked' barley *(uwa)* to **Do Tarap** at 4150m. There are camp sites in grassy meadows south of the village at the confluence of the Tarap Chu and the Doto Chu.

The name Tarap refers to the entire region. The correct name of this village is Do, meaning 'lower end of the valley' in Tibetan, but most local people refer to the village of Do as Do Tarap. The village consists of several clusters of closely packed stone houses with tiny windows. The Ribo Bhumpa gompa above the village was rebuilt in 1955; beside it is the unique 'chorten in a chorten' that contains the remains of a demon killed by Guru Rimpoche. There are paintings inside the chorten representing both Bon-po and Nyingma Buddhism, though the gompa itself is Buddhist. Above Ribo Bhumpa gompa is Mekyem gompa. This gompa is around 100 years old but was restored in the 1930s. It has a large statue of Maitreya Buddha and a richly decorated interior. It is worth visiting the gompas, even though they are not very active. The Bon-po gompa in Shipchhok and the Nyingmapa gompa in Doro, both up the valley of the

Dotu Chu to the east, are unusual destinations that are interesting to visit.

The women of Do Tarap wear elegant Tibetan dress with huge amounts of jewellery and ornate, but cumbersome, silver headgear. The men wear red braid in their hair in the style of Tibetan Khampas. The animals used for ploughing and carrying loads are huge shaggy yaks, not the more docile crossbreeds found in Khumbu. The wind blows fiercely in Tarap from noon to sunset. The houses are smoky from the desert shrubs they burn in the hearth in lieu of firewood.

Day 6: Do Tarap to Tok-khyu High Camp

Tarap is worth exploring, so don't hurry through this region. If you are having altitude problems, continue on to Tok-khyu for a visit and then return down the Tarap valley to Dunai. The crossing of the Baga La and Numa La is a reasonably difficult undertaking and takes you through some wild high country where there are no rescue or communications facilities.

Head west out of Do Tarap village past a cluster of stone houses. Soon you will reach a school building. This is the Crystal Mountain School, a private facility established in 1994 that is funded through a nongovernment organisation (NGO) in Dunai. This is the first serious attempt to bring education to this remote region, and it is having a hard time. Lowland teachers are not happy working in such a harsh, remote environment, and the wooden doors and windows often get appropriated for firewood by local people because it is normally a three day project to fetch a single load of wood in this arid, treeless valley.

Beyond the school a trail leads uphill to **Ga Kar** ('white mountain') village; there is also a lower trail that bypasses the village. Continue up the valley to Trangmar ('red cliff') and Dorje Phorba gompa at 4170m. The gompa may have been built to house a red mask of Guru Dragpo, a terrible form of Guru Rimpoche, brought here a long time ago by a lama from Kham. He also hid Sakya statues and cult objects. The place is richly decorated and has gold-lettered manuscripts in its library. The guardian lives on the first floor.

A bit further on is **Chu Magar**, which means 'don't cross the river', and a small private gompa. A but further on, the trail finally does cross the Tarap Chu (known here as the Thakchio Khola) on a wooden bridge that leads to Mondo at 4170m. Here the valley divides; the northern fork of the Tarap Chu leads to Nangkhong and remote regions of northern Dolpo. The route to the Baga La follows the southern branch past the white Champa Lhakang to **Tok-khyu** village at 4180m.

If you want to declare a holiday, this is an excellent place to do it; there are several places to camp in the hills beyond the village. The Champa Lhakang is worth a visit. It was rebuilt in 1953 and possesses a statue of Maitreya so large that the head goes through a hole in the ceiling. If you are going to cross the pass the following day, it's worth continuing on to another camp site at 4390m by a stream a little more than an hour beyond Tok-khyu. Numerous fat marmots and rabbits live in burrows in the nearby hillsides. The large white building high on the hill and across the valley to the north is Sharring gompa; below it is Joglung gompa. There is a chapel and a library at Joglung, which has been there for at least six generations. Sharring was rebuilt in 1965, using stones from the former temple.

If you are heading for Shey gompa and Inner Dolpo, cross the river at Tok-khyu and follow the trail along the north branch of the Tarap Chu. This route requires a liaison officer and a $700 permit fee. It is a high, difficult and remote route over the 5110m Jengla Bhanjyang into wild country; see the Restricted Areas chapter for details.

Day 7: Tok-khyu High Camp to Pelungtang

It's a long pull over the Numa La, so start early. I crossed in mid-May when there had been a late snowstorm, and we found it rough going in deep snow. We had to make an additional, higher camp in order to cross the pass in the early morning when the snow was still hard. Under normal conditions, however, the pass crossing is reasonably straightforward – just long and high.

From the camp, follow a stream, crossing it on rocks, then climb steeply up a grassy slope to a ridge where there are several mani walls and a chorten at 4580m. In this desolate, improbable location a large *puja* (religious ceremony) is celebrated in July. It is said that there is a hermit monk who lives in a cave below the chorten and spends his life making mani stones. Continue up the ridge to a grassy knoll and a tiny stream at 4930m; this is a possible camp site.

The route is not entirely obvious, but it crosses a small stream and makes a long climb along a moraine to the Numa La at 5318m, a total of about four hours from the high camp (or two hours from the higher camp). From the pass on a clear day you can see Shey Shikar (6139m), Kanjeralwa (the 6612m peak above Phoksumdo Lake) and Dhaulagiri I (8167m).

Descend from the pass into a rocky, U-shaped valley. The trail turns left and you can see, across the valley, Baga La, the next obstacle on the trek. Watch for wildlife, especially blue sheep and snow leopards, in this remote valley. Follow the rocky valley as it descends; the route crosses a large stream and numerous scree slopes and there are several alternative trails. There is a small, rocky camp site at about 4520m and another at 4360m near the foot of the valley. The valley is joined by another large valley from the east and the two streams join to form the Poyon Chu. Follow the river downstream a short distance, then cross it on a combination of rocks and logs and climb again up the south (river left) bank. The trail along the right bank climbs and eventually crosses several passes on yet another route to the restricted region of Saldang and Shey gompa in Inner Dolpo. The trail along the left bank climbs gently, but continually, and the river drops steeply, so you are soon high above the river. After traversing in and out of a few small side valleys, the trail makes a sharp turn to the left, leading into another large side valley. It was from this point in May 1995 that Norbu spotted a snow leopard in the bottom of the valley. It wandered around in the snow on the valley floor, then climbed to a cave on the slopes opposite.

Round the ridge into the valley and climb gently to a good camp site in a meadow at 4465m. This spot is known as **Pelungtang**; *tang* in Tibetan means meadow. The large glaciated peak at the head of the valley is Norbu Kang (6005m).

Day 8: Pelungtang to Dajok Tang

This was a tough day when I crossed the pass in the snow; it's not as difficult when the route is clear. The trail crosses the stream, then climbs a slope above Pelungtang, making its way along the side of several moraines to a large bowl. The trail contours around the bowl on a scree slope to several rough cairns atop the Baga La at 5190m.

Descend from the pass, steeply at first, then more gently, staying high above the right bank of the stream. The trail is well defined in most places, though it sometimes disappears into loose slate-like scree and crosses two large side streams that present a rock-hopping challenge. At 4390m the trail turns a corner and enters a huge valley, making a final descent on steep switchbacks to **Dajok Tang**, 'prayer flag meadow', at 4080m. The stream drops beside the trail in an impressive series of step-like waterfalls. This is truly a spectacular valley, with a large moraine, said to encompass a lake, at its head and numerous Yosemite-like waterfalls shooting off near-vertical rock cliffs. At the foot of the valley are several snow peaks, including Kanjeralwa. If you have energy, you can push on to another camp site 20 minutes below, or even further to camps at the foot of Sonam Kang, 15 minutes beyond that.

Day 9: Dajok Tang to Phoksumdo Lake

Follow a good trail down to a marmot-infested meadow at the foot of a waterfall at 3970m, then descend into a forest of cedars. It's a lovely walk through the trees to a camp site in yak pastures at 3830m near the junction of a stream that descends from Sonam Kang, a 5916m peak to the south. There is a bridge over the Manduwa Khola, but it leads only to Sonam Kang (which is off limits to climbers) and high yak pastures. Trek through more meadows, forests, yak pastures and stone-and-sod herders' huts on a trail that rises high above the river. Eventually the trail emerges into an area of thorny shrubs and descends a bit, then climbs on a high cliffside trail to a ridge at 3780m. There is a good view across the valley to the huge waterfall formed by the Phoksumdo Khola.

The trail levels out again and re-enters forests as it climbs to another crest at 3820m. It then descends gently through a blue pine forest to two Bon-po chortens and the fields of Ringmo at 3730m. It is then a short distance through a forest of birch and pines to the national park camping ground near the shores of **Phoksumdo Lake** at 3728m. See Day 3 of the trek to Phoksumdo Lake for information about the lake and nearby Ringmo village.

Days 10, 11, 12: Phoksumdo Lake to Juphal
Follow the route description (backwards) that is given in the Dunai to Phoksumdo Lake section earlier in the chapter.

Baglung to Dolpo

Duration 13 days	

Duration 13 days
Difficulty Medium to hard
Maximum elevation 4270m
Permit cost US$5 per week plus Rs 650
Season May to October
Hotels None
Summary A long, high and difficult trek across many high passes leads from near Pokhara to Dunai, the gateway to Dolpo. Continue on to Tarap and Phoksumdo Lake.

This is a long, remote, difficult trek with very few facilities along the way. The route is described in detail by George Schaller in *Stones of Silence* and by Peter Matthiessen

in *The Snow Leopard*. There are no hotels beyond Beni, so you will be most comfortable if you take porters and food. With porters the trek takes 12 or 13 days to Dunai. If you add a circuit through Tarap and Phoksumdo Lake, you can make an outstanding 23-day trek. My trekking companion, Bob Peirce, commented that we saw more blue sheep than people on this trek.

Access
The best place to start this trek is Baglung, which is a 73 km drive from Pokhara. Options for travelling the road to Baglung are described in the Baglung to Tatopani section of the Annapurna chapter.

Day 1: Baglung to Ratne Chaur
Trek down from Baglung into the Kali Gandaki valley, reaching the river at a suspension bridge at Pharse at 790m. Follow the trail up the west bank of the river through rice terraces and across landslides to Beldanda. Cross more landslides to Lama Ghara, then continue on to Ratne Chaur, on a shelf above the river at 800m, about four hours from Baglung.

Day 2: Ratne Chaur to Tara Khet
The trail heads upstream below cliffs to Khabara, a small bazaar with traditional tea shops and houses. A bit further the route rounds a corner overlooking the Beni jail, then crosses a new steel bridge to **Beni** itself at an elevation of 770m. Opposite the police post at the south end of town is a lovely temple overgrown with a tree like the temples of Angkor Wat in Cambodia. You can take the bypass route by turning west from the police post, or you can walk north into town for some last-minute shopping in the well-stocked bazaar. If you go into town, turn left at the three-storey *Hotel Dolphin*. Either route takes you to a statue of King Mahendra at the west end of town. The trail heads westwards to the small bazaar of Manglaghat and on to Damara. Another hour of level walking alongside the Myagdi Khola takes you to Kotsangu, also known as

Baglung to Dolpo

0   10   20 km

Chutrini, then past scattered houses to **Singa Bazaar** at 850m.

Most of the people in the Myagdi Khola valley are Magars, though there are some Brahmans and members of other ethnic groups that operate shops and bhattis in the valley. Continue through Rakshe and on to **Tatopani**, named for the small hot spring on the riverbank below the village. The *Kunda Guest House* is among the string of rough stone houses alongside the trail. Continue through another small bazaar, past a small hospital and a third part of Tatopani to a school. Continue past *chautaaras* shaded by

pipal and banyan trees to a suspension bridge, cross it to Jala Keni and climb to Ba Khet. Soon the trail recrosses the river back to the north bank at Simalchaur. Cross a side stream on a suspension bridge and trek through **Tara Khet** on a flagstone-paved trail at 970m. There are good camp sites to be found near Tara Khet.

Day 3: Tara Khet to Danyga Khola
The trail climbs over a small ridge to **Babiyachour**, named after a local grass, *babiyo*, that is woven into ropes. The large stone houses in the village are the offices of

a government agriculture project. The upper part of the village is a substantial bazaar with the tiny *Rabi Guest House*, a medical dispensary, jewellers, tailors and a high school. The trail leads through Naya Bazaar, Sas Dhara and on to **Raato Dhunga**, a small bazaar at 1020m elevation.

The trail drops and follows the riverbank; in the wet season it's necessary to make a long climb over a ridge. Climb from the riverbank across a rock slope where slate is mined to make shingles for roofs. On the opposite bank are the remains of a huge landslide that destroyed much of **Darbang** in 1983. The new village is on the north side of the river and is a large bazaar with silversmiths, tailors, a post office and a watch-repair shop along the flagstone-paved main street. Cross the Myagdi Khola on a large suspension bridge near the school at the west end of town. The trail up the Kharai Khola valley to the west leads to Niskut and several clusters of large villages. The Dhorpatan trail follows the river bank of the Marsyangdi Khola as it turns north to **Danyga Khola** (also known as Phedi), elevation 1125m, at the foot of a steep series of switchbacks. Make camp near the river bank, at the foot of the hill.

Day 4: Danyga Khola to Muna
Cross the Danyga Khola on a big suspension bridge and grind up a series of steep switchbacks. This is best done in the cool of the morning because the first part of the climb is without trees. After about 250m of climbing, some pine trees offer some welcome shade, a tribe of langur monkeys provide a bit of entertainment and Dhaulagiri appears in the distance to brighten the scene. After another hundred metres of climbing, the trail becomes more gentle; turn a corner for a good view of Dhaulagiri IV and V and also Gurja Himal. Traverse a bit, then climb to **Dharapani**, a Magar village with one tiny shop at 1470m. The trail contours up above the village to a crest at 1630m, then drops a bit to **Takam**. The mountain views are great as you traverse around the top of the large village to two shops and a private school. Keep climbing along the side of the hill to

Sibang at 1610m and a shop that advertises that 'all things are available here'. Just above the trail is a camp site for trekkers and a large high school.

Climb over a ridge at 1840m and descend a steep stone stairway to Ghatta Khola, a single shop and the tiny, dingy *Hotel Jaljala* at 1850m. The trail stays fairly level as it traverses fields of corn, wheat and barley to a schoolhouse on a ridge at Paliya Gaon. Pass the small settlement of **Muna**, cross a small suspension bridge, pass a single tea shop and descend to a bridge across the Dara Khola. There is a good camp site by the river.

Day 5: Muna to Jaljala
The trail climbs gently alongside the stream to a suspension bridge at 1830m, then the climb steepens on a newly renovated trail to the Magar village of **Lumsum** at 2100m. In this region you may be able to spot red pandas (*malchaura* in Nepali). A half-hour beyond Lumsum the route crosses the Dhara Khola on an old suspension bridge at 2120m. There is a good camp site near the river if you want to take a break before you begin the long climb to the Jaljala La. The route towards the pass climbs steeply to a small tea shop at 2290m, then through apple orchards, wheat fields, and finally scrub forest to a single house at **Moreni**, 2670m. The peak that is visible peeking over the ridge to the north is Churen Himal, elevation 7371m; Nilgiri and part of Annapurna Himal are also visible in the distance.

Climb through a burned forest to a herders' goth at 2770m, then up the ridge in a forest of rhododendrons inhabited by langur monkeys. It's a long, unrelenting climb up the ridge to a notch at 3350m. The trail climbs a bit further to a crest, then contours to a large meadow at 3390m, surrounded by rhododendron forests and some goths, which makes an excellent camp site. The only water available during the spring season is a tiny spring near the notch on the crest of the ridge.

Day 6: Jaljala to Dhorpatan
The trail continues to climb gently across

meadows. At some point the trail crosses the Jaljala La, but the slope is so gradual that it's not obvious where the actual pass is. From the expanse of meadows on the pass, the trail descends to two stout wooden bridges, then to a stream at 3170m, about 1½ hours from the camp. Follow the stream past herders' huts and a few cultivated fields to a forest of pines and firs and Gurjakot at 3070m. People from Dhorpatan bring their horses here to graze; it's also a depot for mule trains and there is an office for the Dhorpatan Hunting Reserve. The ridiculous design of the bridge over the Simudar Khola provides a short climb on what is otherwise a fairly level trail all the way into Dhorpatan. The level trail is also pretty wet, however, so there are lots of swampy areas to dodge and small streams to cross on precarious logs.

Chantung gompa is on a shelf above a big meadow with grazing horses, cows and buffaloes. A short distance beyond is Chhyantu, the first village in the Dhorpatan Valley at 2990m. The only hotel is the very basic *Hotel Jaljala*. Trek past apple orchards to Tarke Geke Ling gompa and a bit further to the large *Lali Guras Hotel* at 2950m. A trail up the canyon to the north leads to a high route that is a short cut to Dolpo.

There are lots of villages along the way, mostly Tibetan refugee settlements, including the Tibetan Norzin Ling Camp at Bharte. Continue past many scattered stone houses and a small Tibetan school to the office of the Dhorpatan Hunting Reserve. You must pay Rs 650 for entrance into the reserve, which caters to rich hunters who want to bag blue sheep. Inside the hunting reserve office is a collection of skins from various animals that were collected in the region, including blue sheep *(naur* in Tibetan, *bharal* in Nepali), deer *(mirg)* and leopard *(chituwa)*. The leopard skins on display are of common leopard, not snow leopard; the yellow stripe down the centre of the back of the common leopard is the major feature that distinguishes the two. A short distance beyond the office is the defunct **Dhorpatan** airstrip and the *Airport Hotel* at 2830m. The huge Dhorpatan Valley is inhabited by about 300

Tibetan refugees and there are also several Magar settlements around the edge of the basin. The Tibetan settlements can be identified by the prayer flags flying from the houses. *Patan* means 'flat place' in the dialect of western Nepal, and the Dhorpatan Valley is one of the largest flat places in the hills of Nepal. Despite its size, it's not a particularly good place to live. The valley floor is marshy and suited only to grazing, not cultivation, and it's buried in snow during the winter; most people migrate to Kathmandu because of the cold. Camp at the airstrip.

Day 7: Dhorpatan to Takur
In Dhorpatan you begin the second stage of the trek and head north into largely uninhabited country. Many maps of this region are inaccurate in their representation of this stretch of trail – if they show it at all. From the Dhorpatan airport, climb above the houses and reach a crest at 3130m. The trail descends into the beautiful wooded Phagune Khola valley and skirts around the head of it through rhododendron forests, crossing several streams. The trail climbs again gently, then switchbacks to a false summit and keeps climbing to a crest at 3510m. From the crest there are views of the pass far ahead and also a last look back to Dhorpatan.

The trek crosses the tree line and enters a rough wilderness landscape. The route keeps climbing, sometimes steeply, alongside a stream, and then turns up a steep scree-filled draw. There are some treacherous scree slopes to cross as the steep route makes its way up the treeless hillside, finally emerging at a chorten atop the Phagune Dhuri pass at 4061m. From the pass there are great views of Churen Himal and of Putha Hiunchuli, the 'butterfly' mountain.

From the pass the route descends gently to a stream and small camp site at 4000m. The trail makes a long traverse before starting steeply down and traversing a side hill that may be blocked with snow. After a few ups and downs the trail reaches Dupi Neta, a meadow atop a hill at 3810m that offers an excellent camp site with good mountain views. Below Dupi Neta the route re-enters forests and makes steep switchbacks down through the trees to **Takur**, a house and a smoky local-style bhatti in a meadow beside a stream at 3190m.

Day 8: Takur to Pelma

The route now heads west, down the Ghustung Khola valley through a forest of firs and large oaks to a small holy lake at 2980m. The route becomes rougher and you must pick your way among loose rocks as the trail makes its way down alongside the fast-flowing stream to a wooden bridge at 2710m.

The route crosses the bridge and climbs steeply out of the valley through a forest of oaks and rhododendrons, finally emerging on a ridge at 3140m. Follow along the top of the ridge for a long distance, making ups and downs, sometimes in forests and sometimes across meadows. The route skirts around to the south of the ridge on a trail built into the cliff and makes its way to a chautaara sitting on a notch at 2890m. From here the trail descends steep dusty switchbacks to the upper fields of **Pelma** at 2600m. There are camp sites in the fields near this remote and dirty Magar village at 2550m. There is an alternative camp site below the village near the river.

Day 9: Pelma to Dhule

Drop steeply from Pelma to the Pelma Khola, cross on a wooden bridge at 2300m and climb steeply to **Yamakhar** at 2480m. Most of the houses in this village are connected into one sprawling decrepit structure that sits next to the trail. Climb past the barley fields above the village on a steep treeless slope to Bhang Kharka, three houses built into the hillside at 2970m. The trail turns north and continues uphill on a dusty path through scrub oak to a ridge at 3120m. Continue gently down to a simple tea shop near the Gorba Khola at 2930m. Now it's a steep grind up a dusty trail to a crest at 3120m, then more uphill before the trail levels out; it then descends a bit through birch, then fir and rhododendron forest to a stream at 3060m. Climb up a steep ravine on a rocky stream bed to a meadow and rhododendron forest, then keep climbing to **Dhule**, four houses at 3340m. This settlement is the first since Yamakhar and the last until Tarakot. There is a large camp site that is reserved for blue-sheep hunters who helicopter in for sport. You can get a cup of tea, and perhaps a plate of rice, at the very ethnic *Hotel Masta Copila*. It's rumoured that this hotel also specialises in blue-sheep meat.

Day 10: Dhule to Seng Khola

The trail climbs steeply through the forests above Dhule to a ridge at 3790m and then along the ridge to a chautaara where there are outstanding views of Dhaulagiri Himal to the east. The route then cuts across a slope to the north-west, climbing gradually on a good trail to two stone chortens atop the Nautale Bhanjyang at 3961m. Ahead lie the upper reaches of the Seng Khola valley and a spectacular wilderness landscape. Descend steeply, then contour above the Seng Khola, a tributary of the Pelma Khola. The trail makes some ups and downs along the west bank of the river, climbing gradually past a small cave, a ruined hotel and a few pastures. You can camp near the river at 3820m or on the slopes 200m above.

Day 11: Seng Khola to Purpang

There are several goat trails headed up the hill; pick the largest one and make your way up the steep grassy slope to a camp site near a small stream at 4080m. It is along this part of the trail that Peter Matthiessen and George Schaller got lost and climbed the wrong ridge during their trek to Dolpo. To avoid duplicating their error, don't climb the hill to the north-north-west; instead, head generally west to a ridge crest at 4260m. The trail crosses into another side valley and traverses above a small lake. The route becomes more obvious as the trail heads towards the Panidal Pass at 4412m and drops into another alpine basin. Descend to a stream and follow it uphill to its headwaters, then climb further to an indistinct pass at 4525m. Descend to another lake, then head down, cutting across side hills. There's a goat trail that leads off to the left; stay right in a small ravine. Keep heading down, following a stream on a muddy trail that sometimes disappears, to the valley floor where the Saunre Khola has made many meandering channels at 4020m. There's no bridge, so depending on conditions you may be able to rock-hop across the river or you may have to wade it. There are some camping places near the river, but they are muddy, so it's better to climb a bit to **Purpang** at 4050m. There is a stone house with a fancy corrugated iron and steel-truss roof that has collapsed.

Day 12: Purpang to Sahar Tara

Climb steeply to a ridge at 4130m, then follow a stream up the valley to the first pass, marked by two rock cairns at 4340m. Traverse into the next valley, a grassy meadow where people from Tarakot and nearby villages graze their horses. Follow a stream for about half an hour to the foot of the Jangla Bhanjyang at 4270m. The trail climbs a sandy, rocky ravine to four rock cairns atop the Jangla Bhanjyang at 4538m. There are good mountain views from here, including Kanjeralwa, the peak near Phoksumdo Lake.

The trail descends steeply from the pass for the first 400m, then it levels out and makes a high traverse. There is another trail that heads steeply downhill into the trees. This is the short, steep way down the Jangla Khola valley to Dunai; you can see Dunai village far below to the north-west. The Tarakot trail stays high, making some ups and downs as it heads out to a ridge at 4140m. Round the ridge into the next canyon and start down steeply on a good trail to **Tokar**, a meadow and stream at 3740m. The route enters trees at about 3540m and becomes a gentle, wide trail as it descends through pines to a gompa at Tanti, at the top of **Sahar Tara**, elevation 3010m. There is good camping in horse pastures among huge cotoneaster bushes.

This region of the upper Bheri is known in Tibetan as Tichurong. Many people refer to the entire region as Tarakot, though this name correctly applies only to the fortress-like village near the river. The people are Magars, but they practise many Tibetan traditions and have their own language, Kaike, which is spoken only in this region.

Day 13: Sahar Tara to Kanigaon

It's a long day's walk from Sahar Tara to Dunai – in case you are running short of time, are tired, or need to go there to buy supplies. If you have the time, you should make a trip to Tarap and perhaps on to Phoksumdo Lake. The Numa La and Baga La passes are higher than those you have crossed on this trek, but they are less difficult, unless there is snow.

From the camp site in Sahar Tara, descend through corn and millet fields to the main part of Sahar Tara at 2770m. The village is compact and houses are stacked atop each other; some have elaborately carved wooden windows. The people of Tichurong believe that ghosts cannot enter a house if they have to bend over, so all the houses of the village have low ceilings. Beware of getting lost – and of fierce dogs – as you make your way though the narrow alleyways and small courtyards. There is a tiny health post, and somewhere in the village is a shop that sells shoes and a few food items, but it has no sign and is inside a courtyard, so it's hard to find. In Tarakot you may be able to recruit local porters, though the focus of this village's trade is running horse caravans south along the Thulo Bheri to the roadhead at Chaujhari, five days away. Jim Fisher's book *Trans Himalayan Traders* describes this region in detail.

Descend steeply to the village water supply, then contour above fields to Tarakot proper, perched on a ridge at 2550m. From the ridge the trail drops steeply in loose gravel to a stream. There are some good camp sites near a school and wooden bridge at 2500m. Cross a small ridge and climb gently through corn fields that have been scratched out of a field of boulders to a log bridge across the Yalkot Khola at 2520m.

See Day 2 of the trek from Dunai to Tarap earlier in this chapter for details of the route to **Kanigaon**.

Restricted Areas

In October 1991 the Home Ministry announced the opening of the restricted areas in Nepal, a move which was partly a political decision to remove a regulation that was inconsistent with the principles of Nepal's new, democratic constitution. Once the announcement was made, most of the attention was directed at upper Mustang, previously the most inaccessible and firmly controlled area in Nepal. It took several months for the Ministry of Tourism to develop regulations and procedures for the newly opened areas, but by late March 1992 the first foreign trekking groups were allowed into upper Mustang.

Other trekking areas opened in 1991 were Inner Dolpo and Nupri, the region north of Manaslu. The entire region of Dolpo, Mustang and Nupri was first explored by the Tibetan scholar David Snellgrove, and is described in his book *Himalayan Pilgrimage*.

The regulations for the restricted areas were designed primarily to protect the environment and culture of remote regions and to provide security, both for the safety of trekkers and the protection of Nepal's northern border with China. Unfortunately, the emphasis has shifted to the financial aspects of the permit process. It appears that high permit fees will become institutionalised and the need for additional revenue will overshadow efforts to limit the number of tourists.

Fees & Permits

A trek to a restricted area must be arranged as a fully equipped camping trek through a registered trekking company using tents, sherpa staff, cooks and porters. The trekking company arranges the permit through a series of applications, guarantees and letters, a process that requires about two weeks and can be started only 21 days before the arrival of the group. You may not trek alone and there must be at least two trekkers in each group. For some areas there is a limit to the number of trekkers per season. There is no system of advance reservation, and no clear

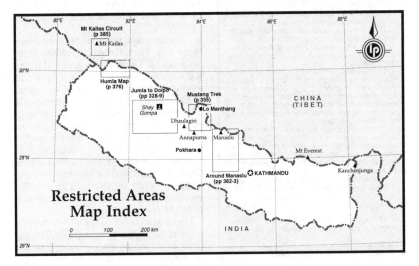

349

Terms & Conditions for Restricted Areas

The company that arranges your trek must agree to abide by the terms and conditions outlined below. The company must agree to be prosecuted as per the laws of the Kingdom of Nepal if it flaunts these terms and conditions.

The terms and conditions under which a trekking company may operate a trek in upper Mustang state:

1. You can operate only groups.
2. You will be responsible for arranging the entire trek from the start to the end of the trek.
3. Unless His Majesty's Government makes other provisions, you must compulsorily take a liaison officer with you in the newly opened areas.
4. You will be responsible for organising the security of the trekking group and, if need be, seek the help of the local police. If you thus need the police's help, you will arrange to meet their personal expenses.
5. You will arrange for medical care and other needs of the trekkers during the trek.
6. You must compulsorily provide solar fuel, electricity, gas, kerosene or a similar alternative fuel to cook food for the trekkers and all others accompanying them. Fuel wood cannot be used.
7. Tin cans, bottles etc necessary for the trek should not be thrown away at random. They should be buried/destroyed at designated sites.
8. You will arrange to ensure that the group travels only on authorised routes and does not break-up into separate groups.
9. You will not allow distribution of money or gifts or charity to local residents and students. If trekkers wish to do so, small parcels can be donated through the Chief District Officer (CDO).
10. Do not take foreigners into religious or cultural sites that are restricted to foreigners.
11. You will not perpetrate or allow any acts that destroy religion, culture or the environment.
12. You will insure all Nepali staff on the trek. Moreover, you will insure or deposit a sum for emergency rescues.
13. Trekking parties to Lo Manthang of the Mustang area must submit to the Tourist Information Service, Jomsom, a copy of the goods and equipment taken with them. Upon returning, you should give them garbage to be dumped at the dumping site, get clearance and submit the same to the Ministry of Tourism.
14. You will provide the liaison officer with food, lodging, trip expenses and Rs 200 (two hundred rupees) per day for the duration of the trek. You will also compulsorily provide the officer necessary items like a sleeping bag, jacket, clothes, boots etc for the duration of the trek.
15. Permission to trek in the Lo Manthang region of Mustang area must be obtained within 21 days of recommendation by the Ministry of Tourism.
16. You must insure the liaison officer for Rs 200,000.
17. You will arrange for the necessary medicines and medical care of the liaison officer. ■

indication of what will happen if the quota is reached the day before you make an application.

Each group is assigned an 'environmental officer' or liaison officer. Despite the fancy name, what you will get is a Nepali policeman or government official whom you must equip, insure and take on the trek. The liaison officer is supposed to handle all the formalities with police and government offices en route.

Mustang Trek

Duration 9 to 14 days
Difficulty Medium to hard
Maximum elevation 4070m
Permit cost US$700 plus Rs 1000
Season May to October
Hotels Only camping treks allowed
Summary Completely closed to foreign trekkers until 1991, Mustang is an ancient Himalayan kingdom. Inside the walled city of Lo Manthang are some of the largest Tibetan Buddhist gompas in Nepal. A difficult trek because of high altitude, exposed terrain and continual strong winds.

In common usage, the name Mustang refers to the arid, Tibet-like region, known to its inhabitants as Lo, at the northern end of the Kali Gandaki. Mustang is probably a Nepali mispronunciation of the name of the capital of Lo, the city of Manthang. The name is pronounced 'moo-staang' and has nothing to do with either the automobile or the horse with a similar name. Officially, Mustang is the name of the district along the Kali Gandaki from the Tibetan border south to Ghasa. The capital of the Mustang district is Jomsom; the restricted area of Tibetan influence is north of Kagbeni, and is generally referred to as upper Mustang.

Upper Mustang consists of two distinct regions: the southern region, with five villages inhabited by people related to the Manangis; and the northern region (the ancient kingdom of Lo), where the language, culture and traditions are almost purely Tibetan. The capital of Lo is named Manthang, which translates from the Tibetan as 'plain of aspiration'. Many texts refer to the capital as Lo Manthang, but this is not strictly correct. Other texts spell the name of the kingdom as Lho, but this is a transliteration of the Tibetan word for 'south' and is also incorrect. Thus the portion of the upper Mustang district north of Samar is Lo and its capital is Manthang. The king of Lo is the Lo Gyelbu, though I use the Nepali term *raja* here. To avoid total confusion with existing maps and texts, I also refer to the capital of Lo as 'Lo Manthang'.

There are many complex issues relating to the development of upper Mustang and the procedures under which trekkers are allowed to visit the area. I have not attempted to address these in detail here. Change and development will come to Lo regardless of the degree of protection that is extended. Despite their isolation, the people of Lo are worldly, well travelled and resourceful. They are essentially Tibetans and are skilful traders, travellers and merchants. One hopes that they can retain their traditions under an influx of tourists, but they are by no means a primitive tribe that must be protected from outside influence. The Annapurna Conservation Area Project (ACAP), the international aid organisation CARE and the American Himalayan Foundation are involved in development, cultural preservation and environmental activities in upper Mustang.

History

Mustang has a long, rich and complex history that makes it one of the most interesting places in Nepal. The early history of Lo is shrouded in legend, myth and mystery, but there are records of events in Lo as early as the 8th century. It is quite likely that the Tibetan poet Milarepa, who lived from 1040 to 1123, visited Lo. Upper Mustang was once part of Ngari, a name for far western Tibet. Ngari was not a true political entity, but rather a loose collection of feudal domains

that also included parts of Dolpo. By the 14th century, much of Ngari, as well as most of what today is western Nepal, was part of the Malla empire governed from the capital at Sinja, near Jumla.

It is generally believed that Ame Pal (Ama-dpal in Tibetan) founded Lo in 1380 and was its first king. The ancestry of the present Mustang raja can be traced 25 generations back to Ame Pal. Ame Pal, or perhaps his father, conquered a large part of the territory in the upper Kali Gandaki and was responsible for the development of the city of Lo Manthang and many gompas. To the west, the Malla empire declined and split into numerous petty hill states. By the 18th century, Jumla had consolidated and reasserted its power. In an effort to develop their domain as a trading centre and to obtain Tibetan goods, the rulers of Jumla turned their attention eastward. In the mid-18th century they assumed control over Lo, from which they extracted an annual tribute.

When he ascended the throne in 1762, Prithvi Narayan Shah began to consolidate what is present-day Nepal. At the time of his death, the kingdom extended from Gorkha eastward to the borders of Sikkim. His descendants directed their efforts westward and by 1789, Jumla had been annexed. The Gorkha armies never actually entered Lo; they recognised the rule of the Mustang raja. Although Mustang became part of Nepal, the raja retained his title and Lo retained a certain amount of autonomy.

Lo maintained its status as a separate principality until 1951. After the Rana rulers were overthrown and King Tribhuvan reestablished the rule of the Shah monarchs on 15 February 1951, Lo was more closely consolidated into Nepal. The raja was given the honorary rank of colonel in the Nepal army.

During the 1960s, after the Dalai Lama had fled to India and Chinese armies established control over Tibet, Mustang was a centre for guerrilla operations against the Chinese. The soldiers were the Khampas, Tibet's most fearsome warriors, who were backed by the CIA (some Khampas were secretly trained in the USA). At the height of the fighting there were at least 6000 Khampas in Mustang and neighbouring border areas. The CIA's support ended in the early 1970s when the USA, under Kissinger and Nixon, initiated new and better relations with the Chinese. The government of Nepal was pressed to take action against the guerrillas and, making use of internal divisions within the Khampa leadership, a bit of treachery and the Dalai Lama's taped advice for his citizens to lay down their arms, it managed to disband the resistance without committing to action the 10,000 Nepali troops that had been sent to the area.

Though Mustang was closed, the government allowed a few researchers into the area. Toni Hagen included Mustang in his survey of the entire kingdom of Nepal, and the Italian scholar Giuseppe Tucci visited in the autumn of 1952. Professor David Snellgrove travelled to the region in 1956 but did not visit Lo Manthang. Longtime Nepal resident Barbara Adams travelled to Mustang during the autumn of 1963. The most complete description of the area is *Mustang, the Forbidden Kingdom*, written by Michel Peissel, who spent several months in the area in the spring of 1964. Dr Harka Bahadur Gurung also visited and wrote about upper Mustang in October 1973. A number of groups legally travelled to upper Mustang during the 1980s by obtaining permission to climb Bhrikuti (6364m), south-east of Lo Manthang. Other than a few special royal guests, the first legal trekkers were allowed into Mustang in March 1992 upon payment of a high fee for a special trekking permit.

Geography

Mustang has been described as a thumb-like part of Nepal extending into Tibet. Yet on the map, it is hardly a bump in Nepal's northern border. This is not the result of an inaccurate description by early writers; the map changed. In 1960 there was a controversy between Nepal and China over the ownership of Mt Everest. This resulted in extended negotiations and the China-Nepal Boundary Treaty of 1963 that completely redefined Nepal's northern frontier. Nepal gained a considerable amount of territory to the east and west of the old boundaries in Mustang, so the protrusion of Mustang into Tibet became much less pronounced. To make matters more confusing, most official maps were not updated until about 1985.

The trek to Lo is through a barren, almost treeless landscape. Strong winds usually howl across the area in the afternoon, generally subsiding at night. Being in the rain shadow of the Himalaya, Lo receives much less rain than the rest of Nepal. During the monsoon the skies are cloudy and there is some rain. In the winter there is usually snow; sometimes as much as 30 or 40 cm accumulates on the ground.

In Lo itself the countryside is similar to the Tibetan plateau with its endless expanses of yellow and grey rolling hills eroded by wind. There is more rain in the lower part of upper Mustang and the hills tend to be great, red, fluted cliffs of tiny, round stones cemented together by mud. Villages are several hours apart and appear in the distance almost as mirages; during the summer season, after the crops are planted, they are green oases in the desert-like landscape.

People & Culture

The people of upper Mustang call themselves Lobas. To be strictly correct, this word would be spelled 'Lopa', meaning 'Lo people', in the same way as Sherpa means 'east people' and Khampa, 'Kham people'. The people of Lo, probably because of regional dialect, pronounce the word with a definite 'b' sound instead of the 'p' sound that the Sherpas and Khampas use. I will follow Lo tradition and spell the word as it is pronounced: 'Loba'; most anthropological texts, however, disagree with this.

House and temple construction throughout the region uses some stone but mostly sun-baked bricks of mud. Astonishing edifices, such as the city wall and the four-storey palace in Lo Manthang, are built in this manner. It is said that there were once large forests in Lo, but now wood for construction is hauled all the way from Jomsom or pruned from poplar trees that are carefully tended in every village.

Religion

The form of Tibetan Buddhism practised in Mustang is primarily that of the Sakyapa sect. This sect was established at Sakya monastery in Tibet and dates from 1073. The Sakyapa sect is more worldly and practical in outlook, and less concerned with metaphysics, than the more predominant Nyingmapa and Gelugpa sects. Sakya monastery is unique for the horizontal grey, white and yellow stripes on its red walls, an identifying feature of Sakyapa structures. Most chortens and gompas in Lo are painted in these colours, which reflect those of the surrounding hills.

Fees, Permits & Formalities

Trekking permits for Mustang cost a minimum of US$700 per person for 10 days; note that this is defined as 10 *days*, not nights, starting and ending at Kagbeni. Extra days are US$70 each. If you wish to travel north of Lo Manthang, even on a day trip, you must buy a 13-day permit for a total of US$910.

ACAP administers trekking in upper Mustang. According to the plan, ACAP also is responsible for channelling a portion of the Mustang trek royalties into development projects in Mustang. Mustang is currently the only restricted area for which any part of the permit fee goes into a special fund.

If you are trekking from Pokhara to Jomsom and continuing to Mustang, you should get an additional normal US$5 per week trekking permit; the US$70 per day permit is required only from Kagbeni northwards. Because of possible delays in Jomsom flights, the entry date on the permit is supposed to have a three-day leeway, though some bureaucrats are not aware of this. Once you start from Kagbeni, you must return within the period of your trek permit, but you need not start on a precise date.

Registration In Jomsom, you must register with the police post and also with the tourist information office across from Om's Home,

just north of the airport. The tourist office will check your permit, equipment, stoves, food and fuel. You should have several lists of group members and equipment available for this purpose. The physical presence of all group members is required at both the police post and the tourist office. Allow at least an hour in both Kagbeni and Jomsom for formalities.

At the conclusion of the trek, you are required to register again with the tourist office and hand over all your rubbish to them for disposal. If the tourist office is satisfied that you have followed all the rules, they will give your liaison officer a letter stating so. This letter is important; any trekking company that does not follow the rules risks being barred from operating treks into restricted areas.

Your liaison officer can register the group with the other checkposts on the trek.

Group Size The rules require that you trek as a member of a group of at least two. You will be much happier if you keep that group as small as possible. Camp sites are small, and a typical trek group of 16 foreigners plus their staff and liaison officer can overwhelm a village.

Maps

US Army Map Service maps NH44-12, NH44-16, NH45-9 and NH45-13 cover upper Mustang. Sheet NH45-9, which covers the top right corner of Lo, has not been reprinted and is virtually unobtainable. The maps are based on surveys made in 1925 and 1926 and are very inaccurate near the northern border of Nepal. They improperly locate several peaks and do not show Tilicho Lake.

The 1989 series *Western Region* map (1:250,000) and *Mustang District* map (1:125,000) produced by the Nepal Ministry of Works & Transport show the current border and are quite accurate, though they do not name the peaks.

Currently, the best available map of the area is Paolo Gondoni's 1:125,000 scale map

RESTRICTED AREAS

entitled *Mustang*, published by Nepa Maps, Kathmandu.

The National Remote Sensing Centre maps with the same keys as the US army series also cover Mustang. These are satellite photos and obviously show geographical features properly, though the features are difficult to interpret. Note also that many annotations in the 1986 edition are not correct; among other errors, Charang is shown in the wrong place.

Mandala Trekking Map series *Jomsom to Mustang* (1:125,000) is a blueprinted map available in Kathmandu.

Books

Mustang – a Lost Tibetan Kingdom, by Michel Peissel, is the first contemporary description of the Lo Manthang region of Mustang, north of Jomsom. *East of Lo Monthang*, by Peter Matthiessen, describes Matthiessen's trek to Mustang and contains many excellent photographs. *Mustang – A Trekking Guide*, by Bob Gibbons & Sian Pritchard-Jones, is a description of a trek to Mustang via the route to Muktinath along the east side of the Mustang Khola.

Other books worth looking out for include the following:

Journey to Mustang, by Giuseppe Tucci
Mustang Bhot in Fragments, by Manjushree Thapa
The Last Forbidden Kingdom: Mustang, Land of Tibetan Buddhism, by Clara Marullo & Vanessa Boeye
The Mollas of Mustang, by David P Jackson

Season

Most of the population departs from Lo on trading expeditions during the winter to avoid the cold and snow. The trekking season, therefore, is from late March until early November. The trek does not go to extremely high elevations, but the cold, dust and unrelenting afternoon winds can make it less pleasant than other treks in Nepal.

Because of the wind and the lack of water, you must always camp in a village, but these are not conveniently spaced, so some days are too short and others too long. There is much less opportunity to vary the itinerary than on most Nepal treks.

Horses

If possible, you should replace your porters with horses from upper Mustang at Jomsom or Kagbeni. Horses carry 40 to 50 kg and cost about Rs 200 per day. Porters demand Rs 200 or 250 per day, so horses are economically competitive with porters. Using horses is also more reliable and environmentally friendly than taking a group of lowland porters into the cold and wind of Mustang, where they will be culturally isolated. By hiring horses from Mustang, you are benefiting the local economy in a culturally sensitive manner. A major advantage of using Mustang horses is that you also gain the services of a local horseman who can serve as a guide and expediter.

Access

The trek I describe here begins and ends in Kagbeni, about two hours walk north of Jomsom. There are daily flights to Jomsom from Pokhara; flights are in the early morning, so you must spend a night in Pokhara en route to Jomsom. The cost of a trip to Mustang escalates severely if you fly in either direction. The airfare from Pokhara to Jomsom is reasonable (US$50) considering you save five days of walking, but you still must calculate the expense of moving your gear to Jomsom. Your food, stoves, tents and fuel, all of which are required by law for a trek to Mustang, must be carried from Pokhara. Once you add the cost of five or six days' porterage plus the salary of camp staff both to and from Jomsom, the trek becomes quite expensive. If you have time, it is very worthwhile to walk from Naya Pul or Baglung, near Pokhara, visit Lo Manthang, trek back to Jomsom and fly or walk back to Pokhara. If you do plan to fly, be aware that Jomsom can occasionally be as bad as the notorious Lukla airstrip in terms of flight delays.

Day 1: Kagbeni to Chele

See Day 6 of the Jomsom trek in the Annapurna Region chapter for information about the facilities in Kagbeni. At the police checkpost at the northern end of the village is a sign saying 'Restricted Area, tourists please do not go beyond this point'. If you have the correct permit for upper Mustang, your liaison officer will complete formalities here and you will be free to enter this long-forbidden region of Nepal.

There is a trail up the east bank of the Kali Gandaki that climbs over many ridges as it heads north. In the dry season, it is possible to trek the entire route up the river along the sand and gravel of the riverbed. This will require at least two, and perhaps many, fords of the several channels of the meandering Kali Gandaki. When Lo people bring their horses to Kagbeni, they travel straight down the centre of the river valley, jumping onto the backs of their horses whenever it is necessary to cross the river. The best solution is to get local advice and then stick to either the high trail or the river-bank route depending on river conditions. It's hard to get back to the high trail if you reach a dead end along the river.

You can see Gompa Kang and some caves on the west bank of the river. Unlike most

gompas in upper Mustang, Gompa Kang is of the Nyingmapa sect. **Tangbe** is alongside the east-bank trail above the river at an elevation of 2990m. Here are the first of the trio of black, white and red chortens that typify upper Mustang. The town is a labyrinth of narrow alleys among whitewashed houses, fields of buckwheat, barley and wheat and apple orchards. Nilgiri (7061m), which dominates the southern skyline from Kagbeni, looms at the foot of the valley.

Chhuksang village is about 1½ hours beyond Tangbe at the confluence of the Narshing Khola and the Kali Gandaki at 2920m. There are three separate parts of this village and some broken castle walls on the surrounding cliffs. Up the Narshing Khola is Tetang, where there is a gompa and a small salt mine.

Across the river from Chhuksang are some spectacular red, eroded, 'organ-pipe' cliffs above the mouths of inaccessible caves. The five villages in this area, Chele, Ghyakar, Chhuksang, Tangbe and Tetang, are inhabited by a culturally unified group of people who call themselves Gurungs and are more closely related to the Manangis than to the Thakalis or Lobas. Note that these five villages are not the Thakali *panchgaon* ('five villages'); those villages – Marpha, Jomsom-Thini, Syang, Chivang and Chherok – are lower on the Kali Gandaki.

Continue north to a huge, red chunk of conglomerate that has fallen from the cliffs above and forms a tunnel through which the Kali Gandaki flows. A steel bridge spans the river just in front of the tunnel. North of here, the Kali Gandaki becomes impassable for those on foot, though the Lobas sometimes travel this route on horseback through a steep, narrow canyon that is dangerous because of falling rocks. There are many ancient caves high on the fluted red cliffs here.

The trek now leaves the Kali Gandaki valley and climbs steeply up a rocky gully to **Chele** at 3030m. This is a small village that boasts upper Mustang's first hotel, the *Nilgiri*, and a shop among the extensive

fields of wheat and barley that blanket the hillside.

There is now a change from the Manangi culture of the five 'Gurung' villages to the Tibetan culture of Lo. Most Lo houses have sheep horns above their doorways and you will see many twigs in the shape of a cross with threads in five colours woven in a diamond-shaped pattern. These are called *zor* and are supposed to capture evil spirits that threaten the population. Being now in a region of Tibetan influence, many people also keep ferocious Tibetan mastiff dogs. Most are chained to houses and their threats are confined to low-pitched barks, but do not treat these animals lightly. If you are surprised by one of these animals on the loose, you can usually keep it at bay by threatening to throw a rock at it. Make a discreet retreat until the owner appears – or until another villager actually does throw a well-aimed stone.

The trading patterns also change in Lo. Despite the fluid political situation, Chinese goods still make their way into Lo. There is more packaged Chinese food available than Nepali or Indian food. Several houses have Chinese wood stoves, porcelain and other articles. Much of the material and decoration for the gompas also comes from Tibet.

Day 2: Chele to Geling
The climb from Chele is up a steep spur to a cairn at 3080m. There is a view of Ghyakar across a huge canyon. A long wall of packed earth encircles Ghyakar and its fields. The climb continues – a long, steep, treeless, waterless slog – along the side of the spectacular, steep canyon to a pass and cairn at 3480m. The trail makes a long, gradual descent to some chortens on a ridge, then descends further on a pleasant trail to **Samar**, surrounded by a grove of poplar trees at 3290m. This is a major stopping place for horse caravans; there are many stables available for hire and there is a hotel catering to locals. The Annapurna Himal, still dominated by Nilgiri, is visible far to the south.

The trail climbs above Samar to a ridge, then descends into a large gorge past a chorten painted in red, black, yellow and white – all pigments made from local rocks. The trail enters another valley filled with juniper trees, crosses a stream, then climbs up to a ridge at 3800m and drops to **Bhena**. It skirts a gorge, climbs slightly to Yamda, then climbs over yet another pass, follows a ridge, then descends to **Shyangmochen**, a tiny settlement with a few tea shops at 3650m.

The trail climbs gently from Shyangmochen to a pass at 3700m and enters another huge east-west valley. There is a trail junction here. The left trail is the direct route to the Nyi La, bypassing Geling. Take the right fork and descend to **Geling** with its poplar trees and extensive fields of barley at 3440m.

Day 3: Geling to Charang
From Geling, the trail climbs gently through fields up the centre of the valley, passing above **Tama Gaon** and its imposing chorten. It rejoins the direct trail and then becomes an unrelenting climb across the head of the valley to the Nyi La at 3950m. This pass is the southern boundary of Lo itself. The descent from the Nyi La is gentle. About half an hour from the pass is a trail junction. The right trail is the direct route to Charang; the left trail leads to Ghami.

The Charang trail descends below the blue, grey and red cliffs across the valley to a steel bridge across the Tangmar Chu river, then climbs past what is perhaps the longest and most impressive stretch of *mani* wall in Nepal. After climbing over another pass at 3770m, the route makes a long, gentle descent to **Charang** at 3490m.

Charang is a maze of fields, willow trees and houses separated by stone walls at the top of the large Charang Chu canyon. The huge, five storey, white *dzong* (Tibetan-style fortress) and red gompa are perched on the edge of the Kali Gandaki gorge at the eastern end of the village. The gompa houses a collection of statues and *thangkas* as well as many large paintings of seated Buddhas. Near the gompa is the house of Maya Bista, which, if you have the nerve to get past the ferocious mastiff at the door, doubles as a hotel and restaurant. There is a camping ground nearby. The village has its own electricity supply; you cross under the pipes of the hydro plant just beyond the village.

Day 4: Charang to Lo Manthang
The trail descends about 125m from Charang, crosses the Charang Chu and climbs steeply up a rocky trail to a cairn on a ridge opposite the village at 3530m, then enters the Tholung valley. The trail turns north and climbs gently to a large, isolated chorten that marks the boundary between Charang and Lo. Still climbing, the trail crosses a stream, then becomes a grand, wide thoroughfare travelling across a desert-like landscape painted in every hue of grey and yellow. Finally, from a ridge at 3850m, there is a view of the walled city of Lo.

A short descent leads onto the 'plain of aspiration' at 3780m. The trail crosses a stream and climbs up onto the plateau of **Lo Manthang** itself at 3730m, crossing an irrigation canal at the southern wall of the city. The only entrance to the city is at the northeastern corner, so circumambulate the wall to the gate where you are sure to find a group of adults and children playing, spinning wool and gossiping.

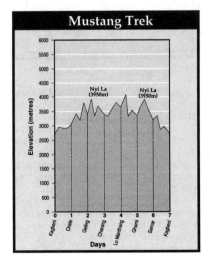

Mustang Trek

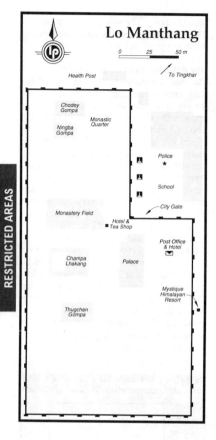

Lo Manthang

0   25   50 m

Health Post

To Tingkhar

Chodey Gompa

Monastic Quarter

Ningba Gompa

Police ★

School

City Gate

Monastery Field

Hotel & Tea Shop

Post Office & Hotel

Champa Lhakang

Palace

Mystique Himalayan Resort

Thugchen Gompa

The whitewashed wall around Lo Manthang resembles a misshapen 'L' with a short vertical arm oriented north-south and a very fat, almost square horizontal arm. The closely packed houses of the city, the palace and temples are in the bottom portion; the vertical part of the 'L' houses the monastic community and two gompas, and this portion of the city wall is painted red.

The school, health post, police checkpost and several important chortens are outside the walls to the north of the gate and east of the monastic part of the city. Peissel described the gates as being closed at night,

but now they remain permanently open. The city contains about 150 houses plus numerous lama residences. The only agricultural land inside the walls is a field, owned by the monastéry, near the city centre.

The wall of Lo Manthang was once more imposing than it is now. In the mid-1980s the raja sold much of the land surrounding the city, and as a result, numerous stables, houses and stone-walled fields now adjoin the wall. Nothing will grow in this arid land without irrigation. A small canal flows around the city, providing sustenance for a few willow trees, and another canal flows under the wall and through the city itself. The surrounding irrigated fields provide one crop a year of wheat, barley, peas or mustard.

Days 5 & 6: In Lo Manthang

Temples There are four major temples within the city walls. Each of these buildings is locked. The villagers feel it necessary to control access to the temples; the caretaker and the key are available only at certain times, and usually only after a bit of negotiation. The standard fee is Rs 100 per person for each gompa that you visit.

The tall **Champa Lhakang** (*lha kang* translates as 'god house') is said to date from the 1420s and is accessible only on the second storey. The central courtyard with its carved wooden pillars has fallen into disrepair. Inside the temple is a huge painted clay statue of Maitreya, the future Buddha, sitting on a pedestal that occupies the entire ground floor. The walls are painted with elaborate mandalas almost two metres in diameter that are in marginally better condition than the paintings in Thugchen gompa.

The red **Thugchen gompa**, near the centre of the city, is a massive assembly hall supported by huge wooden columns dating from the same period as Champa Lhakang. Tucci observed that the same artists had painted frescoes in both temples. There are statues of the deity Sakyamuni surrounded by Avalokitesvara, Vaisravana (the god of wealth) and Padmasambhava. One wall of the temple is completely destroyed; on the other walls are intricate frescoes in various stages of deterioration. The entrance hall contains huge, scowling statues of four Lokapala, the protectors of the cardinal points of the compass.

The other two temples are within the monastic quarter, which is the domain of several large, growling Tibetan mastiffs. Secure the services of a monk before you even attempt to enter this part of the city. The main temple is the **Chodey gompa**, which contains dozens of beautifully crafted small bronze, brass and copper statues, many said to have been cast in Lo Manthang itself. The monks prohibit taking photographs of these statues in an apparent effort to limit interest in them among collectors of stolen art. Nearby is the older assembly hall, which contains little more than the images of the three Sakyapa lamas.

City Life Despite the apparent squalor of Lo Manthang, the city is prosperous and maintains a strong sense of community. Though the people call themselves Lobas, they are Tibetan and practice a sophisticated culture and economy. Before trade with Tibet was disrupted, all of the salt and wool trade on the Kali Gandaki passed through Lo Manthang, and this brought a sizable amount of money to the city. Wealth is now primarily measured in land, horses and social standing, though during the winter many Lobas travel south to India, where they are major players in the sale and distribution of acrylic sweaters manufactured in the Punjabi city of Ludhiana.

The door of most houses opens onto a two storey, open central courtyard. The ground floor is used for storage of food, horse trappings, a pile of dung for fuel and farm implements. A wooden staircase leads to the first storey, which typically has a balcony overlooking the courtyard and doors leading off to living rooms and the kitchen. A notched log leads to the roof, which is surrounded by huge stacks of juniper twigs and firewood. The roof is an important part of the house, used for relaxing or working in the sun. Adorning the roof of most houses are the horns of sheep and yak and, on the palace,

horns that are over 100 years old of extinct Sikkim stags.

Virtually every house has an indoor toilet on the upper floor that drops into a ground-floor chamber. Ashes from the hearth are dumped into the toilet to eliminate smell, and the resulting product is a nutritive, not unpleasant fertiliser. The stoves used in Lo are of a special design. Stoves are a three-armed affair with a 30-cm-high burning chamber that gets roaring like a volcano when fed with yak dung and goat droppings. People rarely burn the wood on the roof for cooking; it is there largely as a show of wealth and for ceremonial occasions.

Raja's Palace The raja's palace is an imposing four-storey building in the centre of the city. It is the home of the present raja, Jigme Parbal Bista, and the queen, or rani, who is from an aristocratic family of Lhasa. The raja is an active horseman and keeps a stable of the best horses in Lo. He also breeds lhasa apso dogs and monstrous Tibetan mastiffs that can be heard barking angrily in the second storey of the palace. Though his duties are largely ceremonial, the raja is respected by the people and consulted about many issues by villagers throughout Lo.

The raja's family name was originally Tandul. It was changed in accordance with a recent tradition in which many people of Tibetan descent 'nepalised' their surnames. This practice is similar to the custom of the 'Matwali Chhetris' of Dolpo, whereby Khampas adopted Hindu surnames. It is also similar to the practice of many Manangis who call themselves Gurungs. Many Lobas use their original Tibetan name, but almost all have a second, Nepali name that was assigned when they enrolled in school.

Places to Stay There are two houses inside the city that provide basic hotel facilities. One hotel is operated by Surendra Bista, and is above the post office in the square across from the palace. The second hotel is primarily a tea shop and drinking establishment, and is in an alley to the right of the entrance gate. Just outside the city wall is the *Mystique*

Himalayan Resort, a nine room hotel with attached bathrooms.

Around Lo Manthang There is a lot to do in Lo Manthang. After visiting the temples in the city, consider hiring a horse to visit some of the other villages in the area. Horses with a saddle covered with a colourful Tibetan carpet are available for Rs 500 per day. The Rs 500 applies whether you use the horse for one hour or from dawn to dusk. Mount and dismount outside the city gate; only the raja may ride a horse within the city walls.

The police do not allow trekkers to travel north of Lo Manthang village unless they have a 13 day, US$910 trekking permit. There are two valleys above Lo Manthang. In the western valley are **Tingkhar**, the site of the raja's summer palace, Kimling, Phuwa and **Namgyal gompa** ('the monastery of victory'). Namgyal, in a spectacular setting atop a desolate ridge, is the newest and most active gompa in Lo. If you have a 13 day permit, you may visit these villages, but you must return to Lo Manthang for the night.

The valley east of Lo Manthang contains **Chosar**, the site of the high school, and Garphu and Nyphu gompas. This is the main trading route to Lhasa, a route that Tucci describes as '... used over the centuries by pilgrims and apostles, robbers and invaders'. The ruins of numerous forts along the trail lend credence to this observation.

Day 7: Lo Manthang to Ghami

There is an opportunity to vary the return route, visiting two villages that you did not see on the trek northwards. From Lo Manthang the trail to Charang heads south; to reach Lo Gekar, turn west along an indistinct trail that passes the irrigated fields of the city.

The trail to Lo Gekar is not a main trading route and the area is crisscrossed with herders' trails, so a local guide is particularly useful here. The trail climbs steadily to a pass marked by a cairn, offering a last glimpse of Lo Manthang. The trail contours across the head of a valley and crosses another ridge, then drops into another large desolate valley. After descending to the valley floor, the route

heads to the west, up the centre of the valley to its head. Cross a ridge at 4070m and traverse across the heads of two more valleys to an indistinct pass. Cross the pass to some meadows and a stream. The trail makes a long rocky descent down a ravine to **Lo Gekar** (which means 'pure virtue of Lo'), then reaches a grassy valley and **Ghar gompa**, in a grove of large trees alongside a stream.

Ghar gompa means 'house temple' and is so named because the structure is built like a house with small, separate rooms. The gompa is decorated with paintings and statues and several large prayer wheels. The primary deities are placed on a brass altar inside a dark alcove; on one wall of the alcove there is a self-emanating statue. The real treasure of Ghar gompa is the hundreds of painted, carved stones displayed on the walls in wooden frames. Snellgrove learned that the lama of Syang, the village south of Jomsom, presented many of the gompa's decorations and often stayed there.

There is no village nearby, but there is a series of quarters for monks and pilgrims near the gompa that provides protection from the wind. The gompa is supplied with electricity via a long transmission line from Marang village. You can see Marang and, below that, Charang in the valley below.

Climb to a ridge, then cross a valley to a

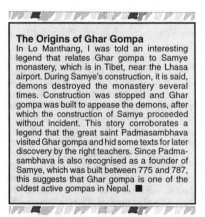

The Origins of Ghar Gompa
In Lo Manthang, I was told an interesting legend that relates Ghar gompa to Samye monastery, which is in Tibet, near the Lhasa airport. During Samye's construction, it is said, demons destroyed the monastery several times. Construction was stopped and Ghar gompa was built to appease the demons, after which the construction of Samye proceeded without incident. This story corroborates a legend that the great saint Padmasambhava visited Ghar gompa and hid some texts for later discovery by the right teachers. Since Padmasambhava is also recognised as a founder of Samye, which was built between 775 and 787, this suggests that Ghar gompa is one of the oldest active gompas in Nepal. ∎

cairn and a pass 200m above Ghar gompa. The route crosses some alpine meadows to a crest, then drops down a steep, eroded gully to the upper part of **Dhakmar**, whose name means 'red crag'. A large stream meanders through this village, making this a particularly pretty valley. Most of the surrounding hills are in pastel shades of grey and yellow, but a huge, red, fluted cliff provides a dramatic contrast. The trail descends alongside the stone walls and fields of the extensive village, then climbs to a ridge. It is a short descent to **Ghami** at 3460m.

Ghami is a large village of whitewashed houses above hectares and hectares of fields. About half of the fields are barren because of problems with the irrigation system. Ghami has a police post and the *Raju Hotel*, which is operated by a grandnephew of the Lo raja. In the winter of 1991, there were rabid dogs in this village. The villagers solved the problem by killing every dog in the locality. The gompa is being restored using local money, and the villagers and lamas are not happy about allowing tourists to visit the gompa. They are fearful of theft of religious objects, and their fears are not unfounded because several old and important thangkas were stolen from the gompa at Geling in early 1992. A small, red nunnery dominates a crag at the far end of the village.

Day 8: Ghami to Samar

From Ghami, follow the direct route to the Nyi La, climbing to a cairn on a ridge and then contouring upwards to meet the trail from Charang. Continue to the pass and descend steeply into the Geling valley. Follow the trail that bypasses Geling to an isolated teahouse, and descend gently to the three houses of **Tama Gaon**. A steep set of switchbacks leads to a stream, then the trail climbs to a huge, painted chorten before rejoining the Geling trail near the ridge, just below a chorten. The remainder of the day is on already-travelled trails back to **Samar**.

Day 9: Samar to Kagbeni

Retrace the upward trail back to the Kali Gandaki and downstream to Kagbeni – hopefully, before your permit expires.

Alternative Route from Lo Manthang to Kagbeni To return to Kagbeni there is another route down the eastern side of the Kali Gandaki valley through Tange and Tetang to Muktinath. These villages are isolated and not frequented by travellers of any kind. Most do not have even basic facilities for porters and are not used to coping with the demands of tourists. Villages are far apart and there is no shelter, except possibly in caves, between them. If you attempt this route, be prepared for at least one long, 10 hour (30-plus km) day. There is no water or vegetation between the few villages on this route.

Around Manaslu

Duration 20 days
Difficulty Medium to hard
Maximum elevation 5100m
Permit cost US$70 per week
Season October to May
Hotels Only camping treks allowed
Summary A long walk up the rough Buri Gandaki valley leads to Nupri, a valley of Tibetan people behind Manaslu. Great mountain scenery, Tibetan culture and a high pass crossing.

This trek was officially opened to tourists in 1991, but mountaineering expeditions have long had access to the area. In 1950 a party led by HW Tilman trekked from Thonje to Bimtang and Colonel Jimmy Roberts crossed the Larkya La looking for an interesting mountain to climb. Manaslu (8156m) was attempted by Japanese expeditions every year from 1952 until 1956, when the first ascent was made. It thus became known as a 'Japanese mountain', and much of the information about the area was available only in Japanese. The Japanese continued to dominate the climbing scene on Manaslu until 1971.

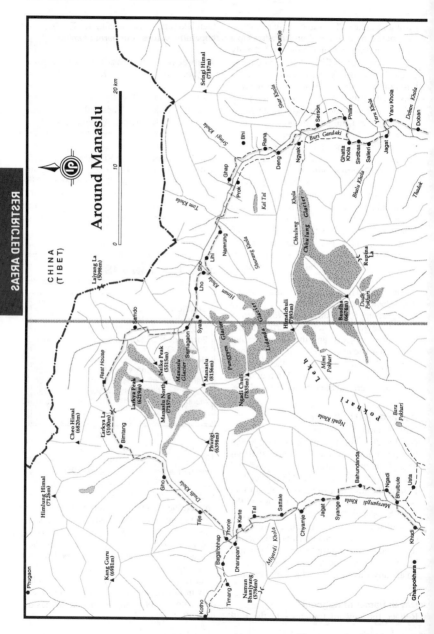

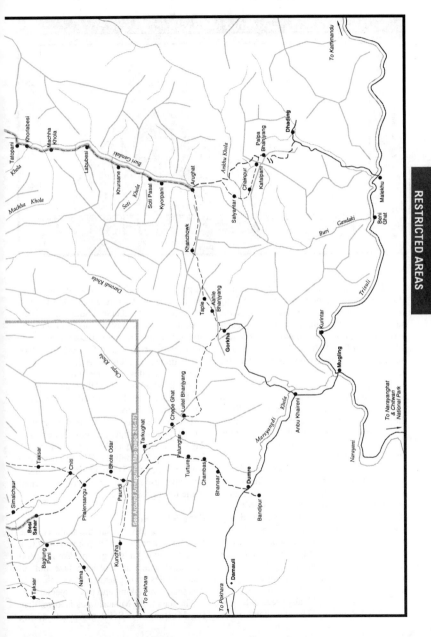

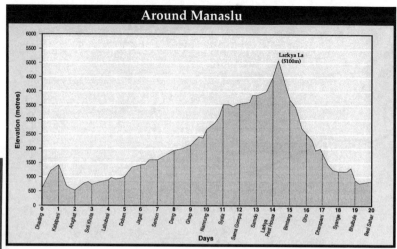

Around Manaslu

RESTRICTED AREAS

A few trekkers, including the peripatetic Hugh Swift, managed to obtain trekking permits for the region, but otherwise this trek has always been the domain of the mountaineering expedition. The book *Honey Hunters of Nepal*, by Eric Valli & Dianne Summers, makes good background reading for this area.

Though the Larkya La is not a difficult pass, the trek around Manaslu is harder than most in Nepal. In many places the walls of the Buri Gandaki valley are perpendicular, so you cannot walk along the bottom of the valley. There is a huge amount of wasted climbing involved during the first part of the trek as you climb up and down over ridges or onto shelves to bypass cliffs. The trail is rough and steep and it often literally hangs on a bluff high above the river. Don't read any further if you have the slightest tendency towards acrophobia. The trek is remote and has no rescue facilities or opportunities to bail out if you are tired. There is only one facility that might conceivably be called a trekkers' hotel, and there are few English signboards between Arughat and Tilje.

The trek is geographically spectacular and culturally fascinating. The inhabitants of the upper Buri Gandaki, a region known as Nupri ('the western mountains'), are direct descendants of Tibetan immigrants. Their speech, dress and customs are almost exclusively Tibetan. There is still continuous trade between Nupri and Tibet; Chinese cigarettes, for example, are found more frequently than Nepali cigarettes. The mountain views in Nupri are sensational, and the crossing of the Larkya La is one of the most dramatic of any pass in the Himalaya.

Because much of this trek is in a region of strong Tibetan influence, most places have Tibetan names in addition to their better known Nepali monikers. Where possible, I have included the Tibetan name in brackets, but have used the more common Nepali name throughout the text.

Fees & Permits

The rules for this trek are the same as those for Mustang and Inner Dolpo: you must trek with a fully organised group; take a liaison (or 'environmental') officer; take out all cans, bottles and 'plastic paper'; use only kerosene for cooking and pay a special fee.

The fee for the Manaslu trek is lower than for Mustang – US$90 per week during

October and November and only US$75 per week during the remainder of the year. There is supposed to be a quota of 400 trekkers per year for this route.

Access
As described here, this trek begins in Dhading, but you can opt to set out from Gorkha or Trisuli Bazaar. All three routes converge at Arughat, two days from Gorkha, three days from Trisuli and one long day from the road above Dhading (at the end of Day 2 in the route description that follows). A road from Dhading to Arughat is under construction.

Gorkha Gorkha is the traditional starting point for treks up the Buri Gandaki. The bus ride from Kathmandu to Gorkha follows the Pokhara road as far as Abu Khaireni, then climbs 24 km to Gorkha. Gorkha is served by buses from Narayanghat, Pokhara and Kathmandu. The cost is Rs 39 from Pokhara and Rs 50 from Kathmandu. There is a road under construction from Gorkha to Aahle Bhanjyang, then it's three days on foot through Taple, Khanchowk and Ganeshtan to Arughat.

Trisuli Bazaar Trisuli Bazaar is an alternative starting point for the Around Manaslu trek. Arughat is a four-day walk from Trisuli along the old route from Kathmandu to Pokhara.

Buses to Trisuli leave from the bus terminal on the Ring Road north of Kathmandu. The first bus leaves at 7 am, costs Rs 32 and takes about five hours to reach Trisuli.

Dhading Dhading provides an excellent starting point for the Manaslu trek and saves a day of walking compared to the trek from Gorkha.

There is no direct bus service to Dhading. From Kathmandu, you need to take a local bus for Pokhara and get off at Malekhu (485m). It is about a two-hour drive to Malekhu. Cross the Trisuli river on a footbridge and take another bus for the remainder of the trip up the 17 km unpaved

road to Dhading Besi. The road follows a stream as it climbs in a steep valley through dense sal forests past Bungchung. Finally the valley opens up as Dhading village comes into view at 670m elevation. The snow peaks of Ganesh Himal are visible to the north. The road beyond Dhading is suitable only for jeeps, so if you are travelling by bus, decamp at Dhading and start climbing along the trail that follows a more direct route than the road.

Day 1: Dhading to Kafalpani
If you are on a public bus, you will end up at the bazaar in Dhading Besi. If you have your own jeep, turn left at the entrance to the village and follow a road upwards. This road will eventually reach Arughat in the Buri Gandaki valley. At present it climbs all the way to the top of the ridge between Dhading and the Buri Gandaki valley, saving a lot of uphill walking. I started trekking from Palpa Bhanjyang, 11 km by road from Dhading Besi, at 1120m. I followed the road for a while, cutting switchbacks. The road heads north over another ridge, but the trail continues level through Nigalpani; there are views of Annapurna II and Manaslu along the route. The trail crests the ridge at Kafalpani (1350m). The major peak groups visible here, from west to east, are the Annapurnas, Manaslu (8156m), Sringi Himal (7187m) and Ganesh Himal (7406m).

Day 2: Kafalpani to Arughat
From the ridge the trek descends gently to **Chainpur**, a village with a few tea shops on a saddle. The trail descends steeply to a stream at 680m, then traverses rice fields before dropping to a long suspension bridge across the Ankhu Khola at 580m. The trail climbs to **Salyantar**, on a flat plateau between the Buri Gandaki and the Ankhu Khola. After a few km of flat walking, the trail enters the valley of the Buri Gandaki.

The trail is flat through forests to Doren and then to **Arughat**, 525m. The village is in two parts, on opposite sides of the Buri Gandaki. The route first enters the eastern part of Arughat, a large, prosperous clean bazaar with hotels and shops selling cloth, food and hardware. There is a trail junction here. Turn west across the bridge over the Buri Gandaki to continue the trek.

From the trail junction descend a set of stone steps to where the village blacksmiths, or *kamis*, ply their trade just beside the eastern end of a big steel suspension bridge. On the western side of the bridge, follow the stone-paved street north through the bazaar to a police checkpost. The trail to Gorkha leads west and the route around Manaslu turns north.

Pass the stone buildings of the hydroelectric power plant and walk through fields of rice and millet to a camp north of Arughat, near Maltar.

Day 3: Arughat to Soti Khola
Continue past forests full of monkeys to Shanti Bazaar, 10 thatched houses, some shops and a shady pipal tree at 630m with a view of Sringi Himal up the valley. The Buri Gandaki valley now becomes steeper and the trek more difficult as the trail crosses the Arkhet Khola, passes through Arkhet (760m) and climbs through fields and over a rock outcrop. Descend to a high, cascading waterfall, then make a long, steep slog up a ridge to **Kyorpani**, a small Magar and Gurung village at 820m. The trail descends to Soti Pasal and, a few minutes beyond, to a good camp by the **Soti Khola** at 710m. There is a good swimming hole and a small waterfall up the Soti Khola just above the trail. A much larger waterfall, with a 60m drop, is visible by climbing upstream. This valley is said to have beehives where honey is harvested in a manner similar to that described in the book *Honey Hunters of Nepal*.

The Gurungs of the Buri Gandaki are primarily farmers, though there are many remnants of a hunting society. You are likely to encounter men with locally made rifles or to hear shots in the woods as the hunt for a deer concludes.

The focus of the region's trade is Gorkha, though many people have never ventured beyond Arughat. Few Gurungs of this region make it into the British army Gurkha regi-

ments. The women often dress elegantly and have extensive collections of jewellery, bangles and saris. The men tend to dress in more simple, locally made clothing, often using cloth woven from nettle fibre. Most men wear a quaint, heavy, brown woollen cape called a *bokkhu*. This versatile garment is usually worn as a coat, but can be used as a hooded raincoat, a sleeping bag, a tent or even a cloak to protect the wearer from bees during a honey hunting expedition.

Day 4: Soti Khola to Labubesi
The trail crosses the bridge and climbs up onto a ridge above huge rapids on the Buri Gandaki before continuing up to **Khursane** and a big Gurung house at 820m. The trail gets a bit precarious as it passes over a big rock and crosses a stream on a single log perched high above it. The rocky trail then weaves its way up and down through large stands of nettles, past two tropical waterfalls and back down to the banks of the Buri Gandaki where a farmer has scratched out a few rice terraces. Trek up again on a steep, rocky trail clinging to the side of a cliff, down and past a few more rice terraces, then up and around to the Gurung village of **Labubesi** at 880m.

Day 5: Labubesi to Doban
The path climbs behind a rocky outcrop to a dilapidated school. The valley opens and the Buri Gandaki meanders among wide gravel bars. The narrow, exposed trail drops to a high, cascading waterfall and wooden bridge, then climbs over another ridge before dropping to the sandy riverbed at 860m. It's just a short walk along the rounded stones of the riverbed before climbing about 110m over a side ridge to avoid a spot where the river changed course and erased the riverside trail. Down again to the river, up over another ridge, then traverse above the river to **Machha Khola** village, above a stream with the same name. You can drop into the village or take the elevated bypass route to a suspension bridge, several tea shops and a camp by the stream at 900m. The Buri Gandaki is spanned by a bridge that provides

access to the area south of Ganesh Himal. Don't cross here.

The trail makes some minor ups and downs and crosses the Thadok Khola, flowing in a rocky ravine, then reaches Khorlabesi. There are two houses, a rudimentary shop, a tea stall and an outside covered restaurant here. The main part of the village is far above, on top of the hill. Climb over a small ridge, then make a very steep climb and descent to a single house. After more ups and downs there is a small trailside hot spring, then the route reaches **Tatopani**, 930m. There is no village at Tatopani, just a stone structure and a single spout of hot water.

From the hot spring the trail climbs over another ridge, then crosses the Buri Gandaki on a suspension bridge in a state of moderate decay. Now on the eastern side of the river, the trail climbs on a wide, well-crafted staircase over a ridge to **Doban**, which boasts a small shop. A long suspension bridge carries the trail over the Doban Khola; the trail reaches the bridge via an interesting cloverleaf approach.

Day 6: Doban to Jagat
The next stretch of trail is under construction, and the stretches where it's not yet finished are pretty rough. Hopefully, by the time you trek here the trail will have been completely rebuilt. The route climbs on a rugged, rocky trail to two tea shops at Duman. After crossing under a big landslide you will eventually find yourself atop a ridge. The river valley widens, and the trail descends to the Buri Gandaki, which is now meandering serenely among gravel bars. At **Yaru Khola**, 1330m, there is a single large house and a good camp site near the river. An old man is trying to eke out a living selling cigarettes, roasted soybeans and beer.

Cross a 93m-long suspension bridge over the Yaru Khola and ascend a wide set of stone stairs, drop to the river and then climb more big stone stairs to **Thado Bharyang**, two houses and a shop next to a bridge. The bridges and trail in this region were constructed as part of a CARE project in 1983.

Cross the Buri Gandaki, climb over a ridge, trek along the river for a while, then climb up to the compact village of **Jagat** at 1410m. Jagat has a beautiful flagstone village square in front of a rudimentary trekkers' hotel. In the village are a shop, a police post and a customs office that assesses duty on goods brought from Tibet. There is a good camp by the Bhalu Khola below Jagat.

Day 7: Jagat to Serson
Either rock-hop across the Bhalu Khola or go upstream and cross the suspension bridge. Climb over a rocky ridge to **Salleri**, a settlement of 10 houses and herders' huts at 1440m. There are good views of Sringi Himal as you continue up along the side of a cliff. The trail descends to Sirdibas (Tara), at 1430m, where a decrepit stone *kani* (arch-shaped chorten) and several mani walls indicate that the trek is now entering a region of Tibetan influence, though the people are still Gurungs. The valley widens a bit as the trail continues up to the stone houses of **Ghatta Khola**. Cross the rock-strewn stream where several mills (*ghatta* in Nepali) spin merrily away. The trail continues upstream to a long suspension bridge that looks just like the Golden Gate bridge in San Francisco. The best route around Manaslu crosses the bridge and follows a new trail on the eastern side of the river.

Cross the bridge and climb up to **Philim** (Dodang) at 1590m. This is a large Gurung village with fields of corn and millet. The trail that climbs through the village and heads up over a ridge leads to Ganesh Himal base camp. The valley behind Ganesh Himal is called Tsum. The people of Tsum are Tibetan; much of their trade is with Tibet, which is across two passes at the head of the Shar Khola ('east river') valley. The Manaslu trail turns north just above the lowest houses in the village and stays fairly level as it traverses millet fields to **Serson**.

Alternative Route via Ngyak The old (west bank) trail goes from Ghatta Khola up to Pangsing, climbs to **Ngyak** (Nyak), a

Gurung village perched high above the river at 2300m, then descends and climbs over another ridge before rejoining the new trail.

Day 8: Serson to Deng

Beyond Serson the route enters a steep, uninhabited gorge. The trail descends grassy slopes dotted with tall pine trees. Cross the Buri Gandaki on a wooden cantilever bridge where the river is at its narrowest. The trail now hangs on a cliff, climbing over ridges and descending to the river. If you have the courage to take your eyes off your feet, you can see the Shar Khola joining the Buri Gandaki on the opposite bank. The trail makes its way up the western side and the valley finally widens, offering a pleasant walk through bamboo forests to the Deng Khola and the tiny village of **Deng** at 1920m. You have now crossed the main Himalayan range. The trail follows the Buri Gandaki valley as it turns from north-south to east-west. This region is known as Kutang and is inhabited primarily by Gurungs who practise Buddhism.

Day 9: Deng to Ghap

A short distance beyond Deng the trail recrosses the Buri Gandaki, onto what is now the north bank, near Rana. There is a rudimentary shop at **Rana** (1980m), near the bridge. Several villagers also have stashes of provisions in their homes; a bit of inquiry will produce almost anything that you might need. Japanese-influenced maps call this village Lana, but the locals insist that the correct name is Rana.

From the bridge the trail climbs a bit to join a trail from Bhi, then heads west up the Buri Gandaki valley. It's level for a bit, then the route climbs on steps past a waterfall. Cross the stream on a crooked wooden bridge, then drop to another stream that flows in a steep, narrow canyon. Contour up and out of the canyon for a view of the Buri Gandaki looking like a tranquil lake above a collection of rocks that form a dam. The trail darts in and out of two ravines, then continues to climb high above the river before dropping into the Sringi Khola valley. There

are a few houses above steep cliffs on the opposite side of the river that are accessible via a bridge that crosses the Buri Gandaki here.

Cross the Sringi Khola on a funky suspension bridge, then climb steeply and traverse above the Buri Gandaki where it flows between vertical rock walls. The trail makes more ups and downs in forests, passing an occasional house or mani wall, then turns a corner and contours to **Ghap** (Tsak). The trail passes through a kani with intricate, well-preserved paintings on the inside, then through corn and wheat fields below Ghap's half-dozen stone houses.

The mani wall in Ghap has particularly elegant carvings said to have been made by a family of stone carvers from Bhi, high on the hillside above. Many of the carvings depict the Buddha in various meditative poses and others are of the Tibetan saint Milarepa, who is said to have travelled and meditated in this valley. The stone in this region is quite hard, so the carvings do not have the deep relief that is typical of mani walls throughout other parts of Nepal and Tibet. The trail from Ghap crosses the Buri Gandaki to the south side on a 26m-long blue steel trestle bridge at 2100m. There are camp sites near the bridge.

Alternative Route via Prok There is a route from Deng to Ghap that stays on the south bank of the river, passing through Prok (2380m) before rejoining the trail at Ghap. Prok has several gompas, and from Prok you can make a side trip to the lake of Kal Tal at 3630m.

Day 10: Ghap to Namrung

Pass more mani stones on the south side of the river, cut across fields and head into the woods. Pass a few houses and three streams in a forest of big firs alive with birds, including the *danphe* or impeyan pheasant, Nepal's colourful national bird. On the north side of the river is the Tom (Tum) Khola, which flows in a deep gorge from Tibet, almost doubling the flow of the Buri Gandaki. Still on the south bank, the trail climbs alongside

STAN ARMINGTON

STAN ARMINGTON

STAN ARMINGTON

Mustang
Top: Tangbe village, in the upper Kali Gandaki valley, on the route to Mustang.
Middle: The village of Ghami and one of the longest mani walls in Nepal.
Bottom: Stacks of juniper wood adorn roofs in the walled city of Lo Manthang.

STAN ARMINGTON

STAN ARMINGTON

STAN ARMINGTON

STAN ARMINGTON

Restricted Areas
Top: The north face of Mt Kailas (Tibet), the most sacred mountain in Asia
Middle Left: An exquisite mani stone carved by a craftsman from Bhi, east of Manaslu
Middle Right: The extensive prayer flags on Dolma La (Mt Kailas)
Bottom: Taklakot, where trekkers to Mt Kailas complete Chinese immigration formalities

the river past two long mani walls to a water-fall. There is a lot of trading between villages in this region and villages higher in the Buri Gandaki valley, and also with Tibet. Most of this trade is by caravans of horses, yaks and yak crossbreeds that stomp the trail into muddy bogs. There are some interesting rock-hopping exercises along this stretch if you want to keep your feet dry. You'll need to climb over a large rock to avoid one big mud hole, then continue up through deep forests of fir and rhododendron.

In the middle of the forest is a wooden bridge that spans the Buri Gandaki. The river has cut through the rock and thunders through a steep, narrow crevice below the bridge. The bridge crossing is made more exciting by the lack of handrails. The trail climbs on the northern side to a big rock cave, then crosses the river again on another wooden bridge under the watchful eyes of a tribe of grey langur monkeys. Back on the south bank, the trail makes a long, serious climb through bamboo and rhododendron forests, finally entering **Namrung** (Namdru) through a stone archway at 2660m. This village has lovely stone houses and a police checkpost that controls access to the upper part of the valley. This is a border police station which takes its work seriously. Your liaison officer will see that the police stamp your trekking permit and take care of the rest of the formalities. The trail drops past a small, dilapidated schoolhouse to the Thorang Khola. There are excellent camps in the forests to the right of the trail, and another part of Namrung lies across a bridge.

Day 11: Namrung to Syala

Beyond Namrung the trek enters the Nupri region. The people of Nupri are all descendants of Tibetan immigrants and most dress in *chubas*, the Tibetan-style wraparound cloak. Climb past a mani wall and the many fields and houses of **Barcham** (Bartsam), then up through a forest of firs, rhododendron and oak to a promontory. The trail passes through a stone arch and enters the closely packed houses and wheat fields of

Lihi at 2900m. There is a gompa on the side of the trail and another above the village.

The stone houses of Lihi exhibit the unusual architecture of this region. They are grouped together like apartments into units of five or six that share a common roof and courtyard. Most roofs are made of heavy wood shingles. Unlike the shingle roofs in other regions of Nepal, these are not piled with rocks to keep them from blowing away. The people say that there are rarely strong winds in this valley.

The trail leaves the village through a kani, then makes a long sweep into a wooded canyon. Cross the Hinan Khola on a double-span cantilever bridge, then huff and puff back up to another kani and the closely packed houses of **Sho**. By this time you will have been hassled by children asking for *shim shim*. This is Tibetan for sweets or candy, and the demands increase from here until you leave the Buri Gandaki valley.

The views now start to get spectacular. Manaslu, Manaslu North (7157m) and Naike Peak appear at the head of the valley. The villages on the opposite side of the river are Shonju and, further to the west, Tong. The trail crosses a small ravine to a big prayer wheel in the middle of the trail, then climbs through more fields to the small settlement of Shrip. The strange-looking platforms in the fields are watchtowers where people sit all night to scare bears away from the crops. The trail climbs past a small stream crowded with dirty kids in tiny chubas collecting water to **Lho** at 3180m. Lho is a big village with a gompa, a rough stone archway at the entrance and a Tibetan-style chorten and huge mani wall at the western end. There's a spectacular view of Manaslu from the kani above Lho.

Drop down to the Damonan Khola, crossing it on a two-span bridge near some mills, then ascend again. The trail follows the north fork of the stream up for a long distance through damp forests on ground that is either muddy or icy, depending on the season. (Don't take the left-hand trail that follows the south fork and ends up at Pung-gyen gompa, the Pungen Glacier and the Manaslu east face

RESTRICTED AREAS

base camp.) Finally the trail emerges onto a plateau at **Syala** (3520m) with a wide vista of Himalchuli, Ngadi Chuli (the Survey of India called this Peak 29, and the locals call it Dhangnang) and Manaslu, known locally as Ghanpurge.

There is a chorten and a small gompa with a huge prayer wheel here. The total deforestation around Syala is shocking. Some time during the last 20 years there was a fire in this forest. This inspired the locals to hack down all the remaining trees, burned or not, to build houses – and the prayer wheel – leaving acres of blackened stumps. The scene is one of almost total desolation.

Day 12: Syala to Sama Gompa

Cross the ridge out of the stream valley to the Buri Gandaki side, trek in and out of the canyon of the Thosang Khola, then descend onto a rock-strewn moraine. Clamber across the boulders and emerge onto a ridge overlooking the extensive pastures and fields of **Samagaon**. Karghi Chhuling gompa is visible in the distance, nestled against a wooded moraine at the far end of the valley. Walk across fields of wheat and buckwheat, past a chorten, to a large yellow kani with bright, well-preserved paintings inside. The extensive village of Samagaon is nestled in the valley at an elevation of 3530m, beyond the kani. Descend to a large collection of mani stones and walk through the village. Many houses have courtyards that overlook the trail, so you become immersed in the domestic affairs of the village during the trek through.

Weaving is a big occupation in Samagaon, and you will see many women working looms as you make your way through hordes of persistent 'shim shim' and 'give me pen' kids. Head west beside the stream that runs through the village and you will eventually pass through a kani and find yourself headed for the gompa. Climb up to the many buildings and residences of the gompa and on to a camp in a large field beyond. When I stayed here we were terrified of the howling winds that we could hear in the distance, though there was no wind in the camp. It took us

until the following day to discover that what we thought was howling wind was only the roar of the Buri Gandaki echoing off the sides of the valley.

Side Trip: Pung-gyen Gompa If you have a day to spare, climb the ridge to the south of Samagaon to the Pung-gyen gompa, which is hidden behind the ridge in front of Manaslu. The Japanese call this Honsansho gompa. It was destroyed by an avalanche during the winter of 1953 after the first Japanese expedition to Manaslu, killing 18 inhabitants, mostly nuns. The villagers believe that the god residing on Manaslu destroyed the gompa to show his wrath for the trespassers, and refused to let the second Japanese expedition to Manaslu climb the mountain in 1954. You can also make a day hike to Birendra Tal, a glacial lake at 3450m.

Day 13: Sama Gompa to Samdo

Descend to the Buri Gandaki, which has now turned north again, and follow it to a bridge over a side stream. There is a trail to the left that leads to the Manaslu base camp. The Larkya La trail passes several mani walls as the valley begins to widen. It's an easy trail on a shelf above the river past juniper and birch forests and the stone huts of **Kermo Kharka**, then it gets rougher as it reaches a ridge where yak trains have ground the trail into mush. Drop off the shelf, cross the river on a wooden bridge and climb steeply onto a promontory between two forks of the river. From a stone arch you can see a large white kani. It looks close, but it will take you a long time before you finally pass through the kani to find **Samdo** nestled behind a ridge at 3780m. There is a mani wall near the small stone-roofed primary school, and the closely packed stone houses of the village extend off to the east. Somewhere in the village a police checkpost lurks, but the police often head for warmer climes during the colder months of the trekking season. A major Tibetan trade route heads east through the village and over the Lajyang La at 5098m to Rhee village in Tibet, a day's walk from here. The people of Samdo feel that they have a proprietary right to the Larkya La and often insist that groups replace their porters with local porters here.

Day 14: Samdo to Larkya Rest House

Descend on a wide, gentle trail from Samdo past many fields to a big, old mani wall and stone archway. Drop to the river, which is now very small and narrow, and cross it on a wooden bridge at 3850m. The Survey of India map shows the village of Larkya Bazaar located here; but this was only a seasonal tent camp, so there is not a house to be seen.

A fine, old mani wall marks the start of the climb to Larkya La. Climb gently through tundra and juniper opposite the huge Larkya Glacier that drops from Manaslu North. After more than an hour of climbing, the trail becomes indistinct. Stay high on the ridge to the right and you will find a trail that crosses the top of two large ravines. The trail gets steeper and climbs the side of a ridge to about 4000m, where there is a viewpoint at the edge of a huge gorge. You can see a single stone house in the distance and a row of abandoned houses, perhaps the remains of the mythical Larkya Bazaar (Babuk), far below. Before the political situation made it impossible, Sherpas from Namche Bazaar used to bring their yaks on a long trip via Tibet, then into Nupri, to trade.

Climb in and out of the gorge and contour to the only shelter on the route to the pass, a **rest house** at 4480m. The stone house is large enough for porters and a kitchen, but there is a real scarcity of flat places to pitch a tent. If you find yourself on a slope, place your clothing under your mattress on the downhill side as a primitive hammock to keep you from falling out of bed all night.

Day 15: Larkya Rest House to Bimtang

The route starts up the ridge in front of the rest house, eventually becoming a long, gentle climb beside a moraine. Cross a small ridge, descend a bit to a lake, and keep climbing the ridge until you reach the top of the moraine at 4700m. The trail becomes rougher and indistinct as it crosses the moraine to the south of steep, grassy slopes.

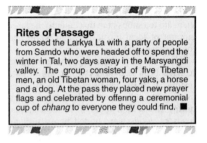

Rites of Passage

I crossed the Larkya La with a party of people from Samdo who were headed off to spend the winter in Tal, two days away in the Marsyangdi valley. The group consisted of five Tibetan men, an old Tibetan woman, four yaks, a horse and a dog. At the pass they placed new prayer flags and celebrated by offering a ceremonial cup of *chhang* to everyone they could find. ■

A few cairns mark the route, but if there is snow you will have a real route-finding problem. Stay on the moraine to a ridge with two cairns; you should be able to see the prayer flags on the pass from here. Descend to four frozen lakes, then make the final steep climb to the pass at 5100m.

It should take three to four hours from the rest house to the **Larkya La**. It is best to make an early start in order to cross the pass safely. It can be extremely cold and windy during the climb, and porters have perished on this pass in snowstorms. The views are tremendous. The peaks to the west of the pass are Himlung Himal (7126m), Cheo Himal (6820m), Gyaji Kung, Kang Guru (6981m) and Annapurna II (7937m).

The descent continues along the top of a moraine to the west, then drops steeply and traverses scree slopes. It makes a long set of steep, rough switchbacks, crosses the moraine and then descends more gently. There is a final long, steep, slippery descent on loose gravel to Taubuche (Dangmoche), another grassy moraine at 4450m – a drop of 650m in little more than an hour. The trail becomes better and easier, descending along the grassy moraine to a small meadow and a spring at 4080m. The trail turns a corner, the valley becomes larger, and the trail heads down to a large meadow, a mani wall and a small rest house. This is **Bimtang**, whose Tibetan name means 'plain of sand', elevation 3720m. The Survey of India maps this place as Bimtakothi; Snellgrove suggests that the ending *kothi*, meaning 'settlement', seems to be the gratuitous addition of some

RESTRICTED AREAS

Nepali informant. From May to October there are tea shops here that cater to the large amount of local traffic between Nupri and the Marsyangdi valley.

The ruins of a much larger building, said to have been two storeys high, are a mute testimony to Bimtang's earlier prominence as a major trading post. Tilman reports that during the season more than 3000 animal loads of goods were traded here. Bimtang was also a Khampa guerrilla staging area during the 1970s. This is a huge valley surrounded by high peaks – we heard many avalanches during the night.

Day 16: Bimtang to Gho

The trail drops from the Bimtang meadow and crosses a glacial stream, the headwaters of the Dudh Khola, on a wooden bridge. Climb over the side of the moraine and descend into a pine and rhododendron forest to **Hompuk** at 3430m.

The walking improves as the trail descends, switchbacking down to a fork of the Dudh Khola, then follows the river through forests to a goth at 3030m. The going stays easy to a stream at 2700m and the fenced fields of **Karache**. The trail crosses a landslide, then goes across fields before making a steep climb over a ridge decorated with prayer flags while the river loops around in a pronounced S shape below. The trail comes off the ridge in a big, sweeping arc down to the river bank at 2580m near a few houses and fields on the opposite side. A short distance beyond is **Gho**, at 2560m, which boasts a real tea shop where our porters gorged themselves on the first *dal bhat* they had eaten in days. At the foot of the valley you can see part of the peak of Lamjung above the Marsyangdi valley.

Day 17: Gho to Dharapani

Continue through fields, over a clear stream, past houses and more fields interspersed with rhododendron and oak forests. Do not cross a suspension bridge that crosses the Dudh Khola; stay on the north bank as you trek into **Tilje** (Tiljet). The first building you reach is the school. Climb over a small ridge

to the stone-paved village street and wind among the closely spaced houses of this large Gurung village to the communal water tap and the primitive *Hotel Samden* at 2300m. Leave the village through a stone arch, cross the Dudh Khola and trek along the river embankment.

As the trail descends through scrub forests, the wall of the Marsyangdi valley looms larger, and finally the houses of Dharapani become visible. Cross a wooden bridge back to the northern side of the Dudh Khola at 1930m and climb up through a chorten-shaped arch and past a mani wall to the *Himlung Hotel* in the centre of **Thonje** (Thangjet). You will need to allow time for your sirdar and liaison officer to contact the police to show off the garbage they collected and obtain a 'clearance certificate' stating that you have fulfilled all the regulations related to restricted areas. The police post is on the paved village street.

To get to **Dharapani**, turn left just beyond the hotel, pass the large, tin-roofed high school and cross a long suspension bridge over the Marsyangdi. You end up at upper Dharapani, elevation 1920m. You would do well to stay here, perhaps on the grounds of the *Dharapani Hotel & Lodge*, to allow completion of the lengthy formalities, or you might trek south 10 minutes to the main part of Dharapani, where the signboards advertise 'comfortable laundries'. There is a telephone in Dharapani; this is the most reliable emergency communication facility if you have trouble on Larkya La.

You are now on the apple pie trail, and the remainder of the trek follows the first days of the Around Annapurna trek in reverse. By now you should be in good shape, and the trail is generally downhill, so you should be able to make a fast trek back to the roadhead.

Day 18: Dharapani to Syange

Trek south through the steepest part of the Marsyangdi Gorge.

Day 19: Syange to Bhulbule

Follow the Marsyangdi south into rice terrace country.

Day 20: Bhulbule to Besi Sahar

Trek to Besi Sahar and arrange transport back to Kathmandu.

Shey Gompa

Duration 5 to 6 days
Difficulty Medium
Maximum elevation 5400m
Permit cost US$700 plus Rs 650
Season May to October
Hotels Only camping treks allowed
Summary Cross high passes from Phoksumdo Lake to the legendary Crystal Mountain and Shey Gompa.

The northern part of Dolpo is usually called Inner Dolpo and has long had an aura of mysticism about it, largely because of the metaphysical discussions of the region in Peter Matthiessen's book *The Snow Leopard*. Shey was closed to foreigners until 1992. One story cites the reason for closure as the large-scale theft of statues from monasteries several years ago.

The description of this trek was provided by Sushil Upadhyay, who made an extended trek in this region, crossing from Phoksumdo Lake to Shey gompa, then over some horrific passes to Kagbeni in the Kali Gandaki valley. Despite the mysticism surrounding Shey and the 'crystal mountain', this is not a popular trek by any means. The harsh terrain, the physical conditioning necessary and the exorbitant fees for visiting this region have deterred most people.

This trek appears on the Jumla to Dolpo map, on pages 328-9 in the Western Nepal chapter.

Fees & Permits

The permit for Shey is as expensive as for Mustang – US$700 for 10 days and US$70 per day thereafter. It becomes especially expensive because the trek only takes five or six days to complete.

Access

The 'restricted' part of this trek starts from Ringmo village at the southern end of Phoksumdo Lake. To visit Shey you need to trek from Dolpo airport in Juphal or make a longer trek from Jumla. See the Western Nepal chapter for information on how to get to Phoksumdo Lake. Once you are at Shey, you can continue to Saldang and trek into Tarap via either of two passes. If you have lots of time, you can keep trekking north, then turn east and cross Cheelmara pass, eventually ending up in Kagbeni after a month of walking.

Day 1: Phoksumdo Lake to Phoksumdo Khola

From Ringmo, at the southern end of Phoksumdo Lake, the trail contours on a rocky ledge as it skirts the western lip of the lake. A precarious trail suspended on a gangway of wood supported on pegs driven into crevices in the rocks signals the remoteness of the area you are about to enter. Beyond a stream, the trail makes a steep climb onto a hillock overlooking the lake. It descends and continues above the lake on an up-and-down trail to a pine forest, then makes a steep descent to the westernmost edge of the lake. Where the Phoksumdo Khola enters the lake, there is a lush meadow that opens up into a long valley. Continue through the valley, crisscrossing the Phoksumdo Khola and avoiding thorn bushes. The valley has steep sides with tundra and occasional boggy marsh underfoot. Camp at a grassy knoll on the bank of the river.

Day 2: Phoksumdo Khola to Snowfields Camp

Continue along the level path that now heads due north through a glacial valley. At the confluence of the Phoksumdo Khola and another mountain stream there is an old wooden bridge. You should take the barely discernible path to the north-east up the valley. There is no trail, as such, so you need to climb over rocks and boulders and ford the stream that rushes down the steep incline of the valley. A long climb brings you to a sheep meadow where the trail veers up a steep ravine. A hard climb to the top brings you to yet another valley where you can see the Kang La, the pass leading to Shey gompa. If you are in good shape and the porters agree, you might make it on to Shey on the same day, or you can camp before the pass in the place that Peter Matthiessen christened 'Snowfields Camp'.

Day 3: Snowfields Camp to Shey Gompa

Climb up the steep hill littered with slate towards the pass. The climb is physically demanding, especially when you slip and slide on the slate dump. From the top of the Kang La at 5400m elevation, you can look down upon a large valley which is bisected by a gushing river. Descend steeply to the valley floor and make a long, meandering trek along the banks of the river, crossing and recrossing it several times. Notice the mud caves on the banks of the river and the hills overlooking the river. A red chorten heralds the gate to Shey gompa. Continue along the path to a large meadow where hairy yaks and hundreds of sheep can be found grazing. There are a few nomads' huts. Cross the river for the final time across a quaint wooden log bridge and climb up to the Shey gompa compound at approximately 4500m.

The gompa itself is not large, and there are no artefacts or paintings of note in its premises, except for an ancient Tibetan scroll that describes the myth of the crystal mountain and Shey gompa. The monk who accompanied our trekking group managed to get hold of this manuscript and read it from cover to cover. According to the book, in a crater in the mountain ranges that dominate Shey gompa, there is a holy lake. When a pilgrim makes nine circumambulations of this lake the water turns into milk. A sip of this milk, and the pilgrim can see Mt Kailas in the distance.

A caretaker lives in a hut adjacent to Shey gompa. To the east of the gompa is the trail that leads to Saldang village, and eventually to Kagbeni via Charkabhot or south to Tarap. To the west of the gompa, a narrow yak trail

climbs up the valley floor to the remote village of Phijergaon.

Humla to Mt Kailas

Duration 20 to 25 days
Difficulty Medium to hard
Maximum elevation 5630m
Permit cost US$90 per week
Season July to October
Hotels Only camping treks allowed
Summary A true pilgrimage. A logistically complex and expensive trek through far north-western Nepal leads to the Tibetan border. Cross the border on foot and drive to holy Mt Kailas, where you gain merit by walking around the mountain.

In May 1993 the governments of Nepal and China reached an accord that allowed the first treks across the border between the two countries. While it had been a route for Nepali pilgrims for years, foreign trekkers were never allowed to trek from Nepal into Tibet. It was possible, however, to bend or ignore the rules. Early British explorers visited Kailas in a variety of disguises, and numerous individual trekkers have managed to make their way from Tibet into Nepal in years past.

Though the *raison d'être* for this trek is theoretically a pilgrimage to Mt Kailas in Tibet, the journey through Humla, Nepal's highest, northernmost and most remote district, is also culturally and scenically rewarding. The people of Limi in northern Humla are Bhotias whose roots are in Tibet and who still enjoy the freedom to graze their animals on the Tibetan plateau. The upper Humla Karnali valley is also populated by Bhotias who trade extensively with Tibet in traditional ways that have totally vanished elsewhere. It is only near Simikot, the district headquarters, that you will encounter people of other ethnic groups, mostly Thakuris and Chhetris.

Because the area covered by this trek encompasses two countries and numerous ethnic groups and religions, most places have two or more names. I have used the most common local name and listed alternate names in parentheses.

A trip to Mt Kailas has always been regarded as a pilgrimage. It satisfies the romantic in us that the pilgrimage to Kailas is a difficult one. Whether you drive for seven days from Lhasa or walk for six days from Simikot, it is still not possible to make a quick, easy visit to Kailas and Manasarovar. You cannot yet travel all the way to Kailas by helicopter or aeroplane. This is certainly as it should be.

History

Humla was once part of the great Malla empire administered from Sinja near Jumla. Until 1787 this empire included Jumla and Purang (Taklakot) and extended as far west as Googay, the 'lost' villages of Toling (Zanda) and Tsaparang on the banks of the Sutlej River in a remote Tibetan valley to the north of the Indian peaks Nanda Devi and Kamet. Taklakot was once part of Nepal; on a map you can see the chunk taken out of the north-west corner of Nepal like a bite.

In Humla the traditional salt-for-grain trade with Tibet continues much as it has for centuries. This trade has virtually ceased in the rest of Nepal because of the import of Indian salt and because China has eliminated many border trading posts in remote regions. The Chinese village of Purang, better known by its Nepali name, Taklakot, is an important trading centre that is a short drive from both the Nepal and India borders. Trade via Taklakot is an important factor in the economy of Humla, which is about a 15 day walk from Surkhet, the nearest roadhead in Nepal.

Taklakot is an extraordinary melting pot of Indian traders and tourists, Chinese and Tibetan traders, Muslim traders from Kashgar, Nepali entrepreneurs trading wool, salt and Indian goods, Chinese government officials and a huge army contingent. Plan on spending at least a day exploring this unusual frontier town.

Fees & Permits

The Nepal portion of this trek is subject to the same regulations as other restricted areas. You must trek as part of an organised group with a liaison officer. The trekking permit fee for the trek from Simikot to the border and back is US$90 for the first week and US$15 per day thereafter. The permit becomes complicated because there is a break in the Nepal trek while you are in Tibet. Normally the immigration office issues two trekking permits with dates 10 days apart, one for the trip to the border and the other for the return. You will also need a double-entry visa or re-entry permit for Nepal in order to avoid complications and excessive visa fees.

You need a specially endorsed Chinese visa if you plan to cross the border. This will be arranged at the same time you organise transport within China. The rules usually prohibit individual travel in Tibet. The border near Taklakot is particularly well controlled and many trekkers, even in organised groups, have been turned back at the border for various reasons. Your liaison officer can stay behind in Nepal or Taklakot while you go to Mt Kailas, though you must continue to provide food, accommodation and salary.

Maps

Maps for this region include *Mid Western Region* 1:250,000, 1989 (HMG Suspension Bridge Division) and *Humla, Nepal* 1:250,000, sheet 44-7 from the National Remote Sensing Centre, 1986.

Books

The following is a list of books which would provide good background reading for this area:

A Mountain in Tibet, by Charles Allen; contains great stories of explorations near Kailas

Himalayan Traders, by Christoph Von Fürer Haimendorf

Kailas – on Pilgrimage to the Sacred Mountain of Tibet, by Russell Johnson & Kerry Moran

Kailas Manasarovar, by Swami Pranavananda; the definitive scholarly documentation of Kailas and Manasarovar

RESTRICTED AREAS

RESTRICTED AREAS

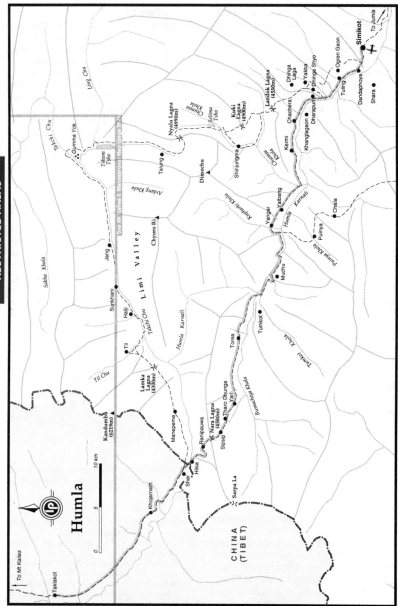

The Sacred Mountain, by John Snelling; an excellent guide to Kailas and accounts of many journeys to the peak

Tibet – a travel survival kit, a Lonely Planet guide by Chris Taylor

To the Navel of the World, by Peter Somerville-Large; an account of travels to Kailas and a trek into Nepal

Trekking in Nepal, West Tibet & Bhutan, by Hugh Swift

Trekking in Tibet, by Gary McCue

Vignettes of Nepal, by Dr Harka Gurung; early travels in Humla

The Way of the White Cloud, by Lama Anagarika Govinda

Spy on the Roof of the World, by Sydney Wignall; a fascinating account of the 1955 Welsh expedition to Gurla Mandata, which doubled as a spy mission for Indian military intelligence

Food & Fuel

It is important to remember that there is a shortage of food in Simikot, so you should arrange to send supplies ahead by plane or porter. The rules state that you must use kerosene for cooking on the trek. Since this is usually not available in Simikot, and cannot be transported by plane, it requires advance planning. There is, however, a reliable supply of kerosene in Taklakot, so you can arrange a porter caravan to bring Chinese kerosene from Taklakot and avoid the long haul from Surkhet.

Season

This trek is possible only in the summer monsoon season from mid-May to late September. The entire region is snowbound in the winter; passes are closed and Taklakot itself is isolated until the snowplough arrives in late March.

Access
Kathmandu to Simikot via Nepalgunj

There is no direct air service from Kathmandu to Simikot. You must first fly 1½ hours to Nepalgunj on the southern border of Nepal, spend the night, and take an early-morning flight to Simikot. See the Western Nepal chapter for suggestions on where to stay in Nepalgunj.

It takes about 50 minutes to fly the 218 km from Nepalgunj to Simikot, almost the entire breadth of Nepal, over a 3800m pass. Look for the 7031m Saipal Himal off the left side of the plane as you approach Simikot; you may also be able to spot Rara Lake some distance off to the right. Simikot (elevation 2910m) is on a ridge high above the Humla

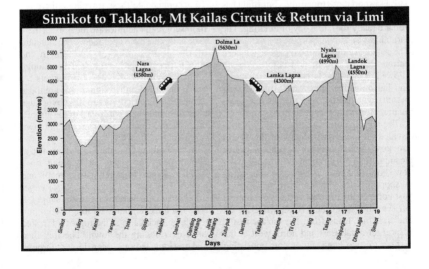

Simikot to Taklakot, Mt Kailas Circuit & Return via Limi

Karnali encircled by high, snow-covered ridges.

Surkhet to Simikot If you want to walk to Simikot, start in Surkhet and walk for about 15 days.

Sher to Taklakot & Darchan (Tibet) The Tibetan plateau is harsh, windy and barren. It makes little sense to walk huge distances in such inhospitable country. If you are headed for Kailas, you should arrange in advance for a vehicle to transport you from the Nepal border at Sher to Taklakot, where Chinese immigration and customs formalities are centred. You will also want to arrange transport for the 100 km drive to Darchan at the foot of Mt Kailas. A travel agent or trekking company in Kathmandu that specialises in Tibet should be able to assist you with this at the same time they arrange your Chinese visa. These sections of the journey are described, respectively, at the end of the Simikot to Taklakot section below and under Access at the beginning of the Mt Kailas Circuit section that follows it.

SIMIKOT TO TAKLAKOT (TIBET)
Day 1: Simikot to Tuling
This is a short day. Hopefully, your flight has arrived in Simikot in the early morning and you are ready for half a day of trekking. The formalities at Simikot airport are extensive. The police examine your baggage and record various bits of information before you are allowed to leave the airport. Then the sirdar and liaison officer must take your trekking permits and passports to the district headquarters for further inspection.

The airstrip dominates the town, which is divided into four parts. South of the airport are government offices, a school, police headquarters, government guesthouse and a few shops. The main bazaar area, consisting of shops, a barber, bank and airline offices is just north of the runway. A few government offices, shops and the RNAC office are on the trail that leads from the bazaar to the airport terminal. East and north-west of the bazaar are two large settlements consisting

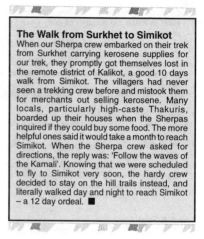

The Walk from Surkhet to Simikot
When our Sherpa crew embarked on their trek from Surkhet carrying kerosene supplies for our trek, they promptly got themselves lost in the remote district of Kalikot, a good 10 days walk from Simikot. The villagers had never seen a trekking crew before and mistook them for merchants out selling kerosene. Many locals, particularly high-caste Thakuris, boarded up their houses when the Sherpas inquired if they could buy some food. The more helpful ones said it would take a month to reach Simikot. When the Sherpa crew asked for directions, the reply was: 'Follow the waves of the Karnali'. Knowing that we were scheduled to fly to Simikot very soon, the hardy crew decided to stay on the hill trails instead, and literally walked day and night to reach Simikot – a 12 day ordeal. ■

of flat-roofed houses, inhabited mostly by Chhetris.

Simikot is the headquarters of Nepal's most remote district, Humla, and the only major village for many days walk. There is a continual stream of 'Humli' people from surrounding villages trading, buying supplies and dealing with various bureaucracies. To accommodate these travellers, there are several tea shops and restaurants and a few rooms for rent. Facilities are local style; there is nothing that even approaches the standard of the poorest trekkers' hotels in the Annapurna or Everest regions. Even though Simikot itself has been open to trekkers for years, the only English signboards are those of airlines. Electricity is supplied by a huge bank of solar panels north-east of the airport; this system provides electricity to the town for about four hours a night.

Start climbing from the Simikot airstrip at 2960m past wheat and barley fields on a rough rocky trail bordered with cannabis and nettles. Trek past the stone houses of upper Simikot and the community water supply. It does not look far, but it's a long, 300m pull to a large rock cairn at the top of a forested ridge overlooking the town. The trek then makes a long, tedious, steep descent through deep forests on a rock-cluttered path with many switchbacks. There are a few tea shops along the way down the hill, but their offerings are pretty spartan. Stay on the main trail that passes above the rooftops of **Dandaphoya**, also known as Mekh; don't take any of the trails that descend into the village itself. The village on the opposite side of the river is Shara. Continue past a single tea shop under a large shady tree. The trail levels out and passes through **Tuling**, also known as Majgaon, a compact Thakuri village at 2270m. The only good camp site in the area is about half an hour beyond the village. At these lower elevations, among unsanitary villages, flies and other tiny bugs are a real nuisance.

Day 2: Tuling to Kermi
The trail is reasonably level, and walnut and apricot trees provide welcome shade. The trail crosses the Yakba Khola, then climbs to a police checkpost and on to **Dharapuri** at 2300m. It's a long, rough traverse across a scree slope to a stream. Below the trail a bridge over the Humla Karnali leads to Khanglagaon, a Thakuri village on the opposite side of the river. This is the last Thakuri village in the valley and the upper limit of rice cultivation.

Stay on the north side of the river as the trail snakes up and down to **Chachera**, a shepherds' camp near a series of three waterfalls at 2350m. It's possible to camp here, but this area, like most possible camps in the valley, is deep in goat droppings thanks to the many caravans that pass by. The trail climbs so steeply that horses and yaks have to be unloaded so that they can scramble up the slope. Climb above the waterfalls and over the ridge past swarms of lizards sunning themselves, and traverse to a tea shop and small camp site at 2520m. Fifteen minutes further is Dhara Kermi, two stone tea shops beside a stream at 2690m. The route bypasses Kermi village itself; the only camp nearby is below the left side of the trail about 10 minutes beyond the village. There is a hot spring about an hour's climb above Kermi and a police post with a radio about 10

minutes beyond the tea shops at Dhara Kermi.

Day 3: Kermi to Yangar
It's a long climb over a ridge into a big valley with walled potato and buckwheat fields. The trail levels out a bit as it traverses through a sparse pine forest to a mani wall and rock cairn on a ridge at 2990m. Make switchbacks down past a meadow to an extensive growth of wild marijuana and nettles on the bank of the Chumsa Khola (also known as the Sale Khola) at 2830m. The trail crosses the stream on an impressive, long suspension bridge built in 1994.

There are several good camp sites alongside the river. Climb a steep, rocky ridge and drop back towards the fast-flowing, light grey waters of the Humla Karnali. Climb over another ridge, then descend to **Yalbang Chaur**, a meadow where goat herders camp beside the river at 2760m. In November there is an annual trade fair, or *mela*, at this site.

Above this sandy meadow the Humla Karnali valley narrows and the sides become quite steep. Climb over two more ridges to **Yalbang** village at 2890m. The trail follows an irrigation canal to a huge rock and two small defunct tea shops just to the north of the village. Yalbang shares a hydroelectric power supply with its neighbour Yangar, a few km away, though the system has been out of operation since 1994. Take the lower, left-hand fork and contour up and around to a house and horse pasture on the ridge. Below, you can see a bridge over the Humla Karnali and a ridiculously steep trail on the opposite side that leads to Puinya (Poyun), the village where Yalbang people live during the summer. This is also a trade route to the once important Humli trading centre of Chala and to Bajura, south of Humla. Climb over another ridge at 2930m and descend gradually to the extensive fields surrounding **Yangar** at 2850m.

Day 4: Yangar to Torea
An old route followed a steep trail over a 3500m ridge, the Illing La, beyond Yangar. Fortunately you can now follow a new, lower

path that avoids the climb. The trail passes through the compact settlement of Yangar, in some places in tunnels beneath houses, then climbs behind a rock spur to a fast-flowing stream. Decline the old trail and instead follow the new route across a long scree slope and out to the end of the ridge before dropping to the river at 2770m. The trail wends its way precariously close to the river on a track built up with rocks and wooden props and along a few stretches where the path was blasted out of the cliff. After more than an hour of ups and downs you will reach a new suspension bridge at 2800m. Cross to the south bank of the Humla Karnali and a big, rocky camp beside the river. Climb to a stream, rock-hop across it and ascend past apricot orchards to a totally defunct kani that marks the entrance to **Muchu** village at 2920m.

The trail passes below the gompa and stone houses of Muchu. Climb through the orchards and fields below the village to a ridge, then drop into a ravine and climb to a chorten on the opposite side. There are a few houses on the ridge and a border police post hidden just behind it. The ridge near the chorten offers a good view of the upper part of the valley and of Tumkot village (also known as Mota gompa) and its large white gompa on the next ridge. The police post is

also the immigration checkpoint, so you must fill in a departure form, present your passport and get stamped out of Nepal.

Enjoy the next easy stretch of trail as it contours down to the Tumkot Khola, follows the rocky stream bed for a short distance, then crosses it on a log bridge. Don't climb the hill westwards towards Tumkot; follow the trail around the foot of the ridge and cross the Bumachiya Khola on a wooden bridge at 2900m. The Humla Karnali disappears into a steep cleft to the north behind a high ridge that provides you with the opportunity to climb uphill for the next two days.

The first part of the climb from the Bumachiya Khola is quite steep. About half an hour up there is an obvious trail junction. Take the lower, left-hand trail. The upper trail, which eventually rejoins the lower one, is a short cut for goats. A bit further on, the route enters a steep, rock-filled gully; it's a long, slow slog up to a ridge at 3270m. The path levels out as it ascends to a cairn at 3310m, then descends gently through juniper trees before climbing again to Palbang, a single teahouse near a stream at 3380m. Palbang has a Nepali name, **Torea**, after the fields of bright yellow mustard *(tori)* that surround it. There's a field above the teahouse that may be available for use as a camp.

Himalayan Barley

At elevations above 3000m barley becomes one of the most important grains. Although cultivated widely at lower elevations, it is less important there because other grains are available. Above 3300m barley assumes a vital role because it is the only grain that thrives at high altitudes. The upward limit of barley cultivation in Nepal is around 4200m in Dolpo and in Dingboche. In the Tingri and Gyantse counties of Tibet it is found as high as 4700m.

After threshing, barley corns are dry roasted and ground into a meal called *sattu* or *tsampa*. The roasting is accomplished by sifting the corns in a basin of hot sand. Tsampa is eaten with tea, milk or yoghurt, sometimes with savoury dishes.

Another common use of barley is to produce the highlanders' beer called *chhang*. Barley, although coarser than wheat, is occasionally mixed with other grains to make bread. It is an extremely nutritious grain with a fairly high protein content, and is considered by Himalayan peoples to be a heat-producing food.

Tibetan-speaking ethnic groups classify the several thousand generic strains of barley into a threefold system. This system is based on the colour of the grain (red, white, black), the length of time the barley needs to ripen (90 to 130 days) and its morphology (bearded, naked, fat grain, slim grain). 'Naked' or 'beardless' Tibetan barley is called *uwa* in Nepali, and regular, 'bearded' barley is *jau*. ∎

Day 5: Torea to Sipsip

From Torea the trail ascends to a stream and a camp site deep in goat droppings, then contours up past fields of amaranth and wild roses to a small cairn at 3660m. Rounding a ridge, you can see the extensive fields of Yari. The trek follows an irrigation canal into the huge valley of the Jhyakthang Chu, marked by a mani wall at 3640m. Climb gently to **Yari**, a compact settlement of stone houses, a police post, a customs office and a schoolhouse just below the trail at 3670m. The police post is the last in Nepal and maintains a register of the comings and goings of both locals and foreigners.

In upper Humla they grow two kinds of millet – finger millet *(kodo)* and common millet *(chinu)* – and two kinds of barley – 'naked' Tibetan barley *(uwa)* and regular 'bearded' barley *(jau)* – plus amaranth *(marcia)*, wheat, buckwheat *(phaphar)*, potatoes and radishes. In the lower parts of Humla they grow winter barley; in higher villages such as Yari, only one crop per year is possible.

To the west of the village a trail leads to Sarpa La, a less-frequented route to Tibet. This is the trail the Khampa leader Wangdi took in 1975 in an attempt to escape into India after the USA removed its support for the Tibetan resistance. He crossed into Tibet at an unmonitored and isolated corner and recrossed into Nepal via Tinkar Pass south of Taklakot, where he was ambushed by the waiting Nepal army.

From Yari the trade route climbs the broad valley to the source of the village's extensive irrigation system. The water is carried in a series of channels and wooden conduits. There's a flat spot where it would be possible to camp at **Tharo Dhunga**, elevation 4000m, but it's better to continue towards the pass to make the following day easier. There's a meadow and stream at 4160m and another meadow, **Sipsip**, near the foot of the pass at 4330m. Despite the remoteness of this location, there is a considerable amount of traffic. You will probably be travelling in the company of several contingents of traders, pilgrims and pack animals (goats, sheep, horses and yaks).

Day 6: Sipsip to Taklakot

There are numerous tracks along the side of the ridge above Sipsip, and all make the same steep, continuous ascent to a huge rock cairn atop the Nara Lagna at 4580m. I measured this pass with both a GPS unit and an altimeter (see the Facts for the Trekker chapter for details on these instruments) and found it to be well below the 4902m elevation shown on the Survey of India and US army maps. In 1979 Dr Harka Gurung correctly identified this discrepancy without the aid of any instruments. Snow usually closes the pass from November to April.

A short distance below the pass you will round a ridge for a view of the Tibetan plateau, the Humla Karnali and the green barley fields of Sher far below. The descent is tolerable as far as Ranipauwa, a hotel in a tent at 4370m. Beyond Ranipauwa the trail consists of steep, loose pebbles. These either wear the bottoms off your boots or provide a natural ball-bearing surface that shoots your feet out from under you. You've done well if you make it down this hill without a few slips and slides. The trail contours around a huge canyon before making a final steep, dusty drop to the Humla Karnali at 3720m. It is a walk of only a few minutes along the river to **Hilsa** – a couple of tents and stone houses surrounded by barley fields.

A stone pillar that marks the Nepal-Tibet border is just across a long Swiss-built suspension bridge, perhaps one of the most informal border crossings in the world. Climb 150m to **Sher** (also called Shera), a Chinese army post at 3860m. If you have made prior arrangements and all goes well, a jeep will be waiting for you to make the 1½-hour drive into Taklakot. All of China is on Beijing time, which is 2¼ hours later than Nepal time, so set your watch accordingly. Because the Ngari region of Tibet is so far west of Beijing, it's dark when you arise at 7 am and light until about 10 pm during the season for this trek in July and August.

Sher is where Humli people sell wood and rice from Nepal. The active illegal trade in wooden beams further helps to deplete Nepal's forest resources. The grain-for-salt

---

A Nightmare Drive in Tibet

Roads in Tibet range from bad to nonexistent. When it does rain in this normally dry region, the river crossings from the Nepal border to Taklakot can look like wild, treacherous truck and jeep cemeteries. The road from Taklakot to Darchan across the Barkha plain can be like driving through the Florida Everglades without the vegetation and alligators. In August 1996, the usual two hour drive into Taklakot from the border took us all night. We were in a Chinese truck with all our gear. While crossing a stream at 10 pm in a downpour, the back wheel got stuck in the muck and started sinking fast. The water rose and boulders rolled downstream beside us. We had to bail out and spend the night in and around a grove of poplar trees above what was now a torrent, and slogged our way into Taklakot the next morning.

There is, however, a mutually beneficial rapport between the tour companies and the Tibetan villagers which keeps the 'roads' open, vehicles moving and avenues of commerce flowing. A Tibetan family took us in for tea and allowed us to pitch our tents in their courtyard next to their snarling mastiff. The next morning at dawn they were down by the river with crowbars and shovels helping us dig out our truck in the receding waters.

Brian Weirum

---

trade is responsible for the thousands of goats you have seen on the trail, each carrying up to 10 kg. Humli people make as many as six or seven trips a year and traders from throughout western Nepal make a single trip each year, exchanging one measure of rice for two measures of salt. Somehow this turns out to be a profitable trip, though it is baffling that it should be.

The Drive from Sher to Taklakot The Chinese border guards in the post on the ridge above the Humla Karnali will want to see your passport and Chinese visa. If you have not made advance arrangements with a Tibetan travel agency for your trip in Tibet, this may be as far as you get. Even the Nepali staff who accompany a trek must have passports and Chinese visas.

From the Nepal border at Sher the road makes a long descent to a stream and some mills, then follows the Humla Karnali to **Khojarnath** at 3790m, 10 km from the border. Khojarnath is the first large village in Tibet and boasts an important gompa of the Sakya sect. This gompa escaped most of the excesses of the Cultural Revolution, though the silver statues and other items described by early travellers have disappeared. The new statues are of Chenresig (Avalokitesvara), Jambyang (Manjushree) and Channadorje (Vajrapani). The monks, familiar with

Indian pilgrims, explain these gods as the Buddhist manifestations of Ram, Laxman and Sita.

Also of interest in the gompa are the stuffed carcasses of a yak, Indian tiger, snow leopard (chen in Tibetan) and wolf (changu) hanging from the ceiling. These are also replacements dating from 1985.

The road climbs over a 4000m pass. Thirteen Humli porters were killed here in July 1993 when a truck carrying two dozen Nepali passengers on top of a load of salt overturned. The route then passes Kangtse, which has a gompa on a nearby hill. Ford the Kangtse Chu and the Gejin Chu and drive on to Gejin and Kirang villages before reaching Taklakot, at 3930m, 26 km from Sher.

Taklakot Taklakot, which the Chinese and Tibetans call Purang, is a large trading centre and is composed of many distinct settlements. The route from Sher enters from the south along a walled road lined with willow trees. This is the Chinese section of town, where you can find the bank, police (including immigration and public security), post office, disco and *Purang Guesthouse* (with its attached 'Happy Drinking Room'). There is a direct dial telephone in the post office. There are two decent restaurants in this part of Taklakot, both with English signboards saying 'dining room'. The more northerly

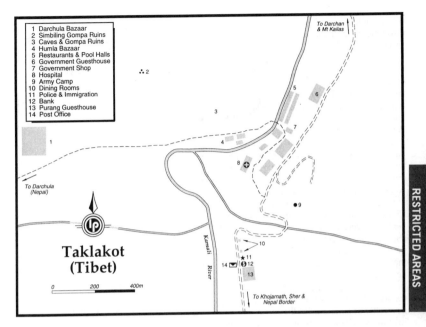

Taklakot (Tibet)

Key:
1 Darchula Bazaar
2 Simbiling Gompa Ruins
3 Caves & Gompa Ruins
4 Humla Bazaar
5 Restaurants & Pool Halls
6 Government Guesthouse
7 Government Shop
8 Hospital
9 Army Camp
10 Dining Rooms
11 Police & Immigration
12 Bank
13 Purang Guesthouse
14 Post Office

To Darchan & Mt Kailas
To Darchula (Nepal)
Karnali River
To Khojarnath, Sher & Nepal Border

0   200   400m

one, apparently run by the army, is better. There are several hole-in-the-wall shops along the road, but for any real purchases you must go to the bazaar near the Karnali River bridge, about a km away. Here you will find more restaurants, an amazing collection of pool parlours, and Chinese-run shops trying to sell polyester clothing to Tibetans, Nepali traders and Indian pilgrims. Nearer the road are at least two department stores that carry pots, pans, TVs and bolts of cloth.

On the opposite side of the Karnali is **Humla Bazaar**, a collection of Nepali hotels, restaurants and small shops. For serious purchases of food and supplies, walk 15 minutes over the hill to **Darchula Bazaar**, an extensive array of shops with mud walls and white canvas roofs. A large trade in Tibetan wool is conducted here; the wool is rolled into huge balls. There is one street for white wool and another street for black wool, as well as streets for Indian tinned food, cloth and necessities such as rice, sugar and flour. The

focus of trade is with the Darchula district of Nepal, several days walk to the south, though many goods from India also appear here. Indians are not allowed the same freedom as Nepalis to trade in Tibet, so Darchula people dominate this market.

As you trek back from Darchula Bazaar you will see the remains of **Simbiling gompa** on the hill overlooking Taklakot. In 1949 Swami Pranavananda described this gompa, housing 170 monks, as the biggest monastery in the region. There is nothing left of Simbiling after the destruction and shelling of the Cultural Revolution except a forlorn mud relic. In the hills along the trail there are caves, one containing the Gokung gompa, and others which are used as houses. Many caves have been equipped with doors and windows and are substantial dwellings. On the hill to the north-west of Taklakot is a huge army base, said to extend far into the mountain in a series of caves. You will meet hundreds of People's Liberation Army

(PLA) soldiers in their baggy green uniforms throughout Taklakot in shops, restaurants and pool parlours.

To the north of the pool parlour street are Tibetan stalls selling goats, yaks, wool and other items of strictly local interest. Sheep are slaughtered by tying their long snouts tightly shut so they suffocate. This somehow absolves the Tibetans of having taken a life. When our sherpas went shopping for meat, a Tibetan astonished them by grabbing a yak-hair rope and lassoing a nearby sheep without rising from his seat. The deal was not consummated, however, since we only wanted a bit of meat, not an entire sheep.

In Taklakot, transactions are conducted in Chinese yuan as well as both Indian and Nepali rupees. There is an unofficial rate of about eight Nepali rupees to the yuan, which the Nepalis call a *sukur*. To my embarrassment, I discovered that the local bank had never heard of travellers' cheques.

The region around Taklakot is dotted with traditional Tibetan settlements that make up a sizeable population. On the full-moon day in August 1993, a festival was held that included lama dancing in front of a huge picture of Chairman Mao. This fair attracted hundreds of people, many dressed in polyester track suits, but also numerous people in traditional Tibetan dress.

MT KAILAS CIRCUIT
Warning
Beware of trekking according to the itinerary described in the Mt Kailas Circuit section and camping at 5200m elevation unless you have spent at least *two nights* at Darchan to acclimatise.

Access
It is a drive of about 100 km from Taklakot to Darchan. From Taklakot the road passes **Toyo**, where the Sikh invader Zorawar Singh was killed in 1841. Beyond Toyo the road climbs past many Tibetan-style settlements and fords a few rivers en route to the Gurla La at 4590m. Just beyond the pass there is a view of Rakshas Tal and, on a clear day, Mt Kailas (6714m). The road descends, passes

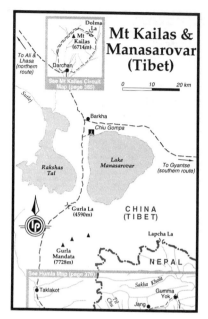

south of **Rakshas Tal**, then crosses the isthmus between the two holy lakes to **Manasarovar**. Two side roads lead to the shores of the lake; the first one ends near a guest house and the next reaches the lake near Chiu gompa. The road traverses the Barkha plain, then climbs and bumps its way to Darchan at 4560m, 2½ hours from Taklakot. Much of the road is an ad hoc route made by drivers who created a path where they saw fit, with only the straight line of telephone poles defining the way. At one point more than 15 parallel lines of vehicle tracks scar the plateau. This drive is best done in the morning; by afternoon the melting snows of Gurla Mandata (7728m) have caused streams to rise so high that fording them may be impossible. Watch for huge jack rabbits and wild asses *(kiang)* along the route.

Darchan Only the top of Mt Kailas is visible from Darchan; you must climb a ridge for a

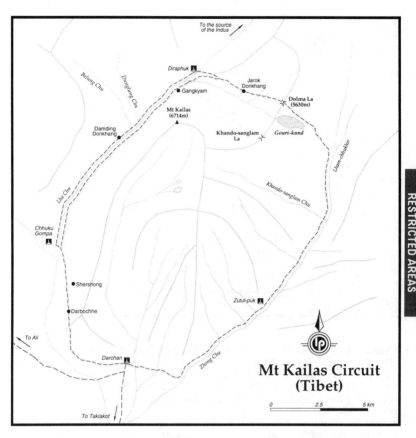

Mt Kailas Circuit
(Tibet)

better view. *Darchan guesthouse* is pretty rough. There is a kitchen where you may be able to get a bowl of noodles, though it takes considerable investigation to find out how and when. Occasionally there is a shop open which sells beer, (sometimes) a few canned goods, miscellaneous useless items, souvenir stickers and enamelled Kailas pins. There is usually a late-evening showing of Chinese and Hindi videos in a tent within the guesthouse compound. Entrance is free; all you need to do is buy a drink. You have a choice of Chinese champagne, Pabst Blue Ribbon beer, Coke and the excellent soft drink Liang

Xibao – a honey-orange concoction. The Dolma Lhakang gompa and some basic Tibetan hotels, shops, outdoor pool parlours and camps are above the compound.

Day 1: Darchan to Damding Donkhang

Trek west from the guesthouse compound high above the Barkha plain to a cairn and prayer flags at 4730m. This is the first of four *chaktsal-gang* ('prostration stations') on the *kora*, or circumambulation, and offers an excellent view of the south face of Kailas and the prominent 'Stairway to Heaven'.

Turn north up the valley of the Lha Chu,

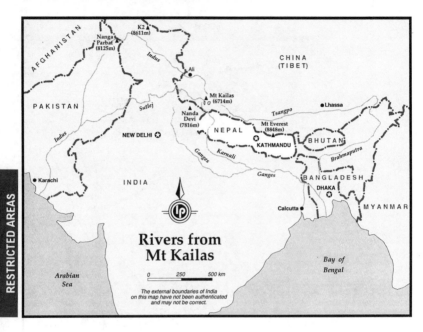

**Rivers from
Mt Kailas**

0   250   500 km

The external boundaries of India
on this map have not been authenticated
and may not be correct.

descending to **Darbochhe**, a tall pole adorned with prayer flags at 4750m. The pole and prayer flags are replaced annually during the Sakya Dawa festival on Buddha's birthday, the full-moon day during the Tibetan month of May/June. Nearby is **Chortenkang-ni**. It is considered an auspicious act to pass through the small archway formed by the two legs of this chorten. The trail continues across the plain to Shershong.

An hour past Shershong is a bridge leading to Chhuku gompa (also known as Nyenri gompa) high on the hillside above. All the monasteries on the Kailas circuit were destroyed during the Cultural Revolution. Chhuku gompa was the first to be rebuilt and contains a few treasures that were rescued from the original gompas. The normal pilgrims' route stays on the east bank of the Lha Chu, but for better views of Kailas, and generally better camp sites, cross the bridge and follow the west bank. The west-bank trail leads across scree slopes to a camp near

Damding Donkhang, a grassy spot at 4890m with a good view of the west face of Kailas.

Day 2: Damding Donkhang to Jarok Donkhang

Cross the side streams Belung Chu and Dunglung Chu on rocks and log bridges as the north face of Kailas comes into view. On the opposite side of the Lha Chu you can see a stone guesthouse and camp. Several groups of nomads tend herds of goats and yaks nearby. Pass their tents carefully; like most Tibetans, they keep ferocious Tibetan mastiff dogs. As you reach the gompa and frugal guesthouse at **Diraphuk**, you are rewarded with a fine view of the north face of Kailas. This is the first night's stop for Indian pilgrims. The three lower hills in front of Kailas from this vantage point are Manjushree, Avalokitesvara and Vajrapani, representing wisdom, kindness and power. The Diraphuk gompa was rebuilt in 1985.

Cross the Lha Chu by a bridge. If you were

The Ngari Region of Tibet

Kailas and Manasarovar are in the Ngari region of Tibet, perhaps the most inaccessible place on earth. Chinese people pronounce 'Ngari' as 'Ali,' so this name has become more or less official. The region's administrative centre is Shiquanhe in Chinese and Senge Khabab ('lion town') in Tibetan. In practice, however, everyone uses the name 'Ali' to refer to the town as well as the district. The town of Ali is a two day drive north-west of Kailas, a dusty five day drive from Lhasa and just as far away from Kashgar in China's Sinkiang province. All of this driving is on roads that are capable of destroying a vehicle in a single trip.

Ngari is populated by Dokpas, nomads who herd sheep, goats and yaks on these desolate plains. Most Dokpas do not have a house; they wander endlessly across the Tibetan plateau, living in yak-hair tents. Ngari is the last frontier of Tibet; even in Taklakot you feel as if you have suddenly been transported back in time. In Ngari, food is either cooked over a yak-dung fire or blasted with a petrol-fuelled blowtorch. There are no buses; if you have not arranged for a travel agency to provide you with a Land Cruiser, your only choice is to hitch a ride (and in Tibet, hitchhikers pay for the ride) in the back of a 1950s-style Chinese truck, probably atop piles of wool and in the company of several families of dusty Tibetans.

Mt Kailas (6714m) is the most sacred mountain in Asia. It is believed to be the physical embodiment of the mythical Mt Meru, said to be the centre of the universe or 'navel of the world'. Mt Meru is often depicted as a mandala, and its image occurs throughout both Buddhist and Hindu parts of Asia. Images of Mt Meru occur as far away as Angkor Wat in Cambodia and Borobadur in Indonesia. Mt Kailas is holy to followers of four religions. To Hindus, Kailas is the abode of Shiva and nearby Manasarovar Lake is the *manas* or soul of Brahma. Tibetans call Kailas Kang Rimpoche. Jains worship it as Mt Ashtapada, the peak from which the religion's founder, Rishabanatha, achieved spiritual liberation. Followers of Bon-po, the ancient pre-Buddhist shamanistic religion of Tibet, revere Kailas as the soul of Tibet.

Manasarovar, at an elevation of 4510m, is more important to Hindus than to Buddhists. Hindu pilgrims make an 85 km circuit around Manasarovar that is made longer and more difficult by marshes and complicated stream crossings. Tibetans, being more pragmatic, often make a circuit of the lake in the winter when the streams are frozen and the route is shorter. Near Manasarovar is another large lake, Rakshas Tal, the 'Demon Lake,' that holds far less spiritual significance.

Another geographical factor that contributes to the mystical aspect of Kailas is that nearby are the headwaters of four major rivers of the Indian subcontinent, the Sutlej, Karnali (a major tributary of the Ganges), Brahmaputra and Indus. The mouths of these rivers are more than 2000 km apart, yet they all have their source within 100 km of Mt Kailas. ■

to trek up the Lha Chu valley you would eventually reach the true source of the Indus. The kora route now makes a serious climb onto a moraine, eventually meeting the trail from the east bank. The trail climbs more gently to **Jarok Donkhang**, a meadow full of fat marmots *(phiya)* at 5210m. This is a good camp that will make the pass crossing easier than it would be if you camped at Diraphuk. It's dangerous to camp higher because of the risk of acclimatisation problems. The snow-covered pass to the right, the Khando-sanglam La, is protected by a lion-faced *dakini* goddess. Pilgrims may cross this difficult pass only on their auspicious 13th circuit of the mountain.

Day 3: Jarok Donkhang to Zutul-puk

Climb past piles of clothing at **Shiva-tsal**,

elevation 5330m. Tibetans leave an article of clothing or a drop of blood here as part of leaving their past life behind them. Continue past thousands of small rock cairns to a large cairn at 5390m and beyond to a stone hut and camp. Just before the rest house is the **Dikpa Karnak**, the sin testing stone. It is said that those without sin can squeeze through the narrow hole between the two boulders, while a sinner, no matter how small, cannot pass through. Beware, it's a *very* small space.

The trail leads across a boulder field and climbs through large rocks to a tiny stream. It is considered auspicious to symbolically wash your past sins away with the holy water of this spring. Climb to a ridge and continue gently on to the **Dolma La** at 5630m. A big boulder on the pass representing the goddess Dolma (better known by her Sanskrit name,

Tara) is festooned with prayer flags and streamers. It is traditional to leave, and take, something as part of the collection of coins, prayer flags, teeth and other offerings attached to the rock. This is the physical and spiritual high point of the kora. Money is pasted to the rock with butter, and pilgrims make the requisite three circumambulations of the rock. This must be the world's largest collection of prayer flags. If you meet Tibetan pilgrims here you will probably be invited to join them for a picnic (complete with alcoholic chhang, which can be lethal at this altitude) in celebration of completing the hardest part of the kora. Most Tibetans do the kora in one day, starting at four or five am, reaching the Dolma La between 10 and 11 am and finishing about 8 or 9 pm. In 1985 the Tyrolean mountaineer Reinhold Messner is reported to have made the fastest kora on record – 45 km in 12 hours.

The trail down the west side of the pass is steep and rocky at first, then begins a series of switchbacks as it passes **Gouri-kund**, the 'lake of mercy', at 5450m. Devout Hindu pilgrims are supposed to break the ice and bathe in its waters. Many more switchbacks lead down to the valley and a stone guest-house alongside the Lham-chhukhir at 5150m. There is a footprint of Buddha, called a *shapje,* nearby. Even though the trail is better and less marshy on the other side, stay on the west side of the river; it becomes too large below to cross back. The trek makes a long, gentle, uninteresting descent of the valley. When crossing the stream of the Khando-sanglam you reach the third prostration station; look upstream for the only view of the east face of Kailas. There are herds of blue sheep on the opposite side of the river.

The **Zutul-puk** gompa, a guesthouse, and camp are further down the valley at 4790m. *Zutul* means miracle and *puk* means cave. This gompa is named after a cave in which the saint Milarepa stayed, meditating and eating only nettles. Among the miracles he performed were adjusting the height of this cave to make it more comfortable. He left his footprint outside, and prints of his head and hand still remain on the inside of the roof. You enter the cave through the gompa. Here the river is known as the Zhong Chu.

Pilgrims to Mt Kailas

The circumambulation of Mt Kailas is an important pilgrimage for Hindus, Buddhists and Jains. Hindus perform a *parikrama*; Buddhists call it a *kora*. You are welcome to do either of these, or simply make a trek around the peak. Tibetan Buddhists believe that a single kora washes away the sins of one life and that 108 circuits secure nirvana in this life. Devout Tibetans often make the 52-km circuit in a single day. Indian pilgrims make the circuit in three days, but this also is rushed, particularly since the circuit, though mostly level, involves the crossing of a 5630m pass. A four day trek is far more enjoyable and rewarding.

An agreement between China and India allows 350 Indians per year to make the pilgrimage to Manasarovar and Kailas. The trip is so important to Hindus that the trips are oversubscribed and the quota is filled by lottery. They trek for nine days through India in order to reach Taklakot.

Hindu and Buddhist pilgrims make a clockwise circuit of the peak. Bon-po tradition is to circumambulate in the opposite direction. As you circle Kailas by the traditional route, you will meet followers of Bon-po making a kora in the opposite direction. When I was at Kailas there was a large contingent of Bon-po pilgrims from faraway Kham and Nakchu. We were astounded at the huge number of adherents to what has been described as an 'ancient pre-Buddhist' religion making the counterclockwise circuit.

The most pious of the pilgrims are those who prostrate themselves around Kailas, lying flat on the ground, then rising, walking to the point that their hands touched and repeating the process. It's an awesome spectacle to meet a group of pilgrims performing this feat.

There is also an 'inner kora' that passes two lakes to the south of Kailas. Tradition dictates that only those who have made 13 circumambulations of Kailas may follow this inner route. This tradition is so important to Tibetans that we were required to assure our hosts that we would not violate the sanctity of this route before they allowed us to proceed to Darchan. ■

Day 4: Zutul-puk to Darchan

Cross a log bridge over a side stream from Kailas, then contour up as the river descends towards the plain. Make a dramatic exit from the river valley onto the plain at the last prostration station (4610m). Rakshas Tal glistens in the distance as you pass mani walls decorated with carved yak skulls. A truck track meets the kora route here, so you could choose to finish the trek at this point. To complete the pilgrimage you should trek a further 1½ hours to Darchan along the edge of the Barkha plain.

TAKLAKOT TO SIMIKOT VIA LIMI

Note that this route is not open to trekkers as of May 1997; it may, however, be open by the time you read this. It is longer and harder than the direct return route to Simikot via Yari. Limi is a remote valley in the north of Humla inhabited by Bhotias. The people of Limi are sophisticated and well-to-do. They trade *pashmina* wool, which retails for about US$400 per kg, in India and export wooden utensils to both Tibet and India. Limi is isolated from the rest of Nepal by snow from November to April, so the primary focus of Limi's trade is the route through Taklakot. For this reason the trails from Limi to Tibet are far better maintained than those to Simikot. The last few days of this trek are tough going over high passes on rough trails. Don't attempt this route unless you are fit and well equipped – nor until the Nepal government finally opens Limi to trekkers.

Day 1: Taklakot to Manepeme

The drive from Taklakot to Sher, described in reverse earlier in this chapter, takes about 1½ hours, so theoretically you will arrive in Sher in time to do some trekking. However, with the time change and customs and immigration formalities, you will probably end up here at night and camp at Sher in a continual upriver wind. Set your watch back 2¼ hours to Nepal time and enjoy reasonable time again.

The Limi trail starts climbing from the salt-trading post where the road ends. If you plan to follow this route, do not descend to the Humla Karnali at Hilsa. By the time you trek there, Nepal may have built an immigration post in Hilsa, so you might have to go down to the river and then climb back into Tibet in order to start walking to Limi. Plan your departure from Sher carefully; it's about four hours from Sher to Manepeme and there is no possible camping place in between.

From the end of the road at 3800m, the trail starts steeply up across a barren slope, crossing unannounced into Nepal. A pole with tattered prayer flags marks a ridge at 4120m and the end of the first steep climb. The trail contours along the side of the ridge high above the Humla Karnali, making minor ups and downs, to a ridge with a stone chorten at 4110m. Follow some switchbacks down, then cut across a slope dotted with scrub juniper. A well-maintained trail crosses a rock slide, then climbs above a recent landslide. Take the upper, new trail over the top of the landslide and drop down to meet the original trail on the opposite side. **Manepeme** is behind a ridge in a large side canyon near a stream at 3970m. It is not an ideal camp because the only flat spaces are deep in goat droppings, as are most camp sites on this trek – though Manepeme is perhaps the worst case. Manepeme is named after a huge stone above the camp site that is carved (now rather faintly) with the mantra *om mani padme hum*.

Day 2: Manepeme to Til Chu

From Manepeme the trail weaves in and out of ravines along the side of the valley, climbing gradually towards the foot of a rock cliff. Ascend along the foot of the cliff, climbing to a ridge at 4070m. The Humla Karnali turns south and flows through a steep gorge towards Muchu. The Limi trail now follows a tributary, the Takchi Chu.

The trail drops into a gully and climbs onto another ridge at 4040m. The trail beyond here looks horrific – winding up a steep rock face onto what looks like a pinnacle. It's not as bad as it looks, just a long, slow series of switchbacks that climb on a well-maintained trail over a ridge at 4120m. Look for blue sheep *(naur)* on the cliffs above. The trail descends from the ridge to Lamka, a stream and some tiny camping places (along with the requisite goat droppings) at 4000m.

Climb steeply again from Lamka to the Lamka Lagna, at 4300m, where there is a first view of the Limi valley and the green fields of Halji in the distance. The trail descends to a tiny stream, then continues down and across a slope. Climb over two rocky ridges and make a short descent to two chortens that mark the end of the ridge above the Til Chu. The houses across the valley are Til gompa; the lowest fields of Til village are also visible below. The main trail descends gently to the stone houses of Til, the first village since Sher, about an hour up the Til Chu at 3700m. To avoid Til, follow a steep trail downhill to join a lower trail that crosses the Til Chu and descends to a super camp site at its confluence with the Takchi Chu, elevation 3580m. Just east of this camp is a large pit lined with stones. This is a snow leopard trap, and there is one near each village in the Limi valley. When a cat has killed local livestock, villagers stake a goat in the pit. The theory is that when a snow leopard jumps in, the overhanging rock walls prevent its escape.

Day 3: Til Chu to Jang

The trail climbs a stone staircase over a rock spur, then drops back down to the Takchi Chu, crossing it on a wooden bridge at 3590m. The trail follows the river along its sandy bank to another bridge that leads back to the north side of the river at 3710m. It's a short walk past barley fields into **Halji** at 3670m. The trail bypasses the village, staying near the river in a pleasant plantation of willow trees. The unpainted stone houses of Halji are surrounded by extensive barley and wheat fields just behind a ridge in a large valley. The houses surround a white gompa that has a single red wall painted with a white inscription of *om mani padme hum* similar to the gompa at Khojarnath. Inside the gompa are numerous recently made statues and paintings. Photography has been prohibited

in the Halji gompa since a recent theft in Khojarnath.

Cross a low ridge that protects Halji from wind, and climb steeply to a ridge at 3850m. From there the descent to the police post at **Sunkhani** (also known as Tayen) at 3830m is a gentle one. There's a reasonably good camp site five minutes beyond Sunkhani and another one 15 minutes beyond that. The valley becomes very rocky as the trail makes ups and downs. A series of irrigated barley fields mark the beginning of **Jang**, also called Jyanga or Jyangba, an impressive stone village with a white gompa at 3930m.

The people of Limi make wooden bowls from pine, birch and maple trees that grow on the south side of the river. You will probably see piles of these bowls drying in the sun. Surprisingly, Limi dominates the entire supply of wooden bowls to Tibet. High-quality bowls are made from the burls of maple trees. The scarcity of these burls in Limi has required people to find alternate sources of supply from Kumaon in northern India, yet the bowls are still manufactured in Limi. Even in Lhasa, wooden bowls from Limi are prized over those made elsewhere.

When I visited Jang, its inhabitants were in the midst of a six-day-long celebration in honour of the birth of a son to one of the families in the village. The parents (in this case represented by the grandfather since the father was off tending his flock of sheep) had to provide food and drink for the entire village – though they were compensated through the ample donations that were offered.

There's a terrific camp 45 minutes further up the trail. Climb gently to two small, white chortens and a snow leopard trap that mark the eastern end of Jang. The river cascades though a narrow defile as it makes a steep drop. At the top of this cascade the route enters the upper portion of the Takchi Chu valley where the river meanders across broad meadows. Jump across a small stream, pass three more chortens and you will arrive at a small stone edifice beside two more chortens at 4070m. The stone wall encloses a small hot spring. You can camp in the meadows nearby and spend the afternoon in the hot spring ridding yourself of the dust of Tibet. The long rows of white stones in the meadow were placed to form a path for an important *rimpoche* from Dehra Dun in India who visited Limi in the summer of 1993.

Day 4: Jang to Talung

Continue across meadows, hopping across a few side streams. A short climb takes you over a rocky ridge, but the trail is mostly level and pleasant. The trail reaches a point that overlooks the river valley, and turns north. The geography is a bit confusing; you trek north along the Takchi Chu to the only bridge, then turn south again. The trail north leads to the Lapcha La, once an important trade route from Limi into Tibet, and one that offers a short cut to Manasarovar Lake. The Chinese emphasis on Taklakot as a trade centre has left this route generally unused, though there is a Nepal police post nearby that controls access to the pass. Turn right before the police post and head down to the river and a wooden bridge at 4160m. The trail rounds a ridge and turns south through country similar to Tibet, with marmots and nettles (the same variety that Milarepa ate). To the south you can see the white sand of a moraine that forms the lake of Tshom Tsho.

Below this plateau was **Gumma Yok**, elevation 4170m, once the most important village of Limi. The village was abandoned many years ago; you can see the remnants of a few buildings here and there.

Climb onto the fine white sand of the moraine and drop to the other side above the huge lake, Tshom Tsho. The best trail bears left across meadows to a bridge over the Ling Chu, though you can wade the stream near the point where it enters the lake if you get lost – or if your feet are hot. Traverse scree slopes above the eastern side of the lake. This huge, U-shaped valley rises in a series of steps created by ancient glaciers. Ascend the first of these into a flat valley at 4320m. Yak and sheep herders from both Humla and Limi have semipermanent settlements with Tibetan-style yak-hair tents at many places in the valley. They are not used to visitors,

but stop and see if you can buy a cup of hot milk (*dudh* in Nepali, *oma* in Tibetan), yoghurt (*dahi*), fresh cottage cheese (*serkum*) or dried cheese (*churpi*). Climb another short, steep slope to the next valley, a pasture and tent camp called **Talung**, at 4380m. You can camp here or half an hour beyond, on the last 'step' in the valley, at 4450m.

Day 5: Talung to Shinjungma

Climb to the next valley and cross the meadows to the foot of the pass. The last of the shepherds' tents are visible at the foot of Dimochu, the huge glaciated peak that dominates the head of the valley. Now the hard work begins as you head east into a rocky valley at the foot of the climb to the pass. Grind your way uphill for about two hours to a collection of cairns and upturned rocks. From here, on a clear day, you can see Mt Kailas. Continue to the pass, Nyalu Lagna, at 4990m, and cross it bearing north-east.

Below the pass the trail makes a U-turn and heads south, descending along the moraine to an attractive high-altitude lake, **Selima Tsho**, at 4570m. Make a long, knee-cracking descent on the moraine that formed the lake, eventually crossing two streams and reaching the valley floor at 4140m. Head east across alpine meadows to a wooden bridge over a large stream that enters from the north-east. When I trekked in this valley, the herders in a nearby camp had just made temporary repairs to the bridge, which looked as though it was going to be washed away at any moment by the fast-flowing, mud-coloured stream.

You are now presented with a choice. There is a steep short cut over a 4900m ridge to the east called the Kuki Lagna, or you can do as our local guide recommended and trek around the edge of the ridge, avoiding the extra climbing. The lazy person's trail follows a rocky route into a birch and rhododendron forest starting around 4050m – the first real vegetation since you left the Humla Karnali on the upward trek. Saipal Himal (7031m) looms in the distance to the south. Descend through forests on a steep trail to a primitive camp near **Shinjungma** at 3850m.

RESTRICTED AREAS

The Chumsa Khola is fast and muddy in the afternoon because of glacial runoff, so it's a lousy water supply. There are a few clear side streams and springs in the area that a local guide can find for you. On the west side of the valley is a terrific rock face that rivals Yosemite Valley in the USA.

Day 6: Shinjungma to Dhinga Laga

Descend further along the wooded Chumsa Khola valley to an inconspicuous trail junction at 3780m. The larger trail (which you do not take) continues down the valley, eventually reaching the Humla Karnali far below near Kermi. It was at the foot of this valley that you probably had lunch in the marijuana fields on the third day out of Simikot.

To go to Simikot, take the smaller, left-hand trail and start uphill. The trail becomes more prominent as it rounds a ridge and ascends through pine, then birch, forests alongside a large stream. Keep climbing through a rocky meadow at 4110m, then to a bridge at 4220m. The trail from Kuki Lagna rejoins the route here. It's another hour of steep climbing to the Landok Lagna, the last major pass on the trek, at 4550m elevation. I crossed this pass in a rainstorm and complete whiteout, so I have no idea what the views are like.

Be careful of the route as you descend. A few minutes below the pass, a cattle trail that looks like the main trail heads down a gully to the left. Don't follow this; stay to the right on an indistinct trail that follows the ridge. The trail moves towards the right side of the ridge, dropping to a tiny stream at 4140m. Continue down the ridge, dropping off the end to a larger stream at 3940m. The trail gets better as it winds its way through a forest of big juniper trees covered with moss. Follow the wide trail down to a stream and a mill, crossing the stream on a wooden bridge at 3710m.

There is no camp here, so keep climbing through oak, birch and rhododendron forest, ferns and wild flowers to a notch in a ridge at 3860m. Head north along the eastern side of the ridge through burned forest, climbing gently to a side ridge at 3890m that leads into a high alpine bowl. Trek downhill to a trail junction. The trail straight ahead leads to the upper part of Dhinga – a summer settlement called **Dhinga Laga**. The right-hand trail leads steeply downhill to a meadow and a small pond surrounded by a forest of blue pines and a good camp site – if the local people agree to allow you to camp in the village grazing land.

Day 7: Dhinga Laga to Simikot

Lace your boots up tightly in preparation for a rough day. From the meadow camp, trek onto the ridge for a view of the huge valley of the Yakba Khola. Turn south on a good trail that heads towards Dhinga Shyo, the lower, winter settlement of Dhinga. Most people of Dhinga have houses in both settlements. About half an hour below the ridge, at an elevation of 3400m, there is another inconspicuous trail on the left that heads downhill. Local people assured us that this is the part of the 'main' trail to Limi, though this is hard to believe as you plummet down through forests, duck under tree limbs, tear your clothing on thorn bushes and dodge stinging nettles. A tough, hot exercise lands you at the Yakba Khola and a bridge at 2630m. You can see Yakba at the foot of the valley some distance upstream.

Follow a narrow, nettle-lined trail downstream, then start uphill. Climb and climb past a few houses at 3010m, eventually cresting the ridge at 3100m. The going is easier now as you walk around the ridge through groves of walnut trees to a tiny stream – the first available potable water and an opportunity for lunch.

The trail passes north above the scattered settlements of **Ogren Gaon**, passing several streams as it makes its way along the rocky slope. You can see the Humla Karnali far below as you ascend to the final ridge of the trek at 3270m. It's only a few minutes walk to the junction of the Humla Karnali trail, and a few more minutes after that to the top of the ridge overlooking **Simikot**. Descend on a gravel trail to the village water supply, then down a clutter of loose rocks to the airport at 2960m.

Other Trekking Areas

As scenic, interesting, culturally enriching and historic as the major treks may be, you should consider a trek to other regions. Although there are restrictions involved with issuing trekking permits, and some areas are still closed to foreigners, there are many places in Nepal that are both fascinating and accessible.

Many trekkers make the mistake of varying their route by attempting a 5500m to 6000m-high pass. Upon reaching the pass they discover that they, their equipment or other members of the party are totally unfit for the cold, high elevation and technical problems that the pass presents. Often the problems force the party to turn back, severely altering their schedule. In the end, they fail to reach their primary goal. It is best to plan to attempt a high pass crossing after achieving the major goal of the trek – usually somewhere on the return route to Kathmandu.

You need not go to a particularly remote region to escape heavily travelled trails. The major trade and trekking routes are the shortest way to a particular destination, but if you allow another few days it is possible to follow less direct, often parallel, routes through villages that are not even on the maps, in areas with less Western contact than the major trails.

In 1984 I visited an area less than a day's walk from an important trekking route. The local people insisted that I was the first trekker who had ever been there. Other foreigners had visited the region, of course, as engineers, doctors and teachers, but none had come there before simply to trek. There must be thousands of similar places in Nepal. Even in the 1990s I have trekked to many places where there were few, if any, other trekkers. Some of those places are described in this book, although others are not. It seems contradictory to leave the congestion of an urban area only to battle crowds in Khumbu and Manang during October, November and April. By choosing an unusual destination during the high season or by going to popular places in the low season, you can recapture some of the spirit of unhurried life in the hills that so entranced early trekkers to Nepal.

On remote or exotic treks a guide is helpful, and it is almost imperative to carry your own food, stove and fuel. In areas that neither trekkers nor local porters frequent, there are no *bhattis*. Food is available, but the time and effort necessary to scrounge out food and accommodation in homes can make progress almost impossible.

KATHMANDU TO POKHARA

Before the Pokhara road was completed in 1971, the only ways to reach Pokhara from Kathmandu were to fly or to walk. The trek from Kathmandu is an easy nine or 10 day trek from Trisuli Bazaar to Begnas Tal, just outside Pokhara. This is the easiest trek in Nepal and has few uphill climbs of any significance. Trekking in a westerly direction, there are many alternatives. A northern route offers a trek close to the mountains – Manaslu (8156m), Himalchuli (7893m), Baudha (6674m) – and a side trip to Bara Pokhari, a fine high-altitude lake. The more direct southern route to Pokhara allows a visit to the ancient town of Gorkha with its large bazaar and fort. This route has the attraction of lower altitudes and avoids the extreme elevation gains and losses common to other treks in Nepal. The views of the Himalaya are good on this trek, but the route never actually gets into the high mountains.

A lot of the interest and remoteness of this trek have vanished because the new road to Gorkha has totally changed the trading habits and culture of the region. Local people hardly ever walk this route now, so the facilities for food and accommodation have degenerated. A few Westerners travel the southern routes, but many parts of the northern regions are both remote and untrammelled by trekkers.

GANESH HIMAL

Between Kathmandu and Pokhara are three major groups of peaks: Ganesh Himal; Manaslu and Himalchuli; and the large Annapurna Himal. You can drive to Dhunche on the same road that leads to the start of the Langtang trek, then either continue driving on the road to Somdang or walk towards Ganesh Himal.

ROLWALING

Rolwaling is the east-west valley below Gauri Shankar (7145m), just south of the Tibetan border. This is an isolated and culturally diverse area, but most treks conclude their visit to Rolwaling by crossing the Tesi Lapcha pass (5755m) into Khumbu. If you must cross this dangerous pass, it is better to cross it from Khumbu into Rolwaling, rather than visit Rolwaling first. There are two reasons for this: well-equipped, willing porters are easier to get in Khumbu than in Rolwaling; and in case of altitude sickness there are better facilities for help if you make your retreat on the Khumbu side rather than back to the isolated villages of Beding or Na in Rolwaling. A second way to visit this region would be to forgo Tesi Lapcha and go only as far as Na, then retrace the route back to Kathmandu.

Tesi Lapcha is particularly dangerous because of frequent rock falls on its western side. The route through the icefall is becoming technically more and more difficult due to the movements of the glacier. The Rolwaling porters operate a Mafia-like system and will not allow outside porters to approach the pass from Rolwaling, forcing parties to accept people from Beding and Na as porters. The local porters either get frightened of the falling rocks and return without notice or demand exorbitant pay once the party is halfway up the pass. There are no facilities at all between Na and Thami. Tesi Lapcha is a true mountaineering project!

The Rolwaling area and Tesi Lapcha are technically closed to foreigners. However, if you obtain a climbing permit for Ramdung, one of the trekking peaks, the immigration office will issue you a trekking permit for Rolwaling.

TILICHO TAL

There is another pass south of Thorung La between Manang and Jomsom. From Manang, the trail goes on to the village of Khangsar, then becomes a goat trail scrambling over moraines to Tilicho Tal (4120m) at the foot of Tilicho Peak (7132m). Herzog's maps depicted Tilicho Tal as the 'great ice lake'. It is usually frozen (except when you decide to trust the ice and walk on it). From the lake, there are several alternative routes, including Meso Kanto Pass (5330m) and another pass a little further north. The trail is difficult and hard to find. One very experienced trekker described the trail as only a figment of someone's imagination – he claimed there was no trail at all. In 1985 a New Zealand trekking group was snowed in near Tilicho Tal. Four sherpas went for help, using the seats of bamboo stools for snowshoes, and were killed in an avalanche.

Thorung La is a good, safe route between Manang and Jomsom. It's better to make a side trip to Tilicho Tal from Manang rather than take all your equipment and porters on the Tilicho Tal trail. One complication of this trek is that the army does not want you wandering through the training exercises they run in the valley east of Jomsom. Enquire in Kathmandu and again in Manang before making plans to cross the Tilicho route. You might cross the pass only to have the army turn you back to Manang an hour before Jomsom.

MUGU

Mugu is a remote region east of Humla and north of Rara Lake. The area is inhabited by people of Tibetan ancestry, and is an old trade route to Tibet. Most of Mugu is closed to trekkers, including the route up the Humla Karnali to Mugugaon, but it is possible to trek north of Rara Lake, cross a pass to Darma and continue to Simikot.

NAR-PHU

The Nar-Phu Valley lies north of Kyupar

village on the way to Manang. This valley, like most of those that lead to the Tibetan border, is generally closed to foreigners. There have been exceptions, and some trekkers have been allowed in if they were engaged in authorised studies. Other trekkers have been admitted upon presentation of a climbing permit for Chulu East. Perhaps it might also be possible to visit the region if you agreed to take a liaison officer, but this is not clearly specified in the regulations.

MILKE DANDA

There is a long, high, forested ridge that divides the Arun and Tamur valleys in eastern Nepal. You can start from Basantpur (see the Kanchenjunga North trek) and make a trek of several days up this ridge, which offers views of Makalu to the west and Kanchenjunga to the east. The Milke Danda ridge eventually ends in some high peaks, so you must retrace your route back down, perhaps dropping off the west side through Chainpur and ending the trek at Tumlingtar.

There are huge forests of rhododendrons along the ridge, making a spring trek an attractive prospect. You may forgo mountain views if you schedule a trek in April to see the rhododendrons in bloom; eastern Nepal in the springtime can often be rainy and cloudy.

AROUND DHAULAGIRI

There is a long, difficult trek around Dhaulagiri (8167m) that starts from Beni on the Kali Gandaki. Follow the Myagdi Khola westwards to Darbang and turn north on a tiny trail that leads through forests into the high country. Much of the route is on snow and glaciers as it crosses French Col (5240m), traverses the head of Hidden Valley and crosses 5155m Dhampus Pass. The trek ends with a steep descent to Marpha and a return to Pokhara, either via the Kali Gandaki valley or over the Ghorapani ridge for a panoramic view of the entire Dhaulagiri massif.

Appendix I – Mountaineering in Nepal

Although this is a book about trekking, a short discussion of mountaineering in Nepal is appropriate. The first trekkers in Nepal were, of course, mountaineers who were either on their way to climb peaks or were exploring routes up unclimbed peaks. There was furious mountaineering activity in Nepal from 1950 to the 1960s, and all the 8000m peaks were climbed during this time.

By the early 1970s the emphasis had shifted to previously impossible feats such as the south face of Annapurna and the south-west face of Everest, both of which were climbed by expeditions led by Chris Bonington. The expeditions in the 1960s and 70s were often well equipped, and sometimes lavish, thanks to sponsorship from governments, foundations, magazines, newspapers, film makers, TV producers and even private companies. Expeditions have become big business and climbers now approach the job with the appropriate degree of seriousness and dedication. It is not uncommon for expeditions to refuse trekkers admission into their base camps. The team members do not have the time or energy to entertain tourists, and there have also been incidents of trekkers taking souvenirs from among the expensive and essential items that often lie around such camps.

There are three seasons for mountaineering in Nepal. The premonsoon season from April to early June was once the only season during which expeditions climbed major peaks. In the 1950s all expeditions were in the 'lull before the storm' period that occurs between the end of the winter winds and the beginning of the monsoon snow. Cold and high winds drove back the Swiss expedition to Mt Everest in 1952 when they attempted to climb the mountain in the autumn. It was not until 1973 that an expedition successfully climbed Everest in autumn. Now the autumn or postmonsoon season of September and October is a period of many successful expeditions.

In 1979 the Ministry of Tourism established a season for winter mountaineering. It is bitterly cold at high elevations from November to February, but recent advances in equipment technology have allowed several teams to accomplish what was thought before to be impossible – a winter ascent of a Himalayan peak. Climbing during the monsoon, from June to August, is not practical from the Nepal side, though the north face of Everest has been climbed during August.

Two organisations control climbing in Nepal. The Ministry of Tourism is responsible for major expeditions and the Nepal Mountaineering Association (NMA) issues permits for the peaks that are open to trekking groups. The type of climbing that appeals to most trekkers is encompassed by the regulations for small peaks.

TREKKING PEAKS

Since 1978 the NMA has had the authority to issue permission for small-scale attempts on 18 peaks. It is not necessary to go through a long application process, hire and equip a liaison officer or organise a huge assault on a major peak in order to try Himalayan mountaineering. The 18 'trekking peaks' provide a large range of difficulty and are situated throughout Nepal.

There is a minimum of formality, requiring only the payment of a fee and the preparation of a simple application. The fee is US$300 for peaks above 6100m and US$200 for peaks less than 6100m. The permit is valid for one month for a group of up to 10 people. An extra US$5 per person is payable if the group exceeds 10 climbers. Because the regulations for climbing a small peak also require an established liaison in Kathmandu (usually a trekking company), it is easiest to use an overseas adventure travel company or a trekking company in Nepal to organise a climb rather than try to do the whole project yourself.

The designation 'trekking peak' is an unfortunate misnomer, because most of the peaks on the list are significant mountaineering challenges. Few of the trekking peaks are 'walk-ups', and some of them, such as Kusum Kangru and Lobuje, can be technically demanding and dangerous. As you think about these 'small' peaks, remember that all of them are higher than any mountain in North America. Before you consider climbing a trekking peak, reread some books on Himalayan expeditions. The weather is often bad and may force you to sit in your tent for days at a time. Usually a well-equipped base camp is necessary, and the ascent of a peak requires one or more high camps that must be established and stocked. Most of the trekking peaks require a minimum of four days to climb, and an ascent can take as long as three weeks.

Bill O'Connor's excellent and comprehensive guidebook, *The Trekking Peaks of Nepal*, is usually available in Kathmandu and in bookshops overseas. The book includes photographs, maps, trekking information and climbing routes on the 18 trekking peaks.

To get a climbing permit for a trekking peak, go to the NMA office (☎ 01-411525, 416278) in Kamal Pokhari, Kathmandu. You must pay the peak fee in foreign currency cash or travellers' cheques. You must also employ a sirdar who is currently registered with the NMA, and if any Nepalis are to climb above base camp, you must insure them and supply them with climbing equipment. A climbing permit does not replace a trekking permit; you need both if you are climbing a trekking peak.

You can buy or rent climbing gear in Kathmandu, saving the expense of air freighting ironmongery around the world. Good mountain tents, stoves, sleeping bags, down clothing and most other expedition necessities are all available for rent. As with trekking gear, the items that might be in short supply are socks, clothing, cooking gas cylinders, boots in large sizes and freeze-dried food.

Peaks which can be climbed under the trekking peak regulations follow.

Annapurna Region

Fluted Peak (6501m) – now Singu Chuli (named for the steep ice slopes that make it difficult to climb); this peak is reached from the Annapurna Sanctuary

Hiunchuli (6441m) – snow, ice and rock; not an easy climb

Mardi Himal (5587m) – five day slog up the Mardi Khola to approach the peak, an outlier of Machhapuchhare

Tent Peak (5500m) – now Tharpu Chuli; climb involves glaciers and crevasses; most people climb the easier Rakshi Peak to the south

Ganesh Himal

Paldor Peak (5928m) – 10 day trek to base camp from Trisuli Bazaar

Langtang Region

Ganja La Chuli (5846m) – now Naya Kangri; involves a snow and rock climb from a base camp either north or south of Ganja La

Manang Region

Chulu East (6584m) – ascent starts after a long approach from Manang; needs one or two high camps

Chulu West (6419m) – route circles Gusang Peak to climb Chulu West from the north; requires at least two high camps

Pisang Peak (6091m) – long snow slog above Pisang village, steep snow at the top. The mountaineering school at Manang uses Pisang Peak for training climbs.

Mt Everest Region

Island Peak (6189m) – now called Imja Tse; involves one steep and exposed 100m ice or snow climb, otherwise a non-technical snow climb

Kwangde (6187m) – north face (seen from Namche) is a difficult climb; southern side (from Lumding Kharka above Ghat) is a moderately technical climb (allow two to three weeks)

Kusum Kangru (6367m) – the most difficult of the trekking peaks

Lobuje East (6119m) – top is exposed and often covered with rotten snow; there's also an exposed knife ridge and some crevasses

Mehra Peak (5820m) – now called Khongma Tse. This is a rock and ice climb that's not difficult from either the Imja valley or Lobuje.

Mera Peak (6476m) – easy snow climb from the Mera La, but sometimes crevasses complicate the route; no villages or food on the approach from Lukla; requires two weeks

Pokhalde (5806m) – short, steep snow climb from the Kongma La above Lobuje

Rowaling Region

Pharchamo (6187m) – steep snow climb on a route subject to avalanches; peak is just above Tesi Lapcha

Ramdung (5925m) – requires a long approach through Rolwaling Valley. A permit for Ramdung allows you to trek into the restricted area of Rolwaling, so many groups that get permits for this peak do not even attempt to climb it.

MOUNTAINEERING EXPEDITIONS

The rules for mountaineering on major peaks require a minimum of six months advance application to the Ministry of Tourism, a liaison officer, a royalty of US$1000 to US$50,000 depending on the elevation of the peak, and endorsement from the government or the national alpine club of the country organising the expedition. There are 87 peaks open for foreign expeditions and another 17 peaks open for joint Nepali-foreign expeditions. Some peaks, such as Mt Everest, are booked many years in advance, while others remain untouched for several seasons.

Further information is usually available through alpine clubs in your own country. Even the most budget-conscious expedition under these regulations would cost at least US$20,000 to cover salary, insurance and equipment for sherpas and a liaison officer, peak fees and other compulsory expenses. If you want an inexpensive climb in Nepal, it is far more reasonable to set your sights on one of the trekking peaks.

Eight of the world's 14 peaks over 8000m are in Nepal. Those outside Nepal include K2 (8611m), Nanga Parbat (8125m), Gasherbrum I (8068m), Gasherbrum II (8035m) and Broad Peak (8047m), all in Pakistan. The remaining 8000m peak is Shisha Pangma (8013m), which is in Tibet, just north of the Nepal-Tibet border.

The following sections summarise the important early climbs on the 8000m peaks of Nepal. For a comprehensive reference on these mountains, climbs and an exhaustive bibliography of books about the Himalaya, I recommend *Sivalaya*, by Louis Baume. Elizabeth Hawley kindly provided the up-to-date statistics on the number of ascents and

deaths. Miss Hawley has lived in Nepal since the 1950s and, in addition to her duties running Sir Edmund Hillary's Himalayan Trust, has maintained an exhaustive record with details of every mountaineering expedition that has climbed on peaks in Nepal.

Mt Everest

Mountaineering and trekking in Nepal has relied heavily on the progress and inspiration developed by various expeditions to Everest. Much of the attraction of Nepal in the early days resulted from the discovery that the highest peak in the world lay within the forbidden and isolated kingdom. Though it was named Mt Everest by the Survey of India in 1856 after Sir George Everest, retired Surveyor-General of India, the peak had been known by other names long before. The Nepalis call it Sagarmatha and the Sherpas call it Chomolungma. The Chinese now call it Qomolangma Feng. Sagarmatha literally means 'head of the sky', the name was invented in 1956 by Babu Ram Acharya, a Nepali historian.

The list of attempts and successes on Everest is one of the classics of mountaineering history. By 1989 there had been 274 ascents of Everest, including several by people who climbed it two or more times. At the end of 1996 the record stood at 391 expeditions, 676 different people had reached the summit (counting the 90 people who have climbed two or more times, it totals 846 ascents), and 147 climbers had been killed. The following section lists all the Everest expeditions until 1982. By 1983 both China and Nepal allowed several expeditions on the mountain at the same time, causing traffic jams, queues for the use of routes and fixed ropes, confusion, squabbles, crowded base camps and the inevitable trashing of the mountain. From 1983 onwards I have listed only the more spectacular or interesting expeditions. For a complete list of Everest ascents and an amazing set of statistics about climbs on the mountain, see the latest edition of *Everest* by Walt Unsworth.

Early Attempts from Tibet The first expeditions to Everest were two British reconnaissance teams that approached the peak through Tibet from Darjeeling. They spent months mapping and exploring the Everest region and ran the first climbing school for Sherpas on the slopes leading to the North Col. On the second expedition George Leigh Mallory named the Western Cwm and declared that Everest was probably impossible to climb from the Nepal side.

The first serious attempt to climb Everest was made in 1922. The expedition, as did all attempts until 1950, climbed the mountain from the north after a long approach march across the plains of Tibet. The highest point reached was 8320m. An avalanche killed seven Sherpas below the North Col.

In 1924 another team of British gentlemen in their tweed suits set off to climb Everest. They didn't have crampons and had a furious argument about whether the use of oxygen was 'sporting'. On this expedition Mallory and Andrew Irvine climbed high on the mountain and never returned. Nobody has ever found out whether they reached the top before they perished.

In 1933 another British expedition reached a height of 8570m, just 275m short of the summit. Frank Smythe's book *Camp Six* is an excellent personal account of this expedition. At the same time a British expedition flew over Everest in two Westland biplanes. This was a spectacular technical achievement at the time and produced many useful photographs.

A year later a strange man named Maurice Wilson flew alone in a small plane from the UK to India, then crossed Tibet to make a solo attempt on Everest. He carried little food, believing that fasting would give him strength; he eventually froze to death on the slopes below the North Col.

In 1935 Eric Shipton led a small expedition as far as the North Col. Tenzing Norgay accompanied this expedition as a porter. The following year another expedition reached a point only slightly above the North Col. In 1938 another famous name associated with Everest came to the fore when HW Tilman led a small expedition in which Eric Shipton reached almost 8300m.

In 1947 Earl Denman, a Canadian, disguised himself as a Tibetan monk, travelled to Everest and made a solo attempt. He quit below the North Col and returned immediately to Darjeeling.

Early Climbs from Nepal After the war Tibet was closed, but Nepal had begun to open its borders. In 1950 Tilman made a peripatetic trip all over Nepal, including a trek from Dharan to Namche Bazaar. His group was the first party of Westerners to visit the Everest region. They made the first ascent of Kala Pattar and walked to the foot of the Khumbu Icefall. In 1951 K Becker-Larson, a Dane, followed the same route as the Tilman party, then crossed into Tibet, reaching the North Col before returning.

The British still considered Everest their mountain, and the Royal Geographical Society and the Alpine Club teamed up to sponsor a serious programme to climb it. Eric Shipton led a reconnaissance in 1951, reaching the Western Cwm at the top of the Khumbu Icefall and proving that Everest was climbable from the south. Nepal allowed only one expedition per year on Everest; in 1952 it was the turn of the Swiss. During this expedition Raymond Lambert and Tenzing Norgay reached a height of almost 8600m. Rushing to beat the British, the Swiss tried again in the autumn but cold and high winds drove them back from a point just above the South Col. In 1953 a huge British expedition, led by John Hunt, finally succeeded. Edmund Hillary and Tenzing Norgay reached the summit of Everest on 29 May 1953.

Climbs after the First Ascent In 1956 the Swiss finally placed four climbers on the summit of Everest and also made the first ascent of Lhotse. The era of large expeditions continued, and in 1960 the first Indian expedition reached a height of 8625m before bad weather forced them to retreat. While the Indians were attempting Everest from the Nepal side, a Chinese expedition made the first ascent from the north. The climb was discredited at first because three members of the team reached the summit at night, but mountaineering history now acknowledges the ascent.

In 1962 Woodrow Wilson Sayre and three others obtained permission to climb Gyachung Kang, then crossed into Tibet and tried to climb Everest without permission. They reached a point above the North Col before returning. Their antics almost jeopardised the US Mt Everest expedition the following year. This large expedition, led by Norman Dyhrenfurth, was successful in placing six people on the summit, including two by the previously unclimbed west ridge. The traffic jam on Everest began two years later when Captain MS Kohli led an Indian team that placed nine climbers on the summit of Everest.

From 1966 to 1968 Nepal was closed to mountaineers. When climbing was again allowed, the Japanese had become interested in Everest and in 1970 a 38 member team placed four climbers on the summit. This was the expedition that included the famous 'ski descent' of Everest. Six Sherpas were killed in the Khumbu Icefall.

Attention now turned to new routes on Everest, especially the south-west face. In 1971 Norman Dyhrenfurth led an ambitious expedition with climbers from 13 nations attempting both the south-west face and the west ridge, finally retreating from a height of 8488m on the face route. Further attempts on the south-west face were made in 1972 by a European expedition and a British expedition led by Chris Bonington.

During the 1970s it seemed that there was an unlimited amount of money available for Everest expeditions. In 1973 a huge Italian expedition placed eight climbers on the summit and two members of a Japanese team made the first successful ascent in autumn. The following year saw an unsuccessful Spanish expedition and a disastrous French attempt on the west ridge that ended when an avalanche killed the leader and five sherpas.

The following year saw some spectacular successes, including the first ascent of Everest by a woman, Junko Tabei, who was

a member of a Japanese expedition. A few days after the Japanese success, a Chinese team placed nine people, including one woman, on the summit. The large survey tripod they erected is still on the top of Everest. The south-west face was finally climbed by a British expedition funded by Barclays Bank and led by Chris Bonington.

Mountaineering continued through the 1970s with numerous successes. In 1978 Everest's largest challenge was overcome when Reinhold Messner and Peter Habeler made the first ascent of the mountain without using oxygen. Climbers began attracting media attention, and in 1978 a gigantic German-French expedition placed 16 climbers on the summit via the South Col and made a live radio broadcast from the 'roof of the world'.

In 1980, after more than 40 years of closure, Tibet was once again accessible to mountaineers. A large and expensive Japanese expedition reached the summit by two different routes from Tibet. In 1980 Reinhold Messner made his second oxygen-less ascent of Everest, this time from the Tibetan side – and alone. Another precedent was set when a 1982 Canadian expedition made live TV transmissions from the mountain.

One of the more unusual accidents on Everest occurred during a 1982 Belgian expedition to the west ridge. One member fell into Tibet and was given up as dead; he eventually made his way back to Kathmandu by bus. The Everest traffic jams reached a new level in 1983 when three Japanese climbers reached the summit via the South Col on the same day that six Americans made the first ascent of the difficult Kangshung face from Tibet.

Nepal now allowed several expeditions on the mountain at the same time and sometimes allowed more than one expedition on the same route. In 1984 there were 14 expeditions, five from Tibet and the rest from Nepal. The first Indian woman and four other climbers reached the summit via the South Col. Five Bulgarians reached the summit via the west ridge; four climbers made a traverse and descended via the south-east ridge.

Climbing from Tibet, Greg Mortimer and Tim McCartney-Snape were the first Australians to reach the summit of Everest.

New Developments By the mid-1980s expeditions had to rely on more and more complex gimmicks to obtain funding for their activities. Everest also became a goal for older and less experienced climbers; the natural result of this was the evolution of guided climbs on the world's highest peak.

In 1985 there were 14 attempts on Everest, but only three were successful. A record 17 climbers from a Norwegian expedition reached the summit via the South Col. Throughout the rest of the 1980s there were many expeditions each year, but few were successful. In the spring of 1988 more than 250 climbers made up a joint Chinese-Nepali-Japanese expedition that traversed the mountain in both directions. The teams met on the summit and made a prime-time live TV broadcast. In autumn, three French teams and American, Korean, Spanish, Czech and New Zealand teams all gathered at base camp. Latecomers were charged for the use of fixed ropes through the icefall. Four French climbers reached the summit and Jean-Marc Boivin jumped off by paraglider, landing at camp two 12 minutes later. During the year a total of 31 climbers reached the summit and nine people died.

In 1991 a group of four hot-air balloonists crossed from Gokyo over the summit of Everest to Tibet in an hour and 20 minutes. The 1992 climbing season saw a queue of climbers waiting at the foot of the Hillary Step, a steep, difficult step on the summit ridge, for their turn to reach the top. A total of 17 expeditions were on the mountain, 13 from the Nepal side, and 58 climbers reached the summit, 32 in a single day. On several occasions sherpa teams set up a route through the icefall and charged a toll for climbers who wished to use it. Several novice mountaineers reached the summit of Everest on guided climbs. The first Nepali woman to climb Everest died on the descent, but she became a national hero.

Nepal has upped the fee for Everest and limited the number of expeditions on the mountain. Each expedition is limited to 10 climbers, though another two may climb if they pay an extra US$5000 each. Climbers who violated rules used to be banned from climbing in Nepal for 10 years; in the autumn of 1993 a British expedition that sent two unauthorised climbers to the summit was fined US$100,000 for the infringement.

The largest tragedy on Everest was in the spring of 1996. Several parties with clients who had paid US$65,000 each to be guided to the top of Everest ended up on the summit at 3 pm, far later than normal. A violent storm blew in and made the descent difficult, and several climbers lost their way in the whiteout and darkness. In the aftermath, eight climbers, including experienced Everest guides Rob Hall and Scott Fischer, perished and several climbers suffered extreme frostbite.

Kanchenjunga
Kanchenjunga, at 8598m, is the third-highest peak in the world and the second-highest in Nepal. It was first climbed by a British team in 1956. The peak consists of four summits. The west summit, Yalung Kang, is 8420m high and some people classify it as a separate 8000m peak. By the end of 1996, 122 people had climbed Kanchenjunga on 69 expeditions and 32 climbers had died on the mountain.

The first Westerner to explore Kanchenjunga was the British botanist JD Hooker, who visited the area twice in 1848 and 1849. Exploration of the Sikkim side of the peak continued with both British and pundit explorers mapping and photographing until 1899. In that year a party led by Douglas Freshfield made a circuit of Kanchenjunga and produced what is still one of the most authoritative maps of the region.

Exploration continued, mostly from the Sikkim side, with expeditions starting from Darjeeling in British India. One of the major contributors to Western knowledge about the region was Dr AM Kellas, who later died in Tibet during the approach march of the 1921 Everest expedition. German expeditions attacked the peak in 1929, 1930 and again in 1931, but none was successful. After the war Sikkim was closed but Nepal was open. In 1955 a team led by Dr Charles Evans approached the peak via the Yalung Glacier. Two teams climbed the peak, stopping just short of the summit to conform to an agreement with the Maharaja of Sikkim that the summit would remain inviolate.

The Japanese now took up the challenge and mounted expeditions in 1967, 1973 and 1974 during which they climbed Yalung Kang. A German expedition climbed Yalung Kang in 1975, and in 1977 an Indian army team mounted the second successful expedition to the main peak of Kanchenjunga.

Lhotse

Lhotse (8501m) was climbed by a Swiss expedition in 1956; its lower peak, Lhotse Shar, 8383m, is sometimes considered a separate 8000m peak. Lhotse, which means 'south peak', is part of the Everest massif, just to the south of Everest. The primary route on Lhotse is via Everest's South Col, but despite the activity on Everest, by 1955 Lhotse was the highest unclimbed peak in the world. Lhotse has had the least climbing activity of any 8000m peak in Nepal. The record in 1996 stood at 83 summiters, 67 expeditions and six deaths.

The first attempt on Lhotse was by an international team in 1955. One member of the party was Erwin Schneider; during this expedition he began work on the first of the series of high-quality 'Schneider maps' of the Everest region. The same Swiss who made the second ascent of Everest in 1956 made the first ascent of Lhotse from a camp just below the South Col.

Lhotse Shar was first climbed by an Austrian expedition in 1970. Various routes on the main peak were attempted by Japanese, South Koreans, Germans, Poles and Italians before the summit was reached again by a German expedition in 1977.

Makalu

Makalu (8463m) was first climbed by a French party in 1955. By 1996, 128 climbers had reached the summit on 113 expeditions; 11 climbers have died in the attempt. The peak was first mapped and photographed from the Tibetan side by the 1921 British Everest reconnaissance. Hillary and Shipton photographed Makalu during a side trip on the 1951 Everest reconnaissance. Hillary and others approached the peak a year later after the failure of their Cho Oyu expedition.

The first attempt on Makalu was in 1954 by a US team, mostly from California, who trekked all the way from the Indian border near Biratnagar. At the same time a British team approached the mountain, but this expedition was abandoned when Hillary became seriously ill and had to be evacuated.

In the autumn of 1954 a French team attempted the peak. In the following spring, successful ascents were made by three teams of French climbers on successive days.

In 1960 a large scientific and mountaineering expedition wintered at the foot of Ama Dablam, occupying the Green and Silver huts. In May 1961, members of the expedition trekked across the Mingbo La and other high passes to the foot of Makalu, where they planned to climb the French route. Sickness stopped the expedition, which became a heroic struggle for survival.

The Japanese climbed Makalu in 1970, another French team climbed it in 1971 and a Yugoslav expedition reached the summit in 1975. In 1976 Spanish and Czechoslovakian teams joined up near the summit.

Dhaulagiri

Dhaulagiri (8167m) was first climbed by the Swiss in 1960. Its name is derived from Sanskrit: *dhavala* means 'white' and *giri* is 'mountain'. The mountain was sighted by British surveyors in India in the early 1800s and was mapped by one of the secret Indian surveyors, the pundits, in 1873, but the region remained largely unknown until a Swiss aerial survey in 1949. In 1996, 254 climbers had summited on 148 expeditions, and 44 climbers had died.

The French Annapurna expedition in 1950 had permission to climb either Annapurna or Dhaulagiri but decided on Annapurna after a reconnaissance of Dhaulagiri. A Swiss party failed in 1953 as did an Argentinian group in 1954.

After four more expeditions had failed, eight members of a Swiss expedition reached the summit in 1960. The climb followed a circuitous route around the mountain from Tukuche, over Dhampus Pass and French Col, to approach the summit from the North-East Col. The expedition was supplied by a Swiss Pilatus Porter aircraft, the 'Yeti', which landed on the North-East Col at 5977m. Near the end of the expedition the plane crashed near Dhampus Pass and the pilots, including the famous Emil Wick, walked down the mountain to Tukuche.

Tragedy struck in 1969 when an avalanche killed seven members of a US expedition on the East Dhaulagiri Glacier. The peak was climbed by the Japanese in 1970, the Americans in 1973 and the Italians in 1976. Captain Emil Wick airdropped supplies to the US expedition from a Pilatus Porter aircraft. Among the delicacies he dropped were two bottles of wine and a live chicken. The Sherpas would not allow the chicken to be killed on the mountain, so it became the expedition pet. It was carried, snow-blind and crippled with frostbitten feet, to Marpha, where it finally ended up in the cooking pot.

Manaslu

Manaslu (8156m) was first climbed in 1956 by a Japanese expedition. Its name comes from the Sanskrit word *manasa*, meaning 'intellect' or 'soul'. This is the same word that is the root of the name of the holy lake Manasarovar near Mt Kailas in Tibet. Just as the British considered Everest to be their mountain, Manaslu has always been a 'Japanese' mountain. The record on Manaslu in 1996 was 149 summiters, 106 expeditions and 47 deaths.

HW Tilman and Jimmy Roberts photographed Manaslu during a trek in 1950, but the first real survey of the peak was made by a Japanese expedition in 1952.

A Japanese team made the first serious attempt on the peak from the Buri Gandaki valley in 1953. When another team followed in 1954, the villagers of Samagaon told them that the first team had been responsible for an avalanche which destroyed a monastery, and refused to let the 1954 expedition climb. The expedition set off to climb Ganesh Himal instead.

Despite a large donation for the rebuilding of the monastery, subsequent Japanese expeditions, including the one that made the first ascent in 1956, took place in an atmosphere of animosity and mistrust. The second successful Japanese expedition was in 1971.

There was a South Korean attempt in 1971, and in April 1972 an avalanche which resulted in the death of five climbers and 10 Sherpas ended the second South Korean expedition. Reinhold Messner made the fourth ascent of Manaslu as a member of a Tyrolean expedition that climbed the peak from the Marsyangdi valley in 1972.

Cho Oyu

Cho Oyu (8153m) was first climbed by Austrians in 1954. It is about 30 km west of Everest at the head of the Gokyo Valley. The mountain was reconnoitred during the 1951 Everest reconnaissance, and a British team led by Eric Shipton attempted the peak in 1952. The first ascent was made in 1954 via the north-west ridge using a route through Tibet from the Nangpa La – not strictly a legal route. An Indian expedition made the second ascent in 1958 and a German ski expedition made the third ascent in 1964. By 1992 a total of 100 expeditions had been made on Cho Oyu. Most of the Nepal-based expeditions had made the illegal approach through Tibet, and the Chinese had dispatched police to try to collect peak permit fees from climbers who crossed the border. The approach to the mountain from both Nepal and Tibet is easy, and the ascent through Tibet is not particularly difficult. Of all Nepal's 8000m peaks, Cho Oyu is second only to Everest in the number of expeditions and successful ascents. In 1996 the record stood at 680 climbers reaching the summit, 229 expeditions and 20 deaths.

Annapurna

Annapurna (8091m) was first climbed by a French expedition in 1950. There are four summits called Annapurna; the entire massif forms a barrier on the northern side of the Pokhara Valley. The main summit of Annapurna is to the west of the Annapurna Sanctuary; Annapurna II is above Chame, about 24 km to the east. Fewer climbers have reached the summit of Annapurna than any other 8000m peak in Nepal. Only 96 climbers on 106 expeditions had reached the summit by the end of 1996; 45 climbers had died on the mountain.

A French expedition led by Maurice Herzog explored the Kali Gandaki valley in 1950. After deciding that Dhaulagiri was too difficult, they turned their attention to climbing Annapurna. Hampered by inaccurate maps, they spent considerable time and effort finding a way to the foot of the mountain. They eventually ascended via the Miristi Khola to the north face and made what was the first ascent of any 8000m peak on June 3, just before the start of the monsoon. The summiters suffered frostbite on the descent and were finally evacuated back to the roadhead in India.

Annapurna was not climbed again until 1970, when a British army expedition followed essentially the same route as Herzog. At the same time Chris Bonington led a successful British expedition to the very steep and difficult south face.

Appendix II – Personal Equipment

The equipment checklist on the following page is based on the experience of many trekkers over the years. I use it myself when preparing to trek to be sure that I don't forget some important item. Everything on the list is useful, and most of it necessary, on a long trek. You can omit many items if your trek does not exceed three weeks in duration or ascend above 4000m. All of this gear (except perhaps the sleeping bag) will pack into a duffel bag that weighs less than 15 kg.

Some gear will not be necessary on your particular trek. You might be lucky enough to trek during a warm spell and never need a down jacket. It might be so cold and rainy that you never wear short pants. These are, however, unusual situations, and it is still important to prepare yourself for both extremes. As you read the checklist, be sure to evaluate whether or not you need a particular item of equipment. More detailed consideration of most items follows. Do not rush out to an equipment shop and buy everything on this list. It works for me and has worked for many other trekkers, but you may decide that many items in this list are unnecessary.

Footwear
Trekking or Running Shoes Proper footwear is the most important item you will bring. Your choice of footwear will depend on the length of the trek and whether or not you will be walking in snow. Tennis or running shoes are good trekking footwear, even for long treks, if there is no snow. You may experience some discomfort in lighter and softer shoes because the trails are usually very rocky and rough. If the soles of your shoes are thin and soft, the rocks can bruise your feet and walking will be painful.

There are numerous brands of lightweight trekking shoes that have stiffer lug soles and are available in both low and high-top models. High-top shoes provide ankle protection, but low-cut shoes are cooler to walk

in. Most trekking shoes are made of a leather and nylon combination and many have Gore-Tex waterproofing, but they are expensive, ranging from US$60 to US$100.

You should try out the shoes you plan to wear on the trek during several hikes (particularly up and down hills) before you come to Nepal. Be sure your shoes provide enough room for your toes. There are many long and steep descents during which short boots can painfully jam your toes (causing the loss of toenails).

Boots and lightweight trekking shoes, both new and used, are available for sale and rent in Kathmandu.

Mountain Trekking Boots Wherever there is snow (likely anywhere above 4000m), proper waterproof boots can become an absolute necessity. If you are travelling with porters, you have the luxury of carrying two sets of shoes and swapping them from time to time. If you are carrying everything yourself, you may have to settle for one or the other.

Camp Shoes Tennis shoes are comfortable to change into for the evening. They can also serve as trail shoes in an emergency. Rubber thongs or shower shoes make a comfortable change at camp during warm weather. They are called *chhapals* in Nepal, and you can buy them in Kathmandu and along most trails. Carry a pair of these in your rucksack, wear them at lunch and in camp and put your shoes and socks in the sun to dry. Fake Teva sport sandals are available in Kathmandu and would be a good choice if you expect to be wading streams.

Socks Good socks are at a premium in Nepal, so bring these with you. There are some heavy, scratchy Tibetan woollen socks available in Kathmandu and Namche Bazaar.

Nylon-wool blend socks are fine, but the

PERSONAL EQUIPMENT CHECKLIST

FOR ALL TREKS

Footwear
- [ ] trekking or running shoes
- [ ] camp shoes or thongs
- [ ] socks – polypropylene

Clothing
- [ ] down or fibre-filled jacket
- [ ] jumper or pile jacket
- [ ] hiking shorts (for men) or skirt
- [ ] waterproof jacket, poncho or umbrella
- [ ] hiking pants
- [ ] T-shirts or blouses
- [ ] underwear
- [ ] sun hat
- [ ] swimwear (optional)

Other Equipment
- [ ] rucksack
- [ ] sleeping bag
- [ ] water bottle
- [ ] torch (flashlight), batteries & bulbs

Miscellaneous Items
- [ ] toilet articles
- [ ] toilet paper & cigarette lighter
- [ ] small knife
- [ ] sunblock (SPF 15-plus)
- [ ] towel
- [ ] laundry soap
- [ ] medical & first-aid kit
- [ ] pre-moistened towelettes
- [ ] sewing kit
- [ ] bandanna

FOR TREKS GOING ABOVE 4000M

Footwear
- [ ] mountain trekking boots
- [ ] socks, wool, to wear with boots
- [ ] socks, light cotton, for under wool socks
- [ ] down booties (optional)

Clothing
- [ ] insulated pants
- [ ] nylon windbreaker
- [ ] nylon wind pants
- [ ] long underwear
- [ ] woollen hat (or balaclava)
- [ ] gloves
- [ ] gaiters

Miscellaneous Items
- [ ] goggles or sunglasses
- [ ] sunblock for lips

OPTIONAL EQUIPMENT

Photography Equipment
- [ ] camera & lenses
- [ ] lens cleaning equipment
- [ ] film (about 20 rolls)

Toys & Navigation Aids
- [ ] GPS unit
- [ ] altimeter
- [ ] thermometer
- [ ] compass

Miscellaneous Items
- [ ] binoculars
- [ ] books to read while waiting for planes & buses
- [ ] If you have a porter, you will need a duffel bag with a padlock, some stuff sacks and lots of plastic bags.
- [ ] A small duffel bag or suitcase to leave your city clothes in is also useful.

new artificial fibre hiking socks (which cost astronomical prices) are the best bet. A number of manufacturers, including Thorlo, Wigwam and Patagonia, make several varieties of hiking socks that are designed to prevent blisters by wicking moisture away from your feet. You will wash your socks several times during a long trek, and pure wool socks dry slowly. Synthetic socks dry in a few hours in the sun – often during a single lunch stop. Three pairs should be

enough unless you are a real procrastinator about washing clothes.

Footwear – high altitude

Wool Socks If you are going to do extensive walking in snow, wool socks are still the best protection against frostbite. A thin cotton liner sock is usually necessary with heavy woollen rag socks.

Down Booties Many people consider these

excess baggage, but they are great to have and not very heavy. If they have a thick sole, preferably with closed-cell foam (Karrimat or ensolite) insulation, they can serve as camp shoes at high elevations. Down booties make a cold night seem a little warmer – somehow your feet seem to feel the cold more than anything else. They're also good for midnight trips outside into the cold. You can buy locally made down booties in Kathmandu.

Clothing
Down-Filled or Fibre-Filled Jacket Down clothing has the advantage of being light and compressible. It will stuff into a small space when packed, yet bulk up when you wear it. You should bring a good jacket on a trek. Most ski jackets are not warm enough and most so-called expedition parkas are too heavy and bulky. The secret is to choose one that will be warm enough even at the coldest expected temperatures, but also comfortable when it is warmer. Don't bring both a heavy and a light down jacket; choose one that will serve both purposes, preferably one with a hood.

Many people try to avoid bringing a down jacket because they are expensive and bulky and the equipment manufacturers are promoting the layering principle, but I wouldn't be without one. On a trek you will have lots of time to sit around and get cold. With the emphasis on wood conservation in Nepal, there is no longer an opportunity to sit around the fireplace in a lodge. On a camping trek, the dining tent can get pretty chilly, and the time between sundown and 'soup ready' is one of the coldest times of day.

Your down jacket can serve many functions on the trek. It will become a pillow at night and will protect fragile items in your backpack or duffel bag. If you are extremely cold at high altitude, wear your down jacket to bed inside your sleeping bag. You don't wear down gear for walking as it rarely gets that cold even at 5000m. Most trekkers leave their down clothing in their duffel bag at lower elevations and only use it during the evening. At higher elevations, carry your jacket and put it on at rest or lunch stops.

Artificial fibre jackets (filled with Polargard, Thinsulate or Fibrefill) are a good substitute for down though somewhat bulkier and heavier, and are much less expensive. Down jackets are expensive. If you don't own a down jacket, you can rent one in Kathmandu, Pokhara or Namche Bazaar.

Jumper or Pile Jacket The layering principle says that two light layers of clothing are better than a single heavy layer. One or two light jumpers (sweaters to North Americans), shirts or polyproplyene, pile or fleece layers are superior to a heavy jacket. Most of the time you will need only a single light garment in the morning and will shed it as soon as you start walking.

Jackets made of polyester pile or fleece come in a variety of styles and thicknesses. They are light, warm (even when wet) and easy to clean. If possible, buy a jacket that uses fleece that is made from recycled plastic bottles. It is possible to rent or buy pile jackets in Kathmandu, though most are made locally with inferior fleece and carry fake brand names. Tibetan woollen jumpers are also for sale in Kathmandu, but they are bulky and scratchy.

Hiking Shorts or Skirts It will often be hot and humid, the trails steep and the wind calm. Long pants pull at the knees and are hot. For hiking at lower elevations, the sherpas usually switch to shorts. It's a good idea. Either 'cutoffs' or fancy hiking shorts with big pockets are fine, but only for men. Skimpy track shorts are culturally unacceptable throughout Nepal.

Villagers giggle at women in shorts, so it's better to wear a skirt, perhaps over a pair of shorts. Many women who have worn skirts on treks are enthusiastic about them. The most obvious reason is the ease in relieving oneself along the trail. There are long stretches where there is little chance to drop out of sight, and a skirt solves the problem. Skirts are also useful when the only place to wash is in a stream crowded with trekkers, villagers and porters. A wrap-around skirt is easy to put on and take off in a tent. Long 'granny' skirts are not good because you will be walking through too much mud to make them practical.

Waterproof Jacket, Poncho or Umbrella

It is likely to rain at some time during your trek. The condensation inside a waterproof jacket can make you even wetter than standing out in the rain. Fancy fabrics such as Gore-Tex are supposed to keep you dry by allowing the jacket to breathe, but in Nepal it's usually so warm, and the hills so steep, that they don't always work as advertised.

One way to keep dry while hiking in the rain is to use a poncho – a large, often hooded, tarp with a hole in the centre for your head. The weather is likely to be warm, even while it's raining, and you can get air circulation with a poncho if you drape it over your rucksack. An inexpensive plastic poncho is often as good as more expensive coated nylon gear. The plastic one is completely waterproof at a fraction of the cost. Nylon ponchos are manufactured in Kathmandu.

The most practical way of keeping dry is an umbrella. This is an excellent substitute for a poncho (except on windy days), and can serve as a sunshade, a walking stick, an emergency toilet shelter and a dog deterrent. Umbrellas with bamboo handles are available in Kathmandu for about US$2, but are bulky and leak black dye over you when they get wet. Collapsible umbrellas are an excellent compromise, although they cannot serve as walking sticks. Imported collapsible umbrellas are available in shops on New Rd and in the supermarket in Kathmandu. An umbrella is necessary in October, April and May and optional for treks in other months.

Sun Hat A hat to keep the sun off your head is an important item, but its design is not critical. Obviously, a hat with a wide brim affords greater protection. Fix a strap that fits under your chin to the hat so it does not blow away in a wind gust. The Nepal Cap House in the shopping centre at the entrance to

Thamel has an amazing assortment of hats to choose from. There are outdoor hat stalls near the immigration office that also offer a selection of locally produced sun hats.

Swimwear Almost nobody older than eight goes without clothing in Nepal or India. You will upset sherpas, porters and an entire village if you skinny dip in a river, stream or hot spring, even to wash. There are many places to swim, although most are ridiculously cold – except along the Arun River in eastern Nepal, where there are some fine swimming holes. There are hot springs in Manang and in Tatopani (literally, 'hot water') on the Jomsom trek. Either bring along swimwear or plan to swim in shorts or a skirt and be prepared to wear them till they dry.

Clothing – high altitude

Insulated Pants Insulated pants of some kind are a real asset on a trek that goes above 4000m. You can bring pile pants, ski warm-up pants or down pants and put them on over your hiking shorts or under a skirt when you stop. You can also wear them to bed for extra warmth when the nights become particularly cold.

Often you will arrive at your camp or hotel at 3 pm and will not dine until 6 pm, so unless you choose to do some exploring, there will be about three hours of sitting around before dinner. In cold weather, insulated pants make these times much more comfortable. Down pants, and sometimes ski warm-up pants, are available for rent in trekking shops in Kathmandu and Namche.

Nylon Windbreaker Strong winds are rare in the places visited by most treks, but a windbreaker is helpful in light wind, light rain and drizzle, when a poncho is really not necessary. If you already have a waterproof jacket as your 'outer layer', you don't need another shell garment. Be sure that your windbreaker breathes, otherwise perspiration cannot evaporate and you will become soaked. A windbreaker is more in the line of emergency gear. If there is a strong wind, you must have it; otherwise, you will probably not use it. If you're rich, or spend a lot of time in the outdoors, a Gore-Tex parka is a good investment.

Nylon Wind Pants Many people use these. The temperature will often be approaching 30°C, and most people prefer to hike in shorts except in the early morning when it is chilly. Wind pants provide the best of both worlds. Wear them over your shorts or under your skirt in the morning, then remove them to hike in lighter gear during the day. Most wind pants have special cuffs that allow you to remove them without taking off your shoes.

If you are going to high elevations, you will truly be 'in the mountains' for several days. Here the weather can change quickly and sometimes dramatically. Although it will often be warm, it can cloud up and become cold and windy very fast – a potential problem if you happen to be wearing shorts. If you carry wind pants, you can just slip them on when it gets cold.

You can substitute ski warm-up pants, or even cotton jogging pants, for both wind pants and down-filled pants. The cost will be lower and there is hardly any sacrifice in versatility or comfort.

Hiking Pants Almost any long pants will do. When it's bitterly cold, you can wear long underwear under them. Many women wear tights under their skirt to stay both warm and culturally correct.

T-Shirts or Blouses You'll spend a lot of time walking in a short-sleeved shirt – what the equipment catalogues call the first layer. Cotton garments are fine, but if you can afford, and find, a synthetic T-shirt, you will be much more comfortable. You will perspire excessively, and a polypropylene or other synthetic (with brand names like Capilene, Thermax and Polartec) shirt wicks the moisture away from your skin. This means that when you put your rucksack on after a rest stop, your back is not cold and damp. The wicking effect also makes a Gore-

Tex parka work better. Strangely, short-sleeved polyester shirts are hard to find in the USA, but they are standard (expensive) fare in Australian outdoor equipment shops.

Long Underwear Long johns are a useful addition to your equipment. A complete set makes a good warm pair of pyjamas and is also useful during late-night emergency trips outside your tent or hotel. Unless the weather is especially horrible, you will not need them to walk in during the day. You could bring only the bottoms and use a woollen shirt for a pyjama top. Cotton underwear is OK, though wool or polyester is much warmer.

Woollen Hat or Balaclava A balaclava is ideal because it can serve as a warm hat or you can roll it down to cover most of your face and neck. You may even need to wear it to bed on cold nights. Because much of your body heat is lost through your head, a warm hat helps keep your entire body warmer. As with jackets, pile and fleece are suitable alternatives to wool.

Gloves Warm ski gloves are suitable for a trek. You might consider taking along a pair of woollen mittens also, just in case your gloves get wet.

Gaiters If your trek visits high elevations, there is a chance of snow and also an opportunity to do some scrambling off the trails. A pair of high gaiters will help to keep your boots and socks cleaner and drier in rough conditions.

Other Equipment
Backpack A backpack or rucksack should have a light internal frame to stiffen the bag and a padded waistband to keep it from bouncing around and to take some weight off your shoulders. There are many advantages to keeping your pack small. Its small size will prevent you from trying to carry too much during the day. It is a good piece of luggage to carry on a plane. A small backpack will fit inside your tent at night without crowding and will not be cumbersome when

you duck through low doorways into houses and temples. Try to find a rucksack that you can lock, or at least one that has a lockable zippered compartment that you can stow valuables in.

If you don't plan to take a porter, you will need a larger pack. This can be either a frame (Kelty type) pack or a large expedition backpack, although a soft pack is more versatile. If you do eventually hand your pack over to a porter, he will certainly stuff it into a bamboo basket called a *doko* and carry it suspended from his forehead with a tumpline called a *naamlo*. A frame pack is difficult for a porter to carry because he will refuse to use the shoulder straps. There is a wide assortment of day packs and backpacks available for sale or rent in Kathmandu.

Sleeping Bag This is one item that you might consider bringing from home. Sleeping bags are readily available for rent in Kathmandu, but the dry-cleaning facilities in Nepal are pretty strange and bags lose their loft quickly during the process. The choice is usually between a clean (old and worn) bag, a dirty (warm) one or an expensive, new one. A cotton liner inside your sleeping bag will keep it clean. You can use the liner instead of a sleeping bag in the lowlands when it's hot.

Most sleeping bags available in Kathmandu are mummy-style expedition bags that rent for less than US$2 a day. It is cold from November to March, even in the lowlands, so a warm sleeping bag is important at these times. A warm sleeping bag is a must at altitudes over 3300m, no matter what the season.

Water Bottle Because you must drink only treated or boiled water, bring a one-litre plastic water bottle that does not leak. During the day your bottle provides the only completely safe source of cold drinking water. If you use iodine, fill your water bottle from streams or water spouts, add the iodine and have cold, safe water half an hour later. It used to be appropriate to fill your water bottle with boiled water at night, let it cool

and then use it the following day. Fuel problems in the hills now make this practice unacceptable.

Many people require two litres of water during the day. If you are one of those, consider a second water bottle. Good water bottles are sometimes hard to find in Kathmandu, but you can always find (leaky) plastic Indian bottles or empty mineral water bottles that will do at a pinch. Metal water bottles are also available, but check before you buy one to be sure it has not been used earlier to carry fuel.

Torch (Flashlight) Almost any torch will do, though many people prefer a headlamp – which is particularly useful for reading or going to the toilet. You can get spare batteries almost anywhere in the hills of Nepal if you bring a torch that uses 'D' cells, and you can often find 'AA' batteries. Larger batteries perform better in the cold than small penlight cells, but of course they are heavier. Indian and Chinese torches and exotic torches left over from expeditions are available in Nepal.

Duffel Bag If you travel with porters, protect your gear with a duffel bag. Several companies make good duffel bags that have a zipper along the side for ease of entry. This is not an item to economise on; get a bag that is durable and has a strong zipper. A duffel 35 cm in diameter and about 75 cm long is large enough to carry your gear and will usually meet the weight limit of porters and domestic flights – typically 15 kg. Army surplus duffel bags are cheaper, but they are inconvenient because they only open from the end, although there is no zipper to jam or break.

If you have porters, they will carry most of your equipment. During the day, you will carry your camera, water bottle, extra clothing and a small first-aid kit in your backpack. Do not overload the backpack, especially on the first day of the trek.

It is impossible to describe how your duffel bag will look after a month on a trek. To find out how it is treated, load a duffel bag with your equipment, take it to the second storey of a building and toss it out a window. Pick it up and shake the contents, then put it in the dirt and stomp on it a few times. Get the idea?

When it rains, your duffel bag will get wet. Porters will leave their loads outside tea shops in the rain while they go inside to keep dry. You should pack your duffel bag in such a way that important items stay dry during rainstorms. A waterproof duffel bag and waterproof nylon or plastic bags inside your bag are both necessary.

Use a small padlock that will fit through the zipper pull and fasten to a ring sewn to the bag. The lock will protect the contents from pilferage during the flight to and from Nepal and will help protect the contents on your trek. It also prevents kids, curious villagers and your porter from opening the bag and picking up something they might think you won't miss. Locally made duffel bags are available in Kathmandu.

Extra Duffel Bag or Suitcase When starting a trek, you will leave your city clothes and other items in the storeroom of your hotel in Kathmandu. Bring a small suitcase or extra duffel bag with a lock to use for this purpose.

Stuff Bags It is unlikely that you will be able to find a completely waterproof duffel bag or backpack. Using coated-nylon stuff bags helps you to separate your gear, thereby lending an element of organisation to the daily chaos in your tent or hotel. Stuff sacks also provide additional protection in case of rain. If you get stuff bags with drawstrings, the addition of spring-loaded clamps will save a lot of frustration trying to untie the knots you tied in too much haste in the morning. You can also use plastic garbage bags, but these are much more fragile. A plastic bag inside each stuff sack is a good bet during the rainy season.

Sunglasses or Goggles The sun reflects brilliantly off snow, making good goggles or sunglasses with side protection essential. At high altitude they are so essential that you should have an extra pair in case of breakage or loss. A pair of regular sunglasses can serve as a spare if you rig a side shield. The lenses should be as dark as possible. At 5000m, the sun is intense and ultraviolet rays can severely damage unprotected eyes. Store your goggles in a metal or hard plastic case as, even in your backpack, it is easy to crush them.

Sunblock During April and May and at high altitudes throughout the year, sunburn can be severe. Use a protective sunblock; those with more sensitive skin need a total sunblock such as zinc oxide cream. Snow glare at high altitude is a real hazard; you'll need a good sunblock, not just suntan lotion.

To protect your lips at high altitude you need a total sunblock such as Dermatone or Labiosan.

Additional Items
There is not much to say about soap, scissors and the like, but a few ideas may help. If there are two people travelling, divide a lot of this material to save weight and bulk.

Laundry soap in bars is available in Kathmandu and along most trails. This avoids an explosion of liquid or powdered soap in your luggage.

Pre-moistened towelettes are great for a last-minute hand wash before dinner. You can avoid many stomach problems by washing frequently. If you bring a supply of these, check the way they are packaged. You can buy them in a plastic container and avoid leaving a trail of foil packets in your wake.

A pair of scissors on your pocket knife is useful. Also bring a sewing kit and some safety pins – lots of uses.

Be sure all your medicines and toiletries are in plastic bottles with screw-on lids. If in doubt, reread the section on the treatment duffel bags receive.

The most visible sign of Western culture in the hills of Nepal is streams of toilet paper littering every camp site. Bring a cigarette lighter or matches so you can burn your used toilet paper.

You might also bring a small shovel or

trowel to dig a toilet hole when you get caught on the trail with no toilet nearby.

Be sure you have the wherewithal to deal with blisters, and carry this with you at all times. It's important to treat blisters as soon as you discover them.

Optional Equipment & Toys
The equipment checklist suggests several items that you might bring on a trek. Do not carry all of them as you will overload your backpack.

Cameras People have brought cameras ranging from tiny Instamatics to heavy Hasselblads. While most trekkers do bring a camera, it is equally enjoyable to trek without one.

A trek is long and dusty. Be sure you have lens caps, lens tissue and a brush to clean the camera and lenses as frequently as possible.

Three lenses – a wide-angle (28 or 35 mm), a standard (50 or 55 mm) and a tele-photo (135 or 200 mm) – are useful if you wish to take advantage of all the photo-graphic opportunities during the trek, but lenses are heavy. Since you will probably carry them in your backpack day after day, you may want to limit your selection. If you must make a choice, you will find a telephoto (or zoom) lens is more useful than a wide-angle, because it will allow you close-up pictures of mountains and portraits of shy people. Be sure to bring a polarising filter. Don't overburden yourself with lots of heavy camera equipment; an ostentatious display of expensive gear invites theft. Insure your camera equipment.

Glossary

ACAP – Annapurna Conservation Area Project, pronounced 'A-cap'

badam – peanut
Bahun – *see* Brahman
baksheesh – a tip or donation
banyan – a species of fig tree, related to the pipal
bari – field where dry crops such as wheat and corn are grown
bazaar – market area; a market town is also called a bazaar
BCE – Before Common Era, a non-Christian representation of years BC
bhanjyang – pass or ridge top
bhat – cooked rice (correct transliteration is *bhaat)*
bhatti – tea shop or small restaurant in the hills
Bhote – Nepali for Tibet
Bhotia – Nepali for Tibetan
bodhi tree – or *bo* tree; a pipal tree under which the Buddha was sitting when he attained enlightenment
Bon-po – the ancient pre-Buddhist animistic religion of Tibet
Brahman – the priest caste of Nepal, also called Bahun

cairn – pile of stones to mark a trail or pass
carom – a game similar to snooker or pool that is played on a small wooden board using checkers instead of billiard balls
chang – north (Tibetan)
chappati – flat unleavened bread, also called *roti*
charpi – toilet
chaur – flat meadow or place for camping (western Nepali)
chautaara – rock wall built as a resting place for porters, almost always near a pipal or banyan tree
chhahara – waterfall
chhang – Tibetan-style beer made from rice, corn or millet; pronounced 'chung'. Lowland people call it *jaand*.

Chhetri – Hindu prince or warrior caste
Chitwan – district in the southern plains of Nepal where Royal Chitwan National Park is located
chiuraa – beaten rice
Chomolungma – the Sherpa name for Mt Everest
chorten – round stone Buddhist monument, often containing relics
chowk – courtyard or square
chu – river (Tibetan)
chuba – Tibetan woollen cloak
Churia – the southernmost range of hills in Nepal, bordering the Terai
col – mountain pass
crevasse – deep fissure in a glacier
cwm – a Welsh word George Mallory used in 1920 to name the high glaciated valley between Everest and Nuptse

dahi – curd or yoghurt
dakshin – south
dal – lentil soup, usually served with rice (correct transliteration is *daal)*
danda – hill (correct transliteration is *daanda)*
Dasain – the week-long autumn festival that worships the goddess Kali
deorali – ridge top
dhami – shaman, sorcerer or medicine man
Dharma – Buddhist teachings
dhindo – paste of wheat, barley and corn; a common meal for hill porters
dhoka – door or gate
dingma – clearing (Tibetan)
Diwali – Indian name of the 'festival of lights' that follows Dasain (called Tihar in Nepal)
doko – woven bamboo basket carried by porters
dudh – milk
durbar – palace
dzong – fort or palace in Tibet
dzopkyo – male crossbreed between a yak and a cow

dzum – female crossbreed between a yak and a cow

gaad – river (western Nepal)
gandaki – river
gaon – village
ghar – house
ghat – place beside a river. A 'burning ghat' is used for cremations.
ghatta – mill, almost always water-driven
ghora – horse
gobar – cow dung. 'Gobar gas' generators are used in the hills to provide combustible gas for lighting and cooking.
gompa – a Tibetan Buddhist temple
gorak – Sherpa name for a raven or large crow
goth – cowshed or hut in a high pasture
GPS – Global Positioning System; a device that calculates position and elevation by reading and decoding signals from satellites
gunsa – winter settlement (Tibetan)
gurkha – Nepali mercenaries who serve in the British and Indian armies
Gurkhali – British army name for the Nepali language
Gurung – people from the western hills, mostly around Pokhara
Guru Rimpoche – founder of Tibetan Buddhism 1250 years ago; also called Ogyan Rimpoche or Padmasambhava

haat – market or hill bazaar in eastern Nepal
himal – Sanskrit word for mountain
HRA – Himalayan Rescue Association

jaat – caste or ethnic group
jhankri – shaman, sorcerer or medicine man
jutho – ritual pollution. Once you have eaten food from a plate, it is *jutho* and no Hindu may eat the remaining food.

Kali – the most terrifying manifestation of the goddess Parvati
Kami – blacksmith caste
kani – an arch over a trail, usually decorated with paintings on the inside (correct transliteration is *kaani*)
kata – a white scarf presented by visitors to a Buddhist lama

Kham – a province in eastern Tibet, home of the Khampas
Khampa – the group of Tibetans best known as guerrilla warriors
khani – mine or quarry
kharka – commonly owned grazing land in the hills
khet – irrigated field for growing rice
khola – river or stream
khorsaani – hot chilli
Khumbu – region near Mt Everest inhabited by Sherpas
kora – Tibetan word for circumambulation of a religious shrine
kosi – one of the seven large rivers in Nepal
Kuhmale – the potter caste
kukhri – traditional curved knife of the Gurkhas
kund – holy lake

la – mountain pass (Tibetan)
lagna – ridge or pass (western Nepal; correct transliteration is *laagna*)
lama – Tibetan Buddhist teacher or priest
lamo – long
lekh – ridge or highlands
lha – god or deity (Tibetan)
lho – south (Tibetan)
Limbu – warrior caste (eastern Nepal)
Loba – people from Lo, the northern part of the Mustang district
Losar – Tibetan or Sherpa new year

maasu – meat
machha – fish
Magar – Tibeto-Burman people related to the Gurungs
Mahabharata – epic war in Hindu mythology
Maitreya – a Buddha who will come in a future era
Malla – royal dynasty of the Kathmandu Valley; also the name of a totally unrelated ancient kingdom in western Nepal
mandir – Nepali word for temple
mani stone – stone carved with the Tibetan Buddhist prayer *om mani padme hum* (the correct transliteration is *maani*)
mantra – prayer formula or chant
mathi – Nepali for up or upper

mela – country fair

mewa – papaya

Milarepa – Tibetan poet and saint (1040-1123)

mithai – candy or sweet

momo – steamed or fried dumplings

moraine – ridge of rocks that a glacier pushed up along its edges (a medial moraine) or at its foot (a terminal moraine)

Musalman – Nepali word for Muslim

naamlo – tumpline used to suspend a load from the forehead

nadi – small stream or river

naike – leader or chief, usually referring to the leader of a team of porters

nak – female yak

nala – stream (the correct transliteration is *naalaa*)

namaste – Nepali greeting, sometimes translated as 'I salute the God in you'

nanglo – round, flat-woven bamboo tray used for cleaning rice; commonly used as a tray for serving meals to trekkers

Newars – people of the Kathmandu Valley

NMA – Nepal Mountaineering Association, responsible for issuing permits for trekking peaks

nup – west (Tibetan), eg Nuptse is the west peak of Everest

Nyingmapa – one of the three Red Hat sects of Tibetan Buddhism

om mani padme hum – sacred Buddhist mantra that roughly translates as 'hail to the jewel in the lotus'

paisa – one one-hundredth of a rupee, but used commonly as a word for money

panch – five

panchayat – the partyless parliamentary system of Nepal until 1990

pani – water

parbat – mountain

pashmina – blanket or shawl made from fine goat's wool

Pharak – Sherpa region south of Khumbu

phedi – foot of a hill

phul – egg

pipal – also known as the bo or bodhi tree, it is the female counterpart of the banyan tree

pokhari – large water tank or lake

prayer flag – long strips of cloth printed with prayers that are 'said' whenever the flag flaps in the wind

prayer wheel – cylindrical wheel inscribed with prayers and containing paper on which are written innumerable prayers. The wheels can be hand-held or as large as three metres high.

puja – religious offering or prayer (pronounced 'poo-ja')

pundits – Indians who were sent into Nepal and Tibet by the Survey of India to secretly gather geographical information

Rai – major ethnic group of eastern Nepal

rajmarg – road or highway, literally 'king's road'

rakshi – distilled spirits made from grain

Rana – hereditary prime ministers who ruled Nepal from 1841 to 1951

rato – red

ri – peak or mountain (Tibetan)

rimpoche – reincarnate lama, usually the abbot of a gompa

RNAC – Royal Nepal Airways Corporation, the government-owned airline

roti – *see* chapatti

SAARC – South Asia Association for Regional Cooperation. This includes the seven countries of Bangladesh, Bhutan, India, Maldives, Nepal, Pakistan and Sri Lanka.

saat – seven

sadhu – wandering Hindu holy man

Sagarmatha – Nepali name for Mt Everest

sahib – term for a Westerner that dates from the time of the British Raj

Sakyamuni – another name for Gautama Buddha

sal – hardwood tree of the Terai and Himalayan foothills

saligram – black fossils of ammonites (sea creatures) from the Jurassic period, proof that the Himalaya was once under water

sangu – bridge

serac – large ice block on a glacier

shar – east (Tibetan)
Sherpa – literally 'people from the east', the Sherpas are Buddhist hill people who are most famed for their work with treks and mountaineering expeditions. With a small 's', sherpa refers to a worker with a trek group.
Sherpani – female Sherpa
Shiva – most powerful Hindu god, the creator and destroyer
sirdar – boss or headman on a trekking or climbing expedition; the role is traditionally filled by a Sherpa
sisnu – stinging nettle
Siwalik – Indian name for the Churia Hills
solja – Tibetan tea flavoured with salt and butter
Solu Khumbu – the district immediately south of Mt Everest, inhabited mostly by Sherpas
sonam – good luck (Tibetan)
STD/ISD – signs you will see on shops offering telephone facilities. Subscriber Trunk Dialling is domestic direct dial and International Subscriber Dialling is international direct dial.
STOL – 'short-take-off-and-landing' aircraft
stupa – hemispherical Buddhist religious structure similar to a chorten
suntala – orange or tangerine

TAAN – Trekking Agents Association of Nepal
tahr – wild mountain goat
tal – lake; the correct transliteration is *taal*
Tamang – Tibeto-Burman ethnic group, most of whom live in the Middle Hills
tamba – copper

tarkari – vegetables
tato – hot
tawa – Tibetan Buddhist monk
tempo – three-wheeled taxi scooter
Terai – flat plains in the south of Nepal
Thakali – people of the Kali Gandaki valley who specialise in running hotels
Thakuri – highest warrior caste from western Nepal
Thamel – the trekkers' and budget travellers' district of Kathmandu
thangka – Tibetan religious painting
thar – species or clan (similar to *jaat*)
Tharu – indigenous people of the Terai
thukpa – noodles, often served in a soup
thulo – big
Tihar – the 'festival of lights' that occurs a week after Dasain
tole – street or quarter of a town or village
tonga – two-wheeled horse-drawn cart
tongba – a drink made from fermented millet seeds
topi – traditional Nepali cap
trisul – trident weapon of Shiva
tsampa – barley flour, a staple food of Tibetans
tsho – lake (Tibetan)

Wai Wai – a brand of instant noodles good for a quick trekking meal. Other popular brands of noodles are Yum Yum and Rara.

yak – main beast of burden and variety of cattle above 3000m elevation
yarsa – fields for crops above the uppermost houses of a village. Its literal translation is *yar* 'summer', *sa* 'ground'.
yeti – the abominable snowman

Index

MAPS

TEXT

LONELY PLANET PHRASEBOOKS

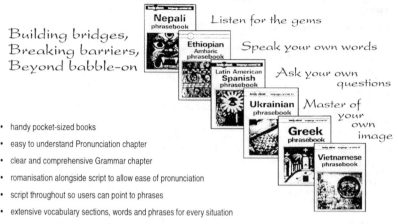

Building bridges,
Breaking barriers,
Beyond babble-on

Listen for the gems

Speak your own words

Ask your own questions

Master of your own image

- handy pocket-sized books
- easy to understand Pronunciation chapter
- clear and comprehensive Grammar chapter
- romanisation alongside script to allow ease of pronunciation
- script throughout so users can point to phrases
- extensive vocabulary sections, words and phrases for every situation
- full of cultural information and tips for the traveller

'...vital for a real DIY spirit and attitude in language learning' – Backpacker

'the phrasebooks have good cultural backgrounders and offer solid advice for challenging situations in remote locations' – San Francisco Examiner

'...they are unbeatable for their coverage of the world's more obscure languages' – The Geographical Magazine

---

Arabic (Egyptian)
Arabic (Moroccan)
Australia
  Australian English, Aboriginal and Torres Strait languages
Baltic States
  Estonian, Latvian, Lithuanian
Bengali
Brazilian
Burmese
Cantonese
Central Asia
Central Europe
  Czech, French, German, Hungarian, Italian and Slovak
Eastern Europe
  Bulgarian, Czech, Hungarian, Polish, Romanian and Slovak
Ethiopian (Amharic)
Fijian
French
German
Greek

Hindi/Urdu
Indonesian
Italian
Japanese
Korean
Lao
Latin American Spanish
Malay
Mandarin
Mediterranean Europe
  Albanian, Croatian, Greek, Italian, Macedonian, Maltese, Serbian and Slovene
Mongolian
Nepali
Papua New Guinea
Pilipino (Tagalog)
Quechua
Russian
Scandinavian Europe
  Danish, Finnish, Icelandic, Norwegian and Swedish

South-East Asia
  Burmese, Indonesian, Khmer, Lao, Malay, Tagalog (Pilipino), Thai and Vietnamese
Spanish (Castilian)
  Basque, Catalan and Galician
Sri Lanka
Swahili
Thai
Thai Hill Tribes
Tibetan
Turkish
Ukrainian
USA
  US English, Vernacular, Native American languages and Hawaiian
Vietnamese
Western Europe
  Basque, Catalan, Dutch, French, German, Irish, Italian, Portuguese, Scottish Gaelic, Spanish (Castilian) and Welsh

---

LONELY PLANET JOURNEYS

JOURNEYS is a unique collection of travel writing – published by the company that understands travel better than anyone else. It is a series for anyone who has ever experienced – or dreamed of – the magical moment when they encountered a strange culture or saw a place for the first time. They are tales to read while you're planning a trip, while you're on the road or while you're in an armchair, in front of a fire.

JOURNEYS books catch the spirit of a place, illuminate a culture, recount a crazy adventure, or introduce a fascinating way of life. They always entertain, and always enrich the experience of travel.

IN RAJASTHAN
Royina Grewal

Indian writer Royina Grewal's travels in Rajasthan take her from tribal villages to flamboyant palaces. Along the way she encounters a multitude of characters: snake charmers, holy men, nomads, astrologers, dispossessed princes, reformed bandits . . . And as she draws out the rarely told stories of farmers' wives, militant maharanis and ambitious schoolgirls, the author skilfully charts the changing place of women in contemporary India. The result is a splendidly evocative mosaic of life in India's most colourful state.

Royina Grewal lives on a farm in Rajasthan, where she and her husband are working to evolve minimal-impact methods of farming. Royina has published two monographs about the need for cultural conservation and development planning. She is also the author of Sacred Virgin, a travel narrative about her journey along the Narmada River, which was published to wide acclaim.

SHOPPING FOR BUDDHAS
Jeff Greenwald

Here in this distant, exotic land, we were compelled to raise the art of shopping to an experience that was, on the one hand, almost Zen – and, on the other hand, tinged with desperation like shopping at Macy's or Bloomingdale's during a one-day-only White Sale.

Shopping for Buddhas is Jeff Greenwald's story of his obsessive search for the perfect Buddha statue. In the backstreets of Kathmandu, he discovers more than he bargained for . . . and his souvenir-hunting turns into an ironic metaphor for the clash between spiritual riches and material greed. Politics, religion and serious shopping collide in this witty account of an enlightening visit to Nepal.

Jeff Greenwald is also the author of Mister Raja's Neighborhood and The Size of the World. His reflections on travel, science and the global community have appeared in the Los Angeles Times, the Washington Post, Wired and a range of other publications. Jeff lives in Oakland, California.

LONELY PLANET TRAVEL ATLASES

Lonely Planet has long been famous for the number and quality of its guidebook maps. Now we've gone one step further and in conjunction with Steinhart Katzir Publishers produced a handy companion series: Lonely Planet travel atlases – maps of a country produced in book form.

Unlike other maps, which look good but lead travellers astray, our travel atlases have been researched on the road by Lonely Planet's experienced team of writers. All details are carefully checked to ensure the atlas corresponds with the equivalent Lonely Planet guidebook.

The handy atlas format means no holes, wrinkles, torn sections or constant folding and unfolding. These atlases can survive long periods on the road, unlike cumbersome fold-out maps. The comprehensive index ensures easy reference.

- full-colour throughout
- maps researched and checked by Lonely Planet authors
- place names correspond with Lonely Planet guidebooks
  – no confusing spelling differences
- legend and travelling information in English, French, German, Japanese and Spanish
- size: 230 x 160 mm

Available now:
Chile & Easter Island • Egypt • India & Bangladesh • Israel & the Palestinian Territories •Jordan, Syria & Lebanon • Kenya • Laos • Portugal • South Africa, Lesotho & Swaziland • Thailand • Turkey • Vietnam • Zimbabwe, Botswana & Namibia

---

LONELY PLANET TV SERIES & VIDEOS

Lonely Planet travel guides have been brought to life on television screens around the world. Like our guides, the programmes are based on the joy of independent travel, and look honestly at some of the most exciting, picturesque and frustrating places in the world. Each show is presented by one of three travellers from Australia, England or the USA and combines an innovative mixture of video, Super-8 film, atmospheric soundscapes and original music.

Videos of each episode – containing additional footage not shown on television – are available from good book and video shops, but the availability of individual videos varies with regional screening schedules.

Video destinations include: Alaska • American Rockies • Australia – The South-East • Baja California & the Copper Canyon • Brazil • Central Asia • Chile & Easter Island • Corsica, Sicily & Sardinia – The Mediterranean Islands • East Africa (Tanzania & Zanzibar) • Ecuador & the Galapagos Islands • Greenland & Iceland • Indonesia • Israel & the Sinai Desert • Jamaica • Japan • La Ruta Maya • Morocco • New York • North India • Pacific Islands (Fiji, Solomon Islands & Vanuatu) • South India • South West China • Turkey • Vietnam • West Africa • Zimbabwe, Botswana & Namibia

The Lonely Planet TV series is produced by:
Pilot Productions
The Old Studio
18 Middle Row
London W10 5AT UK

For video availability and ordering information contact your nearest Lonely Planet office.

Music from the TV series is available on CD & cassette.

PLANET TALK

Lonely Planet's FREE quarterly newsletter

We love hearing from you and think you'd like to hear from us.

When...is the right time to see reindeer in Finland?
Where...can you hear the best palm-wine music in Ghana?
How...do you get from Asunción to Areguá by steam train?
What...is the best way to see India?

For the answer to these and many other questions read PLANET TALK.

Every issue is packed with up-to-date travel news and advice including:

- a letter from Lonely Planet co-founders Tony and Maureen Wheeler
- go behind the scenes on the road with a Lonely Planet author
- feature article on an important and topical travel issue
- a selection of recent letters from travellers
- details on forthcoming Lonely Planet promotions
- complete list of Lonely Planet products

To join our mailing list contact any Lonely Planet office.

Also available: Lonely Planet T-shirts. 100% heavyweight cotton.

LONELY PLANET ONLINE

Get the latest travel information before you leave or while you're on the road

Whether you've just begun planning your next trip, or you're chasing down specific info on currency regulations or visa requirements, check out Lonely Planet Online for up-to-the minute travel information.

As well as travel profiles of your favourite destinations (including maps and photos), you'll find current reports from our researchers and other travellers, updates on health and visas, travel advisories, and discussion of the ecological and political issues you need to be aware of as you travel.

There's also an online travellers' forum where you can share your experience of life on the road, meet travel companions and ask other travellers for their recommendations and advice. We also have plenty of links to other online sites useful to independent travellers.

And of course we have a complete and up-to-date list of all Lonely Planet travel products including guides, phrasebooks, atlases, Journeys and videos and a simple online ordering facility if you can't find the book you want elsewhere.

www.lonelyplanet.com
or
AOL keyword: lp

LONELY PLANET PRODUCTS

Lonely Planet is known worldwide for publishing practical, reliable and no-nonsense travel information in our guides and on our web site. The Lonely Planet list covers just about every accessible part of the world. Currently there are nine series: *travel guides*, *shoestring guides*, *walking guides*, *city guides*, *phrasebooks*, *audio packs*, *travel atlases*, *Journeys – a unique collection of travel writing and Pisces Books - diving and snorkeling guides.*

EUROPE

Amsterdam • Austria • Baltic States phrasebook • Britain • Central Europe on a shoestring • Central Europe phrasebook • Czech & Slovak Republics • Denmark • Dublin • Eastern Europe on a shoestring • Eastern Europe phrasebook • Estonia, Latvia & Lithuania • Finland • France • French phrasebook • Germany • German phrasebook • Greece • Greek phrasebook • Hungary • Iceland, Greenland & the Faroe Islands • Ireland • Italian phrasebook • Italy • Lisbon • London • Mediterranean Europe on a shoestring • Mediterranean Europe phrasebook • Paris • Poland • Portugal • Portugal travel atlas • Prague • Romania & Moldova • Russia, Ukraine & Belarus • Russian phrasebook • Scandinavian & Baltic Europe on a shoestring • Scandinavian Europe phrasebook • Slovenia • Spain • Spanish phrasebook • St Petersburg • Switzerland •Trekking in Spain • Ukrainian phrasebook • Vienna • Walking in Britain • Walking in Italy • Walking in Switzerland • Western Europe on a shoestring • Western Europe phrasebook

Travel Literature: The Olive Grove: Travels in Greece

NORTH AMERICA

Alaska • Backpacking in Alaska • Baja California • California & Nevada • Canada • Chicago • Deep South• Florida • Hawaii • Honolulu • Los Angeles • Mexico • Mexico City • Miami • New England • New Orleans • New York City • New York, New Jersey & Pennsylvania • Pacific Northwest USA • Rocky Mountain States • San Francisco • Southwest USA • USA phrasebook • Washington, DC & the Capital Region

Travel Literature: Drive thru America

CENTRAL AMERICA & THE CARIBBEAN

•Bahamas and Turks & Caicos •Bermuda •Central America on a shoestring • Costa Rica • Cuba •Eastern Caribbean •Guatemala, Belize & Yucatán: La Ruta Maya • Jamaica

SOUTH AMERICA

Argentina, Uruguay & Paraguay • Bolivia • Brazil • Brazilian phrasebook • Buenos Aires • Chile & Easter Island • Chile & Easter Island travel atlas • Colombia • Ecuador & the Galápagos Islands • Latin American Spanish phrasebook • Peru • Quechua phrasebook • Rio de Janeiro • South America on a shoestring • Trekking in the Patagonian Andes • Venezuela

Travel Literature: Full Circle: A South American Journey

ISLANDS OF THE INDIAN OCEAN

Madagascar & Comoros • Maldives• Mauritius, Réunion & Seychelles

AFRICA

Africa - the South • Africa on a shoestring • Arabic (Moroccan) phrasebook • Cairo • Cape Town • Central Africa • East Africa • Egypt • Egypt travel atlas• Ethiopian (Amharic) phrasebook • Kenya • Kenya travel atlas • Malawi, Mozambique & Zambia • Morocco • North Africa • South Africa, Lesotho & Swaziland • South Africa, Lesotho & Swaziland travel atlas • Swahili phrasebook • Tunisia Trekking in East Africa • West Africa • Zimbabwe, Botswana & Namibia • Zimbabwe, Botswana & Namibia travel atlas

Travel Literature: The Rainbird: A Central African Journey • Songs to an African Sunset: A Zimbabwean Story